AFRO-AMERICAN DEMOGRAPHY AND URBAN ISSUES

Recent Titles in
Bibliographies and Indexes in Afro-American and African Studies

Black-Jewish Relations in the United States: A Selected Bibliography
Compiled by Lenwood G. Davis

Black Immigration and Ethnicity in the United States: An Annotated Bibliography
Center for Afroamerican and African Studies, The University of Michigan

Blacks in the American Armed Forces, 1776-1983: A Bibliography
Compiled by Lenwood G. Davis and George Hill

Education of the Black Adult in the United States; An Annotated Bibliography
Compiled by Leo McGee and Harvey G. Neufeldt

A Guide to the Archives of Hampton Institute
Compiled by Fritz J. Malval

A Bibliographical Guide to Black Studies Programs in the United States:
An Annotated Bibliography
Compiled by Lenwood G. Davis and George Hill

Wole Soyinka: A Bibliography of Primary and Secondary Sources
Compiled by James Gibbs, Ketu H. Katrak, and Henry Louis Gates, Jr.

AFRO-AMERICAN DEMOGRAPHY AND URBAN ISSUES

A Bibliography

Compiled by R. A. Obudho and Jeannine B. Scott

Bibliographies and Indexes in Afro-American and African Studies, Number 8

Greenwood Press
Westport, Connecticut • London, England

Z 1361
N 39
O 2 9
1 9 8 5

Library of Congress Cataloging-in-Publication Data

Obudho, Robert A.
  Afro-American demography and urban issues.

  (Bibliographies and indexes in Afro-American and
African studies, ISSN 0742-6925 ; no. 8)
    Includes index.
    1. Afro-Americans—Economic conditions—Bibliography.
2. Afro-Americans—Social conditions—Bibliography.
3. Bibliography—Bibliography—Afro-Americans.
I. Scott, Jeannine B. II. Title. III. Series.
Z1361.N39029 1985   016.3058′96073   85-17752
[E185.8]
ISBN 0-313-24656-4 (lib. bdg. : alk. paper)

Library of Congress Catalog Card Number: 85-17752
ISBN: 0-313-24656-4
ISSN: 0742-6925

First published in 1985

Greenwood Press
A division of Congressional Information Service, Inc.
88 Post Road West
Westport, Connecticut 06881

Printed in the United States of America

∞™

The paper used in this book complies with the
Permanent Paper Standard issued by the National
Information Standards Organization (Z39.48-1984).

10 9 8 7 6 5 4 3 2 1

CONTENTS

FOREWORD

The usefulness of national and topical bibliographies is questioned occasionally because scholarly literature and disciplinary interest usually transcend both the national and disciplinary boundaries. But with Afro-American studies rapidly acquiring an independent, as well as a multi-disciplinary character in such fields as demography, urbanization and regional planning, the geographical extent of these disciplines has become somewhat indistinct. This bibliography has thus been compiled as a research tool in recognition of this academic reality.

Since the 1960s, Afro-American studies have received tremendous impetus in many universities and colleges in the United States. Hardly a month passes without new contributions to the already vast amount of literature on Afro-American demography and urban studies. This development has posed a serious problem in bibliographical control to both the Afro-Americanist and the librarian. The dearth of bibliographies in the field of Afro-American demography and urban studies has complicated, in no small measure, the problems of research in this growing interdisciplinary field. This problem is particularly apparent in the libraries and research centers of Afro-American studies in state and private colleges; most are neither adequately stocked nor provide access to the catalogues of titles available in large university libraries in the United States.

Some significant attempts have been made to improve this state of affairs through the recent and periodic publication of various short bibliographies; however, they do not cover Afro-American studies in general or demography and urban studies in particular. All of these publications almost invariably relate to the whole subject area, or large parts thereof, and do not deal sufficiently with demography and urban issues. In fact, the published bibliographies on Afro-American studies are so limited in scope that they point to only a small portion of the extensive literature in this ever-expanding field. It is to help remedy this situation, insofar as Afro-American demography and urban studies are concerned, that this work has been produced. We strongly encourage others to expand on our work in Afro-American demography and urban studies in order to effectively increase the usefulness of this research tool to students and scholars.

PREFACE

This bibliography is a comprehensive compilation of works that deal with Afro-American demography and urban issues in the United States. In our research and teaching about Afro-Americans, we came across numerous published and unpublished writings, which could help future researchers interested in Afro-American demography and urban studies. The major aim of the bibliography is to serve as a simple and practical tool to individuals interested in all aspects of development planning in the United States, particularly as they relate to the urban demography of Afro-Americans.

Included in this bibliography is a listing of materials that have been published or written on the subject of Afro-American demography and urban issues in the United States, dating as far back as the eighteenth century. The bibliography, therefore, records: academic works, discussion and conference papers, periodical literature, all types of academic theses and dissertations, unclassified public documents, books and edited books. In preparing this bibliography we consulted the periodicals listed in the front matter of this book, as well as other publications on Afro-Americans issued in the United States and around the world.

In order to have easy access to all entries, the bibliography is organized into a sequence from 0001 to 5235 and categorized into nine chapters: bibliography of bibliographies, demography and population; urbanization and disurbanization; housing and residential patterns; ghettoization, slum and squatter settlements; suburbanization and reurbanization; geography and rural studies; and urban and development planning policies. The entries are alphabetized by the last name of the author within each chapter. An author index is included at the back of the book. The individual entries for the bibliographies and books provide: sequence numbers, author, title, place of publication, name of publisher and year of publication. The sequence entry for periodicals and chapters in edited books includes: author, topic, name of the journal or book, volume, month and year of publication, and page numbers. The sequence for public documents includes: sequence number, name of the statutory body, topic, place of publication, publisher, reference code if any and year of publication. Thesis and doctoral dissertations include: sequence number, author, topic, university where it was submitted, and year. And finally, other unpublished manuscripts include: the author, topic, date of publication, and other information that describes the unpublished manuscript. Wherever possible, we have also indicated where the unpublished manuscript is located.

While it is easy to obtain sources from bibliographies, books, articles and public documents, it is not always easy to gain access to academic thesis and doctoral dissertations and other unpublished manuscripts. The inclusion of unpublished manuscrips, therefore, is a very important strength of this bibliography. This bibliography is primarily a informative guide to the literature on demography and urban issues of Afro-Americans. Because bibliographies are never complete, users of this bibliography are advised to look at specialized occasional publications that continue to be published as current and continuing information on Afro-Americans.

As an academic discipline in the United States, Afro-American studies are very new and traditional and usually discrete from other studies. Degree-granting departments began to appear in a few colleges during the 1960s. Prominent journals in the field have only been in circulation for about twenty years. However, social scientists did not really become interested in the demography and urban studies of Afro-Americans until the mid-1960s when the Civil Rights Movement and former President Johnson's Great Society jarred the public consciousness. This bibliography covers much of the pre- and all of the posst-1960s period and focuses on the period from 1960 to 1984. An inventory of the items included in this bibliography is enlightening and reinforces the fact that social scientists' analysis of Afro-Americans increased markedly after the 1960s. The interst peaked in the 1960s and now is declining. It is interesting to note that numerous entries recorded here were written by Afro-Americans, many of whom were actively recruited by graduate departments of major U.S. universities in order to train for a profession which traditionally has been dominated by non-Afro-American.

An examination of this bibliography will reveal that, despite its title, the work is of significant value to policy planners in the United States and to many others including: social scientists, historians, business and marketing professionals, realtors, politicians, and lawyers studying the contemporary United States. Finally, this bibliography is intended to prevent unnecessary duplication of research which often results from the lack of proper knowledge of existing literature.

ACKNOWLEDGMENTS

This volume would not have been possible without the works of the authors. It would be impossible to express our sincere gratitude to all of them because of the limited space. To each and every author named in the Author Index and their respective publishers, we express our thanks.

At the level of preparation, we received support and encouragement from: John Schumaker, Acting Vice President of Research and Educational Development, State University of New York (SUNY) at Albany; John Webb, Dean of the College of Social and Behavioral Sciences, SUNY/Albany; and Seth Spellman, former Chairperson of the Department of African and Afro-American Studies, SUNY/Albany; Vice President Schumaker, by virtue of his intense interest in faculty research activity, supported the preparation of this project by finding the necessary funds for researching and typing the manuscript. Dean Webb and Professor Spellman gave their encouragement and unequivocal moral and financial support during the preparation of this bibliography. Special thanks are also due to Julius Thompson, Department of African and Afro-American Studies, SUNY at Albany and John Logan, Department of Sociology, SUNY at Albany, both of whom carefully checked the entries of accuracy.

Thanks are due to all my former students at Rutgers University and Vassar College and to my present students at SUNY/Albany, who helped us with the library research, typing and proofreading of the manuscript. Special thanks are due to Mahmoud Gheitu, my teaching assistant, and Ellen Oboh, both of whom located, researched and rechecked most of the references. We also acknolwedge the cooperation of the Population Information Program Resource Center at John Hopkins University through the POPLINE.

We must acknowledge the assistance we have received from colleagues at SUNY/Albany Main Library, Rutgers University Libraries, Yale University Libraries, Vassar College Library, Princeton University Libraries, the Amistad Research Center at Dillard University, and the Library of Congress. It is impossible to enumerate the many libraries and curators of collections who have freely given us their time and knowledge and provided us with full use of their facilities. A deep sense of gratitude is felt for their help, and we hereby register our gratitude.

We must also thank various colleagues across America who have constantly fired our interest on the subject of Afro-American demography and urban studies. Special thanks are given to former colleagues in the Department of Africana Studies, Rutgers University and colleagues in the Department of African and Afro-American Studies, Geography, and Regional Planning Department, SUNY/Albany, for their help and encouragement at

various times during the preparation of this bibliography. Last, but by
no means least, we must express our sincere thanks and gratitude to
Benita Lindsay-Jordan, for typing the original drafts and Barbara Savoie
for typing and editing the final copy of this manuscript in camera-ready
form.

While we thank all of the above, we would like to absolve them
of any errors found in this bibliography. All the errors, if any, are
our own responsibility and should be addressed to us.

R.A. Obudho
Editor, African Urban Quarterly
Department of African/Afro-American Studies
State University of New York
1400 Washington Avenue
Albany, New York   12222

UNITED STATES LIBRARIES WITH MAJOR COLLECTIONS OF
PUBLICATIONS ON AFRO-AMERICAN DEMOGRAPHY AND URBAN STUDIES

Benedict College, Starks Library, Taylor and Harden Street, Columbia,
    South Carolina 29204. 28,100 vols. Includes maps, manuscripts,
    pictures, slides.

Bennett College, Thomas F. Holgate Library, Greensboro, North Carolina,
    27420, 1,481 vols.
Bronxville Public Library, 201 Pondfield, Bronxville, New York. Books
    presented in honor of Dr. Ralph J. Bunche by and about Afro-
    Americans.

Columbia University Libraries, Alexander Gumby Collections, New York
    10027.

Detroit Public Library, 5201 Woodward, Detroit, Michigan. 840 vols.
    Includes music, recordings, dance and drama.

Dillard University, Amistad Research Center, New Orleans, Louisiana,
    70122. Geared toward the histories of non-white United States
    ethnic groups.

Dillard University Library, 2601 Gentilly Boulevard, New Orleans,
    Louisiana, 70122. Card index on Afro-Americans in New Orleans
    from newspapers covering 1850-1965.

Divine Word Seminary. St. Augustine Seminary Library, Bay St. Louis,
    Mississippi. 500 vols. Maintained for missionary work by Afro-
    Americans.

Duke University Library, Durham, North Carolina, 27706.

Fisk University Library, Erastus Milo Cravath Memorial Library,
    Nashville, Tennessee, 37203. 10,000 vols. Includes a collection
    of manuscripts. Retricted use: non-circulating.

Fort Valley State College, Henry Alexander Hunt Memorial Library, Fort
    Valley, Georgia, 31301, 861 vols.

Free Library of Philadelphia, Social Science and History Department,
    Negro Collection, Logan Square, Phladelphia, Pennsylvania, 19131.
    900 vols.

Hampton Institute, Collis P. Huntington Memorial Library, George Foster
    Peabody Collection, Hampton, Virginia, 23368. 9,298 vols.

Howard University Library, Afro-American Collection, Washington, D.C.,
    20001. 70,000 vols.
Johnson Publishing Company Library, 1820 South Michigan Avenue, Chicago,
    Illinois. 2,500 vols. Includes African materials.

Livingstone College, Carnegie Library, Salisbury, North Carolina 28144.
    Inclues a Rare Book Room and out-of-print books by and about Afro-
    Americans as well as other miscellaneous rare volumes and first
    editions. Restricted use: non-circulating.

New York Public Library Branch, Schomburg Collection, 103 West 135th
    Street, New York 10027. 33,500 vols. Includes books,
    periodicals, manuscripts, clippings, pictures, prints, records and
    sheet music, which attempt to record the entire experience of
    people of African descent - historical and contemporary.
    Restricted use: materials must be used on the premises.

North Carolina Central University Library, Afro-American Collections,
    Durham, North Carolina, 27707.

Paine College, Warren A. Chandler Library, Augusta, Georgia 30901. 396
    vols. Shelf-list only. Focuses especially on race problems in
    relation to churches in the Old South.

Philander Smith College Library, 812 West 13th Street, Little Rock,
    Arkansas, 72203.

Richard B. Hassison Public Library, 214 South Blount Street, Raleigh,
    North Carolina, 27607. 3,500 vols. Mimeographed bibliographies
    available.

Rust College Library, Magee Memorial Library, Holly Springs,
    Mississippi, 38635. 3,659 vols. Includes books by Afro-Americans.

Rutherford B. Hayes Library, 1337 Hayes Avenue, Fremont, Ohio. 65,000
    vols.

Savannah State College Library, Savannah, Georgia. 1,000 vols.
    Includes pamphlet and clipping file.

Shaw University Library, Raleigh, North Carolina.

Texas Southern University Library, Heartman Collection, 3201 Wheeler, Houston, Texas, 77004. 11,428 vols. Includes maps and photographs.

Tougaloo College, Wastman Library, Tougaloo, Mississippi 39174.

Tuskegee Institute, Hollis Burke Frissell Library, Washington Collection, Tuskegee, Alabama, 36088. 11,000 vols.

University of California/Santa Barbara, Wyles Collection, Goleta, California, 90089. 13,153 vols. Primary emphasis on the Afro-American as a slave, and the implications of slavery and the Civil War.

University of North Carolina/Chapel HIlls, Louis Round Wilson Library, Chapel Hill, North Carolina.

Virginia State College Library, Norfolk Division, 2401 Corprew Avenue, Norfolk, Virginia 23803.

Virginia Union University, William J. Clark Library, 1500 Lombardy Street, Richmond, Virginia, 23220. 1,600 vols.

Wilberforce University, Carnegie Library, Daniel Alexander Paine Collection, Wilberforce, Ohio, 45304. 4,500 vols. Includes manuscripts and pictures.

Xavier University Library, Palmetto and Pine Streets, New Orleans, Louisiana, 70125. Includes manuscrips, maps, pictures, photostats, and microfilm. Restricted use: closed August.

Yale University Library, James Weldon Johnson Memorial Collection of Negro Arts and Letters, New Haven, Connecticut, 06520. Includes manuscripts and pictures.

LIST OF PERIODICALS
CONSULTED ON AFRO-AMERICAN DEMOGRAPHY AND URBAN STUDIES

Acadiensis: Journal of the History of the Atlantic Region (Canada)

Administration and Society

Administrative Science Quarterly

Adventist Heritage

Aerospace Historian

Afro-Americans in New York Life and History

Agricultural History

Alabama Historical Quarterly

Alabama Review Ameriasia Journal

American Archivist

American Art and Antiques

American Art Journal

American Aviation Historical Society Journal

American Bar Association Journal

American Behavioral Scientist

American City

American County Government

American Economic Review

American Heritage

American Historical Review

American History Illustrated

American Hospital Association Newsletter

American Institute of Planners Journal

American Jewish Archives

American Jewish Historical Quarterly

American Jewish History

American Journal of Economics and Sociology

American Journal of Legal History

American Journal of Political Science

American Journal of Sociology

American Literary Realism, 1870-1910

American Literature

American Neptune

American Political Science Review

American Politics Quarterly

American Preservation

American Quarterly

American Review of Canadian Studies

American Scholar

American Sociological Review

American Studies International

American Studies (Lawrence, Kansas)

American Studies (Washington, D.C.) (SEE American Studies International)

American West

Americas: A Quarterly Review of Inter-American Cultural History,
     (Academy of American Franciscan History)

Americas (Organization of American States)

Annals of Iowa

Annals of the American Academy of Political and Social Science

Annals of the Association of American Geographers

Annals of Wyoming

Antioch Review

Appalachian Journal

The Appraisal Journal

Arbitration Journal

Arizona and the West

Arkansas Historical Quarterly

Armenian Review

Art in America

Arts in Society (ceased pub. 1976)

Atlantis: A Women's Studies Journal (Canada)

Audience (ceased pub. 1973)

Aztlan

Baptist History and Heritage

Black Academy Review

Black Dialogue

Black Enterprise

Black Politician

Black Scholar

Black World (Formerly, Negro Digest)

Brigham Young University Studies

Bulletin of the Atomic Scientist (briefly known as Science and Public
    Affairs)

Bulletin of the History of Medicine

Business History Review

Cahiers de Geographie de Quebec (Canada)

California Historical Quarterly SEE California History

California History

Capitol Studies SEE Congressional Studies

Caribbean Review

Catholic Historical Review

Center Magazine

Centerpoint

Change

Chicago History

Chronicle

Chronicles of Oklahoma

Church History

Cincinnati Historical Society Bulletin

City: A Bi-Monthly Review of Urban America

Civil Liberties Review (ceased pub. 1979)

Civil War History

Civil War Times Illustrated

Colorado Magazine

Colorado Quarterly

Commentary

Community Magazine

Compact

Comparative Political Studies

Computers and the Humanities

Concordia Historical Institute Quarterly

Connecticut History

Crisis

Cry California

Curator (American Museum of Natural History)

Current History

Daedalus

Dalhousie Review (Canada)

Daughters of the American Revolution Magazine

Delaware History

Demography

Dialogue: A Journal of Mormon Thought

Dissent

Early American Life

Early American Literature

Ebony

Economic Development and Cultural Change

Economic Geography

Economic Inquiry

Education and Urban Society

Eighteenth-Century Life

Encounter

Environment and Planning

Escribano

Essex Institute Historical Collection

Essence: The Magazine for Today's Black Woman

Ethnic Groups

Ethnicity

Ethnohistory

Explorations

Family Heritage (ceased pub. 1979)

Feminist Studies

Film and History

Filson Club History Quarterly

Florida Historical Quarterly

Focus/Midwest

Foundations: A Baptist Journal of History and Theology

Freedomways: A Quarterly Review of Negro Freedom Movement

Frontiers

Gateway Heritage

Geographical Review

Georgia Historical Quarterly

Georgia Life (ceased pub. 1980)

Georgia Review

Government Publications Review Part A: Research Articles

Great Plains Journal

Growth and Change

Halve Maen

Harvard Educational Review

Harvard Library

Hawaiian Journal of History

Historian

Historic Preservation

Historical Archaelogy

Historical Journal of Massachusetts SEE Historical Journal of
    Massachusetts

Historical Magazine of the Protestant Episcopal Church

Historical Methods

Historical Methods Newsletter SEE Historical Methods

Historical New Hampshire

History of Childhood Quarterly: The Journal of Psychohistory SEE Journal
    of Psychohistory

History of Education Quarterly

History Teacher Horizon

Human Organization

Idaho Heritage (ceased pub. 1978)

Idaho Yesterdays

Indiana Magazine of History

Indiana Social Studies Quarterly

Industrial and Labor Relations Review

Inland Seas

International Migration - Migrants

International Migration Review

International Regional Science Review

International Socialist Review

Jednota Annual Furdek

Jet

Jewish Social Studies

Journal for the Scientific Study of Religion

Journal of Afro-American Issues

Journal of American Folklore

Journal of American History

Journal of Arizona History

Journal of Black Studies

Journal of Business

Journal of Communication

Journal of Conflict Resolution

Journal of Economic History

Journal of Economic Literature

Journal of Ethnic Studies

Journal or Family History: Studies in Family, Kinship, and Demography

Journal of Forest History

Journal of General Education

Journal of Higher Education

Journal of Historical Geography

Journal of Social History

Journal of Social Issues

Journal of Southern History

Journal of Sport History

Journal of Studies on Alcohol

Journal of the American Institute of Planners SEE Journal of the
American Planning Association

Journal of the American Planning Association

Journal of Human Resources

Journal of the American Real Estate and Urban Economics Association

Journal of Regional Science

Journal of Social Issues

Journal of Urban Law

Journal of Urban Planning and Development Division of American Society
of Civil Engineers

Journal of the Folklore Institute

Journal of the History of Medicine and Allied Sciences

Journal of the Illinois State Historical Society

Journal of the Lancaster County Historical Society

Journal of the Rutgers University Library

Journal of the Society of Architectural Historians

Journal of the West

Journal of Urban History

Journalism Quarterly

Judicature

Kansas Historical Quarterly (superseded by Kansas History)

Kansas History

Kansas Quarterly

Kiva

Labor History

Land Economics

Land-Use Controls: A Quarterly Review

Law and Contemporary Problems

Law and Society Review

Liberal Education

Liberator

Library Quarterly

Lincoln Herald

Lituanus

Long Island Forum

Louisiana History

Louisiana Studies SEE Southern Studies: An Interdisciplinary Journal of
    the South

Mankind

Manuscripts

Marine Corps Gazette

Maryland Historian

Maryland Historical Magazine

Massachusetts Historical Society Proceedings

Massachusetts Review

Masterkey

Mennonite Life

Mennonite Quarterly Review

Methodist History

Metropolitan

Metropolitan Management, Transportation and Planning

Michigan Academician

Michigan History

Michigan Jewish History

Mid-American

Midstream

Midwest Quarterly

Midwest Review

Military Affairs

Military Collector and Historian

Milwaukee History

Minnesota History

Mississippi Quarterly

Missouri Historical Review

Missouri Historical Society Bulletin (superseded by Gateway Heritage)

Montana Magazine of History SEE Montana: Magazine of Western History

Montana: Magazine of Western History

Monthly Labor Review

Monthly Review

Municipal Finance

Muhammad Speaks

National Civic Review

Nation's Cities

Nautical Research Journal

Nebraska History

Negro Educational Review

Negro Heritage

Negro History Bulletin

Nevada Historical Society Quarterly

Newberry Library Bulletin (suspended pub. 1979)

New England Galaxy

New England Historical and Genealogical Register

New England Quarterly

New England Social Studies Bulletin

New Jersey History

New Mexico Historical Review

Newport History

New Scholar

New South (superseded by Southern Voices)

New York Affairs

New York Folklore

New York Folklore Quarterly (superseded by New York Folklore)

New York History

New York Historical Society Quarterly

Niagara Frontier

Nineteenth Century Fiction

North Carolina Historical Review

North Dakota History

North Dakota Quarterly

North Jersey Highlander

North Louisiana Historical Association Journal

Northwest Ohio Quarterly: A Journal of History and Civilization

Noticias

Ohio History

Old Northwest

Old-Time New England

Opportunity: A Journal of Negro Life

Oral History Review

Oregon Historical Quarterly

Pacific Historian

Pacific Historical Review

Pacific Northwest Quarterly

Pacific Northwesterner

Pacific Sociological Review

Palimpsest

Panhandle-Plains Historical Review

Pennsylvania Folklife

Pennsylvania History

Pennsylvania Magazine of History and Biography

Perspectives in American History

Pharmacy in History

Phylon

Pioneer America

Policy Studies Journal

Policy Studies Review

Political Science Quarterly

Political Studies (Great Britain)

Politics & Society

Polity

Populations Bulletin

Proceedings of the Academy of Political Science

Proceedings of the American Antiquarian Society

Proceedings of the American Philosophical Society

Progressive Labor

Prologue: The Journal of the National Archives

Psychiatry: Journal for the Study of Interpersonal Process

Public Opinion Quarterly

Public Policy

Publius

Public Administration Review

Public Employee

Public Interest

Public Welfare

Public Works

Quarterly Journal of Economics

Quarterly Journal of Speech

Quarterly Journal of Studies on Alcohol SEE Journal of Studies on
     Alcohol

Quarterly Journal of the Library of Congress

Quarterly Review of Economics and Business

Quarterly Review of Higher Education Among Negroes

Race Relations Law Reporter

Radical America

Radical History Review

Railroad History

Reason

Record

Records of the American Catholic Historical Society of Philadelphia

Regional Studies

Register of the Kentucky Historical Society

Religion in Life (ceased pub. 1980)

Rendezvous

Research Studies

Review of Economics and Statistics

Review of Radical Political Economics

Reviews in American History

Rhode Island History

Rhode Island Jewish Historical Notes

Richmond County History

Rights and Reviews: A Magazine of the Black Power Movement in America

Rochester History

Rocky Mountain Social Science Journal SEE Social Science Journal

Rural Sociology

Science and Society

Sea History

Sepia

Signs: Journal of Women in Culture and Society

Slovakia

Smithsonian

Social Education

Social Forces

Social Policy

Social Problems

Social Science

Social Science History

Social Science Journal

Social Science Quarterly

Social Service Review

Social Work

Societas

Society

Socio-Economic Planning Science

Sociological Analysis

Sociological Inquiry

Sociological Quarterly

Sociology and Social Research

Sociology of Education

Soulbook

Soundings (Nasville, Tennessee)

South Atlantic Quarterly

South Carolina Historical Magazine

South Dakota History

Southern California Quarterly

Southern Economic Journal

Southern Exposure

Southern Humanities Review

Southern Literary Journal

Southern Patriot

Southern Quarterly

Southern Review

Southern Speech Communication Journal

Southern Studies: An Interdisciplinary Journal of the South

Southern Voices (ceased pub. 1974)

Southern Economy and Society

Southern Review

Southern Speech Communication Journal

Southern Studies: An Interdisciplinary Journal of the South

Southern Voices (ceased pub. 1974)

Southwest Economy and Society

Southwest Review

Southwestern Historical Quarterly

Southwestern Social Science Quarterly SEE Social Science Quarterly

State Government

Staten Island Historian

Studies in Comparative International Development

Studies in History and Society (suspended pub. 1977)

Swedish Pioneer Historical Quarterly

Synthesis

Tampa Bay History

Teachers College Record

Teaching Political Science

Technology and Culture

Tennessee Folklore Society Bulletin

Tennessee Historical Quarterly

Tequesta

Texana (ceased pub. 1974)

Theatre Survey: The American Journal of Theatre History

Trans-Action: Social Science and Modern Society

Umoja: A Scholarly Journal of Black Studies

United States Naval Institute Proceedings

University of Ottawa Quarterly

University of Turku, Institute of General History

University of Windsor Review (Canada)

Upper Ohio Valley Historical Review

Urban Affairs Quarterly

Urban and Social Change Review

Urban Data Service

Urban Education

Urban Review

Urban West

Urbanism Past and Present

Utah Historical Quarterly

Vermont History

Virginia Cavalcade

Virginia Magazine of History and Biography

Voice of Negro

Washington Monthly

Welfare in Review

Western City

West Georgia College Studies in Social Sciences

West Tennessee Historical Society Papers

West Virginia History

Western American Literature

Western Folklore

Western Historical Quarterly

Western Illinois Regional Studies

Western Pennsylvania Historical Magazine

Western Political Quarterly

Western States Jewish Historical Quarterly

Westport Historical Quarterly (ceased pub. 1975)

Westways

William and Mary Quarterly

Winterhur Portfolio

Wisconsin Magazine of History

Wisconsin Then and Now (ceased pub. 1979)

Working Papers for a New Society

Working Papers from the Regional Economic History Center

World Affairs

Worldview

Yale Alumni Magazine

Yivo Annual of Jewish Social Science

York State Tradition (ceased pub. 1974)

Youth and Society

AFRO-AMERICAN DEMOGRAPHY

AND

URBAN ISSUES

CHAPTER 1

Bibliography of Bibliographies

0001. Abajian, James de T. Blacks and Their Contributions to the American West: A Bibliography and Union List of Library Holdings Through 1970. Boston: G.K. Hall, 1974.

0002. Abajian, James de T. Blacks in Selected Newspapers, Census and Other Sources. Boston: G.K. Hall, 1977.

0003. Abolition and Emancipation Literature. Annual Report of the American Historical Association for the year 1930. Vol. 3. Washington, D.C.: American Historical Association, 1932.

0004. About Black Americans, Philadelphia: Free Library of Philadelphia, Office of Work with Children, 1970.

0005. About 100 Books: Gateway to Better Group Understandings. New York: American Jewish Committee, Institute of Human Relations, 1970.

0006. Acquisitions in Black Material. Norfolk, VA.: Norfolk Public Library, Minority Materials Committee, 1974.

0007. Adair, Thelma. "Choices, Choices, Choices! Peak Experiences from the Afro-American Heritage." Childhood Education, 47 (April 1970), 355-64.

0008. Addo, Linda D. The Negro in American History: A Selected Bibliography. Greensboro, N.C.: Greensboro Tri-College Consortium, 1970.

0009. Adger, Robert M. Catalogue of Rare Books on Slavery and Negro Authors on Science, History, Poetry, Religion, Biography, etc. New York: Garland, 1982.

0010. Adger, Robert M. Portion of a Catalogue of Rare Books and Pamphlets, Collected by R.M. Adger, Philadelphia, Upon Subject

Relating to the Past Condition of the Colored Race and the Slavery Agitation in this Country. New York: Garland, 1982.

0011. Adinarayaniah, S.P. "Research in Colour Prejudice." British Journal of Psychology. 31 (Jan. 1941), 228-9.

0012. Adler, Patricia. Ethnic and Political Minorities in the Los Angeles Area: A Bibliography of Doctoral Dissertations and Master's Theses at the University of Southern California, 1912-1969. Los Angeles, Cal.: University of Southern California, Department of History, 1970.

0013. Aery, William A. "Negro Problems and Progress." Survey 41:11 (Dec. 14, 1918), 357.

0014. African Bibliographic Center. Black History Viewpoints: A Selected Bibliographic Guide to Resources for Afro-American and African History: 1968. Westport, Connecticut: Negro Universities Press, 1969.

0015. Africans in the U.S., 1961-1962: A Selected Current Reading List Based on Articles Listed in Our Catalogs. Washington, D.C.: African Bibliographic Center, 1964.

0016. Afro-American. Sacramento, Cal.: American River College Library, 1969.

0017. Afro-American and Mexican-American Bibliography: A Selected Guide to Materials in the California State Polytechnic College Library. San Luis Obispo, Cal.: California State Polytechnic College, Dexter Memorial Library, 1969.

0018. "Afro-American Bibliography." The Instructor, 78 (Mar. 1969), 1-10.

0019. Afro-American Culture and History. Cleveland, Ohio: Cleveland Public Library, 1967.

0020. Afro-American Encyclopedia Volumes 1-10. North Miami, Florida Educational Book Publishers, 1974.

0021. "Afro-American History Week." Read, See and Hear 24:5 (Feb. 7, 1975).

0022. Afro-American in Books for Children. Washington, D.C.: District of Columbia Public Library, Children's Service, (1974).

0023. Afro-American, 1553-1906: Author Catalog of the Library Company of Philadelphia and the Historical Society of Pennsylvania. Boston, Mass.: G.K. Hall, 1976.

0024. Afro-American Resources of the El Camino College Library. El

Camino, Cal.: El Camino College Library, 1969.

0025. "Afro-American Studies: A Bibliographic Key for 1976." In: Herman L. Totten. Bibliographic Control of Afro-American Literature, Vol. 2, Eugene Ore.: University of Oregon, School of Librarianship, 1976, 122-59.

0026. Afro-American Studies: A Guide to Resources in the Harvard University Library. Preliminary Edition. Cambridge, Mass.: Harvard University, Houghton Library, 1969.

0027. Agelusto, M. and David Listokin. The Urban Financing Dilemma: Disinvestment-Redlining. Monticello, Illinois: Council of Planning Libraries, Exchange Bibliography No. 892, 1975.

0028. A Guide to Negro Periodical Literature. Published Quarterly in Winston-Salem, North Carolina, 1941-1946.

0029. Airall, Jacqueline. "Finding Afro-American Materials in the Michigan State University Libraries." Readers Advisory Service 1, (1974), 4-7.

0030. Akeroyd, Richard. Bibliographies for Black Studies. Storrs, Conn.: University of Connecticut, Wilbur Cross Library, 1970.

0031. Akeroyd, Richard. Black Voices of the Sixties. Wilbur Cross Library Booklist No. 1. Stores, Conn.: University of Connecticut, Library Committee on Black Studies, 1970.

0032. Akeroyd, Richard. Wilbur Cross Library Black Studies Guide. Storrs, Conn.: University of Connecticut, Wilbur Cross Library.

0033. Akin, Joy. The Feasibility and Actuality of Modern Towns for the Poor in the U.S. Monticello, Illinois: Council of Planning Libraries Exchange Bibliography No. 167, 1970.

0034. All Winds Blow Free: the American Negro in Books For Boys and Girls, A Selected List. Pittsburgh, Pa.: Carnegie Library, 1968.

0035. Allard, Ursula. The Black Man: A Bibliography. St. Paul, Minn.: College of St. Thomas, O'Shaughnessy Library.

0036. Allee, M.H. "Books Negro Children Like." Horn Book 14 (Mar.-Apr.1938), 81-7.

0037. Allen, E.H. "Selected Annotated Bibliography on the Health Education of the Negro." Journal of Negro Education 6(July 1937), 578-87.

0038. Allen, Irving Lewis. Urbanism in the Modern Metropolis: A Classified Bibliography of Selective Sociological Approaches to Urban Ways of Life. Monticello, Illinois: Council of Planning

Libraries, Exchange Bibliography No. 155, 1970.

0039. "American and Foreign Books and Articles Bearing on the Negro." Journal of Negro History 20 (Jan.1935), 100-10.

0040. American Jewish Committee. Institute of Human Relations. The Police and Race Relations. A Selected Bibliography. New York, 1969.

0041. American Missionary Association Archives in Fisk University Library. Nashville, Tenn.: Fisk University, 1947.

0042. American Negro: A Selected Bibliography. Berkeley, Cal.: Berkeley Public Library, 1966.

0043. American Negro and African Studies: A Bibliography on the Special Collections in Carnegie Library, Livingstone College. Salisbury, N.C.: Livingstone College, Carnegie Library, 1968.

0044. American Negro: History and Achievement. Akron, Ohio: Akron Public Library, 1968.

0045. American Negro in Contemporary Society: An Annotated Booklist. Berkeley, Cal.: California Library Association, Young Adult Librarians' Round Table, 1966.

0046. American Negro: Some Recent Titles for Elementary School. Oklahoma City, Ok.: Oklahoma Department of Education, Library Resources Division, 1971.

0047. American Negro: Some Recommended Titles for Secondary Schools. Oklahoma City, Ok.: Oklahoma Department of Education, Library Resources Division, 1971.

0048. American Negro Speaks to Young Americans. Providence, R.I.: Providence Public Library, 1969.

0049. American Negro Writing. Akron, Ohio: Akron Public Library, 1971.

0050. American Studies Program. Rose Bibliography Analytical Guide and Indexes to the Crisis 1910-1960. Volumes 1-3, Westport, Connecticut: Greenwood Press, 1974.

0051. Americans All: An Intercultural Bibliography. New York: Bank Street College of Education, Curriculum, Consultation Service, 1970.

0052. Amoroso, Doreen. List of Materials for Ethnic Studies Laboratory. Tacoma, Wash.: Tacoma Comunnity College, Pearl A. Wanamaker Library, 1970.

0053. Amos, P.E. One Hundred Years of Freedom: A Selected

Bibliography of Books About the American Negro. (Ten Volumes),
Washington D.C.: United Publishing Corp., 1970.

0054. Amos, P.E. One Hundred Years of Freedom: A Selected
Bibliography of Books About the American Negro. Washington,
D.C.: Association for the Study of Negro Life and History,
1963.

0055. Analytical Guide and Indexes to "Alexander's Magazine," 1905-
1909. Westport, Conn.: Greenwood, 1974.

0056. Analytical Guide and Indexes to "The Colored American
Magazine," 1900-1909. Westport, Conn.: Greenwood, 1974.

0057. Analytical Guide and Indexes to "The Crisis: A Record of the
Darker Races," 1910-1960. Westport, Conn.: Greenwood, 1975.

0058. Anderson, Barbara. Afro-American Master's Thesis [Written at
San Francisco State College through 1969.] San Francisco,
Cal.: San Francisco State College, 1969.

0059. Andrew, Ann. Children's Books for and about Blacks.
Ypsilanti, Mich.: Eastern Michigan University Library, 1959.

0060. Andrews, Regina M. Intergroup Relations in the U.S.: A
Compilation of Some Materials and Service Organizations. New
York: Human Rrelations Committee, National Council of Women of
the U.S., 1956.

0061. Annotated Bibliography: Afro-American, Hispano and Amerind
(Abroiginal Indian and Eskimo), Denver, Col.: Colorado
Department of Education, Human Relations Task Force Committee,
1969.

0062. Ansley, Robert E. Discrimination in Housing. Chicago: CPL
Bibliography No. 13, 1979.

0063. Anthony, Elizabeth, V., and Gladys B. Sheppard. Bookshelf of
Negro History. Baltimore, Md.: Roebuck, 1944.

0064. Anthony, Ernestine. The Negro in the North During Wartime:
Select Bibliography, Washington, D.C.: 1945.

0065. Aptheker, Herbert. Annotated Bibliography of the Published
Writings of W.E.B. DuBois. Milwood, New York: Kraus-Thompson,
Org., 1973.

0066. Aptheker, Herbert. "Some Unpublished Writings of W.E.B.
DuBois." Freedomways 5 (Winter 1965), 103-28.

0067. Aptheker, Herbert. "The W.E.B. DuBois Papers." Political
Affairs 45:3 (Mar. 1966), 36-45.

0068. Archibald, Helen A. Negro History and Culture: Selected Material for Use With Children. Chicago: City Missionary Society, 1965.

0069. Armstrong, Douglas, and Marian Dworaczek. A Selected Bibliography on Human and Civil Rights." Toronto, Ont.: Ontario Ministry of Labour, Research Library, 1973.

0070. The Arthur B. Spingarn Collection of Negro Authors. Washington, D.C.: Howard University, Carnegie Library, Moorland Foundation, 1948.

0071. Asher, Robert. "Documents of the Race Riot of East St. Louis". Journal of the Illinois State Historical Society 65:8 (Autumn 1972), 327-36.

0072. Ashford, F.G., et al. Listing of All Books By and About the Negro in the Inman E. Page Library. Jefferson City, Mo.: Lincoln University, Inman E. Page Library, 1976.

0073. Association for the Study of Negro Life and History, International Library of Negro Life and History. Washington D.C.: United Publishing Corp., 1970.

0074. Atkins, H.D. and M.R. Bowles. A Selected Bibliography of Subject Bibliographies in the Fisk University Library. Nashville, Tenn.: Fisk University Library, 1950.

0075. Austin, Mary. "The Negro Problem" The Young Woman Citizen. New York: Women's Press, 1918, 173-4.

0076. "The Availability of Negro Source Material in Philadelphia." Negro History Bulletin 32 (Mar. 1968), 17-18.

0077. Bachus, Edward J. Recent Acquisitions: A List of Books Dealing With The Black Man in America. Saratoga Springs, N.Y.: Skidmore College, Lucy Scribner Library, 1960.

0078. Bailey, Joe H. Black Studies. Denton, Tex.: North Texas State University Library, 1970.

0079. Baker, Augusta B. "The American Negro" American Unity 12:2 (Nov.-Dec. 1953), 17-19.

0080. Bakewell, D.C. Black-Brown Bibliography. Northridge: Cal.: San Fernando Valley State College Library, 1969.

0081. Bakewell, D.C. The Black Experience in the United States: A Bibliography Based on the Collection of the San Fernando Valley State College Library. Northridge, California: San Fernando Valley State College Foundation, 1970.

0082. Baldwin, Lewis V. Resources for the Study of Afro-American

<u>Religion</u>: A Guide to Selected North Shore Libraries.
Evanston, Ill.: Garrett-Evangelical Theological Seminary,
Institue for Black Religious Research, 1980.

0083. Ball, Wendy, and Tony Martin. <u>Rare Afro-Americana: A
Reconstruction of the Adger Library</u>. Boston, Mass.: G.K. Hall,
1981.

0084. Bambrick, Jane. <u>Blacks in America Supplement I: A Bibliography
of the Holdings of the Sarah Byrd Askew Library at William
Paterson College</u>. Wayne, New Jersey: Sarah B. Askew Library,
1977.

0085. Bambrick, Jane. <u>Blacks in America Supplement II: A
Bibliography of the Holdings of the Sarah Byrd Askew Library at
William Paterson College</u>. Wayne, New Jersey: Sarah B. Askew
Library, 1979.

0086. Bambrick, Jane. <u>Blacks in America Supplement III: A
Bibliography of the Holdings of the Sarah Byrd Askew Library at
William Paterson College</u>. Wayne, New Jersey: Sarah B. Askew
Library, 1980.

0087. Bambrick, Jane and Helen Caninie. <u>Blacks in America: A
Bibliography of the Holdings of the Sarah Byrd Askew Library at
William Paterson College</u>. Wayne, New Jersey: Sarah B. Askew
Library, 1976.

0088. Banfield, Beryle. "Bibliograhpy of Afro-American History."
<u>Grade Teacher</u>, 1968, 4-17.

0089. Banks, James A. "Developing Racial Tolerance with Literature on
the Black Inner City." <u>Social Education</u> 34, (May 1970), 549-
52.

0090. Banks, Vera J., et al. <u>Research Data on Minority Groups: An
Annotated Bibliography of Economic Research Service Reports,
1955-1965.</u> Washington, D.C.: U.S. Department of Agriculture
Economic Research Service, 1966.

0091. Barabas, Jean. <u>The Assessment of Minority Groups: An Annotated
Bibliography (with subject index).</u> ERIC Document no. ED 083-
325. Selected Topical Booklists, 84. New York: Science
Associates, 1975.

0092. Barnard, Henry. <u>Slavery, Part I: A Bibliography of the
Microfilm Collection.</u> Sanford, N.C.: Microfilming Corporation
of America, 1980.

0093. Barnes, Nell D. <u>Black Aging: An Annotated Bibliography</u>.
Public Administration Series Bibliography P-167. Monticello,
Ill.: Vance Bibliographies, 1979.

0094.   Barnes, Willard. The Negro in America. Moscow, Idaho:
        University of Idaho Library, 1968.

0095.   Bartlett, John Russell. The Literature of the Rebellion: A
        Catalogue of Books and Pamphlets Relating to the Civil War in
        the U.S., and With Subjects Growing Out of That Event, Together
        With Works on American Slavery and Essays From Reviews and
        Magazines on the Same Subjects. Westport, Connecticut:
        Greenwood Press, 1970.

0096.   Baskin, Wade. Dictionary of Black Culture. Philadelphia,
        Pennsylvania: American Philosophical Library, 1973.

0097.   Bassett, Robert J. Afro-American Collection in the
        Undergraduate Library. Knoxville, Tenn.: University of
        Tennessee, Undergraduate Library, 1970.

0098.   Baxandall, Lee. Africans and Afro-Americans. Marxism and
        Aethetics: A Selective Annotated Bibliography. New York:
        Humanities Press, 1968.

0099.   Baxter, Camille, and Sylvia Lamont. Afro-American Materials in
        the Los Angeles Harbor College Library. Wilmington, Cal.: Los
        Angeles Harbor College Library, 1968.

0100.   Beach, Mark. Desegregated Housing and Interracial
        Neighborhoods: A Bibliographic Guide. Philadelphia, Pa.:
        National Neighbors, 1975.

0101.   Beach, Mark. Interracial Neighborhoods in American Cities.
        Public Administration Series Neighborhoods in American Cities.
        Public Administration Series Bibliography P-352, Monticello,
        Ill.: Vance Bibliographies, 1979.

0102.   Becker, M.L. "A Book Study of American Spirituals." Saturday
        Review Literature, 8 (January 30, 1932), 495.

0103.   Begum, Marcia J. Contributions of the Negro to American Life:
        A List of Books. Providence, R.I.: Providence Public Library,
        1970.

0104.   Bell, Barbara L. Black Biographical Sources: An Annotated
        Bibliography. New Haven, Conn.: Yale University Library,
        Reference Department, 1970.

0105.   Bell, Dorothy, et al. Canadian Black Studies Bibliography.
        Toronto, Ont.: Cross Cultural Learners Workshop, 1971.

0106.   Bengelsdorf, Winnie, et al. Ethnic Studies in Higher
        Education: State of the Art and Bibliography. Washington,
        D.C.: American Association of State Colleges and Universities,
        1972.

0107. Bennett, Elaine C. <u>Calendar of Negro-Related Documents in the Records of the Committee for Congested Production Areas in the National Archives</u>. Prepared for the Committee on Negro Studies of the American Council of Learned Societies. Washington, D.C.: American Council of Learned Societies, 1949.

0108. Bergman, Peter M. "Bibliography of Bibliographies." <u>The Chonological History of the Negro in America</u>. New York: Harper and Row, 1969, 617-24.

0109. Bergman, Peter M. and Jean McCarroll. <u>The Negro in the Congressional Record 1789-1801</u>. New York: Bergman, 1969.

0110. Bergman, Peter M. and Jean McCarroll. <u>The Negro in the Congressional Record</u> 1807-1815. New York: Bergman Publishers, 1970.

0111. Bergman, Peter M. and Jean McCarroll. <u>The Negro in the Congressional Record</u> 1815-1818. New York: Bergman Publishers, 1970.

0112. Bergman, Peter M. and Jean McCarroll. <u>The Negro in the Congressional Record</u> 1818-1819. New York: Bergman Publishers, 1970.

0113. Bergman, Peter M. and Jean McCarroll. <u>The Negro in the Congressional Record</u> 1819-1821. New York: Bergman Publishers, 1970.

0114. Bergman, Peter M. and Jean McCarroll. <u>The Negro in the Congressional Record</u> 1821-1824. New York: Bergman Publishers, 1970.

0115. Berry, Almedius B. <u>Reference Materials On and About the Negro</u>. Syracuse, N.Y.: Syracuse University, School of Library Science, 1945.

0116. Best, Jack L. <u>Records of the Assistant Commissioner for the State of North Carolina Bureau of Refugees, Freedmen, and Abandoned Lands 1865-1870</u>. National Archives Microfilm Publications Pamphlet M843. Washington, D.C.: National Archives and Records Series, General Services Administration, 1973.

0117. Bethel, Elizabeth, et al. <u>Preliminary Checklist of the Records of the Bureau of Refugees, Freedmen, and Abandoned Lands, 1865-1872.</u> Washington, D.C.: National Archives, War Records Office, 1946.

0118. <u>Bibliographic Guide to Black Studies: 1976</u>. Boston: G.K. Hall, 1976.

0119. <u>Bibliographic Guide to Black Studies: 1977</u>. Boston: G.K. Hall,

1977.

0120. Bibliographic Guide to Black Studies: 1978. Boston: G.K. Hall,
        1977.

0121. Bibliographic Guide to Black Studies: 1979. Boston: G.K. Hall,
        1978.

0122. Bibliographic Guide to Black Studies: 1980. Boston: G.K. Hall,
        1979.

0123. Bibliographic Guide to Black Studies: 1981. Boston: G.K. Hall,
        1981.

0124. Bibliographic Guide to Black Studies: 1982. Boston: G.K. Hall,
        1982.

0125. Bibliographic Guide to Black Studies: 1983. Boston: G.K. Hall,
        1983.

0126. Bibliograpical Suggestions for the Study of Negro History.
        Washington, D.C.: Association for the Study of Negro Life and
        History, 1958.

0127. Bibliography and Resource Guide: An Aid to Understanding in
        Intergroup Relations, Negro History and Aspiration, the Civil
        Rights Struggle and the Crisis in Our Cities. Madison, Wis.:
        Wisconsin Department of Industry, Labor and Human
        Relations/Human Rights Division, 1968.

0128. Bibliography for Educational Integration. Baltimore, Md.:
        Urban League, 1954.

0129. Bibliography for Educators: the American Negro. Lansing, Mich.:
        Michigan Education Department, Educational Services Bureau,
        Library Division, 1968.

0130. "Bibliography of African and Afro-American Religions." Black
        Books Bulletin 4 (Spring 1976), 68-71.

0131. Bibliography of African and Afro-American Religions.
        Princeton, N.J.: The Fund for Theological Education, 1971.

0132. Bibliography of Afro-American Culture. Detroit, Mich.: Board
        of Education of the City of Detroit., 1971.

0133. Bibliography of Bibliographies on the Negro Contained in the
        Libraries of the University of Michigan: A Tentative List. Ann
        Arbor, Mich.: University of Michigan, General Library, 1970.

0134. Bibliography of Black Studies Resources in the Library.
        Buffalo, N.Y.: SUNY-Buffalo, Urban Center, 1969.

0135.   Bibliography of Books and Periodicals By and About Blacks in the University of Arkansas Library. Fayetteville, Ark.: University of Arkansas Library, Reference Department, 1970.

0136.   Bibliography of Books By and About Negroes. Jefferson City, Mo.: Lincoln University, Inman E. Page Library, 1970.

0137.   Bibliography of Contributions of Negro Women to American Civilization. New York: Schomburg Library, 1952.

0138.   Bibliography of Doctoral Research on the Negro. Supplement 1967-1977. Ann Arbor, Mich.: University Microfilms, 1978.

0139.   Bibliography of Master's Theses, 1937-1962. Petersburg, Va.: Virginia State College Library, Reference Department, 1963.

0140.   Bibliography of Minorities, Blacks and Mexican-Americans. San Jose, Cal.: San Jose State College, 1968.

0141.   Bibliography of Negro Life. Newark, N.J.: Essex County Community College Library, Readers' Services Department, 1969.

0142.   Bibliography of Published Works by Robert C. Weaver, Secretary, U.S. Department of Housing and Urban Development. Washington, D.C.: U.S. Department of Housing and Urban Development, 1966.

0143.   Bibliography of References and Resource Materials Related to Black Childrearing and Family Life. St. Louis, Mo.: Institute of Black Studies, 1970.

0144.   Bibliography of Required Materials for Teacher Training Centers, Dedicated to the Second International Conference of African People, San Diego, Cal., Aug. 31-Sept. 4, 1972. New York: Conference of African People, Eastern Regional Conference, Action Library, 1972.

0145.   Bibliography of Resource Materials About the American Negro and Other American Minority Groups. Olympia, Wash.: Office of the Superintendent of Public Instruction, 1968.

0146.   Bibliography of Sources By and About Blacks Compiled by the Interns in the Internship Librarian Program. Internship in Ethnic Studies Librarianship. Oct. 21-Dec. 13, 1974. Sponsored by Fisk University Library in Cooperation with the University of Southern California and Oklahoma City University. Nashville, Tenn.: Fisk University Library, 1974.

0147.   Bibliography of Student Movements Protesting Segregation and Discrimination, 1960. Tuskegee, Ala.: Tuskegee Institute, Department of Records and Research, 1961.

0148.   Bibliography of Studies on Negroes, West Virginia Tech Collection. Montgomery, W. Va.: West Virginia Institute of

Technology, 1970.

0149. Bibliography of the Negro Press. Jefferson City, Mo.: Lincoln University, 1946.

0150. "Bibliography on Afro-American History and Culture." Prepared by the Staff, Department of Social Studies, Detroit, Mich., Public Schools. Social Education 33:4 (Apr. 1969), 447-61.

0151. Bibliography on Black Studies. Newark, N.J.: Essex County Community College Library, Readers' Services Department, 1971.

0152. Bibliography on Education of the Negro. Bulletin, 1931, No. 17. Washington, D.C.: U.S. Department of the Interior, Office of Education, 1931.

0153. Bibliography on Fair Employment Practice Law. Los Angeles, Cal.: Los Angeles County Law Library, 1960.

0154. Bibliography on Negro Labor. Washington, D.C.: U.S. Bureau of Statistics, 1937.

0155. Bibliography on Negro Life and History. Lansing, Mich.: Michigan Department of Education, Cooperative Curriculum Program, Committee on Elementary Education, 1969.

0156. "Bibliography on Negro Nursing." National Negro Health News 6 (Apr. - June 1939), 26-7.

0157. Bibliography on Negroes. Rutherford, N.J.: Fairleigh Dickinson University, Messler Library, 1969.

0158. Bibliography on Racism. Department of Health, Education and Welfare. Publication No. 73-9012. Rockville, Md.: U.S. National Institute of Mental Health, Center for Minority Group Mental Health Programs, 1972.

0159. Bibliography on the Negro in Industry. Washington, D.C.: President's Commission on Fair Employment Practice, Division of Review and Analysis, 1972.

0160. Bibliography Part I: The Black American. Walnut, Cal.: Mt. San Antonio College Library, 1969.

0161. Bicknell, Marguerite Elizabeth and Margaret C. McCulloch. Guide to Information about the Negro and Negro-White Adjustment. Memphis, Tenn.: Brunner Printing Co., 1943.

0162. Biddle, Stanton F. Library Resources for Research on Black Families in New York State. Buffalo, N.Y.: Author, 1982.

0163. Biddle, Stanton F. "The Schomburg Center for Research in Black Culture: Documenting the Black Experience." Bulletin of the

New York Public Library 76 (1972), 32-35.

0164. Bigala, John C.B. An Annotated Bibliography for Teaching Afro-American Studies at Secondary and College Levels. Tipsheet no. 5, New York: Columbia University, National Center for Research and Information on Equal Educational Opportunity, 1971.

0165. Bigley, Eleanor, et al. A Bibliography to Promote Better Human Understandings. Washington [State] Education Association, Department of Classroom Teachers, 1953.

0166. Bikshapathi, Adepu. Health and the Urban Poor, A Bibliography. ERIC Document no. ED 114-445. New York: ERIC Clearinghouse on the Urban Disadvantaged, 1978.

0167. Birtha, Jessie M., et al. About Black Americans. Philadelphia, Pa.: Free Library of Philadelphia, 1970.

0168. Bischoff, Phyllis. Ethnic Studies: a Selected Guide to Reference Materials at Berkeley. Berkeley, Cal.: University of California at Berkeley, 1974.

0169. Black. Akron, Ohio: Akron Public Library, 1970.

0170. Black, P.C. Survey of Books By and About the Negro in the U.S. Available in Selected Mississippi Public Libraries. M.A. thesis, Emory University, 1968.

0171. Black America. Baltimore, Md.: Baltimore County Public Library, 1969.

0172. Black America: A Selected Bibliography of Books. New York: Columbia University, Teachers College Library.

0173. Black American. Cleveland, Ohio: Cleveland Public Library, Government, Education and Social Science Department.

0174. Black American: A Selected List of Books at the U.S.A. F.E. Library and W.A.B. Library. Wiesbaden, Germany: Lindsey Air Station Library, Wiesbaden Air Base Library, 1973.

0175. Black American: A Selective Bibliography. Santa Barbara, Cal.: Santa Barbara Public Library, Reference Division, 1971.

0176. Black American, and Africa-Evolutionary Continent: A Compendium in Two Parts. Corning, N.Y.: Arthur A. Houghton, Jr., Library, 1964.

0177. Black American Bibliography: Books about the Black Man in America. Berkeley, Cal.: Berkeley Public Library, 1969.

0178. Black American Culture Bibliography: A List of Books and Periodicals on Black American Culture Located in the Belk

Library. Boone, N.C.: Appalachian State University, Belk
Library, Acquisitions Department, 1972.

0179. Black Americana: A Selected List. East Cleveland, Ohio: East
Cleveland Public Library, 1971.

0180. Black Americana: A Selected List of Recent and Older Books on
Negro Life and Culture from the Collections of the Detroit
Public Library. Detroit, Mich.: Detroit Public Library, 1970.

0181. "Black Americans." Booklist 69 (May 1, 1983), 835-45.

0182. Black and Brown Bibliography: History; A Selected List of Books
Relating to the History of Afro-Americans and Mexican-
Americans. San Bernadino, Cal.: San Bernadino State College,
1970.

0183. Black and Brown Bibliography: Literature, Art, Music, Theatre;
A Selected List of Books Relating to the Culture of Afro-
Americans and Mexican-Americans. San Bernadino, Cal.: San
Bernadino State College Library, 1970.

0184. Black and Brown Bibliography: Philosophy, Social Sciences,
Political Science, Education; A Selected List of Books Relating
to the Culture of Afro-Americans and Mexican-Americans. San
Bernadino, Cal.: San Bernadino State College Library, 1970.

0185. Black and White: What Delight: A List of Books for the Young
Child About Understanding Himself and Others. Raleigh, N.C.:
North Carolina State Library, Library Development Division,
1971.

0186. Black Bibliography. Beloit, Wis.: Beloit College Libraries,
1968.

0187. Black Bibliography. New Brunswick, N.J.: Rutgers University,
Livingston College, Kilmer Area Library, 1973.

0188. Black Bibliography. Salt Lake City, Utah: University of Utah,
Marriott Library, 1974.

0189. Black Bibliography: A Selected List of Books on Africa,
Africans, and Afro-Americans. Long Beach, Cal.: California
State College at Long Beach, 1969.

0190. Black Bibliography: A Selected List of Sources. Little Rock,
Ark.: Arkansas Library Commission, 1970.

0191. Black Bibliography: A Selected Listing from the Law Library.
Salt Lake City, Utah: University of Utah Libraries, n.d.

0192. Black Bibliography for White Students. Nashville, Tenn.: Fisk
University, Amistad Center and Race Relations Department, 1970.

0193. Black Bibliophiles - Preserves of Black History. Washington, D.C.: Howard University, Moorland-Spingarn Research Center, 1982.

0194. "The Black Church in the U.S.: A Resource Guide." Renewals: A Bibliographic Newsletter of the Boston Theological Institute Libraries. 2:4 (Feb. 1979), 1-6.

0195. Black Contributions in the Development of America. Columbus, Ohio: Ohio State Library, 1970.

0196. Black Family and the Black Woman: A Bibliography. Bloomington, Indiana: Indiana University, 1972.

0197. Black Heritage. Jamaica, N.Y.: Queensborough Public Library, 1970.

0198. Black Heritage Resource Guide: A Bibliography of the Negro in Contemporary America. New York: National Council of the Churches of Christ in the U.S.A., Department of Educational Development, 1970.

0199. Black Heritage: The American Experience; A Selected Annotated Bibliography. ERIC Document No. 072-824. Washington, D.C.: Bureau of Naval Personnel, 1970.

0200. Black History. San Francisco, Cal.: San Francisco Unified School District, 1970.

0201. Black History. Westerville, Ohio: Otterbein College, Centennial Library, 1980.

0202. Black History and Other Materials in the Glen Rock Library. Glen Rock, N.J.: Glen Rock Public Library, 1970.

0203. Black History Bibliography. Toledo, Ohio: Toledo Board of Education, Afro-American Resource Center, 1970.

0204. Black History Viewpoints: A Selected Bibliographical Guide to Resources for Afro-American and African History. Westport, Conn.: Negro Universities Press, 1969.

0205. Black in America: Bibliographical Essay. New York: Doubleday, 1971.

0206. Black Index: A Bibliographical Index of Major Studies, Articles and Information Dealing with Black Media Marketing. Arlington, Va.: Sheridan Broadcasting Network, 1980.

0207. Black List. The Concise Reference Guide to Publications and Broadcasting Media of Black America, Africa and the Caribbean. New York: Panther House, 1970.

0208. Black Man in Africa and America. Upper Montclair, N.J.:
       Montclair State College Library, Reference Department, 1970.

0209. Black Man in America: A Selected List of Books. Los Angeles,
       Cal.: Los Angeles Public Library, Young Adult Services, 1969.

0210. Black Man's Past in America: A Selected Reading List.
       Baltimore, Md.: Enoch Pratt Free Library, 1968.

0211. "Black Newspapers Archives." American Libraries 8 (April
       1972), 172.

0212. Black on Black and Other Suggested Reading for Negro History
       Week 1970. Jamaica, N.Y.: Queensborough Public Library, n.d.

0213. Black Perspectives: A Bibliography. New York: Community College
       Press, 1971.

0214. Black Studies. Selected Catalog of National Archives and
       Records Service Microfilm Publications. Washington, D.C.:
       National Archives and Records Service, 1973.

0215. Black Studies: A Selective List of Resources for Teachers. St.
       Louis, Mo.: St. Louis Public Library, 1969.

0216. Black Studies Bibliography. Eugene, Ore.: Lane Community
       College, Learning Resource Center, 1969.

0217. "Black Studies Collection." Australian Library Journal 26
       (Apr. 15, 1977), 92.

0218. Black Studies in the U.S.: A Selected Guide to Research
       Materials in the University of California at Santa Barbara
       Library. Santa Barbara. Cal.: University of California at
       Santa Barbara Library, Reference Department, 1970.

0219. Black Studies: Selected Catalog of National Archives and
       Records Services Microfilm Publication. Washington, D.C.:
       National Archives and Records Services, 1973.

0220. Blackledge, Jacqueline. "The Afro-American in Florida History:
       A Compilation of Materials in Libraries in the Nashville area."
       In Bibliography of Sources by and about Blacks Compiled by
       Interns in the Internship in Black Studies Librarianship
       Program. Nashville, Tenn.: Fisk University Library, 1974, 2-25.

0221. Blackwell, Jean. The Negro in the American Scene: A Selective
       Bibliography. New York: City-Wide Citizens Committee on Harlem,
       1968.

0222. Blaustein, Albert P. Civil Rights and the American Negro; a
       Documentary History. New York: Trident Press, 1968.

0223. Blazek, Ron, et al. The Black Experience: A Bibliography of Bibliographies, 1970-1975. Chicago: American Library Association, Reference and Adult Services Division , 1978.

0224. Blinn, Eleanor. Bibliographies of Current Acquisitions for Black Studies Programs, 1968-1969. San Francisco, Cal.: City College of San Francisco Library, 1970.

0225. Blum, Zahava D., and Peter H. Rossi. Social Class and Poverty: A Selected and Annotated Bibliography. Boston, Mass.: Americam Academy of Arts and Sciences, 1976.

0226. Blum, Zahava D., and Peter H. Rossi. Social Class Research and Images of the Poor: A Bibliographic Review. Baltimore, Md.: Johns Hopkins, Eric Document No. Ed 020-294, 1968.

0227. Blumer, Herbert. " Research on Racial Relations: United States of America." International Social Science Bulletin 10 (1967), 403-47.

0228. Blumfeld, Hans. The Trend to Metropolis: Bibliography. Monticello, Illinois: Council of Planning Librarians Exchange Bibliographies No. 41, 1968.

0229. Bohrn, Harold. Gunnar Myrdal: A Bibliography, 1919-1976. Stockholm, Sweden: Acta Bibliothecae Regiae Stockholmiensis, 1976.

0230. Bolan, Lewis. The Role of Urban Planning in the Residential Integration of Middle Class Negroes and Whites. Exchange Bibliography No. 41. Monticello, Ill.: Council of Planning Librarians, 1968.

0231. Boles, Nancy G. "Notes on Maryland Historical Society Manuscript Collections: Black History Collections." Maryland Historical Magazine 66:1 (Spring 1971), 72-8.

0232. Bolner, James. Racial Imbalance in Public Schools: A Basic Annotated Bibliography. Baton Rouge, La.: Louisiana State University and Agricultural and Mechanical College, 1968.

0233. Boner, Marian D. Poverty and Housing: A Selected Bibliography. Exchange Bibliography No. 128. Monticello, Illinois, Council of Planning Librarians, 1970.

0234. Bontemps, Arna. American Missionary Association Archives in Fisk University Library. Nashville, Tenn.: Fisk University Library, 1947.

0235. Bontemps, Arna. "Special Collections of Negroana." Library Quarterly 14 (July 1944), 187-206.

0236. Booher, D.E. Poverty in an Urban Society. A Bibliography.

Exchange Bibliography No. 246. Monticello, Illinois: Council
of Planning Librarians, No. 246, 1971.

0237. Booker T. Washington. A Register of His Papers in the Library
of Congress. Washington, D. C.: Library of Congress,
Manuscript Division, Reference Department, 1958.

0238. "Books About The Negro." Bulletin of The New York Public
Library: Branch Library Book News 2:9 (Dec. 1925), 131-6.

0239. Books about the Negro People. Spokane, Wash.: Spokane Public
Library, 1968.

0240. "Books and Pamphlets on Negroes and Race Relations." Youth
Leaders Digest 7 (Jan. 1945), 139-43.

0241. Books and the New Era: The Negro. Columbus, Ohio: Methodist
Book Concern 1913.

0242. Books By and About Negroes. Columbia, S.C.: South Carolina
Department of Education, 1969.

0243. Books By and About Negroes, A Special Paperback Collection.
Washington, D.C.: District of Columbia Public Library, 1969.

0244. "Books By and About Negroes, 1943-1944." A Monthly Summary of
Events and Trends in Race Relations 3 (Aug.- Sept. 1945), 64-5.

0245. "Books By and About the American Negro." Library Journal 95
(Jan. 15, 1970), 38.

0246. Books By and About the American Negro: A Selected List for
Young Adults. New York: The New York Public Library, Countee
Cullen Branch, North Manhattan Project, 1966.

0247. Books By and About the Negro: A Selected Bibliography.
Raleigh, N.C.: North Carolina Department of Instruction, 1944.

0248. Books for Multi-Ethnic Studies. Jericho, N.Y.: Nassau County,
N.Y., Board of Cooperative Educational Services, Research and
Development Division, 1970.

0249. "Books, Magazine Articles, Pamphlets, Reports: Covers Housing,
Education, Civil Rights, Etc." Race Relations Law Reporter 5
(Winter 1960), 1287-93.

0250. Books on Africa and the Negro at the 135th Street Branch. New
York: New York Public Library, 1921.

0251. "Books on Minority Groups: Afro-Americans." Catholic Library
World 41:5 (Jan. 1970), 319-21.

0252. Books Transcend Barriers: A Bibliography of Books about Negroes for Elementary School Children. Seattle, Wash.: Seattle Public Schools, 1967.

0253. Boone, Dorothy Deloris. " A Historical Review and a Bibliography of Selected Negro Magazines, 1910-1919." Ed.D. thesis. University of Michigan, 1970.

0254. Booth, Robert S., et al. Culturally Disadvantaged: A Bibliography and Key Word Out-of-Context (KWOC) index. Detroit, Mich.: Wayne State University Press, 1967.

0255. Boubel, Margaret, et al. From Africa to America: A List of Materials in the Chabot College Library Relating to the History of Black People in America. Hayward, Cal.: Chabot College Library, 1969.

0256. Bouknight, L. Marie. Records of the Assistant Commissioner for the State of Mississippi Bureau of Refugees, Freedmen, and Abandoned Lands, 1865-1869. National Archives Microfilm Publications Pamphlet Describing M826. Washington, D.C.: National Archives and Records Service, General Services Administration, 1973.

0257. Boyce, Byrl N., and Sidney Turoff. Minority Groups and Housing: A Bibliography, 1950-1970. Morristown, N.J.: General Learning Press, 1972.

0258. Boyd, Sandra H. Blacks and Religion in America: An Annotated Bibliography of Bibliographies. Cambridge, Mass.: Episcopal Divinity School/Weston School of Theology, 1980.

0259. Brachet, Viviane, et al. Social Stratification and Poverty: A Selected and Annotated Bibliography. Madison, Wis.: University of Wisconsin, Institute for Research on Poverty, 1973.

0260. Bradley, Gladyce Helene. Selected Bibliography on Desegregation and Integration in the Public Schools of the United States. Baltimore, Md.: Morgan State College, 1955.

0261. Braun, Mary, and R. Lawrence Martin. The Negro in American Life: Selected Bibliography of Materials Available in the Ferris State College Library. Big Rapids, Mich.: Ferris State College Library, 1968.

0262. Brawley, Benjamin. Early Negro American: Selections with Bibliographical and Critical Introduction. Chapel Hill: University of North Carolina Press, 1935.

0263. Breyfoyle, Donna and M. Dworaczek. Blacks in Ontario: A Selected Bibliography, 1965-19767. Bibliographic Series No. 8. Ottawa, Ont.: Ontario Ministry of Labour, 1977.

0264. Brickman, W.W. "Light on the Segregation Issue". <u>School and Society</u> 83, (Apr. 14, 1956), 135-6.

0265. Bridges, Hal. <u>Civil War and Reconstruction</u>. Publication No. 5. Washington, D.C.: American Historical Association, Service Center for Teachers of History, 1957.

0266. Brignano, R.C. <u>Black Americans in Autobiography: An Annotated Bibliography of Autobiographies and Autobiographical Books Written since the Civil War.</u> Durham, North Carolina: Duke University Press, 1974.

0267. Brimmer, Andrew F., and Harriett Harper. "Economist's Perception of Minority Problems: A View of Emerging Literature." <u>Journal of Economic Literature</u> 8:3 (Sept. 1970), 783-806.

0268. Briscoe, Dorothy L., et al. <u>A Bibliography of Research on the Negro in Higher Education, 1932-1969.</u> Normal, Ala.: Alabama A & M University, Joseph F. Drake Library, 1970.

0269. Broadhead, Clare A. <u>The Negro Freedom Movement, Past and Present: An Annotated Bibliography</u>. Detroit, Mich.: Wayne County Intermediate School District, Desegregation Advisory Project, 1967.

0270. Brooks, Alexander D., et al. <u>Civil Rights and Liberties in the U.S.: An Annotated Bibliography, With a Selected List of Fiction and the Audio-Visual Materials</u>. New York: Civil Liberties Educational Foundation, 1962.

0271. Brouner, Terre, and Mimi Grindon. <u>Discrimination Today in the U.S.A. Tools of Research: Directory of Human Relations Agencies and Bibliography on Human Rights.</u> Social Action Series 1, No. 8. Purchase, N.Y.: Manhattanville College of the Sacred Heart, Social Action Secretariat, 1961.

0272. Brousseau, Bill, and Carol Klein. <u>Affirmative Action, Equal Employment Opportunity in the Criminal Justice System: A Selected Bibliography.</u> Washington, D.C.: National Institute of Justice, 1980.

0273. Brown, Barbara, et al. <u>The Contemporary Black Woman in Africa and America: A Selected Bibliography of Books and Periodical Articles Published from 1960-1975.</u> Washington, D.C.: Howard University Library, 1975.

0274. Brown, Carol. <u>Afro-American History</u>. Focus: Black American Bibliography Series. Bloomington, Ind.: Indiana University Libraries, 1969.

0275. Brown, H.D. "Brief Survey of the Holdings of Michigan Institutions and Activities in the Field of Negro Life and

History." <u>Negro History Bulletin</u> 26 (October 1962) 5-7.

0276.   Brown, Myland. R.   <u>Bibliography: History of the Negro</u>.
        Orangeburg, S.C.: South Carolina State College, Miller F.
        Whittaker Library, 1962.

0277.   Brown, William Henry. <u>Check List of Negro Newspapers in the</u>
        <u>United States (1827-1946)</u>. Jefferson City Missouri: School of
        Journalism, Lincoln University, 1966.

0278.   Browne, Robert S. <u>Black Economic Development: A Bibliography</u>.
        New York: Afram Associates, 1970.

0279.   Brunner, A.G., and Thomas A. Klein. <u>Minority Enterprise and</u>
        <u>Marketing: An Annotated Bibliography</u>. Monticello, Illinois:
        Council of Planning Librarians, Exchange Bibliography No. 185,
        1971.

0280.   Bryl, Susan, and Erwin K. Welsh.   <u>Black Periodicals and</u>
        <u>Newspapers: A Union List of Holdings in the Libraries of the</u>
        <u>University of Wisconsin and Library of the State Historical</u>
        <u>Society of Wisconsin.</u> Madison, Wis.: University of Wisconsin,
        Memorial Library, 1975.

0281.   Bullock, Julia Amanda. <u>The Role of the Negro in Eighteenth</u>
        <u>Century America: A Bibliography</u>. Boston, Mass.: Simmons
        College School of Library Science, 1942.

0282.   Bullock, Penelope L. <u>The Negro Periodical Press in the United</u>
        <u>States, 1838-1909.</u> Baton Rouge: Louisiana State University
        Press, 1981.

0283.   Burg, N.C. <u>Rural Poverty and Rural Housing: A Bibliography</u>.
        Monticello, Illinois: Council of Planning Librarians Exchange
        Bibliographies, No. 247, 1971.

0284.   Burstein, Rose Ann. <u>Selected List of Black Studies Books</u>
        <u>Currently in the Sarah Lawrence College Library.</u> Bronxville,
        N.Y.: Sarah Lawrence College Library, 1970.

0285.   Bush, Robert D. and Blake Touchstone. "A Survey of Manuscript
        Holdings in the Historic New Orleans Collection." <u>Louisiana</u>
        <u>History</u> 16:1 (1975), 89-96.

0286.   Butterfield, Mary. <u>Civil Rights in the '60s: From Sit-in to</u>
        <u>Black Power.</u> Ypsilanti, Mich.: Eastern Michigan University
        Library, 1980.

0287.   Cabiness, Togo. <u>Books on Negro Life and History</u>. Morristown,
        Tenn.: Morristown College, Carnegie Library, 1968.

0288.   California State College, Long Beach. <u>Library Black</u>
        <u>Bibliography: A Selected List of Books on Africa, Africans and</u>

Afro-Americans, 1969.

0289. Caliver, Ambrose. Sources of Instructional Materials on Negroes. Washington, D.C.: Federal Security Agency, Office of Education, 1944.

0290. Caliver, Ambrose, and Ethyl Graham Greene. Good References on the Life and Education of Negroes. Bibliography no. 68. Washington, D.C.: Office of Education, 1940.

0291. Caliver, Ambrose and Ethyl Graham Greene. Education and Negroes: A Selected Bibliography, 1931-1935. Washington, D.C.: Government Printing Office, 1937.

0292. Calkins, David L. "Nineteenth Century Black History [of Cincinnati]: a Bibliography." Cincinnati Historical Society Bulletin 28:4 (1970), 336-43.

0293. Calloway, Ina Elizabeth. Annotated Bibliograhy of Books in the Trevor Arnett Library Negro Collection Relating to the Civil War. M.S. in L.S. thesis, Atlanta University, 1963.

0294. Cameron, Colin. Attitudes of the Poor and Attitudes Toward the Poor: An Annotated Bibliography. Madison, Wis.: University of Wisconsin, 1973.

0295. Cameron, Colin. Discrimination in Testing Bibliography. Madison, Wis.: University of Wisconsin, Institute for Research on Poverty, 1973.

0296. Cameron, Colin, and Judith Blackstone. Minorities in the Armed Forces: A Selected, Occasionally Annotated Bibliography. Madison, Wis.: University of Wisconsin, Institute for Research on Poverty, 1970.

0297. Cameron, Colin, and Anila Bhatt Menon. Hard Core Unemployment: A Selected, Annotated Bibliography. ERIC Doc. no. ED 038-323. Madison, Wis.: University of Wisconsin, Institute for Research on Poverty, 1969.

0298. Cameron, Colin, et al. Poverty-Related Topics Found in Dissertations. Madison, Wis.: University of Wisconsin, Institute for Research on Poverty, 1976.

0299. Campbell, Agnes. Negro Housing in Towns and Cities, 1927-37. Bull. No. 46. New York: Russell Sage Foundation Library, 1937.

0300. Campbell, D.W. "Black Geneology and the Public Library: A Bibliography." Public Libraries 19 (Spring 1980), 22-4.

0301. Campbell, M.V., and J.A. Hulbert. A Bibliography of Graduate Master's Theses Written at Virginia State College, 1937-49. Petersburg, Va.: Virginia State College, Johnson Memorial

Library, 1949.

0302.   Canadian Black Studies Bibliography.   London, Ontario: n.p.,
        1971.

0303.   Capouya, E.   "Documents of the Struggle for Public Decency."
        Saturday Review 47 (July 25, 1964), 13.

0304.   Cardinale, Susan. Special Issues of Serials About Women.
        Monticello, Illinois: Council of Planning Librarians, Exchange
        Bibliography No. 995, 1976.

0305.   Carey, Elizabeth L., and Corienne K. Robinson.   A Selected List
        of References on Housing for Negroes.   Washington, D.C.:
        National Housing Agency, Federal Public Housing Authority
        Library, 1945.

0306.   Carley, Judith.   Housing: An Element of State Planning.
        Monticello, Illinois: Council of Planning Librarians, Exchange
        Bibliography No. 214, 1966.

0307.   Carlos, Luis.   Black Bibliography 1970.   Monterey, Cal.:
        Monterey Peninsula College Library, 1970.

0308.   Carlson, Alvar W.   "A Bibliography of the Geograhical
        Literature of the American Negro, 1920-1971."   The Virginia
        Geographer VII, (Spring-Summer 1972), 12-18.

0309.   Carlson, K. "Equalizing Educational Opportunities."   Review of
        Educational Research 42 (Fall 1972), 453-75.

0310.   Carmela, Margaret.   The American Negro in Periodicals, 1964-70.
        Convent Station, N.J.: College of St. Elizabeth, Mahoney
        Library, 1970.

0311.   Carmela, Margaret.   The Life and History of Black America.
        Convent Station N.J.: College of St. Elizabeth, Mahoney
        Library, 1970.

0312.   Carmela, Margaret.   Negro Authors. Convent Station, N.J.:
        College of St. Elizabeth, Mahoney Library, 1970.

0313.   Carney, M.   "Doctoral Dissertations and Projects Related to the
        Education of Negroes."   Advanced School Digest 7 (February
        1942). 43-4.

0314.   Carter, Pervis M.   "The Negro in Periodical Literature, 1970-
        1972." Journal of Negro History 63:1 (Jan. 1978), 87-92; 63:2
        (Apr. 1978), 161-89; 63:3 (July. 1978), 262-306.

0315.   Caselli, Ron, et al.   The Minority Experience; A Basic
        Bibliography of American Ethnic Studies.   Santa Rosa, Cal.:
        Sonoma County Superintendent of Schools, 1970.

0316. Cashman, Marc, and Barry Klein. Bibliography of American Ethnology. Eye, N.Y.: Todd Publications, 1976.

0317. Catalog of Books on the War of Rebellion and Slavery, in the Library of the State Historical Society of Wisconsin. Madison, Wis.: State Historical Society of Wisconsin, 1887.

0318. Catalog of Publications, 1964. Washington, D.C.: U.S. Commissions on Civil Rights, 1964.

0319. Catalog of the Negro Collections in the Florida Agricultural and Mechanical University Library and the Florida State University Library. Tallahassee, Fla.: Friends of the F.S.U. Library, 1969.

0320. Catalog of the Old Slave Mart Museum and Library. Charleston, S.C. Boston, Mass.: G.K. Hall, 1978.

0321. Catalogue, Heartman Negro Collection, Texas Southern University. Houston, Tex.: Texas Southern University, 1957.

0322. Catalogue of the Special Negro and African Collection, Vail Memorial Library, Lincoln University. Lincoln, Pa.: Lincoln University, Vail Memorial Library, 1958.

0323. Chambers, Frederick. Black Higher Education in the United States: A Selected Bibliography on Negro Higher Education and Historical Black Colleges and Universities. Westport, Conn.: Greenwood, 1978.

0324. Chandler, Sue. "A Selected Annotated List of Reference Books Reflecting the Black Experience." In E.J. Josey and Ann Allen Shockley, eds. Handbook of Black Librarianship. Littleton, Col.: Libraries Unlimited, 1977, 134–42.

0325. Changing Patterns: the Negro in America. Boston, Mass.: Boston Public Library, 1967.

0326. Chapman, Abraham. The Negro in America's Literature: A Bibliography of Literature by and about the Negro Americans. Stevens Point, Wisconsin State University: Wisconsin Council of Teachers of English. Special Publication, No. 15, 1966.

0327. Cheatham, Mary L. Afro-Americana. Clarksville, Ark.: College of the Ozarks, Dobson Memorial Library, 1969.

0328. The Chicago Afro-American Union Analytic Catalog: An Index to Materials on the Afro-American in the Principal Libraries of Chicago. Boston, Mass.: G.K. Hall, 1972.

0329. Chobanian, Peter, and Eleanor Colbert. A Bibliography in the Lane Library on Black Studies. Ripon, Wis.: Ripon College, Lane Library, 1970.

0330. Christams, Walter. <u>Negroes in Public Affairs and Government.</u> <u>Vol. 1</u> Yonkers, New York: Educational Heritage, 1966.

0331. Christensen, Carol, and Carol Hansen. <u>Minority Groups in the</u> <u>U.S.: A Bibliography of Books in the Bethel College Library.</u> St. Paul, Minn.: Bethel College, 1970.

0332. Christiansen, Dorothy. <u>Busing: A Center for Urban Education</u> <u>Bibliography.</u> ERIC Doc. no. ED 061-378. New York: Center for Urban Education, 1971.

0333. Christiansen, Dorothy. "Desegregation, Integration: References in the Collection of the Library of the Center for Urban Education." <u>The Center Forum</u> (Dec. 23, 1968), 19-20.

0334. Chung, Inso, and Bruce Smithson. <u>Black Bibliography.</u> Hayward, Cal.: California State College at Hayward Library, 1969.

0335. Clark, A. Zane. <u>Afro- and Mexican-Americana, Books and Other</u> <u>Materials in the Library of the Fresno State College Relating</u> <u>to the History, Culture and Problems of Afro-Americans and</u> <u>Mexican-Americans.</u> Fresno, Cal.: California State College at Fresno Library, 1969.

0336. Clark, Vernon L. <u>A Bibliographic Guide to the Study of Black</u> <u>History.</u> ERIC Document no. 094-880. Chapel Hill, N.C.:University of North Carolina, Frank Porter Graham Center, 1974.

0337. Clarke, John Henrik. <u>Black Heritage: A History of Afro-</u> <u>Americans, A Selected Bibliography.</u> New York: WCBS-TV, 1980.

0338. Clarke, John Henrik. "Dimensions of the Black Experience: Bibliography." In LeRoi Jones, (ed.) <u>African Congress: A</u> <u>Documentary of the First Modern Pan African Congress.</u> New York: Morrow, 1972, 436-45.

0339. Clarke, Tobin. <u>Afro-American Heritage. Ethnic Culture Series</u> <u>No. 6.</u> Stockton, Cal.: Stockton-San Joaquin County Library, 1969.

0340. Clapp, James. <u>The Socially Balanced Community Concept.</u> Monticello, Illinois: Council of Planning Librarians, Exchange Bibliography No. 892, 1975.

0341. Clay, Phillip L. <u>Metropolitan Growth and Change: A</u> <u>Bibliography in Metropolitan Differentiation.</u> Monticello, Illinois: Council of Planning Librarians, Exchange Bibliographies No. 1062, 1970.

0342. Clayton, Mayme A., and Kathleen S. Allen. <u>Index to the Afro-</u> <u>American Rare Book Collection</u> [of the Western States Black Research Center, Los Angeles, California.] Denver, Col.:

Information Resources, 1977.

0343. Cleaves, Mary, and Alma L. Gray. A Bibliography of Negro History and Culture for Young Readers. Miles M. Jackson (ed.) Pittsburgh, Pa.: University of Pittsburgh Press, 1968.

0344. Cohen, Iva. Civil Liberties and Civil Rights in the U.S. Today: A Selected Bibliography. New York: American Jewish Committee, 1956.

0345. Cohen, Iva. Intergroup Relations: A Selected Bibliography. New York: American Jewish Committee, 1954.

0346. Cohen, Iva and Diana Bernstein. Civil Rights Today: A Selected Bibliography. New York: American Jewish Committee, 1948.

0347. Cole, Donald B. A Bibliography for the History of Black Americans. Exeter, N.H.: Author, 1960.

0348. Cole, Johnetta B. "Black Woman in America: An Annotated Bibliography." Black Scholar 3:4 (Dec. 1971), 41-53.

0349. Coleman, Maude B. Bibliography and Information on Interracial Programs in the U.S. Harrisburg, Pa.: Pennsylvania Department of Welfare, Bureau of Community Work, 1947.

0350. Collection of Afro-American Literature: Acquisitions List. Boston Mass.: Suffolk University, Museum of Afro-American History, 1979.

0351. Collins, Edward D. Methods of Handling Complaints Against the Source. Chicago, Illinois: CPL Bibliography No. 19, 1979.

0352. Collins, Robert O. and Peter Duignan. Americans in Africa: A Preliminary Guide to American Missionary Archives and Library Manuscript Collections on Africa. Hoover Institution Bibliographical Series: XII. Stanford California: Stanford University, The Hoover Institution on War, Revolution and Peace, 1963.

0353. Collura, Maureen. Afro-American Bibliography. Buffalo, N.Y.: SUNY College at Buffalo, Edward H. Butler, 1971.

0354. Company Experience with the Employment of Negroes. Selected References. Princeton, N.J.: Princeton University, Department of Economics and Social Institutions, Industrial Relations Section No. 60, 1954.

0355. Conover, Helen F. Interracial Relations in the U.S.: A Selected List of References. Washington, D.C.: Library of Congress, General Reference and Bibliography Division, 1945.

0356. Conover, Helen F. Race Relations: Selected References for the

Study of the Integration of Minorities in American Labor. Washington, D.C.: Library of Congress, General Reference and Bibliography Division, 1944.

0357. Contant, Florence. Community Development Corporations: An Annotated Bibliography. Exchange Bibliography No. 530. Monticello, Ill.: Council of Planning Librarians, 1974, 40 pp.

0358. The Contemporary Negro. Harrisburg, Pa.: Pennsylvania State Library, General Library Bureau, 1970.

0359. Cook, Katherine M. and Florence E. Reynolds. The Education of Native and Minority Groups: A Bibliography, 1923-1932. Washington, D.C.: U.S. Department of the Interior, Office of Education, 1933.

0360. Cooke, A.L.   Black Studies. Jackson, Tenn.: Lane College, J.K. Daniels Library, 1965.

0361. Cooke, A.L. Negro Collection. Jackson, Tenn.: Lane College, J.K. Daniels Library, 1965.

0362. Cordasco, Francesco, et al. The Equality of Educational Opportunity: A Bibliography of Selected References. Totowa, N.J.: Littlefield, Adams, 1973.

0363. Cornwell, Sophy and Deborah Williams. Vail Memorial Library: Guide to Reference Books in the Special Negro and African Collections. Lincoln, Pa.: Lincoln University, 1972.

0364. Crayton, James E. "A Case for Afro-American Collections." California Librarian 37:1 (1976), 18-21.

0365. Crisis, Black and White: Negro History, Culture and Protest. Los Angeles, Cal.: Los Angeles Public Library, Community Discussion Program, 1967.

0366. Crisis for Black and White. Pittsburgh, Pa.: Carnegie Library, 1968, 12.

0367. Cromwell, John W. "The American Negro Bibliography of the Year." Papers of the American Negro Academy . . . read at the 19th Annual Meeting of the American Negro Academy . . . Washington, D.C., Dec. 28 and 29, 1915, 73-8.

0368. Crouch, Barry A. "Hidden Sources of Black History: the Texas Freedmen's Bureau as a Case Study." Southwest History Quarterly 83 (Jan. 1980), 211-26.

0369. Crouchett, Lawrence. Bibliography (Topical) on Afro-American History, Culture and Education. Pleasant Hill, Cal.: Diablo Valley College, 1980.

0370. Crouchett, Lawrence. <u>The Negro in U.S. History: A Bibliography of Books, Pamphlets, Periodicals and Articles</u>. Pleasant Hill, Cal.: Diablo Valley College, 1965.

0371. Crumb, Laurence N. <u>Mind and Soul: A Checklist of Sources for Black Studies Available in the Library-Learning Center, University of Wisconsin-Parkside.</u> Kenosha, Wis.: University of Wisconsin-Parkside, 1976.

0372. <u>The Cultural and Historical Contributions of American Minorities: A Bibliography.</u> Buffalo, N.Y.: Buffalo Public Schools, 1967.

0373. <u>Current Books about Negro Life in America</u>. Trenton, N.J.: Free Public Library, Children's Department, 1968.

0374. <u>Current Books about Negroes in America.</u> Trenton, N.J.: Free Public Library, Area Reference Library, Children's Department, 1969.

0375. Curry, Prudence L. <u>Books by and about the Negro available in the George Washington Carver Branch: Supplemented By a List of Books on the Subject at the Main Library</u>. San Antonio, Tex.: San Antonio Public Library, 1941.

0376. Cushman, William Mitchell. <u>Equal Opportunity and the Urban Black: An Analysis of Public Policy and Its Implications for Urban Planning (Abstract and Bibliography)</u>. Monticello, Illinois: Council of Planning Librarians Exchange Bibliography No. 634, 1974.

0377. Dalquist, Janet A. <u>Suomi College Library Black Studies Bibliography.</u> Hancock, Mich.: Suomi College Library.

0378. Dalva, Harry M. et al. <u>Words Like Freedom, A Multi-Cultural Bibliography.</u> Burlingame, Cal.: California Association of School Librarians, Human Relations Committee, 1975.

0379. Daniel, Elenor Murphy, et al. <u>Index to Black Newspapers</u>. Wooster, Ohio: Micro Photography Division, Bell and Howell, 1978.

0380. Daniel, Walter C. <u>Black Journals of the United States</u>. Westport, Conn.: Greenwood, 1982.

0381. Danner, Vinnie M. <u>A Bibliography of Published and Unpublished Materials on the Health Status of Blacks, Minorities and the Poor</u>. Nashville, Tenn.: Center for Health Care Research of Meharry Medical College, 1972.

0382. Dannett, Sylvia G.L. <u>Profiles of Negro Womanhood</u>. New York: M.W. Lads, 1964.

0383. Darden, Joe T. The Ghetto. Monticello, Illinois: Council of Planning Librarians, Exchange Bibliography No. 1310, 1977.

0384. Darden, Joe T. Race, Housing and Residential Segregation: A Selected Bibliography of Basic References. Chicaco: Council of Planning Librarians, Bibliography No. 96, November 1982.

0385. Davis, John P. American Negro Reference Book. Englewood Cliffs, N.J.: Prentice-Hall, 1966.

0386. Davis, Lenwood G. "Bibliographic Material [Housing]." Negro History Bulletin 39 (Apr. 1976), 1-4.

0387. Davis, Lenwood G. The Black Aged in the U.S.: An Annotated Bibliography. Westport, Conn.: Greenwood, 1980.

0388. Davis, Lenwood G. Black Businesses, Employment, Economics and Finance in Urban America: A Selective Bibliography. Exchange Bibliography No. 629. Monticello, Ill.: Council of Planning Librarians, 1974.

0389. Davis, Lenwood G. Black Capitalism in Urban America. Exchange Bibliography No. 630. Monticello, Ill.: Council of Planning Librarians, 1974.

0390. Davis, Lenwood G. The Black Family in the U.S. Exchange Bibliography No. 808-9. Monticello, Ill.: Council of Planning Librarians, 1975.

0391. Davis, Lenwood G. The Black Family in the U.S.: A Selected Bibliography of Annotated Books, Articles and Dissertations on Black Families in America. Westport, Conn.: Greenwood, 1978.

0392. Davis, Lenwood G. The Black Family in Urban Areas of the U.S.: A Bibliography of Published Works. Exchange Bibliography No. 471. Monticello, Ill.: Council of Planning Librarians, 1973.

0393. Davis, Lenwood G. "The Black Woman in America: Autobiographical and Biographical Material." Northwest Journal of African and Black American Studies 2 (Winter 1974), 27-9.

0394. Davis, Lenwood G. The Black Woman in American Society: A Selected Annotated Bibliography. Boston, Mass.: G.K. Hall, 1975.

0395. Davis, Lenwood G. Black Women in the Cities, 1872-1972: A Bibliography of Published Works on the Life and Achievements of Black Women in the Cities in the U.S. Exchange Bibliography No. 336 Monticello, Ill.: Council of Planning Librarians, 1972.

0396. Davis, Lenwood G. Blacks in Politics: An Exploratory Bibliography. Exchange Bibliography No. 926. Monticello,

Ill.: Council of Planning Librarians, 1975.

0397. Davis, Lenwood G. Blacks in Public Administration: A Preliminary Survey. Exchange Bibliography No. 973. Monticello, Ill.: Council of Planning Librarians, 1976.

0398. Davis, Lenwood G. Blacks in the American West: A Working Bibliography. Exchange Bibliography No. 582. Monticello, Ill.: Council of Planning Librarians, 1974.

0399. Davis, Lenwood G. Blacks in the Cities, 1900-1972: A Bibliography. Exchange Bibliography No. 329. Monticello, Ill.: Council of Planning Librarians, 1972.

0400. Davis, Lenwood G. Blacks in the Pacific Northwest, 1788-1972: A Bibliography of Published Works and of Unpublished Source Materials on the Life and Contributions of Black People in the Pacific Northwest. Exchange Bibliography No. 335. Monticello, Il.: Council of Planning Librarians, 1972.

0401. Davis, Lenwood G. Blacks in the State of Ohio, 1800-1976: A Preliminary Survey. Exchange Bibliography No. 1208-1209. Monticello, Ill.: Council of Planning Librarians, 1977.

0402. Davis, Lenwood G. Blacks in the State of Oregon, 1788-1971: A Bibliography of Published Works and of Unpublished Source Materials on the Life and Achievements of Black People in the Beaver State. Exchange Bibliography No. 229. Monticello, Ill.: Council of Planning Librarians, 1971.

0403. Davis, Lenwood G. Blacks in the State of Utah: A Working Bibliography. Exchange Bibliography No. 661. Monticello, Ill.: Council of Planning Librarians, 1974.

0404. Davis, Lenwood G. Crime in the Black Community: An Exploratory Bibliography. Exchange Bibliography No. 852. Monticello, Ill.: Council of Planning Librarians, 1975.

0405. Davis, Lenwood G. Deviant Behavior in the Black Community: An Exploratory Survey. Exchange Bibliography No. 1057. Monticello, Ill.: Council of Planning Librarians, 1976.

0406. Davis, Lenwood G. Ecology of Blacks in the Inner City: An Exploratory Bibliography. Exchange Bibliography No. 785-786. Monticello, Ill.: Council of Planning Librarians, 1974.

0407. Davis, Lenwood G. A History of Black Religion in Northern Areas: A Preliminary Survey. Exchange Bibliography No. 734, Monticello, Ill.: Council of Planning Librarians, 1975.

0408. Davis, Lenwood G. A History of Black Religion in Southern Areas: a Preliminary Survey. Exchange Bibliography No. 733. Monticello, Ill.: Council of Planning Librarians, 1975.

0409. Davis, Lenwood G. A History of Black Self-Help Organizations and Institutions in the U.S., 1776-1976: A Working Bibliography. Exchange Bibliography No. 1207. Monticello, Ill.: Council of Planning Librarians, 1977.

0410. Davis, Lenwood G. A History of Blacks in Higher Education, 1875-1975: A Working Bibliography. Exchange Bibliography No. 720. Monticello, Ill.: Council of Planning Librarians, 1975.

0411. Davis, Lenwood G. A History of Journalism in the Black Community: A Preliminary Survey. Exchange Bibliography No. 862. Monticello, Ill.: Council of Planning Librarians, 1975.

0412. Davis, Lenwood G. A History of Public Health, Health Problems, Facilities and Services in the Black Community: A Working Bibliography. Exchange Bibliography No. 844. Monticello, Ill.: Council of Planning Librarians, 1975.

0413. Davis, Lenwood G. A History of Selected Diseases in the Black Community: A Working Bibliography. Exchange Bibliography No. 1059. Monticello, Ill.: Council of Planning Librarians, 1976.

0414. Davis, Lenwood G. A History of Tuberculosis in the Black Community: A Working Bibliography. Exchange Bibliography No. 859. Monticello, Ill.: Council of Planning Librarians, 1975.

0415. Davis, Lenwood G. Housing in the Black Community: A Selected Bibliography of Published Works on Housing Laws, Problems, Planning and Covenants in the Black Community. Exchange Bibliography No. 925, Monticello, Ill.: Council of Planning Librarians, 1975.

0416. Davis, Lenwood G. Index to Council of Planning Librarians Bibliographies on Blacks, Related to Blacks, on Africa and Related to Africa: Numbers 869-1310. Exchange Bibliography No. 1374. Monticello, Ill.: Council of Planning Librarians, 1977.

0417. Davis, Lenwood G. The Mental Health of the Black Community: An Exploratory Bibliography. Exchange Bibliography No. 958. Monticello, Ill.: Council of Planning Librarians, 1975.

0418. Davis, Lenwood G. Pan-Africanism: A Selected Bibliography. Portland, Ore., 1972.

0419. Davis, Lenwood G. "Pan-Africanism: An Extensive Bibliography." Geneva-Africa [Geneva, Switzerland] 12:1 (Part 2) (Fall 1973), 103-20.

0420. Davis, Lenwood G. A Paul Robeson Research Guide: A Selected Annotated Bibliography. Westport, Conn.: Greenwood, 1982.

0421. Davis, Lenwood G. Poverty and the Black Community: A Preliminary Survey. Exchange Bibliography No. 965.

Monticello, Ill.: Council of Planning Librarians, 1975.

0422. Davis, Lenwood G. Psychology and the Black Community. Exchange Bibliography No. 1060. Monticello, Ill.: Council of Planning Librarians, 1976.

0423. Davis, Lenwood G. Sickle Cell Anemia: A Preliminary Survey. Exchange Bibliography No. 763. Monticello, Ill.: Council of Planning Librarians, 1975.

0424. Davis, Lenwood G. A Working Bibliography on Published Materials on Black studies Programs in the U.S. Exchange Bibliography No. 1213. Monticello, Ill.: Council of Planning Librarians, 1977.

0425. Davis, Lenwood G. and Belinda S. Daniels. Black Athletes in the U.S.: A Bibliography of Books, Articles, Autobiographies and Biographies on Professional Black Athletes in the U.S., 1800-1981. Westport, Conn.: Greenwood, 1981.

0426. Davis, Lenwood G. and Janet Sims. Black Artists in the U.S.: An Annotated Bibliography of Books, Articles and Dissertations on Black Artists, 1779-1979. Westport, Conn.: Greenwood, 1980.

0427. Davis, Lenwood G. and Janet Sims. Marcus Garvey: An Annotated Bibliography. Westport, Conn.: Greenwood, 1980.

0428. Davis, Morris E. and Andrew Roland. The Occupational Health of Black Workers: A Bibliography. Public Administration Series No. 492. Monticello, Ill.: Vance Bibliographies, 1980.

0429. Davis, Nathaniel. Afro-American Studies: A Bibliography of Doctoral Dissertations and Master's Theses Completed at the University of California, Los Angeles, from 1942 to 1980. Los Angeles, Cal.: UCLA Center for Afro-American Studies, 1981.

0430. Davis, Susan E. "Collection Development and the Special Subject Repository [The Schomburg Center for Research in Black Culture]." Bookmark 39:2 (Winter 1981), 100-4.

0431. Davison, Ruth A. and April Legler. Government Publications on the Negro in America, 1948-1968. Focus: Black American Bibliography Series, Bloomington, Ind.: Indiana University Libraries, 1969.

0432. Dawson, John A. Shopping Centers: A Bibliography. Chicago: CPL Bibliography No. 89, 1982.

0433. Deahn, Jean. The American Negro: His History, His Education, His Music, His Family Life and Social Condition, In Politics. Littleton, Col.: Arapahoe Community College Library, 1980.

0434. Democracy Unlimited for America's Minorities. California

Federation for Civic Unity Collection. Los Angeles, Cal.: Los
Angeles Public Library, 1944.

0435. Dengel, Ray E., et al. *Hamilton Library Afro-American
Bibliography*. Edinboro, Pa.: Edinboro State College, Hamilton
Library, 1970.

0436. Denham, Bernard J., et al. *Afro-American Collection Shelf
List*. Stanford, Cal.: Stanford University, Meyer Memorial
Library, 1970.

0437. Deodene, Frank A. and William P. French. *Black American
Fiction Since 1952: A Preliminary Checklist.* Chatham, N.J.:
The Chatham Bookseller, 1970.

0438. Deskins, Donald R. "Geographical Literature on the American
Negro, 1949-1968: A Bibliography." *Professional Geographer*.
21:3 (1969), 145-9.

0439. DeVeaux, Diane. *A Guide to Books and Periodicals about the
Nation of Islam in the Mid-Manhattan Library* (NYPL). New
York: New York Public Library, 1974.

0440. DeWitt, Josephine. *The Black Man's Point of View: A List of
References to Material in the Oakland Free Library*. Oakland,
Cal.: Acorn Club of Oakland, the Oakland Free Library, 1930.

0441. Dickinson, Donald C. "Books in the Field: Black Bibliography."
Wilson Library Bulletin 44 (Oct. 1969), 184-7.

0442. *Dictionary Catalog of the Arthur B. Spingarn Collection of
Negro Authors, Howard University Libraries, Washington, D.C.*
Boston, Mass.: G.K. Hall, 1970.

0443. *Dictionary Catalog of the George Foster Peabody Collection of
Negro Literature and History, Collis P. Huntington Memorial
Library, Hamptom Institute.* Westport, Conn.: Greenwood, 1972.

0444. *Dictionary Catalog of the Jesse E. Moorland Collection of Negro
Life and History, Howard University Libraries, Washington, D.C.*
Boston, Mass.: G.K. Hall, 1970.

0445. *Dictionary Catalog of the Negro Collection of the Fisk
University Library*. Boston, Mass.: G.K. Hall, 1974.

0446. *Dictionary Catalog of the Schomburg Collection of Negro
Literature and History, The New York Public Lirary.* Boston,
Mass.: G.K. Hall, 1962.

0447. *Dictionary Catalog of the Vivian G. Harsh Collection of Afro-
American History and Literature, Chicago Public Library.*
Boston, Mass.: G.K. Hall, 1978.

0448. Dillon, Merton L. "The Abolitionists: A Decade of Historiography, 1959-1969." Journal of Southern History 35 (Nov. 1969), 500-22.

0449. Dimit, R. et al. Community Organization: Urban and Rural Planning and Developement. Monticello, Ill.: Council Planning of Librarians, Exchange Bibliography No. 884, 1975.

0450. Dimitroff, Lillian. Annotated Bibliography of Audio-Visual Materials Related to Iner-City Educational Problems. Chicago, Ill.: Chicago State College Library, 1968.

0451. Dinniman, Andrew E. and Farah E. Rivoir. Guide to Materials on Afro-American Studies in the Francis Harvey Green Library. Westchester, Pa.: Westchester State College Library, 1977.

0452. Directory of Data Sources on Racial and Ethnic Minorities. BLS Bulletin 1879. Washington, D.C.: U.S. Department of Labor, Bureau of Labor Statistics, 1975.

0453. District of Columbia, Public Library, Children's Service. The Afro-American in Books for Children Including Books about Africa and the West Indies, Washington, D.C.: Author, 1969.

0454. Discrimination in Civil Rights: A Selected Bibliography. Lansing, Mich.: Michigan State Library, 1964.

0455. Discrimination in Education: A Selected Bibliography. Chicago, Ill.: American Council on Race Relations, 1948.

0456. Discrimination in Employment: A Selected Bibliography. Chicago, Ill.: American Council on Race Relations, 1949.

0457. "Discrimination in Employment in Defense Industries: Selected Sources of Information." Employment Review 3 (June 1941), 309-11.

0458. Discrimination in Housing, A Selected Bibliography. Chicago, Ill.: American Council on Race Relations, 1948.

0459. "Division of Negro Literature and History, 135th St. Branch, The New York Public Library." Dunbar News (July 30, 1930), 11-17.

0460. Dixon, Elizabeth. Afro-American Resources of the El Camino College Library. Via Torrance, Cal.: El Camino College Library, 1969.

0461. Document and Reference Text (Dart): An Index to Minority Group Employment. Ann Arbor: University of Michigan- Wayne State University, 1967.

0462. Dodd, Don and Alma D. Steading. The History of Black Politics in Alabama: A Preliminary Bibliography. Public Administration Series No. 347. Monticello, Ill.: Vance Bibliographies, 1979.

0463. Donahue, Margaret M., et al. A Selected List of Black Materials in the McKeldin Library, University of Maryland. College Park, Md.: University of Maryland, McKeldin Library.

0464. Donald, David. The Nation in Crisis, 1861-1877. New York: Appleton-Century-Crofts, Golden Trees Bibliographies, 1969.

0465. Dooley, John B. and Lynn Macken. Black Studies: A Selected Bibliography. San Mateo, Cal.: College of San Mateo Library, 1969.

0466. Dorton, Eleanor and Lenwood G. Davis. Juvenile Delinquency in the Black Community. Exchange Bibliography No. 804. Monticello, Ill.: Council of Planning Librarians, 1975.

0467. Doyle, Francis R. Redlining Update: A Supplement to Exchange Bibliography No. 1486. Chicago: CPL Bibliography No. 58, 1981.

0468. Drotning, P.T. A Guide to Negro History in America. New York: Doubleday and Company, 1968.

0469. Drowne, Lawrence, et al. Black Experience: A Bibliography of Books on Black Studies in the Academic Libraries of Brooklyn, N.Y. Brooklyn, N.Y.: Academic Libraries of Brooklyn, 1971.

0470. Du Bois, W.E.B. "Bibliography of Negro Artisan and the Industrial Training of Negroes." The Negrro Artisan. Report of a Social Studie Made Under the Direction of Atlanta University: Together with the Proceedings of the Seventh Conference for the Study of Negro Problems. Held at Atlanta University, on May 27th, 1902, v-vii.

0471. Du Bois, W.E.B. "Bibliography of Negro Health and Physique." The Health and Physique of the Negro American. A Report of Social Study Made Under the Direction of Atlanta University: Together with the Proceedings of the Eleventh Conference for the Study of the Negro Problems, Held at Atlanta University, on May the 29th, 1906. Atlanta, Ga.: Atlanta University Press, 1904, 6-13.

0472. Du Bois, W.E.B. "Select Bibliography of Negro Churches." The Negro Church. Report of a Social Studie Made Under the Direction of Atlanta University; Together with the Proceedings of the 8th Conference for the Study of Negro Problems, Held at Atlanta University, May 26th, 1903. Atlanta, Ga.: Atlanta University Press , 1903, vi-viii.

0473. Du Bois, W.E.B. "A Select Bibliography of Negro Crime." Some Notes on Negro Crime Particularly in Georgia. Report of a Social Made Under the Direction of Atlanta University; Together with the Proceedings of the Ninth Conference for the Study of Negro Problems, Held at Atlanta University, May 24, 1904. Atlanta, Ga.: Atlanta University Press, 1904, vi-viii.

0474. Du Bois, W.E.B. "A Select Bibliography of the American Negro for General Readers." The College-Bred Negro. Report of a Social Study Made Under the Direction of Atlanta University; Together of the Proceedings of the Fifth Conference for the Study of the Negro Problems, Held at Atlanta University, May 29-30, 1900. Atlanta, Ga.: Atlanta University Press, 1900, 6-9.

0475. Du Bois, W.E.B. "A Select Bibliography of the American Negro for General Readers." The Negro Common School. Report of a Social Study Made Under the Direction of Atlanta University; Together with the Proceedings of the Sixth Conference for the Study of the Negro Problems, Held at Atlanta University, on May 28th, 1901. Atlanta, Ga.: Atlanta University Press, 1901, 4-13.

0476. Du Bois, W.E.B. A Selected Bibliography of the Negro American. A Compilation Made Under the Direction of Atlanta University; Together with the Proceedings of the Tenth Conference for the Study of the Negro Problems, Held at Atlanta University, on May 30,1905. Atlanta, Ga.: Atlanta University Press, 1905.

0477. Du Bois, W.E.B. "A Select Bibliography of the Negro American Family." The Negro Family. Report of a Social Study Made Principally by the College Classes of 1909 and 1910 of Atlanta University, under the Patronage of the Trustees of the John F. Slater Fund; Together with the Proceedings of the 13th Annual Conference for the Study of the Negro Problem, Held at Atlanta University on Tuesday, May the 26th, 1908.Atlanta, Ga.: Atlanta University Press, 1908, 6-8.

0478. Du Bois, W.E.B. "Selected Bibliography of Economic Co-operation among Negro Americans." Economic Co-operation among Negro Americans. Report of a Social Study Made by Atlanta University, under the patronage of the Carnegie Institution of Washington, D.C., Together with the Proceedings of the 12th Conference for the Study of the Negro Problems, Held at Atlanta University, on Tuesday, May the 28th, 1907. Atlanta, Ga.: Atlanta University Press, 1907, 6-9.

0479. Du Bois, W.E.B. "A Selected Bibliography of Efforts for Social Betterment among Negro Americans." Efforts for Social Betterment among Negro Americans. Report of a Social Study Made by Atlanta University under the Patronage of the Trustees of the John F. Slater Fund; Together with the Proceedings of the 14th annual Conference for the Study of the Negro Problems Held at Atlanta University on Tuesday, May the 24th, 1909. Atlanta, Ga.: Atlanta University Press, 1909, 7-8.

0480. Du Bois, W.E.B. and Guy B. Johnson. Encyclopedia of the Negro:

Preparatory Volume with Reference Lists and Reports. New York:
Phelps-Stokes Fund, 1945.

0481. Duffert, Gorman L. and Dawn McGaghy. A Bibliography of Items
in the Libraries of Cuyahoga Community College on African and
Afro-American Subjects. Cleveland, Ohio: Cuyahoga Community
College, Metropolitan Campus Library, 1968.

0482. Duffy, Lilliam. Bibliography of Black Studies in the Santa Ana
College Library. Santa Ana, Cal.: Santa Ana College, Neally
Library, 1968.

0483. Duker, Abraham G. "Selected Bibliography [on Negro-Jewish
Relations]." Negro-Jewish Relations in the U.S.: papers and
proceedings of a conference convened by the Conference on
Jewish Social Studies, New York City. New York: Citadel Press,
1966.

0484. Dumond, Dwight Lowell. A Bibliography of Antislavery in
America. Ann Arbor, Mich.: University of Michigan Press, 1961.

0485. Duncan, Margaret. Changing the African Image Through History.
Tacoma Park, Md.: Columbia Union College Library, 1962.

0486. Duncan, Margaret. The Negro in American History and Culture.
Tacoma Park, M.: Columbia Union College Library, 1962.

0487. Dunlap, Mollie E. A Partial Bibliography of the Publications
of the Faculty of College of Education and Industrial Arts,
Wilberforce, Ohio. Yellow Springs, Ohio: The Antioch Press,
1949.

0488. Dunlap, Mollie E. "A Selected Annotated List of Books by and
about the Negro." Negro College Quarterly 3 (March 1945), 40-
5; (June 1945), 94-6; (Sept. 1945), 153-8.

0489. Dunmore, Charlotte. Black Children and their Families. San
Francisco, Cal.: R and E Research Associations, 1976.

0490. Dunmore, Charlotte. Poverty, Participation, Protest, Power and
Black Americans: A Selected Bibliography for Use in Social Work
Education. New York: Council on Social Work Education, 1970.

0491. Durden, Robert F. "Primary Sources for the Study of Afro-
American History [at Duke University]." Gnomon, 1970, 39-42.

0492. Dutton, Penny and Aprodicio A. Laquain. A Selected
Bibliography on Rural-Urban Migrants' Slums and Squatters in
Developing Countries. Monticello, Illinois: Council of
Planning Librarians, Exchange Bibliography No. 82, 1971.

0493. Dvorkin, Bettifae E. Blacks and Mental Health in the U.S.,
1963-1973: A Selected Annotated Bibliography of Journal

Articles. Washington, D.C.: Howard University, Medical-Dental Library, 1974.

0494. Dworaczek, Marian. Human Rights: A Bibliography of Government Documents Held in the Library. Toronto, Ont.: Ontario Ministry of Labour Research Library, 1973.

0495. Eason, V.T. "Annotated Bibliography of Black Theology." In Gayraud S. Wilmore and James H. Cone, eds. Black Theology, A Documentary History. New York: Orbis Books, 1979, 624-37.

0496. Eaton, Elsie M., et al. A Classified Catalogue of the Negro Collection in the Samuel H. Coleman Library, Florida Agricultural and Mechanical University. Tallahassee, Fla.: Florida Agricultural and Mechanical University, 1969.

0497. Editors of Ebony. The Ebony Handbook. Chicago, Ill.: Johnson Publishing Company, 1974.

0498. Ellis, E.M.V. The American Negro: A Selected Checklist of Books. Washington, D.C.: Negro Collection, Howard University, 1968.

0499. Emmer, Pieter C. "The History of the Dutch Slave Trade: A Bibliographic Survey." Journal of Economic History 32 (Sept. 1972), 728-47.

0500. Employment of Minorities, Newark, N.J.: Newark Public Library, 1972.

0501. Epstein, Irene. A Bibliography on the Negro Woman in the U.S.. New York: Jefferson School of Social Science, 1949.

0502. Equal Opportunity: A Bibligraphy of Research on Equal Opportunity in Housing. Washington, D.C.: U.S. Department of Housing and Urban Development Library, 1969.

0503. Equal Opportunity in Employment: Personnel Bibliography. Washington, D.C.: U.S. Civil Service Commission Library, Series No. 29, 1968.

0504. Erikson, Conrad. Black Studies Books. St. Louis, Mo.: Harris Teachers College Library, 1965.

0505. Ernest R. Alexander Collection of Negroana. Nashville, Tenn.: Fisk University, 1945.

0506. Ernst, Robert T. "Geographic Literature of Black America, 1949-1972: A Selected Biliography of Journal Articles, Serial Publications, Theses and Dissertations." In Robert T. Ernst and Lawrence Hugg, eds. Black America: A Geographic Perspective. New York: Doubleday, 1976, 405-25.

0507. Ernst, Robert T. The Geographical Literature of Black America, 1949-1972: A Selected Bibliography of Journal Articles, Serial Publications, Theses and Dissertations. Exchange Bibliography no 492. Monticello, Ill.: Council of Planning Librarians, 1973.

0508. Ernst, Robert T. Negro Migration: a review of the literature. M.A. Thesis, St. Louis University, 1969.

0509. Eshelman, Sylvia N. and Dianna A. Femley. On Being Black: A Bibliography. Cleveland, Ohio: Cleveland Public Library, Mt. Pleasant Branch, 1970.

0510. Ethnic and Cultural Studies: A Bibliography. Baltimore, Md.: Maryland School Media Office, 1978.

0511. Ethnic and Racial Groups in the U.S.: A Selected Bibliography. New York: American Jewish Committee, Institute of Human Relations, 1968.

0512. Ethnic and Racial Minorities in North America: A Selected Bibliography of the Geographical Literature. Exchange Bibliography No. 359-360. Monticello, Ill.: Council of Planning Librarians, 1973.

0513. Evans, Lola. An Annotated Bibliography of the Dated Manuscripts in the Countee Cullen Memorial Collection at Atlanta University. Ph.D. Thesis, Atlanta University, 1959.

0514. Everly, Elaine C. Records of Superintendent of Education for State of Georgia Bureau of Refugees, Freedmen and Abandoned Lands, 1865-1870. Washington, D.C.: U.S. National Archives, 1969.

0515. Everly, Elaine C. Selected Series of Records Issued by Commissioner of Bureau of Refugees, Freedmen and Abandoned Lands, 1865-1872. Washington, D.C.: U.S. National Archives, 1969.

0516. Fairbanks, Helen. Black Workers and the Unions: selected references. Princeton, N.J.: Princeton University, Industrial Relations Section, 1970.

0517. Farber, Evan. Afro-American Studies: reference materials in the Lilly Library. Richmond, Ind.: Earlham College, Lilly Library, 1969.

0518. Faucett, Melba. Books By, About and Relating to Afro-Americans in the Byrne Memorial Library, St. Xavier College: A Bibliography. Chicago, Ill.: St. Xavier College, Byrne Memorial Library.

0519. Fearney, J. Peasant Literature: A Bibliography of Afro-American Nationalism and Social Protest from the Caribbean.

Monticello, Ill.: Council of Planning Librarians, Exchange Bibliography, No. 822, 1975.

0520. Fedink, Simon. Biliography of Publications By and About New York State Division of Human Rights, 1945-1970. New York: New York State Division of Human Rights, 1971, .

0521. Fifteen Topics: on Afroamericana: An Annotated Bibliography. Stockton, Cal.: Relevant Instructional Materials, 1973.

0522. Finney, James E. The Long Road to Now: A Bibliography of Materials Relating to the American Black Man. Farmingdale, N.Y.: Charles W. Clark Co., 1969.

0523. The Fire This Time: Selected Reviews of the Most Significant Books on the Negro in the U.S. New York: United Presbyterian Church in the U.S.A. Board of National Missions, General Department of Mission Strategy and Evangelism, 1967.

0524. Fisher, Edith Maureen. Focusing on Afro/Black American Research: A Guide and Annotated Bibliography to Selected Resources in the University of California, San Diego, Libraries. San Diego, Cal.: University of California at San Diego Libraries, 1975.

0525. Fisher, R.A. "Manuscript Materials Bearing on the Negro in British Archives." Journal of Negro History 27 (Jan. 1942), 83-93.

0526. Fisk University Theses, 1917-1942. Nashville, Tenn.: Fisk University Library, 1942.

0527. Fisk University, Nashville. Library. Dictionary Catalog of the Negro Collection of the Fisk University Library, Nashville, Tennessee. Boston: G.K. Hall, 1960.

0528. Flanders, Teresa. "Equal Employment Opportunity: A Selected Bibliograhy." ALA Library Service to Labor Newsletter 17:1 (Fall 1964), 1-5.

0529. Fleischman, Al. Merritt College Library Guide for Afro-American Studies. Oakland, Cal.: Merritt College Library.

0530. Flesher, Lorna. American Minorities: A Checklist of Bibliographies Published by Government Agencies, 1960-1970. Sacramento, Cal.: California State Library, Government Publications Section, 1970.

0531. Fletcher, Ruth and Beverly Hall. The Black American: A Selected Checklist of Books and Periodicals. Norton, Mass.: Wheaton College Library, 1969.

0532. Focus on Minorities. Washington, D.C.: U.S. Department of

Defense, Army, Library Branch, Special Services Division, 1973.

0533. Foreman, Paul B. and Mozell C. Hill. The Negro in the United States: A Bibliography; A Select Reference and Minimum College Library Resources List. Stillwater, Ok.: Oklahoma A and M College, 1947.

0534. Foster, Joanne. "Books on the American Negro." Senior Scholastic 90 (Feb. 17, 1967), 29.

0535. Foster, William E. "The Harris Collection on Civil War and Slavery [in the Providence, R.I., Public Library]." In Stuart C. Sherman, et al., (eds.) The Special Collections of the Providence Public Library. Providence, R.I.: Providence Public Library, 1968, 12-8.

0536. Found, W. Environment Migration and the Management of Resources Part II: Interregional Migration. Monticello, Ill.: Council of Planning Librarians, Exchange Bibliography, No. 1144, 1976.

0537. Found, W. Environment, Migration and Management of Rural Resources Part III: Farm Economics, Land Use and Spatial Analysis. Monticello, Ill.: Council of Planning Librarians, Exchange Bibliography No. 1145, 1976.

0538. Fralken, Laurie. The Negro Experience in the U.S. Trenton, N.J.: Trenton State College Library, 1969.

0539. Frank, Ilona and Marquerita Breit. A Bibliography of Black Studies. Louisville, Ky.: Bellarmine College Library, 1969.

0540. Frankena, F. Energy and the Poor. Monticello, Ill.: Council of Planning Librarians, Exchange Bibliography No. 1307, 1977.

0541. Fraser, James H. "Black Publishing for Black Children: The Experience of the Sixties and the Seventies." Library Journal 98 (Nov. 15, 1973), 3421-6.

0542. Fraser, Lyn. Bibliography of Publications Relative to Afro-American Studies. Miscellaneous Series No. 10. Greeley, Col.: Colorado State College, Museum of Anthropology, 1969.

0543. Freeman, Leah. The Black Man in American: A Bibliography. Bibliographic Series No. 4. Sacramento, Cal.: Sacramento State College Library, 1969.

0544. Friend, Bruce I. Guide to the Microfilm Record of Selected Documents of Records of the Committee on Fair Employment Practice in the Custody of the National Archives. Glen Rock, N.J.: Microfilming Corporation of America, 1970.

0545. From Negro Protest to Black Revolt: A Selected Working

Bibliography of Negro Writings: 1940-1968, in the U.S. Chicago: Chicago Public Library, George Cleveland Hall Branch, 1963.

0546. From Slavery to Protest: A Bibliography of Afro-American Resources for Pennsylvania Schools. Harrisburg, Pa.: Bureau of General and Academic Education, Social Studies Division, Division of School Libraries, 1968.

0547. Fuller, Sara, et al. Ohio Black History Guide. Columbus, Ohio: Ohio Historical Society, Archives-Library, 1975.

0548. Fuller, Willie J. Blacks in Alabama, 1528-1865. Exchange Bibliography No. 1033. Monticello, Ill.: Council of Planning Librarians, 1976.

0549. Furniss, W. Todd. Colleges and Minority/Poverty Issues: Bibliography and Other Resources. Washington, D.C.: American Council on Education, 1969.

0550. Gagala, Kenneth L. Economics of Minorities: A Guide to Information Sources. Detroit, Mich.: Gale Research, 1976.

0551. Gardner, Henry L. Readings in Contemporary Black Politics: An Annotated Bibliography. Carbondale, Ill.: Southern Illinois University, Public Affairs Research Bureau, 1970.

0552. Garofalo, C. "Black-White Occupational Distribution in Miami During World War I." Prologue 5:2 (1973), 98-101.

0553. Garoogian, Andrew. School Desegregation and "White Flight": A Selected Bibliography. Monticello, Ill.: Vance Bibliographies, 1980.

0554. Garoogian, Andrew. Urban Enterprise Laws: A Selected Review of Literature With Annotations. Chicago: CPL Bibliography No. 101, 1983.

0555. Gary, D.S. "Bibliographical Essay: Black Views on Reconstruction." Journal of Negro History 58 (Jan. 1973), 73-85.

0556. Gaudio, R., et al. Ghetto, A Bibliography. Rochester, N.Y.: St. John Fisher College Library, 1969.

0557. Genovese, E.D. "Cities Within Our Cities". Nation 207 (Aug. 5, 1968), 86-8.

0558. George, Melvin. The City, With A Special Bibliography About Chicago. Elmhurst, Ill.: Elmhurst College, Memorial Library, 1969.

0559. Gerland, P.I. The Afro-American Press and Its Editors. New

York: Arno, 1969.

0560. Gibson, Mary Jane and Sylvia Lyons Render. "Afro-American Experience: a selected list of references by Afro-Americans." Library of Congress Information Bulletin 38 (Feb. 2-16, 1979), 39-44, 49-52, 56-60.

0561. Giordano, Joseph and Grace Pineiro Giordano. The Ethno-Cultural Factors in Mental Health: A Literature Review and Bibliography. New York: Institute on Pluralism and Group Identity of the American Jewish Committee, 1979.

0562. Gittleman, J. The Black Experience in America. South Fallsburg, N.Y.: Sullivan County Community College Library, 1979.

0563. Gleason, E.V. The Southern Negro and the Public Library: A Study of the Government and Administration of Public Library Service to Negroes in the South. Chicago: University of Chicago Press, 1941.

0564. Goetz, Vera C. Afro-American Bibliography. Chicago, Ill.: Malcolm X College Library, 1962.

0565. Goldstein, Samuel. Journals of Negro Interest: A Bibliographic List. Amherst, Mass.: University of Massachusetts Library, 1968.

0566. Goldwater, Walter. Radical Periodicals in America, 1890-1950: A Bibliography with Brief Notes. New Haven, Conn.: Yale University Library, 1966.

0567. Gonzales, Alex S. Minorities and the U.S. Economy. Santa Barbara, Cal.: University of California at Santa Barbara, Library, 1974.

0568. Gordon, Edmund V. An Annotated Bibliography on Higher Education of the Disadvantaged. ERIC Document No. Ed 038-478. New York: Columbia University, Teachers College, The Study of Collegiate Compensatory Programs for Minority Group Youth, 1970.

0569. Gordon, Elizabeth DeLouis. Afro-Americans in [Government] Documents: An Annotated Bibliography. La Jolla, Cal.: University of California at La Jolla, Central University Library, Documents Department, 1974.

0570. Graham, Hugh Davis. A Selected Bibliography of Twentieth Century Southern History with Special Emphasis on Racial Relations especially since 1954. Palo Alto, Cal.: Stanford University, Department of History, 1967.

0571. Gray, Daniel Savage. "Bibliographical Essay: Black Views on

Reconstruction." <u>Journal of Negro History</u> 58:1, (1973), 73–85.

0572. Gregorovich, Andrew. <u>Canadian Ethnic Groups Bibliography: A Selected Bibliography of Ethnocultural Groups in Canada and the Province of Ontario</u>. Toronto, Ont., Canada: Ontario Department of the Provincial Secretary and Citizenship, 1972.

0573. Griffin, A.P.C. <u>List of Discussions of the 14th and 15th Amendments with Special Reference to Negro Sufferage</u>. Washington, D.C., U.S. Library of Congress, Division of Bibliography: Government Printing Office, 1906.

0574. Griffith, George. <u>Bibliography for Race and Ethnic Relations</u>. Bellevue, Neb.: Bellevue College Library, 1973.

0575. Grinstead, Scott E. <u>A Select, Classified and Briefly Annotated List of Two Hundred Fifty Books by or about the Negro Published during the Past Ten Years.</u> Nashville, Tenn.: Fisk University Library, 1939.

0576. Gubert, Betty Kaplan. <u>Early Black Bibliographies, 1863–1918</u>. New York: Garland, 1982.

0577. Gubert, Betty Kaplan. <u>Suggestions and Selected Resources to Begin a Search for Family History</u>. New York: Schomburg Center, The New York Public Library, 1977.

0578. <u>Guide for Teaching the Contribution of the Negro Author to American Literature</u>. San Diego, Cal.: San Diego City Schools, 1969.

0579. <u>Guide to Facts about the Negro</u>. New York: NAACP Training Department, 1970.

0580. <u>Guide to Manuscripts and Archives in the Negro Collection of the Trevor Arnett Library</u>. Atlanta, Ga.: Atlanta University Libraries, 1971.

0581. <u>Guide to Manuscripts and Source Material Relating to the Negro in Massachusetts [from 1827 to 1865 in the Boston Public Library]</u>. Boston, Mass.: U.S. Works Progress Administration, Historical Records Survey, Division of Community Service Programs, 1942.

0582. <u>Guide to Publications By and About Negro Americans</u>. Minneapolis, Minn.: Youth Development Project, 1965.

0583. <u>Guide to Research on Afro–American History and Culture</u>. Northampton, Mass.: Smith College Library, 1972-7.

0584. <u>Guide to Resources for Anti–Poverty Programs: A Selected Bibliography</u>. New York: Federation Employment and Guidance Service, Richard J. Bernhardt Memorial Library, 1965.

0585. Guide to Resources in Afro-American History. Cambridge, Mass.:
MIT Humanities Library, 1977.

0586. Guide to the Literature for Black Studies: Sources in the
Vassar College Library. Poughkeepsie, N.Y.: Vassar College
Library, 1972.

0587. Guss, Margery, et al. Basic Indexing, Bibliographic and
Periodical Services Useful to Students Interested in Ethnic and
Minority Groups. Corvallis, Oregon: Oregon State University,
William Jasper Kerr Library, 1973.

0588. Guzman, Jessie P. "An Annotated List of Books By or Concerning
Negroes in the United States, in Africa and in Latin America.
1938-1946." Negro Year Book: A Review of Events Affecting
Negro Life 1941-1946. Tuskegee, Ala.: Tuskegee Institute,
Department of Records and Research, 1947.

0589. Guzman, Jessie P. Civil Rights and the Negro: A List of
References Relating to Present Day Discussions. Rev. ed.
Tuskegee, Ala.: Tuskegee Institute, Department of Records and
Research, 1950.

0590. Guzman, Jessie P., et al. Desegregation and the Southern
States, 1957. Legal action and voluntary group action.
Tuskegee, Ala.: Tuskegee Institute, Deaprtment of Records and
Reserach, 1958.

0591. Guzman, Jessie P., et al. Negro Yearbook. A Review of
Effecting Negro Life. New York: Wm. H. Wise and Company, Inc.,
1952.

0592. Hackman, Martha. A Library Guide to Afro-American Studies.
Los Angeles, Cal.: California State College, John F. Kennedy
Memorial Library, 1960.

0593. Hadden, J. and Massoti, L.H. Suburbs, Suburbia and
Suburbanization: A Bibliography. Monticello, Ill.: Council of
Planning Librarians, Exchange Bibliography No. 269, 1972.

0594. Haigler, Virgie Biggins, et al. Bibliographies for Negro
History and Culture and Teacher Resources and Teaching
Materials. Englewood, N.J.: Urban League for Bergen County,
Education Committee, 1973.

0595. Hall, Woodrow Wadsworth. A Bibliography of the Tuskegee
Gerrymander Protest: Pamphlets, Magazine and Newspaper Articles
Chronologically Arranged. Tuskegee, Ala.: Tuskegee Institute,
Department of Records and Research, 1960.

0596. Haller, Elizabeth S. American Diversity: A Bibliography of
Resources on Racial and Ethnic Minorities for Pennsylvania
Schools. Harrisburg, Pa.: Pennsylvania Department of

Education, Bureau of General and Academic Education, 1969.

0597. Halliday, Thelma Y. The Negro in Business: Annotated Bibliography. Washington, D.C.: Howard University, Small Business and Development Center, 1969.

0598. Halliday, Thelma Y. The Negro on the Field of Business: An Annotated Bibliography. Washington, D.C.: Howard University, Institute for Minority Business Education, 1970.

0599. Hampton Institute. A Classified Catalogue of the Negro Collection in the Collis P. Huntington Library. Hampton Institute, Hampton, Virginia, 1940.

0600. Hampton Institute. Collis P. Huntington Library. Dictionary Catalogue of the George Peabody Collection of Negro Literature and History. Westport, Conn.: Greenwood, 1972.

0601. Hampton Institute. Historical Books About the Negro Race in the Hampton Institute Library. Hampton, Virginia, 1928.

0602. Hannerz, Ulf. "Research in the Black Ghetto: A Review of the Sixties." Journal of Asian and African Studies [Netherlands] 9:3/4, (1974), 139-59.

0603. Hansen, Anne. A Select Bibliography on Negro History: Books in the Brazoport College Library. Brazoport, Tex.: Brazoport Junior College Library, 1970.

0604. Hansen, P.O. and B. Boehnke. The Spatial Analysis of Crime. Monticello, Ill.: Council of Planning Librarians, Exchange Bibliography No. 1166, 1976.

0605. Haro, Robert P. Affirmative Action in Higher Education: A Selected and Annotated Bibliography. Exchange Bibliography No. 1229. Monticello, Ill.: Council of Planning Librarians, 1977.

0606. Harris, Addie. Afro-American Politicians: A Selected Bibliography. Chicago, Ill.: Association for the Study of Afro-American Life and History, 1981.

0607. Havrilesky, Catherine and Preston Wilcox. A Selected Bibliography on White Institutional Racism. New York: Afram Associates, 1969.

0608. Hayes, Floyd W. "The African Presence in America Before Columbus: A Bibliographic Essay." Black World 22:9 (1973), 4-22.

0609. Hayes, Mary. The Black Experience in America. Washington, D.C.: Trinity College Library, 1974.

0610. Haywood, Terry S. Bibliography of Doctoral Dissertations on

Blacks Accepted in the Ohio State University, 1932-1974.
Author, 1976.

0611. Hazelton, Louise. "Negro: A Bibliography." _North Country Libraries_ 10 (Nov. 1967), 192-4.

0612. Healy, Thomas. _A List of Titles in Black Studies._ Publication No. 69, Potsdam, N.Y.: State University of New York, College at Potsdam, F.W. Crumb Memorial Library, 1969.

0613. Heartmen, C.F. _News Sheet of the Charles F. Heartman Collection of Material Relating to Negro Culture, Printed and in Manuscript._ Hattiesburg, Miss.: 1945.

0614. Heffron, Paul T. "Manuscript Sources in the Library of Congress for a Study of Labor History." _Labor History_ 10 (Fall 1969), 630-8.

0615. Heller, Paul. _An Annotated Bibliography of Black History._ San Francisco, Cal.: Human Rights Commission, 1969.

0616. Helmreich, William B. "Afro-Americans and Africa: anthropoligical and sociological investigations." _Current Bibliography of African Affairs_ 8:3, (1975), 232-44.

0617. Helmreich, William B. _Afro-Americans and Africa: Black Nationalism at the Crossroads._ Westport, Conn.: Greenwood, 1977.

0618. Henderson, Lenneal J. "Black Political Life in the U.S.: A Bibliographic Essay." In Lenneal J. Henderson, Jr., (ed.) _Black Political Life in the U.S.: A First as the Pendulum._ San Francisco, Cal.: Chandler Publications, 1972, 253-69.

0619. _Heritage of the Negro in America: A Bibliography; Books, Records, Tapes, Filmstrips, Film, Pictures._ Lansing, Mich.: Michigan Department of Education, Joint Committee for Media Center Development, 1970.

0620. Hildebrand, Lorraine and Richard S. Aiken. _A Bibliography of Afro-American Print and Non-Print Resources in Libraries of Pierce County, Washington._ Area Urban Coalition, Education Task Froce in cooperation with Pierce County Libraries. Tacoma, Wash.: Tacoma Community College, Pearl A. Wanamaker Library, 1969.

0621. Hill, Mozell C. "Negroes in the U.S.: A Critique of the Periodical Literature." _Social Forces_ 26 (Dec. 1947), 218-23.

0622. Hill, Mozell C. and P.B. Foreman. "The Negro in the U.S.: A Bibliography." _Southwestern Journal_ 2 (Summer 1946), 225-30.

0623. Hill, Marnesta D. _A Bibliography of Black History and_

Literature. New York: Herbert H. Lehman College of the City University of New York, Library, 1971.

0624. Historical Records Survey. District of Columbia. Calendar of the Writing of Frederic Douglass, in the Frederick Douglass Memorial Home, Ancostia, D.C. Washington, D.C.: Historical Records Survey, 1940.

0625. Historical Records Survey. New York City. Calendar of the Manuscripts in the Schomburg Collection of Negro Literature. Located at 135th Street Branch, New York: Public Library, 1942 to 1980.

0626. Hoerder, Dirk. Protest, Direct Action, Repression; Dissent in American Society from Colonial Times to the Present: A Bibliography. Munich, Germany: Verlag Dokumentation, 1977.

0627. Hoerder, Dirk. Violence in the U.S.: Riots, Strikes, Protest and Suppression: A Working Bibliography for Teachers and Students. Berlin, Germany: John F. Kennedy Institut fur Nordamerikastudiern, Freie Universitat Berlin, 1973.

0628. Hogg, Peter C. The African Slave Trade and Its Suppression: A Classified and Annotated Bibliography of Books, Pamphlets and Periodical Articles. London, England: Frank Cass, 1973.

0629. Holmes, Oakley, N. The Complete Annotated Resource Guide to Black American Art: Books, Doctoral Dissertations, Exhibition Catalogues, Periodicals, Films, Slides, Large Prints, Speakers, Filmstrips, Video Tapes, Black Museums, Art Galleries and Much More. Spring Valley, N.Y.: Black Artists in America, 1978.

0630. Homer, D.R. Books About the Negro: An Annotated Bibliography. New York: Praeger, 1966.

0631. Homer, D.R. The Negro in the United States: A List of Significant Books. New York, N.Y.: Public Library, 1965.

0632. Homer, D.R. The Negro: A List of Significant Books. New York: N.Y.: Public Library Press, 1960.

0633. Homer, D.R. "Selected Book List on Negro Life and History." Senior Scholastic 91:14 (January 18, 1968), 14-20.

0634. Homer, D.R. and Evelyn B. Robinson. "The Negro: A Selected Bibliography." New York Public Library Bulletin 59 (Mar. 1955), 133-53.

0635. Homer, D.R. and Ann M. Swartout. Books About the Negro: An Annotated Bibliography. New York: Praeger, 1966.

0636. Hopkins, Lee Bennett. "For and about Afro-Americans: Selected Paperbacks for Children." The Instructor 78 (Nov. 1968), 126-8.

0637. Houston, Helen Ruth. "Contributions of the American Negro to American Culture: A Selected Checklist." Bulletin of Bibliography 26:3 (July-Sept. 1969), 71-9.

0638. Howard, John M. "Sickle Cell Anemia: A Selected Bibliography." Readers Advisory Service 1, (1974), 14-20.

0639. Howard, Sharon M. "Black Reference Books: A Select Bibliography of Retrospective Sources." Bibliography of Sources By and About Blacks Compiled by the Interns in the Internship in Black Studies Librarianship Program. Nashville, Tenn.: Fisk University Libary, 1974, 26-32.

0640. "Howard University Acquires the Most Comprehensive Collection of Works by Negro Authors in the Works [The Spingarn Collection.]" Howard University Bulletin 28 (Jan.-Feb. 1949), 3-5.

0641. Hower, Mentor A. and Roscoe E. Lewis. A Classified Catalogue of the Negro Collection in the Collis P. Huntington Library, Hampton Institute. Compiled by Workers of the Writers' Program of the Works Progress Administration in the State of Virginia. Hampton, Va.: Hampton Normal and Agricultural Institute, 1940.

0642. Howerton, Joseph B. Some Sources of Federal Documentation of Minority Groups in Chicago. Preliminary draft prepared for the Conference on the National Archives and Urban Research. Washington, D.C.: National Archives and Records Service, 1970.

0643. Howie, Marguerite. Interdisciplinary Seminar: An Annotated Bibliography of the Negro in American History. Orangeburg, S.C.: South Carolina State College, Miller F. Whittaker Library, 1970.

0644. Hubbard, Edward E. and Lenwood G. Davis. Suicides in the Black Community: A Preliminary Survey. Monticello, Ill.: Council of Planning Librarians, Exchange Bibliography No. 887, 1975.

0645. Hubbard, Geraldine Hopkins and Julian S. Fowler. "A Classified Catalogue of the Collection of Anti-Slavery Propaganda in the Oberlin College Library." Oberlin College Library Bulletin 2:3, (1932).

0646. Hudson, Gossie Harold. Directory of Black Historians, Ph.D.'s and Others, 1975-1976: essays, commentaries and publications. Monticello, Ill.: Council of Planning Librarians, Exchange Bibliography No. 870/1/2, 1975.

0647. Hume, Mildred and Gayle Marko. Orodha Ya Vitabu: A Bibliography of Afro-American Life. Rev. ed. Minneapolis, Minn.: Minneapolis Public Schools, Board of Education Library, 1980.

0648. Hunt-Bryan, Barbara, et al. _Afro and Afro-American Materials_.
Greensboro, N.C.: Bennett College, Thomas F. Halgate Library,
1972.

0649. Hunterton, C. Stanley, et al. _Busing: Ground Zero in School
Desegregation: A Literature Review with Policy Recommendations_.
ERIC Documentation No. Ed 085-451. Syracuse, N.Y.: Syracuse
University Research Corporation, 1972.

0650. Hutson, Jean Blackwell. "African Materials in the Schomburg
Collection of Negro Literature and History." _African Studies
Bulletin_, 3 (May 1960).

0651. Hutson, Jean Blackwell. "Harlem, a Cultural History: Selected
Bibliography." _The Metropolitan Museum of Art Bulletin_ 27
(Jan. 1969), 280-8.

0652. Hutson, Jean Blackwell. "The Schomburg Collection."
Freedomways 3:3 (Summer 1963), 431-5.

0653. Hymon, Mary Watson, et al. _Bibliography of Resources in the
Afro-American Collection_. Grambling, La.: Grambling College,
A.C. Lewis Memorial Library, 1962.

0654. _Index to Periodical Articles by and about Negroes_. Boston:
G.K. Hall, 1971.

0655. _Index to Periodical Articles by and about Negroes, Cumulated
1960-1970.Compiled by the staffs of the Hallie Q. Brown
Library, Central State University, Ohio, and the Schomburg
Collection, The New York Public Library_. Boston: G.K. Hall,
1971.

0656. _Index to Selected Periodicals. Decennial Cumulation, 1950-1959.
Received in the Hallie Q. Brown Library Central State
University, Ohio_. Boston: G.K. Hall, 1962.

0657. Indiana University. _The Black Family and the Black Woman: A
Bibliography_. Bloomington, Ind.: Afro-American Studies
Department, 1972.

0658. _Insight to the Negro in the United States: A Selected
Bibliography_. Terre Haute, Ind.: Indiana State University,
Cunningham Memorial Library, 1970.

0659. _Interracial Relationships in the U.S.: A Selected List of
References_. Washington, D.C.: Library of Congress, 1945.

0660. _Introduction to Materials for Ethnic Studies in the University
of Southern California Library._ Los Angeles, Cal.: University
of Southern California Library, 1970.

0661. _Inventory of Research in Racial and Cultural Relations_.

Committee on Education, Training and Research in Race Relations
at the University of Chicago, (June 1948 to Summer 1953).

0662. Irwin, Leonard Bertram. Black Studies: A Bibliography for the
Use of Schools, Libraries and the General Reader. Brooklawn,
N.J.: McKinley Publishing Co., 1969.

0663. Ishimatsu, Chiz and Annie Laurie Bezrry. Black Bibliography: A
Selected Listing. Salt Lake City, Utah: University of Utah
Libraries, 1960.

0664. Isika, D. Urban Growth Policy in the United States: A
Bibliographic Guide. Monticello, Ill.: Council of Planning
Librarians, Exchange Bibliography, No. 273, 1972.

0665. Institute of Labor and Industrial Relations, University of
Michigan, Wayne State University. Document and Reference Text:
An Index to Minority Group Employment Information. Ann Arbor,
Mich.: 1967.

0666. Jablonsky, Adelaide. Curriculum and Instruction for Minority
Groups: An Annotated Bibliography of Doctoral Dissertations.
New York: ERIC Clearinghouse on the Urban Disadvantaged, No.
110-587, 1973.

0667. Jablonsky, Adelaide. School Desegregation: An Annotated
Bibliography of Doctoral Dissertations. ERIC Document No. 078-
098. New York: ERIC Clearinghouse on the Urban Disadvantaged,
1973.

0668. Jablonsky, Adelaide. Social and Psychological Studies of
Minority Children and Youth: An Annotated Bibliography of
Doctoral Dissertations. ERIC Document no. ED 110-589. New York:
ERIC Clearinghouse on the Urban Disadvantaged, 1975.

0669. Jackson, Anne. Ethnic Groups: Their Cultures and
Contributions. Little Rock, Ark.: Arkansas State Department of
Education, 1970.

0670. Jackson, Clara O. A Bibliography of Afro-American and Other
American Minorities Represented in Library and Library-Related
Listings. New York: American Institute of Marxist Studies,
1970.

0671. Jackson, Giovanna R. Afro-American Religion and Church and
Race Relations. Focus: Black American Bibliography Series.
Bloomington, Ind.: Indiana Unversity Libraries, 1969.

0672. Jackson, Giovanna R. and Charles E. Sweet. Black Nationalism;
The Negro and the Establishment: Law, Politics and the Courts.
Focus: Black American Bibliography Series. Bloomington, Ind.:
Indiana University Libraries, 1969.

0673. Jackson, Jacqueline Johnson. "A Partial Bibliography on or related to Black Women." Journal of Social and Behavioral Sciences 21:1 (Winter 1975), 90-135.

0674. Jackson, John W. Afro-American Resources. Vallejo, Cal.: Solano Community College Library, 1969.

0675. Jackson, M.M. A Bibliography of Materials by and about Negro Americans for Young Readers. Washington, D.C.: U.S. Office of Education, 1967.

0676. Jackson, M.M. A Bibliography of Negro History and Culture for Young Readers. Pittsburgh, University of Pittsburgh Press, 1969.

0677. Jackson, M.M. Negro History and Culture. Atlanta, Georgia: University of Pittsburgh Pess, 1968.

0678. Jacobs, Donald M. Index to the American Slave. Westport, Conn.: Greenwood, 1931.

0679. Jahn, Janheinz. A Bibliography of Neo-African Literature from Africa, America and the Caribbean. New York: Praeger, 1965.

0680. Jahn, Janheinz. Die neoAfrikanische Literatur: Gesambibliographie Von Dem Anfangen Bis Zur Gegenwart. Dusseldorf, Germany: Diederichs Verlag, 1965.

0681. Jakle, John A. and Cynthia A. Jakle. Ethnic and Racial Minorities in North America: A Selected Bibliography of the Geographical Literature. Exchange Bibliography No. 459/460. Monticello, Ill.: Council of Planning Librarians, 1973.

0682. Jayatilleke, Raja. The Law, the Courts and Minority Group Education: An ERIC/CUE Capsule Bibliography. ERIC Document no. ED 128-497. New York: Columbia University, Teachers College, Institute for Urban and Minority Education, 1976.

0683. Jenkins, Betty Lanier and Susan Phillis. Black Separatism: A Bibliography. Westport, Conn.: Greenwood, 1976.

0684. Jenkins, Betty, et al. Kenneth B. Clark: A Bibliography. New York: Metropolitan Applied Research Center, 1970.

0685. Jenkins, John Julian. Some Contributions of the American Negro Church to the Process of Race Integration: A Bibliography, Washington, D.C.: 1951.

0686. Johnson, Clifton H. A.M.A. [American Missionary Association] Archives as a Source for the Study of American History. New York: AMA of the United Church Board for Homeland Ministries, 1960.

0687.   Johnson, Clifton H. The Negro American: A Selected and
        Annotated Bibliography for High Schools and Junior Colleges.
        Nashville, Tenn.: Amistad Research Center, 1968.

0688.   Johnson, Guy B. Encyclopedia of the Negro: Preparatory Volume
        with Reference Lists and Reports. New York: Phelps-Stokes
        Fund, 1945.

0689.   Johnson, Gary T. Mobility, Residential Locatoin, and Urban
        Change: A Partially Annotated Bibliography. Chicago: CPL
        Bibliography No. 48, 198__.

0690.   Johnson, H.A. Multimedia Materials for Afro-American Studies:
        A Curriculum Orientation and Annotated Bibliography of
        Resources. New York: Bowker, 1971.

0691.   Johnson, James and Frances O. Churchill. "Black and
        Bibliographical." Wilson Library Bulletin 47 (Nov. 1972), 249-
        50.

0692.   Johnson, Jerome W. The Afro-American Experience: A
        Bibliography of Materials Held by the Andersen Library,
        Wisconsin State University, Whitewater. Whitewater, Wisc.:
        Wisconsin State University, Harold Andersen Library, 1969.

0693.   Johnson, Pat Taylor. Black Studies Acquisitions File. Newark,
        Del.: University of Delaware, Hugh M. Morris Library, 1970.

0694.   Johnson, Preston C. and Julia O. Saunders. "The Education of
        Negroes in Virginia: An Annotated Bibliography." Virginia
        State College Gazette 50:1 (Feb. 1944), 1-16.

0695.   Johnson, Vivian R. A Selected Bibliography of the Black
        Experience. Roxbury, Mass.: Afro-American Studies Resource
        Center, Circle Associates, 1971.

0696.   Johnston, Robert. Ethnic Studies. Santa Maria, California:
        Allan Hancock College Library, 1971.

0697.   Jolly, David. Master's Theses, 1932-1945; An Annotated
        Bibliography. Hampton, Va.: Hampton Institute, 1946.

0698.   Jonas, Carol. Bibliography for Afro-American Studies.
        Elmhurst, Ill.: Elmhurst College, Memorial Library, 1970.

0699.   Jones, Betty and Joyce Lacey. Bibliography of Resources: Afro-
        American studies. Norwalk, Conn.: Cerritos College Library,
        1970.

0700.   Jorgensen, Venita McPherson. Negro History: A Selected
        Bibliography of the Afro-American Experience. Riverside, Cal.:
        University of California, Riverside, General Library, 1969.

0701. Julia Davis Collection: Negro and African Life and Culture: A Bibliography. St. Louis, Mo.: St. Louis Public Library, 1971.

0702. Juris, Gail and Ronald Krash. Afro-American Research Bibliography. St. Louis, Mo.: St. Louis University, Pius XII Memorial Library, 1970.

0703. Juris, Gail, et al. Survey of Bibliographic Activities of U.S. Colleges and Universities on Black Studies. St. Louis, Mo.: St. Louis University, Pius XII Memorial Library, 1971.

0704. Justice, J. "American Negro History: A Bibliography of Black Studies Material." California School Libraries 41 (Jan. 1970), 58.

0705. Kain, Mary Ann. Books About the Afro-American. Marshalltown, Iowa: Marshalltown Community College, 1968.

0706. Kaiser, Ernest. "Annotated Bibliography." In Floyd B. Barbour, (ed.) The Black Seventies. Boston, Mass.: Porter Sargent, 1970, 315-25.

0707. Kaiser, Ernest. "Bibliography on Black Education." Freedomways 17:4 (Fourth Quarter 1977), 239-55.

0708. Kaiser, Ernest. "Black History Reference." New York Amsterdam News, (Feb. 23, 1974), D7.

0709. Kaiser, Ernest. "Black Images in the Mass Media: A Bibliography." Freedomways 14:3 (1974), 274-87.

0710. Kaiser, Ernest. "Black Youth: A Bibliography." Freedomways 15:3 (Third Quarter 1975), 226-41.

0711. Kaiser, Ernest. "Library Holdings on Afro-Americans." In E.J. Josey and Ann Allen Shockley, (eds.) Handbook of Black Librarianship. Littleton, Col.: Libraries Unlimited, 1977, 228-45.

0712. Kaiser, Ernest. "Negro History: A Bibliographical Survey." Freedomways 7:4 (Fall 1967), 335-45.

0713. Kaiser, Ernest. "Recently Published Negro Reference and Research Tools." Freedomways 6:4 (Fall 1966), 358-81.

0714. Kantrowitz, Nathan. Racial and Ethnic Residential Segregation: Boston 1830-1970. Annals of the American Academy of Political and Social Science. 1979, 41-54.

0715. Kaplan, Emma N. Guide to Research in Afro-American History and Culture: A Selected and Annotated Bibliography of Materials in the Smith College Library. Northampton, Mass.: Smith College, 1972.

0716. Kaplan, Gubert. Early Black Bibliographies, 1863-1918. New
       York: Garland, 1982.

0717. Katz, William L. Teacher's Guide to American Negro History.
       Chicago: Quadrangle Books, 1968.

0718. Keating, W.D. Rent and Eviction Controls. Monticello, Ill.:
       Council of Planning Librarians, Exchange Bibliography, No.
       1136, 1976.

0719. Kellogg, Jefferson B. "Selected Secondary Sources [on Afro-
       American Studies]" American Quarterly 17:4 (Summer 1979), 25-
       8.

0720. Kelly, Sara. Blacks in America: Selected Holdings of the
       University of Michigan. Dearborn, Mich.: The Library, 1973.

0721. Kemp, Charles H. Blacks in America. Forest Grove, Ore.:
       Pacific University, Harvey W. Scott Memorial Library, 1973.

0722. Kennicott, Patrick. "The Black Revolution in America: A
       Selected Bibliography." In James E. Roever, (ed.) Proceedings:
       Speech Association of America Summer Conference V. New York:
       Speech Association of America, 1969, 125-50.

0723. Kerri, James N. and Anthony Laying. Bibliography of Afro-
       American (Black Studies). Exchange Bibliography no. 657/658.
       Monticello, Ill.: Council of Planning Librarians, 1974.

0724. Kimball, Mark Dennis. A Bibliography of Slavery in the U.S.
       Salt Lake City, Utah: 1965.

0725. King, William M. Black Labor in the Cities: A Selected
       Bibliography. Exchange Bibliography No. 548. Monticello, Ill.:
       Council of Planning Librarians, 1974.

0726. King, William M. Blacks, Crime and Criminal Justice: An
       Introductory Bibliography. Exchange Bibliography No. 570.
       Monticello, Ill.: Council of Planning Librarians, 1974.

0727. King, William M. Health Care and the Black Community: An
       Exploratory Bibliography. Exchange Bibliography No. 555.
       Monticello, Ill.: Council of Planning Librarians, 1974, 16 pp.

0728. King, William M. Urban Racial Violence in the U.S.: An
       Historical and Comparative Bibliography. Exchange Bibliography
       No. 591. Monticello, Ill.: Council of Planning Librarians,
       1974.

0729. Kinton, Jack F. American Ethnic Groups: A Sourcebook. Mt.
       Pleasant, Iowa: Social Science and Sociological Resources,
       1973.

0730. Kinton, Jack F. American Ethnic Groups and the Revival of
       Cultural Pluralism: Evaluative Sourcebook for the 1970's.
       Arora, Ill.: Social Science and Sociological Resource, 1974.

0731. Kirk, Sherri and Glenda Peace. Black Sojourn: A Bibliography.
       Davis, Cal.: University of California at Davis Library,
       Collection Development Section, Ethnic Studies Unit, 1969.

0732. Kirkley, A. Roy. Labor Unions and the Black Experience: A
       Selected Bibliography. New Brunswick, N.J.: Rutgers
       University, Labor Education Center and Library, Institute of
       Management and Labor Relations, University Extension Division,
       1972.

0733. Klotman, Phyllis Rauch and Wilmer H. Baatz. The Black Family
       and the Black Woman: A Bibliography. New York: Arno Press,
       1978.

0734. Klotman, Phyllis Rauch, et al. Black Family and the Black
       Woman: A Bibliography Prepared by the Library Staff and the
       Afro-American Studies Department. Bloomington, Inc.: Indiana
       University Library, 1972.

0735. Knox, Ellis O. "Bibliography [of dissertations by Negroes.]"
       Journal of Negro Education 15 (Spring 1946), 220-30.

0736. Knox, Ellis O. and Mary A. Mortin. "Selected Bibliography [on
       race relations]." Journal of Negro Education 4 (July 1935),
       456-64.

0737. Kolm, Richard. Bibliography of Ethnicity and Ethnic Groups.
       ERIC Document no. ED 090-340. Rockville, Md.: National
       Institute of Mental Health, Center for Studies of Metropolitan
       Problems, 1973.

0738. Kopkin, T.J. Representation of Books by and about American
       Negroes in Georgia Regional Libraries. M.A. thesis, Emory
       University, 1957.

0739. Krash, Ronald, et al. Black America: A Research Bibliography.
       St. Louis, Mo.: St. Louis University, Pius XII Library, 1972.

0740. Krutchkoff, Sonya. The New Negro: A Bibliography for the
       General Reader. New York: Harlem Adult Education Committee,
       1972.

0741. Kugler, Reuben F. Bibliography for Afro-American History. Los
       Angeles, Cal.: California State College at Los Angeles, John F.
       Kennedy Memorial Library, 1970.

0742. Kugler, Reuben F. "Bibliography for Afro-American History."
       Social Studies 60:5 (Oct. 1969), 211-7.

0743. Kuncio, Robert A. Negro History 1553-1903: An Exhibition of Books, Prints and Manuscripts from the Shelves of the Library Company and the Historical Society of Pennsylvania, April 17-July 17, 1969. Philadelphia, Pa.: The Library Company of Philadelphia, 1969

0744. LaBrie, Henry G. The Black Press: A Bibliography. Kennebunkport, Me.: Mercer House Press, 1973.

0745. Lachantere, Diana. "Blacks in California: An Annotated Guide to the Manuscript Sources in the California Historical Society Library." California History 57:3 (Fall 1978), 1-15.

0746. Lancaster, E.M. The Negro in America: A Bibliography Compiled for the American Academy of Arts and Sciences. Cambridge, Massachusetts: Harvard Press, 1966.

0747. Lannon, Maria Mercedes. The Black Man in America: An Overview of Negro History with Bibliography and Basic Book List for K-12. New York: Joseph F. Wagner, 1969.

0748. Lapansky, Phil. Black Voices, 1709-1863: A Selection of Twenty-one Examples of Afro-American Expression and Opinion, from the Shelves of the Library Company of Philadelphia. Prepared for the visit of the Black Studies' Discussion Group, July 12, 1982, by Phil Lapansky. Philadelphia, Pa.: Library Company of Philadelphia, 1982.

0749. Lash, John S. "A Long Hard Look at the Ghetto, A Critical Summary of Literature By and About Negroes in 1956." Phylon 18, (1957), 7-24.

0750. Latimer, Catherine A. The Negro: A Selected Bibliography (1942-1943). New York: New York Vocational High School for Boys, Intercultural Education, 1964.

0751. Leffall, Dolores C. Bibliographic Survey: the Negro in Print; Five-Year Subject Index (1965-1970). Washington, D.C.: Negro Bibliographic and Research Center, 1971.

0752. Leffall, Dolores C. "Bibliography: Books, Bulletins, Pamphlets." Journal of Negro Education 28 (Fall 1959), 454-8.

0753. Leffall, Dolores C. "Bibliography: Books, Bulletins, Pamphlets." Journal of Negro Education 29 (Winter 1960), 59-63.

0754. Leffall, Dolores C. "The Bicentennial and the Afro-American: A Selected Bibliography." Negro History Bulletin 38 (Feb. 1975), 358-61.

0755. Leffall, Dolores C. Black Church: An Annotated Bibliography. Washington, D.C.: Minority Research Center, 1973.

0756. Legislation Affecting Minority Groups: A Selected Bibliography. Chicago, Ill.: American Council on Race Relations, 1973.

0757. Lerner, Gerda. "Bibliographic Notes." Black Women in White America: A Documentary History. New York: Random House, 1972, 615-30.

0758. Lerou, Marion. "Division of Negro Literature, History and Prints, 135th St. Branch, New York Public Library." Mission Fields at Home 6 (Feb. 1934), 71-3.

0759. Lesser, Alexander. "American Negro". In "Bibliography of American Folklore, 1915-1928." Journal of American Folklore 41 (Jan.-Mar. 1928), 47-52.

0760. Lesser, Saal D. "Bibliography on Human Relations Education." Bulletin of the National Association of Secondary School Principals 39 (Mar. 1955), 101-9.

0761. Levtow, Patricia. Black-Jewish Relations in the U.S.: A Selected Annotated List of Books, Pamphlets and Articles. New York: American-Jewish Committee, 1978.

0762. Lewinson, Paul. A Guide to Documents in the National Archives for Negro Studies. Washington, D.C.: American Council of Learned Societies, 1947.

0763. Lewis, Alvin. Bibliography on the Black American. Manhattan, Kan.: Kansas State University, Farrell Library, Minorities Resources and Research Center, 1975.

0764. Lewis, C. Library Services to Special Urban Population Groups, 1970-1974. Monticello, Ill.: Council of Planning Librarians, Exchange Bibliography No. 943, 1975.

0765. Library Materials Written by or about Negroes, including Africa and Island History. Ravenswood, Cal.: Ravenswood City School District Instructional Materials Center, 1968.

0766. Lindgren, William. Afro-American Bibliography. East Peoria, Ill.: Illinois Central College, Sandburg Library, 1968.

0767. Lindsay, Arnett G. "Manuscript Materials Bearing on the Negro in America." Journal of Negro History 27 (Jan. 1942), 94-101.

0768. Lindsay, Crawford Bernard. The Cornell University Special Collection on Slavery: American Publications Through 1840. Ithaca, N.Y.: Ph.D. Thesis, Cornell University, 1949.

0769. Lipscombe, Mildred. The Education of the Afro-American: A Selected Bibliography. Newark, N.J.: Newark Public Library, Education Division, 1968.

0770. List of Additional References on the Anthropology and Ethnography of the Negro Race. Washington, D.C.: Library of Congress, Division of Bibliography, 1916.

0771. "List of Anti-Slavery Periodicals in the May Anti-Slavery Collection." Cornell Library Bulletin 1 (Jan. 1884), 229-32.

0772. List of Books about the Negro for Young Adults. New York: The New York Public Library, Countee Cullen Branch, 1965.

0773. List of Books on the History of Slavery. Washington, D.C.: Library of Congress, 1917.

0774. List of Books on the Negro Question, 1915-1926. Select List of References No. 956. Washington, D.C.: Library of Congress, 1926.

0775. List of Discussions of the 14th and 15th Amendments with Special Reference to Negro Suffrage. Washington, D.C.: Library of Congress, Division of Bibliography, 1906.

0776. A List of Published Books by Members of the Fisk Faculty and Alumni Since 1955. Nashville, Tenn.: Fisk University, Erastus Milo Cravath Memorial Library, 1962.

0777. List of References on the Anthropology and Ethnography of the Negro Race. Washington, D.C.: Library of Congress, 1905.

0778. List of References on the Negro, with Special Reference to Economic and Industrial Conditions. Washington, D.C.: Library of Congress, Division of Bibliography, 1935.

0779. List of References on Negro Education. Washington, D.C.: Library of Congress, 1906.

0780. List of Writings on the Negro in the U.S. (A Selection of Books Published 1915-1929). Washington, D.C.: Library of Congress, Division of Bibliography, 1929.

0781. Lists of Books by and about Negroes Available in the Libraries of the University of North Carolina and Duke University. Chapel Hill: N.C.: University of North Carolina, 1979.

0782. Livingstone College, Salisbury, North Carolina, Carnegie Library. Collectors Item Bibliography on Slavery, the Anti-Slavery Movement, the Civil War and Emancipation. Compiled at Carnegie Library by Louise M. Roundtree, 1966.

0783. Locke, Alaine L. The Negro American. Chicago: American Library Association, 1964.

0784. Logan, Rayford W. "Bibliography of Bibliographies Dealing Directly or Indirectly with the Negro." in W.E.B. Du Bois and

Guy B. Johnson, (eds.) Encyclopedia of the Negro: Preparatory Volume With Reference Lists and Reports. New York: Phelps-Stokes Fund, 1946, 191-8.

0785. Long, Charles. African and Afro-American Religions: A Bibliography. Chicago: University of Chicago Divinity School, 1950.

0786. Lowenfels, Doris B. Selected Reference Materials: The Black Man in America. Purchase, N.Y.: Manhattanville College, Brady Memorial Library, 1960.

0787. Lyells, Ruby E. Stutts. Understanding the Negro: A Short List of Recent Books By and About the Negro, Selected to Give a Background for Understanding What the Negro Thinks in the Present Crisis. Prepared for the Mississippi Council on Interracial Cooperation. Alcorn, Miss.: Alcorn A and M College Library, 1942.

0788. Lytle, E.E. The Geography of Black America. Public Administration Series No. 924. Monticello, Ill.: Vance Bibliographies, 1982.

0789. Maddrell, Jane G. Bibliography of Negro Books Published from January 1, 1948 through July 31, 1949. Kansas City, Kan.: Bibliographical Publishing Co., 1949.

0790. Malcolm X. Bibliographies in Black Studies No. 1. Chicago, Ill.: Chicago Center for Afro-American Studies and Research, 1964.

0791. Mansfield, Stephen. Collections in the Manuscript Division, American Library, the University of Virginia, Containing References to Slavery for the Period from 1820 to 1865. Charlottsville, Va.: University of Virginia, Alderman Library, 1967.

0792. Martin. C.T. The Civil Rights Movement and Publications Relating to the Negro and Race Relations. M.A. Thesis, University of Chicago, 1969.

0793. Masters, Deborah C. A Guide to Research in Black Studies Prepared for the Exhibition on the Black Experience, Feb. 28-Mar. 25, 1977. University Park, Pa.: Pennsylvania State University Libraries, 1978.

0794. Masters, Deborah C. A Guide to Sources in Black Studies in the Pennsylvania State University Libraries. University Park, Pa.: Pennsylvania State University, University Libraries and the Black Studies Program, 1978.

0795. Mather, F.L. Who's Who of the Colored Race: A General Bibliographical Dictionary of Men and Women of African Descent.

Chicago: 1915.

0796. Mathieson, Moira B. and Rita M. Tatis. <u>Understanding Disadvantaged Youth, Their Problems and Potentials: An Annotated Bibliography.</u> ERIC Document No. Ed 044-380. Washington, D.C.: ERIC Clearinghouse on Teacher Education, 1970.

0797. Matthews, Miriam. "The Negro in California from 1781-1810: An Annotated Bibliography." <u>Paper prepared for University of Southern California</u>, Los Angeles, USC, 1944.

0798. Matthews, Miriam. "Selected Bibliography [on Race Relations]." <u>Journal of Educational Sociology</u> 19:3 (Nov. 1945), 198-206.

0799. May, Samuel. "Catalogue of Anti-Slavery Publications in America. In <u>Proceedings of the American Anti-Slavery Society, at its Third Decade, held in the city of Philadelphia. Dec. 3d and 4th, 1863. With an Appendix and a Catalogue of the Anti-Slavery Publications in America, from 1750-1863</u>. New York: American Anti-Slavery Society, 1864, 157-75.

0800. Mazziothi, Donald F. <u>Neighborhood and Neighborhood Planning.</u> Monticello, Ill.: Council of Planning Librarians No. 596, 1974.

0801. McBride, David. <u>The Afro-American in Pennsylvania: A Critical Guide to Sources in the Pennsylvania State Archives.</u> Harrisburg, Pa.: Pennsylvania Historical and Museum Commission, 1973.

0802. McCabe, Jane A. <u>Education and the Afro-American.</u> Focus: Black American Bibliography Series. Bloomington, Ind.: Indiana University Libraries, 1969.

0803. McCabe, William J. <u>Materials Available for Black Studies.</u> South Orange, N.J.: Seton Hall University, McLaughlin Library, 1970.

0804. McCain, Sara B. and Angela Poulos. <u>Negro Culture: A Selected Bibliography</u>. Bowling Green, Ohio: Bowling Green State University Libraries, Bibliographic Research Center, 1968.

0805. McCall, Emmanuel L. "Select Annotated Bibliography on the Black Church." <u>Review and Expositor</u> 70 (1973), 371-6.

0806. MacCann, Donnarie and Gloria Woodard. <u>The Black American in Books for Children: Readings in Racism.</u> Metuchen, N.J.: Scarecrow, 1972.

0807. McCarroll, J. <u>The Negro in the Congressional Record 1824-1827</u>. New York: Bergman Publishers, 1971.

0808. McCarroll, J. <u>The Negro in the Congressional Record 1827-1829</u>.

New York: Bergman Publishers, 1971.

0809. McClure, Daisy, et al. Black Heritage and Horizons: A Booklist. Kokomo, Ind.: Kokomo Public Library, 1969.

0810. McConnell, J. Michael. Bibliography of Books and Other Materials on Negro History and Culture in the Park College Library. Parkville, Mo.: Park College, Carnegie Library, 1970.

0811. McConnell, Ray M. "The Negro Problem". In A Guide to Reading in Social Ethics and Allied Subjects: Lists of Books and Articles Selected and Described for the Use of General Readers; By Teachers in Harvard University. Cambridge, Mass.: Harvard University Press, 1910, 90-9.

0812. McConnell, Ronald C. "The Importance of Records in the National Archives on the History of the Negro." Journal of Negro History 34 (1949) 135-52.

0813. McCrum, Blanche Prichard. Negroes in the Armed Services of the U.S. from the Earliest Times to the Present: A Select List of References. Washington, D.C.: Library of Congress, General Reference and Bibliography Division, 1949.

0814. McDonnell, Robert W. "Selection Sources of Afro-American History: A Bibliographic Discussion." Current Studies in Librarianship (Spring/Fall 1978), 59-70.

0815. McDonough, John. "Manuscript Resources for the Study of Negro Life and History." Quarterly Journal of the Library of Congress 26 (July 1969), 126-48.

0816. McDowell, Jennifer and Milton Loventhal. Black Politics: A Study and Annotated Bibliography of the Mississippi Freedom Democratic Party. Occasional Papers Series no. 3. San Jose, Cal.: Bibliographic Information Center for the Study of Political Science, 1971.

0817. McIlvaine, Eileen. Selected Reference Materials: Black American Studies. New York: Columbia University Libraries, 1971.

0818. MacKay, M.B. and T.M. Maher. "Selected Bibliography on the American Negro." South Dakota Library Bulletin 55 (July 1969), 154-56.

0819. McPheeters, Annie L. Negro Progress in Atlanta, Georgia, 1950-1960: A Selective Bibliography on Human Relations from Four Atlanta Newspapers. Atlanta, Ga.: Atlanta Public Library, West Hunter Branch, 1964.

0820. McPherson, James M., et al. Blacks in America: Bibliographic Essays. Garden City, N.Y.: Doubleday, 1971.

0821. McWhorter, Gerald A. The Political Sociology of the Negro: A Selected Review of the Literature. New York: Anti-Defamation League of B'nai B'rith, 1967.

0822. Meade, Mary Jo, et al. Black and Brown Bibliography. San Bernadino, Cal.: Library, California State College at San Bernardino, 1966.

0823. Meehan, P.J. A Bibliography of the Relation Between Social Networks on Urban Design Phenomena. Monticello, Ill.: Council of Planning Librarians, Exchange Bibliography, 919, 1975.

0824. Melton, J. Gordon. A (First Working) Bibliography of Black Methodism. Evanston, Ill.: Institute for the Study of American Religion, 1970.

0825. Merritt College Library Guide for Afro-American Studies. Oakland, Cal.: Merritt College Library, 1969.

0826. Messner, Stephen D. Minority Groups and Housing: A Selected Bibliography, 1950-1967. Storrs, Conn.: University of Connecticut, Center for Real Estate and Urban Economic Studies, 1969.

0827. Meyer, Jon K. Bibliography on the Urban Crisis: The Behavioral, Psychological and Sociological Aspects of the Urban Crisis. A publication of the U.S. National Clearinghouse for Mental Health Information. Washington, D.C.: National Institute of Mental Health, 1969.

0828. Michalak, Thomas J. Economic Status and Condition of the Negro. Focus: Black American Bibliography Series. Bloomington, Ind.: Indiana University Libraries, 1969.

0829. Mignon, Molly R. Racism in America: A Bibliography of Government Documents and Pamphlets in the Wilson Library, West Washington State College. Bellingham, Wash.: West Washington State College, Mabel Z. Wilson Library, 1970.

0830. Millender, D.H. Real Negroes, Honest Settings, Children and Young Peoples Books About the Negro Life and History. Chicago: American Federation of Teachers, AFL-CIO, 1917.

0831. Miller, Albert Jay. Confrontation, Conflict and Dissent: A Bibliography of a Decade of Controversy, 1960-1970. Metuchen, N.J.: Scarecrow Press, 1972.

0832. Miller, Elizabeth W. The Negro in America: A Bibliography. Compiled for the American Academy of Arts and Sciences. Cambridge, Mass.: Harvard University Press, 1966.

0833. Miller, Joseph C. Slavery: A Comparative Teaching Bibliography. Waltham, Mass.: Crossroads Press, 1978.

0834. Miller, Wayne, et al. A Comprehensive Bibliography for the Study of American Minorities. New York: New York University Press, 1976.

0835. Mills, Annie B. and Mary Lu Yavenditti. The Negro in America: A Selected Bibliography of Books Available in Monteith Library. Alma, Mich.: Alma College, Monteith Library, 1969.

0836. Mills, Hazel E. and Nancy B. Prior. The Negro in the State of Washington, 1788-1969: A Bibliography of Published Works and of Unpublished Source Materials on the Life and Achievements of the Negro in the Evergreen State. Rev. ed. Olympia, Wash.: Washington State Library, 1970.

0837. Mills, Joyce White. The Black World in Literature for Children: A Bibliography of Print and Non-print Materials. Atlanta, Ga.: Atlanta University, School of Library Service, 1975.

0838. Min, Tae H. The Black in America. Pocatello, Id.: Idaho State University Library, 1970.

0839. Minorities and Allied Health: An Annotated Bibliography. Southwest Program Development Corp., 1973.

0840. Minorities and Discrimination in the U.S. with Particular Reference to Employment Practices: A Selected List of Books in the Washington State Library. Olympia, Wash.: Washington State Library, 1967.

0841. Minorities and Intergroup Relations: A Selected Bibliography. Chicago, Ill.: American Council on Race Relations, 1948.

0842. Minority Groups: Bibliography. Salt Lake City, Utah: Utah Board of Education, Office of the State Superintendent of Public Instruction, 1968.

0843. Minority Groups Bibliography. St. Paul, Minn.: Minnesota Department of Education, Division of Instruction, 1968.

0844. Minority Groups/Disadvantaged Youth: A Selected Bibliography. ERIC Document No. ED 074-685. Arlington, Va.: Council for Exceptional Children, 1972.

0845. Minority Groups: Exceptional Child Bibliographic Series. ERIC Document No. 054-575. Arlington, Va.: Council for Exceptional Children, 1971.

0846. Minority Groups in Medicine: Selected Bibliography. DHEW Publication no. (NIH) 72-33. Bethesda, Md.: U.S. National Institute of Health, Division of Physician and Health Professions Education, 1972.

0847. Minority Groups: Selected Bibliographies and References of Materials For Children and Young Adults. Chicago, Ill.: American Library Association, Children's Service and Young Adult Services Division, 1969.

0848. Mitchell, Henry S. and Darryl M. Smaw. A Bibliography of Afro-American History, Ambrose Swasey Library, Colgate Rochester/Bexley Hall/Crozer Seminary, Rochester, N.Y. Rochester, N.Y.: Colgate Rochester/Bexley Hall/Crozer Seminary, Black Church Studies Program, 1971.

0849. Mohr, C.L. "Southern Blacks in the Civil War, a Century of Historiography: Bibliographic Essay." Journal of Negro History 59 (Apr. 1974), 177-95.

0850. Momeni, Jamshid. Demography of Black Population in the United States: an Annotated Bibliography with a Review Essay. Westport, Conn.: Greenwood, 1983.

0851. Montesano, Philip M. San Francisco Black People, 1860-1865: A Bibliographical Essay. San Francisco, 1980.

0852. Morehouse, Jean, et al. Bibliography of the Black. Oswego, N.Y.: SUNY-Oswego, Penfield Library, 1980.

0853. Morris, Effie Lee. Minority Groups: A Bibliography of Books and Pamphlets. San Francisco, Cal.: San Francisco Public Library, Office of Children's Services, 1969.

0854. Mosby, Elizabeth. Bibliography of the Black Studies Collection. Concord, N.C.: Barber-Scotia College Library, 1980.

0855. Moshburn, S. Afro-American History and Culture. Mt. Vernon, Wash.: Skagit Valley College Library, 1980.

0856. Moss, Josephine. Basic Books for Black Studies in Denison University. Granville, Ohio: Denison University, William Howard Doane Library, 1970.

0857. Murphy, Jane and Taylor Pat Johnson. Current Acquisitions in Black Studies. Neward, Del.: University of Delaware, Hugh M. Morris Library, 1970.

0858. Myers, Hector F., et al. Black Child Development in America, 1927-1977: An Annotated Bibliography. Westport, Conn.: Greenwood, 1979.

0859. The NAACP: A Register of Its Records in the Library of Congress. Washington, D.C.: Library of Congress, Manuscript Division, 1972.

0860. NAACP: A Selected Bibliography. New York: the New York Public

Library, Schomburg Collection, 1955.

0861. "Negro." Compiled by the Staff of the Countee Cullen Branch.
First Annual Supplement to the Oct. 1950 List. Branch Library
Book News [The New York Public Library] 28:9 (Nov. 1951), 129-
30.

0862. Negro. Jamestown, N.Y.: Chautauqua - Cattaraugus Public
Library, 1964.

0863. Negro. Milwaukee, Wis.: Milwaukee Public Library, 1960.

0864. "Negro -- A Selected Bibliography." Branch Library Book News
-- Supplement to the Bulletin of the New York Public Library
17:9 (Nov. 1940), 138-56.

0865. "Negro: A Selected Bibliography." Bulletin of The New York
Public Library 54 (Oct. 1950), 471-85.

0866. "Negro-A Selected Bibliograhy." Bulletin of The New York
Public Library; Branch Library Book News 7:2 (Feb. 1930), 18-
30.

0867. "Negro: A Selected Bibliography Including Supplements for 1951-
1953." Branch Library Book News, the New York Public Library
31:2 (Feb. 1954), 18-30.

0868. "Negro--A Selected Bibliography (Part I)." Branch Library Book
News--Supplement to the Bulletin of the New York Public Library
12:4 (Apr. 1935), 66-74.

0869. Negro: A Selected List for School Libraries of Books By or
About the Negro in Africa and America. Nashville, Tenn.:
Tennessee Department of Education, Division of School
Libraries, 1935.

0870. Negro, A Selected Reading List." Branch Library Book News [The
New York Public Library] 23:9 (Nov. 1946), 129-30.

0871. "Negro--A Selected Reading List." Branch Library Book News
[The New York Public Library] 22:2 (Feb. 1945), 39-45.

0872. Negro: A Selected Reading List. Compiled by the Staff of the
135th Street Branch Library, [The New York Public Library].
1949.

0873. Negro American: A Reading List. New York: National Council of
Churches of Christ in the U.S.A., Department of Racial and
Cultural Relations, 1957.

0874. Negro American: A Selected List of Books, Magazines and
Recordings for School Libraries. Nashville, Tenn.: Tennessee
Department of Education, Equal Educational Oppurtunities

Program, 1969.

0875. Negro-American Life and History. Atlanta, Ga.: Georgia Department of Education, Office of Instructional Services, Curriculum Development Division, School Library Services Unit, 1970.

0876. Negro and His Achievements in America: A List of Books Compiled for the American Negro Exposition. Chicago: Chicago Public Library, 1940.

0877. Negro Bibliography. Tacoma, Wash.: Tacoma Public Library, 1960.

0878. Negro Freedom Movement, Past and Present: An Annotated Bibliography. Detroit, Mich.: Wayne County Intermediate School District, Desegragation Advisory Project, 1967.

0879. Negro Heritage Resource Guide: A Bibliography of the Negro in Contemporary America. New York: National Council of Churches of Christ in the U.S.A., Division of Christian Education, 1967.

0880. Negro Housing in Town and Cities, 1927-1937. New York: Russell Sage Foundation Library, 1937.

0881. Negro in American History and Culture: A Bibliography of Sources for Teaching. New York: Union Theological Seminary, Auburn Library, Urban Education Collection, 1965.

0882. Negro in American Life: A Selected Bibliography, 1960-1963. Boston, Mass.: Massachusetts Department of Education, Division of Library Extension, 1963.

0883. Negro in Business: A Bibliography, 1935. Washington, D.C.: U.S.Department of Commerce, Negro Affairs Division, 1935.

0884. Negro in Science: A Selected Bibliography Prepared in the Schomburg Collection. New York: Public Library, 1940.

0885. The Negro in the State of Washington; 1788-1967: A Bibliography of Published Works and Unpublished Source Materials on the Life and Achievements of the Negro in the Evergreen State. Olympia, Wash.: Washington State Library, 1968.

0886. Negro Movement: Past and Present. Detroit, Mich.: Wayne County Intermediate School District, Desegregation Advisory Project, 1967.

0887. Negro Past and Present: An Annotated Bibliography. Mt. Clemens, Mich.: Mt. Clemens Public Library, 1968.

0888. Negroes in Michigan: A Selected Bibliography. Lansing, Mich.: Michigan Bureau of Library Services, 1969.

0889. Nelson, Rose K. *Bibliography of the Negro.* New York: Service Bureau for Intercultural Education, 1969.

0890. Newbacher, G.D. *Low Income Housing Mixing: An Annotated Bibliography.* Monticello, Ill.: Council of Planning Librarians, 1975.

0891. Newby, Corene. *Black America: Past-Present-Future.* Lima, Ohio: Lima Public Library, 1975.

0892. Newby, James E. *Black Authors and Education: An Annotated Bibliography of Books.* Washington, D.C.: University Press of America, 1980.

0893. New Jersey Library Association Bibliographic Committee. *New Jersey and the Negro.* Trenton, N.J.: MacCrellish and Quigley Co., 1967.

0894. New York City Community College. *Black Perspectives: A Bibliography.* New York: Community College Press, 1971.

0895. New York Public Library. *Bibliographic Guide to Black Studies.* Boston: G. K. Hall, 1976.

0896. New York Public Library. *Books About Negro Life for Children.* New York: The Library, 1963.

0897. New York Public Library. *The Negro in the United States: A List of Significant Books.* New York: New York Public Library, 1965.

0898. New York Public Library. *The Negro: A Selected Bibliography.* New York: The Library, 1935.

0899. New York Public Library. *The Negro in the United States: A List of Significant Books.* New York: The Library, 1965.

0900. Newman, Richard. *Black Access: A Bibliography of Afro-American Bibliographies.* Westport, Conn.: Greenwood, 1984.

0901. Newman, Richard. *Black Index: Afro-Americana in Selected Periodicals 1907-1949.* New York: Garland Publishing Inc., 1981.

0902. Newman, Richard. *Black Power: A Bibliography.* Wakefield, Mass.: Community Change, Inc., 1969.

0903. Newman, Richard. "A Preliminary List of Bibliographies on Afro-American Religion." *Newsletter of the Afro-American Religious History Group of the American Academy of Religion* 5:2 (Spring 1981), 8-12.

0904. Newman, Richard. "Some Recent Bibliographic Resources for Black Religion." *Newsletter of the Afro-American Religious*

History Group of the American Academy of Religion 2:1 (Fall 1977), 3-4.

0905. Newspapers and Periodicals by and about Black People: Southeastern Library Holdings. Boston: G.K. Hall, 1979.

0906. Nordie, Margaret. Guide to Afro-American Material in the Carl B. Ylvisaker Library. Moorhead, Minn.: Concordia College, Carl B. Ylvisaker Library.

0907. Norgen, Paul A. Racial Discrimination in Employment. Princeton, N.J.: Princeton University, Industrial Relations Section, 1962.

0908. Oaks, Priscilla S. Minority Studies: A Selective Annotated Bibliography. Boston, Mass.: G.K Hall, 1976.

0909. O'Brien, Gail. Bibliography on Black American Studies. Plattsburgh, N.Y.: SUNY at Plattsburgh, Benjamin F. Feinburg Library, 1965.

0910. Obudho, Constance E. Black-White Racial Attitudes: An Annotated Bibliography. Westport, Conn.: Greenwood, 1976.

0911. O'Hara, Minna. Employment Problems and Opportunities of Minority Groups: The Past, Present and Future of Negroes and Puerto Ricans in the World of Work. New York: Board of Education of the City of New York, Office of the Assistant Superintendent, 1965.

0912. Ohio, Central State College, Wilberforce Library. Index of Periodical Articles By and About Negroes. Boston: G.K. Hall, 1950.

0913. Onderdonk, Dudley. Interracial Housing Since 1970: From Activism to Affirmative Marketing. Chicago: CPL Bibliographies No. 15, 1979.

0914. One Hundred Years of Freedom: A Selected Bibliography of Books About the American Negro. Washington, D.C.: Association for the Study of Negro Life and History, 1968.

0915. Osgood, F.W. A Bibliography for a Program for Continuous Renewal of Our Cities and Metropolitan Regions: A Design for Improved Management, Decision-Making and Action. Monticello, Ill.: Council of Planning Librarians, Exchange Bibliography No. 184, 1971.

0916. Overton, Holda and James Poole. Bibliography on the History of the Negro. Tougaloo, Miss.: Tougaloo College, Eastman Library, 1963.

0917. Oxley, Lawrence A. Bibliography on Negro Labor. Washington,

D.C.: U.S. Bureau of Labor Statistics, 1937.

0918. Padbury, P. The Future: A Bibliography of Issues and Forecasting Techniques. Monticello, Ill.: Council of Planning Librarians, Exchange Bibliography, No. 15, 1970.

0919. Parker, Franklin. "Negro Education in the USA: A Partial Bibliography of Doctoral Dissertations." Negro History Bulletin 24:8 (May 1961), 192.

0920. Parker, Franklin. "Public School Desegregation: A Partial Bibliography of 113 Doctoral Dissertations." Negro History Bulletin 26:7 (Apr. 1963), 225-8.

0921. Parker, Franklin. "School Desegregation: A Partial List of 94 Doctoral Dissertations." Journal of Human Relations 10 (Autumn 1961), 118-24.

0922. Parks, Martha. The Negro: A Selected List for School Librarians of Books by or About the Negroes in Africa and America. Nashville, Tenn.: Tennessee Department of Education, 1941.

0923. Pastorette, Tomma N. Race Relations: Selected References. Maxwell Air Force Base, Ala.: U.S. Department of Defense, Air Force, Air University Library, Special Bibliography No. 200, 1975.

0924. Peabody, Ruth. The Afro-Americans: Their Heritage and Contributions; Education: A Guide to Black Education Materials, A Selected Bibliography. Albany, N.Y.: SUNY at Albany, University Libraries, 1977.

0925. Peabody, Ruth. The Afro-Americans: Their Heritage and Contributions; Reference. Albany, N.Y.: SUNY at Albany, University Libraries, 1975.

0926. Peathe, Lisa R. Slums. Monticello, Ill.: Council of Planning Librarians, Exchange Bibliography No. 15, 1970.

0927. Peebles, J.B. Black Studies: A Dissertation Bibliography; Doctoral Research on the Negro, 1966-1977. Ann Arbor, Mich.: University Microfilms, 1978.

0928. Peebles, J.B. Black Studies: A Dissertation Bibliography. Ann Arbor: University Microfilms, 1982.

0929. Peet, R. "Bibliography on American Poverty." Antipode. 4:2, (December 1980), 84-106.

0930. Pettigrew, T.F. A Profile of the American Negro. Princeton, N.J.: Nostrand, 1964.

0931. Pflieger, E.F. "Bibliography on Afro-American History and Culture." Social Education 33 (Apr. 1969), 447-61.

0932. Phillips, Myrtle R. and C.L. Miller. "A Selected Annotated Bibliography on the Relationship of the Federal Government to Negro Education." Journal of Negro Education 7:3 (July 1938), 468-74.

0933. Phinazee, Annette Hoage. The Georgia Child's Access to Materials Pertaining to American Negroes. Presented at a conference sponsored by the Atlanta University School of Library Service and the Georgia Council on Human Relations. Atlanta, Ga.: Atlanta University School of Library Service, 1968.

0934. Phinazee, Annette Hoage. Materials by and about Negroes. Institute on Materials by and about American Negroes, 1965. Atlanta, Ga.: Atlanta University School of Library Service, 1967.

0935. Phipps, Claire A. Afro-American in the Library of Chico State College. Chico, Cal.: Chico State College Library, 1969.

0936. Piccolo, Vincent and Daniel Dick. Black Studies Library. Worcester, Mass.: Worcester State College Library, 1969.

0937. Pier, Helen Louis and Mary Louisa Spalding. "The Negro: A Selected Bibliography." Monthly Labor Review 22:1 (Jan. 1926), 216-44.

0938. Pilche, W.W. Urban Anthoropology. Monticello, Ill.: Council of Planning Librarians, Exchange Bibliography, No. 944-945, 1975.

0939. Pinto, Patrick R. and J.O. Buchmier. Problems and Issues in the Employment of Minority, Disadvantages and Female Groups: An Annotated Bibliography. Minneapolis, Minn.: University of Minnesota, Industrial Relations Center, 1973.

0940. Ploski, H. Reference Library of Black America. New York: Belwether Publishing Co., 1971.

0941. Ploski, H. and Warner, M. The Negro Almanac. A Reference Work on the Afro-American 1776 (Bicentennial Edition 1976). New York: The Belwether Publishing Company, 1976.

0942. Podlish, Phillip, et al. The Black Experience: the Negro in America, Africa and the World: A Comprehensive, Annotated Subject Bibliography of Works in the University of Toledo Libraries. Toledo, Ohio: University of Toledo, 1969.

0943. Poehlman, Dorothy. Equal Employment Opportunity: Selected References. Washington, D.C.: U.S. Department of

Transportation, Federal Aviation Administration, Library Services Division, 1968.

0944. The Police and Race Relations: A Selected Bibliography. New York: American Jewish Committee, Institute of Human Relations, 1966.

0945. Porter, Dorothy B. Howard University Masters' Theses Submitted in Partial Fulfillment of the Requirements for the Master's Degree at Howard University, 1918-1945. Washington, D.C.: Howard University, Graduate School, 1946.

0946. Porter, Dorothy B. The Negro in American Cities: A Selected and Annotatd Bibliography. Prepared for the National Advisory Commission on Civil Disorders. Washington, D.C.: Howard University Library, 1967.

0947. Porter, Dorothy B. The Negro in the U.S.: A Selected Bibliography. Washington, D.C.: Library of Congress, 1970.

0948. Porter, Dorothy B. The Negro in the United States: A Working Bibliography. Ann Arbor, Mich.: University Microfilms, 1969.

0949. Porter, Dorothy B. Reading List on the Negro in the U.S. and Other Countries. Washington, D.C.: Howard University, Moorland Foundation, 1944.

0950. Porter, Dorothy B. A Selected Bibliography of Bibliographies on the Negro, 1965.

0951. Porter, Dorothy B. A Selected List of Books By and About the Negro. Washington, D.C.: U.S. Department of Commerce, Bureau of Foreign and Domestic Commerce, 1936.

0952. Porter, Dorothy B. and Delores C. Leffall. "Bibliography." Journal of Negro Education 29:2 (Spring 1960), 168-73.

0953. Porter, Jack N. "Black-Jewish Relations: Some Notes on Cross-Cultural Research Plus a Selected Annotated Bibliography." International Review of Sociology (Sept. 1971), 1-9.

0954. Porter, Nancy and Pauline Lilje. A Guide to Washington State University Library Materials for the Black Studies Program. Pullman, Wash.: Washington State University Library, 1969.

0955. Posselt, Jane. Bibliography of Books and Pamphlets in the Middlesex County College Library Which Deal with the Negro in the U.S. Edison, N.J.: Middlesex County College Library, 1969.

0956. Poulos, Angela and Iris Jones. Black Culture: A Selective Bibliography. Bowling Green, Ohio: Bowling Green State University Libraries, Reference Department, 1974.

0957. *Poverty, Rural Poverty and Minority Groups Living in Rural Poverty: An Annotated Bibliography.* ERIC Document No. 041-679. Institute for Rural America. Lexington, Ky.: Spindletop Research Center, 1969.

0958. Powell, Ronald H. *Bibliography for Afro-American Studies.* Largo, Md.: Prince George's Community College Library, 1969.

0959. *Preliminary List of Resource Materials on Minority Groups.* Olympia, Wash.: Washington Department of Education, 1968.

0960. Pressley, Milton M. *Selected Bibliography of Readings and References Regarding Marketing to Black America.* Exchange Bibliography No. 671. Monticello, Ill.: Council of Planning Librarians, 1974.

0961. Preston, Clarence Johnson and Julia O. Saunders. *The Education of Negroes in Virginia: An Annotated Bibliography,* Charlottsville: Archives, 1944.

0962. Preston, M.B. "Blacks and Public Policy: A Selected Bibliography." *Policy Studies Journal* 9 (Spring 1981), 775-84.

0963. *The Prevention and Control of Race Riots: A Bibliography for Police Officers.* Social Adjustment Bibliography No. 1. Los Angeles, Cal.: Los Angeles Public Library, Municipal Reference Library, 1944.

0964. Price, Daniel O. *Changing Characteristics of the Negro Population: A 1960 Census Monograph.* United States Department of Commerce, Washington, D.C.: U.S. Government Printing Office, 1965.

0965. Prince George's County Memorial Library. *Selective List of Governmental Publications About the American Negro.* Hyattsville, Maryland: Prince George's County Memorial Library, 1969.

0966. *Provisional Bibliography on Slavery.* Prepared for the UN Library and UN Ad Hoc Committee on Slavery According to An Outline Supplied by the Sponsors. Washington, D.C.: Library of Congress, General Reference and Bibliography Division, 1950.

0967. Querry, Ronald and Robert E. Fleming. "A Working Bibliography of Black Periodicals." *Studies in Black Literature 3* (Summer 1972), 31-6.

0968. Quigless, Helen, et al. *Black Information Index.* Washington, D.C.: Federal City College, Media Center, 1972.

0969. Quintana, Helena. *A Guide to Ethnic Studies at Zimmerman Library.* Albuquerque, N.M.: University of New Mexico, Zimmerman Library, 1970.

0970. Quintana, Helena, et al. Afro-American Bibliography. Albuquerque, N.M.: University of New Mexico, Zimmerman Library, 1971.

0971. Rabinowitz, Alan. Urban Real Estate Finance 1925-1975. Chicago: CPL Bibliography No. 20, 1980.

0972. The Race Problem in the U.S.: A Brief Bibliographical List. Washington, D.C.: Library of Congress, 1929.

0973. Race Relations Issues in 1961: A Bibliography. New York: NAACP, 1961.

0974. Race Relations, With Special Reference to Employment. Bibliographic Reference List No. 102. Geneva, Switzerland: International Labour Office, Library, 1963.

0975. Race Restrictive Covenants: A Selected List of References. Detroit, Mich.: Detroit Public Library. Distributed by the National Association for the Advancement of Colored People, 1946.

0976. Racism and Education: A Review of Selected Literature Relating to Segregation, Discrimination and Other Aspects of Racism in Education. ERIC Document No. 034-836. Detroit, Mich.: Michigan-Ohio Regional Education Laboratory, 1969.

0977. Racism and Reconstruction: A Selected, Annotated Bibliography of Periodical Articles, 1966 - 1969. Bibliography Series No. 3. Ithaca, N.Y.: Cornell University, John M. Olin Library, Reference Department, 1969.

0978. Rafter, Susan Blacks in Suburbs. Chicago: CPL Bibliography, No. 133, June 1984.

0979. Ragan, Pauline K. and Mary Simonin. Black and Mexican American Aging: A Selected Bibliography. Los Angeles, Cal.: Ethel Percy Andrus Gerontology Center, University of Southern California, 1977.

0980. Randolph, H. Helen. Urban Education Bibliography: An Annotated Listing. New York: Center for Urban Education, 1968.

0981. Raynham, Warner R. Bibliographies Relating Various Areas of Theological Study to the Black Experience in America. Boston, Mass.: Boston Theological Institute, 1973.

0982. Rea, L.M. Transportation and Poverty. Monticello, Ill.: Council of Planning Librarians, Exchange Bibliography 1237, 1977.

0983. Recent Books in the Field of Negro Life and Culture, 1966. Detroit, Mich.: Detroit Public Library, 1966.

0984. Recent Klapper Library Acquisitions in Black Studies. Flushing, N.Y.: Queens College, Paul Klapper Library, 1970.

0985. Reddick, Lawrence D. "Bibliographical Problems in Negro Research." American Council of Learned Societies Bulletin 32 (Sept. 1941), 26-30.

0986. Reddick, Lawrence D. Bibliography: the Afro-American Experience. Nashville, Tenn.: Fisk University, Workshop on Negro Culture, 1969.

0987. Reddick, Lawrence D. "Library Facilities for Research in Negro Colleges." Quarterly Review of Higher Education Among Negroes 8:3 (July 1940), 127-9.

0988. Reddick, Lawrence D. "Select Bibliography" [of studies on Negro Colleges]. Journal of Educational Sociology 19 (April 1946), 512-6.

0989. Reichard, Max. The Black Man in St. Louis: A Preliminary Bibliography. Exchange Bibliography No. 574. Monticello, Ill.: Council of Planning Librarians, 1974.

0990. Reid, Ira De Augustine. Negro Youth, Their Social and Economic Backgrounds: A Selected Bibliography of Unpublished Studies, 1900-1938. Washington, D.C.: American Youth Commission of the American Council on Education, 1939.

0991. Research on the Disadvantaged: An Annotated List of Relevant E.T.S. Studies, 1951-1969. ERIC Document no. ED 037-392. Princeton, N.J.: Educational Testing Service, 1969.

0992. Research on Racial Relations. Amsterdam, Netherlands: United Nations, UNESCO, 1966.

0993. Rhodes, Barbara and Verena Larson. A Selected Listing of Materials Held by the Texas A and M University Library Relative to the Black Man in America. College Station, Tex.: Texas A and M University Library, 1969.

0994. Rhodes, Lelia G., et al. Classified Bibliography of the Afro-American Collection and Selected Works on Africa in the Library. Compiled for the National Evaluative Conference in Black Studies. Sponsored by the Institute for the Study of the History, Life and Culture of Black People. Jackson, Miss.: Jackson State College, 1971.

0995. Richardson, J.M. The Negro in the Reconstruction of Florida, 1865-1877. Tallahassee, Florida State University, 1965.

0996. Richardson, Marilyn. Black Women and Religion: A Bibliography. Boston: G.K. Hall, 1980.

0997. Richter, Edward, et al. *An Introductory Bibliography of Black Studies Resources in the Eastern New Mexico University Library.* Portales, N.M.: Eastern New Mexico University, 1970.

0998. Rosenberg, Arnold S. *Bibliography for a Black Studies Minor.* Danbury, Conn.: Western Connecticut State College Library, 1971.

0999. Ross, Frank Alexander and Louise Venable Kennedy. *A Bibliography of Negro Migration.* New York: Columbia University Press, 1934, 251.

1000. Rountree, Louise. *American Negro and African Studies: A Bibliography on the Special Collections in Carnegie Library.* Salisbury, N.C.: Livingstone College, 1968.

1001. Rountree, Louise. *Collector's Itemized Bibliography on Slavery, the Anti-Slavery Movement and Emancipation.* Salisbury, N.C.: Livingstone College, Carnegie Library, 1966.

1002. Rowell, Gordon A. *Bibliography of Books on the Black Experience in the USA Available in Manhattan Bech and Mid-Brooklyn Libraries.* New York: Kingsborough Community College of CUNY, 1969.

1003. Rutgers University, Main Library. *The Negro and New Jersey; A Checklist of Books, Pamphlets, Official Publications, Broadsides and Dissertations, 1754-1964, in the Rutgers University Library.* New Brunswick, New Jersey: Library, 1965.

1004. Rutstein, Joel and Patricia Peabody. *Black Studies on Campus: A Bibliographic Approach.* Durham, N.C.: University of New Hampshire, Ezekiel W. Dimond Library, 1969.

1005. Sampson, F.A. and W.C. Breckenridge. "Bibliography of Slavery in Missouri." *Missouri Historical Review* 2 (April 1908), 233-44.

1006. Sandhu, Manmohan Singh. *Race Relations and Group Relations: A Selected Research Bibliography.* Jackson, Miss.: Jackson State University, 1977.

1007. Sanford, Marvin. *A Bibliography on the Revolutionary Approach to the Negro Question in America.* Mena, Ark.: Commonwealth College Library, 1937.

1008. Sarah Byrd Askew Library. *Curriculum Materials: the Black Experience in Books for Children and Young People, A Selective Bibliography.* Wayne, N.J.: William Paterson College, 1984.

1009. Schatz, Walter. *Directory of Afro-American Resources.* New York: R.R. Bowker Co., 1970.

1010. Scherer, Lester. "Bibliography: Dissertations in Afro-American Religion." _Newsletter of the Afro-American Religious History Group of the American Academy of Religion_ 2:2 (Spring 1978), 4-16.

1011. Schlachter, Gail and Donna Belli. _Blacks in an Urban Environment: A Selected Annotated Bibliography of Reference Sources._ Exchange Bibliography No. 819. Monticello, Ill.: Council of Planning Librarians, 1975.

1012. Schlachter, Gail and Donna Belli. _Minorities and Women: A Guide to the Reference Literature in the Social Sciences._ Los Angeles, Cal.: References Services Press, 1977.

1013. Schneider, Joyce B. _A Selected List of Periodicals Relating to Negroes, with Holdings in the Libraries of Yale University._ New Haven, Conn.: Yale University, 1970.

1014. Schor, Joel and Cecil Harvey. _A List of References for the History of Black Americans in Agriculture, 1619-1974._ Davis, Cal.: University of California at Davis, Agricultural Historical Center, 1975.

1015. Scott, Nancy, et al. _Black American: A Selected, Classified and Partially Annotated List of Books, Periodicals and Audiovisual Materials in the Gettysburg College Library._ Gettysburg, Pa.: Gettysburg College, Schmucker Memorial Library, 1970.

1016. _Segregation and Desegregation in American Education._ 2nd ed. Bibliography No. 18. Gainesville, Fla.: University of Florida, College of Education Library, 1956.

1017. _Selected Bibliography By and About Minority Groups._ Frankfort, Ky.: Kentucky Department of Education, Division of Instructional Services, School Library Services, 1966.

1018. _Selected Bibliography of Books on Race Relations and the Negro._ New York: NAACP, 1960.

1019. _Selected Bibliography of Government Publications About the American Negro. Prepared for Negro History Week 1969._ Hyattsville, Md.: Prince George's County Memorial Library, Oxon Hill Branch, Reference Department, 1969.

1020. "Selected Bibliography of Negro History Material." _Negro Digest_ 16 (Feb. 1967), 81-2.

1021. "Selected Bibliography of Studies of Negro Education." _Journal of Negro Education_ 5 (July 1936), 534.

1022. _Selected Bibliography on Discrimination in Housing._ Sacramento, Cal.: California State Library, Law Library, 1964.

1023. Selected Bibliography on the Negro. New York: National Urban League, Department of Research and Community Projects, 1937.

1024. Selected Guide to Materials on Black Studies. Detroit, Mich.: Wayne State University Library, 1971.

1025. Selected List of Books By and About the Negro. Washington, D.C.: Howard University, Carnegie Library, Moorland Foundation, 1940.

1026. Selected List of Books By and About the Negro, 1950-1956. Raleigh, N.C.: Richard B. Harrison Public Library, 1957.

1027. Selected List of References Relating to Desegregation and Integration, 1949 to June 1955. Tuskegee, Ala.: Tuskegee Institute, Department of Records and Research, 1955.

1028. Selected List of References Relating to Discrimination and Segregation in Education, 1949 to June 1955. Tuskegee, Ala.: Tuskegee Institute, Department of Records and Research, 1955.

1029. Selected List of References on the Negro Question. Washington, D.C.: Library of Congress, 1903.

1030. Selected Negro Reference Books and Bibliographic: An Annotated Guide. Amherst, Mass.: University of Massachusetts Library, Reference Department, 1969.

1031. Selected Reference on Housing for Minorities. Racial Relations Service Documents. Series F. Bibliographies, No. 1. Washington, D.C.: National Housing Agency, Office of the Administration, 1946.

1032. Selected Reference on Housing of Minorities. Washington, D.C.: U.S. Housing and Home Finance Agency, Office of the Administrator, Racial Relations Service, 1950.

1033. Selected Texts of Afro-American History (U.S.A.). Santa Barbara, Cal.: University of California at Santa Barbara, Center for Black Studies, 1977.

1034. Selected Titles on Afro-American and African Collections. Atlanta, Ga.: Southern Association of Colleges and Schools, Education Improvement Project Staff, 1969.

1035. Sernett, Milton. Geographical Literature on Black America: A Selected Bibliography (including some items of historical interest). Syracuse, N.Y.: Syracuse University, 1980, 3 pp.

1036. Shafer, Ann M. and Rosen E. Longfellow. Fiar Share Housing: A Bibliography. Chicago: CPL Bibliography No. 38, 1980.

1037. Shannon, Magdaline O. New York Urban Statistics. Monticello,

Ill.: Council of Planning Librarians, Exchange Bibliography No.
873, 1975.

1038.   Sharma, Prakash. <u>Slum and Ghetto Studies</u>. Monticello, Ill.:
Council of Planning Librarians, Exchange Bibliography No. 573,
1974.

1039.   Sherwood, Margaret. <u>Devices to Assist the Handicapped's Use of
Automobiles: An Annotated Bibliography</u>. Chicago: CPL
Bibliography No. 24, 1980.

1040.   Shevory, Joan. <u>The American Negro: A List of Books in the
Jamestown Community College Library.</u> Jamestown, N.Y.:
Jamestown Community College Library, 1970.

1041.   Shilling, Barbara. <u>Exclusionary Zoning: Restrictive
Definitions of Family: An Annotated Bibliography</u>. Chicago: CPL
Bibliography No. 31, 1980.

1042.   Shockley, Ann Allen. "Concise Selected Bibliography of Books
and Periodicals for an Initial Afro-American Library." <u>A
Handbook for the Administration of Special Negro Collections</u>.
Nashville, Tenn.: Fisk University Library, 1970, 57-63.

1043.   Shumsky, N. and Timosky C. <u>Urban America.</u> Santa Barbara,
Cal.: ABC-Clio, 1983.

1044.   Sieg, Vera. <u>The Negro Problem: A Bibliography.</u> Madison, Wis.:
Wisconsin Free Library Commission, 1908.

1045.   Sieg, Vera. "The Negro Problem: A Bibliography," in Betty
Kaplan Gubert. <u>Early Black Bibliographies, 1863-1918</u>. New
York: Garland, 1982, 271-92.

1046.   Siegel, Judith A. <u>Racial Discrimination in Housing.</u> Exchange
Bibliography No. 1201. Monticello, Ill.: Council of Planning
Librarians, 1977.

1047.   Simmie, J.M. <u>The Sociology of Town Planning: A Bibliography</u>.
Monticello, Ill.: Council of Planning Librarians, Exchange
Bibliography, No. 1039-1040, 1976.

1048.   Sinclair, Donald A. <u>The Negro in New Jersey: A Checklist of
Books, Pamphlets, Official Publications, Broadsides and
Dissertations, 1754-1964, in the Rutgers University Library.</u>
New Brunswick, N.J.: Rutgers University Library, 1965.

1049.   Sinclair, Donald A. <u>New Jersey and the Negro: A Bibliography,
1716-1966</u>. Bibliography Committee of the New Jersey Library
Association. Trenton, N.J.: Trenton Free Public Library, 1967.

1050.   Slevin, Ann D. <u>A Selection of Holdings on the Afro-American</u>.
Princeton, N.J.: Princeton University, Firestone Memorial

Library, 1967.

1051. Sloan, I.J. The American Negro: A Chronology and Fact Book. New York: Oceana, 1965.

1052. Sloan, I.J. The Blacks in America 1492-1977. A Chronology and Fact Book. New York: Oceana 1975.

1053. Smith, Bonnie L. and Agnes Hammond. Afro-American Archives in California and the West. San Marcos, Cal.: Palomar College, Phil H. Putnam Library, 1968.

1054. Smith, Bonnie L. and Agnes Hammond. The Afro-American: His Life and History; A Bibliography of Works in the Palomar College Library. San Marcos, Cal.: Palomar College, Phil H. Putnam Library, 1969.

1055. Smith, Dwight L. "Afro-American History: A Bibliographic Survey and Suggestion." Paper read at Association for the Study of Afro-American Life and History, New York, 1973.

1056. Smith, Dwight L. Afro-American History: A Bibliography, Vol. 1, Santa Barbara, Cal.: ABC-CLIO, 1974.

1057. Smith, Dwight L. Afro-American History: A Bibliography, Vol. 2, Santa Barbara, Cal.: ABC-CLIO, 1981.

1058. Smith, Dwight L. Afro-American History, Vol. 3: A Bibliography. Santa Barbara, Cal.: ABC-Clio, 1984.

1059. Smith, Jessie Carney. Black Academic Libraries and Research Collections: An Historical Survey. Westport, Conn.: Greenwood, 1977.

1060. Smith, Jessie Carney. Ethnic Genealogy: A Research Guide. Wesport, Conn.: Greenwood, 1983.

1061. Smith, Jessie Carney. Handbook for the Study of the Black Bibliography. Nashville, Tenn.: Fisk University Library, 1971.

1062. Smith, Jessie Carney. "The Research Collections in Negro Life and Culture at Fisk University." Paper Read at the Workshop on Bibliographic and Other Resources for a Study of the American Negro, Washington, D.C.: Howard University, 1968.

1063. Smith, John David. Black Slavery in the Americas: An Interdisciplinary Bibliography, 1865-1980. Westport, Conn.: Greenwood, 1982, 2 vols.

1064. Smythe, M.M. The Black American Reference Book. Englewood Cliffs, N.J.: Prentice-Hall, 1982.

1065. Snowden, George. Negro Political Behavior: A Bibliography.

Bloomington, Ind.: Indiana University, Department of
Government, 1941.

1066. Snyder, Joann and Michele Johnson. Black Studies Bibliography.
St. Mary's City, Md.: St. Mary's College of Maryland.

1067. Sollars, Werner. Bibliographic Guide to Afro-American Studies
(based on the holdings of the library). Berlin, Germany: Free
University of Berlin, John F. Kennedy Institute for North
American Studies, Library, 1972.

1068. Sollars, Werner. "Black Studies in the U.S.: A Bibliography."
Jahrbuch fur Amerikastudien 16 (1971), 213-22.

1069. Some Books About the Negro. Atlanta, Ga.: Atlanta Public
Library, Children's Department, 1967.

1070. Some Recent Books on Negro History and Literature: A
Bibliography for Groups of All Ages. New York: National
Federation of Settlements and Neighborhood Centers, 1968.

1071. Some Significant Books on Afro-American History and Culture.
Philadelphia, Pa.: Free Library of Philadelphia, 1968.

1072. Sotendahl, Audrey. Selected Bibliography of Books on the Negro
in America. Utica, N.Y.: Mohawk Valley Community College,
1969.

1073. Source Material on the Urban Negro in the US, 1910-1937: A List
of Selected Data. New York: National Urban League, 1937.

1074. Sowell, Thomas. Bibliography of American Ethnic Groups.
Washington, D.C.: Urban Institution, ERIC Document no. ED 129-
708, 1976.

1075. Spencer, Mary E.G. and Jane Humbertson. Black Studies: A
Bibliography. Hagerstown, Md.: Hagerstown Junior College,
1962.

1076. Spivey, Lydia L. The Negro in America: A Selected Bibliography
of Material in the Public Library of Charlotte and Mecklenburg
County. Charlotte, N.C.: Public Library of Charlotte and
Mecklenburg County, 1970.

1077. Spradling, M.M. In Black and White, Afro-American in Print: A
Guide to Africans and American Who Have Made Contributions to
the United States of America. Kalamazoo, Mich.: Kalamazoo
Public Library, 1976.

1078. Sprangler, Earl. Bibliography of Negro History. Minneapolis,
Ross and Haines, 1973.

1079. Sprangler, Earl. Bibliography of Negro History: Selected and

Annotated Entries, General and Minnesota. Minneapolis, Minn.: Ross and Haines, 1963.

1080. Stanke, Michael J. "New York Black Abolitionist Bibliography." Afro-Americans in New York Life and History 3:1 (1979), 45-50.

1081. Stanke, Michael J. and Barbara L. Stanke. "Black Abolitionist [Editorial] Project." The Schomburg Center for Research in Black Culture Journal 1:2 (Spring 1977), 4-5.

1082. Starbuck, J.C. LEAA and Criminal Justice Planning. Monticello, Ill.: Council of Planning Librarians, Exchange Bibliography No. 1100, 1976.

1083. Stetler, Henry G. Inter-Group Relations Bibliography: A Selected List of Books, Periodicals and Resource Agencies in Inter-Group Relations, Including a Special Section Devoted to Connecticut Studies. Hartford, Conn.: Connecticut State Inter-Racial Commission, 1947.

1084. Stevens, Jocelyn E. and Pennie E. Perry. Bibliography of Master's Theses, 1946-1967, North Carolina College at Durham. Durham, N.C.: North Carolina Central University, James E. Shepart Memorial Library, 1948.

1085. Stoots, C.F. Local Housing Authorities. Monticello, Ill.: Council of Planning Librarians, Exchange Bibliography, no. 135, 1970.

1086. Strache, Neil E., et al. Black Periodicals and Newspapers: A Union List of Holdings in the Libraries of the University of Wisconsin and the Library of the Historical Society of Wisconsin. Madison, Wis.: State Historical Society of Wisconsin, 1979.

1087. Suggs, Susan. Selected Bibliographies Relating to Black Studies in the Robert W. Woodruff Library. Atlanta, Ga.: Emory University, Robert W. Woodruff Library, 1980.

1088. Suzuki, Peter T. Minority Groups Aged in America: A Comprehensive Bibliography of Recent Publications on Blacks, Mexican Americans, Native Americans, Chinese and Japanese. Exchange Bibliography No. 816 Monticello, Ill.: Council of Planning Librarians, 1975.

1089. Sweet, Charles E. and Giovanna R. Jackson. The Negro and the Establishment: Law, Politics and the Courts/Black Nationalism. Focus: Black American Bibliography Series. Bloomington, Ind.: Indiana University, 1969.

1090. Swisher, Robert, et al. Black American Bibliography/Black American Scientists/Black Americans in Public Affairs. Bloomington, Ind.: Indiana University, 1969.

1091. Szabo, Andrew. Afro-American Bibliography: A List of Books, Documents and Periodicals on Black-American Culture Located in the San Diego State College Library. San Diego, Cal.: San Diego State College Library, 1970.

1092. Tackaberry, M. Liguori and Anne Bernice Whalen. Bibliography of Books and Other Material on Negro History and Culture in the Fontbonne College Library. St. Louis, Mo.: Fontbonne College Library, 1964.

1093. Takle, John A. and Cynthia A. Takle. Ethnic and Racial Minorities in North America: A Selected Bibliography on the Geographical Literature. Exchange Bibliography No. 459-460. Monticello, Ill.: Council of Planning Librarians, 1973.

1094. Tacoma Area Urban Coalition, Education Task Force. A Bibliography of Afro-American Print and Non-Print Resources in Libraries of Pierce County. Washington Tacoma: Tacoma County College Library, 1969.

1095. Talbot, F. Housing Rehabilitation: A Joint County-City Cooperative Program for Selected Bibliography. Monticello, Ill.: Council of Planning Librarians, Exchange Bibliography, no. 981, 1976.

1096. Tannenbaum, Earl. Insight: the Negro in the U.S., A Selected Bibliography. Terre Haute, Ind.: Indiana State University, Cunningham Memorial Library, 1970.

1097. Tanneyhill, Ann. Bibliography on the Negro and National Defense. New York: National Urban League, 1941.

1098. Taylor, Barbara and Margaret Mattern. A Guide to Afro-American Resources in University of Rochester Libraries. Rochester, N.Y.: University of Rochester, Rush Rhees Library and the Center for Afro-American Studies, 1971.

1099. Taylor, David Vassar. Blacks in Minnesota: A Preliminary Guide to Historical Sources. Minneapolis, Minn.: Minnesota Historical Society, 1976.

1100. Texas Southern University, Library Heartman Negro Collection. Catalog: Heartman Negro Collection. Houston, Texas Southern University Library, 1956.

1101. Thaden, J.F. and Walter E. Freeman. A Partial Bibliography on the American Negro: Books and Their Call Numbers in the Library of Michigan State University as of Sept. 1, 1962. East Lansing, Mich.: Michigan State University Library, Institute for Community Development and Services, 1962.

1102. Thompson, Bryan. Ethnic Groups in Urban Areas: A Community Formation and Growth: A Selected Bibliography. Monticello,

Ill.: Council of Planning Librarians, Exchange Bibliography
No. 202, 1971.

1103. Thompson, Edgar T. The Plantation: A Bibliography.
Washington, D.C.: Pan American Union, Social Science Section,
Department of Cultural Affairs, 1957.

1104. Thompson, Edgar T. and Alma Thompson. Race and Religion: A
Descriptive Bibliography Compiled with Special Reference to
Relations Between Whites and Negroes in the United States.
Chapel Hill: University of North Carolina Press, 1949.

1105. Thompson, Lawrence Sidney. The Southern Black, Slave and Free:
A Bibliography of Anti- and Pro-Slavery Books and Pamphlets and
of Social and Economic Conditions in the Southern States from
the Beginnings to 1950. Troy, N.Y.: Whitson Publishing Co.,
1970.

1106. Thompson, Lucille Smith and Alma Smith Jacobs. The Negro in
Montana, 1800-1945: A Selected Bibliography. Helena, Mont.:
Montana State Library, 1970.

1107. Thompson, Marilyn. Afro-American Studies. Downers Grove,
Ill.: George Williams College Library, 1970.

1108. Thorne, Kathleen, et al. Minorities in America: A List of
Books on Blacks and Mexican-Americans in the San Jose State
College Library. San Jose, Cal.: San Jose State College
Library, 1969.

1109. Thorpe, E. Black History and Organic Perspective: An Essay to
Introduce the Directory and Bibliography Nos. 870-872.
Monticello, Ill.: Council of Planning Librarians, Exchange
Bibliography, No. 869, 1975.

1110. Tilghman, Levin. A Selected List of Reference Sources in Afro-
American Studies. Tampa, Fla.: University of South Florida
Library, 1976.

1111. Tolmachev, Mirjana. The Contemporary Negro: A Selected
Bibliography of Recent Material in the Pennsylvania State
Library. Harrisburg, Pa.: Pennsylvania State Library, General
Library Bureau, 1970.

1112. Tompkins, Dorothy Campbell. Poverty Studies in the Sixties: A
Bibliography. Berkeley, Cal.: University of California at
Berkeley, 1970.

1113. Trainor, Juliette. A Bibliography of Holdings of the Paterson
College Library Relating to Black Studies. Wayne, N.J.:
William Paterson College of New Jersey, Sarah Byrd Askew
Library, 1970.

1114. Trattner, W. and W. Andrew Achembaum. _Social Welfare in America: An Annotated Bibliography._ Westport, Conn.: Westview Press, 1983.

1115. Treworgy, M.L. _Negroes in the United States: A Bibliography of Materials for Schools Approvable Purchase in Pennsylvania Under N.D.E.A. Provisions. With Supplement of Recent Materials on other American Minority Peoples._ University Park, Pa.: State University School Series no. 1, 1967.

1116. Trumpeter, Margo and Kathryn Scarich. _The Black Community and Champaign-Urbana [Ill.]: A Preliminary Subject List._ Urbana, Ill.: University of Illinois Library, 1970.

1117. Trusty, Lance. _Black America: A Bibliography of the Holdings of the Purdue University, Calumet Campus._ Hammond, Indiana: Purdue University Calumet Campus, 1976.

1118. Turner, Gladys. _Black People in the U.S._ Chicago, Ill.: Roosevelt University, Murray Green Library, 1970.

1119. Tynes, H.A. "Negro Bibliography." _New York Teacher_ 3 (May 1938), 22-3.

1120. Tyson, Edwin L. _Africa and the Blacks: A Bibliography._ San Jose, Cal.: San Jose City College Library, 1938.

1121. _Understanding Minorities: A Multi-Ethnic Bibliography._ Oklahoma City, Ok.: Oklahoma City Public Schools, School Media Services, 1969.

1122. U.S. Bureau of Census. _1869-1969 Books About Black Experience in America._ Washington, D.C.: Government Printing Office, 1969.

1123. U.S. Bureau of the Census, Department of Commerce. _Negroes in the United States._ Washington, D.C.: Government Printing Office, 1915.

1124. U.S. Bureau of Labor Statistics. _Black Americans: A Decade of Occupational Change._ Washington, D.C.: Government Printing Office, 1972.

1125. U.S. Bureau of Labor Statistics. _Work Attitudes of Disadvantaged Black Men: A Methodological Inquiry._ Washington, D.C.: Government Printing Office, 1972.

1126. U.S. Civil Service Commission. _Equal Opportunity in Employment._ Wasington, D.C.: Government Printing Office, 1971.

1127. U.S. Civil Service Commission. _Equal Opportunity in Employment._ Washington, D.C.: Government Printing Office, 1977.

1128. U.S. Commission on Civil Rights. Home Ownership for Lower Income Families: A Report on the Racial and Ethnic Impact of the Section 235 Program. Washington, D.C.: Government Printing Office, 1971.

1129. U.S. Employment Service. A Bibliography of Negro Labor. Washington, D.C.: Office of Negro Field Service, 1938.

1130. U.S. Library of Congress. Introduction to Africa: A Selective Guide to Background Reading. Washington, D.C.: University Press of Washington, 1952.

1131. U.S. Library of Congress. List of Discussion of the 14th and 15th Amendments with Special Reference to Negro Sufferage. Washington, D.C.: Government Printing Office, 1906.

1132. U.S. Library of Congress. Select List of References on the Negro Question: Compiled under the Direction of A.P.C. Griffin. Washington, D.C.: Government Printing Office, 1903.

1133. U.S. National Institute of Mental Health. Center for Minority Group Mental Health Programs. Bibliography on racism. Washington, D.C.: Government Printing office, 1972.

1134. U.S. Navy Department. General Library Services Branch. Black Heritage: the American Experience. Washington, D.C.: Human Resources Development Project Office, Bureau of Naval Research, 1972.

1135. U.S. Works Project Administration. The American Negro: A Selected Reading List. Hackensack, N.J.: 1937.

1136. Urban America. One year later: An Assessment of the Nation's Response to the Crisis Described by the National Advisory Commission on Civil Disorders. New York: Praeger, 1969.

1137. Vernon, Harriet. Bibliography of Books and Periodicals By and About Negroes. Fayetteville, Ark.: University of Arkansas Library, 1979.

1138. Viet, Jean. Selected Documentation for the Study of Race Relations. Paris, France: UNESCO, 1958.

1139. Von Furstenberg, George M., et al. Discrimination in Employment: A Selected Bibliography. Exchange Bibliography No. 298. Monticello, Ill.: Council of Planning Librarians, 1972.

1140. Von Furstenberg, George M., et al. Discrimination in Housing: A Selected Bibliography. Exchange Bibliography No. 297, Monticello, Ill.: Council of Planning Librarians, 1972.

1141. Wade, Mary Pius. A Bibliography of Negro Periodical Publications and Some Other Periodicals Containing Articles on

the Black Experience. Baltimore, Md.: Mt. Providence Junior
College Library, 1972.

1142. Wade, Mary Pius. Books in Black Studies. Baltimore, Md.: Mt.
Providence Junior College Library, 1973.

1143. Wakstein, A.M. A Bibliography of Urban History. Monticello,
Ill.: Council of Planning Librarians, Exchange Bibliography No.
987, 1975.

1144. Walker, Cornelia A. and F.F. Greene. African and African
American History and Culture: A Comprehensive Bibliography.
Franfort, Ky.: Kentucky State College, Blazer Library, 1972.

1145. Walker, Robert A. A Beginning Bookshelf for Teaching Afro-
American Culture. Champaign-Urbana, Ill.: University of
Illinois, 1969.

1146. Wallace, Patricia and Helen Lacy. Black Studies: A
Bibliography. Seattle, Wash.: Shoreline Community College,
1969.

1147. Walters, Mary Dawson. Afro-Americana: A Comprehensive
Bibliography of Resource Materials in the Ohio State University
Libraries By or About Black Americans. Columbus, Ohio: Ohio
State University Libraries, Office of Educational Services,
1969.

1148. Walters, Mary Dawson. Black History Holdings of the Ohio State
Libraries: A Partial List. Columbus, Ohio: Ohio State
University Libraries, 1969.

1149. Walton, Hanes. The Study and Analysis of Black Politics: A
Bibliography. Metuchen, N.J.: Scarecrow, 1973.

1150. Waltzer, K. "Urban America: Boiling Pot and Melting Pot."
Review in American History. 7:2 (1979), 241-246.

1151. Weed, Perry E. American Ethnic Groups. Monticello, Ill.:
Council of Planning Librarians, Exchange Bibliography, no.
1158, 1976.

1152. Weed, Perry L. Ethnicity and American Group Life: A
Bibliography. New York: Institute for Human Relations, ERIC
Document No. Ed 073-208, 1972.

1153. Weinberg, Meyer. The Education of the Poor and Minority
Children: A World Bibliography. Westport, Conn.: Greenwood,
1981.

1154. Weinberg, Meyer. School Integration: A Comprehensive
Classified Bibliography of 3,100 References. Chicago, Ill.:
Integrated Education Associates, 1967.

1155. Weintraub, Irwin. Black Agriculturists in the U.S. (1865-1973): An Annotated Bibliography. University Park, Penn.: Pennsylvania State University Libraries, Office of the Dean, 1976.

1156. Weir, Birdie, et al. Black Material for the Public Schools: A Study Guide Published by CEMBA, Alabama Center for Higher Education. Normal, Ala.: Alabama A and M University, Joseph F. Drake Library, 1976.

1157. Wells, Marion. Materials for Afro-American Studies in Drake Memorial Library. Brockport, N.Y.: SUNY, College at Brockport, Drake Memorial Library, 1970.

1158. Welsh, Erwin K. Afro-American Bibliography: A Lecture Given to the Institute on African and Afro-American Studies. Madison, Wis.: University of Wisconsin, 1970.

1159. Welsh, Erwin K. The Negro in the United States: A Research Guide. Bloomington: Indiana University Press, 1966.

1160. Wesley, Charles H. "An Aspect of Bibliography and Research in Negro History." Negro History Bulletin 29:3 (Dec. 1965), 51.

1161. West, Earle H. A Bibliography of Doctoral Research on the Negro, 1933-1966. Ann Arbor, Mich.: University Microfilms, 1969.

1162. West, Earle H. A Bibliography of Doctoral Research on the Negro, 1967-1969. Ann Arbor, Mich.: Michigan State University, University Microfilms, 1970.

1163. Westmoorland, G.T. An Annotated Guide to Basic Reference Books on the Black American Experience. Wilmington, Delaware: Scholarly Resoures, 1974.

1164. Wheelbarger, Johnny J. "Black Religion: A Bibliography of Fisk University Library Materials Relating to Various Aspects of Black Religious Life." Bibliographies of Sources by and about Blacks Compiled by the Interns in the Internship in Black Studies Librarianship Program. Nashville, Tenn.: Fisk University Library, 1974, 70-96.

1165. White, Anthony G. Discrimination in Housing Loans -- Redlining: A Selected Bibliography. Exchange Bibliography No. 977. Monticello, Ill.: Council of Planning Librarians, 1976.

1166. Whitney, P.B. America's Third World Guide: A Guide to Bibliographic Resources in the Library of the University of California at Berkeley. Berkeley, California: University of California Library, 1970.

1167. Wiehe, Emma L., et al. Black Bibliography. Menomonie, Wis.:

Stout State University, Robert L. Pierce Library, 1970.

1168. Wilkinson, Doris Y. "Toward a Positive Frame of Reference for Analysis of Black Families: A Selected Bibliography." Journal of Marriage and the Family 40 (Nov. 1978), 707–8.

1169. Williams, Daniel T. Eight Negro Bibliographies. New York: Kraus Reprint, 1970.

1170. Williams, Daniel T. The Black Muslims in the United States: A Selected Bibliography. Tuskegee, Ala.: Frissell Library, Tuskegee Institute, 1964.

1171. Williams, D.E. The Political Economy of Black Community Development: A Research Bibliography. Monticello, Ill.: Council of Planning Librarians, Exchange Bibliography No. 457, 1972.

1172. Williams, Ethel L. Afro–American Religious Studies: A Comprehensive Bibliography with Locations in American Libraries. Merachen, N.J.: Scarecrow, 1972.

1173. Williams, Ethel L. and Christeon, F. Brown. The Howard University Bibliography of African and Afro–American Religious Studies. Williamston, Delaware: Scholarly Resources, 1977.

1174. Williams, Ethel L. and Clifton L. Brown. Afro–American Religious Studies: A Comprehensive Bibliography with Locations in American Libraries. Metuchen, N.J.: Scarecrow, 1975.

1175. Williams, Ethel L. and Clifton L. Brown. The Howard University Bibliography of African and Afro–American Religious Studies (with locations in American Libraries). Wilmington, Del.: Scholarly Resources, 1979.

1176. Williams, Frederick and Rita C. Naremore. Language and Poverty: An Annotated Bibliography. Madison, Wis.: University of Wisconsin, Institute for Research on Poverty, 1967.

1177. Williams, G.W. History of the Negro Race in America from 1619 to 1880. New York: G.P. Putnam's Sons, 1883.

1178. Williams, Oliver. American Black Women in the Arts and Social Sciences: A Bibliography Survey. Metachun, N.J.: Scarecrow, 1973.

1179. Williams, Oliver. "A Bibliography of Works Written by American Black Women." CLA Journal, (1972), 1–7.

1180. Wills, Gordon. Racial Minorities: A Bibliography. Marion, Ind.: Marion College Library, 1970.

1181. Windley, L.A. Runaway Slave Adverbs: A Documentary History from 1730–1790. Westport, Conn.: Greenwood, 1983.

1182. Winters, William R., et al. Minority Enterprise and Marketing: An Annotated Bibliography. Monticello, Ill.: Council of Planning Librarians, Exchange Bibliography No. 185, 1971.

1183. Wisdom, Aline Crawley. Bibliography of Materials on Afro-American Culture in Citrus College Library. Azusa, Cal.: Citrus College Library, 1965.

1184. Wood, Vivian. Selected Reference Sources for Afro-American Studies at Kilmer Area Library. New Brunswick, N.J.: Rutgers University, Livingston College, Kilmer Area Library, 1978.

1185. Woods, Hortense. Bibliography of the Negro History Collection of the Vernon Branch Library. Los Angeles, Cal.: Los Angeles Public Library, Vernon Branch, 1973.

1186. Woods, Joyce V. Selected Bibliography on the Black Experience. Lafayette, Ind.: Purdue University Libraries, 1970.

1187. Work, Monroe N. A Bibliography of the Negro in Africa and America. New York: H.W. Wilson, 1928.

1188. Worsham, John P. A Bibliographical Guide to the Black Literature in Planning and Urban Studies Periodicals, 1970–1978. Monticello, Ill.: Vance Bibliograhies, Public Administration Series No. 299, 1979.

1189. Wright, Jerome. Black Background – 1966. Monterey, Cal.: Monterey Peninsula College Library, 1967.

1190. Wynar, L.R. Encyclopedia Directory of Ethnical Newspapers and Periodicals in the United States. Littleton, Colorado: Libraries Unlimited, 1972.

1191. Yale University. Library. A Selected List of Periodicals Relating to Negroes, with Holdings in the Libraries of Yale University. New Haven, Connecticut: The Library, 1970.

1192. Yelton, Donald C. A Survey of the Special Negro Collection and Related Resources of the Vail Memorial Library of Lincoln University. Lincoln University, Penn.: Lincoln University, 1964.

1193. Young, Pauline. "The American Negro: A Bibliography for School Libraries." Wilson Bulletin 7 (May 1935), 563.

1194. Zaretsky, Irving I. and Cynthia Shambaugh. Spirit Possession and Spirit Mediumship in Africa and Afro-America: An Annotated Bibliography. New York: Garland, 1978.

1195. Zunz, O. "The Organization of the American City in the Late

Nineteenth Century: Ethnic Structure and Spatial Arrangement in Detroit." <u>Journal of Urban History</u>, 3:4 (1977) 443-466.

CHAPTER 2

Demography and Population

1196. Abbott, E.M. "The Negro Woman and the South." <u>Outlook</u>,
       77:165-8 (May 21, 1904), 165-8.

1197. Abernathy, J.R., et al. "Estimates of Induced Abortion in
       Urban North Carolina." <u>Demography</u> 7:1 (1970), 19-29.

1198. Acevedo, Z. "Abortion in Early America." <u>Women and Health</u>, 4:2
       (1979), 159-167.

1199. Allen, James Egert. "An Appearance of Genocide: A Review of
       Governmental Family Planning Program Policies." <u>Perspectives in
       Biology and Medicine</u> 20:2 (1977), 300-306.

1200. Allison, Thomas W. "Population Movements in Chicago." <u>Journal
       of Social Forces</u> 2, (May 1924), 529-533.

1201. Alonso, W. <u>The Systems Inter-Metropolitan Population Flows</u>.
       Berkeley: University of California, Institute of Urban and
       Regional Development, 1971.

1202. Altenderfer, Marion E. and Beatrice Crowther. "Relationship
       Between Infant Mortality and Socio-Economic Factors in Urban
       Areas," <u>Public Health Reports</u>, 64, (March 18, 1949), 331-339.

1203. American Negro Reference Book. <u>The Negro Population in U.S.A.</u>
       Englewood Cliffs, N.J.: Prentice Hall, 1965.

1204. Anderson, J.E. "Planning of Births: Differences Between Blacks
       and Whites in the United States." <u>Phylon</u> 38:3, (1977) 282-296.

1205. Anderson, J.E. and Jack Smith. "Planned and Unplanned
       Fertility in a Metropolitan Area: Black and White Differences."
       <u>Family Planning Perspectives</u> 7:6, (1975) 281-285.

1206. Anderson, S.G. et al. "Maternal Mortality in North Carolina,

1966-1970." North Carolina Medical Journal 33: 11 (1972), 949-952.

1207. Anonymous. "Alabama Halts Sterilization of Retarded Youngsters." Jet 44: 21 (1973), 23.

1208. Anonymous. "Black Organizations Strongly Support Family Planning, but Oppose any Form of Coercion Incentives." Family Planning Perspective 8:1 (1976), 27.

1209. Anonymous. "Blacks View Limitations on Number in the Family as Genocide Effort by U.S." Jet, 40 (August 1975), 20-21.

1210. Anonymous. "Expectation of Life Among Non-Whites: Metropolitan Life." Insurance Company Statistical Bulletin, (March 1977), 5-7.

1211. Anonymous. "Federal Judge Sets Rules for Alabama Sterilizations." Jet, 45 (1974: 18), 5.

1212. Anonymous. "First Black Woman Heads Center for Family Planning." Jet 43: 17, (1973), 20.

1213. Anonymous. "Genocide: Cash-or-sterilization Plans Comes Under Fire." Jet 44 (1973:22), 24-25.

1214. Anonymous. "Is Birth Control a Menace to Negroes?" Jet, 19 (August 1954), 52-55.

1215. Anonymous. "Poor Should Have an Option for Sterilization: Expert." Jet 45: 6 (1973), 15.

1216. Anonymous. "Rules will not Stop Sterilization: HEW" Jet 44:23 (1973), 5.

1217. Anonymous. "The Sinister Side of Sterilization." South African Medical Journal 53(2):38-39. January 14, 1978.

1218. Anonymous. "Sterilization of Females Resumes in Alabama." Jet 46 (1974), 25.

1219. Anonymous. "Strict Sterilization Rules Proposed by HEW Officials." Jet 45:3 (1973), 68.

1220. Anonymous. U.S. Women Marrying Later, Having Babies Later, Spacing Them Further Apart than in Earlier Years." Family Planning Perspectives 10:5 (September 1978), 302.

1221. Anonymous. "U.S. Women Marrying Later, Having Babies Later, Spacing Them Further Apart than in Earlier Years." Family Planning Perspectives, 10:6 (October 1978), 411.

1222. Anonymous. "Use of Abortion by Poor is High." Obstetrics and

Geonocology News, 7: 7 (1972), 39.

1223. Anonymous. "ZPG for Blacks Without Health Care Plan is Termed Genocidal." _Obstetrics and Gyneocology News_, 8:9 (1973), 5.

1224. "Another Negro Exodus to the North", _Literary Digest_, (February 1923), 18.

1225. Armstrong, R.J. _A Study of Infant Mortality from Linked Records by Birth Weight, Period of Gestation, and Other Variables._ HEW, National Center for Health Statistics, DHEW Publication No. PHS 79-1055. Washington D.C.: Government Printing Office, 1972.

1226. Arnold, C.B. "A Condom Distribution Program for Adolescent Males." In: _Readings in Family Planning: A Challenge to the Health Professions._ D.V. McCalister, V. Thiessen and M. McDermott (eds.) St. Louis, Missouri: Mosby., 1978, 138-145.

1227. Arnold, C.B., et al. "Needed Research on Demographic Aspects of the Black Community," _Milbank Memorial Fund Quarterly_, 48, (April 1970), 311-344.

1228. Ashe, C. "Abortion . . . or Genocide?" _Liberator_, 10:8 (1970) 4-9.

1229. Attah, E.B. "Racial Aspects of Zero Population Growth." _Science_, 80: 4091 (1973), 1143-1151.

1230. Aug, R.G. and Thomas Bright. "Study of Wed and Unwed Motherhood in Adolescents and Young Adults." _Journal of American Academy of Child Psychiatry_ 9, (October 1970), 577-594.

1231. Bagnall, Robert W. "The Labor Problem and Negro Migration." _Southern Workman_, 49 (November 1920), 518-23.

1232. Bahr, Howard M. _Racial Differentiation in American Metropolitan Areas._ San Antonia: University of Texas, 1965.

1233. Bailey, R.T. "Arkansas Therapeutic Abortions." _Journal of the Arkansas Medical Society_, 71:3 (1974), 134-137.

1234. Bailey, R.W. "United States. The New Disenfranchisement: The Census, The Undercount, and Black Power in Electoral Politics." In: _Black People and the 1980 Census. Vol. 1: Proceedings From a Conference on the Population Undercount._ Illinois Council for Black Studies, Chicago, Ill., United States, 1980.

1235. Baird, J.T. and L.G. Quinlivan. _Parity and Hypertension. Vital and Health Statistics Series 11, No. 38._ Washington, D.C.: Government Printing Office, 1972.

1236. Baker, Ray Staunard. "Negro Goes North." _World's Work_, 34: (1917), 414-419.

1237. Baldwin, George J. "The Migration: A Southern View." _Opportunity_, Vol. II, (June 1924), 183.

1238. Baldwin, William H. "Adolescent Pregnancy and Childbearing – An Overview". _Seminars in Perinatology_ (January 1981), 1-8.

1239. Baldwin, William H. "Adolescent Sexual and Reproductive Behavior." In: Berman, P.W. and E.R. Ramey, (ed.) _Women: A Developmental Perspective: Proceedings of a Research Conference._ Bethesda, Maryland: U.S. Department of Health and Human Services, Public Health Service, National Institute of Health, 1982, 375-385.

1240. Basu, R. _The Effects of Aging on Residential Changes and Mobility of the Low Income Elderly: A Case Study from Allegheny County, Pennsylvania._ Unpublished Ph.D. Thesis, University of Pittsburgh, 1978.

1241. Baughman, E. Earl. _Black Americans_. New York: Academic Press, 1971.

1242. Bauman, K.E. "Birth Rates." in J.R. Udry (ed.), _The Media and Family Planning._ Cambridge, Mass.: Ballinger, 1972, 147-153.

1243. Bauman, K.E. and J.R. Udry. "The Difference in Unwanted Births Between Blacks and Whites." _Demography_ 10: 3 (1973), 315-328.

1244. Bauman, K.E. and J.R. Udry. "Powerlessness and Regularity of Contraception in an Urban Negro Male Sample: A Research Note." _Journal of Marriage and the Family_, 34:1 (1972), 112-114.

1245. Beales, LaVerne. "Negro Enumeration of 1920." _Scientific American_, XIV, (April 1922), 253-60.

1246. Bean, F.D. and C.H. Wood. "Ethnic Variations in the Relationship Between Income and Fertility." _Demography_, 11 (November 1974), 629-640.

1247. Bean, F.D. and J.P. Marcum. "Differential Fertility and the Minority Group Status Hypothesis: An Assessment and Review." in F.D. Bean and W.P. Friskie (eds.), _The Demography of Racial Ethnic Groups._ New York: Academic Press, 1978.

1248. Beasley, J.D. and R.F. Frankowski. "Utilization of a Family Planning Program by the Poor Population in the Metropolitan Area." United States: _Milbank Memorial Fund Quarterly_, 48:2 (1970) 241-268.

1249. Beasley, J.D. and R.F. Frankowski. "United States: Utilization of a Family Planning Program in a Metropolitan Area." _Studies in Family Planning_ 1:59 (1970) 7-16.

1250. Beasley, J.D. et al. "Attitudes and Knowledge Relevant to

Family Planning Among the New Orleans Negro Woman." _American Journal of Public Health,_ 56: 11 (1942), 1847–1857.

1251. Beasley, J.D. et al. "Louisiana Family Planning." _American Journal of Public Health_, 61: 9 (1971), 1812–1825.

1252. Beckman, L.J. "The Relationship Between Sex Roles, Fertility and Family Size." _Psychology of Women Quarterly._ 4:1 (Fall 1979), 43–6.

1253. Beebe, G.W. _Contraception and Fertility in the Southern Appalachians._ Baltimore: Williams and Wilkins, 1942.

1254. Bell, Robert R. _Premarital Sex in a Changing Society._ Englewood Cliffs, New Jersey: Prentice-Hall, 1966.

1255. Bernard, Jessie. _Marriage and Family Among Negroes._ Englewood Cliffs, New Jersey: Prentice-Hall, 1966.

1256. Bernstein, I.M. _The Relationships of Psychiatric Symptoms Among Lower Socio-economic Post Hospitalized Negro Schizophrenics to Certain Demographic Variables._ Unpublished Ph.D. Thesis, New York University, 1968.

1257. Berry, Brian J.L. and P.J. Scwind. "Information on Entropy in Migrant Flows." _Geographical Analysis_, (January 1969), 5–14.

1258. Berry, W.E. "Furor Mounts Over Sterilization of Blacks." _Jet_, 44: 19 (1973), 20–21.

1259. Bianchi, S.M. _Household Composition and Racial Inequality: 1960–1976._ Unpublished Ph.D. Thesis, University of Michigan, 1978.

1260. Biggar, J.C. "Racial Differences in the Determinants of Prospective Mobility." _American Statistical Association, Proceedings of the Social Science Section_. Washington, D.C., 1968, 14–28.

1261. Billingsley, Andrew. _Black Families in White America._ Englewood Cliffs, New Jersey: Prentice-Hall, 1968.

1262. Binkin, N., et al. _Illegal Abortion Deaths in the United States: Why They Are Still Occuring._ A Paper presented at the 109th Annual Meetings of the American Public Health Association, Los Angeles, California, November 2, 1981.

1263. "Black Teenage Pregnancy: Values or What?" _Paper Presented at American Public Health Association Annual Meeting_, New York, November 1979.

1264. Blackman, W.F. "Movement of Negro Population in the Last Decade", _Yale Review_, 10 (1962), 428.

1265. Blair, A.O. "A Comparison of Negro and White Fertility Attitudes." In D.J. Bogue (ed.), Sociological Contributions to Family Planning Research. Chicago: University of Chicago, Community and Family Study Center, 1968, 1-35.

1266. Blake, J. "Elective Abortion and Our Reluctant Citizenry: Research on Public Opinion in the United States." in Osofsky, H.J. and J.D. Osofsky (eds.) The Abortion Experience: Psychological and Medical Impact, Hagerstown, Maryland: Harper and Row, 1973, 447-465.

1267. Blake R.R. et al. Beliefs and Attitudes About Contraception Among the Poor. Chapel Hill, NC: Carolina Population Center, Monograph No. 5, 1969.

1268. Blanco, C. "The Determinants of Interstate Population Movements." Journal of Regional Science, 5 (Summer 1963), 77-84.

1269. Bleiweis, P.R., et al. "Health Characteristics of Migrant Agricultural Workers in Three Florida Counties." Journal of Community Health 3:1 (1977), 32-43.

1270. Blevins, A.L. Rural Urban Migration of Poor Anglos, Mexicans, and Negroes. Unpublished Ph.D. Thesis, The University of Texas at Austin, 1970.

1271. Blum, H.F. "Is Sunlight a Factor in the Geographical Distribution of Human Skin Color." The Geographical Review, 49, (October 1969), 557-81.

1272. Blum, Zahava D., et al. Migration and Household Composition: A Comparison Between Blacks and Non-Blacks. Baltimore, Md.: Center for the Study of Social Organization of Schools, The Johns Hopkins University, Report No. 77, August, 1970.

1273. Blumstein, B.A., et al. "Blood Pressure Changes and Oral Contraceptive Use: A Study of 2676 Black Women in the Southeastern United States." American Journal of Epidemiology, 112:4 (October 1980), 539-52.

1274. Boddy, J.M. "Getting at the True Causes of the Migration of Negro Labor From the South." Economic World (1918), 333.

1275. Bodnar, J.E. "The Immigrant and the American in the American City." Journal of Urban History, 3:2 (1977), 241-247.

1276. Bodnar, J.E. "The Impact of the "New Immigration" on the Black Worker: Steelton, Pennsylvania, 1880-1920." Labor History, 17: 2 (1976), 214-229.

1277. Bodnar, J.E. "Socialization and Adaptation: Immigrant Families in Scranton, 1880-1920." Pennsylvania History, 43: 2 (1976),

147-162.

1278. Bodnar, J.E., et al. "Migration, Kinship and Urban Adjustment: Blacks and Poles in Pittsburgh, 1900-1930." Journal of American History, 6: 3 (1979), 548-565.

1279. Bogue, Donald J. "A Long-term Solution to the AFDC Problem: Prevention of Unwanted Pregnancies." Social Service Review, 49: 4 (1975), 539-552.

1280. Bogue, Donald J. Components of Population Change in Standard Metropolitan Areas. Oxford, Ohio: Scripps Foundation, Miami University Population Center, University of Chicago, 1957.

1281. Bogue, Donald J. "Family Planning the Negro Ghettoes of Chicago." Milbank Memorial Fund Quarterly, 48: 2 (1970), 283-299.

1282. Bogue, Donald J. "The Geography of Recent Population Trends in the United States." Annals, 44: (1954), 124-134.

1283. Bogue, Donald J. and Dandekar, D.P. Population Trends and Prospects for the Chicago Northwestern Indiana Consolidated Metropolitan Area: 1960-1990. Population Research Training Center, University of Chicago, March 1962.

1284. Bogue, Donald J. et al. "A New Estimate of the Nero Population and Negro Vital Rates in the U.S., 1930-1960." Demography, 1: 1 (1964), 339-358.

1285. Bohm, R.A. The Determinants of Non-White Male Employment Growth and Migration in Behavior in Large United States Cities. Harvard University, Unpublished Ph.D. Thesis, Washington, D.C., 1970.

1286. Bontemps, Arna and Jack Conroy. Any Place But Here. New York: Hillard Wang, 1966.

1287. Bourne, J.P. and R.W. Rochat. Association Between Prenatal Infant Mortality and Family Planning in Rural Georgia. Paper Presented at the Thirteenth Annual Meeting of the Association of Planned Parenthood Physicians, Los Angeles, California, April 17, 1975.

1288. Bousefield, M.O. "Negro Public Health Work Needs Birth Control." Birth Control Review. 16: 6 (1932), 170-171.

1289. Bowles, G.K. and J.D. Tarver. Net Migration of the Population 1950-1960 by Age, Sex and Color. Washington D.C.: Government Printing Office, 1965.

1290. Bracken, M.B.; T.R. Holford. "Induced Abortion and Congental Malformations in Offspring of Subsequent Pregnancies." American

Journal of Epidemiology, 109: 4 (1979), 425-432.

1291. Bradley, F.J. "Black Caucus Raps About Planned Genocide of Blacks." _Jet_, 38: 18, 14-18.

1292. Brandon, D.G. _Migration of Negroes in the United States, 1910-1947_. Ph.D. Dissertation Thesis, Columbia University, 1949.

1293. Breed, Warren. "Suicide, Migration, and Race: A Study of Cases in New Orleans,"_Journal of Social Issues_, 20, (January 1966), 30-43.

1294. Bressler, T. and N.R. McKenney. _Negro Population: March 1964._ U.S. Bureau of the Census. Current Population Reports, Population Characteristics, Series P-20, No. 142. Washington, D.C.: Government Printing Office, 1965.

1295. Bronstein, E.S. and Lentz, D. "Characteristics of Vasectomy Patients Utilizing a Mobile Unit in Georgia." _Journal of the Medical Association_, Georgia, 62: (April 1974), 110-113.

1296. Brookfield, H.C. and Tatham, M.A. "The Distribution of Racial Groups in Durham." _The Geographical Review_, 47 (January, 1972), 4-19.

1297. Brotman, H.B. "Facts and Figures on Older Americans." _Administration on Aging_ 2:3, (1971), 2-12.

1298. Brotman, H.B. "Facts and Figures on Older Americans." _Administration on Aging_, 3: 3 (1972), 15-20.

1299. Brotman, H.B. "Facts and Figures on Older Americans: State Trends, 1960-1970." _Administration on Aging_, 6 (1974), 4-5.

1300. Broude, Jeffrey E. _A Survey of 1960 Negro Occupational Patterns in Standard Metropolitan Statistical Area by Region, Total Population and Percentage Negro._ M. Sc. Thesis, University of California, Los Angeles, 1971.

1301. Brown, Frederick J. _The Northward Movement of the Colored Population: A Statistical Study_. Baltimore: Cushing, 1897.

1302. Brown, Phil H. "Negro Labor Moves Northward". _Opportunity Negro Life_ 1 (1923), 5-6.

1303. Bryant, Nathaniel H. _Black Migration and the Settlement of the Puget Sound Country._ Master's Thesis, University of Washington, 1972.

1304. Brye, D.L. _European Migration and Ethnicity in the United States and Canada._ Santa Barbara, Cal.: ABC-Clio, 1983.

1305. Buenker, John D. "Dynamics of Chicago Ethnic Politics, 1900-

1930". Journal of the Illinois State Historical Society, 67:2 (1974), 175–199.

1306. Bufford, C.B. The Distribution of Negroes in Maryland, 1850–1860. Washington, D.C.: Catholic University of America, Master's Thesis, 1965.

1307. Bumpass, L.L. and H.B. Presser. "Contraceptive Sterilization in the U.S.: 1965 and 1970." Demography, 9: 4 (1972), 531–548.

1308. Burnham, D. Black-White Differentials in Illegitimacy: An Examination of the Effects of Socio-Economic Differences, Marital Stability and Educational Attainment. Unpublished Ph.D. Thesis, Florida State University, 1977.

1309. Butts, J.B. Perceptions of the Experience of Tubal Ligation: An Exploratory Study in Fertility Control Among Twenty Low Income Black Women. Unpublished Ph.D. Thesis, Columbia University, 1969.

1310. Butts, J.B. Adolescent Sexuality and the Impact of Teenage Pregnancy for a Black Perspective. Washington D.C.: George Washington University, Institute of Educational Leadership, Family Impact Seminar, 1979.

1311. Cade, Toni. "The Pill: Genocide or Liberation." In: Toni Cade (ed.), The Black Woman: An Anthology. New York: Signet Books, 1970, 162–169.

1312. Cahill, Edward E. "Migration and the Decline of Negro Population in Rural and Non-Metropolitan Areas." Phylon 35:3, (1974) 283–292.

1313. Cain, Glen G. and Andriana Weininger. "Economic Determinants of Fertility: Results from Cross-Sectional Aggregate Data". Demography 10 (May 1973): 205–233.

1314. Calef, Wesley C. and Howard J. Nelson. "Distribution of Negro Population in the United States". Geographical Review 46 (January 1956) 82–97.

1315. Calloway, Josephine S. "Negro Migration: Effects on Home Life." Southern Workman 46: (1917), 132–140.

1316. Campbell, Arthur A. "Fertility and Family Planning Among Non-white Married Couples in the United States." Eugenics Quarterly 12:3, (1965) 124–131.

1317. Campbell, Rex R. and Johnson, Daniel M. Propositions on Internal Counterstream Migration. Paper Presented at the Population Tribune 1974, Non-Governmental Forum - World Population Conference, Bucharest, Romania, August 1974.

1318. Campbell, Rex R. and Johnson, Daniel M. "Propositions on Counterstream Migration," _Rural Sociology_ 41 (Spring 1978), 127-45.

1319. Campbell, Rex R. and Peter R. Robertson. _Negroes in Missouri: A Compilation of Statistical Data from the 1960 United States Census of Population_. Jefferson City, Missouri: Missouri Commission on Human Rights, 1967.

1320. Campbell, Rex. R., et al. "Counterstream Migration of Black People to the South: Data from the 1970 Public Use Sample," _Review of Public Use Data_ 3 (Jan. 1975), 13-21.

1321. Campbell, Rex R., et al. "Return Migration of Black People to the South," _Rural Sociology_, 39:4, (1974), 514-527.

1322. Carter, Bernard. _An Investigation of the Black Population Concentration in the Ohio-Mississippi River Confluence Area of Illinois._ Southern Illinois University, Carbondale, Master's Thesis, 1969.

1323. Carter, Elmer A. "Eugenics for the Black." _Birth Control Reviews_ 16:6, (1932), 169-170.

1324. Carter, Hugh and Paul C. Glick. "Trends and Current Patterns of Marital Status Among Non-white Persons." _Demography_ 3: (1966), 276-288.

1325. Cates, Willard. "Legal Abortion: Are American Black Women Healthier Because of It?" _Phylon_ 38:3, (1977), 267-281.

1326. Chabot, Marion J, et al. "Urbanization and Differentials in White and Non-White Infant Mortality". _Pediatrics_ 56:5, (1975), 777-781.

1327. Champion, P. "A Pilot Study of the Success or Failure of Low Income Negro Families in the Use of Birth Control." In: Donald J. Bogue (ed.) _Sociological Contributions to Family Planning Research_. Chicago: University of Chicago, Community and Family Study Center, (1967), 112-128.

1328. Charles, Alan and Susan Alexander. "Abortion for Poor and Non-white Women: A Denial of Equal Protection?" _The Hastings Law Journal_ 23 (November 1971), 147-169.

1329. Chase, Helen C. "Registration Completeness and International Comparisons of Infant Mortality." _Demography_ 6:4, (1969), 425-433.

1330. Chase, Helen C. _Study of Infant Mortality From Linked Records: Comparison of Neonatal Mortality from Two Cohort Studies._ Paper presented at the Population Association of American

Annual Conference, Philadelphia, Penn., 1972.

1331. Chase, Helen C. and F.G. Nelson. "Education of Mother, Medical Care and Condition of Infant." American Journal of Public Health 63: 27-40.

1332. Chasteen, R.R. "Barriers to Birth Control." In E.R. Chasteen: The Case for Compulsory Birth Control. Englewood Cliffs, N.J.: Prentice-Hall, 1971; 125-147.

1333. Clark, Howard L. "Growth of Negro Population in the United States and Trend of Migration from the South Since 1860. Economic Conditions the Reason Negroes are Leaving South." Manufactuing Research 83: (1923), 14-20.

1334. Clark, John T. "The Migrant in Pittsburgh. A Story of the Pittsburgh Urban League." Opportunity, (1923), 308.

1335. Clark, Samuel D., et al. "Sex, Contraception and Parenthood: Experience and Attitudes Among Urban Black Young Men" Family Planning Perspectives 16:2 (March/April 1984), 77-86.

1336. Clark, W.A.V. "Patterns of Black Intraurban Mobility and Restricted Relocation Opportunities, in Harold M. Rose (ed.) Perspectives in Geography 2: Geography of the Ghetto. DeKalb: Northern Illinois University Press, 1972.

1337. Clemence, Theodore G. "Residential Segregation in the Mid-Sixties," Demography 4:2, (1967), 562-568.

1338. Coale, A. and N.W. Rives. "A Statistical Reconstruction of the Black Population of the United States 1880-1970: Estimates of True Numbers by Age and Sex, Birth Rates, and Total Fertility." Population Index 39, (1973), 3-36.

1339. Cochrane, Carl M., et al. "Motivational Determinants of Family Planning Clinic Attendance." Journal of Psychology 84 (May 1968), 33-43.

1340. Coe, Paul F. "Nonwhite Population Increases in Metropolitan Areas." Journal of the American Statistical Association 50 (June 1955), 283-308.

1341. Coe, Paul F. "The Non-White Population Surge to our Cities," Land Economics, 35 (August 1959), 195-210.

1342. Cohen, Patricia, et al. "The Effect of Teenaged Motherhood and Maternal Age on Offspring Intelligence." Social Biology 27:2 (1980), 138-154.

1343. Coles, Robert. The South Goes North, Children of Crises. Boston: Little Brown, 1971).

1344. Combs, M.W. and S. Welch. "Blacks, Whites, Attitudes Toward Abortion," Public Opinion Quarterly. 46:4, (Winter 1982), 510-20.

1345. Commission on Human Relations. Philadelphia's Negro Population - Facts on Housing. Philadelphia: The Commission, October 1953.

1346. Coney, Rosemary S. "Demographic Components of Growth in White, Black, and Puerto Rican Female-Headed Families: Comparison of the Cutright and Ross/Sawhill Methodologies." Social Science Research 8 (June 1979), 144-158.

1347. Cooper, A.J., et al. "Biochemical Polymorphic Traits in a U.S. White and Negro Population." American Journal of Human Genetics 15:4, (1968), 420-428.

1348. Cowhig, James D. "The Negro Population of the United States, March 1967." Welfare in Review 7 (January-February 1967), 14-16.

1349. Cowles, Wylda, et al. "Health and Communication in a Negro Census Tract," Social Problems, 10, (Winter 1963), 228-236.

1350. Cox, Oliver C. "Sex Ratio and Marital Status Among Negroes." American Sociological Review 5 (Fall 1940), 937-947.

1351. Craigie, David William. Causes and Consequences of Black-White Residential Differentiation in American Central Cities: A Longitudinal Analysis 1950-1970. Tucson: The University of Arizona, Unpublished Ph.D., 1977.

1352. Craven, Erma C. "Abortion, Poverty and Black Genocide: Gifts to the Poor?" In: Thomas W. Higlers and Dennis J. Horan (eds.)Abortion and Social Justice. New York: Sheed and Ward. 1972, 231-243.

1353. Cummings, John. Negro Population: 1790-1915. Washington, D.C.: Government Printing Office, 1918.

1354. Curry, James P. and Gayle D. Scriven. "The Relationship Between Apartment Living and Fertility for Blacks, Mexican-Americans, and Other Americans in Racine, Wisconsin." Demography 15:4, (1978), 477-485.

1355. Cutler, W.B., et al. "Infertility and Age at First Coitus: A Possible Relationship." Journal of Biosocial Science 11:4, (1979), 425-432.

1356. Cutright, P. "Teenage Illegitimacy: An Exchange." Family Planning Perspectives 6:3. (1974), 132-133.

1357. Cutright, P. and F.S. Jaffe. Impact of Family Planning

Programs on Fertility: the U.S. Experience. New York: Preager.
1977.

1358. Daily, E.F. and N. Nicholas. "Tubal Ligations on General
Service Patients Seen by Peer-Level Family Planning Counselors
in Thirty New York City Voluntary and Municipality Hospitals."
American Journal of Obstetrics and Gynecology, 123: 6, (1957),
656-659.

1359. Daliwal, M.S. Preferences in the Size of Family Among Senior
Girls in Black Segregatd High Schools in South, Central and
Western Parts of Mississippi. Unpublished Ph.D. Thesis, Utah
State University, 1970.

1360. Damon, A. "Race and Ethnic Group Disease." Social Biology,
16: 2 (1969), 69-80.

1361. Dancy, J.C. "The Negro in Michigan." Michigan History
Magazine, 24, (1940), 1-8.

1362. Darty, W.A. and C.B. Turner. "Attitudes Toward Family
Planning: A Comparison Between Northern and Southern Black
Americans: A Preliminary Report." Advances in Planned
Parenthood, 7 (1973), 13-20.

1363. Darity, W.A. and C.B. Turner. "Family Planning, Race
Consciousness, and the Fear of Race Genocide." American Journal
of Public Health, 62: 1 (1972), 1454-1459.

1364. Darity, W.A. and C.B. Turner. Research Findings Related to
Sterilization: Attitudes of Black Americans. Paper Presented
at the Fifty-First Annual Meetings of the American
Oorthpsychiatric Association, San Franciso, California, April
8-12, 1974.

1365. Darity, W.A., et al. "An Exploratory Study on Barriers to
Family Planning: Race Consciouness and Fears of Black Genocide
as a Basis." Advances in Planned Parenthood, 7 (1972), 20-32.

1366. Darity, W.A., et al. "Race Consciousness and Fears of Black
Genocide as Barriers to Family Planning." in K.C.W. Kammayer
(ed.) Population Studies: Selected Essays and Research.
Chicago: Rand McNally, 1975, 433-447.

1367. Darney, P.D. "Fertility Decline and Participation in Georgia's
Family Planning Program: Temporal and Areal Associations.
"Studies in Family Planning, 6: 6 (1975), 156-165.

1368. Darney, P.D. "A Statewide Family Planning Program's Effect on
Fertility." in J.R. Udry and E.E. Huyck (eds.), The Demographic
Evaluation of Domestic Family Planning Programs: Proceedings of
a Research Workshop. Cambridge, MA: Ballinger, 1975, 85-89.

1369. Davis, C.S. and Gary L. Fowler. "The Disadvantaged Female Household Head: Migrants form Indianapolis."Southeastern Geoographer, 11: 2 (1971), 113-120.

1370. Davis, C.S. and Gary L. Fowler. "The Disadvantaged Urban Migrant in Indianapolis." Economic Geography, 48: 2 (1972), 157-175.

1371. Davis, D. "Reverse Black Migration to Metropolitan or Non-Metropolitan Areas, "Black Americans and Urban Society, edited by D. Deskins in Monography Series, Center for Afro-American and African Studies, the University of Michigan, 1984.

1372. Davis, R. "The Significance of the Black Population Undercount in the Production and Use of Health and Mortality Rates." In Volume 1 Black People and the 1980 Census. Proceedings from a Conference on Population Undercount. Chicago: Illinois Council for Black Studies, 1981, 630-640.

1373. Davis, R. A Statistical Analysis of the Current Reported Increase in the Black Suicide Rate. Ph.D Thesis, Washington State University, 1975.

1374. Davis R. "United States. The Significance of the Black Population Undercount in the Production and Use of Health and Mortality Rates." In: Black People and the 1980 Census. Vol.1: Proceedings from a Conference on the Population Undercount. Illinois Council for Black Studies, Chicago: United States, 1980: 630-640.

1375. Day, C.B. and E.A. Hooton. A Study of Some Negro and White Families in the United States. Cambridge: Peabody Museum, Harvard University, 1932.

1376. Daymont, Thomas N. Parameters of Racial Discrimination in the Late 1960's. Madison: The University of Wisconsin, Ph.D Thesis, 1978.

1377. Daymont, Thomas N. "Racial Equity or Racial Equality." Demography. (1980) 17:4, 379-393.

1378. Deasy, L.C. and O.W. Quinn. "The Urban Negro and Adoption of Children." Child Welfare 41 (November 1962), 40-47.

1379. DeLaubenfels, David J. "Australoids, Negroids, and Negroes: A Suggested Explanation for Their Disjunct Distributions. Annals of the Association, 48 (March 1968), 42-50.

1380. Delcampo, R.L., et al. "Premarital Sexual Permissiveness and Contraception Knowledge; A Biracial Comparison of College Students." Journal of Sex Research, 12: 3 (1976), 180-192.

1381. Demeny, P. and P. Gingrich. "A Reconstruction of Negro-White

Mortality Differentials in the United States." Demography, 4: 2 (1967), 820-837.

1382. Deskins, Donald R. Residential Mobility of Negro Occupational Groups in Detroit 1837-1965. Ph.D Thesis, The University of Michigan, 1971.

1383. Dewey, P. "Moving North: Migration of Negroes." Phylon, 28 (1967), 61.

1384. Dicker R.C., et al. "Hysterectomy Among Women of Reproductive Age: Trends in the United States, 1970-1978." Journal of American Medical Association 248:3 (July 16, 1982), 323-7.

1385. Dillingham, H.C. and D. Sly. "The Mechanical Cotton Picker, Negro Migration and Integration Movement." Human Organization, 25: (Winter 1966), 346.

1386. Dixon, R.D. "The Absence of Birth Order Correlations Among Unwed and Married Black First-Conceptors." Journal of Sex Research, (August 1980) 16:3, 238-44.

1387. Dlugacz, Y.D. The Prosperity to Move: A Sociological Analysis of the Process of Moving Among Whites and Blacks. Ph.D. Thesis. City Univeristy of New York, 1979.

1388. Donald, Henderson H. "Negro Migration 1916-1918." The Journal of Negro History, 6: (October 1921), 178-181.

1389. Dott, A.B. and A.T. Fort. "The Effect of Maternal Demographic Factors on Infant Mortality Study. Part I." The American Journal of Obstetrics and Gynecology, 13: 8 (1975), 847-853.

1390. Douglas, Frederick. "Negro Exodus, 1879." American Journal of Social Sciences 11 (1880), 1.

1391. DuBois, W.E.B. "Black Folk and Birth Control." Birth Control Review, 16: 6 (1932), 166-167.

1392. DuBois, W.E.B. "Migration of Negroes". Crisis 14 (1917), 63-6.

1393. DuBois, W.E.B. Mortality Among Negroes in Cities, Together with Proceedings of the 1st Conference for the Study of Negro Problems. Atlanta: Atlanta University, 1899.

1394. DuBois, W.E.B. The Philadelphia Negro: A Social Study. New York: Shocken Books, 1967.

1395. Duncan, Otis D. and Beverly Duncan. The Negro Population of Chicago, A Study of Residential Succession. Chicago: University of Chicago Press, 1957.

1396. Dunn, J.E. and D.F. Austin. "Cancer Epidemology in the San Francisco Bay Area." In Epidemology and Cancer Registries in the Pacific Basin. Washington, D.C.: Government Printing Office, 1977, 93-98.

1397. Dyer, D.R. "The Place of Origin of Florida's Population." Annals of the Association of American Geographers, 42 (1952), 283-294.

1398. Eblen, J.E. "Growth of the Black Population in the Ante Bellum America, 1820-1860." Population Studies, 26 (1972), 273-289.

1399. Eblen, J.E. "New Estimates of the Vital Rates of the United States Black Population During the Nineteenth Century." Demography, 11: 2 (1974), 301-319.

1400. Eckard, E. "Teenagers Who Used Organized Family Planning Services," United States, 1978. Vital and Health Statistics. Series 13: Data from the National Health Survey. 1981. August; 57:1-18.

1401. Eckard, E. "Wanted and Unwanted Births Reports by Mothers 15-44 Years of Age: United States, 1976." Advance Data 56: (January 24), 1-10.

1402. "Economic Causes of the Negro Exodus," Library Digest, 78, (1923), 14-15.

1403. Edelman, M.W. United States Portrait of Inequality: Black and White Children in America. Washington, D.C.: Children's Defense Fund, United States, 1980.

1404. Edwards, G. Franklin, "Community and Class Realities: The Ordeal of Change, Deadalus. 95 (1962), 1-23.

1405. Edwards, G. Franklin. "Marriage and Family Life Among Negroes", Journal of Negro Education. 32, (Fall 1963), 451-564.

1406. Edwards, G. Franklin. "Marital Status and General Family Characteristics of the Non-White Population," Journal of Negro Education. 22:2, (1953), 280-296.

1407. Edwards, G. Franklin. "Marital Status and General Family Characteristics of the Non-White Population of the United States." Journal of Negro Education, 22: 3 (1953), 296-312.

1408. Eichenbaum, J.J. Magic, Mobility and Minorities in the Urban Drama. Ann Arbor: Ph.D. Thesis, University of Michigan, 1972.

1409. Ellifson, K.W. and J. Irwin. Black Minister's Attitudes Toward Population Size and Control." Sociological Analysis 38: 3 (1977), 252-257.

1410. Ellis, C.A. The Relationships of Selected Variables to the Use/Nonuse of Contraceptives Among Undergraduate College and University Students. Knoxville: University of Tennessee, Ph.D. Thesis, 1982.

1411. Emlen, J.T. Report of the National Conference on Migration. National Urban League Papers, Washington, D.C.: Library of Congress, January 1917.

1412. Engerman, S. "Black Fertility and Family Structure in the U.S., 1880-1940." Journal of Family History, 2: 2 (1977), 117-138.

1413. Engerman, S. "Changes in the Black Fertility, 1880-1940." in Hereven, T. and Vinovkis, M.A. (eds.). Family and Population in Nineteenth Century America. Princeton: Princeton University Press, 1978, 14-20.

1414. Epstein, Abraham. The Negro Migrant in Pittsburgh. New York: Arno Press, 1969.

1415. Erhardt, C.L. et al. "Seasonal Patterns of Conception in New York City." American Journal of Public Health, (November 1971), 2246-2258.

1416. Erhardt, C.L. and Helen C. Chase. "Ethnic Group, Education of Mother and Birth Weight." American Journal of Public Health 63, (1973) 17-26.

1417. Ernest, R.T. Negro Migration: A Review of the Literature. Master's Thesis, St. Louis University, 1969.

1418. Ewer, Gibbs, J.O. "Relationship with Putative Father and Use of Contraception in a Population of Black Ghetto Adolescent Mothers." Public Health Reports 90: 5 (1975), 417-423.

1419. "Exodus of Negro" Opportunity, 4 (1926), 399.

1420. Ezzard, N.V., et al. Race Specific Patterns of Abortion United States, 1972-1978. A Paper Presented at the 109th Annual Meetings of the American Public Health Association, Los Angeles, California: November 3, 1981.

1421. Ezzard, N.V. et al. "Race-Specific Patterns of Abortions Used by American Teenagers." American Journal of Public Health. 1982, 72:8, 809-14.

1422. Ezzard, N.V.; et al. "Response [to Haleand Pickett Letter Concerning Comparison of Age-Specific and Race-Specific Abortion Ratios]". American Journal of Public Health. 73:4, (1983), 453-4.

1423. Faber Bernard Lewis. Intra-Urban Residential Mobility as a Determinant of the Integration of Urban Residents. Brown

University, Unpublished Ph.D. thesis, 1973.

1424. Falk R. et al. "Personality Factors Related to Black Teenage Pregnancy and Abortion." Psychology of Women Quarterly. 5:5, (1981), 737-46.

1425. Family Planning Digest. "Georgia Program: Black Fertility Drops When Service Offered." Family Planning Digest 2:6, (1973), 7.

1426. Family Planning Digest. "1970 National Fertility Study; Over 1960s Decade Unwanted Births Declined, Fertility Gap Between Poor and More Affluent Reduced." Family Planning Digest 1:6, (1972) 9-12.

1427. Farley, Reynolds. "The Changing Distribution of Negroes Within Metropolitan Areas: The Emergence of Black Suburbs." American Journal of Sociology 75: (1970), 512-529.

1428. Farley, Reynolds. "The Demographic Rates and Social Institutions of the Nineteenth-Century Negro Population: A Stable Population Analysis." Demography 2, (1955), 386-398.

1429. Farley, Reynolds. "Differentials in Negro Fertility." In Reynolds Farley (ed.): Growth of the Black Population: A Study of Demographic Trends. Chicago: Markham, 1970, 101-120.

1430. Farley, Reynolds. "Family Types and Family Headship: A Comparison of Trends Among Blacks and Whites." The Journal of Human Resources 6:3, (1971), 275-296.

1431. Farley, Reynolds. "Fertility Among Urban Blacks." Milbank Memorial Fund Quarterly 48:2, (1970), 183-206.

1432. Farley, Reynolds. "Fertility and Mortality Trends Among Blacks in the United States." In: Demographic and Social Aspects of Population Growth and the American Future, Research Reports, Volume 1. Charles F. Westoff and Robert Parke, Jr. (eds.), New York: Plenum, 1972, 111-118.

1433. Farley, Reynolds. Growth of the Black Population: A Study of Demographic Trends. Chicago: Markham, 1970.

1434. Farley, Reynolds. "Indications of Recent Demographic Change Among Blacks." Social Biology 18:4, (1971), 341-357.

1435. Farley, Reynolds. "The Quality of Demographic Data for Nonwhites." Demography 5:1, (1960), 1-10.

1436. Farley, Reynolds. "Recent Changes in Negro Fertility." In: Growth of the Black Population: A Study of Demographic Trends. Chicago: Markham, 1970, 76-100.

1437. Farley, Reynolds. "Recent Changes in Negro Fertility." Demography 3:1, 188-203.

1438. Farley, Reynolds. "The Urbanization of Negroes in the United States," Journal of Social History. Spring 1968, 4-12.

1439. Farley, Reynolds and Albert I. Hermalin. "Family Stability: A Comparison of Trends Between Blacks and Whites." American Sociological Review 36:1, (1971), 1-17.

1440. Farley, Reynolds and Albert Hermalin. "The 1960s: A Decade of Progress for Blacks?" Demography 9:2, 1972, 353-370.

1441. Farrel, W.C. and Marvin P. Dawkins. "Determinants of Genocide Fear in a Rural Texas Community: A Research Note." American Journal of Public Health 69:6, 1979, 605-607.

1442. Fawcett, B.E. The Moral Development of Black Adolescents and Its Relationship to Contraceptive Use. Ann Arbor, Michigan, University Microfilms International, 1981.

1443. Feagin, Joe R. "The Kinship Ties of Negro Urbanities," Social Science Quarterly, 49, (December 1968), 4-14.

1444. Ferebee, D. Boulding. "Planned Parenthood as a Public Health Measure for the Negro Race." Human Fertility 7:1, (1942), 7-10.

1445. Ferster, Elyce Z. "Eliminating the Unfit: Is Sterilization the Answer?" Ohio State Law Journal 27:4, (1966), 591-633.

1446. Fisch, Maria Alba. Internal Versus External Ego Orientation and Family Planning Effectivness Among Poor Black Women. New York: Unpublished Ph.D. Dissertation, Columbia University, 1960.

1447. Fischman, S. et al. "The Impact of Family Planning Classes on Contraceptive Knowledge, Acceptance and Use." Health Education Monographs 2:3, (1974), 246-259.

1448. Fisher, Constance. "The Negro Social Worker Evaluates Birth Control." Birth Control Review 16:6, (1932), 174-175.

1449. Fisher, Isaac. "Negro Migration, An Opportunity for Bi-Racial Statemanship in the South". National Conference Social Work Procedures, (1924), 75-82.

1450. Fleming, Walter L. "'Pap' Singleton, The Moses of the Colored Exodus," American Journal of Sociology 15 (July 1909), 61-82.

1451. Fligstein, Neil David. Going North, Migration of Blacks and Whites From the South, 1900 to 1950. New York: Academic Press, 1981.

1452. Fligstein, Neil David. Migration from Counties of the South. 1900-1950. A Social Historical, and Demographic Account. Ph.D.1978 The University of Wisconsin, Madison.

1453. Ford, K. "Contraceptive Practice Among U.S. Couples." Forum 1:2, (1978), 5-7.

1454. Ford, K. "Contraceptive Use in the United States, 1973-1976." Family Planning Perspectives 10:5, (1978), 264-269.

1455. Ford, K. "Contraceptive Utilization in the United States: 1973-5 and 1976." Advance Data 36: (1978), 1-12.

1456. Ford, K. "Contraceptive Use. in United States Since 1970." In: Ross J.A., (ed.) International Encyclopedia of Population. Vol. 1. New York: Free Press, 1982, 1-8.

1457. Fortson, B. and William Pickens. "Negro Migration: A Debate", Forum 72 (1924), 563-607.

1458. Frazier, E. Franklin. "An Analysis of Statistics on Negro Illegitimacy in the United States." Social Forces 11 (December 1932), 249-257.

1459. Frazier, E. Franklin. Bourgeoisie. New York: The Free Press, 1957.

1460. Frazier, E. Franklin. "The Negro and Birth Control." Birth Control Review 17:3, (1933), 68-70.

1461. Frazier, E. Franklin. The Negro Family in Chicago. Chicago: University of Chicago Press, 1932.

1462. Frazier, E. Franklin. The Negro Family in the United States. Chicago, University of Chicago Press, 1939.

1463. Frazier, E. Franklin. The Negro Family in the United States. Chicago: University of Chicago Press, 1966.

1464. Freeman, John Esten. A Social and Demographic Analysis of Urban Racial Violence, Boulder, Colorado: Unpublished Ph.D. Dissertation, University of Colorado, 1969.

1465. Freeman, M.G. et al. "Indigent Negro and Caucasian Birth Weight-Gestational Age Tables." Pediatrics 46:1, (1970), 9-15.

1466. Frey, William H. Black Movement to the Suburbs : Potentials and Prospects for Metropolitan-wide Integration, Discussion Paper No. 452-77, Madison: Univesity of Wisconsin, Institute for Research on Poverty, December 1977.

1467. Frey, William H. White Flight and Central City Loss: Application of An Analytic Migration Framework. Madison

University of Wisconsin, Institute for Research on Poverty,
November 1977.

1468. Fried, E.S. and J.R. Udry. "Normative Pressures on Fertility
Planning." Population and Environment 3:3, (1980), 199-209.

1469. Frisbee, W. Parker and Lisa Neidert. "Inequality and the
Relative Size of Minority Populations: A Comparative Analysis."
American Journal of Sociology 82:5, (1977), 1007-1030.

1470. Furstenburg, Frank, F. "Attitudes Toward Abortion Among Young
Blacks." Studies in Family Planning 3:4, (1972), 66-69.

1471. Furstenburg, Frank F. et al. "The Origins of the Female-Headed
Black Family: The Impact of the Urban Experience." Journal of
Interdisciplinary History 6:2, (1975), 211-233.

1472. Gallagher, Ursula M. "Adoption, Current Trends," Welfare in
Review. Washington, D. C.: U. S. Department of Health,
Education and Welfare, (February 5, 1967), 1-4.

1473. Gallaway, Lowell E. et al. "The Distribution Of The Immigrant
Population In The United States, An Economic Analysis."
Explorations in Economic History, 11:3, (1974), 213-226.

1474. Galle, Omar R. and Karl E. Taeuber. "Metropolitan Migration
and Intervening Opportunities." American Sociological Review.
31, (February 1966), 5-13.

1475. Garn, S.M. et al. No Ifs, Ands, or Buts, an Essay On the
Maternal Smoking Effect. Paper Presented at the Symposium in
Honor of Dr. Olaf Mickelson, East Lansing, Michigan. June 17,
1977.

1476. Garvin, Charles H. "The Negro Doctor's Task." Birth Control
Review 16:9, (1932), 269-270.

1477. Gaston, Juanita. The Changing Residential Pattern Of Blacks In
Battle Creek, Michigan: A Study In Historical Geography. East
Lansing: Ph.D. Thesis, Michigan State University, 1977.

1478. Gebhard, P.H. et al. "Negro Woman." In: P.H. Gebhard et al.
(eds.) Birth and Abortion. New York: Harper, 1958, 153-167.

1479. Gebhard, P.H. et al. "The Prison Woman: Three Studies." In
P.H. Gebhard et al. (eds.) Pregnancy, Birth and Abortion. New
York: Harper, (1958), 168-188.

1480. Geerken, Michael and Walter R. Gove. "Race, Sex, and Marital
Status: Their Effect on Mortality." Social Problems 21 (April
1974), 567-579.

1481. George, Kochuparampil M. Family Structure and Fertility Among

Lower Class Negroes: A Study in Social Demography. Unpublished Doctoral Dissertation. University of Kentucky, 1970.

1482. Geruson, Richard Thomas. Migration in the New York City Area Since the Civil War: A Descriptive, Analytical and Comparative Study. Unpublished Ph.D. Dissertation. University of Pennsylvania, 1973.

1483. Gettys, J.O. et al. "A Review of Family Health's Latest Evaluation of the Demographic Impact of the Louisiana Family Planning Program." Journal of the Louisiana State Medical Society 126:3, (1974), 81-88.

1484. Gill, Flora Davidov. Economics and the Black Exodus: An Analysis of Negro Emigration from the Southern United States, 1910-1970. Unpublished Ph.D. Dissertation. Stanford University, 1975.

1485. Gill, Flora Davidov. "The Long and Short in Migration Descisions: An American Case Study." Australian Economic Papers. 19:35, (1980), 278-290.

1486. Ginn, Doris O. "Demographic Patterns of Afro-American Speech" in R.A. Obudho (ed.) Afro-Americans and the City. Albany, New York: State University of New York Press, 1984.

1487. Ginzberg, Eli and Dale L. Hiestrand. Mobility in the Negro Community. Washington, D.C.: United States Commission on Civil Rights, CLearinghouse Publication No. 11, June 1968.

1488. Gispert, M. and R. Falk. "Sexual Experimentation and Pregnancy in Young Black Adolescents." American Journal of Obstetrics and Gynecology 126:4, (1976), 459-466.

1489. Glass, Leonard et al. "Effects of Legalized Abortion on Neonatal Mortality and Obstetrical Morbidity at Harlem Hospital Center." American Journal of Public Health 64, (1974), 717-718.

1490. Glenn, Norval D. "The Relative Size of the Negro Population and Negro Occupational Status." Social Forces 43, (1964), 42-49.

1491. Glick, Paul C. "A Demographic Picture of Black Families." In: Harriet Pipes McAdoo (ed.) Black Families. Beverly Hills: Sage, 1981, 106-126.

1492. Glick, Paul C. "Marriage and Marital Stability Among Blacks." Milbank Memorial Fund Quarterly 48:2, (Part 2), (1970), 99-116.

1493. Godfrey, Daniel Douglas. The Utilization of Selected Services by Household Types, White and Black, in Region Q, North Carolina. Unpublished Ph.D. Dissertation. Cornell University,

1975.

1494. Godkin, Edward L. "Negro Exodus, 1879." Nation, 28:242, (1879), 386.

1495. Gold, Edwin M. et al. "Therapeutic Abortions in New York City: A 20-Year Review." American Journal of Public Health 55:7, (1965), 964-972.

1496. Goldscheider, Calvin and P.R. Uhlenberg. "Minority Group Status and Fertility." American Journal of Sociology 74 (January 1969), 361-372.

1497. Goldsmith, S. et al. "A Study of Teenage Contraceptors: Their Sexual Knowledge, Attitudes and Use of Contraceptives." Advances in Planned Parenthood 7: (1972), 33-46.

1498. Goodrich, Carter et al. Migration and Economic Opportunity: The Report of the Study of Population Redistribution. Philadelphia: University of Philadelphia Press, 1936.

1499. Gottlieb, Peter. Making Their Own Way: Southern Blacks' Migration to Pittsburgh, 1916-30. Unpublished Ph.D. Dissertation. University of Pittsburgh, 1977.

1500. Goyer, Doreen S. and Elaine Domschke. The Handbook of National Population Census, Latin America and the Caribbean, North America, and Oceania. Westport, Conn.: Greenwood, 1982.

1501. Grabow, Steve. Migration of Blacks and Whites: A Focus on Outlying Neighborhoods of Cincinnati, Ohio. University of Cincinnati, M.A. Thesis, Cincinnati, Ohio, 1974.

1502. Graves, W.L. and Barbara Robinson Bradshaw. "Early Reconception and Contraceptive Use Among Black Teenage Girls After an Illegitimate Birth." American Journal of Public Health 65:7, (1975), 738-740.

1503. Graves, W.L. and Barbara Robinson Bradshaw. "Some Social and Attitudinal Factors Associated with Contraceptive Choice Among Low Income Black Teenagers after an Illegitimate Birth." Advances in Planned Parenthood 9:2, (1974), 28-33.

1504. Gray, Willia Bower. Residential Patterns and Associates Socioeconomic Characteristics of Black Populations of Varying City-Suburban Locations Within the San Francisco Area: A Census Based Analysis with Emphasis on Black Suburbanized Populations of 1970. D.S.W. 1975 University of California: Berkeley.

1505. Greenwood, Michael J. and P.J. Gormely. "A Comparison of the Determinants of White and Nonwhite Interstate Migration." Demography 8:1, (1971), 141-155.

1506. Gregory, Dick. "My Answer to Genocide: Bitter Comic Prescribes Big Families as Effective Black Protect." _Ebony_ 26 (October 1971), 66-72.

1507. Grenz, Suzanne M. "The Exodusters of 1879: St. Louis and Kansas City Responses." _Missouri Historical Review_ 73:1, (1978), 54-70.

1508. Grier, Eunice S. _Understanding Washington's Changing Population_. Washington, D.C.: Washington Center for Metropolitan Studies, 1961.

1509. Grindstaff, Carl Forest. _Migration and Mississippi._ Unpublished Ph.D. Dissertation. University of Massachusetts, 1970.

1510. Grindstaff, Carl Forest. "Trends and Incidence of Childlessness by Race: Indicators of Black Progress Over Three Decades." _Sociological Focus_ 9:3, (1970), 265-284.

1511. Groff, William. _An Analysis of White and Negro Fertility Differences._ Unpublished Ph.D. Disssertation. Brown University, 1968.

1512. Groh, George. _The Black Migration: The Journey to Urban America_. New York: Weybright and Talley, 1972.

1513. Groves, Paul A. "The Hidden Population: Washington Alley Dwellers in the Late Nineteenth Century." _Professional Geographer_. 26:3, (1974), 270-276.

1514. Guidotti, R.J. et al. "Fatal Amniotic Fluid Emolism During Legally Induced Abortion, United States, 1972 to 1978." _American Journal of Obstetrics and Gynecology_. 141:3, (October 1981), 257-61.

1515. Gustavos, Susan and K.G. Mommsen. "Black-White Differences in Family Size Preferences Among Youth." _Pacific Sociological Review_ 16:1, (1973), 107-119.

1516. Gutman, H.G. "Persistent Myths about the Afro-American Family." In: _The American Family in Social-Historical Perspective_, edited by Michael Gordon. New York, N.Y.: St. Martin's, (1978), 467-489.

1517. Hale, C.B. and G.E. Pickett. "On Comparison of Age- and Race-Specific Abortion Ratios." _American Journal of Public Health_. 73:4, (April 1983), 453.

1518. Hale, C.B. and S.C. O'Neil. _Southern Black and White Women Who Seek Abortion: A Comparative Analysis._ Paper Presented at the 107th Annual Meetings of the American Public Health Association, New York, November 4-9, 1979.

1519. Hale, C.B. et al. Infant Mortality Differentials in Alabama, 1976-1978. Paper Presented at the American Public Health Association Annual Meetings, New York, November 1979.

1520. Hamilton, Horace. "Continuity and Change in Southern Migration." In John C. McKinney and Edgar T. Thompson (eds.) The South in Continuity and Change. Durham, N.C.: Duke University Press, 1965, 8-12.

1521. Hamilton, Horace. "Effects of Census Errors on the Measurement of Net Migration." Demography. 3:2 (1966), 395-415.

1522. Hamilton, Horace. "The Negro Leaves the South." Demography. 1:1 (1964), 273-95.

1523. Hamilton, Horace. "The Negro Leaves the South." In Helen M. Hughes (ed.) Population Growth and the Complex Society. Boston: Allyn and Bacon, 1972, 1-10.

1524. Hamilton, Horace. "Population Pressures and Other Factors Affecting Net Rural-Urban Migration." In Joseph J. Spengler and Otis D. Duncan (eds.)Demographic Analysis: Selected Readings. Glencoe, Illinois: The Free Press, 1963, 15-24.

1525. "Hampton and Negro Migration." Southern Workman 46: (1917), 330-1.

1526. Hampton, Robert L. "Husband's Characteristics and Marital Disruption in Black Families." The Sociological Quarterly 20 (Spring 1979), 255-266.

1527. Haney, C.A. et al. "Legitimacy, Illegitimacy, and Live Birth Ratios in a Black Population." Journal of Health and Social Behavior 13:3, (1972), 303-310.

1528. Haney, C.A. et al. "The Value Stretch Hypothesis: Family Size Preferences in a Black Population." Social Problems 21:2, (1973), 206-220.

1529. Hansen, Christian M. "The Pediatrician and Family Planning in a Very Poor Community: An Appraisal of Experiences in the Tufts Delta Health Center, Bolivar County, Mississippi." Clinical Pediatrics 11:6, (1972), 319-323.

1530. Hansen, H. et al. "School Achievement: Risk Factor in Teenage Pregnancies?" American Journal of Public Health 68:8, (1978), 753-758.

1531. Hare, Nathan. "Recent Trends in the Occupational Mobility of Negroes, 1930-1960: An Intracohort Analysis." Social Forces 44 (December 1965): 166-173.

1532. Harig, T.J. et al. Excessive Fertility Among a Black Inner-

City Population. Paper presented at the Second Annual Meeting of the World Population Society and International Population Conference. Washington, D.C.: November 1975.

1533. Harper, Roland M. "Ante-Bellum Census Enumerations in Florida." Florida Historical Society Quarterly 6:42, (July 1927), 47-53.

1534. Harrier, Keith D. "Population Change Trends in Large U.S. Metropolitan Areas, 1960-1970: A Review." Journal of Geography, 72, (1973), 19-30.

1535. Harris, Abram L. "Negro Migration to the North." Current History 20 (1924), 921-5.

1536. Harris, H.L.. "Health of the Negro Family in Chicago, Illinois." Opportunity, 5, (September 1927), 258-260.

1537. Harris, H.L. "Negro Mortality Rates in Chicago," Social Service Review I (March 1927), 58-77.

1538. Harris, Leroy E. The Other Side of the Freeway: A Study of Settlement Patterns of Negroes and Mexican-Americans in San Diego, California. Carnegie-Mellon University, Unpublished Doctor of Arts Thesis, 1974.

1539. Harris W.G.; Turner, et al. Black Family Planning: Attitudes of Leaders and a General Sample. Presented at the 39th Annual Meeting of the American Psychological Association, Los Angeles, California, August 26, 1981.

1540. Harrison, Algea. "Attitudes Toward Procreation Among Black Adults." In: Harriet Pipe McAdoo (ed.) Black Families. London: Sage, (1981), 199-208.

1541. Hart, John Fraser. "Censal Year of Maximum Negro Population in the Easter United States." Annals of the Association of American Geographers. 41 (June 1959), 183-184.

1542. Hart, John Fraser. "The Changing Distribution of the American Negro." Annals of the Association of American Geographers. 50:3, (1960), 242-266.

1543. Hart, John Fraser. "Negro Migration in the United States." Annals of the Association of American Geographers. 48, (1959), 268.

1544. Hauser, Philip M. "Demographic and Social Factors in the Poverty of the Negro." In: The Disadvantaged Poor: Education and Employment. Washington, D.C.: Chamber of Commerce of the United States. Task Force on Economic Growth and Opportunity, 1966, 229-261.

1545. Hauser, Philip M. "Demographic Factors in the Integration of the Negro." Daedalus 94 (1965), 847–877.

1546. Hauser, Robert M. and David L. Featherman. "White–Nonwhite Difference? in Occupational Mobility Among Men in the United States, 1962–1977." Demography 11: 2 (May 1974), 247–65.

1547. Hawkins, Homer C. "Trends in Black Migration from 1863 to 1960". Phylon 34:2 (1973), 140–152.

1548. Hayes, Laurence J.W. The Negro Federal Government Worker, Washington, D.C.: The Graduate School, Howard University, 1941.

1549. Haynes, George E. "Movement of Negroes from the Country to the City." So. Workman 43 (1913), 23.

1550. Haynes, George E. The Negro at Work in New York, unpublished Ph.D. Dissertation, Columbia University, 1912.

1551. Haynes, George E. The Negro at Work During the World War and During Reconstruction, Washington, D.C.: Government Printing Office, 1921.

1552. Haynes, George E. "Negro Migration." Opportunity, (October 1924), 273.

1553. Haynes, George E. "Negro Migration and Its Effects on Family and Community Life in the North." National Conference of Social Work (1924), 62–75.

1554. Heath, L.L. et al. "A Research Note on Children Viewed as Contributors to Marital Stability: The Relationships to Birth Control Use, Ideal and Expected Family Size." Journal of Marriage and the Family 36:2, (1974), 304–306.

1555. Heath, Marilyn S. "A Study of the Threshold Negro Population of Ohio 1950–1970." M.A. Thesis, Bowling Green State University, Bowling Green, Ohio, 1973.

1556. Hecht, P.K. and P. Cutright. "Racial Differences in Infant Mortality Rates: United States, 1969." Social Forces 57:4, (1979), 1180–1193.

1557. Hefner, James A. Black Employment in a Southern 'Progressive' City: The Atlanta Experience, unpublished Ph.D. Dissertation, University of Colorado, 1971.

1558. Hellwig, David J. "Black Meets Black: Afro–American Reactions to West Indian Immigrants in the 1920's." South Atlantic Quarterly 77:2, (1978), 206–224.

1559. Hendershot, G.E. "Trends in Breast Feeding." Advance Data 59 (March 1980), 1–3.

1560. Hendershot, G.E. "Work During Pregnancy and Subsequent Hospitalization of Mothers and Infants: Evidence from the National Survey of Family Growth." Public Health Reports 94:5, (1979), 425-431.

1561. Hendershot, G.E. and K.E. Bauman. "Coitus-Related Cervical Cancer Risk Factors; Trends and Differentials in Racial and Religious Groups. American Journal of Public Health. 73:3, (March 1983), 299-301.

1562. Hendershot, G.E. and K.E. Bauman. Use of Services for Family Planning and Infertility: United States. Vital and Health Statistics. Series 23: Data from the National Survey of Family Growth. (December 1981), 1-15.

1563. Henderson, Donald. "The Negro Migration, 1916-1918," Journal of Negro History, 5 (October 1921), 4-12.

1564. Hendricks, L.E. An Analysis of Two Select Populations of Black Unmarried Fathers, Vol. F: Final Report. Washington, D.C., Howard University, Institute for Urban Affairs and Research, Mental Health Research and Development Center, April 1981.

1565. Hendricks, L.E. "Black Unwed Adolescent Fathers." Urban Research Review 6:1, (1980), 7-9.

1566. Hendricks, L.E. Suggestions for Reaching Unmarried Black Adolescent Fathers. Prepared from a paper presented at Child Welfare Legue of America's 1982 Eastern Regional Training Conference, Baltimore, Maryland. Also in Child Welfare. 62:2, (March/April 1983), 141-6.

1567. Hendricks, L.E. "Unmarried Black Adolescent Fathers' Attitudes Toward Abortion, Contraception, and Sexuality: A Preliminary Report." Journal of Adolescent Health Care. 2:3, (March 1982), 199-203.

1568. Hendricks, L.E. "Unwed Adolescent Fathers: Problems They Face and Their Sources of Social Support." Adolescence. 15:60, (Winter 1980), 861-9.

1569. Hendricks, L.E. and T. Montgomery. "A Limited Population of Unmarried Adolescent Fathers: A Preliminary Report of Their Views on Fatherhood and the Relationsihp with the Mothers of Their Children." Adolescence. 18:69, (Spring 1983), 201-10.

1570. Henri, F. Black Migration: Movement North 1900-1920. New York: Doubleday, 1975.

1571. Henson, D. and R. Tarone. "An Epidemiologic Study of Cancer of the Cervix, Vagina, and Vulva." American Journal of Obstetrics and Gynecology 129:5 (1977), 525-532.

1572. Herbst, Alma. The Negro in the Slaughtering and Meat-Packing Industry in Chicago, Boston: Houghton Mifflin, 1932.

1573. Herson, J. et al. "Comprehensive Family Planning Services to an Urban Black Community." Journal of the National Medical Association 67:1 (1973), 61-65.

1574. Hickok, Floyd Clinton. The Distribution and Demographic Character of the Major Minorities in California, 1970. California State University, Fullerton, unpublished M.A.Thesis, 1975.

1575. Hicks, Florence J. Variables Associated with Participation of a Group of Nonwhite Mothers in a Selected Health Department Birth Control Program. Unpublished Ph.D. Dissertation. University of Maryland, 1970.

1576. Hicks, Nancy. "Sterilization of Black Mother of the Stirs Aiken, S.C." The New York Times (August 1, 1973), 27.

1577. Hill, A.C. and F.S. Jaffe. "Negro Fertility and Family Size Preference." In: Talcott Parsons and Kenneth Clark (eds.) The Negro American. New York: The Daedalus Library, (1965), 205-224.

1578. Hill, E.L. and J.W. Eliot. "Black Physicians' Experience With Abortion Requests and Opinion About Abortion Law Change in Michigan." Journal of the National Medical Association 64:1, (1972), 52-58.

1579. Hill, Herbert. "Demographic Change and Racial Ghettoes: The Crisis of American Cities." Journal of Urban Law, 44 (Winter 1966), 231-285.

1580. Hill, J.G. "Birth Control Usage Among Abortion Patients." Journal of the Kansas Medical Society, (June 1972), 293-301.

1581. Hill, Joseph A. "Recent Northward Migration of the Negro." Monthly Labor Report, 18:475, 88 (March 1924).

1582. Hill, M.S. and M. Ponza. Poverty Across Generations: Is Welfare Dependency a Pathology Passed from One Generation to the Next? Presented at the 52nd Annual Meeting of the Population Association of America, Pittsburgh, Pennsylvania, April 14-16, 1983.

1583. Hill, Richard J. and Calvin J. Larson. "Variability of Ghetto Organizations." In Thomas D. Sherrand, (ed.) Social Welfare and Urban Problems. New York: Columbia University Press, 1968, 132-160.

1584. Hill, Robert. Black Families: Their Strengths and Stability. Washington, D.C.: Research Department, National Urban League,

1972.

1585. Hill, T. Edward. The Negro in West Virginia. Bureau of Negro Welfare and Statistics of the State of West Virginia. 1925-26 Charleston, West Virginia: Bureau of Welfare and Statistics, 1926.

1586. Hillery, George A. "The Negro in New Orleans: A Functional Analysis of Demographic Data." American Sociological Review 22:2, (1957), 183-188.

1587. Hiltner, John. "Negro Migration in a Section of Toledo, Ohio." Annals of the Association of American Geographers, 48, (March 1967), 177.

1588. Himes, Joseph S. "Some Characteristics of the Migration of Blacks in the United States." Social Biology 18:4, (1971), 359-366.

1589. Hirsch, M.B. et al. "Desired Family Size of Young American Women, 1971 and 1976." In: In G.E. Hendershot and P.J. Placek (eds.) Predicting Fertility: Demographic Studies of Birth Expectations. Lexington, Massachusetts: D.C. Heath, 1981, 4-15.

1590. Hodge, Patricia Leavey and Philip M. Hauser. The Challenges of America's Metropolitan Population Outlook - 1960 to 1985. Washington, D.C.: Government Printing Office, 1968.

1591. Hodson, Cora B. "An Instrument in Race Progress." Birth Control Review 17:4 (1933), 105-16.

1592. Hoeppner, M. Early Adolescent Childbearing: Some Social Implications. Santa Monica, California: The Rand Corporation, 1977.

1593. Hofferth, S.L. High School, Occupational Choice and Sex Equity. [Revised version of Working Paper 1303-01, "High school experience in the attainment process of non-college boys and girls: when and why did their paths diverge?"] Washington, D.C.: The Urban Institute and Working Paper; 1303-02, September, 1980.

1594. Hofferth, S.L. and K.A. Moore. "Early Child Bearing and Later Economic Well-Being." American Sociological Review 44:5, (1979), 784-815.

1595. Hogan, D.P. and E.M. Kitagawa. Family Factors in the Fertility of Black Adolescents. Presented at the 52nd Annual Meeting of the Population Association of America, Pittsburgh, Pennsylvania, April 14-16.

1596. Holmes, S.J. "The Negro Birth Rate." Birth Control Review

16:6 (1932) 172-173.

1597. Hope, John H. "How Can the South Meet the Negro Migration Movement?" Manufacturers Record (1923), 495.

1598. Hout, Michael. "Age Structure, Unwanted Fertility, and the Association Between Racial Composition and Family Planning Programs: A Comment on Wright." Social Forces 57:4 (1979), 1387-1392.

1599. Howell, E.M. "A Study of Reported Therapeutic Abortion in North Carolina." American Journal of Public Health 65:5 (1975), 480-483.

1600. Hudgins, John. "Is Birth Control Genocide?" The Black Scholar 4:3 (1972), 34-37.

1601. Hughes, Blanche R. Abortion: Perception and Contemporary Genocide Myth: A Comparative Study Among Low-Income Pregnant Black and Puerto Rican Women. Unpublished Ph.D. Dissertation. New York University, 1973.

1602. Hull, Herbert. "Demographic Changes and Racial Ghettos: The Crisis of American Cities." Journal of Urban Law, 44 (Winter 1966), 231-285.

1603. Hunt, Eleanor P. "Infant Mortality and Poverty Areas," Welfare in Review 5 (August-September 1967), 1-12.

1604. Hutchins, F.L. "Teenage Pregnancy and the Black Community." Journal of the National Medical Association. 70:11 (1978), 857-9.

1605. Huyck, Earl E. "White-Nonwhite Differentials: Overview and Implications." Demography 3:2, (1966), 548-565.

1606. Ibom, Godfrey Gamili. A Dynamic Quasi-Stochastic Model for Forecasting Population Distribution of Residential Black Pupils in Suburbia Ph.D. 1973 the Ohio State University.

1607. Illinois Council for Black Studies. Black People and the 1980 Census. Volume 1: Proceedings from a Conference on the Population Undercount. Chicago: Illinois Council for Black Studies, 1980.

1608. Jackson, J.A. Migration. Cambridge: Cambridge University Press, 1969.

1609. Jackson, E.J. "Two Projects in Rural North Carolina, U.S.A." In: P.W. Blair (ed.) Health Needs of the World's Poor Women. Washington, D.C.: Equity Policy Center, 1981, 142-5.

1610. Jackson, Eureal Grant. "Some Tendencies in Demograhic Trends in Maryland, 1950-1956." Journal of Negro Education 26 (Fall 1957), 514-519.

1611. Jackson, Giles B. and Webster D. Davis. The Industrial History of the Negro Race in the United States, Richmond, Virginia, 1908.

1612. Jaffe, F.S. "Family Planning and Poverty." Journal of Marriage and the Family 26:4 (1964), 467-470.

1613. Jaffe, F.S. and P. Cutright. "Short-Term Benefits and Costs of U.S. Family Planning Programs, 1970-1975." Family Planning Perspectives 9:2, (1977), 77-80.

1614. Jakobovits, Antal et al. "Early Intrauterine Development: I1. The Rate of Growth in Black and Central American Populations Between 10 and 20 Week's Gestation." Pediatrics 58:6, (1976), 833-841.

1615. Jiobu, Robert M. "Urban Determinants of Racial Differentiation in Infant Mortality." Demography 9:4, (1972), 603-615.

1616. Johnson, Charles S. "The Negro Population of Waterbury, Connecticut." Opportunity 1 (1923), 298-303.

1617. Johnson, Charles S. "Some Economic Aspects of Negro Migrations." Opportunity (1927), 297-9.

1618. Johnson, Charles S. "Substitution of Negro Labor for European Immigration Labor." National Conference Social Work (1926), 317-27.

1619. Johnson, Charles S. "When the Negro Migrates North." World To-morrow 6 (1923), 139-40.

1620. Johnson, Charles S. "How Much is the Migration a Flight from Persecution?" Opportunity I (September 1923), 1-10.

1621. Johnson, Charles S. "A Question of Negro Health." Birth Control Review 16:6 (1932), 167-169.

1622. Johnson, Daniel M. Black Return Migration to a Southern Metropolis: Birmingham, Alabama. Ph.D. Dissertation, University of Missouri, 1973.

1623. Johnson, Daniel M. and Rex R. Campbell. Black Migration in America: A Social Demographic History. Durham: Duke University Press, 1981.

1624. Johnson, Daniel M. et al. Black Migration to the South: Primary and Return Migrants; Paper Presented at the Annual Meeting of the Rural Sociological Society in Montreal, Canada, August, 1974.

1625. Johnson, Guy B. "The Negro Migration and Its Consequences." Journal of Social Forces 2 (March, 1924), 404-408.

1626. Johnson, J. and Stanley D. Brunn. "Spatial and Behavioral Aspects of the Counterstream Migration of Blacks to the South." Scripta Series in Geography. In: In Stanley D. Brunn and James O. Wheeler (eds.) The American Metropolitan System: Present and Future. New York: Halsted, 1980, 59-76.

1627. Johnson, J.D. "The Migration and the Census of 1920." Opportunity, 1 (August 1923), 235-8.

1628. Johnson, Leon Boulin. Black Migration, Spatial Organization and Perception and Philadelphia's Urban Environment, 1638-1930. M.A. Thesis, University of Washington, Seattle, WA, 1973.

1629. Johnson, Leanor Boulin and Robert E. Staples. "Family Planning and the Young Minority Male: A Pilot Project." The Family Coordinator 28 (October 1979), 535-543.

1630. Johnson, N.E. "Minority Group Status and the Fertility of Black America, 1970: A New Look." American Journal of Sociology 84:6 (1979), 1386-1400.

1631. Johnson, N.E. "A Response to Rindfuss." American Journal of Sociology. 86:2 (1980), 375-7.

1632. Johnson, N.E. "Minority-Group Status and the Fertility of Black Americans, 1970: A New Look." American Journal of Sociology 84:6 (May 1980), 1386-1400.

1633. Johnson, Robert E. "Legal Abortion: Is It Genocide or Blessing in Disguise?" Jet 43 (March 22, 1973), 12-19.

1634. Jones, C. "Population Issues and the Black Community." In V. Gray and E. Bergman (eds.) Political Issues in U.S. Population Policy. Lexington, Massachusetts: D.C. Heath, 1974, 151-166.

1635. Jones, Donald W. Migration and Urban Unemployment in Dualistic Economic Development. Chicago: Department of Geography the University of Chicago, 1975.

1636. Jones, Eugene Kinckle. "Negroes, North and South: A Contrast." Mississippi Review 45 (1922), 479-82.

1637. Jones, Eugene Kinckle. "Negro in the North." Current History 15 (1922), 969-974.

1638. Jones, Eugene Kinckle. "Negro Migration in New York State," Oppurtunity 5 (January 1926), 7-11.

1639. Jones, Marcus Earl. Black Migration in the United States with

Emphasis on Selected Central Cities. Ph.D. 1978 Southern
Illinois University at Carbondale.

1640. Jones, Marcus Earl. Black Migration in the United States with
Selected Emphasis on Selected Central Cities. Saratoga,
California: Century Twenty-One Publishers, 1980.

1641. Jones, Thomas Jesse. "Negro Population in the United States."
Annals of American Association of Geographers. 49: (1913),
317-9.

1642. Jones, Thomas Jesse. Negroes and the Census of 1910. Hampton,
VA.: Hampton Normal and Agricultural Institute, 1912.

1643. Journal of Negro History. "The Negro Migration of 1916-1918" 6,
(1926), 383-398.

1644. Journal of Negro History. "The Negro in the Reconstruction of
Virginia: The Migration" 11, (1926), 327-346.

1645. Journal of Negro History. "The Redistribution of the Negro
Population of the United States," 51, (1966), 155-173.

1646. Journal of Negro History. "Statutory Means of Impeding
Migration of the Negro." 22, (1937), 148-162.

1647. Journal of Negro History. "Turner's Safety Valve and Free
Negro Westward Migration." 50, (1965), 185-197.

1648. Kahlil, Brother. "Eugenics, Birth Control and Black Man."
Black News 27 (14 January 1971), 20-21.

1649. Kammeyer, K.C.W. et al. "Family Planning Services and the
Distribution of Black Americans." Social Problems 21:5, (1974)
674-690.

1650. Kammeyer, K.C.W. et al. "Family Planning Services and the
Distribution of Black Americans." In Kenneth C. W. Kammeyer
(ed.) Population Studies: Selected Essays and Research.
Chicago: Rand McNally, 1975, 475-499.

1651. Kantner, J.F. and M. Zelnik. "United States: Exploratory
Studies of Negro Family Formation--Common Conceptions About
Birth Control." Studies in Family Planning 47, (1969), 10-13.

1652. Karashkevych, Boris. The Postwar Fertility of the American
Negro. Unpublished Ph.D. Dissertation. New York University,
1964.

1653. Kariel, Herbert G. "Selected Factors Areally Associated with
Population Growth Due to Net Migration." Annals of the
Association of American Geographers (June 1963), 210-23.

1654. Kaun, David E. "Negro Migration and Unemployment." The Journal of Human Resources 5: 2 (Spring 1970), 191-207.

1655. Kellam, S.G. et al. "The Long-Term Evolution of the Family Structure of Teenage and Older Mothers. Journal of Marriage and the Family 44:3, (August 1982), 539-54.

1656. Kellogg, John. "Negro Urban Clusters in the Post-Bellum South". Geographical Review 67:3, (1977), 310-321.

1657. Kelsey, J.L. "A Review of the Epidemiology of Human Breast Cancer." Epidemiological Reviews. (1979), 74-109.

1658. Kennard, Gail. "Sterilization Abuse," Essence 5 (October 1974) 66-67.

1659. Kennedy, Louise V. The Negro Peasant Turns Cityward. New York: Columbia University Press, 1930.

1660. Kephart, William and Thomas P. Monahan. "Desertion and Divorce in Philadelphia." American Sociological Review 17 (December 1952), 719-727.

1661. King, Allan G. and R. White. "Demographic Influences on Labor Force Rates of Black Males." Monthly Labor Review 99 (November 1976), 42-43.

1662. Kirksey, H. "United States: The Black Undercount and Political Issues." In: Black People and the 1980 Census. Vol. 1: Proceedings from a Conference on the Population Undercount. Illinois Council for Black Studies, Chicago, Ill., United States, 1980.

1663. Kiser, C.V. "Fertility Trends and Differentials Among Nonwhites in the United States." Milbank Memorial Fund Quarterly 46 (April 1958), 190-195.

1664. Kiser, Clyde V. and Myrna E. Frank. " Factors Associated with Low Fertility of Nonwhite Women of College Attainment." Milbank Memorial Fund Quarterly 45 (1967), 427-449.

1665. Kiser, Clyde V. "Fertility of Harlem Negroes." Milbank Memorial Fund Quarterly 13:3 (1935), 273-285.

1666. Kitagawa, Evelyn M. and P.M. Hauser. " Differential Mortality by Race, Nativity, Country of Origin, Marital Status, and Parity." In: Evelyn M. Kitagawa and Philip M. Hauser (Eds.) Differential Mortality in the United States: A Study in Socioeconomic Epidemiology. Cambridge, Massachusetts: Harvard University Press, 1973, 93-113.

1667. Klebba, A. Joan et al. Mortality Trends: Age, Color, Sex, United States 1950-1969. Washington, D.C.: Government

Printing Office, 1973.

1668. Klove, Robert C. "Urban and Metropolitan Population Trends and Patterns." Annals of the Association of American Geographers. 44, (1954), 222.

1669. Klungness, Paul H. Negro Population Density and Agricultural Changes: the Case of North Carolina. M.A. Thesis, Syracuse University, Syracuse, 1970.

1670. Knuth, Clarence Paul Edward. Early Immigration and Current Residential Patterns of Negroes in Southwestern Michigan. Ph.D. 1969 The University of Michigan.

1671. Koo, H.P. et al. Long-term Marital Disruption, Fertility, and Socioeconomic Achievement Associated with Adolescent Childbearing. Presented at the 109th Annual Meeting of the Americal Public Health Association, Los Angeles, California, November 1, 1981.

1672. Koren, Barry. Residential Mobility in a Potentially Changing Neighborhood: A Study of Household Moving and Staying in the Aftermath of a School Conflict. Ph.D. 1978 the University of Wisconsin - Madison.

1673. Kovar, Mary Grace. "Mortality of Black Infants in the United States." Phylon 38 (December 1977), 370-397.

1674. Kozol, Jonathan. Death at an Early Age. Boston: Houghton Mifflin, 1967.

1675. Kramer, M.J. "Legal Abortion Among New York City Residents: An Analysis According to Socioeconomic and Demographic Charcteristics." Family Planning Perspectives 7:3, (1975), 128-137.

1676. Kriesberg, Louis. Mothers in Poverty: A Study of Fatherless Families. Chicago: Aldine, 1970.

1677. Kritz, Mary M. and Douglas Gurak. "Ethnicity and Fertility in the United States: An Analysis of 1970 Public Use Sample Data." Review of Public Data Use 4 (May 1976), 12-23.

1678. Kronus, S. "Fertility Control in the Rural South: A Pretest." In: Donald J. Bogue (ed.) Sociological Contributions to Family Planning Research. Chicago: University of Chicago, Community and Family Study Center, 1967, 129-160.

1679. Kulikoff, K. "The Beginnings of the Afro-American Family in Maryland." In Michael Gordon (Ed.) The American Family in Social-Historical Perspective New York: St. Martin's Press, 1978, 444-466.

1680. Lamman, J.T. et al. "Reduced Delivery Rates of Immature and Premature Infants Following Liberalization of New York State Abortion Law." Pediatric Research 7:4, (1973), 289.

1681. Lammermeier, Paul J. "The Urban Black Family of the Nineteenth Century: A Study of Black Family Structure in the Ohio Valley, 1850-1880." Journal of Marriage and the Family 35:3, (1973), 440-456.

1682. Lampman, Robert. The Low Income Population and Economic Growth. Study Paper No. 12. Washington, D. C.: United States Congress Joint Economic Committee, 1959.

1683. Lanctot, C.A. Apparent Increase in the Popularity of NFP in the U.S.A. (from 1973-1976) from National Family Planning Surveys. Washington, D.C.: IFFLP Memorandum, January 14, 1980.

1684. Landis, Paul H. "Internal Migration by Subsidy," Social Forces 22 (December 1943), 183-87.

1685. Landon, Fred. "The Negro Migration to Canada After the Passing of the Fugitive Slave Act." Journal of Negro History 5, (1920), 22-36.

1686. Langley, W.M. and C.B. Hale. Family Composition, Socioeconomic Status, Sexual and Contraceptive Knowledge, Attitudes, and Practices Among Black Adolescent Females. Presented at the 109th Annual Meeting of the American Public Health Association, Los Angeles, California, November 2, 1981.

1687. Lansing, John B. et al. "Negro-White Differences in Geographic Mobility." The Geographic Mobility of Labor. Ann Arbor, Michigan: Institute of Social Research, University of Michigan, 1967.

1688. Lantz, Herman and L. Hendrix. "The Free Black Family at the Time of the U.S. Census: Some Implications." International Journal of Sociology of the Family 7:1, (1977), 37-44.

1689. Lantz, Herman and L. Hendrix. "Black Fertility and Black Family in the Nineteenth Century: Re-examination of the Past." Journal of Family History 3:3, (1978), 251-261.

1690. Leavy, Zad and Jerome M. Kummer. "Abortion and the Population Crisis: Therapeutic Abortion and the Law: Some New Approaches." Ohio State Journal 27:4, (1966), 647-678.

1691. Lee, Anne S. and Everett Lee. "The Future Fertility of the American Negro." Social Forces 37:3, (1959), 228-231.

1692. Lee, Anne S. and G.K. Bowles. "Contributions of Rural Migrants to the Urban Occupational Structure." Agricultural Economic Research 26:2 (1974), 25-32.

1693. Lee, Anne S. and G. K. Bowles. "Policy Implications of the Movement of Black Out of the Rural South." Phylon 35:3, (1974), 332-339.

1694. Lee, Everett. Migration and the Convergence of White and Negro Rates of Mental Disease. In: Proceedings of the Worlds Population Conference, Belgrade, August 30 to September 10, 1965. Volume 2: Selected Papers and Summaries: Fertility, Family Planning, Mortality. New York: United Nations. Department of Economic and Social Affairs, 1967, 410-413.

1695. Lee, Everett S. and Anne S. Lee. "The Differential Fertility of the American Negro." American Sociological Review 17:4, (1952), 437-447.

1696. Lees, Hannah. "The Negro Response to Birth Control." The Reporter 34:10, (1966), 46-47.

1697. Lester, Julius. "Birth Control and Blacks." In Julius Lester (ed.) Revolutionary Notes. New York: Richard W. Baron, 1969, 140-43.

1698. Levin, David E. Negro Migration from Georgia: A Gravity Model Approach. M.A. Thesis, Temple University, Philadelphia, PA, 1973.

1699. Lewis, Julian. "Can the Negro Afford Birth Control." Negro Digest 3 (May 1945); 19-22.

1700. Lewis, Lawrence Thomas. Some Migration Models: Their Applicability to Negro Urban Migration. Unpublished Ph.D. Dissertion. Clark University, 1971.

1701. Lewis, T.B. "Fertility Trends and the Community: A Consumer's Point of View." Journal of Medical Education 44:11, (1969), 93-97.

1702. Lieberson, Stanley. "Selective Black Migration from the South: A Historical View." In Frank D. Bean and W.P. Frisbee (eds.) The Demography of Racial and Ethnic Groups. New York: Academic Press, (1978), 119-141.

1703. Lieberson, Stanley. "A Reconsideration of the Income Differences Found Between Migrants and Northern- Born Blacks." American Journal of Sociology 83: (1978), 940-966.

1704. Lieberson, Stanley and C.A. Wilkenson. "A Comparison Between Northern and Southern Blacks Residing in the North." Demography 13:2, (1976), 199-224.

1705. Liebow, Elliot. "Attitudes Toward Marriage and Family Among Black Males in Tally's Corner." In: Demographic Aspects of the Black Community, Milbank Memorial Fund Quarterly 48:2, (1970),

151-165.

1706. Lief, T. Parrish. The Decision to Migrate: Black College Graduates and Their Tendency to Leave New Orleans. Unpublished Ph. D. Dissertation. Tulane University, 1970.

1707. Lindsey, Kay. "Birth Control and the Black Woman." Essence 1 (October 1970), 56-57.

1708. Linn, M.W. et al. "Fertility Related Attitudes of Minority Mothers with Large and Small Families." Journal of Applied Social Psychology 8:1, (1978), 1-14.

1709. Littlewood, Thomas B. "Birth Rates in the Bayous...the Sage of Joe Beasley." In T.B. Littlewood (ed.) The Politics of Population Control. Notre Dame, Indiana: University of Notre Dame Press, 1977, 88-106.

1710. Littlewood, Thomas B. "Black Genocide and Homewood-Brushton." In T.B. Littlewood (ed.) The Politics of Population Control. Notre Dame, Indiana: University of Notre Dame Press, 1977, 69-87.

1711. Littlewood, Thomas B. "Prelude to Change Black Birth Rates...and the Powerhouse." In T.B. Littlewood (ed.) The Politics of Population Control. Notre Dame, Indiana: University of Notre Dame Press, 1977, 12-24.

1712. Littlewood, Thomas B. "Teen Sex: Double Standards of Feasibility." In T.B. Littlewood (ed.) The Politics of Population Control. Notre Dame, Indiana: University of Notre Dame Press, 1977, 133-143.

1713. Locke, Alain. The New Negro. New York: Albert and Charles Boni, 1925.

1714. Long, Larry. "Interregional Migration of the Poor: Some Recent Changes," Current Population Peports. Washington, D.C.: Government Printing Office, 1978.

1715. Long, Larry H. and K.A. Hansen. "Trends in Return Migration to the South." Demography 12 (November 1975), 601-14.

1716. Long, Larry H. and K.A. Hansen. "Selectivity of Black Migration to the South." Rural Sociology 42 (1977), 317-331.

1717. Long, Larry H. and L.R. Heltman. "Migration and Income Differences Between Black and White Men in the North." American Journal of Sociology 80 (1975), 1391-1409.

1718. Lorimer, Frank and Dorothy S. Jones. "The Demographic Characteristics of the Negro Populations in the United States." Journal of Negro Education 22:3, (1953), 250-254.

1719. Loth, David and Harold Fleming. Integration North and South, New York: The Fund for the Republic, 1956.

1720. Lowry, Mark II. "Population and Race in Mississippi, 1940-1960." Annals of the Association of American Geographers. 51 (September 1971), 576-88.

1721. Lowry, Mark II. Population and Socioeconomic Well Being in Mississippi. Master's Thesis, Syracuse University, 1968.

1722. Luna, Telesforo W. Changes in the Distribution Pattern of Negro Population in the United States. Master's Thesis, Clark University, 1956.

1723. Lunde, A.S. Recent Trends in White-Nonwhite Fertility in the United States. In: International Union for Scientific Study of Population (IUSSP). International Population Conference. Volume 3. Liege, Belgium, IUSSP, (1969), 2062-2073.

1724. Lunde, A.S. "White-Nonwhite Fertility Differentials in the United States." Health, Education, and Welfare Indicators (September 1965), 23-28.

1725. Lundgren, Terry Dennis. Comparative Study Of All Negro Ghettoes In The United States. Ph.D. 1976 The Ohio State University.

1726. "Lure of the North for Negroes." Survey 28 (1917), 27.

1727. Lurie, M. and E. Rayack. "Racial Differences in Migration and Job Search: A Case Study." Southern Economic Journal. 33, (1966), 91-95.

1728. Macri, J.M. "Maternal Sreum Alpha-Fetoprotein and Low Birth Weight (Letter)." Lancet 1 (1978), 660.

1729. Madans, J.H. et al. "Differences Among Hospitals as a Source of Excess Neonatal Mortality: The District of Columbia, 1970-1978." Journal of Community Health 7:2, (1981), 103-117.

1730. Malone, Erwin Lionel. The Phenomenon of Increasing Uniformity in Unrelated Areas of the United States: An Investigation Into Industrial and Sociological Patterns and Trends in Certain States of the United States, 1870 to 1950. Ph.D. 1957 Columbia University, 1957.

1731. Mare, R.D.M. and S.K. Matsumoto. Socio-Economic Effects on Child Mortality in the United States. Paper presented at the Annual Meetings of the Population Association of America, Denver, Colorado, 1980, April 10-12.

1732. Marsh, Robert E. "Negro-White Differences in Geographic Mobility." United States Social Security Bulletin 30 (May

1967), 8-19.

1733. Marschall, Charles K. <u>The Exodus: Its Effect Upon the People of the South, Colored Labor Not Indispensable.</u> An Address delivered before the Board of Directors of the American Colonization Society, January 21, 1880. Washington: Colonization Rooms, 1880.

1734. Marshall, Harvey H. and John M. Stahura. "Black and White Population Growth in American Suburbs: Transition or Parallel Development?" <u>Social Forces</u> 58 :1, (September 1979), 305-27.

1735. Matthews, Diller G. <u>The Distribution of the Negro Population of the District of Columbia, 1800-1960.</u> Master's Thesis. Catholic University of America, 1967.

1736. Maurer, Neil. "A Minority Rendered Less 'Invisible'," <u>City: Magazine of Urban Life and Environment</u>, 5:2, (March-April 1971), 11-12.

1737. Maurer, Neil. "The Scope and Causes of Black Migration," <u>City: Magazine of Urban Life and Environment</u>, 5:2, (March-April 1972), 11.

1738. May, W.H. et al. "Maternal Deaths from Ectopic Pregnancy in the South Atlantic Region, 1960 Through 1976." <u>American Journal of Obstetrics and Gynecology</u> 132:2, (1978), 140-147.

1739. Mayhew, Bruce H. "Behavioral Observability and Compliance with Religious Proscriptions on Birth Control." <u>Social Forces</u> 7:1, (1968), 60-71.

1740. Mayo, Selz C. and C.H. Hamilton. "Current Population Trends in the South." <u>Social Forces</u> 42:1, (1963), 77-88.

1741. Mayo, Selz C. and C.H. Hamilton. "The Rural Negro Population of the South in Transition." <u>Phylon</u> 24:2, (1963), 160-171.

1742. McCormick, E.P. <u>Attitudes Toward Abortion Among Women Undergoing Legally Induced Abortions.</u> Paper Presented at the Annual Meetings of the Population Association of America, New Orleans, Louisiana, April 1973.

1743. McCormick, E.P. <u>Attutides Toward Abortion: Experiences of Selected Black and White Women.</u> Lexington, Massachusetts: D.C. Heath, 1975.

1744. McFalls, J.A. "The Impact of VD on the Fertility of Black Populatiion, 1880-1950." <u>Social Biology</u> 20:1, (1973), 2-19.

1745. McFalls, J.A. and G.S. Masnick. "Birth Control and the Fertility of the U.S. Black Population, 1880-1980." <u>Journal of Family History</u> 6:1, (1981), 89-106.

1746. McGhee, James D. "The Black Teenager: An Endangered Species" in James D. Williams (ed.) The State of Black America 1982, New York: National Urban League 1982, 171-196.

1747. McKay, R.B. One-Child Families and Atypical Sex Ratios in an Elite Black Community: Class Contrasts in Black Family Size. Paper presented at the American Association for the Advancement of Science Annual Meetings, New York, January 25, 1975.

1748. McKee, Jesse O. "A Geographical Analysis of the Origin, Diffusion, and Spatial Dsitribution of the Black American in the United States." Southern Quarterly 12:3, (1974), 203-216.

1749. McKenney, N.R. Negro Population: March 1966. U.S. Bureau of the Census, Current Population Reports, Series P-20, No. 168. Washington, D.C.: Government Printing Office, 1967.

1750. McKenney, N.R. Socioeconomic Fertility Differentials of the Negro Population in the District of Columbia: 1960 and 1950. M.A. The American University, 1964.

1751. McKenney, N.R. "United States Studying the Black Experience with the 1980 Census." In: Black People and the 1980 Census. Vol. 1: Proceedings From a Conference on the Population Undercount. Chicago: Illinois Council for Black Studies, 1980, 517-533.

1752. McKenney, N.R. et al. The Social and Economic Status of the Black Population in the United States, 1972. U.S. Bureau of the Census, Current Population Reports, Series P-23, No. 46. Washington, D.C.: Government Printing Office, 1973.

1753. McKenney, N.R. et al. The Social and Economic Status of the Black Population in the United States, 1973. U.S. Bureau of the Census, Current Population Reports, Series P-23, No. 48. Washington, D.C.: Government Printing Office, 1974.

1754. McKenney, N.R. et al. The Social and Economic Status of the Black Population in the United States, 1973. U.S. Bureau of the Census, Current Population Reports, Series P-23, No. 54. Washington, D.C.: Government Printing Office, 1975.

1755. McWorter, G.A. "Racism and the Numbers Game: Black People and the 1980 Census." Black Scholar, 11, (1980), 61-71.

1756. McWorter, G.A. "United States Racism and the Numbers Game: A Critique of the Census Underenumeration of Black People and a Proposal for Action." In: Black People and the 1980 Census. Vol.1: Proceedings from a Conference on the Population Undercount. Chicago: Illinois Council for Black Studies, 1980.

1757. Meade, Anthony Carl. The Residential Segregation of Population Characteristics in the Atlanta Standard Metropolitan

Statistical Area: 1960. Ph.D. 1971 The University of Tennessee.

1758. Meeker, Edward. "Mortality Trends of Southern Blacks, 1859–1910: Some Preliminary Findings." Explorations in Economic History 13:1, (1976), 13–42.

1759. Menken, James A. "Teenage Childbearing: Its Medical Aspects and Implications for the United States Population." In Charles F. Westoff and Robert Parke, Jr. (eds.).: Demographic and Social Aspects of Population Growth. Washington, D.C.: Commission on Population Growth and the American Future, Research Reports, Volume 1, 1972, 331–354.

1760. Meyer, David R. "Classification of SMSA's Based upon Characteristics of their Nonwhite Populations." In Brian J.L. Berry (ed.) Classification of Cities: New Methods and Evolving Uses. New York: International City Managers Association and Resources for the Future, 1971, 14–21.

1761. Michielutte, R. et al. "Early Sexual Experiences and Pregnancy Wastage in Two Cultures." Journal of Comparative Family Studies 4:2, (1973), 225–238.

1762. Middleton, H.C. "Negro Migration." Manufacturers Record 5 (1923), 78–80.

1763. Mikel, Linda L. Group Membership and Migration: A Comparison of Negro and White Migration from Mississippi. Master's thesis, Indiana University, 1970.

1764. Miller, Kelly. "Enumeration Errors in Negro Population." Scientific Monthly 14 (1922), 168–77.

1765. Miller, Kelly. "The Expansion of the Negro Population." Forum 32: (1902), 671–9.

1766. Miller, A.R. "The Black Migrant: Changing Origins, Changing Characteristics." In Papers on the Demography of Black Americans. Atlanta, Georgia: Atlanta University. W.E.B. Dubois Institute for the Study of the American Black, 1974.

1767. Miller, Brenda Kaye. Racial Change in an Urban Residential Area: A Geographical Analysis of Wilkinsburg, Pennsylvania. Ph.D. 1979 University of Pittsburgh 1979.

1768. Miller, Joseph. The Social Determinants of Women's Attitudes Toward Abortion: 1970 Analysis. University of Wisconsin. Madison, Unpublished Report, 1973.

1769. Misra, B.D. "A Comparison of Husbands' and Wives' Attitudes Toward Family Planning." Journal of Family Welfare 12:4, (1966), 9–23.

1770. Misra, B.D. "Correlates of Males' Attitudes Towards Family Planning." In Donald J. Bogue (ed.) Sociological Contributions to Family Planning Research. Chicago: University of Chicago, Community and Family Study Center, (1967), 161-271.

1771. Momeni, Jamshid. "Black Demography: A Review Essay" in Jamshid Momeni Demography of the Black Population in the United states: An Annotated Bibliography with a Review Essay. Westport, Conn.: Greenwood, 1983, 3-32.

1772. Monahan, Thomas P. "Interracial Marriage: Data for Philadelphia and Pennsylvania." Demography 7:3, (1970), 287-299.

1773. Moore, K.A. and S.B. Caldwell. "The Determinants of Out-of-Wedlock Fertility: Data Analysis." In S.B. Caldwell (ed.) Out-of-Wedlock Pregnancy and Childbearing. Washington, D.C.: Urban Institute. Working Paper 992-02, 1976, 88-157.

1774. Morehead, J.E. "Intrauterine Device Retention: A Study of Selected Social-Psychological Aspects." American Journal of Public Health 65:7, (1975), 720-730.

1775. Morris, N.M. et al. "Reduction of Low Birth Weight Rates by the Prevention of Unwanted Pregnancies." Family Planning Resume 1:1, (1977), 252-253.

1776. Morrison, Joseph L. "Illegitimacy, Sterilization, and Racism: A North Carolina Case History." The Social Service Review 39:1, (1965), 1-10.

1777. Mosher, W.D. "Reproductive Impairments Among Currently Married Couples: United States, 1976." Advance Data 55, (1981), 1-11.

1778. Mosher, W.D. and C.F Westoff. "Trends in Contraceptive Practice: United States, 1965-76." Vital and Health Statistics. Series 23, Data from the National Survey of Family Growth. 10: (1982), 1-47.

1779. Mossell, S.T. "Standard of Living Among 100 Negroes and Their Families in Philadelphia." Annals of American Academy (1921), 173-218.

1780. Mott, F.L. and D. Shapiro. "Complementarity of Work and Fertility Among Young American Mothers." Population Studies. 37:2, (July 1983), 239-52.

1781. Murray, Edward and Edwin Hedge. Growth Center Population Redistribution, 1980-2000. Washington, D.C.: Urban Land Institute, 1972.

1782. Namerow, P.B. and J.E. Jones. Ethnic Variation in Adolescent

Use of a Contraceptive Service. Presented at the 109th Annual Meeting of the American Public Health Association, Los Angeles, California, November 1-5, 1981.

1783. "National Conference on Negro Migration." Nation 104, (1927), 149.

1784. National Urban League. Economic and Social Status of the Negro in the United States. New York: National Urban League, 1961.

1785. "Negro in New England." Harvard Graduate Magazine, 34: (1926), 538-49.

1786. "Negro Migrant." Opportunity 2 (August 1924), 250.

1787. "Negro Migration." New Republic 7 (July 1, 1916), 213-214.

1793. "New Negro Migration." Survey 45 (February 26, 1921), 752.

1794. "New Northward Migration." Survey 50 (June 1, 1923), 297-8.

1788. "Negro Migration Causing Revolution in South." New York Times, May 6, 1923, 876-77.

1789. "Negro Moving North. Literary Digest 53 (October 7, 1916), 877-8.

1790. "Negro's Place in the South." Opportunity, 1 (July 1923), 220.

1791. "Negroes As Workers: A Page of Comment." Opportunity (Journal of Negro Life 4 (March 1926), 90.

1792. "Negroes at Work in the United States." Opportunity 1 (July 1923), 216.

1793. "New Negro Migration." Survey 45 (February 26, 1921), 752.

1794. "New Northward Migration." Survey 50 (June 1, 1923), 297-8.

1795. Norton, E.H. "Population Growth and the Future of Black Folk." The Crisis (May 1973), 151-153.

1796. O'Connell, M. "Comparative Estimates of Teenage Illegitimacy in the United States, 1940-44 to 1970-74." Demography 17:1, (1980), 13-23.

1797. Okun, Bernard. "Secular Trends in the Birth Ratio of Negroes, By Selected States, and for the United States, 1870-1950." In: Trends in Birth Rates in the United States Since 1870. Baltimore: Johns Hopkins Press, 1958, 102-156.

1798. Oppel, W. and S. Wolf. "Liberalized Abortion and Birth Rate

Changes in Baltimore." American Journal of Public Health 63:5, (1973), 405-408.

1799. Orshansky, Mollie. "Who's Who Among the Poor: A Demographic View of Poverty." Social Security Bulletin 28:7, (1965), 3-32.

1800. Ory, H.W. et al. Mortality Among Young Black Contraceptive Users (Working Draft). ENG Public Health Service, Centers for Disease Control, Center for Health Promotion and Education, Atlanta, Georgia, 1960.

1801. Ory, H.W. et al. "Mortality Among Young Black Women Using Contraceptives." Journal of the American Medical Association. 251:8 (February 1984), 1044-1048.

1802. Ovington, Mary White. Half a Man: The Status of the Negro in New York. New York: Longmans, 1911.

1803. Padgett, Herbert R. Florida's Migratory Workers, unpublished M.A. thesis, Florida State University, 1951.

1804. Pakter, J. and F. Nelson. "Abortion in New York City: the First Nine Months." Family Planning Perspectives 3:3, (1971), 5-12.

1805. Palmer, Dewey. "Moving North: Migration of Negroes during World War I." Phylon 28 (1967), 61.

1806. Parson, Talcott et al. The Negro American. Boston: Houghton Mifflin, 1966.

1807. Pathak, Chittaranjan. "A Spatial Analysis of Urban Population Distribution in Raleigh, North Carolina." Southeastern Geographer, 4 (1964), 41-50.

1808. Patterson, William L. (ed.) We Charge Genocide: The Crime of Government Against the Negro People. New York: International Publishers, 1970.

1809. Pearl, R. "Contraception and Fertility in 4945 Married Women: A Second Report on a Study of Family Limitation." Human Biology 6:2, (1934), 355-401.

1810. Pearl, R. "Fertility and Contraception in Urban Whites and Negroes." Science 83 (May 1936), 503-506.

1811. Pearl, R. "The Effects Upon Natural Fertility of Contraceptive Efforts." In R. Pearl (ed.) The Natural History of Population. New York: Oxford University Press, 1939, 198-248.

1812. Peirce, Neal R. "Teen-age Pregnancies Cloud Blacks' Future," Los Angeles Times, (June 30, 1982), 1-10.

1813. Pettigrew, Thomas F. "Demographic Correlates of Border-State Desegregation." American Sociological Review, 22 (December 1957), 683-689.

1814. Pettigrew, Thomas F. and Richard M. Cramer. "The Demography of Desegregation." Journal of Social Issues, 15 (October 1959), 61-71.

1815. Petty, John and F. Leonard. Factorial Ecology of the Los Angeles - Long Beach Black Population. Unpublished Ph.D. The University of Wisconsin - Milwaukee, 1976.

1816. Pfifer, Alan. "Don't Forget the Children". American Demographics, (September 1979), 32-37.

1817. Philliber S.G. and E.H. Graham. Age of Mother: Its Impact on Mother-Child Interaction Patterns. Presented at the 107th Annual Meeting of the American Public Health Association, New York, November 1979.

1818. Philliber, S.G. and P.B. Namerow. A Comparison of Response to Adolescent-Oriented and Traditional Contraceptive Programs. Presented at the 51st Annual Meeting of the Population Association of America, San Diego, California, April 29-May 1, 1982.

1819. Phillips, Coy T. "Population Distribution and Trends in North Carolina." Journal of Geography. 55, (1956), 182-193.

1820. Phillips, J.H. and G.E. Burch. "A Review of Cardiovascular Diseases in the White and Negro Races." Medicine 39: (1960), 241-288.

1821. Philpel, Harriet F. "Birth Control and a New Birth of Freedom." Ohio State Law Journal 27:4, (1966), 679-690.

1822. Pick, J.B. "Correlates of Fertility and Mortality in Low-Migration Standard Metropolitan Statistical Areas." Social Biology 24:1, (1977), 69-83.

1823. Pinkney, Alphonse. "Characteristics of the [Black] Population." In Alphonso Pinkney (ed.) Black Americans. Englewood Cliffs, N.J.: Prentice-Hall, 1975.

1824. Pleck, Elizabeth H. Black Migration and Poverty: Boston, 1865-1900. New York: Academic Press, 1979.

1825. Pleck, Elizabeth H. Black Migration to Boston in the Late Nineteenth Century. Published Ph.D. Dissertation. Brandeis University, 1974.

1826. Pohlman, Vernon C. and Robert H. Walsh. "Black Minority Racial Status and Fertility in the United States, 1970." Sociological

Focus 8:2, (1975), 97–108.

1827. Polgar, S. and F. Rothstein. "Research Report: Family Planning and Conjugal Roles in New York City Poverty Areas." _Social Science and Medicine_ 4: (1970), 135–139.

1828. Pomeroy, R. and A. Torres. "Family Planning Practices of Low Income Women in Two Communities." _American Journal of Public Health_ 672 (1972), 1123–1129.

1829. Pope, Hallowell. "Unwed Mothers and Their Sex Partners." _Journal of Marriage and the Family_ 29:3 (1967), 555–567.

1830. Population Reference Bureau. "Family Size and the Black American." _Population Bulletin_ 30:4 (1975), 1–29.

1831. Pratt, W.F. _Sterilization in the United States: Preliminary Findings from the National Survey of Family Growth, 1973._ Paper Presented at the Annual Meetings of the Population Association of America, Seattle, Washington, April 17–19, 1975.

1832. Price, Daniel O. _Changing Characteristics of the Negro Population: A 1960 Census Monograph_. Washington, D.C.: Government Printing Office, 1969.

1833. Price, Daniel O. "Examination of Two Sources of Error in the Estimation of Net Migration." _Journal of American Statistical Association_. 50 (September, 1955), 689–700.

1834. Price, Daniel O. "Marital Patterns and Household Composition." In: _Changing Characteristics of the Negro Population: A 1960 Census Monograph_, by Daniel O. Price. Washington, D.C.: U. S. Bureau of the Census: Government Printing Office, 1961, 219–240.

1835. Price, Daniel O. "Non-White Migrants to and from Selected Cities." _American Journal of Sociology_. 44:2, (September 1948), 196–201.

1836. Price, Daniel O. "Rural to Urban Migration of Mexican Americans, Negroes and Anglos." _International Migration Review_ 5 (1971), 281–291.

1837. Presser, H.B. "The Timing of the First Birth, Female Roles and Black Fertility." _Milbank Memorial Fund Quarterly_ 49:3 (1971), 329–361.

1838. Presser, H.B. and L.L. Bumpass. "The Acceptability of Contraceptive Sterilization Among U.S. Couples: 1970." _Family Planning Perspectives_ 4:4 (1972), 18–26.

1839. Presser, H.B. and L.L. Bumpass. "Demographic and Social Aspects of Contraceptive Sterilization in the United States: 1965 - 1970." In _Demographic and Social Aspects of Population_

Growth. Commission on Population and the American Future Research Reports, Volume 1. Washington, D.C.: Government Printing Office, 1972, 505-568.

1840. Purdy, Lawson. "Negro Migration in the United States." American Journal of Economics and Sociology. 13 (July 1954), 357-62.

1841. Ram, Bali. Instability of Unions and Black Fertility in the United States. Unpublished Ph.D. Dissertation. The Ohio State University, 1975.

1842. Ram, Bali. "Regional-Subcultural Explanation of Black Fertility in the United States." Population Studies 30:3 (1976), 553-559.

1843. Ramjoue, George. The Negro in Utah: A Geographical Study in Population. Master's Thesis. University of Utah, 1968.

1844. Ramond, Richard. "Determinants of Non-white Migration During the 1950s." The American Journal of Economics and Sociology. 31 (1972): 9-20.

1845. Rao, S.L.N. "On Long-Term Mortality Trends in the United States, 1850-1968." Demography 10:3 (1973), 405-419.

1846. Rao, V.V. and V.N. Rao. "Family Size and Sex Preference of Children: A Bi-Racial Comparison." Adolescence. 16:62 (1981), 385-401.

1847. Rauch, Sister Delores. Impact of Population Changes in the Central Area of Milwaukee upon Catholic Parochial Schools, 1940-1970. Master's Thesis, University of Wisconsin, Milwaukee, 1968.

1848. Redford, Myron H. and Edgar K. Marcuse. Legal Abortions in Washington State: An Analysis of the First Year Experience. Seattle, Washington: Battelle Human Affairs Research Center, Population Study Center, 1973.

1849. Reed, Ruth. Negro Illegitimacy in New York City. New York Columbia University Press, 1926.

1850. Reid, J. "Black America in the 1980s." Population Bulletin. 37:4 (December 1982), 1-39.

1851. Reid, Ira deAugustine. The Negro Immigrant, His Background, Characteristics and Social Adjustment, 1899-1937. New York: Columbia University, 1939.

1852. Reid, Ira deAugustine. The Negro Population of Elizabeth, New Jersey: A Survey of Its Economic and Social Condition. National Urban League, Department of Research, for the

Elizabeth Interracial Committee, 1930.

1853. Reid, Ira deAugustine. The Negro Population of Denver, Colorado: A Survey of Its Economic and Social Status. National Urban League, Department of Research and Investigations, New York, 1929.

1854. Reid, Ira deAugustine. Social Conditions of the Negro in the Hill District of Pittsburgh. General Committee on the Hill Survey, Pittsburgh, 1930.

1855. Reid, Ira deAugustine. Twenty-Four Hundred Negro Families in Harlem. New York Urban League, New York, 1927.

1856. Richards, Eugene S. The Effects of the Negro's Migration to Southern California Since 1920 Upon His Sociocultural Patterns. University of Southern California, 1941.

1857. Riemer, Robert J. Child-Spacing and Economic Behavior in a Black Community. Unpublished Ph.D. Dissertation. University of Notre Dame, 1971.

1858. Rindfuss, R.R. Fertility Rates for Racial and Social Subpopulations within the United States: 1945-1969. University of Wisconsin, Center for Demography and Ecology. Working Paper Series, 1976.

1859. Rindfuss, R.R. "Minority Status and Fertility Revisited -- Again: A Comment on Johnson." American Journal of Sociology, 86:2 (September 1980), 372-5.

1860. Rindfuss, R.R. and J.A. Sweet. Postwar Fertility Trends and Differentials in the United States. New York: Academic Press, 1977.

1861. Rischaner, Robert Danton. The Impact of the Welfare System on Black Migration and Marital Stability. Unpublished Ph.D. Dissertation. Columbia Universitym 1971.

1862. Ritchey, P. Neal. "The Fertility of Negroes Without Southern Experience: A Re-examination of the 1960 GAF study Findings with 1967 SEO Data." Population Studies 27:1 (1973), 127-134.

1863. Ritchey, P. Neal. "The Effect of Minority Group Status on Fertility: A Re-examination of Concepts." Population Studies 29:2 (1975), 249-257.

1864. Roberts, R.E. and Everett S. Lee. "Minority Group Status and Fertility Revisited." American Journal of Sociology 80 (September 1974), 503-523.

1865. Rockwood, H.L. "The Effect of Negro Migration on Community Health in Cleveland," National Conference of Social Work,

Proceedings (1926), 238-244.

1866. Rochat, R.W. "Regional Variation in Sterility, United States: 1970." Advances in Planned Parenthood 11: (1977), 1-11.

1867. Rochat, R.W. "Pap Smear Screening: Has it Lowered Cervical Cancer Mortality Among Black Americans?" Phylon 38:4 (1977), 429-447.

1868. Rochat, R.W., et al. "The Effect of Family Planning in Georgia on Fertility in Selected Rural Counties." Excerpta Medica International Congress Series, 224 (1971), 6-14.

1869. Rochat, R.W., et al. "Program Evaluation." In A.W. Isenman, E.G. Knox, and L.B. Tyrer (eds.) Seminar in Family Planning. Chicago: American College of Obstetricians and Gynecologists, 1971, 90-92.

1870. Robinson, Henry S. "Some Aspects of the Free Negro Population of Washington, D.C, 1800-1862." Maryland Historical Magazine 64: (1969), 43-64.

1871. Roge, M.J., et al. Female Adolescents: Factors Differentiating Early-, Middle-, Late- and Never-Contraceptors. Presented at the 88th Annual Meeting of the American Psychological Association, Montreal, Quebec, Canada, September 1-5, 1980.

1872. Roghmann, Klaus J. "The Impact of the New York State Abortion Law on Black and White Fertility in Upstate New York." International Journal of Epidemiology 4:1 (1975), 45-49.

1873. Rose, G. "Cardiovascular Mortality Among Negroes," Archives of Environmental Health, 5 (November 1962), 412-414.

1874. Rose, Harold. "Metropolitan Miami's Changing Negro Population, 1950-1960." Economic Geography. 40 (1964), 221-38.

1875. Rose, Harold. "Migration and the Changing Status of Black Americans." Geographical Review. 61:2 (1971), 297-299.

1876. Rose, John Carter. "Census and Negroes." Nation 525 (1891), 32.

1877. Rose, John Carter. "The Census of Races at South." Nation 73 (1901), 24.

1878. Rose, John Carter. "Growth of the Negro Population." Nation 73, (1901), 31-33.

1879. Rose, John Carter. "Negroes and Whites, Ratios for Eleven Decades." Nation 73 (1901), 39.

1880. Roseman, Curtis C. and Prentice L. Knight. "Residential

Environment and Migration Behavior of Urban Blacks."
Professional Geographer. 27:2 (1975), 160–165.

1881. Rosen, R.H., et al. "Contraception, Abortion, and Self-Concept." *Journal of Population*. 2:2 (1979); 118–39.

1882. Rosenwaike, Ira and Robert J. Melton. "Abortion and Fertility in Maryland, 1960–1971." *Demography* 11:3 (1974), 377–395.

1883. Ross, J. "United States: The Chicago Fertility Control Studies." *Studies in Family Planning* 1:15 (1966), 1–8.

1884. Rubin, E. "The Sex Ratio at Birth." *American Statistician* 21:4 (1967), 45–48.

1885. Rubin, Morton. "The Negro Wish to Move: the Boston Case." *Journal of Social Issues* 15 (October 1959), 4–13.

1886. Rush, D. "Respiratory Symptoms in a Group of American Secondary School Students: The Overwhelming Association with Cigarette Smoking." *International Journal of Epidemiology* 3:2 (1974), 153–165.

1887. Rush, D. and E.H. Kass. "Maternal Smoking: A Reassessment of the Association of Perinatal Mortality." *American Journal of Epidemiology* 96:3 (1972), 183–196.

1888. Russell, Cheryl. "The Minority Entrepreneur," *American Demographics*, 3:6 (1981), 18–20.

1889. Russi, Peter H. *Why Families Move*. Glencoe, Illinois: Glencoe Free Press, 1955.

1890. Ruzek, S.B. "Sterilization." In S.B. Ruzek (ed.) *The Women's Health Movement: Feminist Alternatives to Medical Control*. New York: Praeger, 1978, 46–47.

1891. Ryan, G.M. and P.J. Sweeney. "Attitudes of Adolescents Toward Pregnancy and Contraception." *American Journal of Obstetrics and Gynecology* 136:3 (1980), 358–366.

1892. Ryan, G.M. and J.M. Schneider. "Teenage Obstetric Complications." *Clinical Obstetrics and Gynecology* 21:4 (1978), 1191–1197.

1893. Ryder, N.B. and Charles F. Westoff. "Fertility Planning Status: United States, 1965." *Demography* 6:4 (1969), 435–444.

1894. Ryder, N.B. and Charles F. Westoff. "Racial, Religious, and Socioeconomic Differences in Fertility." In: *Reproduction in the United States, 1965*. Princeton, N.J.: Princeton University Press, (1971), 53–95.

1895. Ryder, N.B. and Charles F. Westoff. "Use of Oral Contraception in the United States." Science 153:3741 (1966), 1199-1205.

1896. Rydman, Edward J. Factors Related to Family Planning Among Lower Class Negroes. Unpublished Ph.D. Dissertation. Ohio State University, 1965.

1897. Ryser, P.E. and W.H. Spillane. "The Effect of Education and Significant Others Upon the Contraceptive Behavior of Married Men." Journal of Biosocial Science 6:3 (1974), 305-314.

1898. Salisbury, L. and A.G. Blackwell. Petition to Alelviate Domestic Infant Formula Misuse and Provide Informed Infant Feeding Choice: An Administrative Petition to the United States Food and Drug Administration and Department of Health and Human Services. Unpublished. San Francisco California: Public Advocates, Inc., 1981.

1899. Samdani, Ghulam Mohammad. Migration and Modernization: A Study of Changing Values and Behavior Among Former Migrants From the Rural South to Upstate New York. Unpublished Ph.D. Dissertation. Cornell University, 1970.

1900. Sanger, Margaret. "Love or Babies: Must Negro Mothers Choose?" Negro Digest 4:1 (1946), 3-8.

1901. Sardon, J.P. "La Progression de la Sterilization aux Etats-Unis [The Advancement of Sterilization in the United States]." Population 31:2 (1976), 492-498.

1902. Sarvis, B. and H. Rodman. "Black Genocide." In: The Abortion Controversy, by B. Sarvis and H. Rodman. New York: Columbia University Press, 1974, 173-187.

1903. Sarvis, Betty and Human Rodman. "Social and Cultural Aspects of Abortion: Class and Race." In: The Abortion Controversy, by Betty Sarvis and Human Rodman. New York: Columbia University Press, 1974, 153-172.

1904. Sastry, K.R. Female Work Participation and Work-Motivated Contraception. Unpublished Ph.D. Dissertation. University of North Carolina, 1973.

1905. Saveland, Walt and Paul C. Glick. "First-Marriage Decrement Tables by Color and Sex for the United States in 1958-60." Demography 6:3 (1969), 243-260.

1906. Schmid, Calvin F. and Charles E. Nobbe. "Socioeconomic Differentials Among Nonwhite Races in the State of Washington." Demography 2: (1969), 549-566.

1907. Schottenfeld, D. "The Epidemiology of Cancer: An Overview." Cancer 47:5 (1981), 1095-1108.

1908. Schulder, Diane and F. Kennedy. "Black Genocide." In Diane Schulder and Floryne Kennedy (eds.) Abortion Rap. New York: McGraw Hill, 1971, 151-161.

1909. Schuyler, George S. "Quantity or Quality." Birth Control Review 16:6 (1982), 165-166.

1910. Scott, Emmett J. "Letters of Negro Migrants of 1916-1918," Journal of Negro History, 4: 3 and 4 (July and October 1919), 291-340, and 412-465.

1911. Scott, Emmett J. Negro Migration During the War. New York: Arno Press, 1969.

1912. Scroggs, W.O. "Interstate Migration and Negro Population." Journal of Political Economy 25 (December 1917), 1034-1043.

1913. Selig, Suzanne Mae. Selected Characteristics of Cities and the Difference in Mortality Between Urban Blacks and Whites. Unpublished Ph.D. Dissertation. University of Cincinnati, 1976.

1914. Sewell, Lemuel T. "The Negro Wants Birth Control." Birth Control Review 17:3 (1933), 131.

1915. Shah, F., et al. "Unprotected Intercourse Among Unwed Teenagers." Family Planning Perspectives 7:1 (1975), 39-44.

1916. Shelton, J.D. Induced Abortion: George. Paper Presented at the 24th Annual Epidemic Intelligence Service Conference, Center for Disease Control, Atlanta, Georgia, April 21-25, 1975.

1917. Shelton, J.D. "The Contraception-To-Conception Ratio: A Tool For Measuring Success of Family Planning Programs in Reaching Very Young Teenagers." Advances in Planned Parenthood 13: (1978), 1-7.

1918. Sherline, D.M. and R.A. Davidson. "Adolescent Pregnancy: the Jackson, Mississippi Experience." American Journal of Obstetrics and Gynecology 132:3 (October 1, 1978), 245-255.

1919. Shin, Eui Hang. Migration Differentials of the Nonwhite Population : United States, 1955-1960. Unpublished Ph.D. Dissertation, University of Pennsylvania, 1971.

1920. Shin, Eui Hang. "Black-White Differentials in Infant Mortality in the South, 1940-1970." Demography 12:1 (1975), 1-19.

1921. Shin, Eui Hang. "Effects of Migration on the Educational Level of the Black Resident Population at the Origin and Destination, 1955-1960, and 1965-1970." Demography 15:1 (1978), 41-56.

1922. Shin, Eui Hang. "Correlates of Intercounty Variations in Net Migration Rates of Blacks in the Deep South, 1960–1970." Rural Sociology 44 (Spring 1979), 39–55.

1923. "Sickle Cell and the Pill: Birth Control Pills Dangerous to Black Women," Ramparts, (February 1972), 1–16.

1924. Siegel, E., et al. "Measurement of Need and Utilization Rates for a Public Family Planning Program." American Journal of Public Health 59:8 (1969), 1322–1330.

1925. Siegel, J.S. "Natality, Mortality, and Growth Prospects of the Negro Population of the United States." Journal of Negro Education 22:3 (1953), 255–279.

1926. Siegel, J.S. "Prospective Trends in the Size and Structure of the Elderly Population, Impact of Mortality Trends, and Some Implications." In: United State Congress. House of Representatives. Select Committee on Aging. Consequences of Changing U.S. Population: Demographics of Aging. Volume 1. Hearings, May 24, 1978. Washington, D.C.: Government Printing Office, 1978, 76–121.

1927. Sims, Newell L. "Hostage to the White Man." Birth Control Review 17:7–8 (1932), 214–215.

1928. Singer, A., et al. "Contraceptives and Cervical Carcinoma." British Medical Journal, 4 (1969), 108.

1929. Sinnette, Calvin H. "Genocide and Black Ecology." Freedomways 12:1 (1972), 4–46.

1930. Sinquefield, J.C. "The Effects of Personal Efficacy on Resistance to Family Planning." In J.C. Sinquefeidl (ed.) A Social-Psychological Study of Resistance in Family Planning in Rural Alabama. Chicago: University of Chicago, Community and Family Study Center, 1974, 20–32.

1931. Sinquefield, J.C. "Family Factors in Resistance of Family Planning." In A Social-Psychological Study of Resistance to Family Planning in Rural Alabama. Chicago: University of Chicago, Community and Family Study Center, 1974, 33–46.

1932. Sinquefield, J.C. Source of Resistance to Innovation." In: A Social-Psychological Study of Resistance to Family Planning in Rural Alabama. Chicago: University of Chicago, Community and Family Study Center, 1974, 1–19.

1933. Slater, Jack. "Sterilization: Newest Threat to the Poor." Ebony 28:12 (1973), 150–156.

1934. Sly, David F. "Minority Group Status and Fertility: An Extension of Goldscheider and Uhlenberg." American Journal of

Sociology 76:3 (1970), 443-459.

1935. Sly, David F. and Dillingham, Harry C. "The Mechanical Cotton Picker; Negro Migration, and the Integration Movement." In Richard Frucht (ed.) _Black Society in the New World_. Toronto: Random House, 1971, 10-15.

1936. Smith, Mary. "Birth Control and the Negro Woman." _Ebony_ 23 (March 1968), 29-37.

1937. Smith, T. Lynn. "The Changing Number and Distribution of the Aged Negro Population in the U.S." _Phylon_ 18 (Fall 1957), 339-354.

1938. Smith, T. Lynn. "The Redistribution of the Negro Population of the United States, 1910-1960." _Journal of Negro History_ 51:3 (1966), 155-173.

1939. Social Science Institute. "Negro Internal Migration, 1940-1943: An Estimate. Social Science Institute, Fisk University." _A Monthly Summary of Events and Trends in Race Relations_ 1:2 (1943), 10-12.

1940. Sohardjo, Sri P. _Toward a Socioeconomic Model of Migratoin and Fertility._ Unpublished Ph.D. Dissertation. The Florida State University, 1981.

1941. Spain, Daphne G. _The Effects of Intrametropolitan Mobility on Racial Residential Segregation._ Ph.D. University of Massachusetts, 1977.

1942. Spain, Daphne G. and Larry H. Long. _Black Movers to the Suburbs: Are They Moving to Predominantly White Neighborhoods?_ Washington, D.C., U.S. Bureau of the Census, 1981.

1943. Spanier, Graham B. and Paul C. Glick. "Mate Selection Differentials Between White and Blacks in the United States." _Social Forces_ 58:3 (1980), 707-725.

1944. Spear, Alden, et al. _Residential Mobility, Migration, and Metropolitan Change_. Cambridge, Massachusetts: Ballinger, 1976.

1945. Spencer, G. _The Contributions of Childlessness and Non-Marriage to Racial and Ethnic Differences in American Fertility._ Paper presented at Population Association of American Annual Meeting, April 9-12, 1980.

1946. Spiers, P.S. "Father's Age and Infant Mortality." _Social Biology_ 19:3 (1972), 275-284.

1947. Stangler, Gary J., et al. _Black Return Migration to Two Non-Metropolitan Areas of the South,_ paper presented at the Rural

Sociological Society meeting of the Southern Association of Agricultural Scientists, New Orleans, Louisiana. February 1975.

1948. Stearns, R. Prescott. Factors Related to Fertility Values of Low-Income Black Males: A Case Study. Miami, Ohio: Unpublished Ph.D. Dissertation. Case Western Reserve University, 1974.

1949. Sterns, R.S. and Garland, T.N. Factors Affecting Contraceptive Use and Nonuse Among Adolescents. Presented at the Annual Meeting of the National Council on Family Relations, Boston, Massachusetts, August, 1979.

1950. Stevenson, C.S. and C.C. Yang. "Septic Abortion with Shock." Obstetrics and Gynecology 83:9 (1962), 1229-1239.

1951. Stewart, Douglas E. Questions and Answers About the Charge of "Genocide" as it Relates to Planned Parenthood-World Population, its Affiliates, and the Provision and Expansion of Private and Publicly Sponsored Family Planning Programs in the U.S. New York: Planned Parenthood-World Population, 1969.

1952. Stewart, Douglas E. "Population, Environment, and Minority Groups." In Noel Hinrichs (ed.) Population, Environment and People. New York: McGraw Hill, 1971, 104-112.

1953. Still, William. Underground Railroad. Philadelphia, Pa.: Porter and Coates, 1872.

1954. Stinner, William and G.F. DeYong. "Southern Negro Migration: Social and Economic Components of an Ecological Model." Demography 7:4 (1969), 455-471.

1955. Stokes, C. Shannon, et al. "Race, Education, and Fertility: A Comparison of Black-White Reproductive Behavior." Phylon 38:2 (1977), 160-169.

1956. Stycos, J.M. "Some Minority Opinions on Birth Control." In: Population Policy and Ethics: the American Experience. New York: Irvington Publishers, 1977, 169-196.

1957. Sutherland, R.L. A Profile of the Negro American. Princetown: D. VanNostrand, 1964.

1958. Sutton, G.F. "Assessing Mortality and Morbidity Disadvantages of the Black Population of the United States." Social Biology 18: (1971), 369-383.

1959. Sutton, G.F. "Measuring the Effects of Race Differentials in Mortality Upon Surviving Family Members." Demography 14:4 (1977), 419-430.

1960. Sutton, G.F. "Mortality Differences by Race and Sex:

Consequences for Families." In Frank D. Bean and W.P. Frisbie (eds.) The Demography of Racial and Ethnic Groups. New York: Academic Press, 1978, 301-314.

1961. Swartz, D.P. "The Harlem Hospital Center Experience." In: The Abortion Experience: Psychological and Medical Impact. H.J. Osofsky and J.D. Osofsky (eds.). Hagerstown, Maryland: Harper and Row, 1973, 94-121.

1962. Sweet, J.A. Comparisons of Own Children Marital Fertility Estimates Using 1970 Decennial Census, 1976 Survey of Income and Education, and 1970 and 1976 CPS Data. Madison, Wis: University of Wisconsin, Center for Demography and Ecology, 1981

1963. Sweet, J.A. and R.R. Rindfuss. Those Ubiquitous Fertility Trends: United States, 1945-1979. Madison, Wisconsin: University of Wisconsin, Center for Demography and Ecology, 1981.

1964. Sweet, James A. and L.L. Bumpass. "Differentials in Marital Instability of the Black Population, 1970." Phylon 35:3 (1974), 323-331.

1965. Swift, Hildegarde. The Railroad to Freedom. New York, 1932.

1966. Taeuber, Conrad and Irene B. Taeuber. The Changing Population of the United States. New York: Wiley, 1958.

1967. Taeuber, Irene B. "Change and Transition in the Black Population of the United States." Population Index 34 (April-June 1968), 121-141.

1968. Taeuber, Irene B. "Migration, Mobility and the Assimilation of the Negro." American Negro at Mid-Century, Population Bulletin, (November 1958), 1-15.

1969. Taeuber, Karl E. "Negro Population and Housing: Demographic Aspects of a Social Accounting Scheme." In: Race and the Social Sciences. Irwin Katz and Patricia Gurin (eds.). New York: Basic Books, 1969, 145-193.

1970. Taeuber, Karl E. and Alma F. Taeuber. "The Changing Character of Negro Migration." American Journal of Sociology 70:4 (1965), 429-441.

1971. Taeuber, Karl E. and Alma F. Taeuber. "The Negro As An Immigrant Omeup: Recent Trends in Racial and Ethnic Segregation in Chicago." American Journal of Sociology 69, (January 1964), 374-382.

1972. Taeuber, Karl E. and Alma F. Taeuber. "The Negro Population in the United States." In John P. Davis (ed.) The American Negro

Reference Book. ᵞnglewood Cliffs, N.J.: Prentice-Hall, 1966, 100.

1973. Taeuber, Karl E. and Alma F. Taeuber. "White Migration and Socioeconomic Differences Between Cities and Suburbs." American Sociological Review, 29 (October 1964), 1-15.

1974. Teele, James E. and W.M. Schmidt. "Illegitimacy and Race: National and Local Trends." Milbank Memorial Fund Quarterly 48:2 (1970), 127-145.

1975. Thomas, Wesley Wyman. Intra-Urban Migration and the Racial Transition of Residential Areas: A Behavioral Approach. Unpublished Ph.D. Dissertation. University of Cincinnati, 1975.

1976. Thomas, Wesley Wyman. Intra-Urban Migration and the Racial Transition of Residential Areas: A Behavioral Approach. Ph.D. 1975 University of Cincinnati, 1953.

1977. Thomlinson, R. "The Structure of Population." In R. Thomlinson (ed.) Demographic Problems: Controversy Over Population Control. Encino, California: Dikenson, 1975, 192-214.

1978. Thompson, Charles H. "The Relative Status of the Negro Population in the United States." Journal of Negro Education 22:3 (1953), 221-451.

1979. Thompson, K.S. "A Comparison of Black and White Adolescents' Beliefs About Having Children." Journal of Marriage and the Family 42:1 (1980), 133-139.

1980. Thompson, M. Cordell. "Genocide: Black Youngsters Sterilized by Alabama Agency." Jet 4:17 (1973), 12-15.

1981. Thompson, Robert A. "The Social Dynamics in the Demographic Trends and the Housing Minority Group." Phylon, 196 (1958), 31-4.

1982. Thompson, S.J. Change in Maternal Attitudes During Pregnancy. Paper Presented at the American Public Health Association Annual Meetings, New York, November 1979.

1983. Thorpe, C. "Social Status and the Pill at a Black Woman's College." College Student Journal 6:2 (1973), 66-73.

1984. Tietze, C. "Legal Abortions in the United States: Rates and Ratios by Race and Age, 1972-1974." Family Planning Perspectives 9:1 (1977), 12-15.

1985. Tilly, C., "Race and Migration to the American City," in J.Q. Wilson (ed.) The Metropolitan Enigma, Cambridge,

Massachusetts: Harvard University Press, 1968.

1986. Tobin, P., et al. "Value of Children and Fertility Behavior in a Tri-Racial, Rural County." Journal of Comparative Family Studies 6 (Spring 1975), 46-55.

1987. Tolnay, Stewart E. "Black Fertility in Decline: Urban Differentials in 1900." Social Biology 27:4 (1980), 249-260.

1988. Tolnay, Stewart E. The Fertility of Black Americans in 1900. Unpublished Ph.D. Dissertation. University of Washington, 1981.

1989. Tolnay, Stewart E. "Trends in Total and Marital Fertility for Black Americans, 1886-1899." Demography 18:4 (1981), 443-463.

1990. Tower, J. Allen. "The Negro Exodus from the South." Annals of the Association of American Geographers. 45 (1955), 301-303.

1991. Treadwell, Mary. "Is Abortion Black Genocide?" Family Planning Perspectives. 4:1 (1972), 4-5.

1992. Trigg, Martelle Daisy. Differential Mobility Among Black and White Physicians in the State of Tennessee. Unpublished Ph.D. Dissertation. The University of Tennessee, 1972.

1993. Trussell, J. and Jane Menken. "Early Childbearing and Subsequent Fertility." Family Planning Perspectives 10:4 (1978), 209-218.

1994. Tucker, Charles J. "Changes in Age Composition of the Rural Black Population of the South 1950 to 1970." Phylon 35:3 (1974), 268-275.

1995. Turner, C.B. and W. A. Darity. "Fears of Genocide Among Black Americans as Reelated to Age, Sex, and Region." American Journal of Public Health 63:12 (1973), 1029-1034.

1996. Turner, C.B. and Darity W.A. "Black Couples and Birth Control: Knowledge, Attitudes, and Reported Practices." International Quarterly of Community Health Education. 1:1, 1980-1981; 29-47.

1997. Turner, S. M. and R.T. Jones. Behavior Modification in Black Population: Psychosocial Issues and Empirical Findings. New York: Plenum, 1982.

1998. Udry, J. Richard. "Age at Menarche, at First Intercourse, and at First Pregnancy." Journal of Biosocial Science 11:4 (1979), 433-441.

1999. Udry, J. Richard. "Marital Instability by Race, Sex, Education, and Occupation Using 1960 Census Date," American Journal of Sociology. 72 (September 1966), 203-209.

2000. Udry, J. Richard and K.E. Bauman. "Unwanted Fertility and the Use of Contraception." Health Services Report 88:8 (1973), 730-732.

2001. Uhlenberg, Peter. "Marital Instability Among Mexian Americans: Following the Patterns of Black?" Social Problems 20:2 (1972), 49-56.

2002. U.S. Bureau of the Census. Afro-American Blacks 1970 to 1982: A Statistical View by William C. Mortney and Dwight L. Johnson. Washington, D.C.: Government Printing Office, 1983.

2003. U.S. Bureau of the Census. The Social and Economic Status of the Black Population in the United States, 1971. Washington, D.C.: Government Printing Office, 1972, 29-31.

2004. U.S. Bureau of the Census. "Differences Between Income of White and Negro Husband-Wife Families are Relatively Small Outside the South," U.S. Department of Commerce News, February 19, 1971, 1-10.

2005. U.S. Bureau of the Census. Distribution of the Negro Population. 1960 Census of Population, Supplementary Reports. Washington, D.C.: Government Printing Office, 1960.

2006. U.S. Bureau of the Census. Distribution of the Negro Population, by County. Census of Population, Supplementary Report, Series PC (s1)-1. Washington, D.C.: Government Printing Office, 1970.

2007. U.S. Bureau of the Census. "Educational Attainment: March 1970," Current Population Reports, Population Characteristics. Series P-20, No. 207, November 30, 1970.

2008. U.S. Bureau of the Census. "Fertility." In: Characteristics of American Children and Youth: 1976. Current Population Reports: Special Studies, Series P-23, No. 66. Washington, D.C.: Government Printing Office, 1977.

2009. U.S. Bureau of the Census. "Fertility Indicators: 1970," Current Population Reports, Special Studies. Series P-23, No. 36, April 16, 1971.

2010. U.S. Bureau of the Census. Fertility of American Women: June 1975. Current Population Reports: Population Characteristics, Series P-20 No. 301. Washington, D.C.: Government Printing Office, 1976.

2011. U.S. Bureau of the Census. Fertility of American Women: June 1976. Current Population Reports: Population Characteristics, Series P-20, No. 308. Washington, D.C.: Government Printing Office, 1977.

2012. U.S. Bureau of the Census. "Income in 1969 of Families and Persons in the United States," Current Population Reports, Consumer Income. Series P-60, No. 75, December 14, 1970.

2013. U.S. Bureau of the Census. Marital Status and Living Arrangements: March 1975. Current Population Reports, Population Characteristics, Series P-20, No. 287. Washington, D.C.: Government Printing Office, 1975.

2014. U.S. Bureau of the Census. Measuring the Quality of Housing: An Appraisal of the Census Statistics and Methods. Washington, D.C.: Government Printing Office, 1967.

2015. U.S. Bureau of the Census. "Median Family Income Up in 1970," Current Population Reports, Consumer Income. Washington, D.C.: Series P-60 No. 78, May 20, 1971.

2016. U.S. Bureau of the Census. Negroes in the United States, 1920-1932 (Washington, D.C.: Government Printing Office, 1935), pp. 10-11, 14-15.

2017. U.S. Bureau of the Census. Negro Population. Census of Population, Subject Reports, PC (2)-1B. Washington, D.C.: Government Printing Office, 1970.

2018. U.S. Bureau of the Census. Negro Population: March 1965. Current Populations Reports, Series P-20, No. 155. Washington, D.C.: Government Printing Office, 1966.

2019. U.S. Bureau of the Census. Negro Population: March 1967. Current Population Reports, Population Characteristics, Series P-20, No. 175. Washington, D.C.: Government Printing Office, 1968.

2020. U.S. Bureau of the Census. Negro Population in Selected Places and Selected Counties. Supplementary Report, Series PC (s1)-2. Washington, D.C.: Government Printing Office, 1971.

2021. U.S. Bureau of the Census. Population Profile of the United States, 1975. Current Population Reports, Series P-20, No. 292, Washington, D.C.: Government Printing Office, 1976.

2022. U.S. Bureau of the Census. "Population Profile of These United States, 1979. Current Population Reports" Population Characteristics 350 (1980), 1-52.

2023. U.S. Bureau of the Census. Poverty Areas in the 100 Largest Metropolitan Areas, 1960 Census of Population, Supplementary Reports PC(S1)-54. Washington, D.C.: Government Printing Office, November 13, 1967.

2024. U.S. Bureau of the Census. "Poverty Increases by 1.2 Million in 1970," Current Population Reports, Consumer Income. Series

P-60 No. 77, May 7, 1971.

2025. U.S. Bureau of the Census. "Probabilities of Marriage, Divorce and Remarriage," Current Population Reports, Special Studies. Series P-23, No. 32, July 29, 1970.

2026. U.S. Bureau of the Census. Recent Trends in Social and Economic Conditions of Negroes in the United States. Government Printing Office, Washington, 1968.

2027. U.S. Bureau of the Census. Recent Trends in Social and Economic Conditions of Negroes in the United States. Washington, D.C.: Government Printing Office, Current Population Report, p. 23, No. 27, January 1969.

2028. U.S. Bureau of the Census. "Selected Characteristics of Persons and Families, March 1970." Current Population Reports, Population Characteristics. Series P-20, No. 204, July 13, 1970.

2029. U.S. Bureau of the Census. "The Social and Economic Status of Negroes in the United States, 1969," Current Population Reports, Special Studies. Series P-23, No. 29, and BLS Report No. 375.

2030. U.S. Bureau of the Census. The Social and Economic Status of the Black Population in the United States: An Historical View, 1790-1978. Current Population Reports: Special Studies, Series P-20, No. 80. Washington, D.C.: Government Printing Office, 1979.

2031. U.S. Bureau of the Census. Social and Economic Conditions of Negroes in the United States. Washington, D.C.: Government Printing Office, 1967.

2032. U.S. Bureau of the Census. The Social and Economic Status of the Black Population, Subject Reports, PC (2)-1B. Washington, D.C.: Government Printing Office, 1973.

2033. U.S. Bureau of the Census. The Social and Economic Status of the Black Population in the United States. Current Population Reports, Special Studies, Series P-23, No. 48. Washington, D.C.: Government Printing Office, 1973.

2034. U.S. Bureau of the Census. "The Social and Economic Status of Negroes in the United States, 1970," Current Population Reports, Special Studies. Series P-23, No. 38 and BLS Report No. 394.

2035. U.S. Bureau of the Census. Supplementary Reports, Race of the Population by States: 1980, PC80-S1-3, issued July, 1981. Washington, D.C.: Government Printing Office, 1981.

2037. U.S. Bureau of the Census. <u>Trends in Social and Economic Conditions in Metropolitan Areas.</u> Washington, D.C.: Government Printing Office, Current Population Report, p. 23, No. 27, February 7, 1969.

2037. U.S. Bureau of the Census. <u>Trends in Social and Economic Conditions of Negroes in the United States.</u> Washington, D.C.: Government Printing Office, 1969.

2038. U.S. Bureau of the Census and U.S. Bureau of the Labor Statistics. <u>Social and Economic Conditions of Negros in the United States. BLS Report No.332. Current Population Reports:, Series P-23, No. 24.</u> Washington D.C.: Government Printing Office, 1967.

2039. U.S. Bureau of the Census and U.S. Bureau of the Labor Statistics. <u>The Social and Economic Status of Negroes in the United States, 1970. BLS Report No. 394. Current Population Reports, Series P-23, No. 38.</u> Washington, D.C.: Government Printing Office, 1971.

2040. U.S. Center for Disease Control, Family Planning Evaluation Division. Abortion Surveillance. Atlanta, Georgia: Center for Disease Control, Family Planning Evaluation Division, 1974.

2041. U.S. Center of Disease Control. "Unintended Teenage Childbearing: United States, 1974." <u>Morbidity and Mortality Weekly Report</u> 27:16 (1978), 131-132.

2042. U.S. Congress House. <u>Select Committee on National Defense Migration, Hearing, 77th Cong., 2nd sess..</u> Washington, D.C.: Government Printing Office, 1942.

2043. U.S. Department of Commerce. Press Release Entitled, <u>Twelve States Have Black Populations of 1 Million or More, 1980 Census Shows, issued May 1981.</u> Washington, D.C.: Government Printing Office, 1981.

2044. U.S. Department of Commerce. <u>The Social and Economic Status of the Black Population in the United States: An Historical View, 1790-1978.</u> Washington, D.C.: Government Printing Office, 1979.

2045. U.S. Department of Commerce. <u>Negroes in the United States, 1920-1932,</u> Washington, D.C.: U.S. Government Printing Office, 1935.

2046. U.S. Department of Commerce. <u>Negro Population in Selected Places and Counties.</u> Supplementary Report, Washington, D.C.: Government Printing Office, 1971.

2047. U.S. Department of Commerce. <u>The Social and Economic Status of the Black Population in the United States, 1971,</u> Washington, D.C.: U.S. Government Printing Office, July 1972.

2048. U.S. Department of Commerce. The Social and Economic Status of the Black Population in the United States, 1972. Current Population Reports. Series P-23, No. 46, Special Studies. Washington, D.C.: Government Printing Office, 1972.

2049. U.S. Department of Commerce. The Social and Economic Status of the Black Population in the United States, 1790-1978. Current Population Reports, Special Studies, Series P-23, No. 80, Washington, D.C.: Government Printing Office, 1979.

2050. U.S. Department of Commerce. Statistical Abstract of the United States: 1978. Washington, D.C.: Government Printing Office, 1978.

2051. U.S. Department of Health. "Who's Who Among the Poor: A Demographic View of Poverty." Social Security Bulletin, July 1965.

2052. U.S. Department of Labor. Negroes in the United States: Their Economic and Social Situation. Bulletin No. 1511. Washington, D.C.: Government Printing Office, 1966.

2053. U.S. Department of Labor. Negro Migration in 1916-1917. New York: Negro Universities Press, 1969.

2054. U.S. Department of Labor. Negro Employment in the South. Volume I: The Houston Labor Market. Manpower Research Monograph No. 23. Washington, D.C.: U.S. Government Printing Office, 1971.

2055. U.S. Department of Labor. Black Americans: A Decade of Occupational Changes. Publication No. 1731. Washington, D.C.: Government Printing Office, 1972.

2056. U.S. Housing and Home Finance Agency. Intergroup Relations Service. Fair Housing Laws: Summaries and Text of State and Municipal Laws. Washington, D.C.: Housing and Home Finance Agency, Office of the Administrator, for sale by the Superintendent of Documents, Government Printing Office, 1965.

2057. United States, Joint Center for Political Studies, Blacks on the Move: A Decade of Demographic Change, Washington, D.C.: 1982.

2058. U.S. Office of Program Policy. Our Non-White Population and Its Housing: The Changes Between 1950 and 1960. Washington, D.C.: Government Printing Office, 1963.

2059. Valanis, B.M., and D. Rush. "A Partial Explanation of Superior Birth Weights Among Foreign-Born Women." Social Biology 26:3 (1979), 198-210.

2060. Valien, Preston. "General Demographic Characteristics of the

Negro Population in the United States." _Journal of Negro Education_, 32 (Fall 1963), 329-336.

2061. Valien, Preston. "The Growth and Distribution of Negro Population in the United States." _Journal of Negro Education_ 22:3 (1953), 242-249.

2062. Valien, Preston. _Southern Negro Internal Migration Between 1935 and 1940: Its Direction, Distance and Demographic Effects._ University of Wisconsin, 1947.

2063. Valien, Preston. "Overview of Demographic Trends and Characteristics by Color." _Milbank Memorial Fund Quarterly_ 48:2, Part 2 (1970), 21-37.

2064. Valien, Preston and A. Fitzgerald. " Attitudes of the Negro Mother Toward Birth Control." _American Journal of Sociology_ 55 (1949), 279-283.

2065. Valien, Preston and Ruth E. Vaughan. "Birth Control Attitudes and Practices of Negro Mothers." _Sociology and Social Research_ 35:6 (1951), 1-5.

2066. Vanderkamp, J. "Return Migration: Its Significance and Behavior", _Western Economic Journal_, 10:10 (1972), 460-465.

2067. Van Arsdol, Maurice D. and Leo A. Schuerman. "Redistribution and Assimilation of Ethnic Populations: The Los Angeles Case." _Demography_ 8:4 (1971), 459-480.

2068. Vann, A. "United States The Census and Black Elected Officials." In: _Black People and the 1980 Census. Vol. 1: Proceedings From a Conference on the Population Undercount._ Illinois Council for Black Studies, Chicago, Ill., United States, 1980.

2069. Vasantkumar, N.J.C. _Age Patterns of Mortality of American Blacks, 1940 to 1970._ Unpublished Ph.D. Dissertation. Princeton University, 1978.

2070. Vaughan, B., et al. "Contraceptive Efficacy Among Married Women Aged 15-44. Vital and Health Statistics." Series 23: _Data from the National Survey of Family Growth._ 5 (May 1980), 1-62.

2071. Vavra, Helen M. and Linda J. Querec. _A Study of Infant Mortality from Linked Records by Age of Mother, Total-Birth Order, and Other Variables: United States, 1960 Live Birth Cohort._ U.S. Department of Health, Education and Welfare, National Center for Health Statistics, Publication No. HRA 74-1851. Washington, D.C.: Government Printing Office, 1973.

2072. Veena, Sneh Bebarta. _The Movement of Blacks from Central_

Cities to Rings in the Metropolitan Areas of the United States. Ph.D. University of Georgia, 1979.

2073. Ventura, Stephanie J. Trends and Differentials in Births to Unmarried Women: United States, 1970-76. U.,S. Department of Health and Human Services, National Center for Health Statistics, 1980.

2074. Vernarelli, Michael Joseph. Locational Distortion and Black Ghetto Expansion. Ph.D. State University of New York at Binghamton, 1978.

2075. Villie, Charles Vert. Socio-Economic and Ethnic Areas of Syracuse, New York. Ph.D. Syracuse, University, 1957.

2076. Vincent, Clark E., et al. "Abortion Attitudes of Poverty-Level Blacks." Seminars in Psychiatry 2:3 (1970), 309-317.

2077. Vincent, Clark E., et al. "Familial and Generational Patterns of Illegitimacy." Journal of Marriage and the Family 31:5 (1969), 659-667.

2078. Wacker, Peter O. "The Changing Geography of Black Population of New Jersey, 1810-1860: A Preliminary View." Proceedings, III (1971), 174-78.

2079. Walters, Ronald. "Population Control and the Black Community." The Black Scholar 5:8 (1974), 45-51.

2080. Watson, Franklin J. "A Comparison of Negro and White Populations, Connecticut: 1940-1960." Phylon 29 (Summer 1968), 142-155.

2081. Watson, Ora Vesta Russell. A Comparative Demographic Analysis of Two Louisiana Cities: Baton Rouge and Shreveport. Ph.D. The Louisiana State University and Agricultural and Mechanical College, 1956.

2082. Weaver, Robert C. "Economic Factors in Negro Migration -- Past and Future," Social Forces, 18 (October 1939), 90-101.

2083. Weaver, Robert C. "Non-White Population Movements in Urban Ghettos," Phylon. 20 (Fall 1959), 1-5.

2084. Weaver, Robert C. Our Non-white Population and Its Housing. Housing and Home Finance Agency, U.S. Government Printing Office, Washington, D.C., 1963.

2085. Weisbord, R.G. "Birth Control and the Black American: A Matter of Genocide?" Demography 10:4 (1973), 571-590.

2086. Weisbord, R.G. "Birth Control as Black Genocide: Fact of Paranoia?" In: Genocide? Birth Control and the Black American, by R.G. Weisbord. Westport, Connecticut, Greenwood, 1975, 3-10.

2087. Weisbord, R.G. "Black Sexuality and the Racial Threat." In: Genocide? Birth Control and the Black American, by R.G. Weisbord. Westport, Connecticut, Greenwood, 1975, 25-40.

2088. Weisbord, R.G. "Blacks on the Distaff Side." In: Genocide? Birth Control and the Black American, by R.G. Weisbord. Westport, Connecticut, Greenwood, 1975, 110-123.

2089. Weisbord, R.G. "Coercion and Society's Parasites." In: Genocide? Birth Control and the Black American, by R.G. Weisbord. Westport, Connecticut, Greenwood, 1975, 137-157.

2090. Weisbord, R.G. "Concluding Thoughts." In: Genocide? Birth control and the Black American, by R.G. Weisbord. Westport, Connecticut, Greenwood, 1975, 176-187.

2091. Weisbord, R.G. "The Meaning of Genocide." In: Genocide? Birth Control and the Black American, by R.G. Weisbord. Westport, Connecticut, Greenwood, 1975, 11-24.

2092. Weisbord, R.G. "Reservations Among the Most Reasonable." In: Genocide? Birth Control and the Black American, by R.G. Weisbord. Westport, Connecticut: Greenwood, 1975, 124-136.

2093. Weisbord, R.G. "Sterilization, Genocide, and the Black American." In: Genocide? Birth Control and the Black American, by R.G. Weisbord. Westport, Connecticut, Greenwood, 1975, 158-175.

2094. Weiss, Leonard and J.G. Williamson. "Black Education, Earnings, and Inter-Regional Migration: Some New Evidence." American Economic Review 62 (1972), 382-383.

2095. Weller, Robert H. "The Differential Attainment of Family Size Goals by Race." Population Studies 33:1 (1979), 157-164.

2096. Werton, Pamela C. Sociodramatic Play Among Three and Four Year Old Black Children. Unpublished Ed.D. Dissertation. Ball State University, 1975.

2097. West, Herbert Lee. Urban Life and Spatial Distribution of Blacks in Baltimore, Maryland. Ph.D. University of Minnesota), 1974.

2098. Westoff, Charles F. and Norman B. Ryder. "The Structure of Attitudes Toward Abortion." Milbank Memorial Fund Quarterly 47:1 (1979), 1-5.

2099. Westoff, Charles F. and Norman B. Ryder. "Contraceptive Practice Among Urban Blacks in the United States, 1965."

Milbank Memorial Fund Quarterly 48:2 (1970), 215-233.

2100. Westoff, L.A. and C.F. Westoff. "Black Fertility and Contraception: From African Tribes to American Plantations." In L.A. Westoff and C.F. Westoff (eds.) From Now to Zero: Fertility, Contraception, and Abortion in America. Boston: Little, Brown, and Company, 1971, 234-277.

2101. Wheeler, James A. and Stanley D. Brunn. "Negro Migration into Rural Southwestern Michigan." The Geographical Review, 48 (April 1968), 214-30.

2102. Whalpton, Pascal, et al. Fertility and Family Planning in the United States. Princeton, New Jersey: Princeton University Press, 1966.

2103. White, L.K. "A Note on Racial Differences in the Effect of Female Economic Opportunity on Marriage Rates." Demography. 18:3 (1981), 349-354.

2104. White, Walter F. "The Success of Negro Migration," Crisis (January 1920), 112-15.

2105. Wienker, Curtis Wakefield. The Influences of Culture and Demography on the Population Biology of a Non-Isolate: The Colored People of McNary, Arizona. Unpublished Ph.D. Dissertation. The University of Arizona, 1975.

2106. Wilkie, Jane Riblett. "The Black Urban Population of the Pre-Civil War South." Phylon 37:3 (1976), 250-262.

2107. Wilkinson, Doris Y. "Toward a Positive Frame of Reference of Analysis of Black Families: A Selected Bibliography." Journal of Marriage and the Family 40 (November 1978), 707-708.

2108. Williams, Barbara A. "Family Planning and the Black Perspective." Essence 4 (September 1973), 18.

2109. Williams, Dorothy Slade. Ecology of Negro Communities in Los Angeles County: 1940-1959. Ph.D. University of Southern California, 1961.

2110. Williams, L. "Census Data in Research, Teaching, and Studying the Conditions of Black Women." In: Black People and the 1980 Census. Vol. 1: Proceedings From a Conference on the Population Undercount. Chicago: Illinois Council for Black Studies, United States, 1980.

2111. Willie, Charles V. The Family Life of Black People. Columbus, Ohio: Charles Merril, 1970.

2112. Willie, Charles V. and W.B. Rothney. "Racial, Ethnic, and Income Factors in the Epidemiology of Neonatal Mortality."

American Sociological Review 27:4 (1962), 522-526.

2113. Wilson, Franklin D. and Karl E. Taeuber. "Residential and School Segregation: Some Tests of their Associatoin." In Franklin D. Bean and W. Parker Frisbie (eds.) _The Demography of Racial and Ethnic Groups_. New York: Academic Press, 1978, 51-78.

2114. Wilson, R.W. and Danchik, K.M. "A Comparison of 'Black' and 'Other White' Data from the National Health Interview Survey and Mortality Statistics". In: _American Statistical Association, 1980 Proceedings of the Social Statistics Section._ Washington, D.C.: American Statistical Association, Social Statistics Section, 1981, 429-433.

2115. Wolfer, S.R. and E.L. Ferguson. "The Physician's Influence on the Nonacceptance of Birth Control." In D.V. McCalister, V. Thiessen, and M. McDermott (eds.) _Readings in Family Planning: A Challenge to the Health Professions._ St. Louis, Missouri: Mosby, 226-230.

2116. Woodruff, James F. "Some Characteristics of the Alabama Slave Population in 1850." _The Geographical Review_, 42 (July 1962), 379-88.

2117. Woodruff, James F. "Study of the Characteristics of the Alabama Slave Population in 1850." _Annals of the Association of American Geographers_, 42 (September 1962), 370.

2118. Woodside, Moya. _Sterilization in North Carolina: A Sociological and Psychological Study._ Chapel Hill: University of North Carolina Press, 1950.

2119. Woodson, Carter Godwin. _A Century of Negro Migration._ New York: Russell and Russell, 1969.

2120. Woodson, Carter Godwin. _A Century of Negro Migration._ Washington, D.C.: The Association for the Study of Negro Life and History, 1918.

2121. Woofter, Thomas Jackson, et al. _Negro Housing in Cities._ New York: Doubleday, 1928.

2122. Woofter, Thomas Jackson, et al. _Negro Housing in Philadelphia._ Philadelphia: Friends' Committee on Interests of the Colored Race and Whittier Center, 1927.

2123. Woofter, Thomas Jackson. _Negro Migration._ New York: W.D. Gray, 1920.

2124. Woofter, Thomas Jackson. _Negro Migration. Changes in Rural Organization and Population of the Cotton Belt._ New York: W.D. Gray, 1940.

2125. Wright, Gerald C. "Racism and the Availability of Family Planning Services in the United States." Social Forces 56:4 (1977), 1087-1098.

2126. Wright, N.H. "Vital Statistic and Census Tract Data Used to Evaluate Family Planning." Public Health Reports 85:5 (1970), 383-389.

2127. Wynder, E.L. et al. "A Study of the Epidemiology of Cancer of the Breast." Cancer 13:3 (1960), 559-601.

2128. Zabin, L.S. et al. Ages of Physical Maturatoin and First Intercourse in Black Teenage Males and Females. Presented at the Annual Meeting of the American Public Health Association, Montreal, Canada, November 18, 1982.

2129. Zelinsky, Wilbur. "The Population Geography of the Free Negro in Ante-Bellum America." Population Studies, III (March 1950): 386-401.

2130. Zelinsky, Wilbur. Population Patterns in Georgia. Ph.D. Dissertation, University of California, Berkeley, 1953.

2131. Zelnik, Melvin. "Fertility of the American Negro in 1830 and 1850." Population Studies 20:1 (1966), 77-83.

2132. Zelnik, Melvin. "Socioeconomic and Seasonal Variations in Births." Milbank Memorial Fund Quarterly 47:1 (1969), 59-165.

2133. Zelnik, M. and J.F. Kantner. "United States: Exploratory Studies of Negro Family Formation -- Factors Relating to Illegitimacy." Studies in Family Planning 60 (1970), 5-9.

2134. Zelnik, M. and J.F. Kantner. "Some Preliminary Observations on Pre-Adult Fertility and Family Formation." Studies in Family Planning 3:4 (1972), 59-65.

2135. Zelnick, M. and J.F. Kantner. "Sexuality, Contraception and Pregnancy Among Young Unwed Females in the United States." In Charles F. Westoff and Robert Parke (eds.) Demographic and Social Aspects of Population Growth and the American Future, Research Reports, Volume 1. Washington, D.C.: Government Printing Office, 1972, 359-374.

2136. Zelnik, M., and J.F. Kantner. "United States: Exploratory Studies of Negro Family Formation: Factors Relating to Illegitimacy." In D.V. McCallister, V. Thiessen, and M. McDermott (eds.) Readings in Family Planning: A Challenge to the Health Professions. St Louis, Missouri: Mosby, 1973, 196-204.

2137. Zelnik, M., and J.F. Kantner. "First Pregnancies to Women Aged 15-19: 1976 and 1971." Family Planning Perspectives 10:1

(1978), 11-20.

CHAPTER 3

Urbanization and Disurbanization

2138. A Report of Attitudes of Negroes in Various Cities. Prepared
      for the Senate Subcommittee on Executive Reorganization by John
      K. Kraft, privately circulated, 1966.

2139. Abbott, Edith H. The Tenements of Chicago 1908-1935. Chicago:
      University of Chicago Press, 1936.

2140. Abrams, Charles. The City is the Frontier. New York: Harper,
      1965.

2141. Adams, John S. Contemporary Metropolitan America: Twenty
      Vignettes. Cambridge, Ma: Ballinger, 1976.

2142. Adamson, John C. The Relationship Between the Commuting
      Problems and Job Oppurtunities for Negroes in the City of Terre
      Haute, Indiana. M.A. thesis, Indiana University, 1972.

2143. Adjei-Barwuah, Barfuor. Socio-Economic Regions in the
      Louisiana Ghetto. Ph.D. Indiana University, 1972.

2144. Akin, Edward N. "When a Minority Becomes the Majority." In
      Edward N. Akin (ed.) Blacks in Jacksonville Politics, 1887-
      1907. Westport, Conn.: Greenwood, 1970, 44-60.

2145. Alex, Nicholas. Black in Blue; A Study of the Negro Policeman.
      New York: Appleton-Century-Crofts, 1969.

2146. Alilunas, Leo. "Statutory Means of Impending Emigration of the
      Negro," Journal of Negro History, 22:2 (April 1937), 148-62.

2147. Allen, A. "The Urban Setting. IV. The Black City Dweller--
      Mental Health Needs and Services," Rhode Island Medical Journal
      53 (May 1970), 267-70.

2148. Allen James Egert. "The Negro in New York." New York
      Exposition: Historical Quarterly 53:2 (1964), 123-145.

2149. Allen, Rodney F. and Charles H. Adair. Violence and Riots in Urban America. Worthington, Ohio: C. A. Jones, 1969.

2150. Allen, Thomas H. "Mass Media Patterns in a Negro Ghetto." Journalism Quarterly, 45 (Autumn 1968), 525-528.

2151. Allison, Thomas W. "Population Movements in Chicago." Journal of Social Forces, 2 (1924), 329-33.

2152. Alston, John P. "The Black Population in Urbanized Areas, 1960." Journal of Black Studies 1 (June 1971), 435-442.

2153. Altschuler, Alan A. Community Control: The Black Demand for Participation in Large American Cities. Indianapolis: Bobbs-Merrill, 1970.

2154. "Anatomy of a Riot." Journal of Urban Law 45 (Spring-Summer 1968).

2155. Anderson, Marc B. Racial Discrimination in Detroit: A Spatial Analysis of Racism. Wayne State University, Master's Thesis, 1969.

2156. Anderson, Theodore R. "Intermetropolitan: A Correlation Analysis," American Journal of Sociology, 59 (March, 1960), 459-62.

2157. Aptheker, Herbert. "The Watts Ghetto Uprising, Part I," Political Affairs, 44 (October 1965), 16-29.

2158. Archibald, Helen A. "Notes on the Culture of the Urban Negro Child." Religious Education, 62 (July 1967), 321-326.

2159. Arnold, Benjamin William. "Concerning the Negroes of the City of Lynchburg, Virginia." Southern Historical Association Publication, 10 (1906), 19-38.

2160. Ashby, William M. "What Happened at Carteret?", Opportunity, 4 (June 1926), 191-192.

2161. Asher, Robert. "Documents of the East St. Louis Race Riot," Journal of the Illinois State Historical Society 65 (Autumn 1972), 327-336.

2162. Bahr, Howard Miner. Racial Differentiation in American Metropolitan Areas. Unpublished Ph.D. Thesis, The University of Texas at Austin, 1965.

2163. Baldwin, William H. "Negro in Cities," The Standard 13 (February 1927), 174-81.

2164. Banfield, Edward C. The Unheavenly City Revisited. Boston: Little Brown, 1974.

2165. Barnes, Annie S. "The Black Beauty Parlor Complex in a Southern City." Phylon 36:2 (1975), 149-154.

2166. Baron, Harold M. and Bennett Hymer. "The Negro Worker in the Chicago Labor Movement," in Julius Jacobson (ed.) The Negro and the American Labor Movement, Garden City, New York: Anchor Books, 1968, 232-85.

2167. Beard, Virginia Harison. A Study of Aging Among a Successful, Urban Black Population. Ph.D. Saint Louis University, 1976.

2168. Bearwood, Robert. "Southern Roots of Urban Crisis: Forced Off the Farms Into Destitution, Thousands of Negroes Migrate to Northern Slums." Fortune 78 (August 1968), 80-84.

2169. Bederman, Sanford. "The Stratification of 'Quality Life' in the Black Community of Atlanta, Georgia." Southeastern Geographer 14:1 (1974), 26-37.

2170. Bell, Wendell and Ernest M. Willis. "The Segregation of Negroes in American Cities: A Comparison Analysis." Social and Economic Studies 4 (March 1957), 59-75.

2171. Bellisfield, G. "White Attitudes Toward Racial Integration and the Urban Riots in the 1960's". Public Opinion Quarterly 36 (Winter 1972-1973), 579-584.

2172. Benet, James. "Bussing in Berkeley: Neither Calamity Nor Cure All." City: Magazine of Urban Life and Environment 4:1 (1970), 17-20.

2173. Bercouici, Konrad. Around the World in New York. New York: Century, 1924.

2174. Bercouici, Konrad. "The Black Blocks of Manhattan." Harper, 149 (1924), 613-623.

2175. Bercouici, Konrad. "The Rhythm of Harlem," Survey, 53 (1925), 379.

2176. Berry, Brian J.L., et al. "Attitudes Towards Integration: The Role of Status in Community Response to Neighborhood Change." In Barry Schwartz (ed.) The Changing Face of the Suburbs. Chicago: University of Chicago Press, 1976, 221-64.

2177. Berry, Edwin C., et al. The Racial Aspects of Urban Planning: An Urban League Critique of the Chicago Comprehensive Plan. Chicago: Chicago Urban League, 1968.

2178. Berry, Theodore M. "The Negro in Cincinnati Industries," Opportunity 8 (December 1930), 361-63.

2179. Berson, Lenora E. Case Study of a Riot: The Philadelphia

Story. New York: Institute of Human Relations Press, 1966.

2180. Bethune, Mary McLeod. "The Problems of the City Dweller", Opportunity 3 (1925), 54.

2181. Betten, Neil and Raymond A. Mohl. "The Evolution of Racism in an Industrial City, 1906-1940: A Case Study of Gary, Indiana." Journal of Negro History 59:1 (1974), 51-64.

2182. Billingsley, Andrew. "Family Functioning in the Low-Income Black Community," Social Casework. 50 (1966), 563-572.

2183. Billingsley, Andrew and Amy Tate Billingsley. "Illegitimacy and Patterns of Negro Family Life," in Robert W. Roberts (ed.) The Unwed Mother. New York: Harper and Row, 1966.

2184. Billingsley, Andrew and Amy Tate Billingsley. "Negro Family Life in America," Social Service Review. 39 (September 1965), 310-319.

2185. Binder, Carroll. "Chicago and the New Negro". Studies in a Great Community's Changing Race Relations. Chicago Daily News (March 1927), 15-18.

2186. Bittker, B.I. "The Case of the Checker-Board Ordinance: An Experiment in Race Relations." Yale Law Journal, 71 (July 1962), 1387-1423.

2187. "Black Cities: Colonies or States?" The Black Scholar (April 1970), 1-10.

2188. Black, W. Joseph. "Renewed Negro and Urban Renewal." Architectural Forum, 128 (June 1968), 60-67.

2189. Blair, Lewis H. A Southern Prophecy: The Prosperity of the South Dependent Upon the Elevation of the Negro (1889). Boston: Little, Brown, 1964.

2190. Blake, Virginia, et al. College and Community: A Study of Interaction in Chicago, Urbana: University of Illinois, Department of Urban Planning, 1967.

2191. Blalock, H.M. "Urbanization and Discrimination in the South." Social Problems 7 (Fall 1959), 146-152.

2193. Blauner, Robert. "The Dilemma of the Black Revolt," Journal of Housing 24 (December 1967), 603.

2193. Blauner, Robert. "Internal Coloialism and Ghetto Revolt." Social Problems 16 (Spring 1969), 393-408.

2194. Blauner, Robert. "Whitewash Over Watts: The Failure of the McCone Commission Report," Trans-action 54:3 (March-April

1966), 3-9.

2195. Block, Carl E. "Communicating with the Urban Poor: An Exploratory Inquiry." Journalism Quarterly 47 (Spring 1970), 3-11.

2196. Block, Herman. "Employment Status of the New York Negro in Retrospect," Phylon 20 (December 1959), 327-44.

2197. Blood, Robert. "Negro-White Differences in Blue-Collar Marriages in a Northern Metropolis," Social Forces 48 (September 1969), 59-64.

2198. Blumberg, Leonard and Robert R. Bell. "Urban Migration and Kinship Ties," Social Problems 6 (Spring 1959), 328-333.

2199. Boggs, James. "Blacks in the Cities: Agenda for the 70's." Black Scholar, 4:3 (November-December 1972), 50-61.

2200. Boggs, James. The American Revolution, New York: Monthly Review Press, 1963.

2201. Boggs, Vernon William. A Swedish Dilemma: Scandinavian Prostitutes and Black Pimps. Ph.D. City University of New York, 1979.

2202. Bogue, Donald J. Components of Population Change in Standard Metropolitan Areas. Oxford, Ohio: Scripps Foundation, 1957.

2203. Bogue, Donald J., et al. "A New Estimate of the Negro Population and Negro Vital Rates in the United States, 1930-1960," Demography. 1:1 (1964), 20-30.

2204. Bogue, Grant. "Racial Separation in a Small Northern City." Interracial Review, 39 (January 1966), 15-22.

2205. Bontemps, Arna and Jack Conroy. Anyplace But Here. New York: Hillard Wang, 1966.

2206. Boskin, Joseph. "A History of Urban Racial Conflicts in the Twentieth Century," in Audry Rawitscher (ed.) Riots in the City: An Addendum to the McCone Commission Report. Los Angeles: 1967, 1-24.

2207. Boskin, Joseph. "The Revolt of the Urban Ghettos, 1964-1967." Annals of the American Academy of Political and Social Science 382 (March 1969), 1-14.

2208. Boskin, Joseph and V. Pilson. "Los Angeles Riot of 1965: A Medical Profile of an Urban Crisis," Pacific Historical Review 39 (August 1970), 353-365.

2209. Boskin, Joseph and Fred Krinsky. Urban Racial Violence in the

<u>Twentieth Century.</u> Beverly Hills: Glencoe Press, 1969.

2210. Boulding, Kenneth E., et al. (eds.). <u>Transferes in an Urbanized Economy: Theories and Effects of the Grants Economy.</u> Belmont, California: Wadsworth, 1972.

2211. Bowen, Harry W. <u>The Persuasive Efficacy of Negro Non-Violent Resistance.</u> University of Pittsburgh, Unpublished Ph.D. Thesis, 1962.

2212. Bowen, Louise D. "Colored People of Chicago." <u>Survey</u> 31 (1913), 117-20.

2213. Bowes, John Elliott. <u>Information Control Behaviors and the Political Effectiveness of Low Income Urban Blacks</u>. Ph.D. Michigan State University, 1971.

2214. Bragaw, Donald H. "Status of Negroes in a Southern Port City in the Progressive Era." <u>Florida History Quarterly</u> 51:3 (1973), 281-302.

2215. Brandt, Lilian. "The Negroes of St. Louis." <u>American Statistics Assocation Publication</u> 8 (1903), 203-268.

2216. Brandt, Lilian. "Negroes of St. Louis." <u>Southern Workman</u> 34 (1904), 223-7.

2217. Brisbane, Robert H. <u>The Rise of Protest Movement Among Negroes Since 1900</u>. Cambridge, Massachusetts: Harvard University Press, 1949.

2218. Brooks, Michael P. and Michael A. Stegman. "Urban Social Policy, Race and the Education of Planners." <u>Journal of the American Institute of Planners</u>, 34 (September 1968), 275-286.

2219. Brooks, Thomas R. "Drumbeats in Detroit," <u>Dissent</u> (January-February 1970), 16-25.

2220. Broude, Jeffrey E. <u>A Survey of 1960 Negro Occupational Patterns in Standard Metropolitan Statistical Area by Region, Total Population and Percentage Negro</u>. Master's Thesis, University of California, Los Angeles, 1971.

2221. Brown, Claude. "Harlem, My Harlmem." <u>Dissent</u> 8 (1961), 371-382.

2222. Brown, Claude, et al. "Harlem's America." <u>The New Leader</u>, 49 (September 26, 1966), 1-5.

2223. Brown, Letitia W. "Residential Patterns of Negroes in the District of Columbia, 1800-1860." <u>Columbia Historical Society Records</u> 77 (1969-1970), 14-21.

2224. Brown, Thomas Edwards. "Sex Education and Life in the Negro Ghetto." *Pastoral Psychology* 19 (May 1968), 45-54.

2225. Brown, William H. *Class Aspects of Residential Development and Choice in the Oakland Black Community.* Ph.D. Dissertation, University of California, Berkeley, CA., 1970.

2226. Brownell, Blaine and David R. Goldfield. *The City in Southern History: The Growth of Urban Civilization in the South.* Port Washington, New York: Kennikat, 1977.

2227. Brownlee, W. Elliott. "The Economics of Urban Slavery." *Review in American History* 5:2 (1977), 230-235.

2228. Brunner, W.F. "The Negro Health Problem in Southern Cities," *American Journal of Public Health* 5 (1915), 183-190.

2229. Brunson, Rose Toomer. *Socialization Experiences and Socio-Economic Characteristics of Urban Negroes as Related to Use of Selected Southern Foods and Medical Remedies.* Ph.D. Michigan State University, 1962.

2230. Bulkley, William L. "The Industrial Condition of the Negro in New York City," *Annals* 27 (May 1906), 590-96.

2231. Bullock, Henry A. *Pathways to the Houston Negro Market.* Ann Arbor, Michigan: J.W. Edwards, 1957.

2232. Bullock, Paul. *Watts: The Aftermath, An Inside View of the Ghetto By the People of Watts.* New York: Grove, 1969.

2233. Bullough, Bonnie Louise. "Alienation in the Ghetto," *American Journal of Sociology* 72 (1960), 469-478.

2234. Bunche, Ralph J. "The Negro in the Political Life of the United States," *The Journal of Negro Education* 10 (July 1941), 579-81.

2235. Burgess, Ernest W. "Residential Segregation in American Cities." *The Annals of the American Academy of Political and Social Science*, 130 (November, 1928), 20-29.

2236. Burgess, Ernest W. and Harvey J. Locke. "The Negro Family," in *The Family*. New York: American Book Company, 1945, 148-179.

2237. Burgess, Ernest W. and Donald J. Bogue. *Contributions to Urban Sociology.* Chicago: University of Chicago Press, 1964.

2238. "Business Labor and Jobs in the Ghetto: A Staff Survey." *Issues in Industrial Society* 1 (1969), 3-18.

2239. Butler, George O. "The Black Worker in Industry, Agriculture, Domestic, and Personal Service," *Journal of Negro Education*

8:3 (July 1939), 416-29.

2240. Butts, J.W. and Dorothy Jones. "The Underlying Causes of the Elaine Riot of 1919," Arkansas Historical Quarterly 20 (Spring 1961), 95-104.

2241. Byrd, Frank. "Harlem's Employment Situation," Crisis 38 (May 1931), 160-61.

2242. Byrn, Robert M. "Urban Law Enforcement: A Plea from the Ghetto," Criminal Law Bulletin 5 (April 1969), 125-136.

2243. Byrne, Dennis Michael. Analysis of Time Allocation Patterns of Inner-City Blacks. Unpublished Ph.D. Thesis, University of Notre Dame, 1975.

2244. Caine, Augustus F. Patterns of Negro Protest: A Structural-Functional Analysis. Michigan State University, Unpublished Ph.D. Thesis, 1964.

2245. California, State of. Governor's Commission on the Los Angeles Riots. Transcripts, depositions, consultants reports, and selected documents. Los Angeles, 1965.

2246. California, State of. California Governor's Commission on the Los Angeles Riots. Violence in the City-An End or a Beginning? Los Angeles, 1965.

2247. California, State of. Division of Fair Employment Practices. Negroes and Mexican Americans in South and East Los Angeles: Changes Between 1960 and 1965 in Population, Employment, Income and Family Status. San Francisco, 1966.

2248. Camerota, Michael. "Westfield's Black Community, 1755-1905." Historical Journal of Western Massachusetts 5:1 (1976), 17-27.

2249. Campbell, A. and H. Schuman. "Racial Attitudes in Fifteen American Cities," in Supplemental Studies for the National Advisory Commission on Civil Disorders. Washington, D.C.: Government Printing Office, 1969.

2250. Capeci, Dominic Joseph. The Harlem Riot of 1943, unpublished Ph.D. Dissertation, University of California, Riverside, 1970.

2251. Caplan, Nathan S. and Jeffrey M. Paige. "Study of Ghetto Rioters," Scientific American (August 1968), 10-20.

2252. Carey, George W. "The Regional Interpretation of Manhattan Population and Housing Patterns Through Factor Analysis." Geographical Review 56 (1966), 551-569.

2253. Carey, George W., et al. "Educational and Demographic Factors in the Urban Geography of Washington, D.C." Geographical Review

58 (1968), 515-537.

2254. Carlson, David B. "The New Urbanites: Nature and Dimensions," Architectural Forum (June 1960), 1-10.

2255. Carpenter, Niles. Nationality, Color and Economic Opportunity in the City of Buffalo. Buffalo, New York: University of Buffalo Press, 1927.

2256. Carter, Dan T. Scottsboro, A Tragedy of the American South. Baton Rouge: Louisiana State University Press, 1969.

2257. Carter, Wilmoth A. "Negro Main Street as a Symbol of Discrimination." Phylon 21 (Fall 1960), 234-242.

2258. Carter, Wilmoth A. The Urban Negro in the South. New York: Vantage, 1962.

2259. Case, Fred E. Minority Families in the Metropolis. Los Angeles: Report No. 8. University of California, 1966.

2260. "Causes of the Chicago Race Riot." Worlds Work 45 (December 1922), 131-344.

2261. Cayton, Horace and St. Clair Drake. Black Metropolis: A Study of Negro Life in a Northern City. New York: Harper and Row, 1962.

2262. Charity Organization Society. The Negro in the Cities of the North. New York: Charity Organization Society, 1905.

2263. Cherry, Frank T. Southern In-Migrant Negroes in North Lawndale. Chicago, 1949-59: A Study of Internal Migration and Adjustment. Chicago: University of Chicago Press, 1966.

2264. Chicago, City of. Mayor's Commission on Human Relations. The Trumbull Park Homes Disturbances, A Chronological Report. August 4, 1953 to June 30, 1955. Chicago, 1955.

2265. Chicago, City of. Commission on Race Relations. The Negro in Chicago: A Study of Race Relations and a Race Riot in Chicago. New York: Arno Press, 1968.

2266. Chicago, City of. Commission on Race Relations. The Negro in Chicago Chicago: University of Chicago Press, 1922.

2267. Chicago Race Riot. Symposium. Chicago: Great Western Publishing Co., 1919.

2268. Chitoka, Richard A. and Michael C. Moran. Riot in the Cities; An Analytical Symposium on the Causes and Effects. Rutherford, New Jersey: Fairleigh Dickinson University Press, 1970.

2269. Christian, Charles M. The Impact of Industrial Relocations from the Black Community of Chicago Upon Job Opportunities and Residential Mobility of the Central City Workforce. Ph.D. University of Illinois at Urbana-Champaign, 1975.

2270. City-Wide Citizens Committee on Harlem. Report of the Subcommittee on Housing 1942.

2271. Clark, Dennis. The Ghetto Game: Racial Conflicts in the City. New York: Sheed Ward, 1962.

2272. Clark, John T. "The Migrant in Pittsburgh. A Story of the Pittsburgh Urban League." Opportunity 1:3 (1923), 308.

2273. Clark, John T. "When the Negro Resident Organizes." Opportunity (June 1934), 168-70.

2274. Clark, Kenneth B. The Negro Protest. Boston: Beacon Press, 1963.

2275. Clark, Kenneth B. "Group Violence: A Preliminary Study of the Attitudinal Pattern of Its Acceptance and Rejection - A Study of the 1943 Harlem Riots." Journal of Social Psychology 19 (August 1944), 319-337.

2276. Clark, Kennneth B. Dark Ghetto; Dilemmas of Social Power. New York: Harper & Row, 1965.

2277. Clark, Kenneth B. "The Negro and the Urban Crisis." In Kermit Gordon (ed.) Agenda for the Nation Washington, D.C.: Brookings Institution, 1968, 117-140.

2278. Clark, LeRoy D. "Minority Lawyer: Link to the Ghetto." American Bar Association Journal 55 (January 1969), 61-64.

2279. Clark, Peter B. The Black Brigade of Cincinnati. New York: Arno, 1975.

2280. Clarke, John Henrik. Harlem: A Community in Transition. New York: Citadel, 1964.

2281. Coe, Paul F. "The Non-White Population Surge to Our Cities." Land Economics 35 (August 1959), 195-210.

2282. Coe, Paul F. Non-White Population Increases in Metropolitan Areas." Journal of American Statistical Association, 50 (June 1955), 283-308.

2283. Cobb, Robert W. Black Settlement in Silverton, Ohio, 1960-1967: A Spatial Diffusion Process. Ph.D. Dissertation, State University of New York at Buffalo, 1971.

2284. Cohen, Jerry and William S. Murphy. Burn, Baby, Burn! The Los

Angeles Race Riot, August, 1965. New York: Dutton, 1966.

2285. Cohen, N.E. "The Los Angeles Riot Study." Social Work 12 (October 1967), 14-21.

2286. Cohen, N.E. (ed.) The Los Angeles Riots: A Socio-Psychological Study. New York: Praeger, 1970.

2287. Colasanto, Diane Lee. The Prospects for Racial Integration in Neighborhoods: An Analysis of Residential Preferences in the Detroit Metropolitan Area. Ph.D. the University of Michigan, 1977.

2288. Colenutt, Robert J. "Do Alternatives Exist for Central Cities?" In Harold M. Rose (ed.) Geography of the Ghetto, Perspectives in Geography, Vol. II. Dekalb, Illinois: Northern Illinois University Press, 1972, 40-50.

2289. Coles, Howard W. The Cradle of Freedom: A History of the Negro in Rochester, Western New York and Canada. New York: Oxford, 1941.

2290. Coles, Robert. The Image is You. Boston: Houghton Mifflin, 1969.

2291. Coles, Robert. "Like It Is In The Alley." Daedalus 97 (Fall 1968), 1315-1330.

2292. Coles, Robert. "Maybe God Will Come and Clean Up This Mess." Atlantic 220 (October 1967), 103-106.

2293. Collins, G.L. "The City Within the City. St. Cyprian's Parish." Outlook 84 (1906), 274-277.

2294. Collins, Keith E. Black Los Angeles: The Maturing of the Ghetto, 1940-1950. Ph.D. Thesis University of California, San Diego, 1975.

2295. Commission on Human Relations. Philadelphia's Negro Population Facts on Housing. Philadelphia: The Commission (1953).

2296. Commission on Integroup Relations. Negroes in the City of New York. New York: Commission on Intergroup Relations, 1961.

2297. Commission on Race and Housing. Where Shall We Live? Berkeley, University of California Press, 1958.

2298. Comstock, A.P. "Chicago Housing Conditions: The Problem of the Negro." American Journal of Sociology 18 (1912), 241-57.

2299. "Condition of the Negro in Various Cities." Bulletin Department of Labor 10 (1897), 257-369.

2300. Conley, Paul B. and Stanley K. Bigman. "Acquaintance with Municipal Government Health Services in a Low-Income Urban Population," American Journal of Public Health 52 (November 1962), 1877-1886.

2301. Connery, Robert H. (ed.) Urban Riots. New York: Vintage Books, 1969.

2302. Cottingham, Clement. Race, Poverty and the Urban Underclass. MA, Lexington: Bellinger, 1982.

2303. Cottingham, Phoebe H. "Black Income and Metropolitan Residential Disperson." Urban Affairs Quarterly 10 (1975), 273-96.

2304. Courant, Paul J. and John Yinger. "On Models of Racial Prejudice and Urban Residential Structure." Journal of Urban Economics 4 (1977), 272-91.

2305. Cowgill, Donald D. "Segregation for Metropolitan Areas," American Sociological Review 27 (June 1962), 400-402.

2306. Cowgill, Donald D. "Trends on Residential Segregation of Non-Whites in American Cities, 1940-1950." American Sociological Review 21 (February 1956), 43-47.

2307. Coyers, James E., et al. Black Youth in a Southern Metropolis. Atlanta, Georgia: Southern Regional Council, 1968.

2308. Craig, David William. "Recreational Activity Patterns in a Small Negro Urban Community: The Role of the Cultural Base." Economic Geography 38 (January 1972), 107-15.

2309. Craigie, David William. Causes and Consequences of Black-White Residential Differentiation in American Central Cities: A Longitudinal Analysis 1950-1970. Ph.D. The University of Arizona, 1977.

2310. Cressey, Paul F. The Succession of Cultural Groups in the City of Chicago. Unpublished Ph.D. Thesis, University of Chicago, 1930.

2311. Creveling, Harold F. "Mapping Cultural Groups in an American Industrial City." Annals 53 (June 1953), 162-63.

2312. Creveling, Harold F. Mapping Cultural Groups in an American Industrial City." Economic Geography 90 (July 1964), 221-38.

2313. Crew, Spencer R. Black Life in Secondary Cities: A Comparative Analysis of the Black Communities of Camden and Elizabeth, New Jersey, 1860-1920. Ph.D. Rutgers University the State University of New Jersey, 1978.

2314. Crockett, Norman L. *The Black Towns* Lawrence, Kansas: The Regents Press of Kansas, 1979.

2315. Crosby, Alexander L. *In These Ten Cities: How Minorities are Roused in Ten Communities of the U.S.* Washington, D.C.: Published for Public Affairs Committee, March 1951.

2316. Crossland, William August. *Industrial Conditions Among Negroes in St. Louis.* St. Louis, Mo.: Mendle Printing Co., 1914.

2317. Crouthamel, James L. "The Springfield Race Riot of 1908," *Journal of Negro History* 45:3 (July 1960), 164-181.

2318. Crowe, Charles. "Racial Massacre in Atlanta, September 22, 1906," *Journal of Negro History* 54:2 (April 1969), 150-173.

2319. Crowe, Charles. "Racial Violence and Social Reform--Origins of the Atlanta Riot of 1906," *Journal of Negro History* 53:3 (July 1968), 234-256.

2320. Crump, Spencer. *Black Riots in Los Angeles: The Story of The Watts Tragedy.* Los Angeles: Trans-Anglo Books, 1966.

2321. Curran, Barbara W. *Getting By With a Little Help From My Firends: Informal Networks Among Older Black and White Urban Women Below the Poverty Line.* Ph.D. The University of Arizona, 1978.

2322. Curtis, C. Michael. "Travels with Mr. Charlie: Journalists Look at the Black American Ghetto." *Atlantic* 224 (August 1969), 31-38.

2323. Curtis, Rep. Thomas B. *Supplementary View, in the U.S. Congress, Senate Joint Economic Committee, Report: Employment and Manpower Problems in the Cities--Implication of the Report of the National Advisory Commission on Civil Disorders,* 90th Congress, 2nd Session, Report No. 1568. Washington, D.C.: U.S. Government Printing Office, September 16, 1968.

2324. Cushman, William Mitchell. *Equal Opportunity and the Urban Black: An Analysis of Public Policy and Its Implications for Urban Planning.* Ph.D. University of Washington, 1973.

2325. Czaja, Ronald. *Social and Political Participation of Blacks and Whites in a Metropolitan Area: A Test of Three Perspectives.* Ph.D. University of Illinois at Chicago Circle, 1976.

2326. Dabney, Lillian Gertrude. *The History of Schools for Negroes in the District of Columbia: 1806-1947.* Washington, D.C.: Catholic University of American Press, 1949.

2327. Dabney, Wendell P. *Cincinnati's Colored Citizens: Historical,*

Sociological and Biographical. Cincinnati: Dabney, 1926.

2328. Danella, Rose Decarlo. Racial Balance Policy in Utica: A Case Study. Ph.D. Syracuse University, 1975.

2329. Daniels, Douglas H. "Looking for a Home: The Travelcraft Skills of San Francisco's Pioneer Black Residents." Umoja 1:2 (1977), 49-70.

2330. Daniels, John. In Freedom's Birthplace; A Study of the Boston Negroes. Boston: Houghton Mifflin, 1914.

2331. Danielson, M.N. "Differentiation, Segregation, and Political Fragmentation in the American Metropolis." In A.E.K. Nash (ed.) Governance and Population. Washington, D.C.: Commission on Population Growth and the American Future, Research Reports, Vol. 4, 1972, 143-76.

2332. Davies, Christopher Shane. The Effect of Transportation on the Employment Distribution of Negro Residents within the Indianapolis Standard Statistical Area. Ph.D. Dissertation, Indiana University, Bloomington, IN., 1970.

2333. Davies, Christopher Shane. "The Reverse Commuter Transit Problem in Indianapolis." In Harold M. Rose (ed.) Geography of the Ghetto, Perspectives in Geography Vol. II. Dekalb, Illinois: Northern Illinois University Press, 1972, 45-60.

2334. Davies, Christopher Shane and Gary L. Fowler. "The Disadvantaged Urban Migrant in Indianapolis." Economic Geography 48:2 (1972), 157-175.

2335. Death, Colin Edward. Patterns of Participation and Exclusion: A Poor Italian and Black Urban Community and Its Response to a Federal Poverty Program. Ph.D. Thesis, University of Pittsburgh, 1970.

2336. Deskins, Donald R. Negro Settlement in Ann Arbor, unpublished M.A. Thesis, The University of Michigan, 1963.

2337. Deskins, Donald R. "Race as an Element in the Intra-City Regionalization of Atlanta's Population." Southeastern Geographer 11:2 (1971), 90-100.

2338. Deskins, Donald R. "Race, Residence, and Workplace in Detroit, 1800-1965." Economic Geography. 48:1 (1967), 79-94.

2339. Deskins, Donald R. Residential Mobility of Negro Occupational Groups in Detroit, 1837-1965. Ph.D. Dissertation, University of Michigan, Ann Arbor, MI., 1971.

2340. Deskins, Donald R. "The Urbanization of Jobs and Minority Employment." Economic Geography 52:4 (1976), 348-362.

2341. Detroit Bureau of Governmental Research. The Negro in Detroit. Detroit: DBGR, 1926.

2342. Detroit, City of. Public Library, Department of Social Science. Detroit Race Riot, June 1943. Detroit: The City, 1946.

2343. DeVise, Pierre. "The Urbanization of Jobs and Minority Employment." Economic Geography 54:4 (1976), 100-115.

2344. Dillard, James H. "Conditions in Harlem." Crisis 33 (1926), 21-22.

2345. Dimensions of Poverty in New York City. New York: Mayor's Council on Poverty, March 23, 1964.

2346. Dixon, Vernon John. A Determination of Investment Priorities in Urban Black Communities: Bedford-Stuyvesant. Ph.D. Princeton University, 1973.

2347. Dobson, Kenneth E. Journey to Work Patterns of Black Federal Employees in Early Twentieth Century Washington, D.C. M.A. Thesis, University of Maryland, College Park, MD., 1975.

2348. Dollard, John. Caste and Class in a Southern Town. New Haven: State University Press, 1937.

2349. Downs, Anthony. "Alternative Futures for the American Ghetto." Daedalus, 97 (Fall 1968), 1331-1378.

2350. Downs, Bryan T. "A Critical Re-Examination of the Social and Political Characteristics of Riot Cities," Social Science Quarterly 51 (September 1970), 349-360.

2351. Downs, Bryan T. "Social and Political Characteristics of Riot Cities: A Comparative Study," Social Science Quarterly, 49 (December 1968), 504-520.

2352. Drake, St. Clair and R. Horace Cayton. Black Metropolis: A Study of Negro Life in a Northern City. New York: Harper and Row, 1962.

2353. DuBois, W.E.B. Darkwater. New York: Shocken Books, 1969.

2354. DuBois, W.E.B. The Negro American Family. Cambridge, Massachusetts: MIT Press, 1970.

2355. DuBois, W.E.B. Philadelphia Negro. Philadelphia: University of Pennsylvania Press, 1899.

2356. DuBois, W.E.B. Some Notes on Negroes in New York City. Atlanta, 1903.

2357. DuBois, W.E.B. "Upholding of Black Durham." World's Work 23 (1912), 334-8.

2358. DuBois, W.E.B., and Martha Gruening. The Massacre of East St. Louis: an Account of an Investigation for the National Association for the Advancement of Colored People. New York: National Association for the Advancement of Colored People, 1917.

2359. Dubovsky, Melvyn. When Workers Organize: New York City in the Progressive Era. Amherst, Mass.: University of Massachusetts Press, 1968.

2360. Dulaney, William L. "The Negro and the City," Journal of Negro Education 31 (Spring 1962), 198-201.

2361. Duncan, Otis D. and Albert J. Reiss. Social Characteristics of Urban and Rural Communities. Amherst, Mass.: University of Massachusetts Press, 1968.

2362. Duncan, Otis D. and Beverly Duncan. The Negro Population of Chicago: A Study of Residential Succession. Chicago: University of Chicago Press, 1957.

2363. DuToit, Brian M. and Helen I. Safa. Migration and Urbanization: Models and Adaptive Strategies. Paris: Mouton, 1975.

2364. Dyckoff, E.F. "A Negro City in New York." Outlook 108:9 (1914), 149-54.

2365. Dynes, Russell R. and E.L. Quarantelli. "Urban Civil Disturbances: Organizational Change and Group Emergence," American Behavioral Scientist 16 (January 1973), 304-439.

2366. Dynes, Russell R. and E.L. Quarantelli. "What Looting in Civil Disturbances Really Means," Trans-action 5 (May 1968), 9-14.

2367. "East St. Louis Riots." Congressional Record 56 (July 6, 1918), 9573-9581.

2368. Edwards, Ozzie L. "Patterns of Residential Segregation Within a Metropolitan Ghetto." Demography 7 (May 1970), 10-20.

2369. Edwards, Paul K. The Southern Urban Negro as a Consumer. New York: Prentice-Hall, 1932.

2370. Eichenbaum, Jacob J. Magic, Mobility and Minorities in the Urban Drama. Ph.D. Dissertation, University of Michigan, Ann Arbor, MI., 1972.

2371. Eisinger, P.K. "Conditions of Protest Behavior in American Cities," American Political Science Review, 67 (March 1973),

11-28.

2372. Elwang, William Wilson. The Negro of Columbia, Missouri: Cover Study of the Race Problems. University of Missouri, Department of Sociology, 1904.

2373. Emlet, John T. "Movement for the Betterment of the Negro in Philadelphia." Annals of American Academy of Geographers 49 (1913), 81-92.

2374. Emlet, John T. "Negro Immigration in Philadelphia." Southern Workman 46 (1917), 555-557.

2375. Epstein, Abraham. The Negro Migrant in Pittsburgh. Pittsburgh: University of Pittsburgh Press, 1918.

2376. Erickson, Rodney A. and Theodore K. Miller. "Race and Resources in Large American Cities: An Examination of Introduction and Interregional Variations." Urban Affairs Quarterly 13 (July 1978), 401-20.

2377. Ernst, Robert T. Factors of Isolation and Interaction in an All-Black City: Kinlock, Missouri. Ph.D. Dissertation, University of Florida, Gainsville, Florida, 1973.

2378. Ervin, James M. The Participation of the Negro in the Community Life of Los Angeles. San Francisco: R.E. Research Associates, 1973.

2379. Evans, William. "Federal Housing Brings Segregation to Buffalo." Opportunity 124 (April 1942), 106-110.

2380. Etzkowits, Henry and Gerald M. Schaflander. Ghetto Crisis: Riots of Reconciliation. Boston: Little, Brown, 1969.

2381. Everett, John R. "The Decentralization Fiasco and Out Ghetto Schools." The Atlantic Monthly 22 (1960), 71-73.

2382. Fainstein, Norman and Susan Fainstein. Urban Political Movements: The Search for Power by Minority Groups in American Cities. Englewood Cliffs, New Jersey: Prentice-Hall, 1974.

2383. Fantini, Mario, et al. Community Control and the Urban School. New York: Praeger, 1969.

2384. Farley, Dorothy Anne. A Comparative Study of the Perspective of Health and Social Needs of Selected Poor Held by Black Ghetto Dwellers and Health Planners: Implications for Planning of Nursing Services. Ph.D. Thesis, Boston University School of Nursing, 1971.

2385. Farley, Reynolds. "The Changing Distribution of Negroes Within

Metropolitan Areas: The Emergence of Black Suburbs." American Journal of Sociology 75 (January 1970): 512-29.

2386. Farley, Reynolds. Recent Changes in the Social and Economic Status of Blacks in the U.S.: Three Steps Forward and One Backward. Paper presneted at the Ethnicity and Race in the Last Quarter of the Twentieth Century, State University of New York at Albany, Albany, New York, 1984.

2387. Farley, Reynolds. "The Urbanization of Negroes in the United States." Journal of Social History. (Spring 1968): 241-258.

2388. Farley, Reynolds and Karl E. Taeuber. "Population Trends and Residential Segregation Since 1960: Special Censuses for 13 Cities Reveal Increasing Concentration of Highly Segregated Negroes." Science 159 (March 1, 1968), 953-956.

2389. Farley, Reynolds, et al. "'Chocolate City, Vanilla Suburbs': Will the Trend Toward Racially Separate Communities Continue?" Social Science Research 7 (December 1978), 319-44.

2390. Fauset, Arthur Huff. Black Gods of the Metropolis: Negro Religious Cults of the Urban North. Philadelphia: University of Pennsylvania Press, 1971.

2391. Favor, Homer E. The Effects of Racial Changes in Occupancy Patterns Upon Property Values in Baltimore. Pittsburgh: University of Pittsburgh, 1960.

2392. Feldstein, Sylvan G. and Bernard Mackler. School Desegregation and the Law in New York City: The Case of In Re Skipwirth. New York: Center for Urban Education, May 1968.

2393. Feagin, Joe R. "Social Sources of Support for Violence and Non-Violence in a Negro Ghetto." Social Problems 15 (Spring 1968), 432-400.

2394. Feagin, Joe R. and Paul B. Sheatsley. "Ghetto Resident Appraisals of a Riot." Public Opinion Quarterly 32 (Fall 1968), 352-362.

2395. Fleming, Karl Henshaw. The 1967 Milwaukee Riot: A Historical and Comparative Analysis, unpublished Ph.D. Dissertation, Syracuse University, 1970.

2396. Franklin, Hardy Rogers. The Relationship Between Adult Communication Practices and Public Library Use in a Northern, Urban Black Ghetto. Ph.D. Thesis, Rutgers University, The State University of New Jersey, New Brunswick, New Jersey, 1971.

2397. Frazier, E. Franklin. "An Analysis of Statistics on Negro Illegitimacy in the United States" Social Forces 11 (1932),

249-257.

2398. Frazier, E. Franklin. Black Bourgeoisie. Glencoe, Illinois: The Free Press, 1957.

2399. Frazier, E. Franklin. "Chicago: A Cross-Section of Negro Life." Opportunity 7 (March 1939), 70-73.

2400. Frazier, E. Franklin. "Ethnic Family Patterns: The Negro Family in the United States," American Journal of Sociology 53 (May 1948), 435-438.

2401. Frazier, E. Franklin. "The Impact of Urban Civilization Upon Negro Family Life," American Sociological Review 2 (August 1937), 604-618.

2402. Frazier, E. Franklin. "The Impact of Urban Civilization Upon Negro Family Life." In G. Franklin Edwards (ed.) E. Franklin Frazier on Race Relations: Selected Writings. Chicago: University of Chicago Press, 1968, 50-69.

2403. Frazier, E. Franklin. The Negro Family in Chicago. Chicago: University of Chicago Press, 1932.

2404. Frazier, E. Franklin. "The Negro Family in Chicago." In E.W. Burgess and D.J. Bogue (eds.) Contributions to Urban Sociology. Chicago: University of Chicago Press, 1964, 404-418.

2405. Frazier, E. Franklin. The Negro Family in the United States. Chicago: University of Chicago Press, 1966.

2406. Frazier, E. Franklin. "Negro Harlem: An Ecological Study." American Journal of Sociology 43 (August 1937), 30-40.

2407. Frazier, E. Franklin. "Negro in the Industrial South." Nation 125 (1927), 83-4.

2408. Frazier, E. Franklin. "Occupational Classes Among Negroes in Cities," The American Journal of Sociology 35 (March 1970) 718-738.

2409. Frazier, E. Franklin. On Race Relation: Selected Writings. Chicago: University of Chicago Press, 1968.

2410. Frazier, E. Franklin. "Some Effects of the Depression on the Negro in Northern Cities," Science and Society 2 (Fall 1938), 604-618.

2411. Frazier, E. Franklin. "The Urban Ordeal of Negroes." Negro Digest 12 (December 1962), 26-32.

2412. Freeman, Edward Barnes. Church and Community Interaction in an Urban Area of Deterioration and Racial Change: A Case Study of

the Twenty-Third and Broadway Baptist Church, Louisville,
Kentucky. The Southern Baptist Theological Seminary, Ph.D.
Thesis, 1978.

2413. Frey, Williams. White Flight and Central-City Loss:
Application of an Analytic Migration Framework. Madison:
University of Wisconsin, Institute for Research on Poverty,
November 1977.

2414. Frieden, Bernard. "Toward Equality of Urban Opportunity."
Journal of American Institute of Planners 31:4 (1965), 320-30.

2415. Friesma, H. Paul. "Black Control of Central Cities: The Hollow
Prize." Journal of the American Institute of Planners 35
(1969), 75-9.

2416. Frishman, Joshua A. "Southern City." Midstream 7 (1961), 39-
63.

2417. Frueh, Linda K. A Factor Analytic Investigation of the
Internal Structure of the Black Community in Detroit. Master's
Thesis, Western Illinois University, 1971.

2418. Frumkin, Robert M. "Race, Occupation and Social Class in New
York." Journal of Negro Education 27 (1958), 62-65.

2419. Fuller, Ross. Negro Voting Patterns in Akron, Ohio. M.A.
Thesis, Kent State University, Kent, Ohio, 1968.

2420. Furstenberg, F.F., et al. "The Origins of the Female-Headed
Black Family: The Impact of the Urban Experience." Journal of
Interdisciplinary History 6:2 (1975), 211-233.

2421. Fusfeld, Daniel. The Basic Economics of the Urban Racial
Crisis. New York: Holt, Rinehart and Winston, 1973.

2422. Gale, Stephen and David M. Katzman. "Black Communities: A
Program for Interdisciplinary Research." In Harold M. Rose
(ed.) Geography of the Ghetto. Perspectives in Geography, Vol.
II. Dekalb, Illinois: Northern Illinois University Press,
1972, 42-59.

2423. Gallagher, Eugene Francis. Provision for Education Practices
and Facilities in an Era of Urban Renewal. Ph.D. Saint Louis
University, 1963.

2424. Gappert, Gary and Harold M. Rose. The Social Economy of
Cities. Beverly Hills: Sage, 1975.

2425. Gans, Herbert J. "The Ghetto Rebellions and Urban Class
Conflict." Academy of Political Science, Proceedings 29 (July
1968), 42-51.

2426. Gaston, Juanita. The Changing Residential Pattern of Blacks in Battle Creek, Michigan: A Study in Historical Geography. Ph.D. Dissertation, Michigan State University, East Lansing, Michigan, 1977.

2427. George, Paul S. "Colored Town: Miami's Black Community, 1896-1930." Florida Historical Quarterly 56:4 (1978), 3432-447.

2428. Gerlach, Don R. "Black Arson in Albany, New York: November 1973." Journal of Black Studies 7:3 (1977), 301-312.

2429. Gibson, T. "Anti-Negro Riots in Atlanta," Harper's Weekly 50 (October 13, 1906), 1457-1459.

2430. Giese, Vincent. Revolution in the City. Notre Dame, Indiana: Fides Publishers, 1961.

2431. Gilbert, Ben W. Ten Blocks From the United House: Anatomy of the Washington Riots of 1968. New York: Praeger, 1968.

2432. Gilbert, Carol Mary. Correlates of Occupational Goal-Oriented Behaviors and Attitudes Among Urban, Low Income, Black, Adolescent Boys. Ph.D. Thesis, Harvard University, 1975.

2433. Gimlin, Hoyt. New Towns. Washington, D.C.: Editorial Research Reports, November 6, 1968.

2434. Gitelman, Paul Jay. Morale, Self-Concept and Social Integration: A Comparative Study of Black and Jewish Aged, Urban Poor. Ph.D. Rutgers University, the State University of New Jersey, 1976.

2435. Glaser, Daniel. Crime in the City. New York: Harper and Row, 1970.

2436. Glazer, Nathan. "Ghetto Crisis." Encounter 29 (November 1967), 15-22.

2437. Glazer, Nathan. "On 'Opening Up' the Suburbs." Habitat International Land 5:1-2 (1980), 175-80.

2438. Glazer, Nathan. "Race and the Suburbs". U.S. News and World Report (October 10, 1966), 76-78.

2439. Glazer, Nathan. "The Real Task in America's Cities." New Society 11 (March 21, 1968), 406-408.

2440. Glazer, Nathan. "Slums and Ethnicity." In Thomas R. Sherrard (ed.) Social Welfare and Urban Problems. New York: Columbia University Press, 1968, 84-112.

2441. Goering, John M. "Neighborhood Tipping and Racial Transition: A Review of Social Science Evidence." Journal of the American

Institute of Planners 44:1 (1978), 68-78.

2442. Gold, N.N. "The Mismatch of Jobs and Low-Income People in Metropolitan Areas and Its Implications for the Center City Poor." In S.M. Mazie (ed.)Population, Distribution and Policy. Washington, D.C.: Commission on Population Growth and the American Future, Future, Research Reports, 1972, 441-86.

2443. Gold, H.R. and Armstrong, B.K. A Preliminary Study of Interracial Conditions in Chicago. New York: Home Missions Council, 1920.

2444. Goldstein, Gernard. Low Income Youth in Urban Areas: A Critical Review of the Literature. New York: Holt, Rinehart and Winston, 1967.

2445. Goldstein, Rhoda L. (ed.) Black Life and Culture in the United States. New York: Thomas Y. Crowell, 1971.

2446. Gordon, Joan. The Poor in Harlem: Social Functoining in the Underclass. Office of the Mayor, Indepartment Neighorhood Service Center, New York, July 31, 1965.

2447. Graham, Leroy. Baltimore: The Nineteenth Century Black Capital. Washington, D.C.: University Press of America, 1982.

2448. Graham, Todd P. Ethnic Concentrations and Socio-Political Patterns of Syracuse and Rochester, New York, 1946-1962. Master's Thesis, Syracuse University, 1965.

2449. Grant, R.T. The Black Man Comes to the City: A Documentary Account from the Great Migration to the Great Depression, 1915-1930. Chicago: Nelson-Hall, 1972.

2450. Gray, Willia Bowser. Residential Pattern and Associated Socio-Economic Characteristics of Black Populations of Varying City-Suburban Locations Within the San Francisco Area: A Census Based Analysis with Emphasis on Black Suburbanized Populations of 1970. Unpublished D.SW. Dissertation, University of California, Berkeley, 1975.

2451. Graves, J.T. and W.E.B. DuBois. "Tragedy at Atlanta", World To-Day 11 (November 1906), 1169-1175.

2452. Green, Constance McLaughlin. The Secret City: A History of Race Relations in the Nation's Capital. Princeton: Princeton University Press, 1967.

2453. Greene, Lorenzo Johnston. Employment of Negroes in the District of Columbia. Washington, D.C.: Association for the Study of Negro Life and History, 1967.

2454. Greer, Scott and Ann Lennarson Creer, (eds.) Neighborhood and

Ghetto: The Local Area in Large-Scale Society. New York: Basic Books, 1974.

2455. Gregor, A. James and D. Angus McPherson. "Racial Attitudes Among White and Negro Children in Deep-South Standard Metropolitan Area." Journal of Social Psychology 63 (1966), 95-106.

2456. Grier, Eunice. "Factors Hindering Integration in American Urban Areas." Journal of Intergroup Relations 2 (Fall 1961), 293-301.

2457. Grier, Eunice. The Impact of Race on Neighborhood in the Metropolitan Setting. Washington, D.C.: Washington Center for Metropolitan Studies, 1961.

2458. Griffin, Bobby. An Analysis of Journey to Work Patterns of an All-Black Town: A Case of Glenarden, Maryland. M.A. Thesis, University of Cincinnati, Cincinnati, Ohio, 1973.

2459. Grimshaw, Allen D. A Study of Social Violence: Urban Race Riots in the United States. Unpublished Ph.D. Dissertation, University of Pennsylvania, 1959.

2460. Grodzins, Morton. The Metropolitan Area as a Racial Problem. Pittsburgh: University of Pittsburgh Press, 1958.

2461. Grodzins, Morton. "Metropolitan Segregation" Scientific American 198 (October 1957), 33-49.

2462. Gunn, Karen Sue. An Exploratory Analysis of Urban Black Heroin Patterns: The Role of Community Types, Sex Status and Support Systems. Ph.D. Thesis, The University of Michigan, 1979.

2463. Handlin, Oscar. The Newcomers: Negroes and Puerto Ricans in a Changing Metropolis. Cambridge: Harvard University Press, 1959.

2464. "Harlem". Fortune 78 (July 1939), 168-70.

2465. Harmon, John. Cognitions of Cincinnati, Ohio Neighborhoods: The Views of Black and White University Students. M.A. Thesis, University of Cincinnati, Cincinnati, Ohio, 1974.

2466. Harries, Keith D. An Analysis of Inter-Ethnic Variations in Commercial Land-Use in Los Angeles. Ph.D. Dissertation, University of California, Los Angeles, 1969.

2467. Harries, Keith D. "Ethnic Variations in the Los Angeles Business District." Annals of the Association of American Geographers 61:4 (1971), 36-543.

2468. Harries, Keith D. "Population Change Trends in Large U.S.

Metropolitan Areas, 1960-1970: A Review." <u>Journal of Geography</u> 72 (1973), 19-30.

2469. Harrington, Michael. "Harlem Today." <u>Dissent</u> 8 (1961), 371-382.

2470. Harris, Leroy. <u>The Other Side of the Freeway: A Study in the Settlement Pattern of Negroes and Mexican Americans in San Diego, California</u>. Ph.D. Dissertation, Department of Social Work, Carnegie-Mellon University, Pittsburgh, PA, 1974.

2471. Harris, William. "Work and the Family in Black Atlanta, 1880." <u>Journal of Social History</u> 9:3 (1976), 319-330.

2472. Hart, John Fraser. "Functions and Occupation Structures of Cities of the American South." <u>Annals of the Association of American Geographers</u> 45 (1955), 269-286.

2473. Harvey, Diane. The Terri, Augusta's Black Enclave. <u>Richmond County History</u> 5:2 (1973), 60-75.

2474. Harwood, Edwin. "Urbanism as a Way of Negro Life," in William McCord (ed.) <u>Life Styles in the Black Ghetto.</u> New York: Norton, 1969, 14-25.

2475. Hatcher, Richard G. "The Black City Crisis." <u>The Black Scholar</u> 1:6 (April 1970), 54-62.

2476. Hawley, Amos H. and Vincent P. Rock (eds.). <u>Segregation in Residential Areas, Papers on Racial and Socioeconomic Factors in Choice of Housing.</u> Washington, D.C.: National Academy of Sciences, 1973.

2477. Hawley, Langston T. "Negro Employment in the Birmingham Metropolitan Area," in <u>Selected Studies of Negro Employment in the South</u>. Washington, D.C.: National Planning Association, 1955, 100-115.

2478. Haynes, George E. "Conditions Among Negroes in Cities," <u>Annals of the Association of American Geographers</u> 49 (1913), 105-19.

2479. Haynes, George E. "Migration of Negroes into Northern Cities." <u>National Conference Social Work</u> (1917), 494-7.

2480. Haynes, George E. <u>Negro Migration in 1916-17</u>. Washington, D.C.: Government Printing Office, 1919.

2481. Haynes, George E. <u>Negro Newcomers in Detroit</u>. New York: Home Missions Council, 1918.

2482. Heller, Charles and Anthony Redente. "Residential Location and Attitudes Toward Mixed Race Neighborhoods in Kalamazoo,

Michigan." _Journal of Geography_ 72:3 (1973), 15-25.

2483. Henry, Curtis Charles. _The Spatial Interaction of Black Families in Suburban Cities in the Bay Area: A Study of Black Subsystem Linkage._ Ph.D. Thesis, University of California, Berkeley, 1978.

2484. Hepler, Mark Kerby. _Color, Crime and the City,_ unpublished Ph.D. Dissertation, Rice University, 1972.

2485. Hepler, Mark. _Urban Negro Crime._ Unpublished Ph.D. Dissertation, Rice University, 1968.

2486. Hershberg, Theodore, et al. "A Tale of Three Cities: Blacks and Immigrants in Philadelphia: 1850-1880, 1930 and 1970." _The Annals of the American Academy of Political and Social Science_ (January 1969), 55-81.

2487. Hewes, Laurence I. and William Y. Bell. _Intergroup Reltions in San Diego._ San Diego: American Council on Race Relations, 1946.

2488. Hill, Herbert. "Demographic Change and Racial Ghettos: The Crisis of American Cities." _Journal of Urban Law_ 44 (Winter 1966), 231-285.

2489. Hill, Herbert. "Job Crisis in the Urban North," _Crisis_ 72 (November 1965), 565-72.

2490. Hill, Mozell C. "The Metropolis and Juvenile Delinquency Among Negroes," _Journal of Negro Education_ 28 (1959), 277-285.

2491. Hill, Mozell C. "The All-Negro Communities of Oklahoma: The Natural History of a Social Movement." _The Journal of Negro History_ 31 (July 1964), 254-68.

2492. Himes, J.S. "Forty Years of Negro Life in Columbus, Ohio., 1900-1940." _Journal of Negro History_ 27 (April 1942), 25-34.

2493. Himes, J.S. _The Negro Delinquent in Columbus, 1935,_ unpublished Ph.D. Dissertation, Ohio State University, 1938.

2494. Himes, J.S. and Margaret Hamelett. "The Assessment of Adjustment of Aged Negro Women in a Southern City" _Phylon_ 23 (1962), 139-47.

2495. Hirsch, Arnold Richard. _Making the Second Ghetto: Race and Housing in Chicago, 1940-1960._ Ph.D. Thesis, University of Illinois at Chicago Circle, 1978.

2496. Hirsch, Carl. _Primary Group Supports Among A Sample of Elderly Black And White Ethnic Residents Of Urban, Working-Class Neighborhoods._ Ph.D. Thesis, The Pennsylvania State

University, 1979.

2497. Holdemaker, Sally B. The Spatial Patterns of Negroes and White Middle Class: St. Louis, Missouri, 1960. Master's Thesis, Southern Illinois University, Edwardsville, 1971.

2498. Holman, C.W. "Race Riots in Chicago." Outlook 122 (1919), 566-7.

2499. Holmes, Jack D.L. "The Effects of the Memphis Race Riot of 1866," West Tennessee Historical Society Papers 12 (1958), 58-79.

2500. Holmes, Jack D.L. "The Underlying Causes of the Memphis Race Riot of 1866," Tennessee Historical Quarterly 17 (September 1958), 194-221.

2501. Humphrey, N.D. "Race Riots and Detroit Social Agencies," Compass (March 1945), 20-23.

2502. Hunter, Chester L. "Private Integrated Housing in a Moderate Size Northern City." Social Problems 7 (Winter 1959), 195-209.

2503. Hunter, Chester L. "A Research Report on Integrated Housing in a Small Northern City." Journal of Intergroup Relations 3 (Winter 1961-62), 65-79.

2504. Ikemma, W.N. "Revitalizing Inner City Minority Communities," Urbanism Past and Present 4 (1977), 11-18.

2505. Institute of Government and Public Affairs. Los Angeles Riot Study. Los Angeles: University of California, 1967.

2506. Isaacs, Reginald R. "Are Urban Neighborhoods Possible?: Journal of Housing 5 (July 1948), 177-80.

2507. Jackson, Kenneth T. The Ku Klux Klan in the City, 1915-1930. New York: Oxford University Press, 1967.

2508. Jackson, Luther P. "The Free Negroes of Petersburg, Virginia," The Journal of Negro History 12:3 (July 1927), 14-21.

2509. Jackson, T.A. Technical Job Opportunities for Neroes in the Atlanta Metropolitan Area, unpublished Ph.D. Dissertation, University of Tennessee, 1962.

2510. Jacobs, Paul. Prelude to Riot, A View of Urban America from the Bottom. New York: Random House, 1967.

2511. Jakubs, John Francis. Ghetto Dispersal and Suburban Reaction. Ph.D. Thesis, The Ohio State University, 1974.

2512. Jefferson, Richard R. "Negro Employment in St. Louis War

Production," _Opportunity_ 22 (Summer 1944), 116-19.

2513. Jeffress, Philip W. _The Negro in the Urban Transit Industry_.
Philadelphia: University of Pennsylvania Press, 1970.

2514. Johnson, Charles S. "The Black Worker in the City." _Survey_.
(March 1925), 637.

2515. Johnson, Charles S. _The Shadow of the Plantation_. Chicago:
University of Chicago Press, 1966.

2516. Johnson, Charles S. "The Negro Population of Waterbury,
Connecticut." _Opportunity_ (1923), 298-303.

2517. Johnson, Charles S. "Black Workers and the City." _Survey_ 53
(1925), 641.

2518. Johnson, Charles S., et al. _The Negro War Worker in San
Francisco_. San Francisco: San Francisco YWCA, 1944.

2519. Johnson, James Weldon. _Black Manhattan_. New York: Alfred A.
Knopf, 1930.

2520. Johnson, James Weldon. "The Making of Harlem," _Survey_ 53
(1925), 635.

2521. Johnson, Lawrence E. _The Negro Community in Droville,
California._ Master's Thesis, Chicago State College, 1970.

2522. Johnson, Philip A. _Call Me Neighbor, Call Me Friend; the Case
History of the Integration of a Neighborhood on Chicago's South
Side._ Garden City, New York: Doubleday and Company, 1965.

2523. Johnstone, J.W.C. "Youth Gangs and Black Suburbs." _Pacific
Sociological Review_ 24:3 (1981), 355-75.

2524. Jones, Adrian Harold. _A Methodology for Analyzing Urban
Rioting in the United States (1964-1966)_. Washington, D.C.:
unpublished Ph.D. Thesis, The American University, 1972.

2525. Jones, E.D. "Urban Conditions in Harlem." _Outlook_ 109 (1915),
597.

2526. Jones, Eugene Kinckle. "Negro City in New York." _Outlook_ 109
(1915), 597.

2527. Jones, William Henry. _Recreation and Amusement Among Negroes in
Washington, D.C.: A Sociological Analysis of the Negro in An
Urban Environment_. Washington, D.C., 1927.

2528. Jones, William Henry. _The Housing of Negroes in Washington,
D.C.: A Study in Human Ecology._ Washington: Howard University
Press, 1929.

2529. Jordan, Kenneth Allen. The Geography of Consumer Economics Among Black Americans in Oakland: A Cultural Behavioral Perspective, Ph.D. Dissertation, University of California, Berkeley, CA., 1977.

2530. Justice, B. Violence in the City. Fort Worth, Texas: Christian University Press, 1969.

2531. Kantrowitz, Nathan. Ethnic and Racial Segregation in the New York Metropolis: Residential patterns Among White Ethnic Groups, Blacks and Puerto Ricans. New York: Praeger, 1973.

2532. Kantrowitz, Nathan. "Negro and Puerto Rican Populations of New York City in the Twentieth Century." Studies in Urban Geograhy I (1969), 1-20.

2533. Karmin, Monroe W. "Racial Tinderbox: A Federal Study Finds Unrest Among Negroes Rising in Many Cities." Wall Street Journal January 5, 1966.

2534. Katzelson, Ira. Black Men, White Cities: Race, Politics and Migration in the United States. 1969. New York: Oxford University Press, 1973.

2535. Kegan, Frank. Blacktown, U.S.A.. New York: Little, 1971.

2536. Keil, Charles. Urban Blues. Chicago: University of Chicago Press, 1966.

2537. Keller, Suazanne. "The Social World of the Urban Slum Child." American Journal of Orthopsychiatry 33 (October 1963), 823-831.

2538. Kellogg, John. "Negro Urban Clusters in the Postbellum South," Geographical Review (1977), 310-21.

2539. Kendall, Paul L. Westwood, Dayton, Ohio: An Urban Geographic Study of Racial Transition. Master's Thesis, Miami University, 1968.

2540. Kenyon, James B. "Patterns of Residential Integration in the Bicultural Western City." Professional Geographer 28:1 (1976), 40-44.

2541. Kephart, W.M. "Integration of Negroes into the Urban Police Force." Journal of Criminal Law, Criminology and Police Science 45 (September-October 1954), 325-333.

2542. Kephart, W.M. Racial Factors and Urban Law Enforcement. Philadelphia: University of Pennsylvania Press, 1957.

2543. Kerbert, Linda K. "Abolitionists and Amalgamators: The New York City Race Riots of 1834," New York History 48 (January 1967), 28-39.

2544. Killian, Lewis M. and Charles M. Grigg. "Rank Order of Discrimination of Negroes and Whites in a Southern City." Social Forces 39 (March 1961), 235-239.

2545. Killian, Lewis M. and Charles M. Grigg. "Urbanism, Race, and Anomia." American Journal of Sociology 67 (May 1962), 661-665.

2546. King, Charles E. "The Process of Social Stratification Among an Urban Southern Minority Population." Social Forces 41 (May 1953), 352-355.

2547. Kiser, Clyde Vernon. Sea Island to City: A Study of St. Helena Islanders in Harlem and Other Urban Centers. New York: Columbia University Press, 1932.

2548. Kleiner, R.J. and Henry Louis Taylor. Social Status and Aspirations in Philadelphia's Negro Population. New York: Bureau of Publications, Teachers College, Columbia University, 1960.

2549. Klopf, Gordon J. and Israel A. Luster (eds.). Integrating the Urban School. New York: Columbia University Teachers College Press, 1968.

2550. Knapp, Robert B. Social Integration in Urban Communities: A Guide for Educational Planning. New York: Bureau of Publications, Teachers College, Columbia University, 1960.

2551. Knight, Charles Louis. Negro Housing in Certain Viriginia Cities. Richmond, Va.: W. Byrd, 1927.

2552. Kraft, John F. Attitude of Negroes in Various Cities. New York, 1966.

2553. Kramer, John and Walter Ingo. "Politics in an All-Negro City." Urban Affairs Quarterly 3 (September 1968), 66-87.

2554. Krantz, Sheldon and William D. Kramer. "The Urban Crisis and Crime," Boston University Law Review 50 (Summer 1970), 343-359.

2555. Kristol, Irving. "The Negro Today is Like the Immigrant Yesterday," New York Times Magazine (September 11, 1966). 1-10.

2556. Lachman, Sheldon and Benjamin Singer. The Detroit Riot of July 1967. Detroit: Behavioral Research Institute, 1968.

2557. Ladner, Joyce and Walter W. Stafford. "Black Repression in the Cities." The Black Scholar 1:6 (April 1970), 38-52.

2558. Lamb, Richard. Growth Characteristics of Urban Places with Population 10,000-50,000, 1960-1970. Chicago: University of

Chicago, Center for Urban Studies, 1974.

2559. Lamb, Richard. Metropolitan Impacts on Rural America. Chicago: Department of Geography, The University of Chicago, 1975.

2560. Lambing, Mary L. Brooks. A Study of Retired Older Negroes in an Urban Setting. Ph.D. Thesis, The University of Florida, 1970.

2561. Landes, Ruth. "Negro Jews in Harlem." Jewish Journal of Sociology (December 1967), 175-190.

2562. Lane, Roger. Policing the City, Boston 1822-1885. Cambridge, Massachusetts: Harvard University Press, 1967.

2563. Lane, Winthrop. "Ambushed in the City: The Grim Side of Harlem." Survey 53 (1925), 692.

2564. Lasker, Bruno. "The Negro in Detroit." Survey 58: (1927), 72-73.

2565. Laurenti, Luigi. Property Values and Race: Studies in Seven Cities. Berkeley: University of California Press, 1960.

2566. Lee, Elliot D. "Will We Lose Harlem?" Black Enterprise 11:11 (1981), 191-98.

2567. Lee, George. "Negroes in a Medium-Sized Metropolis Pennsylvania - A Case Study." Journal of Negro Education 37 (Fall 1968), 397-400.

2568. Leinward, Gerald. The Negro in the City. New York: Washington Square Press, 1968.

2569. Leonard, O. "East St. Louis Pogrom," Survey 38 (July 14, 1917), 331-333.

2570. Leonard, O. and Washington B. Forrester. "Welcoming Southern Negroes: East St. Louis and Detroit: A Contrast," Survey 38 (1917), 331-334.

2571. Lerner, Max. "The Negro American and His City: Person in Place in Culture." Daedalus 97 (Fall 1968), 1390-1408.

2572. Levine, Marvin J. The Untapped Human Resource: The Urban Negro and Employment Equality. Morristown, New Jersey: General Learning Press, 1972.

2573. Lewis, Hylan. Blackways of Kent. Chapel Hill, North Carolina: University of North Carolina Press, 1955.

2574. Lewis, Hylan and Hill Mozell. "Desegregation, Integration, and the Negro Community," Annals of the American Academy of Political and Social Science 24 (March 1956), 116-23.

2575. Lewis, Terry E. Frenchtown: A Geographic Survey of an All-Negro Business District in Tallahassee, Florida. M.A. Thesis, Florida State University, Tallahassee, Florida, 1960.

2576. Lewis, Walter B. Problems of the Negro in the City. Washington, D.C.: U.S. Department of Housing and Urban Development, 1968.

2577. Ley, David Frederick. The Black Inner City as Frontier Outpost: Images and Behavior of a Philadelphia Neighborhood. Ph.D. Dissertation, The Pennsylvania State University, University Park, PA., 1972.

2578. Ley, David Frederick. The Black Inner City as Frontier Outpot: Images and Behavior of a Philadelphia Neighborhood. Washington, D.C.: Association of American Geographers, 1974.

2579. Lieberson, Stanley. Ethnic Patterns in American Cities. New York: The Free Press, 1963.

2580. Lieberson, Stanley. "Suburbs and Ethnic Residential Patterns." American Journal of Sociology 22 (May 1962), 673-681.

2581. Lieham, Elliott. Tally's Corner: A Study of Negro Streetcorner Men. Boston: Little, Brown, 1967.

2582. Lightfoot, Robert M. Negro Crime in a Small Urban Community. Charlottesville, Virginia: University of Virginia, 1934.

2583. Lincoln, James H. The Anatomy of a Riot: A Detroit Judge's Report. New York: McGraw-Hill, 1968.

2584. Linsay, Arnett G. "The Economic Conditions of the Negroes of New York Prior to 1861," Journal of Negro History 6:2 (April 1921), 190-99.

2585. Locke, Hubert G. The Detroit Riot of 1967. Detroit: Wayne State University Press, 1969.

2586. Long, Larry H. "How the Racial Composition of Cities Changes." Land Economics 41:3 (August 1975), 258-67.

2587. Lowe, Jeanne R. Cities in a Race with Time: Progress and Poverty in America's Renewing Cities. New York: Random House, 1967.

2588. Lowman, Ruth M. Delinquency Among Negroes in Pittsburgh, unpublished M.A. Thesis, Carnegie Institute of Technology, 1924.

2589. Lowry, Ira S. Migration and Metropolitan Growth: Two Analytical Models. San Francisco: Chandler Publishing Co., 1966.

2590. Lubeck, Dennis Russell. University City: A Suburban Community's Response to Civil Rights, 1959-1970. Ph.D. Thesis, Saint Louis University, 1978.

2591. Lupsha, Peter A. "On Theories of Urban Violence," Urban Affairs Quarterly 4 (March 1969), 273-296.

2592. Lyle, Jerolyn R. Differences in the Occupational Standing of Negroes Among Industries and Cities, unpublished Ph.D. Dissertation, University of Maryland, 1970.

2593. Lyles, Lionel D. An Historical-Urban Geographical Analysis of Black Neighborhood Development in Denver, 1860-1970. Ph.D. Dissertation, University of Colorado, Boulder, CO., 1977.

2594. Lynch, Hollis R. The Black Urban Condition. New York: Thomas Y. Crowell, 1973.

2595. Manly, A.L. "Where Negroes Live in Philadelphia," Opportunity (May 1923), 10.

2596. Manoni, Mary. Bedford-Stuyvesant: The Anatomy of a Central City Community. New York: Quadrangle, 1973.

2597. Marge, Gail B. A Functional Analysis of Land Use Patterns in the Negro Shopping Areas of Raleigh and Charlotte, North Carolina. Master's Thesis, University of North Carolina, 1969.

2598. Mark, Mary Louise. Negroes in Columbus. Columbus, Ohio. State University Studies, Graduate School Series in Social Science No. 2, Ohio State University Press, 1928.

2599. Marshall, Thurgood. "The Gestapo in Detroit," Crisis (August 1943), 232-33.

2600. Martineau, William Henry. Patterns of Social Participation and a Sense of Powerlessness Among Urban Blacks. Ph.D. Thesis, University of Notre Dame, 1971.

2601. Marston, Wilfred George. Population Redistribution and Socioeconomic Differentiation Within Negro Areas of American Cities: A Comparative Analysis. Unpublished Ph.D. Dissertation, University of Washington, 1966.

2602. Massa, Ann. "Black Women in the 'White City'." Journal of American Studies 8:3 (1974), 319-337.

2603. Mason, Elliott James. An Exploratory Teacher Attitude Study of Social Issues Associated with the Development of Positive

Ethnic Identity in Black Inner-City Youth. Ph.D. Thesis, California School of Professional Psychology, Los Angeles, 1974.

2604. Masotti, Louis H. and Donald R. Bowen, (eds.) *Riots and Rebellion Civil Violence in the Urban Community.* Beverly Hills: Sage, 1968.

2605. Massotti, Louis H. and Jerome R. Corsi. *Shoot-Out in Cleveland: Black Militants and the Police, July 23, 1968.* New York: Praeger, 1969.

2606. Maxey, Alva. "The Block Club Movement in Chicago." *Phylon* 18 (Summer 1957), 124-131.

2607. Maynard, Joan. "Black Urban Culture." *Historic Preservation* 25:1 (1973), 28-30.

2608. Mayor's Commission on Conditions in Harlem. *The Negro in Harlem: A Report on Social and Economic Conditions Responsible for the Outbreak of March 19, 1935.* New York: Municipal Archives, unpublished, 1936.

2609. McCague, James. *The Second Rebellion: The Story of the New York City Draft Riots of 1863.* New York: Dial, 1968.

2610. McCord, William and John Howard. "Negro Opinions in Three Riot Cities". *American Behavioral Scientist* 11 (March 1968), 24-27.

2611. McDaniel, Paula and Nicholas Babchuk. "Negro Conceptions of White People in a Northeastern City." *Phylon* 21 (Spring 1960), 19.

2612. McElroy, Jerome L. and Larry D. Singell. "Riot and Nonriot Cities, An Examination of Structural Contours," *Urban Affairs Quarterly* 8 (March 1973), 281-302.

2613. McKay, Claude. *Harlem: Negro Metropolis.* New York: Dutton, 1940.

2614. McMillen, Thomas Leonard. *The Urban Riot: Dimensions of Empirical Theory,* unpublished Ph.D. Dissertation, University of Kansas, 1970.

2615. McQueen, Albert James. *A Study of Anomie Among Lower Class Negro Migrants.* Ph.D. Thesis, The University of Michigan, 1959.

2616. Meade, A. Carl. *The Residential Segregation of Population Characteristics in the Atlanta Metrpolitan Statistical Area: 1960.* Unpublished Ph.D. Dissertation. The University of Tennessee, 1971.

2617. Meadow, Kathryn P. "Negro-White Differences Among Newcomers to a Transitional Urban Area," Journal of Intergroup Relations 3 (1962), 320-330.

2618. Meier, August and David Lewis. "History of the Negro Upper Class in Atlanta, Georgia, 1890-1958," Journal of Negro Education (Spring 1959), 300-310..

2619. Mensah, Anthony Jacob. Social Commitment: A Study to Determine An Effective Participation for Urban Universities in Poverty Programs in America's Turbulent Cities, Special Reference to the people of Milwaukee's Inner City-North-The Negro Community. ED.D. Thesis, Marquette University, 1968.

2620. Meyer, David R. "Classification of SMSA's Based Upon Characteristics of Their Non-White Populations." In Brian J.L. Berry (ed.) Classification of Cities: New Methods of Evolving Uses. New York: International City Managers Association and Resources for the Future, 1971.

2621. Meyer, Douglas K. The Changing Negro Residential Patterns in Lansing, Michigan, 1850-1969. Ph.D. Dissertation, Michigan State University, 1970.

2622. Meyer, J.R., et al. "Race and the Urban Transportation Problems." The Urban Transportation Problem. Cambridge, Massachusetts: Harvard University Press, 1965, 145-167.

2623. Meyer, Philip. "Miami Negroes. A Study in Depth." Miami Herald (1960), 50-55.

2624. Meyer, Philip. A Survey of Attitudes of Detroit Negroes after the Riot of 1967. Detroit, Michigan: Detroit Urban League, 1969.

2625. Meyerson, Martin, et al. Housing, People and Cities. New York: McGraw-Hill, 1962.

2626. Michigan, State of. Governor's Committee to Investigate Riot Occuring in Detroit, June 21, 1943, Final Report. Lansing, Michigan: August 11, 1943.

2627. Midura, Edmund M. (ed.). Blacks and Whites: The Urban Communication Crisis. Washington, D.C.: Acropolis, 1971.

2628. Miles, Norman Kenneth. Home at Last, Urbanization of Black Migrants in Detroit, 1916-1929. Ph.D. Thesis, The University of Michigan, 1978.

2629. Miller, Brenda Kaye. Racial Change in an Urban Residential Area: A Geographical Analysis of Wilkinsburg, Pennsylvania. Unpublished Ph.D. Dissertation. University of Pittsburgh, 1979.

2630. Miller, Kelly. "The City Negro." Workman 31 (1902), 217.

2631. Miller, M. Sammy. "Slavery in An Urban Area-District of Columbia." Negro History Bulletin 37:5 (1974), 293-295.

2632. Mincieli, Michael. "New York City: Why Not Riot?" New City 6 (May 1968), 9-14.

2633. Minor, Richard C. The Negro in Columbus, Ohio. Columbus: Ohio State University, 1937.

2634. Molotch, Harvey. Managed Integration: Dilemmas of Doing Good in the City. Berkeley: University of California, 1972.

2635. Montesano, Philip M. "San Francisco Black Churches in the Early 1860's: Political Pressure Group." California History Quarterly 52:2 (1973), 145-152.

2636. Moore, Mordean T. The Mental Health Problems and Treatment of Black Women In An Urban Community Mental Health Center. Ph.D. Thesis, Brandeis University, The F. Heller Graduate School for Advanced Studies in Social Welfare, 1979.

2637. Moore, Maurice and James McKeown. A Study of Integrated Living in Chicago. Chicago: Community and Family Study Center of the University of Chicago, 1968.

2638. Moore, William Franklin. Status of the Negro in Cleveland. Ph.D. Thesis, The Ohio State University, 1953.

2639. Mossell, Sadie Tanner. "Standard of Living Among 100 Negro Migrant Families in Philadelphia." Annals American Academy (1921), 173-218.

2640. Mottl, Tahi Lani. Social Conflict and Social Movements: An Exploratory Study of the Black Community of Boston Attempting to Change the Boston Public Schools. Ph.D. Thesis, Brandeis University, 1976.

2641. Mugge, Robert. Negro Migrants in Atlanta. University of Chicago, 1957.

2642. Nash, Roderick W. "The Christiana Riot: An Evaluation of Its National Significance," Journal of the Lancaster County Historical Society 65 (Spring 1961), 65-91.

2643. Nathan, Winfred B. Health Conditions in North Harlem 1923-1927. Social Research Series No. 2. New York: National Tuberculosis Association, 1932.

2644. National Association of Social Workers and Washington Center for Metropolitan Studies. The Public Welfare Crisis in the Nation's Capital, A Call to the Conscience of the Community.

Washington, D.C., 1963.

2645. National Urban League. Unemployment Among Negroes. Data on 25 Industrial Cities. New York: National Urban League, 1930.

2646. Needham, Maurice d'Arlan. Negro Orleanian: Status and Stake in a City's Economy and Housing. New Orleans: Tulane Publications, 1962.

2647. The Negro and the City. New York: Time-Life Books, 1968.

2648. The Negro in Chicago: A Study of Race Relations and a Race Riot. Chicago: University of Chicago Press, 1922.

2649. "The Negro in San Francisco," San Francisco Chronicle (November 6, 1950), 4-8.

2650. "Negro Segregation adopted by St. Louis." Survey 35:8 (1916), 694.

2651. "Negro Segregation in Cities." Chautauquan 62 (1911), 11-13.

2652. "Negro Segregation in St. Louis." Literary Digest 52 (1916), 702.

2653. Newman, Bernard J. Housing in the City Negro. Philadelphia: The Whittier Center, 1915.

2654. Newman, Dorothy K. "The Negro's Journey to the City - Part I." Monthly Labor Review 88 (May 1965), 502-507.

2655. Nichols, Woodrow Wilson. "The Evolution of an All-Black Town: The Case Study of Roosevelt City, Alabama?" Professional Geographer 26:3 (1974), 298-302.

2656. Nichols, Woodrow Wilson. A Spatio-Perspective Analysis of the Effect of the Santa Monica and Simi Valley Freeways on Two Selected Black Residential Areas in Los Angeles County. Ph.D. Dissertation, University of California at Los Angeles, 1973.

2657. Niederhoffer, Arthur. Behind the Shield: The Police in Urban Society. New York: Doubleday, 1967.

2658. Noble, M.W. "Negroes in Washington, D.C." Chautauquan 4 (1892), 183.

2659. Noel, Donald L. Correlates of Anti-White Prejudice: Attitude of Negroes in Four American Cities. Unpublished Ph.D. Thesis, Cornell University, 1961.

2660. Nordsiek, Evelyn M. The Residential Location and Mobility of Blacks in Indianapolis, 1850-1880. M.A. Thesis, University of Maryland, College Park, MD., 1975.

2661. Northwood, L.K. Urban Desegregation: Negro Pioneers and Their White Neighbors. Seattle: University of Washington, 1965.

2662. Northwood, L.K. and Ernest A.T. Barth. Urban Desegregation: Negro Pioneers and Their White Neighbors. Seattle: University of Washington Press, 1965.

2663. Oberschall, Anthony. "The Los Angeles Riot of August 1965," Social Problems 15 (Winter 1968), 322-341.

2664. O'Connor, Michael J. The Measurement and Significance of Racial Residential Barriers in Atlanta, 1890-1970. Department of Geography, University of Georgia, Athens, GA., 1977.

2665. Omari, Thompson P. Urban Adjustment of Rural Southern Negro Migrants in Beloit, Wisconsin. University of Wisconsin, 1955.

2666. Orlansky, Harold. "The Harlem Riot: A Study in Mass Frustration." Social Analysis (1943), 5.

2667. Osborn, Donald D. Negro Employment in St. Louis, 1966, Carbondale: Southern Illinois University Press, 1968.

2668. Oskison, J. "Negroes in the Cities of the Nation." Nation 81 (1905), 273.

2669. Osofsky, Gilbert. Harlem: The Making of a Ghetto. New York: Harper Torchbooks, 1966.

2670. Ottley, Roi and William J. Weatherby, (eds.) The Negro in New York, An Informal Social History. New York: Oceana Publications, 1967.

2671. Paaswell, R.E. and M. Izadi. Mobility of Inner City Residents, Department of Civil Engineering, State University of New York at Buffalo, 1920.

2672. Palmer, E.N. "Discrimination in Urban Employment," American Journal of Sociology 52 (January 1947), 357-61.

2673. Palmieri, Victor H. Hard Facts About the Future of Our Cities, Los Angeles County Commission on Human Relations, November 1965.

2674. Palmieri, Victor H., et al. Race and City. Washington, D.C.: Center for the Study of Democratic Institutions, January-February, 1967.

2675. Parker, Russell D. "The Black Community in a Company Town: Alcoa, Tennessee, 1919-1939." Tennessee Historical Quarterly 37:2 (1978), 203-221.

2676. Parker, Seymour and Robert Kleiner. Mental Illness in the

Urban Negro Community. New York: The Free Press, 1966.

2677. Parris, Guichard and Lester Brooks. Blacks in the City: A History of the Urban League. New York: Little, 1971.

2678. Patterson, William L. (ed.) We Charge Genocide: The Crime of Government Against the Negro People. New York: International Publishers, 1970.

2679. Perlman, Laura. "Black Employment in Houston," Manpower 3 (May 1971), 25-29.

2680. Perry, Welhelmina Elaine. The Urban Negro with Special Reference to The Universalism - Particularism Pattern Variable. Ph.D. Thesis, The University of Texas at Austin, 1967.

2681. Pettigrew, Thomas F. "Negro American Personality: Why Isn't More Known?" Journal of Social Issues 20 (1964), 4-23.

2682. Pettigrew, Thomas F. "Racial Issues in Urban America," in Bernard J. Frieden and William W. Wash (eds.). Shaping an Urban Future. Cambridge, Massachusetts: MIT Press, 1966, 47-94.

2683. Pettyjohn, Leonard. Changing Structures of Selected Retail Activities in a Racially Changing Neighborhood. M.S. Thesis, University of Wisconsin of Milwaukee, Milwaukee, WI., 1967.

2684. Pettyjohn, Leonard F. Factorial Ecology of the Los Angeles - Long Beach Black Population. Unpublished Ph.D. Dissertation. The University of Wisconsin, Milwaukee, 1976.

2685. Piven, Francis and Richard Howard. "Black Control of Cities," The New Republic (October 27, 1967), 19-21.

2686. Piven, Francis and Richard Howard. "The Case Against Urban Desegregation: Although Efforts at Integration Have Produced Significant Gains in Some Areas, They Have Worked Against the Interests of Urban Negro Poor in Housing and Education," Social Work 12 (January 1967), 12-21.

2687. Pollack, Neuman F. The Impact of Racial Composition on Urban Policies: The Linkages Between Environment and Policy Commitments from 1950 to 1970. Ph.D. Thesis, The Florida State University, 1974.

2688. Porter, William A. Analysis of the Residential Structure of Underprivileged Black Neighborhoods: A Case of Manhattan, Kansas. M.A. Thesis, Kansas State University, Manhattan, KS., 1973.

2689. Powe, Alphonso S. The Role of Negro Pressure Groups in Interracial Integration in Durham City, North Carolina. New

York University, 1954.

2690. Pred, Allan. "Business Thoroughfares as Expressions of Urban Negro Culture." Economic Geography 39 (July 1963), 217-233.

2691. Price, Daniel. "Urbanization of the Blacks," Milbank Memorial Fund Quarterly 48 (April 1963), 217-230.

2692. Price, Thomas A. Negro Store-Front Churches in San Francisco: A Study of Their Distribution in Selected Neighborhoods. M.A. Thesis, San Francisco State College, San Francisco, CA., 1968.

2693. Provine, Dorothy. "The Economic Position of Free Blacks in the District of Columbia, 1800-1860." Journal of Negro History 58:1 (1973), 61-72.

2694. Pruitt, Shirley. "Ethnic and Racial Composition of Selected Cleveland Neighborhoods." Social Science 43 (June 1968), 160-174.

2695. Radford, J.P. Patterns of Nonwhite Segregation in Washington, D.C. in the Late Nineteenth Century. M.A. Thesis, University of Maryland, College Park, MD., 1967.

2696. Ragland, John Marshall. "The Negro in Detroit." Southern Workman 53 (1923), 534-540.

2697. Raine, Walter J. Los Angeles Riot Study: The Ghetto Merchant Survey. Los Angeles: Institute of Government and Public Affairs, 1967.

2698. Ransom, Robert Morgan. The Effects of Race and Data Collection Techniques on the Response Rates of Inner-City Residents. Ph.D. 1979 The Ohio State University, 1979.

2699. Rauch, Delores. Impact of Population Changes in the Central Area of Milwaukee upon Catholic Parochial Schools, 1940-1970. Master's Thesis, University of Wisconsin, Milwaukee, 1968.

2700. Raymond, W.W. "The Negro in New Brunswick," Neith I:1 (February 1903), 1-10.

2701. Reichard, Maximilian. "Black and White on the Urban Frontier, The St. Louis Community in Transition, 1800-1830." Missouri Historical Society Bulletin 33:1 (1976), 3-17.

2702. Reid, Ira DeA. "Mirrors of Harlem-Investigations and Problems of America's Largest Colored Community." Journal of Social Issues 5 (1927), 628-634.

2703. Reid, John D. "Black Urbanization of the South." Phylon 35:3 (1974), 259-267.

2704. Rex, John and Robert Moore. Race, Community and Conflict: A Study of Sparkbrook. New York: Oxford Press, 1959.

2705. Ridley, F.R. "The Negro in Boston". Our Boston 3 (1927), 15-20.

2706. Ritter, Frederic A. "Toward a Geography of the Negro in the City." Journal of Negro Geography 70 (March 1971), 150-56.

2707. Robb, Frederick H. (ed.) The Negro in Chicago 1879-1927, Intercollegian Wonder Book. Chicago: Washington Intercollegiate Club of Chicago, 1927.

2708. Robins, Lee N., et al. "Drinking Behavior of Young Urban Negro Men," Quarterly Journal of Studies on Alcohol 29 (September 1968), 657-684.

2709. Robinson, Leonard. Negro Street Society: A Study of Racial Adjustment in Two Southern Urban Communities. Altheus: Ohio State University, 1950.

2710. Robinson, Welford C. Race and Spatial Interaction Patterns in Baltimore City. Ph.D. Dissertation, Rutgers University, New Brunswick, NJ., 1973.

2711. Roof, W.C. "Southern Birth and Racial Residential Segregation: The Case of Northern Cities," American Journal of Sociology 86 (1980): 350-358.

2712. Rose, Harold. "The All-Black Town: Suburban Prototype or Urban Slum?" In People and Politics in Urban Society. Beverly Hills: Sage, 1972, 397-431.

2713. Rose, Harold. "The All-Negro Town: Its Evolution and Function." Geographical Review. 55 (1965), 362-381.

2714. Rose, Harold. The Black Ghetto: A Spatial Perspective. New York: McGraw-Hill, 1973.

2715. Roseman, Curtis C. and Henry W. Bullamore. "Factorial Ecologies of Urban Black Communities." In Harold M. Rose (ed.) Geography of the Ghetto, Perspectives in Geography. Vol. II. Dekalb, Illinois: Northern Illinois University Press, 1972.

2716. Roseman, Curtis C. and Prentice L. Knight. "Residential Environment and Migration Behavior of Urban Blacks." Professional Geographer. 27:2 (1975), 160-165.

2717. Rudwick, Elliott M. Race Riot at East St. Louis, July 2, 1917. Carbondale: Southern Illinois University Press, 1964.

2718. Sagay, Anirejuoritse. An Inquiry into the Economic-Demographic Causes of Black Poverty in the Urban Southeast of the United

States. Ph.D. Thesis, University of Pittsburgh, 1975.

2719. Salter, Paul S. and Robert C. Mings. "A Geographical Aspect of the 1968 Miami Racial Disturbances: A Preliminary Investigation." The Professional Geographer 21 (May 1969), 79-86.

2720. Sanders, Ralph S. Spatial Trends in Age Structure Changes within the Cleveland Ghetto: 1940-1965. Master's Thesis, Pennsylvania State University, 1968.

2721. Sanders, Ralph and John S. Adams. "Age Structure in Expanding Ghetto-Space; Cleveland, Ohio, 1940-1965." Southeastern Geographer 11 (November 1971), 121-32.

2722. Scheiner, Seth M. Negro Mecca: A History of the Negro in New York City, 1865-1920. New York: New York University Press, 1965.

2723. Schieber, Sylvester Joseph. An Analysis of Child Care Utilization in a Black, Low Income, Urban Environment. Ph.D. Thesis, University of Notre Dame, 1974.

2724. Schietinger, E.F. "Racial Succession and Changing Property Values in Residential Chicago." in E.W. Burgess and D.J. Bogue (eds.) Contributions to Urban Sociology. Chicago: University of Chicago Press, 1964, 80-90.

2725. Schmid, Calvn F. and Wayne W. McVey. Growth and Distribution of Minority Races in Seattle, Washington. Seattle: Seattle Public Schools, 1964.

2726. Schnore, Leo F. Class and Race in Cities and Suburbs. Chicago: Markham Publishing Company, 1972.

2727. Schnore, Leo F. "Social Class Segregation Among Non-Whites in Metropolitan Centers." Demography II (1965), 126-33.

2728. Schnore, Leo F. and Harry Sharp. "Racial Changes in Metropolitan Areas, 1950-1960." Social Forces 41 (March 1963), 247-53.

2729. Schnore, Leo F. and Philip C. Evenson. "Segregation in Southern Cities." American Journal of Sociology 72 (July 1966), 58-67.

2730. Schuler, Edgar A. "The Houston Race Riot, 1917," Journal of Negro History 29 (July 1944), 300-338.

2731. Schussheim, Morton J. The Modest Commitment to Cities. Lexington, Massachussetts: D.C. Heath and Company, 1974.

2732. Schweninger, Loren. "The Free-Slave Phenomenon: James P.

Thomas and the Black Community in Ante-Bellum Nashville."
Civil War History 22:4 (1976), 293–307.

2733. Scott, Estelle H. _Occupational Changes Among Negroes in
Chicago_. Chicago: Works Projects Administration, 1939.

2734. Sears, David O. and T.M. Tomlinson. "Riot Ideology in Los
Angeles: A Study of Negro Attitudes." _Social Science Quarterly_
49 (December 1968), 485–603.

2735. Sears, David O. and John B. McConaughy. "Participation in The
Los Angeles Riot," _Social Problems_ 17 (Summer 1969), 3–20.

2736. Sears, David O. and John B. McConaughy. _Politics of Violence:
The Watts Riot._ Boston: Houghton Mifflin, 1972.

2737. Seelbach, Wayne Clement. _Filial Responsibility and Morale
Among Elderly Black and White Urbanites: A Normative and
Behavioral Analysis._ (Ph.D. Thesis, The Pennsylvania State
University, 1976.

2738. "Segregation of the White and Negro Races in Cities: Types of
Ordinances." _South Atlantic Quarterly_ 13 (1914), 1–18.

2739. "Segregation Ordinances Prohibiting Acquisition of Residence
Property by Negroes or White Respectively in Certain Blocks of
Cities." _Central Law_ 1:85 (1911), 422–3.

2740. Seman, Paul. _Structure and Spatial Distribution of Black-Owned
Businesses in Columbia, South Carolina, 1900–1976._ M.A.
Thesis, University of South Carolina, Columbia, South Carolina,
1977.

2741. Shannon, Lyle W. and Magdaline Shannon. _Minority Migrants in
the Urban Community: Mexican American and Negro Adjustment to
Industrial Society._ Beverly Hills: Sage, 1973.

2742. Shapiro, Fred G. and James W. Sullivan. _Race Riot New York._
New York: Crowell, 1964.

2743. Sharp, Harry and Leo F. Schnore. "The Changing Color
Composition of Metropolitan Areas." _Land Economics_ 28 (May
1962), 169–85.

2744. Sherman, Eugene Garfield. _Urbanization and Florida's Negro
Population: A Case Study._ Ph.D. Thesis, Purdue University,
1968.

2745. Sherman, Richard B. _The Negro and the City._ Englewood Cliffs,
New Jersey: Prentice-Hall, 1970.

2746. Shogan, Robert and Tom Craig. _The Detroit Race Riot._
Philadelphia: Chilton Books, 1964.

2747. Silberman, Charles. Crisis in Black and White. New York: Vantage Books, 1964.

2748. Silberman, Charles. "The City and the Negro." Fortune 65 (March 1962), 88.

2749. Silberman, Charles E. "The Deepening Crisis in Metropolis," Journal of Intergroup Relations 4 (Summer 1965), 119-131.

2750. Singell, Larry D. "The Socio-Economic Causes of the Recent Urban Disorders: Some Empirical Evidence," Land Ecomonics 47 (August 1971), 225-234.

2751. Sitkoff, Harvard. "The Detroit Race Riot of 1943," Michigan History 53 (Fall 1969), 183-194.

2752. Slattery, J.R. "Negroes in Baltimore". Catholic World 66 (1898), 519.

2753. Smith, Barton A. and Carol O. Wilson. An Analysis of the Concept and Use of Segregation Indices and Their Implications for Public Policy, U.S. Department of Housing and Urban Development, Washington, D.C., 1977.

2754. Smith, Paul Alan. Negro Settlement in Los Angeles, California, 1890-1930. M.A. Thesis, California State University of Northridge, Northridge, CA., 1973.

2755. Smith, Ralph V., et al. Community Interaction and Racial Interaction in the Detroit Area: An Ecological Analysis. Ypsilanti, Michigan: Eastern Michigan University, 1967.

2756. Sneed, H.P. "Negroes in New Orleans." Nation 78:3 (1904), 30.

2757. Snyder, Roger. An Analysis of Travel Patterns from Selected Neighborhoods in Detroit. Master's Thesis, Wayne State University, 1970.

2758. Somers, Dale A. "Black and White in New Orleans: A Study in Urban Race Relations, 1865-1900." Journal of Southern History 40:1 (1974), 19-42.

2759. Sonenblum, Sidney, et al. Local Government Program Budgeting for Urban Health Care Services. Los Angeles: University of California, 1973.

2760. Sorenson, Annemette, et al. "Indexes of Racial Rsidential Segregation for 109 Cities in the United States, 1940 to 1970." Sociological Focus (April 1975): 125-42.

2761. Spear, Allan H. Black Chicago: The Making of a Negro Ghetto, 1890-1920. Chicago: University of Chicago Press, 1967.

2762. Speed, J. Gilmer. "The Negro in New York." Harp 44 (1900), 249-50.

2763. Stavisky, L.P. "Industrialism in Ante Bellum Charleston," Journal of Negro History 36:3 (July 1951), 302-22.

2764. Stegman, Michael A. Housing Investment in the Inner-City: The Dynamics of Decline; A Study of Baltimore, Maryland, 1968-1970. Cambridge, Massachusetts: MIT Press, 1972.

2765. Stephenson, Gilbert Thomas. "Segregation of the White and Negro Races in Cities by Legislation." National Municipal Review 3 (1914), 496-504.

2766. Sternlieb, George and James Hughes. "The Changing Demography of The Central City," Scientific American 243 (August 1980), 48-53.

2767. Sternlieb, George and Robert W. Lake. "Aging Suburbs and Black Home Ownership." Annals of the American Academy of Political and Social Science 422 (November, 1975), 105-17.

2768. Stevens, Stanley Carlson. The Urban Racial Border: Chicago 1960. Ph.D. Thesis, University of Illinois at Urbana-Champaign, 1972.

2769. Straits, Bruce C. "Residential Movements Among Negroes and Whites in Chicago." Social Service Quarterly 49 (December 1968), 573-592.

2770. Strickland, Arvah E. History of the Chicago Urban League. Urbana: University of Illinois Press, 1966.

2771. Strecher, Victor G. Police- Community Relations, Urban Riots, and the Quality of Life in Cities. Ph.D. Thesis, Washington University, 1968.

2772. "Study Names of Riot-Prone Cities." Public Management 50 (January 1968), 2-14.

2773. Sullivan, Margaret Lo Piccolo. St. Louis Ethnic Neighborhoods, 1850-1930: An Introduction. Missouri Historical Society Bulletin 33:2 (1977), 64-76.

2774. Sumka, Howard J. "Racial Segregation in Small North Carolina Cities." Southeastern Geographer 17:1 (1977), 58-75.

2775. Swados, Harvey. When Black and White Live Together, in Rockdale Village, New York City. New York: 1966.

2776. Taeuber, Conrad. "The Growth of the Black Metropolitan Population." In: Papers on the Demography of Black Americans. Atlanta, Georgia: Atlanta University. W.E.B. Dubios Institute for the Study of the American Black, 1974, 30-40.

2777. Taeuber, Karl E. and Alma F. Taeuber. Negroes in Cities: Residential Segregation and Neighborhood Change. Chicago: Aldine, 1965.

2778. Taeuber, Karl E. and Alma F. Taeuber. "White Migration and Socioeconomic Differences Between Cities and Suburbs." American Sociological Review 29 (October 1964), 1-20.

2779. Tanganyi, Z. Review of Blacks in Suburbs by Thomas A. Clark. Annals of Regional Science 16:1 (1982), 96-97.

2780. Taylor, Henry Louis. The Building of a Black Industrial Suburb: The Lincoln Heights, Ohio Story. Ph.D. Thesis, State University of New York at Buffalo, 1979.

2781. Thernstrom, Stephen. The Other Bostonians: Poverty and Progress in the American Metropolis. Cambridge, Massachusetts: Harvard University Press, 1973.

2782. "Thirty-four Percent Increase in Suburban Black Tied to Incomes and New Laws." New York Times 3 (December, 1978).

2783. Thomas, Gerald Eugene. Hope Versus No Hope: A Pivotal Question in Adult Development for the Afro-American In The Urban North. Ph.D. Thesis, The University of Wisconsin-Madison, 1974.

2784. Thomas, Herbert A. "Victims of Circumstance: Negroes in a Southern Town, 1865-1880." Register of the Kentucky Historical Society 71:3 (1973), 253-271.

2785. Thomas, William J. "American's Changing Suburbans". Editorial Research Report (August 17, 1979), 583-600.

2786. Todd, William J. Factor Analytic Black-White Polarization in Milwaukee, 1950-1970. M.A. Thesis, Indiana State University, Terre Haute, Indiana, 1972.

2787. Trubowitz, Julius. Changing the Racial Attitudes of Children: The Effects of an Activity Group Program In New York City Schools. New York: Praeger, 1969.

2788. Trubowtiz, Sidney. A Handbook for Teaching in the Ghetto School. New York: Quadrangle, 1968.

2789. Tucker, Jackson and John D. Reid. "Urban Growth and Redistribution of the Black Urban American by Size of City, 1950 to 1970." In: Papers on the Demography of Black Americans. Atlanta, Georgia: Atlanta University, W.E.B. DuBois Institute for the Study of the American Black, 1972, 52-62.

2790. United Community Services of Metropolitan Boston. Black and

White in Boston: A Report Based on the Community Research Project. Boston: United Community Services of Metrpolitan Boston, 1968.

2791. U.S. Bureau of the Census. Poverty Areas in the 100 Largest Metropolitan Areas. 1960 Census of Population, Supplementary Reports PC(S1)-54. Washington, D.C.: Government Printing Office, November 13, 1967.

2792. U.S. Congress. House of Representatives. Memphis Riots and Massacres. Washington, D.C.: Government Printing Office, 1867.

2793. U.S. Congress. House Committee on New Orleans Riots. Report on the New Orleans Riots. Washington, D.C.: Government Printing Office, 1867.

2794. U.S. Congress, Joint Economic Committee. Employment and Manpower Problems in the Cities: Implications of the Report of the National Advisory Committee on Civil Disorders, Hearings Ninetieth Congress, Second Session, May 28, 29 and June 4, 5, 6, 1968, Washington, D.C.: Government Printing Office, 1968.

2795. U.S. Department of Comerce press release entitled, "Eight of Ten U.S. Cities With Largest Black Population Gained Blacks, 1980 Census Shows," Issued August 1981.

2796. U.S. Department of Housing and Urban Development. Problems of the Negro in the City, address by Walter B. Lewis, Washington, D.C.: Government Printing Office, April 20, 1968.

2797. U.S. Department of Labor, Manpower Administration. The Detroit Riot: A Profile of 500 Prisoners. Washington, D.C.: Government Printing Office, 1968.

2798. U.S. House: Special Committee on East St. Louis Riots. House Document 1231. Washington, D.C.: U.S. Government Printing Office, 1918.

2799. U.S. Manpower Administration. Civil Rights in the Urban Crisis. Washington, D.C.: Government Printing Office, 1968.

2800. U.S. National Commission on Urban Problems. The Large Poor Family--a Housing Gap, by Walter Smart and Others. Research Report No. 4. Washington, D.C.: Government Printing Office, 1968.

2801. U.S. National Youth Administration. Job Opportunities for Negro Youth in Columbus. Columbus, Ohio, June 1938.

2802. U.S. President's National Advisory Panel on Insurance in Riot-Affected Areas. Meeting of the Insurance Crisis of Our Cities, A Report. Washington, D.C.: Government Printing Office, 1968.

2803. Urban League of Cleveland and The National Urban League. Cleveland Operation Equality. Research Report No. 1, covering operations from January 1967 to December 1968. New York: National Urban League, 1968.

2804. "Urban Racial Violence in the United States: Changing Ecological Considerations." American Journal of Sociology 66 (1960), 109-119.

2805. "Urban Violence and Disorders". American Behavioral Scientist (March-April 1968), 1-55.

2806. Utley, Roi and William J. Weatherly. The Negro in New York. New York: Oceana, 1967.

2807. Varady, David. Ethnic Minorities in Urban Areas: A Case of Racially Changing Communities. Boston, Mass: Martinus Nijhoff, 1979.

2808. Viteritti, Joseph Peter. The Old Public Administration Reconsidered The Allocation of Jobs and Services to Minorities in New York City. Ph.D. Thesis, City University of New York, 1978.

2809. Vroman, Mary Elizabeth. Harlem Summer. New York: Putnam, 1967.

2810. Wade, Richard C. Slavery in the Cities: The South, 1820-1860. New York: Oxford University Press, 1964.

2811. Wakin, E. Portrait of a Middle-Class Negro Family at the Edge of Harlem. New York: Morrow, 1965.

2812. Walker, Earl. The Impact of Urban Renewal on the Los Angeles Subcommunity of Sawtelle. Master's Thesis, University of California, Los Angeles, 1968.

2813. Walker, Jack Lamar. "Negro Voting in Atlanta." Phylon 24 (1963), 1-10.

2814. Walker, Jack Lamar. Protest and Negotiation: A Study of Negro Political Leaders in a Southern City. Ph.D. Thesis, The University of Iowa, 1963.

2815. Watkins, Ralph Richard. Black Buffalo 1920-1927. Ph.D. Thesis, State University of New York at Buffalo, 1978.

2816. Watson, James Milton. Violence in the Ghetto: A Critical Comparison of Three Theories of Black Urban Unrest. Ph.D. Thesis, University of California, Los Angeles, 1973.

2817. Watson, Ora Vesta Russell. A Comparative Demographic Analysis of Two Louisiana Cities: Baton Rouge and Shreveport. Ph.D.

Dissertation, Louisiana State University, 1956.

2818. Watts, Lewis Gould. _Attitudes Toward Moving of Middle-Income Negro Families Facing Urban Renewal._ Ph.D. Thesis, Brandeis University, 1964.

2819. Weaver, Robert C. _Dilemmas of Urban America._ Cambridge: Harvard University Press, 1966.

2820. Weaver, Robert C. _The Urban Complex: Human Values in Urban Life._ Garden City, New York: Doubleday, 1964.

2821. Weissbourd, Bernard. _Segregation, Subsidies, and Megalopolis._ Occasional Paper No. 1 on the City. Center for the Study of Democratic Institutions, Santa Barbara, California, 1964.

2822. Weller, Charles Frederick. _Neglected Neighbors: Stories of Life in the Alleys, Tenements and Shanties of the National Capital._ Philadelphia: John C. Winston, 1960.

2823. West, Herbert Lee. _Urban Life and Spatial Distribution of Blacks in Baltimore, Maryland._ Unpublished Ph.D. Dissertation. University of Minnesota, 1974.

2824. Wetzel, James R. and Susan S. Holland. "Poverty Areas of Our Major Cities: The Employment Situation of Negro and White Workers in Metropolitan Areas Compared In A Special Labor Force Report." _Monthly Labor Review_ 89 (1966), 1105-1111.

2825. Wheeler, James O. "The Spatial Interaction of Blacks in Metropolitan Areas." _Southeastern Geographer_ 11 (November 1971), 101-12.

2826. Wheeler, Raymond H. _The Relationship Between Negro Invasion and Property Prices in Grand Rapids, Michigan._ University of Michigan, 1962.

2827. Wienker, Curtis W. "McNary: A Predominantly Black Company Town in Arizona". _Negro Historical Bulletin_ 37:5 (1974), 282-285.

2828. Wilkie, Jane Riblett. "Urbanization and Re-urbanization of the Black Population Before the Civil War," _Demography_ 13:3 (1976), 311-328.

2829. Williams, Lee E. and Lee E. Williams. _Anatomy of Four Race Riots: Racial Conflict in Knoxville, Elaine (Ark.), Tulsa and Chicago._ Jackson, Mississippi: University and College Press of Mississippi, 1972.

2830. Williams, Lillian Serece. _The Development of a Black Community: Buffalo, New York, 1900-1940._ Ph.D. Thesis, State University of New York at Buffalo, 1979.

2831. Williams, Ora Lee Bates. The Black Hustler: A Three Generation Study. Ph.D. Thesis, United States International University, 1974.

2832. Williams, William James. Attacking Poverty in the Watts Area: Small Business Development Under the Economic Opportunity Act of 1964. D.P.A., University of Southern California, 1966.

2833. Williams, William James. The State of Black America, 1983. New York: National Urban League, 1984.

2834. Willie, Charles Vert. Socio-Economic and Ethnic Areas of Syracuse, New York. Unpublished Ph.D. Dissertation. Syracuse University, 1957.

2835. Wilson, Bobby McClain. The Influence of Church Participation on the Behavior in Space of Black Rural Migrants Within Bedford-Stuyvesant: A Social Space Analysis. Ph.D. Thesis, Clark University, 1974.

2836. Wilson, James Q. (ed.) The Metropolitan Enigma: Inquiries into the Nature and Dimensions of America's "Urban Crisis." Washington, D.C.: Chamber of Commerce of the United States, Task Force on Economic Growth and Opportunity, 1967.

2837. Wilson, Robert Arthur. Three Urban Neighborhoods: A Study of Anomie and Militancy. Ph.D. Temple University, 1971.

2838. Winters, Wilda Glasgow. Black Mothers in Urban Schools: A Study of Participation and Alienation. Ph.D. Thesis, Yale University, 1975.

2839. Wolf, Eleanor P. Changing Neighborhood: A Study of Racial Transition. Ph.D. Thesis, Wayne State University, 1959.

2840. Wolf, Eleanor P. "Class and Race in the Changing City: Searching for New Solutions for Old Problems." in Leo Schore (ed.) Social Science and the City. New York: Praeger, 1968.

2841. Wolfe, Jacqueline. The Changing Pattern of Residence of the Negro in Pittsburgh, Pennsylvania, 1930-1960. Master's Thesis, University of Pittsburgh, 1964.

2842. Wolfgang, Marion E. "Urban Crime," in James Q. Wilson (ed.) The Metropolitan Enigma: Inquiries into the Nature and Dimensions of America's Urban Crisis, Cambridge, Massachusetts: Harvard University Press, 1968, 245-281.

2843. Woodson, Carter G. "The Negroes of Cincinnati Prior to the Civil War," Journal of Negro History I:1 (January 1916), 1-22.

2844. Woofter, Thomas Jackson. "Negro Migration to Cities, Maps." Survey 59 (1928), 657-9.

2845. Woofter, Thomas Jackson, et al. <u>Negro Problems in Cities</u>. New York: Doubleday, 1928.

2846. Wright, Nathan. <u>Black Power and Urban Unrest</u>. New York: Hawthorn Books, 1968.

2847. Yamamoto, Kinzo. <u>Assimilation of Migrant Negroes in the District of Columbia: A Study of the Effect of Length of Residence on Urban Life Adjustment.</u> Ph.D. Thesis, The Pennsylvania State University, 1971.

2848. Yinger, John. "Racial Prejudice and Racial Residential Segregation in an Urban Model." <u>Journal of Urban Economics</u> 3 (October 1976): 383-96.

2849. Young, Whitney. "The Case for Urban Integration." <u>Social Work</u> 12 (July 1967), 12-17.

2850. Zimmer, Bash G. "The Adjustment of Negroes in a Northern Industrial Community." <u>Social Problems</u> 9 (Spring 1962), 378-386.

CHAPTER 4

Housing and Residential Patterns

2851. Abrams, Charles. "Living in Harmony." Oppurtunity (1946), 116-18.

2852. Abrams, Charles. "Homes for Aryans Only." Commentary 6 (1947), 421-27.

2853. Abrams, Charles. "The Segregation Threat in Housing." Commentary 7 (February 1949), 123-131.

2854. Abrams, Charles. Forbidden Neighbors: A Study of Prejudice in Housing. New York: Harper & Brothers. 1955.

2855. Abrams, Charles. "The Housing Problem and the Negro." Daedalus 95 (1966), 64-76.

2856. Ackerman, Susan Rose. "Racism and Urban Structure." Journal of Urban Economics 2 (1975), 85-103.

2857. Adams, Samuel L. Blueprint for Segregation: A Survey of Atlanta Housing. Atlanta: Southern Regional Council, 1967.

2858. Alfred, Stephen J. and Charles R. Marcoux. "Impact of a Community Association on Integrated Suburban Housing Patters." Cleveland State Law Review 19 (1970), 90-99.

2859. Alienikoff, Alexander. "Racial Steering: The Real Estate Broker and Title VIII." The Yale Law Journal 6 (1976), 808-825.

2860. Aloi, Frank and Arthur Abba Goldberg. "Racial and Economic Exclusionary Zoning: The Beginning of the End?" Urban Law Annual, (1971), 9-62.

2861. Aloi, Frank and Arthur Abba Goldberg. "Racial and Economic Segregation by Zoning: Death Knell for Home Race?" University of Toledo Law Review 65 (1969), 1-15.

2862. Anderson, Marc B. _Racial Discrimination in Detroit: A Spatial Analysis of Racism._ Unpublished Masters Thesis, Wayne State University, 1969.

2863. Arter, Rhetta M. _Wins Pilot Preview: Report of An Action-Research, Demonstration Project on the Process of Acheiving Equal Housing Oppurtunities, Womans Integrating Neighborhood Services, Sponsored by the Educational Foundation of National Council of Negro Women._ New York, Research and Action Associates, 1961.

2864. Ashby, William M. "No Jim Crow in Springfield Federal Housing." _Opportunity_ 188 (June 1942), 170-71.

2865. Atelsek, Frank J. et al. "Neighborhood Reactions to Isolated Negro Residents: An Alternative to Invasion and Succession." _American Sociological Review_ 18:5 (October 1953), 1-20.

2866. Babcock, Richard F. _The Zoning Game._ Madison: The University of Wisconsin Press, 1966.

2867. Bacon, Robert. "Racial and Ethnic Redistribution in Denver, Colorado 1960-1970." _Ohio Geographers: Recent Research Themes_ 3 (1975), 1-19.

2868. Bahr, Howard Miner and J.P. Gibbs. "Racial Differentiation in American Metropolitan Areas." _Social Forces_ 45 (June 1967), 521-532.

2869. Baldwell, George. _Segregation: A Social Account._ Denver: Colorado Civil Rights Commission.

2870. Ball, William B. "Housing and the Negro." _America_ 119 (July 6, 1968), 11-13.

2871. Banfield, Edward C. and Morton Grodzins. _Government and Housing in Metropolitan Areas._ New York: McGraw Hill, 1958.

2872. Barresi, Charles M. "Racial Transition in an Urban Neighborhood." _Growth and Change_ 3 (1972), 16-22.

2873. Barresi, Charles M. "The Role of the Real Estate Agent in Residential Location." _Sociological Focus_ 1 (Summer 1968), 58-71.

2874. Barth, Ernest A.T. and Sue March. "A Research Note on the Subject of Minority Housing." _Journal of Intergroup Relations_ 3 (Fall 1982), 314-319.

2875. Bartell, Jeffrey B. et al. "Mediation of Civil Rights Disputes: Open Housing in Milwaukee." _Wisconsin Law Review_ (1968), 1127-1191.

2876. Bauer, Catherine. "Good Neighborhoods." Annals of the American Academy of Political and Social Science (November 1945), 104-15.

2877. Baum, Daniel J. Toward a Free Housing Market. Coral Gables, Fla.: University of Miami Press, 1971.

2878. Beauchamp, A. "Processual Indices of Segregation: Some Preliminary Comments." Behavioral Science 11 (1966), 190-192.

2879. Bederman, Sanford. "The Stratification of 'Quality of Life' in the Black Community of Atlanta, Georgia." Southeastern Geographer 14:1 (1974), 26-37.

2880. Beehler, George W. "Colored Occupancy Raises Values." Review of the Society of Residential Appraisers 12 (1945), 3-6.

2881. Bell, Wendell. "Comment on Congill's 'Trends in Residential Segregation of Nonwhites." American Sociological Review 22 (April 1957), 221-222.

2882. Bell, Wendell. "A Probability Model for the Measurement of Ecological Segregation." Social Forces 32 (May 1954), 357-364.

2883. Bell, Wendell and Ernest M. Willis. "The Segregation of Negroes in American Cities." Social and Economic Studies 6 (1957), 59-75.

2884. "Benign Quotas: A Plan for Integrated Private Housing." Yale Law Journal 70 (November 1966), 126-134.

2885. Bennett, Don C. "Segregation and Racial Interaction." Annals of the Association of American Geographers 62 (1973), 48-57.

2886. Berg, Irving. Racial Discrimination in Housing: A Study in Quest for Governmental Access By Minority Interest Groups, 1945-1962. Ph.D. Thesis, The University of Florida, 1967.

2887. Berger, Stephen D. The Social Consequences of Residential Segregation of the Urban American Negro. New York: Metropolitan Applied Research Center, 1970.

2888. Bergman, E.M. Eliminating Exclusionary Zoning: Reconciling Workplace and Residence in Suburban Areas. Cambridge, Massachusetts: Ballinger, 1974.

2889. Berry, Brian J.L. Commercial Structure and Commercial Blight. Department of Geography, University of Chicago, Research paper No. 85, 1963.

2890. Berry, Brian J.L. Comparative Mortality Experience of Small Business in Four Chicago Communities. Center for Urban Studies, University of Chicago, 1966.

2891. Berry, Brian J.L. The Open Housing Question: Race and Housing in Chicago, 1966-1976. Cambridge, Ma.: Ballinger, 1979.

2892. Berry, Brian J.L. Race and Housing: The Chicago Experience 1960-1975. Cambridge, MA.: Ballinger, 1967.

2893. Berry, Brian J.L. et al. "Attitudes Toward Inegration: The Role of Status in Community Response to Racial Change." In B. Schwartz (ed.) The Changing Face of the Suburbs. Chicago: The University of Chicago Press, 1976, 221-264.

2894. Birath, John F. "Judicial Review of Public Housing Admissions." Urban Law Annual (1971), 228-233.

2895. Blair, Rima Nancy. Housing Environment Choices and Acceptance of Racial Mixture. Ph.D. Thesis, New York University, 1979.

2896. Blanford, John B. The Need for Low-Rent Housing, Speech Before Annual Conference of the National Urban League Columbus, Ohio: Urban League, 1944.

2897. Blumberg, Leonard. "Segregated Housing, Marginal Location and the Crisis of Confidence." Phylon 25 (Winter 1964), 321-330.

2898. Bogen, David S. and Richard Flacon. "The Use of Racial Statistics in Fair Housing Cases." Maryland Law Review 34 (1974), 59-85.

2899. Boles, Alan. "Black Homeowning." New Republic 161 (December 12, 1969), 7-9.

2900. Bontemps, Arna and Jack Conroy. Anyplace But Here. New York: Hill and Wang, 1966.

2901. Boswell, T.D. "Residential Patterns of Puerto Ricans in New York City." Geographical Review 66 (1976), 92-93.

2902. Bowen, David Warren. Andrew Johnson and the Negro. Ph.D. Thesis, The University of Tennessee, 1976.

2903. Bradburn, Norman M. et al. Racial Integration in American Neighborhoods. Chicago: National Opinion Research Center, 1970.

2904. Bradburn, Norman M. et al. Side by Side: Integrated Neighborhoods in America. Chicago: Quadrangle, 1971.

2905. Bradshaw, Barbara Robinson and Edward L. Holmgren. "Open Occupancy and Open Minds: A Study of Realtors." Interracial Review 39 (April 1966), 92-95.

2906. Branscomb, A.W. "Analysis of Attempts to Prohibit Racial Discrimination in the Sale and Rental of Publicly Assisted

Private Housing." George Washington Law Review 28 (April 1960), 758-778.

2907. Breckinridge, Sophonisba Preston. "Color Line in the Housing Problem." Survey 29 (1913), 575-6.

2908. Brenner, Bernard. Racial Integration and City Planning. Unpublished Master's Thesis, Massachusetts Institute of Technology, Department of City Planning, 1958.

2909. Brown, Jud. "The Whiting of Society Hill: Black Families Refuse Eviction." The Drummer 230 (February 1973), 1-6.

2910. Brown, Letitia W. "Residential Patterns of Negroes in the District of Columbia, 1900-1960." Columbia Historical Society Records 77 (1969-1970), 1-10.

2911. Brown, William Henry. Class Aspects of Residential Development and Choice in the Oakland Black Community. Ph.D. Thesis, University of California, Berkeley, 1970.

2912. Brown, William Henry. "Access to Housing: The Role of the Real Estate Industry." Economic Geography 48:1 (1972), 66-78.

2913. Brunn, Stanley D. and Wayne L. Huffman. "The Spatial Response of Negroes and Whites Toward Open Housing: The Flint Referendum." Annals of the Association of American Geographers 60 (March 1970), 18-36.

2914. Brunn, Stanley D. et al. "Some Spatial Considerations of the Flint Open Housing Referendum." Proceedings (1969), 26-31.

2915. Bullard, Robert D. "Housing and the Quality of Life in the Urban Community: A Focus on the Dynamic Factors Affecting Blacks in the Housing Market." Journal of Social and Behavioral Sciences 25:2 (1979), 46-52.

2916. Bullard, Robert D. and D.L. Tryman. "Competition for Decent Housing: A Focus on Housing Discrimination Complaints in a Sunbelt City." The Journal of Ethnic Studies 7 (Winter 1980), 51-63.

2917. Bullard, R.D. and Odessa Pierce. "Black Housing Patterns in a Southern Metropolis: Competition for Housing in a Shrinking Market." The Black Scholar 2 (November/December 1979), 60-67.

2918. Bullough, Bonnie Louise. Social-Psychological Barriers to Housing Desegregation. Los Angeles: Graduate School of Business Administration, University of California, 1969.

2919. Bullough, Bonnie Louise. Alienation Among Middle Class Negroes: Social-Psychological Factors Influencing Housing Desegregation. Ph.D. Thesis, University of California, Los

Angeles, 1968.

2920. Bunte, Frederick Joseph. _An Inquiry Into the Decline in the Number of Blacks Entering the Teaching Profession._ Ph.D. Thesis, The Ohio State University, 1972.

2921. Bunzel, Joseph H. _Negro Housing Needs in Pittsburgh and Alleghany County_ Pittsburgh Housing Association, 1946.

2922. Burby, Raymond and Shirley F. Weiss. _Public Policy for Suburban Integration: The Case for New Communities._ Chapel Hill, NC.: Center for Urban and Regional Studies, 1977.

2923. Burgess, Ernest W. "Residential Segregation in American Cities." _Annals of the American Academy of Political and Social Science_ 440 (November 1938), 106-115.

2924. Butler, Edmond B. "Race Relations and Public Housing." _Interracial Review_ (March 1947), 38-40.

2925. Caplan, Eleanor and Eleanor Wolfe. "Factors Affecting Racial Change in Two Middle-Income Housing Areas." _Phylon_ 21:3 (Fall 1960), 1-10.

2926. Carey, George W. "The Regional Interpretation of Manhattan Population and Housing Patterns through Factor Analysis." _Geographical Review._ 56 (1966), 551-569.

2927. Carey, T.C. et al. "Analysis of Recent Housing Discrimination Cases." _Journal of Urban Law_ 52 (1975), 897-911.

2928. Carlson, David B. "The New Urbanites: Nature and Dimensions." _Architectural Forum._ (June 1960), 11-21.

2929. Carper, Laura. "The Negro Family and the Moynihan Report." _Dissent_. (March-April, 1966), 1-5.

2930. Carper, Laura. _Racism and the Class Struggle._ New York: Monthly Review Press, 1970.

2931. Casey, Stephen C. "The Effect of Race on Opinions of Housing and Neighborhood Quality." In George Sternlieb and James W. Hughes (eds.) _America's Housing: Prospects and Problems_. New Brunswick, New Jersey: Center for Urban Policy Research, Rutgers University, 1980, 485-542.

2932. Casstevens, T.W. _Politics, Housing and Race Relations: California's Rumford Act and Proposition 14_. Berkeley: Institute of Governmental Studies, University of California, 1967.

2933. Casstevens, T.W. "California's Rumford Act and Proposition 14." In L.W. Eley and T. Casstevens (eds.) _The Politics of_

Fair Housing Legislation: State and Local Case Studies. San Francisco, CA.: Chandler, 1983, 284-351.

2934. Cayton, Horace R. "Negro Housing in Chicago", Social Action (April 15, 1940), 1-5.

2935. Cayton, Horace R. and George S. Mitchell. Black Workers and the New Unions. Chapel Hill: University of North Carolina Press, 1939.

2936. Chicago, City of. Mayor's Commission on Human Relations. The Trumbull Park Homes Disturbance; A Chronological Report, August 4, 1953 to June 30, 1955. Chicago: Mayor's Office, 1955.

2937. Christian, Charles M. The Impact of Industrial Relations from the Black Community Upon Job Opportunities and Residential Mobility of the Central Workforce. Ph.D. Dissertation, University of Illinois, Urbana, Ill., 1975.

2938. Christian, Charles M. Social Areas and Spatial Change in the Black Community of Chicago: 1950-1960. University of Illinois, Urbana. Occasional Publications of the Department of Geography 2, 1972.

2939. Chudacof, Howard P. "New Look at Ethnic Neighborhoods-- Residential Dispersion and Concept of Visibility in a Medium- Sized City." Journal of American History 60 (1973), 76-93.

2940. Citizen's Housing Council of New York. Harlem Housing. New York: City of New York, 1939.

2941. City-Wide Citizens Committee on Harlem. Report of the Subcommittee on Housing. New York: City of New York, 1942.

2942. Clark, Henry. The Church and Residential Desegregation; A Case Study of an Open Housing Covenant Campaign. New Haven: College and University Press, 1965.

2943. Clark, John T. "When the Negro Resident Organizes." Opportunity (June 1934), 168-70.

2944. Clark, R.E. "Negro Home Life and Standards of Living." Annals of the American Academy of Political and Social Science 49 (September 1913), 147-163.

2945. Clemence, Theodore. "Residential Segregation in the Mid- Sixties." Demography 4 (1976), 562-568.

2946. Coburn, Frances E. Housing of Nonwhites in Grand Rapids Michigan. Grand Rapids: Grand Rapids Urban League, 1965.

2947. Cohen, Benjamin I. "Another Theory of Residential Segregation." Land Economics 47 (August 1971), 319-339.

2948. Colasanto, Diane Lee. The Prospects for Racial Integration in Neighborhoods: An Analysis of Residential Preferences In The Detroit Metropolitan Area. Ph.D. Thesis, The University of Michigan, 1977.

2949. Collison, Peter. "Immigrants and Residence." Sociology 1 (September 1967), 277-292.

2950. Collison, Peter and J.M. Mogey. "Residence and Social Class in Oxford." American Journal of Sociology 74 (May 1959), 599-605.

2951. Commission on Human Relations. Philadelphia's Negro Population--Facts on Housing. Philadelphia: The Commission, October 1953.

2952. Commission on Human Relations. Some Factors Affecting Housing Desegregation. City of Philadelphia, Philadelphia, 1962.

2953. Commission on Race and Housing. Where Shall We Live? Report Conclusions From a Three-Year Study of Racial Discrimination in Housing. Berkeley and Los Angeles: University of California Press, 1958.

2954. Committee on Quality in Intergroup Relations, Inc. Survey of Home Builder's Opinions on Impact of a Possible Executive Anti-Discrimination Order. An Analysis Prepared for National Association of Home Builders. Arlington, Virginia: C-E-I-R, Inc., June 1962.

2955. Comparative Cost Analysis of White, Non-White and Puerto Rican Families in the New York Metropolitan Area. New York: State Commission on Civil Rights, 1968.

2956. Comptroller General of the United States. Stronger Federal Enforcements Needed to Uphold Fair Housing Laws. Washington, D.C.: General Accounting Office, 1978.

2957. Comstock, A.P. "Chicago Housing Conditions; The Problem of the Negro." American Journal of Sociology 18 (1912), 241-57.

2958. Congress of Industrial Organizations. Facing the Job of Housing Negroes, 1945.

2959. Connecticut, State of. Commission on Civil Rights. Racial Integration in Public Housing Projects in Conecticut. Prepared by Henry G. Stetler, Supervisor, Research Division. Hartford, 1955.

2960. Connecticut, State of. Commission on Civil Rights. Racial integration in Private Residential Neighborhoods in Connecticut by Henry G. Stetler, Supervisor, Research Division. Hartford, 1957.

2961. Cooper, Gary Douglas. The Economics of Ghetto Expansion: A Study of Residential Segregation. Ph.D. Thesis, The Florida State University, 1975.

2962. Cortese, Charles F. et al. "Further Consideration on the Methodological Analysis of Segregation Indexes." American Sociological Review 41 (August 1976), 630-637.

2963. Cosner, Eugene P. Human Rights and the Realtor. Chicago: National Association of Real Estate Boards, 1963.

2964. Cottingham, Phoebe H. Black Income and Metropolitan Residential Dispersion. Urban Affairs Quarterly 10:3 (1975), 273-196.

2965. Couper, Mary and Timothy Brindley. "Housing Classes and Housing Values." Sociological Review 23 (1975), 563-576.

2966. Courant, Paul N. "Racial Prejudice in a Search Model of the Urban Housing Market." Journal of Urban Economics 5 (1978), 329-45.

2967. Courant, Paul N. Economic Aspects of Racial Prejudice in Urban Housing Markets. Ph.D. Dissertation, Princeton University, 1973.

2968. Courant, Paul N. and John Yinger. "On Models of Racial Prejudice and Urban Rsidential Structure." Journal of Urban Economics 4 (1977), 272-91.

2969. "Courts and Coercion - Enjoining Federal Funding to Eliminate Segregation of Public Housing." Iowa Law Review 58 (1973), 1283-1303.

2970. Cowgill, Donald O. "In Defense of a Segregation Index." American Sociological Review 28 (June 1963), 453-454.

2971. Cowgill, Donald O. "Segregation Scores for Metropolitan Areas." American Sociological Review 27 (June 1962), 400-402.

2972. Cowgill, Donald O. "Trends in Residential Segregation of Non Whites in American Cities 1940-1950." American Sociological Review 21 (February 1956), 43-47.

2973. Cowgill, Donald O. and Mary S. Cowgill. "An Index of Segregation Based on Block Statistics." American Sociological Review 16 (December 1957), 825-831.

2974. Craigie, David William. Causes and Consequences of Black-White Residential Differentiation in American Central Cities: A Longitudinal Analysis 1950-1970. Unpublished Ph.D. Dissertation. The University of Arizona, 1977.

2975. Crosby, Alexander L. How to End Discrimination in Housing. New York: The New York State Committee on Discrimination in Housing.

2976. Crosby, Alexander L. In These Ten Cities: How Minorities are Housed in Ten Communities of the U.S. Washington, D.C.: Published for Public Affairs Committee, 1959.

2977. Cuomo, Mario. Forest Hills Diary: The Crisis of Low Income Housing. New York: Random House, 1974.

2978. Cybrinsky, Roman A. "Social Aspects of Neighborhood Change." Annals of the American Academy of Political and Social Science. 61:1 (1978), 17-33.

2979. Daams, Gerrit. Summary of Segregation, Discrimination, and Open Housing. Kent: Ohio, Kent State University Press, 1965.

2980. Daniels, Charles B. "The Influence of Racial Segregation on Housing Prices." Journal of Urban Economics 2 (April 1975), 105-122.

2981. Daniels, Charles B. An Investigation of the Influence of Racial Segregation on Housing Prices in the Oakland, California Housing Market. Ph.D. Thesis, Stanford University, 1973.

2982. Danielson, M.N. "Differentiation, Segregation and Political Fragmentation in the American Metropolis." In A.E.K. Nash (ed.) Governance and Population: The Governmental Implications of Population Change,. Washington, D.C.: Commission on Population Growth and the American Future, Research Reports 4, 1972, 143-176.

2983. Darden, Joe T. Afro Americans in Pittsburgh: The Residential Segregation of a People. Lexington, MA.: D.C. Heath and Co., 1973.

2984. Darden, Joe T. "Black Residential Segregation: Impact of State Licensing Laws." Journal of Black Studies 12 (June 1982), 415-426.

2985. Darden, Joe T. "Black Residential Segregation in Michigan Cities in the Nineteenth Century." In Richard Thomas and Homer Hawkins (eds.) Minorities in Urban Michigan. Lansing: Michigan Historical Society, 1978, 20-27.

2986. Darden, Joe T. "Lending Practices and Policies Affecting the American Metropolitan System" in The American Metropolitan System: Present and Future. Edited by Stanley D. Brunn and James O. Wheeler. New York: V.H. Winston and Sons, 1980.

2987. Darden, Joe T. "Residential Segregation of Blacks in Detroit, 1960-1970." International Journal of Comparative Sociology 17

(1976), 84-91.

2988. Darden, Joe T. "Residential Segregation of Blacks in Flint, Michigan, 1950-1970." _Resources in Education_. ERIC Document No. ED 12596, November 1976.

2989. Darden, Joe T. "The Residential Segregation of Blacks in Medium Size Cities of Michigan." _Journal of Social and Behavioral Sciences_ 22 (Winter 1976), 60-66.

2990. Darden, Joe T. "Residential Segregation of Afro-Americans in Pittsburgh, 1960-1970." _Journal of Social and Behavioral Sciences_ 20 (Winter 1974), 72-77.

2991. Darden, Joe T. "Residential Segregation of Blacks in the Suburbs: The Michigan Example." _Geographical Survey_ 5 (1976), 7-16.

2992. Darden, Joe T. _The Spatial Dynamics of Residential Segregation of Afro-Americans in Pittsburgh_ Ph.D. Thesis, University of Pittsburgh, 1972.

2993. Darden, Joe T. and Jane B. Haney. "Measuring Adaptation: Migration Status and Residential Segregation Among Anglos, Blacks and Chicanos." _East Lakes Geographer_ 13 (June 1978), 20-33.

2994. Darden, Joe T. and Arthur Tabachneck. "Algorithm 8: Graphic and Mathematical Descriptions of Inequality, Dissimilarity, Segregation, or Concentration." _Environment and Planning A_ 12 (1980), 227-234.

2995. Davis, Dewitt and Emilio Casetti. "Do Black Students Wish to Live in Integra-Socially Homogeneous Neighborhoods? A Questionnaire Analysis." _Economic Geography_ 54:3 (1978), 197-210.

2996. Davis, F. James. "Effects of Freeway Displacement on Racial Housing Segregation in a Northern City." _Phylon_ 26 (Fall 1965), 209-215.

2997. Davis, J.T. "Sources of Variation in Housing Values in Washington, D.C." _Geographical Analysis_ 3 (January 1971), 63-76.

2998. Davis, Jane E. "Over-Crowded and Defective Housing in the Rural District." _Southern Workman_ 44 (1915), 454.

2999. Davison, R.B. "The Distribution of Immigrant Groups in London." _Race_ 5 (1963), 56-69.

3000. Deakin, Nicholas. "Residential Segregation in Britain: A Comparative Note." _Race_ 6 (July 1964), 18-33.

3001. DeFriese, Gordon H. and W. Scott Ford. "Open Occupancy - What the Whites Say, What They Do." _Trans-action_ 5 (April 1968), 53-56.

3002. Dempsey, Travis J. "How Whites Are Taking Back Black Neighborhoods." _Ebony_ (September 1979), 20-30.

3003. Denton, John H. _Apartheid American Style_. Berkeley, California: Diablo Press, 1967.

3004. Denton, John H. _Race and Property_. Berkeley, California: Diablo Press, 1964.

3005. Deskins, Donald Richard. "Race, Residence, and Workplace in Detroit, 1880 to 1965." _Economic Geography_ 48 (1972), 79-94.

3006. Deskins, Donald Richard. _Residential Mobility of Negro Occupational Groups in Detroit 1837-1965._ Ph.D. Thesis, The University of Michigan, 1971.

3007. Deskins, Donald Richard. "Residential Mobility of Negro Occupational Groups in Detroit, 1837-1965." _Michigan Geographical Publication #5._ Department of Geography, University of Michigan, Ann Arbor, MI, 1971.

3008. Deutsch, Morton and Mary Evans Collins. _Interracial Housing in Minneapolis_. Minneapolis: University of Minnesota Press, 1950.

3009. Deutsch, Morton and Mary Evans Collins. _Interracial Housing: A Psychological Evaluaton of a Social Experiment._ Minneapolis: University of Minnesota Press, 1951.

3010. Deutsch, Morton et al. "New Housing Which Is Available To All Groups Without Discrimination." In _Studies of Interracial Housing_. New York: Research Center for Human Relations, New York University, 1952.

3011. "Development of Open Occupancy Laws: A Survey on Legislation Against Discrimination in Housing ." Milwaukee Bar Association Gavel, 24 (September 1963), 13-20.

3012. DiMartino, David R. _Residential Mobility in the Racial Transition Zone: A Trend Surface Analysis of Home-Ownership Turnover in Columbus, Ohio._ Ph.D. Dissertation, Syracuse University, Syracuse, NY, 1975.

3013. "Discrimination in Employment and Housing: Private Enforcement Provisions of the Civil Rights Act of 1964 and 1963." _Harvard Law Review_ 82 (February 1969), 834-8.

3014. Dorsen, Norman. _Housing for the Poor: Rights and Remedies_. New York: New York University School of Law, 1967.

3015. Downs, Anthony. "Residential Segregation: Its Effects on Education." Education Digest 36 (April 1971), 12-15.

3016. Driedger, L. and G. Church. "Residential Segregation and Institutional Completeness—Comparison of Ethnic Minorities." Canadian Review of Sociology and Anthropology 11 (1974), 30-52.

3017. Dudas, John J. and David B. Lonbrake. "Problems and Future Directions of Residential Integration: The Local Application of Federally Funded Programs in Dade County, Florida." Southeastern Geographer 11:2 (November 1971), 158-168.

3018. "Due Process and the Poor in Public Housing." Harvard Law Journal 15 (1969), 422.

3019. Dumont, New Jersey Fair Housing Committee. Discrimination in the Twin Boroughs: A Report to the Residents and Officials of Dumont and Bergenfield, New Jersey. Milford: Fair Housing Committee of Dumont, Bergenfield and New Milford, 1965.

3020. Duncan, Beverly and Philip M. Hauser. Housing a Metropolis-Chicago. New York: Free Press, 1960.

3021. Duncan, Otis and Beverly Duncan. Contributions to the Theory of Segregation Indexes. Urban Analysis Report No. 14, Chicago. Chicago Community Inventory, University of Chicago, 1953.

3022. Duncan, Otis and Beverly Duncan. "Measuring Segregation." American Sociological Review 28 (Feruary 1963), 133.

3023. Duncan, Otis and Beverly Duncan. "A Methodological Analysis of Segregation Indexes." American Sociological Review 20 (April 1955), 210-217.

3024. Duncan, Otis Dudley and Beverly Duncan. The Negro Population of Chicago: A Study of Residential Succession. Chicago: University of Chicago Press, 1957.

3025. Duncan, Otis and Beverly Duncan. "Residential Distribution and Occupational Stratification." American Journal of Sociology 60 (March 1955), 493-503.

3026. Duncan, Otis and Stanley Liberson. "Ethnic Segregation and Assimilation." American Journal of Sociology 64 (January 1959), 364-374.

3027. Duncan, Margaret, et al. "Redlining Practices, Racial Resegregation, and Urban Decay-Neighborhood Housing Services as a Viable Alternative." Urban Lawyer 7 (1975), 510-539.

3028. Dworkin, Rosalind J. "Segregation in Suburbia." In Raymond W. Mack (ed.) Our Children's Burden. New York: Random House, 1968, 190-234.

3029. Dytkoff, E.F. "Negro City in New York." Outlook 108 (1914), 949-954.

3030. Edwards Ozzie L. "Patterns of Residential Segregation Within a Metropolitan Ghetto." Demography 7 (May 1970), 185-193.

3031. Eggers, Frederick J. et al. Background Information and Initial Findings of Housing Market Practices Survey. Washington, D.C.: U.S. Department of Housing and Urban Development, April 17, 1978.

3032. Eichler, Edward P. Race and Housing: An Interview with Edward P. Eichler, President, Eichler Homes, Inc. New York: Fund for the Republic, 1964.

3033. Eisenberg, Lawrence D. "Uncle Tom's Multi-Color Subdivision - Constitutional Restrictions on Racial Discrimination by Developers." Cornell Law Review 53 (January 1968), 314-324.

3034. Eley, L.W. "Fair Housing Laws--Unfair Housing Practices." Transaction 31 (1967), 428-438.

3035. Eley, L.W. and T.W. Casstevens (eds.) The Politics of Fair Housing Legislation: State and Local Case Studies. San Francisco, CA: Chandler, 1968.

3036. Elliott, Deborah M. and Barbara F. Gluckman. "The Impact of the Pittsburgh Fair Housing Ordinance: A Pilot Study." Journal of Intergroup Relations 5:1 (Autumn 1966), 75-85.

3037. Erbe, B.M. "Race and Socio-Economic Segregation." American Sociological Review 40 (1975), 801-812.

3038. Erbies, Richard A. Housing Problems of Our Spanish Heritage Population. Monticello, IL: Council of Planning Librarians Exchange Bibliography 1274, 1977.

3039. Erskine, H.G. "The Polls: Negro Housing." Public Opinion Quarterly 31 (1967), 482-498.

3040. Evans, Williams L. Race and Fear and Housing in a Typical American Community. New York: National Urban League, 1946.

3041. Evans, William L. "Federal Housing Brings Segregation in Buffalo." Opportunity 124 (April 1942), 106-10.

3042. Fair Housing Council of Metropolitan Washington, D.C. Negro Military Servicemen and Racial Discrimination in Housing. Washington, D.C.: Metropolitan Housing Program of the American Friends Service Committee, 1966.

3043. Falk, David and Herbert M. Franklin. Equal Housing Opportunity: The Unfinished Federal Agenda. Washington, D.C.:

The Potomac Institute, Inc., 1977.

3044. Farley, Reynolds. "Residential Segregation and Its
Implications for School Integration." Law and Contemporary
3045. PsoblemsR29n61975),"R64idential Segregation in Urbanized Areas
of the United States in 1970: An Analysis of Social Class and
Racial Difference." Demography 14 (November 1977), 497-518.

3046. Farley, Reynolds and Karl E. Taeuber. "Population Trends and
Residential Segregation Since 1960." Science 159 (March 1,
1968), 953-956.

3047. Fauman, S. "Housing Discrimination, Changing Neighborhoods,
and Public Schools." The Journal of Social Issues 13 (1957),
21-30.

3048. Favor, Homer Eli. The Effects of Racial Changes in Occupancy
Patterns Upon Property Values in Baltimore. Ph.D. Thesis,
University of Pittsburgh, 1960.

3049. "The Federal Fair Housing Requirements: Title VIII of the 1968
Civil Rights Act." Duke Law Journal 1969 (August 1969), 733-
771.

3050. Federal Housing Administration. Materials for FHA Offices on
Minority Group Housing. Washington, D.C.: Government Printing
Office, 1946.

3051. Federal Public Housing Authority. Experience in Public Housing
Projects Jointly Occupied by Negro, White and Other Tenants,
Washington, D.C.: Government Printing Office, 1944.

3052. Federal Public Housing Authority. Public Housing Available for
Negroes, as of July 31, 1944, Report S-602, Statistics
Division, Washington, D.C.: Government Printing Office, 1945.

3053. Federal Public Housing Authority. Public Housing Available for
Negroes, as of October 31, 1945, Report S-602, Statistics
Division, Washington, D.C.: Government Printing Office, 1946.

3054. Federal Public Housing Authority. Public Housing Available
for Negroes, as of August 31, 1946, Report S-602, Statistics
Division, Washington, D.C.: Government Printing Office, 1947.

3055. The Federation of Neighborhood Association of Chicago.
Restrictive Covenants. Chicago: The Federation, 1944.

3056. Fine, J. et al. "The Residential Segregation of Occupational
Groups in Central Cities and Suburbs." Demography 8 (Feruary
1971), 91-101.

3057. Fischer, Roger A. "Racial Segregation in Antebellum New Orleans." *American Historical Review* 74 (1969), 926-937.

3058. Fisher, Ernest McKinley. *Principles of Real Estate Practice*. New York: Macmillan, 1923.

3059. Fishbein, Annette. *The Expansion of Negro Residential Areas in Chicago, 1950-1960*. Chicago: University of Chicago, 1963.

3060. Fly, Jerry and George R. Reinhart. "Racial Separation During the 1970's: The Case of Birmingham." *Social Forces* 58:4 (1980), 1255-1262.

3061. Foley, Donald. "Institutional and Contextual Factors Affecting the Housing Choices of Minority Residents." In Amos H. Hawley and Vincent P. Rock (eds.) *Segregation in Residential Areas*. Washington, D.C.: National Academy of Sciences 1973, 168-81.

3062. Foote, Nelson N. *Housing Choices and Housing Constraints.* New York: McGraw-Hill, 1960.

3063. Foote, Nelson N et al. *Housing Choices and Housing Constraints*. New York: McGraw-Hill, 1960.

3064. Ford, James. *Slums and Housing, With Special Reference to New York City*. Camridge, Massachusetts: Harvard University Press, 1936.

3065. Forman, E.M.S. "Ethnic and Income Housing--Occupancy Patterns of Federal Moderate-Income Neighborhoods of New York City." *Environment and Planning* 8:6 (1976), 707-714.

3066. Franklin, John Hope. "Another Kind of City: A Study of Racial Transition and Property Values." in *Studies of the Urban Poor*. Edited by I. Deutscher and E. Thompson, New York: Basic Books, 1967, 47-56.

3067. Freeman, Linton C. and M.H. Sunshine. *Patterns of Residential Segregation*. Cambridge, MA: Schenkman, 1970.

3068. Freeman, Linton C. and M.H. Sunshine. *Residential Segregation Patterns*. Boston: Schenkman and Company, 1980.

3069. Fried, Joseph P. *Housing Crisis U.S.A.* New York: Praeger, 1971.

3070. Frieden, Bernard J. *The Future of Old Neighborhoods: Rebuilding for a Changing Population.* Cambridge, MIT Press, 1964.

3071. Frieden, Bernard J. "Blacks in Suburbia: the Myth of Better Opportunities" in L. Wingo (ed.) *Minority Perspectives*. Baltimore: Johns Hopkins University Press, 1972, 31-49.

3072. Friedman, Lawrence M. Government and Slum Housing: A Century of Frustration. Chicago: Rand McNally, 1968.

3073. Friedman, Linton C. "Public Housing and the Poor: An Overview." California Law Review (1966), 642.

3074. Frey, William H. Black Movement to the Suburbs: Potentials and Prospects for Metropolitan-Wide Integration. Madison: Institute for Research on Poverty, University of Wisconsin, December 1977.

3075. Frey, William H. "Black In-Migration, White Flight, and The Changing Economic Base of the Central City." American Journal of Sociology 85:6 (1980), 1396-1417.

3076. Fulton, Robert L. Russell Woods: A Study of a Neighborhoods's Initial Response to Negro Invasion. Wayne State University, 1960.

3077. Galster, George C. Preferences for Neighborhood Racial Composition. Unpublished Report Prepared for the U.S. Department of Housing and Urban Development, Washington, D.C.: 1978.

3078. "Gallup Poll. Opposition of Negroes As Neighbors Decreases." Washington Post, (May 28, 1965), p. A2.

3079. Gamberg, Herbert Victor. White Perceptions of Negro Race and Class as Factors in the Racial Residential Process. Ph.D. Thesis, Princeton University, 1964.

3080. Gardner, Major. "Race Segregation in Cities." Kentucky Law Journal 29 (January 1941), 213-219.

3081. Gaston, Juanita. The Changing Residential Pattern of Blacks in Battle Creek, Michigan: A Study in Historical Geography. Ph.D. Dissertation, Michigan State University, East Lansing, Michigan, 1977.

3082. Gelber, Steven Michael. Black Men and Businessmen: Business Attitudes Toward Negro Employment, 1945-1967. Ph.D. Thesis, The University of Wisconsin Madison, 1972.

3083. Ginger, A.F. "Little Democracy -- Housing for America's Minorities in 1960." Lawyers Guild Review 20 (Spring 1960), 6-17.

3084. Glasserg, Susan Spiegel. "Legal Control of Blocktrusting." Urban Law Annual (1972), 145-170.

3085. Glantz, F.B. and N.J. Delaney. "Changes in Non-White Residential Patterns in Large Metropolitan Areas, 1960-1970." New England Economic Review (March-April 1973), 2-13.

3086. Glazer, Nathan and Davis McEntire (eds.) _Studies In Housing and Minority Groups_. Berkeley: University of California Press, 1960.

3087. Glazer, Nathan and Davis McEntire (eds.) _Studies in Housing and Minority Groups_. Los Angeles: University of California Press, 1963.

3088. Glazer, Nathan and Daniel P. Moynihan. _Beyond the Melting Pot_. Cambridge, Massachusetts: Harvard University Press, 1970.

3089. Goering, John M. "Neighborhood Tipping and Racial Transition: A Review of Social Science Evidence." _Journal of the American Institute of Planners_ 44:1 (1978), 68-78.

3090. Gold, N.N. "The Mismatch of Jobs and Low-Income People in Metropolitan Areas and its Implications for the Center-City Poor". In Sim Mazie (ed.) _Population, Distribution and Policy_. Washington, D.C.: Commission on Population Growth and the American Future, Research Reports, 1972, 441-86.

3091. Goldblatt, Harold S. _Westchester Real Estate Brokers, Builders, Bankers and Negro Home Buyers_. A Report to the Housing Council of the Urban League of Westchester County, Inc. on Opportunities for Private Open-Occupancy Housing in Westchester. White Plains, New York, 1954.

3092. Goldblatt, Harold S. and F. Cromein. "The Effective Social Reach of the Fair Housing Practices Law of the City of New York." _Social Problems_ 9:4 (Spring 1962), 365-370.

3093. Goldner, William. _New Housing for Negroes: Recent Experience_. Research Report No. 12. Berkeley: Real Estate Research Program, University of California, 1958.

3094. "Good Neighbors." _Architecture Forum,_ (January 1946), 16-18.

3095. Goodman, Emily J. _The Tenant Survival Book._ Indianapolis Bobbs-Merrill Company, 1972.

3096. Gordon, A. et al. "The Social Class Basis of Ethnic Residential Segregation: The Canadian Case." _American Journal of Sociology_ 77 (1971), 491-510.

3097. Governor's Interracial Commission. _The Negro and Home in Minnesota._ Minneapolis: The Commission, June, 1947.

3098. Gray, George. _Housing and Citizenship: A Study of Low-Income Housing._ New York: Reinhold, 1937.

3099. Grayson, George W. and Cindy L. Wedel. "Open Housing: How to Get Around the Law." _The New Republic,_ (June 22, 1968), 15-16.

3100. Green, Robert L. et al. Discrimination and the Welfare of Urban Minorities. Springfeild, IL: Charles Thomas Publications, 1981.

3101. Green, Sidney. "Public Housing Promotes Civic Unity." Journal of Housing, (July 1946), 136.

3102. Greene, Kenneth Roger. Black Demands for Open Housing: The Responses of Three City Governments. Ph.D. Thesis, Michigan State University, 1971.

3103. Grier, Eunice. Buyers of Interracial Housing: A Study of the Market for Concord Park. Philadelphia: Institute for Urban Studies, University of Pennsylvania, 1957.

3104. Grier, Eunice. Civil Rights and Land Development:Background on Housing for Negroes in Cleveland, Ohio. Washington,D.C.: Washington Center for Metropolitan Studies, 1966.

3105. Grier, Eunice. "Factors Hindering Integration In America's Urban Areas." Journal of Intergroup Relations 2 (Autumn 1960), 293-301.

3106. Grier, Eunice. "Research Needs in the Field of Housing and Race." Journal of Intergroup Relations 1 (Summer 1960), 21-31.

3107. Grier, Eunice and George W. Grier. Case Studies in Racially Mixed Area. 3 Vol. Washington, D.C.: Washington Center for Metropolitan Studies, 1962.

3108. Grier, Eunice and George W. Grier. Discrimination in Housing: A Handbook of Fact. New York: Anti-Defamation League of B'nai B'rith, 1960.

3109. Grier, Eunice and George W. Grier. "Equality and Beyond: Housing Segregation in the Great Society." In Talcott Parsons and Kenneth Clark (eds.) The Negro American. Boston: Houghton Mifflin, 1955, 52-554.

3110. Grier, Eunice and George W. Grier. "Equality and Beyond: Housing Segregation in The Great Society." Daedalus 95 (Winter 1966), 77-106.

3111. Grier, Eunice and George W. Grier. Privately Developed Interracial Housing. Los Angeles: University of California Press, 1960.

3112. Grier, George W. "Negro Ghettos and Federal Housing Policy." Law and Contemporary Problems 32 (1967), 550-560.

3113. Grier, George and Eunice Grier. Equality and Beyond: Housing Segregation and the Goals of Great Society. Chicago: Quadrangle Books, 1966.

3114. Grier, George and Eunice Grier. The Impact of Race on Neighborhood or the Metropolitan Setting. Washington, D.C.: Washington Center for Metropolitan Studies, May 1961.

3115. Grier, George and Eunice Grier. The Negro Migration: Doubled Populations in a Decade Pose Urgent Problems for Northern Cities. Housing Yearbook. Washington, D.C.: National Housing Conference, 1960.

3116. Grier, George and Eunice Grier. "Obstacles to Desegregation in America's Urban Areas." Race 11 (July 1964), 3-17.

3117. Grier, Goerge and Eunice Grier. Racial Violence in the United States. Chicago: University of Chicago Press, 1969.

3118. Grier, George and Eunice Grier. In Search of Housing: A Study of Experiences of Negro Professional and Technical Personnel in New York State. Albany, New York: State Commission Against Discrimination, 1958.

3119. Grisby, William G. Housing Markets and Public Policy. Philadelphia: University of Philadelphia Press, 1963.

3120. Grodzins, Morton. "Metropolitan Segregation." Scientific American 197 (October 1957), 33-41.

3121. Grodzins, Morton. The Metropolitan Area As A Racial Problem. Pittsburgh: University of Pittsburgh Press, 1958.

3122. Groner, Isaac and David Jelfeld. "Race Discrimination in Housing." The Yale Law Journal 57 (1948), 426-458.

3123. Guest, Avery M. and James Weed. "Ethnic Residential Segregation: Patterns of Change." American Journal of Sociology 81 (March 1976, 1088-1111.

3124. Guest, Avery M. and James J. Zuiches. "Another Look at Residential Turnover in Urban Neighborhoods: A Note on Racial Change in a Stable Community by Harvey Molotch." American Journal of Sociology 77 (1971), 457-467.

3125. Haar, Charles Monroe. Housing the Poor in Suburbia: Public Policy at the Grass Roots. Camridge, Massachusetts: Ballinger Publishing Company, 1973.

3126. Haar, Charles Monroe. Federal Credit and Private Housing: The Mass Financing Dilemma. New York: McGraw Hill, 1960.

3127. Haar, Charles Monroe and D.S. Iatridas. Housing the Poor in Suburbia: Public Policy at the Grass Roots. Cambridge, Massachusetts: Ballinger, 1974.

3128. Hadden, Kenneth and Thomas Werling. Residential Segreation in

Metropolitan Connecticut: 1970. Storrs, CT: Agricultural Experiment Station Bulletin 434, February 1975.

3129. Harding, Robert R. "Housing Discrimination as a Basis for Interdistrict School Desegregation Remedies," The Yale Law Journal 93:2 (December 1983), 340-361.

3130. Harmon, John. Cognitions of Cincinatti, Ohio Neighborhoods: The View of Black and White University Students. M.A. Thesis, University of Cincinatti, Cincinatti, Ohio, 1974.

3131. Harris, Leroy. The Other Side of the Freeway: A Study in the Settlement Pattern of Negroes and Mexican Americans in San Diego, California. Ph.D. Dissertation, Department of Social Work, Carnegie-Mellon University, Pittsburgh, PA, 1974.

3132. Hartman, Chester W. Housing: Private Failure, Public Needs, Testimony before the U. S. Joint Economic Committee, U.S. 90th Congress, 1st Session, Subcommittee on Urban Affairs, October 4, 1967.

3133. Hartman, Chester W. Low-Income Housing in the Boston Area: Needs and Proposals. Boston, Mass.: Prepared by Housing Advisory Research Committee, Massachusetts Committee on Discrimination in Housing, July 1964.

3134. Harvey, David., Social Justice and the City. Baltimore: John Hopkins University Press, 1973.

3135. Hastie, W.H. A Relic of Slavery: A Study of the Causes, Effects, and Parameters of American Residential Discrimination. Unpublished term paper, Department of City and Regional Planning, University of California, Berkeley, 1970.

3136. Hauser, Philip. "Demographic Factors in the Integration of the Negro." Daedalus 94 (Fall 1965), 847-877.

3137. Hawley, Amos H. Dispersion Versus Segregation: Apropos of a Solution of Race Problem. Papers of the Michigan Academy of Science, Arts, and Letters, 30 (1944), 667-674.

3138. Hawley, Amos H. and Vincent R. Rock (eds.) Segregation in Residential Areas. Washington, D.C.: National Academy of Sciences, 1973.

3139. Heller, Charles F. and A.L. Redente. "Residential Location and White Attitudes Toward Mixed-Race Neighborhoods in Kalamazoo, Michigan." Journal of Geography 72:3 (1973), 15-25.

3140. Helper, Rose. The Racial Practices of Real Estate Institutions in Selected Areas of Chicago. Unpublished Ph.D. Thesis, University of Chicago, 1958.

3141. Helper, Rose. _Racial Policies and Practices of Real Estate Brokers,_ Minneapolis: University of Minnesota Press, 1969.

3142. Hendon, William S. "Discrimination against Negro Homeowners in Property Tax Assessment" _American Journal of Economics and Sociology_ 27 (April 1968) 125-132.

3143. Herbers, John. "Census Data Reveals 70's Legacy: Poor Cities and Richer Suburbs," _New York Times_ (February 27, 1983), 28.

3144. Hermalin, Albert and Reynolds Farley. "The Potential for Residential Integration in Cities and Suburbs: Implications for the Busing Controversy." _American Sociological Review_ 38 (1973), 595-610.

3145. Hermsmyer, Rex. _An Analysis of Housing for Blacks in Edwardsville, Illinois._ M.A. Thesis, Southern Illinois University, Edwardsville, Ill., 1972.

3146. Hesslink, George K. _Black Neighbors: Negroes in a Northern Rural Community._ Indianapolis, Indiana: Bobbs-Merrill, 1968.

3147. Heurmann, Leonard. _The Definition and Analysis of Stable Integration._ Ph.D. Thesis, University of Pennsylvania, Department of City and Regional Planning, 1973.

3148. "Homeownership for the Poor: Tenant Condominiums, The Housing and Urban Development Act of 1968, and the Rockefeller Program." _Cornell Law Quarterly_ 54 (1969), 811.

3149. Horne, F.S. "Interracial Housing in the United States." _Phylon_ 12 (April 1958), 13-20.

3150. Hornseth, Richard. "A Note on the Measurement of Ecological Segregation by Julius Jahn, Calvin F. Schmid, and Clarence Schrag." _American Sociological Review_ 12 (October 1947), 603-604.

3151. Horowitz, Carl F. "Racial Steering and the 'Captive' Real Estate Broker" in R.A. Obudho (ed.) _Afro-Americans and the City._ Albany, New York: State University of New York Press, 1984.

3152. Housing and Home Finance Agency. _The Housing of Negro Veterans,_ Washington, D.C.: Government Printing Office, 1948.

3153. "Housing and Minorities." _Phylon_ 19 (Summer 1958), 8-124.

3154. _Housing and Welfare: Report of Survey._ Washington, D.C.: Government Printing Office, 1940.

3155. Housing Assistance Council. _Housing of Minorities in Rural America: An Analysis of Farmers Home Administration Rural_

Housing Loans to Minorities for the Period 1971-1975.
Washington, D.C.: May 1, 1976.

3156. "Housing of Colored People in Chicago." City Club Bulletin 12
(August 18, 1919), 169-170. '

3157. "Housing the Migrants". Opportunity 1 (1923), 290.

3158. Hunt, Chester L. "A Research Report on Integration Housing in
a Small Northern City." Journal of Intergroup Relations 3
(Winter 1961-62), 65-79.

3159. Hunt, Chester L. "Private Integrated Housing in a Medium Size
Northern City." Social Problems 7 (Winter 1959-60), 196-209.

3160. Hutchinson, Peter M. Accessibility and Segregation, Their
Effects on the Employment of the Urban Poor. Ph.D.
Dissertation, University of Pittsburgh, 1972.

3161. Hyman, H.H. and P.B. Sheatsley. "Attitudes Toward
Desegregation." Scientific American 211 (July 1964), 16-23.

3162. Hyman, H.H. and P.B. Sheatsley. "A Research Report on
Integrated Housing in a Small Northern City." Journal of
Intergroup Relations 3 (Winter 1961-1962), 65-79.

3163. Ianni, Francis. "Residential and Occupational Mobility as
Indeces of the Acculturation of an Ethnic Group." Social
Forces 36 (October 1957), 65-72.

3164. "Injunction Against the Recording of Deeds Containing Racial
Covenants." Maryland Law Review 34 (1974), 403-419.

3165. "Integration in Housing." Lawyer's Guild Review. (Spring
1958), 4-8.

3166. "Iron Ring in Housing." Crisis (July 1940), 205-10.

3167. Isaacs, Reginald R. "The Neighborhood Unit as an Instrument
for Segregation." Journal of Housing 5: 7 & 8 (July and August
1948), 177-180 and 215-219.

3168. Isaacs, Reginald R. "Are Urban Neighborhoods Possible?"
Journal of Housing 5 (July 1948), 177-180.

3169. Iskander, Michel G. "The Neighborhood Approach." Journal of
Integroup Relations 3 (Winter 1961-1962), 80-86.

3170. Jackson, Hubert M. "Public Housing and Minority Groups."
Phylon (1958), 21-30.

3171. Jackson, Peter and Susan Smith (eds.) Social Interaction and
Ethnic Segregation. New York: Academic Press, 1982.

3172. Jahn, Julius A. "The Measurement of Ecological Segregation: Derivation of an Index Based on the Criterion of Reproducibility." American Sociological Review 15 (February 1960), 100–104.

3173. Jahn, Julius, et al. "Rejoinder to Dr. Hornseth's Note on the Measurement of Ecological Segregation." American Sociological Review 13 (April 1948), 216–217.

3174. Jahn, Julius A. Principles and Methods of Area Sampling Applied to a Survey of Employment, Housing and Place of Residence of White and Non–White Ethnic Groups in Seattle, Washington, from July to October, 1947. University of Washington, 1949.

3175. Jahoda, Marie and Patricia West. "Race Relations in Public Housing." Journal of Social Issues 7 (1951), 132–39.

3176. Jahoda, Marie and Patricia West. "Race Relations in Public Housing" Journal of Personality and Social Psychology 17 (1971), 250–258.

3177. Jakubs, J. "Residential Segregation: The Taeuber Index Reconsidered." Journal of Regional Science 17 (1977), 281–283.

3178. Janson, Carl–Gunnar. "On Segreation." Plan 31 (1977), 110–119.

3179. Jefferson, Alphine Wade. Housing Discrimination and Community Response in North Lawndale (Chicago), Illinois 1948–1978. Ph.D. Thesis, Duke University, 1979.

3180. Jenks, Jeffrey. Minorities: Where Do They Live? Prepared for the Central States Anthropological Society Meeting. April 3, 1975, Detroit, Michigan. Detroit: Research and Planning Division, Michigan Department of Civil Rights, 1975.

3181. Johnson, Charles S. Patterns of Negro Segregation. New York: Harper & Bros, 1943.

3182. Johnson, James A. The Impact of Court Ordered Desegreation on Student Enrollment and Residential Patterns in the Jefferson County, Kentucky Public School District: An Interim Report. Louisville, KY: Jefferson County Education Consortium, May 31, 1977.

3183. Johnson, Philip A. Call Me Neighbor, Call Me Friend; the Case History of the Integration of a Neighborhood on Chicago's South Side. Garden City, New York: Doubleday and Company, Inc., 1965.

3184. Johnson, Reginald A. A Documented Report on Housing. New York: National Urban League, 1955.

3185. Johnson, Reginald A. Racial Bias and Housing. New York: National Urban League, 1963.

3186. Johnston, R.J. Urban Residential Patterns. London: Bell & Sons, 1971.

3187. Johnston, R.J. "Towards A General Model of Intra-Urban Residential Patterns: Some Cross Cultural Observations." Progress in Geograhy 4 (1972), 83-124.

3188. Jones, William H. The Housing of Negroes in Washington, D.C.: The Study in Human Ecology. Washington, D.C.: Howard University.

3189. Kain, John F. "Effects of Housing Segregation on Urban Development." In Savings and Residential Financing. 1969 Conference Proceedings, U.S. Savings and Loan League, Chicago, 1969.

3190. Kain, John F. "Housing Segregation, Negro Employment, and Metropolitan Decentralization." Quarterly Journal of Economics 82 (May 1968), 175-197.

3191. Kain, John F. "Housing Segregation, Negro Employment and Metropolitan Decentralization: Rejoinder." Quarterly Journal of Economics 85 (February 1970), 161-162.

3192. Kain, John F. "Measuring the Value of Housing Quality." Journal of the American Statistical Association 5 (June 1970), 532-48.

3193. Kain, John F. Race, Ethnicity, and Residential Location. Department of City and Regional Planning, Harvard University, Cambridge, Massachusetts, June 1975.

3194. Kain, John F. Theories of Residential Location and Realities of Race. Discussion Paper No. 47. Harvard University Program on Regional and Urban Economics, June, 1969.

3195. Kain, John F. and John M. Quigley. "Housing Market Discrimination, Home-Ownership, and Savings Behavior." American Economic Review 62 (1972), 263-277.

3196. Kain, John F. and John M. Quigley. Housing Markets and Racial Discrimination. New York: National Bureau of Economic Research, 1975.

3197. Kantrowitz, Nathan. Ethnic and Racial Segregation in the New York Metropolis, New York: Praeger, 1973.

3198. Kantrowitz, Nathan. "Ethnic and Racial Segregation in the New York Metropolis, 1960." American Journal of Sociology 74 (1969), 685-695.

3199. Kantrowitz, Nathan. "The Index of Dissimilarity: A Measurement of Residential Segregation for Historical Analysis." Historical Methods Newsletter 7 (September 1974), 285-289.

3200. Keith, Nathaniel S. Housing America's Low and Moderate Income Families; Progress and Problems Under Post Programs, Progress Under Federal Act of 1968. Washington, D.C.: Government Printing Office, 1968.

3201. Kelleher, D.T. "Neighborhood Schools and Racial Residential Segregation." Educational Forum 39 (1975), 209-215.

3202. Kelley, Joseph B. Racial Integration Policies of the New York City Housing Authority, 1959-1961. D.S.W. Columbia University, 1963.

3203. Kenyon, J.B. "Patterns of Residential Integration in a Bi-Cultural Western City." Professional Geographer 28 (1976), 40-44.

3204. Kerchhoff, Richard. "A Study of Racially Changing Neighborhoods." Merrill Palmer Quarterly 4 (Fall 1957), 15-49.

3205. Kiang, Y.C. "The Distribution of Ethnic Groups in Chicago." American Journal of Sociology 74 (1968), 292-295.

3206. Killingsworth, Mark R. "Desegregating Public Housing." New Leader 51 (October 7, 1963), 13-14.

3207. King, A.T. and P. Mieszkowski. "Racial Discrimination, Segregation and the Price of Housing." Journal of Political Economy 81 (1973), 590-606.

3208. King, Arthur E. "Mortgage Money and Housing." Opportunity 3 (1923), 360.

3209. King, Morton B. "Residential Desegregation." Journal of Intergroup Relations 4 (Autumn 1965), 253-258.

3210. King, Thomas. An Estimate of Racial Discrimination in Rental Housing. New Haven, Connecticut: Cowles Foundation for Research in Economics at Yale University, 1971.

3211. Kirschenbaum, Alan. "Spatial Clustering, Segregation and Urban Planning: A Methodological Approach." Urban Studies 11 (1974), 323-327.

3212. Knight, Charles L. Negro Housing in Certain Virginia Cities. Richmond, Virginia: William Byrd Press, 1927.

3213. Kolben, A.A. Enforcing Open Housing: An Evaluation of Recent Legislation and Decision. New York: New York Urban League, 1969.

3214. Kopkind, Andrew. "Civil Rights and Housing." New Statesman 72 (September 16, 1966), 360-361.

3215. Koren, Barry. Residential Mobility in a Potentially Changing Neighborhood: A Study of Household Moving and Staying in the Aftermath of a School Conflict. Unpublished Ph.D. Dissertation. University of Wisconsin, Madison, 1978.

3216. Krasner, Barbara. "Open Housing and the Black Community." Renewal 7 (March 1967), 16-18.

3217. Kraus, Henry. In The City Was A Garden A Housing Project Chronicle. New York: Renaissance Press, 1951.

3218. Krislof, Frank S. Urban Housing Needs Through the 1980's: An Analysis and Projection. Washington, D.C.: Government Printing Office, 1968.

3219. Ladd, M.W. "Effect of Integration on Property Values." American Economic Review 52 (September 1962), 801-808.

3220. Laessig, Robert Ernest. Racial Disparities in Urban Housing Quality. Ph.D. Cornell University, 1971.

3221. Lake, Robert W. The New Suburbanites: Race and Housing in the Suburbs. New Brunswick, Rutgers University, Center for Urban Research, 1981.

3222. Lake, Robert W. Race, Status, and Neighborhood Behavioral Aspects of the Ecology of Racial Residential Change. M.A. Thesis, University of Chicago, Chicago, Illinois, 1972.

3223. Lang, Marvin. Historic Settlement and Residential Segregation in Rural Neighborhoods of Jasper County, Mississippi. Unpublished Ph.D. Dissertation East Lansing, Michigan: Michigan State University, Department of Geography, 1979.

3224. Langendorf, Richard. "Residential Desegregation Potential." Journal of the American Institute of Planners 35 (March 1969), 90-95.

3225. Langton, J. "Residential Patterns in Pre-Industrial Cities-- Some Case Studies from 17th Century Britain." Institute of British Geograhers Transactions 65 (1975), 1-27.

3226. Lansing, John B., et al. New Homes and Poor People: A Study of Chain Moves. Ann Arbor, Michigan: University of Michigan, Institute for Social Research, 1969.

3227. Lapham, Victoria Cannon. Price Differences for Black and White Housing. Ph.D. Southern Methodist University, 1970.

3228. Laurenti, Luigi. Property Values and Race: Studies in Seven

<u>Cities.</u> Berkeley: University of California Press, 1960.

3229. Lauter, Sylvia. <u>The Racial Gap, 1955-1965 in Employment, Health and Housing</u>. New York: The National Urban League, 1967.

3230. Lawyers Guild Review. <u>Integration in Housing.</u> New York: National Lawyers Guild, 1958.

3231. Lazin, F.A. "Federal Low Income Housing Assistance Programs and Racial Segregation--Leased Public Housing." <u>Public Policy</u> 24 (1976), 337-360.

3232. Leacock, E., et al. <u>Toward Integration in Suburban Housing: The Bridgeview Study.</u> New York: Anti-Defamation League of B'Nai B'rith, 1965.

3233. Leaman, Samuel Hardy. <u>A Study of Housing Decisions by Negro Home Owners and Negro Renters.</u> Chapel Hill: University of North Carolina, Department of City and Regional Planning, 1967.

3234. Leasure, J. William and David H. Stern. "A Note on Housing Segregation Indexes." <u>Social Forces</u> 46 (March 1968), 406-407.

3235. LeBlanc, N.E. "Race, Housing, and Government." <u>Vanderbilt Law Review</u> 26 (1973), 487-507.

3236. Lee, Douglas B. <u>An Analysis and Descritpion of Residential Segregation, An Application of Centrographic Techniques to the Study of Spatial Distribution of Ethnic Groups in Cities.</u> Ithaca, New York: Center for Housing and Environmental Studies, Division of Urban Studies. Cornell University, 1965.

3237. Lee, Douglas B. <u>Analysis and Description of Residential Segregation.</u> Unpublished M.A. Thesis, Cornell University, 1966.

3238. Lee, Trevor R. "Ethnic and Social Class Factors in Residential Segreation: Some Implications for Dispersal." <u>Environment and Planning</u> 5 (1973), 477-490.

3239. Lee, Trevor R. <u>Socio-economic Considerations in the Residential Segregation of Ethnic and Racial Groups.</u> London School of Economics Graduate School of Geography Discussion Paper, 43 (1972), 1-15.

3240. Lehman, M.W. "Discrimination in F.H.A. Home Financing." <u>Chicago Bar Record</u> 40 (May 1959), 375-379.

3241. Lehman, M.W. "Must I Sell My House to a Negro?" Chicago Bar Record, 42 (March 1961), 283-288.

3242. Leigh, Wilhemina A. <u>Housing and Black Affordability</u>. Washington, D.C.: National Urban League Research Development,

1982.

3243. Leung, Lee. "Patterns of Residential Segregation: A Case Study." Great Plains - Rocky Mountain Geographical Journal 4 (1975), 87-93.

3244. Levin, Arthur J. and John Silard. Metropolitan Housing Desegregation. Washington, D.C.: The Potomac Institute, January 1966.

3245. Lewis, Horacio D. I Might As Well Move to the Moon: A Case Study on Housing Discrimination and a Legal Manual. Bloomington, IN.: Indiana University Press, 1974.

3246. Lewis, Hylan and Mozell Hill. "Desegregation, Integration and the Negro Community." Annals of the American Academy of Political and Social Sciences 304 (March 1956), 116-123.

3247. Lieberson, Stanley. "An Asymmetrical Approach to Segregation." In Ceri Peach, et al. (eds.) Segregation in Cities. London: Croom Helm, 1981, 61-82.

3248. Lieberson, Stanley. Ethnic Patterns in American Cities. New York: The Free Press of Glencoe, 1963.

3249. Lieberson, Stanley. "The Impact of Residential Segregation on Ethnic Assimilation." Social Forces 40 (October 1961), 52-57.

3250. Lieberson, Stanley and Donna K. Carter. "Temporal Changes and Urban Differences in Residential Segregation: A Reconsideration." American Journal of Sociology 88 (September 1982), 296-310.

3251. Lilley, W. "Housing Report: Romney Faces Political Perils with Plan to Integrate Suburbs." National Journal 2 (October 17, 1970), 2251-2263.

3252. Linder, Leo J. "The Social Results of Segregation in Housing." Lawyer's Guild Review 18 (Spring 1958), 2-11.

3253. Lipsky, Michael. Protest in City Politics, Rent Strikes, Housing and the Power of the Poor. Chicago: Rand McNally, 1970.

3254. Lipsky, Michael. "Rent Strikes: Poor Man's Weapon." Transaction 6 (February 1969), 10-15.

3255. Logan, John R. and Linda Stearns. Trends in Racial Segregation: A Caution on the Index of Dissimilarity. Paper presented at the 1980 Annual Meeting of the American Sociological Association, 1980.

3256. Long, Herman Hodge and Charles S. Johnson. People vs.

Property; Race Restrictive Covenants in Housing. Nashville: Fisk University Press, 1947.

3257. Long, Larry H. and Daphne Spain. Racial Succession in Individual Housing Units. Current Population Reports, Special Studies, Series P-23, No. 71. Washington, D.C.: U.S. Government Printing Office, 1979.

3258. Lopez, Manuel M. "Patterns of Interethnic Residential Segregation in the Urban Southwest, 1960-1970." Social Science Quarterly 62:1 (March 1981), 50-63.

3259. Lovett, Edward P. "Housing and Racial Prejudice 1966-1968." HUD Challenge 4 (1973), 6-11.

3260. Lowry, Ira S. Welfare Housing in New York City. New York: Rand, 1972.

3261. Lowry, Mark. "Racial Segregation: A Geographical Adaptation and Analysis." Journal of Geography 71 (January 1972), 28-40.

3262. Lyles, Lionel D. An Historical - Urban Geographical Analysis of Black Neighborhood Development in Denver, 1960-1970. Ph.D. Dissertation, University of Colorado, Boulder, Colorado, 1977.

3263. MacDonald, K.I. "Residential Segregation in United States Cities: A Comment." Social Forces 55 (September 1976), 85-88.

3264. MacErbe, Brigitt. "Race and Socioeconomic Segregation." American Sociological Review 40 (1975), 801-12.

3265. Madden, J. Patrick. "Poverty by Color and Residence -- Projections to 1975 and 1980." American Journal of Agricultural Economics 50 (December 1969), 1399-1412.

3266. Maher, C.A. "Spatial Patterns in Uran Housing Markets: Filtering in Toronto, 1953-1971." Canadian Geographer 18 (1974), 108-124.

3267. Mandelbaum, Joel. "Race Discrimination in Home Buying Resists Rough Laws." New York Times (December 3, 1972), B 11-17.

3268. Mandell, Richard. Report of Housing Problems in Williamantic. Williamantic, Connecticut: Windham Area Community Action Program, Inc., July 1969.

3269. Marantz, Janet K., et al. Discrimination in Rural Housing: Economic and Social Analysis of Six Selected Markets. Lexington, MA: Lexington Books, 1976.

3270. Marcuse, Peter. "Black Housing: A New Approach for Planners." Connection 6 (1969) 95-125.

3271. Margavio, Anthony Victor. Residential Segregation in New Orleans: A Statistical Analysis of Census Data. Ph.D. Thesis, The Louisiana State University and Agricultural and Mechanical College, 1968.

3272. Marshall, Harvey and Robert Jiobu. "Residential Segregation in United States Cities: Rejoinder." Social Forces 55 (1976), 89-92.

3273. Marshall, Harvey and John M. Stahura. "Determinants of Black Suburbanization: Regional and Suburban Size Category Patterns." The Sociological Quarterly 20:2 (1979), 237-253.

3274. Martin, A.J. "Segregating Residences of Negroes." Michigan Law Review 32 (April 1934), 721-742.

3275. Martin, Peter W. The Ill-Housed; Cases and Materials on Tenants' Rights in Private and Public Housing. Minneola, New York: Foundation Press, 1971.

3276. Maslen, Sidney. "Relocation in the Southeastern Region During the Process of Urban Renewal." Phylon 19 (Spring 1958), 70-71.

3277. Massey, S. Douglas. "On the Measurement of Segregation as a Random Variable." American Sociological Review 44 (1979), 587-590.

3278. Massey, S. Douglas. "Residential Segregation and Spatial Distribution of a Non-Labor Force Population: The Needy, Elderly and Disabled." Economic Geography 56:3 (1980), 190-200.

3279. Matre, Marc and Mindiola Tatcho. "Residential Segregation in Southwestern Metropolitan Areas: 1970." Sociological Focus 14 (January 1981), 15-31.

3280. Maxiarz, Thomas J. "A Factorial Ecology of Cincinnati's Black Residential Areas." Ohio Geographers: Recent Research Theme 2 (1974), 1-11.

3281. Maxwell, Lawrence. Segregation by Income in Residential Areas of Large U.S. Cities. Ph.D. Dissertation, University of California, Los Angeles, 1972.

3282. Mayer, Albert J. "Race and Private Housing: A Social Problem and a Challenge to Understanding Human Behavior." Journal of Social Issues 13 (1957), 253-273.

3283. Mayer, Albert J. The Urgent Future: People, Housing, City, Region. New York: McGraw-Hill, 1967.

3284. Mayo, Mary Lou. Residential Patterns and Their Socio-Economic Correlates: A Study of Blacks in Westchester County, New York. Ph.D. Thesis, Fordham University, 1974.

3285. Mayor's Statement on Open Housing Ordinance Given Before Common Council Judiciary Committee, October 16, 1967, Milwaukee.

3286. Mayor's Statement to the Legislature of the State of New York in Support of a Tax Program for New York City. New York, March 11, 1966.

3287. McAllister, Ronald J., et al. "Residential Mobility of Blacks and Whites: A National Longitudinal Survey." American Journal of Sociology 77:3 (1971), 445-457.

3288. McCarroll, Thomas. "CEDCO: Chicago's Catalyst for Change." Black Enterprise 12:4 (1982), 59-63.

3289. McClellan, Grant S. Crisis in Urban Housing. New York: Wilson, 1974.

3290. McEntire, Davis. Residence and Race; Final and Comprehensive Report to the Commission on Race and Housing. Berkeley, University of California Press, 1960.

3291. McEntire, Davis. "Government and Racial Discrimination in Housing." Journal of Social Issues 13 (Fall 1957), 60-87.

3292. McEvoy, D. and T.P. Jones. "More on Race and Space." Area 11:3 (1979), 222-223.

3293. McGovney, D.O. "Racial Residential Segregation by State Court Enforcement of Restrictive Agreements, Covenants or Conditions in Deeds is Un-Constitutional." California Law Review (March 1945), 4-39.

3294. McKee, James B. "Changing Patterns of Race and Housing: A Toledo Study." Social Forces 41 (1963), 253-60.

3295. McKee, James B. "Changing Patterns of Race and Housing: A Toledo Study." Social Forces 43 (March 1961), 353-360.

3296. McKenna, J.P. and H.D. Werner. "The Housing Market in Integrating Areas." Annals of Regional Science 4 (December 1970), 127-133.

3297. McTigue, Geraldine. "Patterns of Residence: Housing Distribution by Color in Two Louisiana Towns, 1860-1880." Louisiana Studies 15:4 (1976), 345-388.

3298. Meade, Anthony. "The Distribution of Segregation in Atlanta." Social Forces 51 (December 1972), 182-192.

3299. Meere, Bernard and Edward Freeman. "The Impact of Negro Neighbors on White Home Owners." Social Forces 45 (September 1966), 11-19.

3300. Mercer, John. "Housing Quality and the Ghetto." In Harold M. Rose (ed.) Geography of the Ghetto. Perspectives in Geography. Vol. II. Dekalb, Illinois: Northern Illinois University Press, 1972.

3301. Mercer, N.A. "Discrimination in Rental Housing: A Study of Resistance of Landlords to Non-White Tenants." Phylon 23 (1962), 45-47.

3302. Messner, Stephen D. Minority Groups and Housing: A Seleted Bibliography, 1950-1967. Storrs, Connecticut: University of Connecticut Press, 1968.

3303. Metropolitan, Philadelphia Housing Program of American Friends Service Committee, and Fair Housing Council of Delaware Valley. Looking for a House? Look Everywhere: A Guide to Metroplitan Philadelphia Communities. Philadelphia, Housing Information Service in Cooperation with the Author, 1960.

3304. "Metropolitan Segregation." Scientific American (October 1957), 33-41.

3305. Meyer, Douglas K. "Spatiotemporal Trends of Racial Residential Change." Land Economics 48 (1972), 62-65.

3306. Meyer, David R. "Interurban Differences in Black Housing Quality." Annals, Association of American Geographers 63 (1973), 347-352.

3307. Meyer, David R. "Implications of Some Recommended Alternative Urban Strategies for Black Residential Choice." In Harold M. Rose (ed.) Geography of the Ghetto: Perspectives in Geography. Vol. II. Dekalb, Illinois: Northern Illinois University Press, 1972.

3308. Meyer, David R. Spatial Variation of Black Households in Cities Within a Residential Choice Framework. Ph.D. Dissertation, University of Chicago, published as Department of Geography, Research Paper No. 129, 1970.

3309. Meyerson, Martin, et al. Housing, People and Cities. New York: McGraw Hill Co., 1962.

3310. Meyerson, Martin and Edward C. Banfield. Politics, Planning, and the Public Interest: The Case of Public Housing in Chicago. Glencoe, Illinois, Free Press, 1955.

3311. Mieszkowski, Peter. Studies of Prejudice and Discrimination in Urban Housing Markets. Boston: Federal Reserve Bank, 1979.

3312. Miles, Guy H. Some Factors in Minority Housing Patterns in Minneapolis. Final Report. Minneapolis: North Star Research and Development Institute, 1966.

3313. Milgram, Morris. "Commercial Development of Integrated Housing," Journal of Intergroup Relations 1:3 (Summer 1960), 1-10.

3314. Milgram, Morris. Good Neighborhood: the Challenge of Open Housing. New York: W.W. Norton, 1977.

3315. Milgram, Morris. Developing Open Communities. New York: Association Press, 1963.

3316. Milgram, Morris and Roger Beilson. Recommendations to Promote Racial Integration in Housing. New York: New York Planned Communities, Inc., 1968.

3317. Millen, James S. "Factors Affecting Racial Mixing in Residential Areas." In Amos H. Hawley and Vincent P. Rock (eds.) Segregation in Residential Areas. Washington, D.C.: National Academy of Sciences, 1973.

3318. Miller, L. "Government's Responsibility for Residential Segregation." In J. Denton (ed.) Race and Property. Berkeley, California: Diablo Press, 1964, 58-76.

3319. Miller, Vincent P.. "De Facto Segregation and Residential Stability in Pittsburgh's Last Burroughs." Pennsylvania Geographer 11 (1973), 19-25.

3320. Mitchell, Robert E. and Richard A. Smith. "Race and Housing: A Review and Comments on the Context and Effects of Federal Policy." Annals of the American Academy of Political and Social Science 441 (January 1979), 168-85.

3321. Molotch, Harvey. "Reply to Guest and Zuuiches: Another Look at Residential Turnover in Urban Neighborhoods." American Journal of Sociology 77 (1971), 468-471.

3322. Molotch, Harvey. "Racial Integration In a Transition Community." American Sociological Review 34 (1969), 878-893.

3323. Molotch, Harvey. Managed Integration. Berkeley: University of California Press, 1972.

3324. Mooney, Joseph B. "Housing Segregation, Negro Employment and Metropolitan Decentralization: An Alternative Perspective." Quarterly Journal of Economics 83 (May 1969), 299-311.

3325. Moore, Joan W. and Frank G. Mittelbach. Mexican American Study Project: Residential Segregation in the Urban Southwest. Los Angeles: University of California Advance Report 4, June 1966.

3326. Moore, Maurice and James McKeown. A Study of Integrated Living in Chicago. Chicago: Community and Family Study Center of the University of Chicago, 1968.

3327. Morgan, Barrie S. "Metropolitan Area Characteristics and Occupational Segregation." Transactions, Institute of British Geographers 5:2 (1980), 174-184.

3328. Morgan, Barrie S. Social Status Segregation in Comparative Perspective: The Case of the United Kingdom and United States. London: University of London King's College. Department of Geography, 1976.

3329. Morgan, Barrie S. "The Segregation of Socio-Economic Groups in Urban Areas: A Comparative Analysis." Urban Studies 12 (1975), 47-60.

3330. Morgan, Barrie S. and John Norbury. "Some Further Observations on the Index of Residential Differentiation." Demography 18 (1981), 251-256.

3331. Morner, Mognus. "The Theory and Practice of Racial Segregation in Colonial Spanish America." Proceedings of the Thirty-Second International Congress of Americanists (Copenhagen 1958), 708-713.

3332. Morris, D.C. "Racial Attitudes of White Residents in Integrated and Segregated Neighborhoods." Sociological Focus 6 (1973), 74-94.

3333. Mortgage Bankers Association of America, Committee on Financing Minority Housing. Report to the Board of Directors. Chicago: The Author, 1955.

3334. Moyer, Albert A. The Black Owned Boarding Home: A Primary Housing Resource for Former Mental Hospital Patients. Ph.D. Thesis, Union Graduate School - East, 1977.

3335. Musial, John J. The Measurement and Analysis of Residential Segregation in Metropolitan Areas. Detroit, MI: Detroit Commission on Community Relations, 1963.

3336. Musial, John J. Midwestern Minority Housing Markets: A Special Report. Detroit: Advance Mortgage Corporation, 1964.

3337. Muth, Richard F. "Residential Segregation and Discrimination." In M. Van Furstenberg, et al. (eds.) Patterns of Racial Discrimination in Housing. Lexington, MA: D.C. Heath, 1974.

3338. Myers, Samuel L. and Kenneth E. Phillips. "Housing Segregation and Black Employment: Another Look at the Ghetto Dispersal Strategy," American Economic Review 69 (1979), 298-302.

3339. Nance, Frederic D. Patterns of Negro Residential Segregation in Five Northern Cities. Unpublished Master's Thesis, Syracuse University, Department of Sociology, 1951.

3340. National Academy of Sciences, Freedom of Choice in Housing: Opportunities and Constraints. Washington, D.C., 1972.

3341. National Association for the Advancement of Colored People. Memorandum Concerning Present Discriminatory Practices of Federal Housing Administration, October 26, 1944.

3342. National Association of Intergroup Relations Officers (NAIRO). Report of Commission on Housing and Family Life -- 1955. Detroit: NAIRO, 1956.

3343. National Association of Real Estate Boards (NAREB). New Release No. 78. Washington, D.C.: NAREB, November 15, 1944.

3344. National Association of Real Estate Boards. Realtor Work for Negro Housing. Washington, D.C.: NAREB, October 24, 1944.

3345. National Association of Realtors. Realtors Guide to Practice Equal Opportunity in Housing. Chicago: National Association of Realtors, 1976.

3346. National Association of Realtors. Affirmative Marketing Handbook. Chicago: National Association of Realtors, 1975.

3347. National Comittee Against Discrimination in Housing (NCADH). Jobs and Housing: A Study of Employment and Housing Opportunities for Racial Minorities in Suburban Areas of the New York Metropolitan Area. New York: NCADH, 1970.

3348. National Committee Against Discrimination in Housing (NCADH). Freedom of Residence. New York: NCADH, 1963.

3349. National Committee Against Discrimination in Housing. Guide to Fair Housing Law Enforcement. Washington, D.C.: U.S. Department of Housing and Urban Development, 1964.

3350. National Committee Against Discrimination in Housing. The Impact of Housing Patterns on Job Opportunities. New York: NCADH, 1968.

3351. National Committee Against Discrimination In Housing Brotherhood-in-Action Housing Conference. Affirmative Action to Achieve Integration: A Report Based on the NCADH Brotherhood-in-Action Housing Conference. New York: NCADH, 1966.

3352. National Committee Against Discrimination in Housing. How Will Equal Opportunity Fare Under the New Housing and Community Development Art. Washington, D.C., NCADH, 1974.

3353. National Committee on Segregation in the Nation's Capital. Segregation in Washington. Washington, D.C.: The Committee, 1948.

3354. National Housing Agency. Negro Share of Priority War Housing--
Private and Public as of December 31, 1944. Washington, D.C.:
Office of Principal Housing Analyst, May 1, 1945.

3355. National Public Housing Conference (NPHC). Race Relations in
Housing Policy. Washington, D.C.: NPHC, 1940.

3356. National Urban League. Racial Problems in Housing. New York:
National Urban League, 1944.

3357. National Urban League. Unemployment Among Negroes . . . Data
on 25 Industrial Cities. New York: National Urban League,
1930.

3358. National Urban League. A Documented Report on Housing. New
York: National Urban League, 1955.

3359. Needham, Maurice d'Arlan. Negro Orleanian: Status and Stake in
a City's Economy and Housing. New Orleans: Tulane
Publications, 1962.

3360. "Negro Faces Housing Test in Major Shift to Suburbs." The New
York Times (July 9, 1961), 1.

3361. "Negro Segregation Adopted by St. Louis". Survey 35 (1916),
694.

3362. "Negro Segregation in Cities." Chautauquan 62 (1911), 11-13.

3363. "Negro Segregation in St. Louis." Literary Digest 52 (1916),
6702.

3364. "Negro's Right of Residence." Literary Digest 55 (1917), 17-
18.

3365. Nelson, Susan Caroline. Housing Discrimination and Black
Employment Opportunities. Ph.D. Thesis, Princeton University,
1976.

3366. Nesbitt, George B. "Misconceptions in the Movement for Civil
Rights in Housing." Journal of Intergroup Relations 2 (Winter
1960-1961), 61-67.

3367. Nesbitt, George B. and Marian P. Yankauser. "The Potential for
Equalizing Housing Opportunity in the Nation's Capital."
Journal of Intergroup Relations 4 (Winter 1962-1963), 73-97.

3368. Newbacher, Gary D. Low Income Housing Mixing: An Annotated
Bibliography. Monticello, Ill.: Council of Planning
Librarians, 1975.

3369. Newman, Bernard J. Housing in the City Negro. Philadelphia:
Whittier Center, 1915.

3370. Newman, Bernard J. "The Housing of Negro Immigrants in Pennsylvania." Opportunity 2 (1924), 46-48.

3371. New York, State of. State Commission for Human Rights. In Search of Housing: A Study of Experiences of Negro Professional and Technical Personnel in New York State by Eunice and George Grier. Albany, New York: State Commission Against Discrimination, 1958.

3372. Nichols, Woodrow W. "Residence - Shopping Place Separation of Black Communities," in R.A. Obudho (ed.) Afro-Americans and the City. Albany, New York: State University of New York Press, 1984.

3373. Noe, Kaye Sizer. The Fair Housing Movement: An Overview and a Case Study. College Park, Maryland, 1965.

3374. Nordsiek, Evelyn M. The Residential Location and Mobility of Blacks in Indianapolis, 1850-1880. M.A. Thesis, University of Maryland, College Page, MD, 1975.

3375. Northwood, Lawrence K. Urban Desegregation: Negro Pioneers and Their White Neighbors. Seattle, University of Washinton, 1965.

3376. Northwood, Lawrence K. and Ernest A.T. Barth. Urban Desegregation: Negro Pioneers and Their White Neighbors. Seattle: School of Social Work, Department of Sociology, University of Washington, 1966.

3377. Oakland-Kenwood Property Owners' Association. President's Annual Report for the year 1944 Chicago, 1945.

3378. O'Connell, George Edward. Residential Segregation by Racial-Ethnic Background and Socio-Economic Status in Four Standard Metropolitan Statistical Areas, 1970. Ph.D. Thesis, University of Minnesota, 1974.

3379. O'Connor, Michael James. The Measurement and Significance of Racial Residential Barriers in Atlanta, 1890-1970. Ph.D. Thesis, University of Georgia, 1977.

3380. Onderdonk, Dudley, et al. Integration in Housing: A Plan for Racial Diversity. Forest Park, IL: Planning Division, 1977.

3381. Openshaw, H. Race and Residence: An Analysis of Property Values in Transitional Areas, Atlanta, Georgia, 1960-1971. Georgia State University, School of Business Administration, Atlanta, GA, Monograph No. 53, 1973.

3382. "Ordinance Segregating Whites and Blacks Into Separate "Communities" Within City Upheld." Yale Law Journal 36 (1926), 274-5..

3383. Orfield, Gary. "Federal Agencies and Urban Segregation: Steps Toward Coordinated Action." In Gary Orfield and William L. Taylor (eds.) Racial Segregation: Two Policy Views. New York: The Ford Foundation, 1979, 6-44.

3384. Paderanga, Cayetano Woo, Jr. Racial Preferences and Housing Prices: The Case of San Mateo County, California. Ph.D. Thesis, Stanford University, 1979.

3385. Page, Alfred N. "Race and Property Values." Appraised Journal 36 (July 1968), 334-341.

3386. Page, Alfred N. and Warren P. Seyfried. "Urban Housing and Racial Integration," In Urban Analysis: Readings in Housing and Urban Development. Glenview, Illinois: Scott, Foresman, and Company, 1970.

3387. Palmer, Stuart H. The Role of the Real Estate Agent in the Structuring of Residential Areas: A Study in Social Control. Unpublished Ph.D. Thesis, Yale University, 1955.

3388. Palmore, Erdman. "Integration and Property Values in Washington, D.C." Phylon 27 (Spring 1968), 15-19.

3389. Palmore, Erdman and John Howe. "Residential Integration and Property Values." Social Problems 10 (Summer 1962), 52-55.

3390. Park, Woo-Suh. An Empirical Analysis of the Rental Housing Market, The Borough of Manhattan, New York: Do Blacks Pay More Than Whites? Ph.D. Thesis, New York University, 1979.

3391. Pascal, Anthony H. The Economics of Housing Segregation. Santa Monica, CA: Rand Corporation, 1967.

3392. Pascal, Anthony H. The Economics of Housing Segregation. Ph.D. Thesis, Columbia University, 1967.

3393. Patterson, John. "Racial Inequality in Federal Housing Programs: A Welfare Geography Approach." Southeastern Geographer 19:2 (1979), 114-126.

3394. Paulus, Virginia. Housing: A Bibliography: 1960-1972. New York: AMS Press, 1974.

3395. Peach, Ceri. "Ethnic Segregation and Intermarriage." Annals, Association of American Geographers 70:3 (1980), 371-381.

3396. Pearce, Diana M. Black, White and Many Shades of Gray: Real Estate Brokers and Their Racial Practices. Ph.D. Thesis, University of Michigan, 1976.

3397. Pearce, Diana M. "Gatekeepers and Homeseekers: Institutional Patterns in Racial Stearing." Social Problems 26 (February

1979):325–42.

3398. Pearlman, Kenneth. "The Closing Door: The Supreme Court and Residential Segregation." Journal of the American Institute of Planners. 44:2 (April 1978), 160–69.

3399. Pettigrew, Thomas F. "Attitudes on Race and Housing: A Social-Psychological View." In Amos H. Hawley and Vincent P. Rock (eds.) Segregation in Residential Areas. Washington, D.C.: National Academy of Sciences, 1973, 21–84.

3400. Pettigrew, Thomas F. "Black and White Attitudes Toward Race and Housing." In T.F. Pettigrew (ed.) Racial Discrimination in the United States. New York: Harper and Row, 1975, 10–20.

3401. Pettigrew, Thomas F. "Racial Change and the Intrametropolitan Distribution of Black Americans," in Arthur P. Solomon (ed.), The Prospective City: Economic, Population, Energy, and Environmental Developments. Cambridge, Mass.: MIT Press, 1980, 52–79.

3402. Phares, Donald. "Racial Transition and Residential Property Values." Annals of Regional Science 5 (1972), 152–160.

3403. Pinkerto, J.R. The Residential Redistribution of Socio-Economic Strata in Metropolitan Areas. Unpublished Ph.D. Dissertation, University of Wisconsin, Madison, 1965.

3404. Poole, M.A. and F. Boal. "Religious Residential Segregation in Belfast in Mid 1969: A Multi-Level Approach." In B.D. Clark and M.B. Gleave (eds.) Social Patterns in Cities. London: Institute of British Geographer's Special Publication, 5, 1973.

3405. Popenoe, D. "Urban Residential Differentiation: Overview of Patterns, Trends, and Problems." Sociological Inquiry 43 (1973), 35–56.

3406. Porter, William A. Analysis of the Residential Structure of Underprivileged Black Neighborhoods: A Case of Manhattan, Kansas. M.A. Thesis, Kansas State University, Manhattan, KS, 1973.

3407. Portes, A. "Dilemma of a Golden Exile: Integration of Cuban Refugee Families in Milwaukee." American Sociological Review 34 (1969), 505–518.

3408. Poston, Dudley and Jeffrey Passel. "Texas Population in 1970: Racial Residential Segregation in Cities." Texas Business Review 46 (July 1972), 1–6.

3409. Potomac Institute. The Federal Role in Equal Housing Opportunity: An Affirmative Program to Implement Executive Order 11063. Prepared by Arthur J. Levin, Staff Director,

Washington, D.C.: The Institute, 1964.

3410. Potomac Institute. A Guide to Equal Opportunity in Housing. Washington, D.C.: The Author, 1964.

3411. Powers, Mary G. "Class, Ethnicity, and Residence in Metropolitan America." Demography 5 (1968), 443-448.

3412. President's Conference on Home Building and Home Ownership. Negro Housing; Report of the Committee on Negro Housing, Nannie H. Burroughs, Chairman; Prepared for the Committee by Charles S. Johnson; edited by John M. Gries and James Ford Washington. Washington, D.C.: Government Printing Office, 1932.

3413. Price, William L. Factors Influencing and Pertaining to the Housing Mobility of Negroes in Metropolitan Detroit. Detroit Urban League, 1957.

3414. Property Values in Louisville's Changing Neighborhoods: Analyzing the Effect of Minority Entry on Real Estate Values. Frankfort, Kentucky: Commission on Human Rights, August 1967.

3415. Pynocs, Jon, et al. (ed.) Housing Urban America. Chicago: Aldine Publishing Company, 1973.

3416. Quimby, Harriet. "Better Homes for Negroes." Southern Workman 34 (1905), 505.

3417. Rabkin, Sol. A Landmark Decision on Segregation in Housing. Jones vs. Meyer. New York: Anti-Defamation League of B'nai B'rith, 1969.

3418. "Racial Discrimination in the Private Housing Sector Five Years After." Maryland Law Review 33 (1973), 289-326.

3419. "Racial Discrimination by State Leasee as State Action." Iowa Law Review 47 (Spring 1962), 716.

3420. "Racial Discrimination in Housing." University of Pennsylvania Law Review 107 (February 1959), 515-550.

3421. "Racial Restriction in Leaseholds." University of Florida Law Review 11 (Fall 1958), 344-351.

3422. "Racially Restrictive Covenants in Deeds." Georgia Bar Journal 25 (November 1962), 232-238.

3423. Radford, John P. "Delicate Space: Race and Residence in Charleston, South Carolina, 1860-1880." West Georgia College Studies in the Social Sciences 16 (1977), 17-37.

3424. Radford, John P. "Race and Residence in Charleston, South Carolina, 1860-1880." Essays on the Human Geography of the

Southeastern United States. No. 16. Carrolltown, GA: West Georgia College Studies in the Social Sciences, 1977.

3425. Rapkin, Chester. Market Experience and Occupancy Patterns in Interracial Housing Developments. Philadelphia: University of Pennsylvania, Institute of Urban Studies, July, 1957.

3426. Rapkin, Chester. "Price Discrimination Against Negroes in Rental Housing Markets." in Essays in Urban Land Economics. Los Angeles: Real Estate Research Center, University of California, 1966.

3427. Rapkin, Chester and William G. Grigsby. The Demand for Housing in Eastwick: A Presentation of Estimates and Forecasts, Including Methods and Techniques for Analyzing the Housing Market in a Large Scale Open Occupancy Redevelopment Area. Philadelphia: Redevelopment Authority of the City of Philadelphia, 1960.

3428. Rapkin, Chester and William G. Grigsby. The Demand for Housing in Racially Mixed Areas: A Study of the Nature of Neighborhood Change. Berkeley: University of California Press, 1960.

3429. Rasmussen, Gerald. Let's Open The Doors in Des Moines: The Story of the Campaign to Get Signatures on a Statement of Conscience. Des Moines: 1959.

3430. Reeb, Donald J. (ed.) Housing the Poor. New York: Praeger, 1973.

3431. Regional Plan Association. "Segregation and Opportunity in the Region's Housing." Regional Plan News 104 (July 1979), 4-8.

3432. Reid, Clifford E. "Measuring Residential Decentralization of Blacks and Whites." Urban Studies 14 (October 1977), 353-358.

3433. Reid, Margaret Y. Housing and Income. Chicago: University of Chicago Press, 1962.

3434. Reiner, T.A. "Racial Segregation: A Comment." Journal of Regional Science 12 (1972), 137-148.

3435. Rice, R.L. "Residential Segregation by Law." The Journal of Southern History 34 (1968), 194-199.

3436. Rich, J.M. "Municipal Boundaries in a Discriminatory Housing Market - An Example of Racial Leapfrogging." Urban Studies 21:1 (February 1984), 31-40.

3437. Rich, Richard. "Neglected Issues in the Study of Urban Service Distributions: A Research Agenda." Urban Studies 16 (1979) 143-156.

3438. Richardson, Ann. The Availability of Apartments for African Diplomats. Washington, D.C.: Bureau of Social Science Research, Inc., 1963.

3439. Richmond, Anthony. Ethnic Residential Segregation in Metropolitan Toronto. Toronto: Institute for Behavioral Research, York University, 1972.

3440. Riis, Jacob A. How The Other Half Lives: Studies Among the Tenements of New York. New York: Sagamore Press, 1957.

3441. "Riots: What Happened to Public Housing in Newark, Detroit and San Francisco," Journal of Housing 24 (August 1967), 371-78.

3442. Roberts, Richard J. "Fair Housing Laws: A Tool for Racial Equality." Social Order 12 (January 1962), 20-34.

3443. Roberts, Richard J. The Emergence of a Civil Right: Anti-Discrimination Legislation in Private Housing in the United States. Ph.D. Thesis, Saint Louis University, 1961.

3444. Robinson, Corienne K. "Relationship Between Condition of Dwellings and Rentals, by Race." Journal of Land and Public Utility Economics (August 1946), 296-302.

3445. Roof, Wade Clark. "Residential Segregation of Blacks and Racial Inequality in Southern Cities: Toward a Causal Model." Social Problems 19 (Winter 1972), 393-407.

3446. Roof, Wade Clark. "Southern Birth and Racial Residential Segregation: The Case of Northern Cities." American Journal of Sociology 86:2 (1980), 350-358.

3447. Roof, Wade Clark. "Race and Residence: The Shifting Base of American Race Relations." In Norman R. Yetman and Hoy Steele (eds.) Majority and Minority Relations: The Dynamics of Race and Ethnicity in American Life. Boston: Allyn & Bacon, 1981.

3448. Roof, Wade Clark. "Race and Residence: The Shifting Basis of American Race Relations." Annals of the American Academy of Politial and Social Sciences 441 (1979), 1-12.

3449. Roof, Wade Clark and Thomas L. Van Valey. "Residential Segregation and Social Differentiation in American Urban Areas." Social Forces 51 (September 1972), 87-91.

3450. Roof, Wade Clark, et al. "Residential Segregation in Southern Cities: 1970." Social Forces 55 (September 1976), 58-71.

3451. Rose, Harold M. "Inconsistencies in Attitudes Toward Negro Housing." Social Problems 8 (Spring 1961), 286.

3452. Rose, Harold. "The Problem of Segregated Housing and The

Applied Social Researcher." Social Problems 12 (Fall 1964), 241-247.

3453. Rose, Harold M. Social Processes in the City: Race and Urban Residential Choice. Washington, D.C.: Association of American Geographers, Commission on College Geography, Resource paper No. 6, 1969.

3454. Rose, Harold M. Social Processes in the City: Race and Urban Residential Choice. Commission on College Geography Resource Paper No. 6. Association of American Geographers, Washington, D.C., 1969.

3455. Rose, Harold M. "The Spatial Development of Black Residential Subsystems," Economic Geography 48 (1972), 44-65.

3456. Rose, Harold M., et al. "Neighborhood Reactions to Isolated Negro Residents: An Alternative in Invasion and Succession." American Sociological Review 18 (October 1953), 497-507.

3457. Roseman, D.M. "May Operative Builders of F.H.A. Housing Be Barred from Discriminating Against Purchasers on Basis of Race." Boston Bar Journal 3 (December 1959), 21-24.

3458. Rosen, H.M. and D.H. Rosen. But Not Next Door. New York: I. Obolenshy, 1962.

3459. Rosenberg, Terry J. Residence, Employment and Mobility of Puerto Ricans in New York City. Chicago: University of Chicago, Department of Geography, Research Paper No. 141, 1974.

3460. Rosenberg, Terry J. and Robert Lake. "Toward a Revised Model of Residential Segregation and Success: Puerto Ricans in New York 1960-1970." American Journal of Sociology 81 (March 1976), 1142-1150.

3461. Roshco, Bernard. "The Integration Problem and Public Housing." New Leader 43 (July 4-11, 1960), 10-13.

3462. Ross, Myron H. "Prices, Segregation and Racial Harmony." Journal of Black Studies 2 (December 1971), 225-243.

3463. Rosser, Lawrence B. Ending the Dual Racial Market in Real Estate: A Proposal to Create a Metropolitan Wide Unitary Real Estate Marketing System for Sales and Rentals. Washington, D.C.: National Committee Against Discrimination in Housing, 1975.

3464. Rowley, Gwyn. "Geography, Segregation and American Urban Society." Geojournal 4:4 (1980), 349-357.

3465. Rubinowitz, Leonard S. Low-Income Housing: Suburban Strategies. Cambridge, Massachusetts: Ballinger, 1974.

3466. Runnion, D.A. "Civil Rights: Attorney's Fees Held Part of an Effective Remedy Against Racial Discrimination in Housing." Journal of Public Law 21 (1972), 223-237.

3467. Russell Sage Foundation. Negro Housing in Towns and Cities, 1927-1937. New York: Russell Sage Foundation, 1937.

3468. Rutledge, Edward. "Housing Bias in the College Community." Journal of Intergroup Relations 1 (Fall 1960), 30-39.

3469. Rutledge, Edward. Site Selection, Costs and Interracial Housing. Detroit: National Association of Intergroup Relations. New York, 1956.

3470. Sacks, Sadelle R. Annual Housing Report. Balmont Massachusetts: Fair Housing Incorporated, 1963.

3471. Saks, J.H. and Sol Rabkin. "Racial and Religious Discrimination in Housing: A Report of Legal Progress." Iowa Law Review 45 (Spring 1960), 488-524.

3472. Sakumoto, Raymond E. "Residential Segregation in a Multi-Ethnic Metropolis: Honolulu." In S. Greet, et al. (eds.) The New Urbanization. New York: St. Martin, 1968, 169-178.

3473. Salling, Mark J. "Residential Preferences in Three Neighborhoods of Different Racial Composition." East Lakes Geographer 10 (1976), 91-109.

3474. Saltman, Juliet. "Housing Discrimination: Policy Research, Methods and Results." Annals of the American Academy of Political and Social Science 441 (January 1979), 186-96.

3475. Saltman, Juliet. Open Housing: Dynamics of a Social Movement. New York: Praeger, 1978.

3476. Saltman, Juliet. "Implementing Open Housing Laws Through Social Action." Journal of Applied Behavioral Science 11 (1975), 39-61.

3477. Schafer, Robert. Racial Discrimination in the Boston Housing Market. Cambridge, MA: Harvard University, City and Regional Planning Department, Discussion Paper D-76-6, 1976.

3478. Schafer, Robert. "Racial Discrimination in the Boston Housing Market." Journal of Urban Economics 6 (April 1979), 176-96.

3479. Schechter, Alan H. "Impact of Open Housing Laws on Suburban Realtors." Urban Affairs Quarterly 8 (June 1973), 439-63.

3480. Schelling, Thomas C. "The Process of Residential Segregation: Neighborhood Tipping." In Anthony Pascal (ed.) Racial Discrimination in Economic Life. Lexington, MA: D.C. Heath,

1972.

3481. Schermer, G. and Arthur J. Levin. Housing Guide to Equal Opportunity: Affirmative Practices for Integrated Housing. Washington, D.C.: Potomac Institute, 1968.

3482. Schiltz, Michael E. "Interracial Housing." Social Order 11 (June 1961), 276-279.

3483. Schietinger, Egbert F. "Racial Succession and Changing Property Values in Residential Chicago." In E.W. Burgess and D.J. Bogue (eds.) Contributions to Urban Sociology. Chicago: University of Chicago Press, 1964.

3484. Schietinger, Egbert F. Racial Succession and Changing Property Values In Residential Chicago. Chicago: University of Chicago Press, 1953.

3485. Schnare, Ann B. Externalities, Segregation and Housing Prices. Washington, D.C.: The Urban Institute, 1974.

3486. Schnare, Ann B. The Persistence of Racial Segregation in Housing. Washington, D.C.: the Urban Institute, 1978.

3487. Schnare, Ann B. "Racial and Ethnic Price Differentials in a Urban Housing Market." Urban Studies 13 (1976), 107-120.

3488. Schnare, Ann B. Residential Segregation by Race in United States Metropolitan Areas: An Analysis Across Cities and Over Time. Washington, D.C.: Urban Institute, February 1977.

3489. Schnare, Ann B. "Trends in Residential Segregation by Race." Journal of Urban Economics 7 (May 1980), 293-301.

3490. Schnare, Ann B. and Raymond J. Struyk. "An Analysis of Ghetto Housing Prices Over Time." In Gregory K. Ingram (ed.) Residential Location and Urban Housing Markets. New York: National Bureau of Economic Research, 1977, 95-133.

3491. Schnell, George. "Pennsylvania's Black Population: A Study of Recent Spatial Trends." Pennsylvania Geographer 11 (1973), 3-11.

3492. Schnelling, Thomas C. "Dynamic Models of Segregation." Journal of Mathematical Sociology 1 (1971), 143-186.

3493. Schnelling, Thomas C. Models of Segregation. Santa Monica, CA: The Rand Corporation, May 1969.

3494. Schnore, Leo F. "Social Class Segregation Among Non-Whites in Metropolitan Centers." Demography 2 (1965), 126-133.

3495. Schnore, Leo F. and Philip Evenson. "Segregation in Southern

Cities." <u>American Journal of Sociology</u> 72 (July 1966), 58-67.

3496. Schnore, Leo F. and J.R. Pinderton. "Residential Redistribution of Socioeconomic Strata in Metropolitan Areas." <u>Demography</u> 3 (1966), 491-499.

3497. Schoenberg, Sandra and Charles Bailey. "The Symbolic Meaning of An Elite Black Community: The Ville in St. Louis." <u>Missouri Historical Society Bulletin</u> 33:2 (1977),94-102.

3498. Schorr, Alvin Louis. <u>Slums and Social Insecurity, An Appraisal of the Effectiveness of Housing Policies in Helping to Eliminate Poverty in the United States.</u> Washington, D.C.: Government Printing Office, 1963.

3499. Schwirian, F.P. and J. Rica-Velasco. "The Residential Distribution of Status Groups in Puerto Rico's Metropolitan Areas." <u>Demography</u> 8 (1971), 81-90.

3500. Schwulst, Earl . <u>Race and Housing: The Basic American Dilemma</u>. Address by Earl B. Schmulst before the National Urban League and the Urban League of Greater New York on April 1959.

3501. Sears, David W. and David Faytell. "Black Residential Segregation in American Metropolitan Regions: Some Changes During the 1960-1970 Decade." <u>Review of Public Data Use</u> 2 (July 1974), 35-40.

3502. "The Segregation of the Negro in Separate Residence Districts. Note to State versus Garry, Indiana." <u>Harvard Law Review</u> 27 (1914), 270-71.

3503. "Segregation of the White and Negro Races in Cities; Types of Ordinances." <u>South Atlantic</u> 13 (1914), 1-11.

3504. "Segregation of the White and Negro Races in Rural Communities of North Carolina." <u>South Atlantic Quarterly</u> 13 (1914), 107-17.

3505. "Segregation Ordinance. Harris versus City of Louisville, KY.177 S.W. 471 Carey versus City of Atlanta, GA." <u>University of Pennsylvania Law Review</u> 63 (1916), 895.

3506. "Segregation Ordinances Prohibiting Acquisition of Residence Property by Negroes or Whites Rspectively in Certain Blocks in Cities." <u>Central Law Journal</u> 85 (1914), 422-3.

3507. Seligman, Herbert. "A Protest Against Ghetto Conditions." <u>Current History</u> 25 (1926), 831-833.

3508. "Separating Residence of White and Colored Races." <u>Chicago Legeislative News</u> 46 (1913), 167-8.

3509. Setlow, Marcie L. <u>Metropolitan Open Housing Ordinance in</u>

Illinois: Their Effectiveness as a Deterrant to Segregated Housing. Master's Thesis, University of Chicago, 1968.

3510. Shaffer, Helen B. Interracial Housing. Washington, D.C.: Editorial Research Reports, 1963.

3511. Shannon, Gary W. Residential Distribution and Travel Patterns: A Case Study of Detroit Elementary School Teachers. M.A. Thesis, University of Michigan, Ann Arbor, Michigan, 1965.

3512. Shuman, Sara. "Differential Rents for White and Negro Families." Journal of Housing (August 1946), 167-74.

3513. Simkus, Albert A. "Residential Segregation by Occupation and Race in Ten Urbanized Areas, 1950-1970." American Sociological Review 43 (February 1978), 81-93.

3514. Simmons, James W. "Changing Residence in the City: A Review of Intraurban Mobility." The Geographical Review 58 (October 1968), 622-51.

3515. Simpson, George and John M. Yinger. Racial and Cultural Minorities: An Analysis of Prejudice and Discrimination. New York: Harper & Row, 1972.

3516. Smart, Walter. The Large Poor Family: A Housing Gap. Washington, D.C.: National Commisson on Urban Problems, 1968.

3517. Smith, Bulkeley. "The Differential Residential Segregation of Working Class Negroes in New Have." American Sociological Review 24 (August 1959), 529-537.

3518. Smith, Bulkeley. "The Reshuffling Phenomenon: A Pattern of Residence of Unsegregated Negroes." American Sociological Review 24 (February 1959), 77-79.

3519. Smith, Christopher Beck. Private Residential Integration in a Northern City: A Further Analysis of the Interracial Contact Hypothesis Ph.D. Thesis, University of Notre Dame, 1977.

3520. Smith, Lella. Apartment Integration in Suburban Washington: A Survey of the Effect of Admitting Negro Tenants to Apartments Previously Closed To Them. Washington, D.C.: Metropolitan Washington Housing Program, American Friends Service Committee, June 1967.

3521. Smith, Richard A. "An Analysis of Black Occupancy of Mobile Homes." Journal of the American Institute of Planners 2:4 (October 1976), 410-18.

3522. Snyder, D. and P.M. Hudis. "Occupational Income and Effects of Minority Competition and Segregation: Re-Analysis and Some New Evidence." American Sociological Review 41 (1975), 309-324.

3523. Solomon, Arthur P. Housing the Urban Poor: A Critical Evaluation of Federal Housing Policy. Cambridge, Massachusetts: MIT Press, 1974.

3524. Sorenson, Annemette, et al. "Indexes of Racial Residential Segregation for 109 Cities in the United States, 1940-1970." Sociological Focus 8 (April 1975), 124-142.

3525. Spain, Daphne G. "Race Relations and Residential Segregation in New Orleans: Two Centuries of Paradox." Annals of the American Academy of Political and Social Sciences 441 (1979), 82-96.

3526. Spain, Daphne G. The Effects of Intrametropolitan Mobility on Racial Residential Segregation. Unpublished Ph.D. Thesis. University of Massachusetts, 1977.

3527. Spain, Daphne G., et al. Housing Successions Among blacks and Whites in Cities and Suburbs. U.S. Bureau of the Census, Current Population Reports, Special Studies, Series P-23, No. 101. Washington, D.C.: U.S. Government Printing Office, 1980.

3528. Spaulding, Charles B. "Housing Problems of Minority Groups in Los Angeles." Annals of the American Academy of Political and Social Sciences, November 1946, 220-25.

3529. Spiegel, Allen David. Housing and Related Patterns of Middle Income Negroes. Ph.D. Brandeis University, 1969.

3530. Stafford, Walter William. An Analysis of Grants and Public Housing Units Approved for Municipalities by the Department of Housing and Urban Development 1965-1970 and Their Relationships to the Black Population. Ph.D. Thesis, University of Pittsburgh, 1973.

3531. Statura, M. "Determinants of Change in the Distribution of Blacks Across Suburbs." Sociological Quarterly 24:3 (1983), 79-93.

3532. Stegman, Michael A. Housing Investment in the Inner-City: The Dynamics of Decline; A Study of Baltimore, Maryland, 1968-1970. Cambridge, Massachusetts, MIT Press, 1972.

3533. Stephens, J.D. and R.I. Wittick. "Institutional Unit for Simulating Urban Residential Segregation." Professonal Geographer 27 (1975), 340-346.

3534. Stephenson, Gilbert Thomas. "Segregation of the White and Negro Races in Cities by Legislation." National Municipal Review 3 (1914), 496-504.

3535. Sternlieb, George S. The Ecology of Welfare, Housing and the Welfare Crisis in New York City. New Brunswick, New Jersey:

Transaction Books, 1973.

3536. Sternlieb, George S. _Abandonment and Rehabilitation: What Is To Be Done?_ New Brunswick, New Jersey: Rutgers University, 1970.

3537. Sternlieb, George S. (ed.) _Housing, 1971-1972, An AMS Anthology._ New York, AMS Press, 1974.

3538. Sternlieb, George S. and Robert W. Lake. "Aging Suburbs and Black Homeownership." _Annals of the American Academy of Political and Social Science_ 422 (November 1975); 105-17.

3539. Stetler, Henry. _Racial Integration in Private Interracial Neighborhoods in Connecticut._ Hartford, CT: Commission on Human Rights, 1957.

3540. Stetler, Henry. _Racial Integration by Public Housing Projects in Connecticut._ Hartford, Connecticut: Connecticut Commission on Civil Rights, 1950.

3541. Steward, J.E. "Racial Discrimination in Public Housing: Rights and Remedies." _University of Chicago Law Review_ 41 (1974), 582-603.

3542. Stone, Michael. "The Housing Crisis, Mortgage Lending, and Class Struggle." In Richard Peet's (ed.) _Radical Geography._ Chicago: Maaroufa Press, 1977, 14-20.

3543. Straits, Bruce C. "Residential Movement Among Negroes and Whites in Chicago." _Social Science Quarterly_ 49 (December 1968), 5-7.

3544. Straszhe, M.R. "Housing Market Discrimination and Black Housing Consumption." _Quarterly Journal of Economics_ 88 (1974), 19-43.

3545. Stubbs, A.C. and F. Drew. "Representative Housing of Three Ethnic Groups in Texas." _Housing Educators Journal_ (1975), 7-15.

3546. Sudman, S., et al. "The Extent and Characteristics of Racially Integrated Housing in the United States." _Journal of Business_ 42 (January 1969), 50-87.

3547. Sumka, Howard Jeffrey. _Racial Discrimination in Urban Rental Housing: An Analysis of Southern Nonmetropolitan Markets With Implications For Demand Side Housing Assistance._ Ph.D. Thesis, The University of North Carolina at Chapel Hill, 1976.

3548. Swados, Harvey. _When Black and White Live Together, in Rockdale Village, New York City._ New York, 1966.

3549. Taeuber, Alma F. A Comparative Urban Analysis of Negro Residential Succession. Chicago: University of Chicago Press, 1962.

3550. Taeuber, Alma F. and Karl E. Taeuber. "The Negro as an Immigrant Group: Recent Trends in Racial and Ethnic Segregation in Chicago." American Journal of Sociology 69 (January 1964), 374-382.

3551. Taeuber, Karl E. "On Assessing Segregation Indexes." American Sociological Review 28 (June 1963), 453-454.

3552. Taeuber, Karl E. "The Effect of Income Redistribution on Racial Residential Segregation." Urban Affairs Quarterly 4 (September 1968), 5-14.

3553. Taeuber, Karl E. Negroes in Cities: Residential Segregation and Neighborhood Change. Chicago: Aldine, 1965.

3554. Taeuber, Karl E. "Negro Population and Housing: Demographic Aspects of a Social Accounting Scheme." In Irwin Katz and Patricia Gurin (eds.) Race and the Social Sciences. New York: Basic Books, 1969, 145-193.

3555. Taeuber, Karl E. "Negro Residential Segregation: Trends and Measurement." Social Problems 12 (Summer 1964), 42-50.

3556. Taeuber, Karl E. Patterns of Negro-White Residential Segregation. Santa Monica, CA.: The Rand Corporation, 1970.

3557. Taeuber, Karl E. "Patterns of Negro-White Residential Segregation." The Milbank Memorial Fund Quarterly 48 (April 1970), 69-84.

3558. Taeuber, Karl E. "The Problem of Residential Segregation." Proceedings of the Academy of Political Science 29 (1968), 101-110.

3559. Taeuber, Karl E. "The Problem of Residential Segregation." In R.H. Connery (ed.) Urban Riots. New York: Vintage Press, 1969, 101-110.

3560. Taeuber, Karl E. "Racial Segregation: The Persisting Dilemma." Annals of the American Academy of Political and Social Science 422 (November 1975), 87-96.

3561. Taeuber, Karl E. "Residential Segregation." Scientific American 213 (August 1965), 12-19.

3562. Taeuber, Karl E. Residential Segregation by Color in the United States Cities, 1940 and 1950: A Comparative Analysis. Harvard University, 1960.

3563. Taeuber, Karl E. "Trends in Residential Segregation of Non-Whites in American Cities, 1940-1950." *American Sociological Review* 16 (February 1956), 825-883.

3564. Taeuber, Karl E. and Alma Taeuber. "A Practitioner's Perspective on the Index of Dissimilarity." *American Sociological Review* 41 (1976), 884-889.

3565. Tata, Robert, et al. "Defensible Space in a Housing Project: A Case Study from a South Florida Ghetto." *Professional Geograher*. 27:3 (1975), 297-303.

3566. Taylor, D. Garth. "Housing, Neighborhoods, and Race Relations: Recent Survey Evidence." *Annals of the American Academy of Political and Social Science* 441 (January 1979), 26-40.

3567. Taylor, William L. "Mounting a Concerted Federal Attack on Urban Segregation: A Preliminary Exploration." In Gary Orfield and William L. Taylor (eds.) *Racial Segregation: Two Policy Views*. New York: The Ford Foundation, 1979, 45-68.

3568. Tebbel, Robert. *The Slum Markets*. New York: Dial Press, 1963.

3569. "Thirty-Four Percent Increase in Suburban Blacks Tied to Incomes and New Laws." *New York Times*, December 3, 1978.

3570. Thomas, Trevor. *San Francisco's Housing Market - Open or Closed?* San Francisco: Council for Civic Unity, 1960.

3571. Thomas, Wesley W. *Intra-Urban Migration and the Racial Transition of Residential Areas: A Behavioral Approach.* M.A. Thesis, University of Cincinnati, Cincinnati, Ohio, 1975.

3572. Thomas, William V. "America's Changing Suburbs." *Editorial Research Reports* (August 17, 1979), 583-600.

3573. Thompson, Robert A. "The Social Dynamics of Demographic Trends and the Housing of Minority Groups." *Phylon* 19 (Spring 1958), 31-43.

3574. Tillman, James A. "The Quest for Identity and Status. Facets of the Desegregation Process in the Upper Midwest." *Phylon* 22 (Winter 1961), 329-339.

3575. Tillman, James A. *Not by Prayer Alone: A Report on the Greater Minneapolis Interfaith Fair Housing Program*. Philadelphia: United Church Press, 1964.

3576. Tilly, Charles, et al. *Race and Residence in Wilmington, Delaware.* New York: Bureau of Publications, Teachers College, Columbia University, 1965.

3577. Tumin, Melvin. *Segregation and Desegregation: A Digest of*

Recent Research. Princeton, NJ: Princeton University Press, 1958.

3578.   Tyler, Poyntz (ed.) City and Suburan Housing. New York: H.W. Wilson Company, 1957.

3579.   U.S. Bureau of the Census. Measuring the Quality of Housing: An Appraisal of the Census Statistics and Methods. Government Printing Office, Washington, 1967.

3580.   U.S. Bureau of the Census. Problems of the Negro in the City, address by Walter B. Lewis. Government Printing Office, Washington, April 20, 1968.

3581.   U.S. Bureau of the Census. Equal Opportunity in Housing; a Series of Case Studies. Prepared by Office of Program Policy and Intergroup Relations Service. Washington, D.C.: Government Printing Office, 1969.

3582.   U.S. Bureau of the Census. Our Non-White Population and Its Housing: The Changes Between 1950 and 1960. Washington, D.C.: Government Printing Office, 1963.

3583.   U.S. Bureau of the Census. Senior Citizens and How They Live: An Analysis of 1960 Census Data. Report prepared by the Statistical Reports Staff. Washington, D.C.: Housing and Home Finance Agency, Office of the Administrator, 1962-1963.

3584.   U.S. Commission on Civil Rights. Civil Rights U.S.A.: Housing in Washington, D.C. Washington, D.C.: Commission on Civil Rights, 1962.

3585.   U.S. Commission on Civil Rights. Family Housing and the Negro Serviceman. 1964 Staff Report. Washington, D.C.: Commission on Civil Rights, 1965.

3586.   U.S. Commission on Civil Rights. Family Housing and the Negro Serviceman: 1963 Staff Report. Washington, D.C.: Government Printing Office, 1963.

3587.   U.S. Commission on Civil Rights. The Federal Fair Housing Enforcement Effort. Washington, D.C.: Government Printing Office, 1979.

3588.   U.S. Commission on Civil Rights. The Federal Civil Rights Enforcement Effort: One Year Later. Washington, D.C.: Government Printing Office, 1971 a.

3589.   U.S. Commission on Civil Rights. Federal Civil Rights Enforcement Effort. Washington, D.C.: Government Printing Office, 1970.

3590.   U.S. Commission on Civil Rights. Home Ownership for Lower

Income Families. Washington, D.C.: Government Printing
Office, 1971 b.

3591. U.S. Commission on Civil Rights. Housing. A Report of the
Commission, Washington, D.C.: Government Printing Office, 1961.

3592. U.S. Commission on Civil Rights. Housing in Washington:
Hearings. Washington, D.C.: Government Printing Office, 1962.

3593. U.S. Commission on Civil Rights. Understanding Fair Housing.
Washington, D.C.: United States Government Printing Office,
1973.

3594. U.S. Congress. Senate. Committee on Banking and Curency.
Fair Housing Act of 1967. Hearings before the Subcommittee on
Housing and Urban Affairs of the United States Senate, 19th
Congress, 1st session on S. 1358. S. 2114, and S. 2280.
Relating to Civil Rights and Housing. Washington, D.C.:
Government Printing Office, 1967.

3595. U.S. Congress. Senate Committee on Human Resources.
Desegregation and Cities: The Trends and Policy Choices. 95th
Congress, 1st Session, 1977.

3596. U.S. Congress. House. Committee on the Judiciary. Equal
Opportunity in Housing. Washington, D.C.: Government Printing
Office, June 1977.

3597. U.S. Department of Commerce. Hearings Before the U.S.
Commission on Civil Rights. Washington, D.C.: 1971.

3598. U.S. Department of Housing and Urban Development. Fair Housing
and the Real Estate Industry. Washington, D.C.: Government
Printing Office, 1975.

3599. U.S. Department of Housing and Urban Develoment. Fair Housing:
An American Right/Right for Americans. Washington, D.C.:
Government Printing Office, June 1977.

3600. U.S. Department of Housing and Urban Development. Measuring
Racial Discrimination in American Housing Markets.
Washington, D.C.: Office of Policy Development and Research,
1979.

3601. U.S. Department of Housing and Urban Development. The Role of
the Real Estate Sector in Neighborhood Change. Washington,
D.C.: Office of Policy Development and Research, U.S.
Department of Housing and Urban Development, 1979.

3602. U.S. Housing and Home Finance Agency. Intergroup Relations
Service. Fair Housing Laws: Summaries and Text of State and
Municipal Laws. Washington, D.C.: Government Printing Office,
1965.

3603. U.S. Department of Housing and Urban Development, HUD. In-Cities Experimental Housing Research and Development Project, Phase I Composite Report, User Needs, March 1969.

3604. U.S. Housing and Home Finance Agency Office of Program Policy. Our Non-White Population and Its Housing the Changes Between 1950 and 1960. Washington, Government Printing Office, 1963.

3605. U.S. Department of Commerce and Labor. Conditions of Living Among the Poor. Washington, D.C.: Government Printing Office, 1966.

3606. U.S. National Commission on Urban Problems. The Large Poor Family--A Housing Gap. Washington, D.C.: Government Printing Office, 1968.

3607. United Community Services of Metropolitan Boston. Black and White in Boston: A Report Based on the Community Research Project. Boston: United Community Services of Metropolitan Boston, 1968.

3608. Urban League of Greater Cincinnati. Is Yours A Changing Neighborhood? Cincinnati: Urban League of Greater Cincinnati, 1959.

3609. "Urban Negro: Focus on the Housing Crisis", Real Estate Reporter and Building News (October 1945), 12-14.

3610. Urban Law Annual Editorial Staff. "Eviction of Tenants in Public Housing Projects." Urban Law Annual 2 (1969), 162-65.

3611. Urban Systems Research and Engineering, Inc. The Barriers to Equal Opportunity in Rural Housing Markets. A Report for the Department of Housing and Urban Development, Office of Policy Development and Research. Vol. 1, Analysis and Findings, January 1977.

3612. Usher, R.G. "Negro Segregation in St. Louis." New Republic 6 (1916), 176-178.

3613. Uyeki, Eugene S. "Residential Distribution and Stratification, 1950-1960." American Journal of Sociology 69 (March 1964), 491-498.

3614. Uyeki, Eugene S. Occupation and Residence: Cleveland 1940-1970. Paper presented at the Annual Meeting of the American Sociological Association, San Francisco, 1975.

3615. Vandell, Kerry D. and Bennett Harrison. "Racial Transition Among Neighborhoods: A Simulation Model Incorporating Institutional Parameters." Journal of Urban Economics 5 (1978), 441-70.

3616. Van Valey, Thomas L., et al. "Measuring Residential Segregation in American Cities: Problems of Inter-City Comparison." Urban Affairs Quarterly 11 (1976), 453-468.

3617. Van Valey, Thomas L., et al. "Trends in Residential Segregation: 1960-1970." American Journal of Sociology 82 (January 1977), 826-844.

3618. Vaughn, Garrett Allan. "Some Recent Evidence on Supply of Urban Housing to Non-Whites from Neighborhoods Undergoing Racial Change." Journal of Economics and Business 25 (1972), 53-61.

3619. Vaughn, Garrett Allan. "Role of Residential Racial Segregation in Causing and Perpetuating Inferior Housing for Lower Income Non-Whites." Journal of Economics and Business 27 (1975), 248-253.

3620. Vaughn, Garrett Alan. A Comparison of White and Non-White Metrpolitan Low-Income Housing. Ph.D. Thesis, Duke University, 1970.

3621. Velie, Lester. "Housing: Detroit's Time Bomb." Collier's (November 23, 1946), 14-15.

3622. Villenneave, Paul Y. "Changes Overtime in the Residential and Occupational Structures of an Urban Ethnic Minority." In Robert Leigh (ed.) Contemporary Geography: Western Viewpoints. British Columbia Geographical Series 12, 1971, 115-128.

3623. Vinton, Warren Jay. Conference on Housing the Economically and Socially Disadvantaged Groups in the Population. Chicago: Metrpolitan Housing and Planning Council of Chicago in Cooperation with ACTION, Inc. of New York, 1960.

3624. Vogel, Kenneth Robert. Exclusionary Zoning and the Provision of Local Public Services: An Economic Analysis of Southern Burlington County NAACP V. Township of Mount Laurel. Ph.D. Thesis, University of Pennsylvania, 1977.

3625. Vose, Clement. Caucasians Only: The Supreme Court, the NAACP, and the Restrictive Covenant Cases. Berkeley: University of California Press, 1959.

3626. Wallace, David A. Residential Concentration of Negroes in Chicago. Unpublished Ph.D. Dissertation, Harvard University, 1953.

3627. Warfield, D. and G. Laurent. A Study of the Economic Potential of Baltimore Black Families for Living in the Suburban Baltimore Area. Baltimore, MD: Baltimore Neighborhoods, Inc., 1972.

3628. Weatherby, Norman Lee. Racial Segregation in Dallas Public Housing: 1970-1976. M.A. Thesis, North Texas State University, 1978, 234.

3629. Weaver, Robert C. "Chicago--A City of Covenants." Crisis (March 1946), 75-78, 93.

3630. Weaver, Robert C. "The Effect of Anti-Discrimination Legislation Upon the FHA--and VA--Insured Housing Market in New York State." Land Economics 31:4 (November 1955), 303-13.

3631. Weaver, Robert C. Hemmed In. New York: American Council on Race Relations, 1945.

3632. Weaver, Robert C. "Housing in a Democracy." Annals of the American Academy of Political and Social Sciences (March 1946), 95-105.

3633. Weaver, Robert C. "Integration in Public and Private Housing." Annals of the American Academy of Political and Social Sciences 30 (March 1956), 86-97.

3634. Weaver, Robert C. "The Negro in a Program of Public Housing." Opportunity (July 1938), 198-203.

3635. Weaver, Robert C. "Non-White Population Movements and Urban Ghettos." Phylon 20 (Summer 1959), 235-241.

3636. Weaver, Robert. Our Nonwhite Population and Its Housing. Housing and Home Finance Agency. Washington, D.C.: Government Printing Office, 1963.

3637. Weaver, Robert C. "Race Restrictive Housing Covenants." Journal of Land and Public Utility Economics, (August 1944), 183-93.

3638. Weaver, Robert C. "A Tool for Democratic Housing." Crisis (February 1947), 47-48.

3639. Weber, Michael P. "Residential and Occupational Patterns of Ethnic Minorities in Nineteenth Century Pittsburgh." Pennsylvania History 44:4 (1977), 317-334.

3640. Wedel, C. "Open Housing: How to Get Around the Law." New Republic (June 22, 1968.)

3641. Weinstein, E.A. and P.N. Geisel. "Family Decision Making Over Desegregation." Sociometry 25 (March 1962), 21-29.

3642. Weissbourd, Bernard. Segregation, Subsidies, and Megalopolis. Santa Barbara, California: Center for the Study of Democratic Institutions, 1964.

3643.   Wellenback, Shirley. Segregation 1975: Residential Patterns and Possibilities for New Negro Households in the Philadelphia Region. Philadelphia: Philadelphia Housing Association, November, 1967.

3644.   Weller, Charles Frederick. Neglected Neighbors; Stories of Life in the Alleys, Tenements and Shanties of the National Capital. Philadelphia: John C. Winston, 1965.

3645.   West Virginia, State of. Bureau of Negro Welfare and Statistics. Negro Housing Survey of Charleston, Keystone, Kimball, Wheeling and Williamson. West Virginia: Bureau of Negro Welfare and Statistics, 1964.

3646.   Wheaton, William L. (ed.) Urban Housing. New York: The Free Press, 1966.

3647.   Wheeler, Raymond Harry. The Relationship Between Negro Invasion and Property Prices in Grand Rapids, Michigan. Ph.D. Thesis, The University of Michigan, 1962.

3648.   Wilkins, Arthur H. The Residential Distribution of Occupation Groups in Middle-Sized Cities of the United States in 1950. Unpublished Ph.D. Dissertation, University of Chicago, 1956.

3649.   Williams, Josephine J. "Another Commentary on So-Called Segregation Indices." American Sociological Review 13 (June 1948), 298-304.

3650.   Williams, Norman and Edward Wacks. "Segregation of Residential Areas Along Economic Lines: Lionshead Lake Revisited." Wisconsin Law Review 3 (1969), 827-847.

3651.   Williams, Oliver P. and Kent Eklund. "Segregation in a Fragmented Context: 1950-1970." In Kevin Cox (ed.) Urbanization and Conflict in Market Societies. Chicago: Maaroufa Press, 1978, 213-228.

3652.   Williamson, Sall. The Origins of Segregation. Lexington, MA: D.C. Heath, 1968.

3653.   Wilner, David and Rosabell Walkley. "Residential Proximity and Intergroup Relations in Public Housing Projects." Journal of Social Issues 8 (1952), 45-70.

3654.   Wilner, David, et al. Human Relations in Interracial Housing: A Study of the Contact Hypothesis. Minneapolis: University of Minnesota Press, 1955.

3655.   Wilson, Allan B. "Residential Segregation of Social Classes and Aspiration of High School Boys." In Seymour Martin Lipset and Reinhard Bendix (eds.) Class, Status and Power. New York: The Free Press, 1966, 335-342.

3656. Wilson, Allan B. The Effect of Residential Segregation Upon Educational Achievement and Aspiration. Unpublished Ph.D. Dissertation, University of California, Berkeley, 1961.

3657. Wilson, Bobby McClain. "Black Housing Opportunities in Birmingham, Alabama." Southeastern Geographer 17:1 (1977), 49-57.

3658. Wilson, Franklin D. and Karl E. Taeuber. Residential and School Segregation: Some Tests of Their Association. Madison, WI: Institute for Research on Poverty, University of Wisconsin, 1978.

3659. Winder, A.F. "White Attitudes Toward Negro-White Integration in an Area of Changing Racial Composition." American Psychologist 7 (1952), 330-331.

3660. Winer, M.L. White Resistance and Negro Insistence: An Ecological Analysis of Urban Desegregation. Unpublished honors thesis, Department of Social Relations, Harvard University, 1965.

3661. Winiecke, L. "Appeal of Age Segregated Housing to Elderly Poor." International Journal of Aging and Human Development 4 (1973), 293-306.

3662. Winsborough, Haliman H., et al. Models of Change in Residential Segregation 1940-1970. Paper presented at the Annual meeting of the Population Association of America, Seattle, 1975.

3663. Winship, Christopher. "A Re-evaluation of Indexes of Residential Segregation." Social Forces 55 (June 1977), 1958-1966.

3664. Wolf, Eleanor P. Changing Neighborhood: A Study of Racial Transition. Detroit: Wayne State University Press, 1959.

3665. Wolf, Eleanor P. "Housing Opportunities and Residential Decision." In The Purchase and Sale of Housing: Constitutional Rights and Human Values. St. Louis: Washington University, 1967.

3666. Wolf, Eleanor P. "The Tipping-Point in Racially Changing Neighborhoods." Journal of the American Institute of Planners 29:3 (1963), 217-22.

3667. Wolf, Eleanor P. "Racial Transition in a Middle-Class Area." Journal of Intergroup Relations 1 (Summer 1960), 75-81.

3668. Wolf, George T. and Donald L. Shiver. "De-facto Segregation in Low-Rent Public Housing." Urban Law Annual 1 (1968), 174-96.

3669. Wolfe, Jacqueline. The Changing Pattern of Residence of the Negro in Pittsburgh, Pennsylvania, 1930-1960. Master's Thesis, University of Pittsburgh, 1964.

3670. Wolff, Reinhold Paul. Negro Housing in the Miami Area: Effects of the Postwar Building Boom. Miami: Bureau of Business and Economic Research, University of Miami, 1951.

3671. Wood, Elizabeth. A New Look at the Balanced Neighborhood: A Study and Recommendation. New York: Citizen's Housing and Planning Council of New York, 1960.

3672. Woofter, Thomas J., et al. Negro Problems in Cities. New York: Doubleday, 1928.

3673. Woofter, Thomas J. and Madge Headly Priest. Negro Housing in Philadelphia. Philadelphia: Friends' Committee on Interests of the Colored Race and Whittier Center, 1927.

3674. Works, E. "Residence in Integrated and Segregated Housing and Improvements in Self-Concepts of Negroes." Sociology and Social Research 46 (April 1962), 294-301.

3675. Yancey, William L. "Architecture, Interaction and Social Control: The Case of a Large-Scale Public Housing Project," Environment and Behavior 3 (1971), 3-21.

3676. Yankauer, Alfred. "The Relationship of Fetal and Infant Mortality to Residential Segregation." American Sociological Review 15 (October 1950), 644-648.

3677. Yankauer, Marian P. and M.B. Sunderhauf. "Housing: Equal Opportunity to Choose Where One Shall Live." Journal of Negro Education, 1963 Yearbook 32:4 (1963), 402-14.

3678. Yinger, John. A Model of Discrimination by Lanlords. Madison, WI: Institute for Research on Poverty, University of Wisconsin. Discussion Paper No. 259, 1975.

3679. Yinger, John. Racial Prejudice and Locational Equilibrium in an Urban Area. Discussion Paper 251. Madison, WI: Institute for Research on Poverty, University of Wisconsin, 1975.

3680. Yinger, John. An Analysis of Discrimination by Real Estate Brokers, Discussion Paper 252-75. Madison, Wisconsin: Institute for Research on Poverty, University of Wisconsin, 1975.

3681. Yinger, John. "The Black-White Price Differential in Housing: Some Further Evidence." Land Economics 54 (May 1978), 187-206.

3682. Yinger, John. "Prejudice and Discrimination in the Urban Housing Market." In Peter Mieszkowski and Mahlon Straszheim (eds.) Current Issues in Urban Economics. Baltimore, Maryland: John Hopkins University Press, 1979, 430-468.

3683. Yinger, John. "Racial Prejudice and Racial Residential Segregation in an Urban Model." Journal of Urban Economics 3 (October 1976), 383-96.

3684. Yinger, John. Three Essays on the Economics of Discrimination in Housing. Ph.D. Princeton University, 1974.

3685. Zelder, Raymond E. "Racial Segregation in Urban Housing Markets." Journal of Regional Science 10 (1970), 93-105.

3686. Zelder, Raymond E. "Residential Desegregation: Can Nothing Be Accomplished?" Urban Affairs Quarterly 5:3 (March 1970), 265-77.

3687. Zonn, Leo Edward. Residential Search Patterns of Black Urban Households: A Spatial Behavioral View. Ph.D. Dissertation, University of Wisconsin at Milwaukee, Milwaukee, WI, 1975.

CHAPTER 5

Ghettoization, Slum and Squatter Settlements

3688. Abudu, Margaret J.G. Black Ghetto Violence as Communication: A
       Case Study of Non-Conventional Political Protest. Indiana
       University, Ph.D. Dissertation, 1971.

3689. Adams, Arvil V. and Gilbert Nestal. "Interregional Migration,
       Education and Poverty in the Urban Ghetto: Another Look at
       Black-White Earnings Differentials." Review of Economics and
       Statistics 58 (May 1976), 156-166.

3690. Adams, John B. and Robert Sanders. "Urban Residential
       Structure and the Location of Stress in Ghettos." Earth and
       Mineral Sciences 38 (January 1968), 29-32.

3691. Adjei-Barwuah, Barfour. Socio-Economic Regions in the
       Louisville Ghetto. Indiana University, Ph.D. Dissertation,
       1972.

3692. Adjei-Barwuah, B. and Harold M. Rose. "Some Comparative
       Aspects of the West African Zongo and the Black American
       Ghetto." In Harold M. Rose (ed.) Geography of the Ghetto.
       Perspectives in Geography. Vol. II, Dekalb, Illinois: Northern
       Illinois University Press, 1972.

3693. Adrian, Charles R. "The States and the Ghettos." In Roland
       Warren (ed.) Politics and the Ghettos. New York: Atherton,
       1969, 82-83.

3694. Aldrich, Howard E. "Employment Opportunities for Blacks in the
       Black Ghetto: The Role of White-Owned Businesses." American
       Journal of Sociology 78 (1973), 1403-1425.

3695. Allen, Louis L. "Making Capitalism Work in the Ghettos."
       Harvard Business Review (May-June 1969), 83-92.

3696. Anchor, Shirley. Mexican Americans in a Dallas Barrio.

Tucson: University of Arizona Press, 1978.

3697. Atkinson, Paul, et al. "Creating a Company of Unequals: Sources of Occupational Stratification in a Ghetto Community Mental Health Center." Sociology of Work and Occupation 4 (August 1977), 1-18.

3698. Armbrister, Trevor. "White Cop in the Black Ghetto." Saturday Evening Post 241 (November 16, 1968), 26-29.

3699. Asinof, E. "Ghetto Doctor; Multipurpose Medical Center in Compton, California," Today's Health 50 (April 1972), 52-56.

3700. Bailey, Robert M. "The Cutting Edge of the City's Expanding Ghetto." Planning (ASPO) 40 (1974), 10-13.

3701. Barrera, Mario, et al. "The Barrio as an Internal Colony." In People and Politics in Urban Society. Beverly Hills: Sage Publications, 1972, 465-498.

3702. Bartles-Smith, Douglas. Urban Ghetto Guildford: Lutterwork Press, 1976.

3703. Barton, Allen H. "The Columbia Crisis: Campus, Vietnam, and the Ghetto." Public Opinion Quarterly 32 (Fall 1968), 333-351.

3704. Battle, Sol. Ghetto '68. New York: New World Press, 1968.

3705. Bauman, Gerald and Ruth Grimes. Psychiatric Rehabilitation in the Ghetto: An Educational Approach. Lexington, Mass.: D.C. Heath, 1974.

3706. Bauman, John F. "Poverty in the Urban Ghetto." Current History (November 1970), 283-289.

3707. Bell, Carolyn S. Economics of the Ghetto. New York: Pegasus, 1970.

3708. Bergsman, Joel. "Alternatives to the Non-Gilded Ghetto: Notes on Different Goals and Strategies." Public Policy 19 (Spring 1971), 309-321.

3709. Berk, Richard A. The Role of Ghetto Retail Merchants in Civil Disorders. Ph.D. Dissertation, Johns Hopkins University, 1970.

3710. Berk, Richard A., et al. "Black Ghetto Violence: A Case Study Inquiry of Four Los Angeles Riot Event Types." Social Problems 19 (Winter 1972), 408-426.

3711. Berkowitz, William R. "Socioeconomic Indicator Changes in Ghetto Riot Tracts." Urban Affairs Quarterly 10 (September 1974), 69-94.

3712. Berndt, Harry E. New Rules in the Ghetto: The Community Development Corporation and Urban Poverty. Westport, Conn.: Greenwood, 1977.

3713. Bernstein, Betty J. "What Happened to Ghetto Medicine in New York State?" American Journal of Public Health 61 (July 1971), 1287-1293.

3714. Berry, Brian J.L. "Monitoring Trends, Forecasting Change and Evaluating Goal Achievements: The Ghetto v. Desegregation Issue in Chicago as a Case Study." In M. Chisholm, et al. (eds.) Regional Forecasting. London: Buttersworth, 1971.

3715. Berry, Brian J.L. "Ghetto Expansion and Single Family Housing Prices, 1968-1972." Journal of Urban Economics 3 (October 1976), 397-423.

3716. Berson, Lenora E. "Strategies: The Young Militants Challenge Philadelphia's Effort to Cool the Ghettos with Patronage and Police." The City 2 (January 1968), 2-5.

3717. Bienen, Henry. "Violence in the Ghetto," in Violence and Social Change. Chicago: University of Chicago Press, 1968, 13-38.

3718. Binstock, Robert. "The Ghettos, the New Left and Some Dangerous Fallacies." In Roland L. Warren (ed.) Politics and the Ghettos. New York: Atherton, 1969, 191-196.

3719. Blair, Thomas L. Retreat to the Ghetto: The End of a Dream? New York: Hill & Wang, 1977.

3720. Blassingame, John W. "Before the Ghetto: The Making of the Black Community in Savannah, Georgia, 1865-1880." Journal of Social History 6 (1973), 469-481.

3721. Blauner, Robert. "Internal Colonialism and Ghetto Revolt." Social Problems 16 (Spring 1969), 393-408.

3722. Blauner, Robert. "Internal Colonialism and the Ghetto Revolt." In Joe T. Darden (ed.) The Ghetto: Readings with Interpretations. Port Washington, New York: Kennikat, 1981, 111-128.

3723. Blaut, J.M. "The Ghetto as an Internal Neocolony." Antipode 6:1 (1974), 37-42.

3724. Blaut, J.M. "Assimilation versus Ghettoization." Antipode (1983), 37-42.

3725. Blaut, J.M. "Assimilation and Ghettoization." In R.A. Obudho (ed.) Afro-Americans and the City. Albany, New York: State University at New York, 1984.

3726. Bloom, Gordon F. "Black Capitalism in Ghetto Supermarkets: Problems and Prospects." _Industrial Management Review_ 2 (Spring 1970), 37–48.

3727. Bloom, Solomon. "Dictator of the Lodz Ghetto." _Commentary_ 7 (January–June 1949), 111–122.

3728. Blumberg, Leonard and Michael Lalli. "Little Ghettos: A Study of Negroes in the Suburbs." _Phylon_ 27 (1966), 117–131.

3729. Boesel, David Paul. _The Ghetto Riots, 1964–1968,_ unpublished Ph.D. Dissertation, Cornell University, 1972.

3730. Boesel, David Paul. "An Analysis of the Ghetto Riots." In David Boesel and Peter Rossi (eds.) _Cities Under Seige: An Anatomy of the Ghetto Riots, 1964–1968_. New York: Basic Books, 1971, 324–342.

3731. Boesel, David Paul. "The Liberal Society, Black Youths, and Ghetto Riots." _Psychiatry_ (May 1970), 265–281.

3732. Boesel, David Paul and Peter Rossi (eds.) _Cities Under Seige: An Anatomy of the Ghetto Riots._ New York: Basic Books, 1971.

3733. Bogue, Donald J. "Family Planning in the Negro Ghettos of Chicago." _Milbank Memorial Fund Quarterly_ 48 (April 1970), 283–307.

3734. Boskin, Joseph. "The Revolt of the Urban Ghettos." _Annals of the American Academy of Political and Social Science_ 382 (March 1969), 1–14.

3735. Boskin, Joseph. "Violence in the Ghettos: A Consensus of Attitudes." _New Mexico Quarterly_ 37 (Winter 1968), 317–334.

3736. Boyce, Ronald R. _Is There a Geographically Based Solution to the Problems of the Negro Ghetto._ British Columbia, Canada: Department of Geography, University of Victoria, _Geographic_ 2 Western Geographic Series, 1973.

3737. Bracy, John H., et al. (eds.) _The Rise of the Ghetto_. Belmont, California: Wadsworth, 1971.

3738. Brown, James K. and Seymour Lusterman. _Business and the Development of Ghetto Enterprise_. New York: Conference Board, 1971.

3739. Browne, Robert S. "Building Viable Ghettos," In James Blumstein and Eddie Martin (eds.) _The Urban Scene in the Seventies_. Nashville: Vanderbilt University, 1974, 229–237.

3740. Browne, Robert S. "Cash Flows in a Ghetto Community." _Review of Black Political Economy_ 1 (Winter/Spring 1971), 28–39.

3741. Bryne, D. "Allocation, The Council Ghetto, and the Political Economy of Housing." Antipode 8 (March 1976), 24-29.

3742. Bullington, Bruce. Heroin Use in the Barrio. Lexington, Mass.: D.C. Heath, 1977.

3743. Bullough, Bonnie Louise. "Alienation in the Ghetto." American Journal of Sociology 72 (March 1967), 469-479.

3744. Campbell, Robert. The Chasm: The Life and Death of a Great Experiment in Ghetto Education. Boston: Houghton Mifflin, 1974.

3745. Canfield, Roger B. Black Ghetto Riots and Campus Disorders. San Francisco: R and E Research Associates, 1973.

3746. Caplan, Nathan S. "The New Ghetto Man: A Review of Recent Empirical Studies." Journal of Social Issues (1970), 59-73.

3747. Caplan, Nathan S. and J.M. Paige. "A Study of Ghetto Rioters." Scientific American 219 (1968), 19-25.

3748. Carey, George W. "Density, Crowding, Stress and the Ghetto." American Behavioral Scientist 15 (1972), 495-509.

3749. Carr, Homer B. Before the Ghetto: A Study of Detroit Negroes in the 1890's. M.A. Thesis, Wayne State University, 1968.

3750. Cervantes, Alfonso J. "To Prevent a Chain of Super Watts: Rioting in the Ghettos of Our Great Cities Threatens to Become Epidemic Unless Business Takes a Greater Initiative." Harvard Business Review 45 (September–Octoer 1967),55-65.

3751. Chisholm, Shirley. "Ghetto Power in Action: The Value of Positive Political Action." In Marvyn Dymally (ed.) The Black Politician: His Struggle for Power. Scituate, Mass.: Duxbury, 1971, 40-42 and 123-131.

3752. Clark, Dennis. The Ghetto Game: Racial Conflicts in the City. New York:Sheed and Ward, 1962.

3753. Clark, Dennis. "Immigrant Enclaves in Our Cities," in Joe T. Darden (ed.) The Ghetto Readings With Interpretations. Port Washington, New York: Kennikat, 1981, 59-73.

3754. Clark, Kenneth B. Dark Ghetto: Dilemma of Social Power. New York: Harper and Row, 1965.

3755. Clark, Kenneth B. Youth in the Ghetto. New York: Harlem Youth Opportunities Unlimited, 1964.

3756. Clark, John Henrik. "Revolt in the Ghettos; An Essay-Review of Five Books and Pamphlets on Race Riots, Historical and Recent, in Various Cities in the United Staes," Freedomways 7 (Winter 1967), 34-41.

3757. Clark, M.F. "A Hospital for the Black Ghetto," Hospital Progress 50 (February 1969), 49-52.

3758. Clark, W.V.A. and C.R. Hansell. "The Expansion of the Negro Ghetto in Milwaukee." Tijdschirft voor Economische en Social Geografie 61 (1970), 267-277.

3759. Clarke, M.M. Black-White Ghettos: Quality of Life in the Atlantic Inner City. Oak Ridge National Laboratory, December 25, 1971.

3760. Clinard, Marshall B. Slums and Community Development: Experiments in Self-Help. New York: The Free Press, 1966.

3761. Cloward, Richard A. and Richard M. Elman. "Advocacy in the Ghetto." Transaction (December 1966), 27-35.

3762. Collins, Keith E. Black Los Angeles: The Maturing of the Ghetto 1940-1950. Sarasota, Florida: Century Twenty-One, 1980.

3763. Connally, Harold X. A Ghetto Grows in Brooklyn. New York: New York University Press, 1977.

3764. Cooper, John L. The Police and the Ghetto. Port Wasington, New York: Kennikat Press, 1979.

3765. Crawford, Thomas J. "Police Perception of Ghetto Hostility." In Richard L. Hershel and Robert Silverman (eds.) Perception in Criminology. New York: Columbia University Press, 1975.

3766. Darden, Joe T. "A Bibliographic Guide for the Study of the Ghetto." In Joe T. Darden (ed.) The Ghetto: Readings with Interpretations. Port Washington, NY: Kennikat Press, 1981, 227-240.

3767. Darden, Joe T. "Definitions of Ghetto: Concensus versus Nonconcensus." In Joe T. Darden (ed.) The Ghetto: Readings with Interpretations. Port Washington, New York: Kennikat Press Press, 1981, 5-14.

3768. Darden, Joe T. "Environmental Perception by Ghetto Youths in Pittsburgh." In Joe T. Darden (ed.) The Ghetto: Readings with Interpretations. Port Washinton, New York: Kennikat, 1981, 174-180.

3769. Darden, Joe T. "Environmental Perception by Ghetto Youth in Pittsburgh." Pennsylvania Geographer (April 1970), 19-22.

3770. Darden, Joe T. "The Quality of Life in a Black Ghetto: A Geographic View." Pennsylvania Geographer 12 (Novemer 1974),

3-8.

3771. Darden, Joe T. "The Quality of Life in Black Ghetto: A Geographical View." In Joe T. Darden (ed.) The Ghetto: Readings with Interpretations. Port Washinton, New York: Kennikat, 1981, 27-31.

3772. Davies, Shane and David L. Hutt. "Impact of Ghettoization on Black Employment." Economic Geography 48 (1972), 421-427.

3773. Davis, James W. "Decentralization, Citizen Participation and Ghetto Health." American Behavioral Scientist 15 (September-October 1971), 94-107.

3774. Deskins, Donald R. Interaction Patterns and the Spatial Form of the Ghetto. Evanston: Department of Geography, Northwestern University, 1969.

3775. Deskins, Donald R. "The Black Subcommunity: A Microcosm," in Joe T. Darden (ed.) The Ghetto Readings with Interpretations. Port Washington, New York: Kennikat, 1981, 32-56.

3776. Different Strokes: Pathways to Maturity in the Boston Ghetto: A Report to the Ford Foundation. Boulder: Westview Press, 1976.

3777. Doeringer, Peter B. Ghetto Labor Markets: Problems and Programs, Program on Regional and Urban Economics, Discussion Paper No. 35, Harvard University, 1968.

3778. Doeringer, Peter B. "Manpower Programs for Ghetto Labor Markets." In Proceedings of the 21st Annual Winter Meeting, Industrial Relations Research Association Madison, Wis.: n.p., 1969, 257-267.

3779. Dollard, John. Caste and Class in a Southern Town. New Haven: Yale University Press, 1937.

3780. Donaldson, Loraine and Raymond S. Strangways. "Can Ghetto Groceries Price Competitively and Make a Profit?" Journal of Buinsess 46 (January 1973), 61-66.

3781. Downs, Anthony. "Alternative Futures for the American Ghetto." Daedalus 97 (Fall 1968), 1331-1378.

3782. Drake, St. Clair and Horace R. Cayton. Black Metropolis. New York: Harcourt Brace, 1945.

3783. Drotning, Phillip T. and Wesley, W. South. Up From the Ghetto. New York: Cowles Book, 1970.

3784. Dumpson, James R. "Fantasy and Reality in the Ghetto Problem." In Roland L. Warren (ed.) Politics and The Ghettos. New York: Atherton, 1969, 71-79.

3785. Edel, Matthew. "Development vs. Dispersal: Approaches to Ghetto Poverty." In Matthew Edel and Jerome Rothenberg (eds.) Readings in Urban Economics. New York: Macmillan, 1972.

3786. Edwards, O.L. "Patterns of Residential Segregation Within a Metropolitan Ghetto." Demography 7 (May 1970), 185-193.

3787. Eiben, Crowell. "Insurers Invest in the Ghetto." Civil Rights Digest 1 (Summer 1968), 11-15.

3788. Elam, Lloyd C. "What Does the Ghetto Want from Medicine?" In John Norman (ed.) Medicine in the Ghetto. New York: Appleton-Century-Crofts, 1969, 14-20.

3789. Elgie, Robert. "Rural Immigration, Urban Ghettoization and Their Consequence." Antipode 2 (December 1970), 35-54.

3790. Eripps, Thomas R. "Movies in the Ghetto, B.P. (Before Poitier)." Negro Digest 18 (February 1969), 21-32.

3791. Ettore, E.M. "Women, Urban Social Movements and the Lesbian Ghetto." International Journal of Urban and Regional Research 2 (October 1978), 499-520.

3792. Evans, Lelia. "Neo-Colonialism and Development of the Black Ghetto: Model Cities." Black Lines: A Journal of Black Studies 1 (1970), 17-26.

3793. Everett, John R. "The Decentralization Fiasco and Our Ghetto Schools." Atlantic Monthly 222 (December 1968), 71-73.

3794. Etzkowitz, H. and O.M. Shaflander. Ghetto Crisis: Riots or Reconciliation. Boston: Little, Brown, 1969.

3795. Farrell, Gregory R. "Resources for Transforming the Ghetto." In Alvin Toffler (ed.) The Schoolhouse in the City. New York: Praeger, 1968, 86-96.

3796. Farrell, Walter. Intra-Urban Mobility and Environmental Perception in a Black Middle-Class Ghetto: A Case Study in Flint, Michigan. Ph.D. Dissertation, Department of Geography, Michigan State University, 1974.

3797. Farrell, Walter and Stanley Brunn D. "Intraurban Mobility and Neighborhood Perception in Flint's Black Middle-Class Ghetto." East Lakes Geographer 13 (June 1978), 4-19.

3798. Feagin, Joe R. Ghetto Social Structure: A Study of Black Bostonians. San Francisco: R. and E. Associates, 1975.

3799. Feagin, Joe R. "Social Sources of Support for Violence and Non-Violence in a Negro Ghetto." Social Problems 15 (Spring 1968), 432-441.

3800. Feagin, Joe R. and Paul B. Sheatsley. "Ghetto Resident Appraisals of a Riot." Public Opinion Quarterly 32 (Fall 1968), 352–362.

3801. Feagin, Joe R. and Harlan Hahn. Ghetto Revolts: The Politics of Violence in American Cities. New York: Macmillan, 1973.

3802. Foley, Eugene. The Achieving Ghetto. Washington, D.C.: National Press, 1968.

3803. Ford, James. Slums and Housing, With Special Reference to New York City. Cambridge, Massachusetts: Harvard University Press, 1936.

3804. Ford, Lawrence and Ernst Griffin. "The Ghettoization of Paradise." The Geographical Review 69 (April 1979), 140–158.

3805. Forman, Robert. Black Ghettos, White Ghettos and Slums. New York: Prentice-Hall, 1972.

3806. Foster, Madison. "Black Organizing: The Need for a Conceptual Model of the Ghetto." Catalyst: A Socialist Journal of the Social Services 1 (1978), 76–90.

3807. Fowler, Gary L. "Poverty and the Black Ghetto in the United States." Geograhical Review 63:1 (1973), 106–108.

3808. Frankel, Barbara. Childbirth in the Ghetto: Folk Beliefs of Negro Women in a North Philadelphia Hospital Ward. San Francisco: R and E Research Associates, 1977.

3809. Franklin, Vincent P. "Ghetto on Their Minds: Afro-American Historiography and the City." Afro-Americans in New York Life and History 1:1 (1977), 111–119.

3810. Fried, Marc and Peggy Gleicher. "Some Sources of Residential Satisfaction in an Urban Slum." Journal of the American Institute of Planners (November 1961), 305–15.

3811. Friedman, Lawrence M. Government and Slum Housing: A Century of Frustration. Chicago: Rand McNally, 1968.

3812. Funnye, Clarence. Black Power and Deghettoization: A Retreat to Reality. Washington, D.C.: The National Committee Against Discrimination in Housing, Inc., 1969.

3813. Funnye, Clarence. Deghettoization: Specifics for Planning and an Examination of Elements of Urban Opportunity in New York City. Brooklyn: Idea Plan Associates, 1966.

3814. Fusfeld, Daniel R. "Transfer Payments and the Ghetto Economy." In Kenneth Boulding, et al. (eds.) Transfers in an Uranized Economy. Belmont: Wadsworth Publishing, 1973, 78–92.

3815. Fusfeld, Daniel R. "The Economy of Urban Ghetto." In Joe T. Darden (ed.) The Ghetto: Readings With Interpretations. Port Washington, New York: Kennikat, 1981, 131-158.

3816. Fusfeld, Daniel R. "The Economy of the Urban Ghetto." In John P. Crecine (ed.) Financing the Metropolis. Beverly Hills: Sage, 1970, 369-399.

3817. Gans, Herbert. "The Ghetto Rebellions and Urban Class Conflict." In R. H. Connery (ed.) Urban Riots: Violence and Social Change. New York: Vantage Press, 1969, 45-54.

3818. Gardner, Burleigh B., et al. The Effect of Busing Ghetto Children Into White Suburban Schools. Washington, D.C.: ERIC Ed. 048-389, 1970.

3819. Garrity, John T. "Red Ink for Ghetto Industries." Harvard Business Review 171 (May-June 1968), 158-161.

3820. Geschwender, James A. Black Revolt: the Civil Rights Movement, Ghetto Uprisings and Separatism. Englewood Cliffs, New Jersey: Prentice-Hall, 1971.

3821. Glickman, Elliott B. and Vera M. Jones. "Consumer Legislation and the Ghetto." Journal of Urban Law 45 (1969), 705-712.

3822. Goldberg, Louis. "Ghetto Riots and Others: The Faces of Civil Disorder in 1967." Journal of Peace Research 5 (1968), 116-131.

3823. Goldfield, David R. "The Black Ghetto: A Tragic Sameness." Journal of Urban History 3 (May 1977), 361-371.

3824. Goldfield, David, et al. The Enduring Ghetto. Philadelphia: Lippincott, 1973.

3825. Goldfarb, Ronald. Jails: The Ultimate Ghetto. New York: Anchor, 1975.

3826. Gordon, D.M. Class, Productivity and the Ghetto. Ph.D. Dissertation, Harvard University, 1971.

3827. Gordon, D.M. A Graph Theoretic Approach to the Ghetto Marketplace. Paper presented at 41st Annual Meeting of the Operations Research Society of America, Atlantic City, N.J.: November 1972.

3828. Gordon, Gregory and Albert Swanson. Chicago: Evolution of a Ghetto. Chicago: Home Investment Fund, 1976.

3829. Gregorovius, Ferdinand A. The Ghetto and the Jews of Rome. New York: Schocken Books, 1948.

3830. Greer, Scott A. Neighborhood and Ghetto: The Local Area in Large-Scale Society. New York: Basic Books, 1974.

3831. Grier, George C. "The Negro Ghettoes and Federal Housig Policy." Law and Contemporary Problems 32 (Summer 1967), 550-560.

3832. Groves, W.E. "Police in the Ghetto." In J.S. Goodman (ed.) Perspectives on Urban Politics. Boston: Allyn and Bacon, 1970, 169-198.

3833. Groves, W.E. Supplemental Studies for the National Adivsory Commission on Civil Disorders. Washington, D.C.: Government Printing Office, 1968.

3834. Groves, Paul A. and Edward Muller. Preliminary Inquiry into the Emergence of Negro Ghettos: The Comparative Analysis of Washington, D.C. and Baltimore in the Late Nineteenth Century. Paper presented at the Annual Meeting of the Association of American Geographers, Kansas City, 1972.

3835. Hahn, Harlan. "Cops and Rioters; Ghetto Perceptions of Social Conflict and Control," American Behavioral Scientist, 13 (May/July 1970), 761-779.

3836. Hahn, Harlan. "Black Separatists: Attitudes and Objectives in a Riot Torn Ghetto." Journal of Black Studies (September 1970), 35-53.

3837. Hahn, Harlan. "Ghetto Sentiments on Violence." Science and Society 33 (Spring 1969), 197-208.

3838. Hahn, Harlan. "Violence: The View from the Ghetto." Mental Hygiene 53 (October 1969), 509-512.

3839. Hammerz, Ulf. "Harlem Diary." Ramparts 3 (October 1964), 14-28.

3840. Hammerz, Ulf. "Roots of Black Manhood: Sex, Socialization and Culture in the Ghettos of American Cities." Transaction (October 1969), 12-22.

3841. Hammerz, Ulf. Soulside: Inquiries into Ghetto Culture and Community. New York: Columbia University Press, 1969.

3842. Hammerz, Ulf. Southside: An Inquiry into Ghetto Culture. New York: Columbia University Press, 1969.

3843. Hansell, C.R. and W.A.V. Clark. "The Expansion of the Negro Ghetto in Milwaukee," Tydschrift Voor Economishe in Sociale Geografie 61 (1970), 267-277.

3844. Hansell, C.R. and W.A.V. Clark. "The Expansion of the Negro

Ghetto in Milwaukee: A Description and Simulation Model" in Joe T. Darden (ed) The Ghetto: Readings with Interpretations Port Washington, New York: Kennikat, 1981, 81-88.

3845. Hapgood, Hutchines. "The Picturesque Ghetto." Century 94 (July 1917), 469-473.

3846. Hapgood, Hutchines. The Spirit of the Ghetto: Studies of Three Jewish Quarter in New York. New York: Funk and Wagnalls, 1909.

3847. Hapgood, Hutchiness, et al. The Spirit of the Ghetto. New York: Funk and Wagnalls, 1965.

3848. Hardy, Richard T. and John G. Cull. Climbing Ghetto Walls. Springfield, Ill.: Charles C. Thomas, 1973.

3849. Harris, Donald. "The Black Ghetto as Colony: A Theoretical Critique and Alternative Formulation." Review of Black Political Economy 2 (1972), 3-33.

3850. Harrison, Bennett. "Education and Underemployment in the Urban Ghetto." In D.M. Gordon (ed.) Problems in Political Economy. Lexington, Mass.: D.C. Health, 1971, 81-190.

3851. Harrison, Bennett. "Ghetto Economic Development: A Survey." Journal of Economic Literature (March 1974), 1-36.

3852. Harrison, Bennett. "Suburbanization and Ghetto Dispersal: A Critique of Conventional Wisdom." In Mavis Mann Reeves and Parris Glendening (eds.) Controversies of State and Local Government. Boston: Allyn and Bacon, 1971.

3853. Harrison, Bennett. Education, Training and the Urban Ghetto. Baltimore: Johns Hopkins University Press, 1972.

3854. Harrison, N. "Education and Earnings in the Urban Ghetto." American Economist (Spring 1970), 12-22.

3855. Harvey, David. "Revolutionary and Counter-Revolutionary Theory in Geography and the Problem of Ghetto Formation." Antipode 4 (July 1972), 1-13.

3856. Harvey, David. "Revolutionary and Counter-Revolutionary Theory in Geography and the Problem of Ghetto Formation." In Harold M. Rose Geography of the Ghetto: Perspectives in Geography. Dekalb, Illinois: Northern Illinois University Press, 1972.

3857. Harwood, Edwin. "Youth Unemployment: A Tale of Two Ghettos." Public Interest 17 (Fall 1969), 78-87.

3858. Hayden, Tom. Rebellion in Newark: Official Violence and Ghetto Response. New York: Random House, 1967.

3859. Headrrick, W.C. "Race Riots: Segregated Slums," Current History, 5 (September 1943), 30-34.

3860. Hefner, James. "Ghetto Economic Development- Content and Character of the Literature." Review of Black Political Economy 1 (1971), 43-71.

3861. Heilburn, James and Stanislaw Wellisz. "An Economic Program for the Ghetto." Proceedings of the Academy of Political Science 29 (1968), 72-85.

3862. Heilburn, James and R.R. Conant. "Profitability and Size of Firm as Evidence of Dualism in the Black Ghetto." Urban Affairs Quarterly 7 (March 1972), 251-284.

3863. Heins, Marjorie. Strictly Ghetto Property. Berkeley: Ramparts Press, 1972.

3864. Henderson, William L. and L.C. Ledebur. "The Viable Alternative for Black Economic Development (Three Programs: Jobs and Training, Black Capitalism, Ghetto Eradication or Dispersal)," Public Policy 18 (Spring 1969), 429-449.

3865. Hesse-Biber, Sharlene. "The Ethnic Ghetto as Private Welfare: A Case of Southern Italian Immigration to the United States, 1880-1914." Urban and Social Change Review 12 (Summer 1979), 9-15.

3866. Hicks, Charles, et al. "Black Ghettos and Uncertain Futures." Faculty Research Journal (January 1971), 18-25.

3867. Hill, Richard J. and Calvin J. Larson. "Variability of Ghetto Organizations." In Thomas D. Sherrard (ed.) Social Welfare and Urban Problems. New York: Columbia University Press, 1968, 132-160.

3868. Hill, Richard J. and Calvin J. Larson. "Differential Ghetto Organization." Phylon (Fall 1971), 302-311.

3869. Hill, Herbert. "Demographic Change and Racial Ghettos: The Crisis of American Cities." Journal of Urban Law 44 (Winter 1966), 231-285.

3870. Hinckley, Katherine. "The Bang and the Whimper: Model Cities and Ghetto Opinion." Urban Affairs Quarterly 13 (December 1977), 131-150.

3871. Hippler, Arther. Hunter's Point: A Black Ghetto. New York: Basic Books, 1974.

3872. Hirsch, Arnold. Making the Second Ghetto: Race and Housing in Chicago, 1940-1960. Ph.D. Dissertation, University of Illinois, Chicago Circle, 1978.

3873. Hodgart, Robert L. The Process of Expansion of the Negro Ghetto in Cities of the Northern United States: A Study of Cleveland, Ohio. M.A. Thesis, Pennsylvania State University, 1969.

3874. Humphrey, Norman D. "Black Ghetto in Detroit." Christian Century (January 15, 1947), 78-79.

3875. Hull, Herbert. "Demographic Changes and Racial Ghettos: The Crisis of American Cities." Journal of Urban Law 44 (Winter 1966), 231-285.

3876. Hunter, David E. The Slums: Challenge and Response. New York: Free Press, 1964.

3877. Ingram, Gregory. "An Analysis of Ghetto Housing Prices Over Time." In Residential Location and Urban Housing Markets. Cambridge: Ballinger, 1979.

3878. Ipcar, Charles. The Ghetto: a Critique of Conceptual Approaches. Department of Geography, Michigan State University, 1971.

3879. Jakubs, John Francis. Ghetto Dispersion and Suburban Reaction. Ph.D. Dissertation, The Ohio State University, Columbus, Ohio, 1974.

3880. Johnson, E.T. "The Delivery of Health Care in the Ghetto." Journal of National Medical Association 61 (1969), 263-270.

3881. Jones, Clinton. "Impact of Local Elections Systems on Black Political Representations" in Joe T. Darden (ed.) The Ghetto: Readings with Interpretation. Port Washington, New York: Kennikat Press, 1981, 182-90.

3882. Jones, Delmos J. "Incipient Organizations and Organizational Failures in an Urban Ghetto." Urban Anthropology 1 (Spring 1972), 51-67.

3883. Jones, Mary Gardner. The Revolution of Rising Expectations: The Ghettos Challenge to American Business. Address before the 34th Annual Meeting of the National Association of Food Chains, November 16, 1967.

3884. Kain, John F. "The Big Cities Big Problem: The Growth of Huge Racial Ghettos Exacerbates Already Existing Problems Ranging From Finance to Transportation." Challenge 15 (September-October 1966), 4-8.

3885. Kain, John F. Coping with Ghetto Unemployment. Cambridge: Harvard University Press, 1968.

3886. Kain, John F. "Coping with Ghetto Unemployment." Journal of the American Institute of Planners 35 (March 1969), 80–89.

3887. Kain, John F. The Effect of the Ghetto on the Distribution and Level of Non-White Employment in Urban Areas. Santa Monica, Cal.: Rand Corporation Bulletin, 1965.

3888. Kain, John F. and Joseph Persky. "Alternatives to the Gilded Ghetto," Public Interest 14 (Winter 1969), 74–87.

3889. Kain, John F. and Joseph J. Perskey. "Alternatives to the Gilded Ghetto" in Joe T. Darden (ed.) The Ghetto: Readings with Interpretations. Port Washington, New York: Kennikat, 1981, 212–224.

3890. Kapsis, Robert. "Black Ghetto Diversity and Anomie: A Sociopolitical View." American Journal of Sociology 83 (March 1978), 1132–1153.

3891. Karpel, Craig. "Ghetto Fraud on the Installment Plan." New York 2 (May 26, 1969), 24–32.

3892. Katzman, David M. Before the Ghetto: Black Detroit in the Nineteenth Century. Urbana: University of Illinois Press, 1973.

3893. Kelly, Gregory P. "The Westside: The Making of a Ghetto." The Lansing Star (August 30, 1978), 4.

3894. Kegels, S. Stephen. "A Field Experimental Attempt to Change Beliefs and Behavior of Women in an Urban Ghetto." Journal of Health and Social Behavior 10 (June 1969), 115–125.

3895. Kern, Clifford R. Racial Discrimination and the Price of Ghetto Housing in City and Suburb: Some Recent Evidence. Cambridge: Department of City and Regional Planning, Harvard University Discussion Paper No. D 77-2, March 1977.

3896. Kilson, Martin. "Political Change in the Negro Ghetto, 1900–1940's." In Nathan I. Huggins, et al. (eds.) Key Issues in the Afro-American Experience, 167–192.

3897. Kochman, Thomas. "Rapping in the Ghetto." Transaction 6 (February 1969), 26–35.

3898. Koestler, Frances A. "Puritt-Igoe: Survival in a Concrete Ghetto." Social Work 12 (October 1967), 3–14.

3899. Komorowski, Conrad. "The Detroit Ghetto Uprisings," Political Affairs 46 (September 1967), 12–24.

3900. Kramer, Judith and Seymour Leventman. Children of the Gilded Ghetto. New Haven: Yale University Press, 1961.

3901. Krout, Maurice H. "A Community in Flux, The Chicago Ghetto Resurveyed." Social Forces 5 (1926), 273-282.

3902. Kuhn, M.W. and P.E. Mason. Isla Vista, a Ghetto Model. Paper presented at the Association of Pacific Coast Geographers, Victoria, British Columbia, 1971.

3903. Kupchick, George J. "Environmental Health in the Ghetto." American Journal of Public Health 59 (February 1969), 220-225.

3904. Kusmer, Kenneth L. A Ghetto Takes Shape: Black Cleveland, 1870-1930. Urbana: University of Illinois Press, 1976.

3905. Labov, William. "A Note on the Relation of Reading Failure to Peer Group Status in Urban Ghettos." Florida Reporter (1969), 54-57.

3906. Labrie, Peter. "Black Central Cities: Dispersals or Rebuilding", in Joe T. Darden (ed.) The Ghetto: Readings with Interpretations. Port Washington, New York: Kennikat, 1981, 193-211.

3907. Labrie, Peter. "Black Central Cities: Dispersal or Rebuilding." Review of Black Political Economy 1 (Winter-Spring 1971), 78-99.

3908. Laguerre, Michel. "Internal Dependency: The Structural Position of the Black Ghetto in American Society." Journal of Ethnic Studies 6 (Winter 1979), 29-44.

3909. Lammermeier, Paul J. "Cincinnati's Black Community: The Origins of a ghetto, 1870-1880." In John Bracey, et al. (eds.) The Rise of the Ghetto. Belmont: Wadsworth Publishing Co., 1971, 24-28.

3910. Lanneti, Luisi. "Law and the Demise of the Urban Ghetto," Catholic Lawyer 15 (1969), 39-55.

3911. Lawrence, Paul R. "Organization Development in the Black Ghetto." In Richard S. Rosenbloom and Robin Morris (eds.) Social Innovation in the City: New Enterprises for Community Development. Cambridge, Massachusetts: Harvard University Press, 1969, 109-119.

3912. Leah, Daniel. "All Colored - But Not Much Different: Films Made for Negro Ghetto Audiences, 1913-1928." Phylon 36 (September 1975), 321-339.

3913. Levey, Burton. "Cops in the Ghetto: a Problem of the Police System". In Louis H. Massotti and Don R. Bowen Riots and Rebellion: Civil Violence in the Urban Community. Beverly Hills, Sage, 1968.

3914. Levin, Henry M. "Why Ghetto Schools Fail." _Saturday Review_ (March 21, 1970), 68-69.

3915. Levine, Charles "Black Entrepreneurship in the Ghetto: A Recruitment Strategy." _Land Economics_ 48 (August 1972), 269-273.

3916. Levitan, Sar A. and Robert Taggart. "Developing Business in the Ghetto." _Conference Board Record_ (July 1969), 13-21.

3917. Levitan, Sar A., et al. _Economic Opportunity in the Ghetto: The Partnership of Government and Business_. Baltimore: Johns Hopkins University Press, 1970.

3918. Levy, Burton. "Cops in the Ghetto: A Problem of the Police System," _American Behavioral Scientist_ 11 (March 1968), 31-34.

3919. Levy, Burton. "Cops in the Ghetto." In Louis Masotti and Don R. Bowen (eds.) _Riots and Rebellion: Civil Violence in the Urban Community_. Beverly Hills: Sage, 1968, 347-358.

3920. Levy, Gerald. _Ghetto School: Class Welfare in an Elementary School._ New York: Pegasus Publishing, 1970.

3921. Lightfoot, Claude M. _Ghetto Rebellion to Black Liberation_. New York: International Publishers, 1968.

3922. Llewellyn, J.B. "The Problem of Business Operations in the Ghetto." In _Minority Business Development._ Boston: Federal Research Bank of Boston, 1976.

3923. Lofland, J. "The Youth Ghetto". _Journal of Higher Education_ 39 (1968), 131-143.

3924. Long, Norton E. "Politics and Ghetto Perceptuation." In Roland L. Warren (ed.) _Politics and the Ghettos_. New York: Atherton Press, 1969, 31-43.

3925. Loury, Glenn C. "The Minimum Border Length Hypothesis Does Not Explain the Shape of Black Ghettos." _Journal of Urban Economics_ 5 (April 1978), 147-153.

3926. Luchterhand, E. and L. Weller. "Social Class and the Desegregation Movement: A Study of Parent's Decisions in a Negro Ghetto." _Social Problems_ 13 (Summer 1965), 83-88.

3927. Lundgren, Terry Dennis. _Comparative Study of All Negro Ghettos in the United States._ Unpublished Ph.D. Dissertation. The Ohio State University, 1976.

3928. Lyons, S.R. "Political Socialization of Ghetto Children: Efficacy and Cynicism." _Journal of Politics_ 32 (May 1970), 288-304.

3929. Mackler, Bernard. "Grouping in the Ghetto." Education and Urban Society 2 (1969), 80-96.

3930. Marcus, Burton H. "Similarity of Ghetto and Non-Ghetto Food Costs." Journal of Marketing Research 6 (August 1969), 365-368.

3931. Mark, Ber. Uprising in the Warsaw Ghetto. New YOrk: Schocken Books, 1975.

3932. Martin, Marcine. Barrio and Ghetto Delimination: A Carto-Analytic Approach. M.A. Thesis, University of California of Los Angeles, 1975.

3933. Mason, Peter F. "Some Characteristics of a Youth Ghetto in Boulder, Colorado." Journal of Geography (December 1972), 526-533.

3934. Mason, Peter F. "Some Spacial and Locational Relationships Relevant to Youth Ghetto Disorder." Proceedings of the Association of American Geographers 5 (1973), 165-169.

3935. Mayer, John E. and Aaron Rosenblatt. "Encounters with Danger: Social Workers in the Ghetto." Sociology of Work and Occupations 2 and 3 (August 1975), 227-246.

3936. McColl, Robert W. "Vietnam, Cuba and the Ghetto." In David A. Lanegian and Risa Palm (eds.) Invitation to Geography. New York: McGraw Hill, 1973, 112-117.

3937. McColl, Robert W. "Creating Ghettos: Manipulating Social Space in the Real World and the Classroom." Journal of Geography 71 (November 1972), 496-502.

3938. McCord, William, et al. Life Styles in the Black Ghetto. New York: W.W. Norton, 1969.

3939. McLaurin, Dunbar S. Ghetto Economic Development and Industrialization Plan. New York: Human Resources Adminstration, April 1968.

3940. Mefer, August and Elliott Rudwick. From Plantation to Ghetto. New York: Hill and Wang, 1970.

3941. Meister, Richard. The Black Ghetto: Promised Land or Colony. Lexington, Mass.: D.C. Heath, 1972.

3942. Mellor, Earl F. "A Case Study: Costs and Benefits of Public Goods and Expenditures for a Ghetto." In Kenneth Boulding, et al. (eds.) Transfers in an Urbanized Economy. Belmont: Wadsworth, 1973, 38-57.

3943. Mercer, John. "Housing Quality and the Ghetto." In Harold M.

Rose (ed.) Geography of the Ghetto. Dekalb: Northern Illinois University Press, 1972, 144–167.

3944. Mercer, John. Monopoly Profits and Ghetto Food Merchants: An Empirical Test. Unpublished paper, Columbia University, 1973.

3945. Meyer, David R. Spatial Variation of Black Urban Households. Chicago: University of Chicago Press, Department of Geography Research Paper No. 129, 1970.

3946. Milio, Nancy. "Project in a Negro Ghetto." American Journal of Nursing 67 (May 1967), 1006–1010.

3947. Miller, Henry. "Social Work in the Black Ghetto: The New Colonialism." Social Work 14 (July 1969), 65–76.

3948. Miller, Kenneth, H. "Community Organizations in the Ghetto." In Richard S. Rosenblum and Robin Morris (eds.) Social Innovation in the City: New Enterprises for Community Development. Cambridge, Massachusetts: Harvard University Press, 1969, 97–108.

3949. Miller, Thomas V. Ghetto Fever. Milwaukee: Bruce Publishing, 1968.

3950. Minuchin, Salvadore, et al. Families of the Slums: An Exploration of Their Structure and Treatment. New York: Basic Books, 1967.

3951. Moore, Wilfred B. The Vertical Ghetto. New York: Random House, 1969.

3952. Morgan, Gordon Daniel. The Ghetto College Student: A Descriptive Essay on College Youth from the Inner City. Iowa City: American College Testing Program, 1970.

3953. Morrill, Richard L. "The Negro Ghetto: Problems and Alternatives." Geographical Review 55 (1965), 339–361.

3954. Morrill, Richard L. "The Persistence of the Black Ghetto as Spatial Separation." Southeastern Geographer 11 (November 1971), 149–156.

3955. Morrill, Richard L. "A Geographic Perspective of the Black Ghetto." In Harold M. Rose (ed.) Geography of the Ghetto. DeKalb: Northern Illinois University Press, 1972, 28–58.

3956. Muller, Thomas J. The Ghetto of Indifference. Nashville: Abingdon Press, 1966.

3957. Murphy, Arthur W. NAACP Legal Defense and Educational Fund, Inc. Materials for Conference on Slum Housing Remedies in New York City, New York 1966.

3958. Myers, Samuel L. "The Economics of Crime in the Urban Ghetto."
       The Review of Black Political Economy 9 (Fall 1978), 43-59.

3959. Nash, William W. and Chester W. Hartman. "Laissez-Faire in the
       Slums", The Reproter (February 25, 1965), 53.

3960. National Advisory Commission on Civil Disorders. "Comparing
       the Immigrant and Negro Experience." In Joe T. Darden (ed.) The
       Ghetto: Readings with Interpretations. Port Washington, New
       York: Kennikat Press, 74-78.

3961. National Committee Against Discrimination in Housing. "Black
       Unemployment in the Ghetto." In Thomas Pettigrew (ed.) Racial
       Discrimination in the United States. New York: Harper and Row,
       1975, 152-158.

3962. Nelson, Richard R. The Moon and the Ghetto. New York: W.W.
       Norton, 1977.

3963. Nesbitt, George A. "Breakup the Black Ghetto." Crisis 56
       (February 1969), 48-50.

3964. Norman, John C. Medicine in the Ghetto. New York: Appleton-
       Century-Crofts, 1969.

3965. "Oakland Presents Its Case for Salvaging a Ghetto,"
       Architectural Forum 125 (April 1967), 42-45.

3966. Oakland, W.H., et al. "Ghetto Multipliers: A Case Study of
       Hough." Journal of Regional Science 11 (1971), 337-345.

3967. O'Loughlin, John. "Malapportionment and Gerrymandering in the
       Ghetto." In John S. Adams (ed.) Urban Policy Making and
       Metropolitan Dynamics. Cambridge: Ballinger Publishing Co.,
       1978.

3968. Osofsky, Gilbert. "The Enduring Ghetto." Journal of American
       History (September 1968), 243-255.

3969. Osofsky, Gilbert. Harlem: The Making of a Ghetto. New York:
       Harper and Row, 1966.

3970. Palley, Marian Lief, et al. "Subcommunity Leadership in a
       Black Ghetto: A Study of Newark, New Jersey." Urban Affairs
       Quarterly 5:3 (March 1970), 291-312.

3971. Panker, G.J. Black Nationalism and Prospects for Violence in
       the Ghetto. Santa Monica: Rand Corporation, 1969.

3972. Partridge, William. The Hippie Ghetto: The Natural History of
       a Subculture. New York: Holt, Rinehart and Winston, 1973.

3973. Percy, Charles H. Building the New America. Developing

Practical Programs for Enterprise in the Ghetto: The New Capitalism, American Management Association Briefing Session. New York: December 18, 1968.

3974.   Philpott, Thomas L. The Slum and the Ghetto: Neighborhood Deterioration and Middle-Class Reform, Chicago, 1880-1930. New York: Oxford University Press, 1978.

3975.   Price, William A. "Economics of the Negro Ghetto." National Guardian (September 3, 1966), 4.

3976.   Radzialowski, Thaddeus. "The View from a Polish Ghetto: Some Observations on The First One Hundred Years in Detroit." Ethnicity 1 (July 1974), 125-150.

3977.   Raine, Walter J. The Ghetto Merchant Survey. A Report Prepared for the Office of Economic Opportunity, Nathan E. Cohen, Coordinator. Los Angeles: University of California, Institute of Government and Public Affairs (June 1, 1967).

3978.   Rainwater, Lee. Behind Ghetto Walls. Chicago: Aldine, 1971.

3979.   Rainwater, Lee. Family Design. Chicago: Aldine, 1964.

3980.   Rainwater, Lee.   Soul. Chicago: Aldine, 1970.

3981.   Ramirez, Manuel. "Identity Crisis in the Barrios." In Edward Simer (ed.) Pain and Promise. New York: New American Library, 1972, 57-60.

3982.   Rasmussen, Karl R. "The Multi-Ordered Urban Area: A Ghetto." Phylon (Fall 1968), 282-290.

3983.   Raspberry, William. "Should Ghettoese Be Accepted?" Today's Education 59 (April 1970) 30-31 and 61-62.

3984.   Rein, Martin. "Social Stability and Black Ghettos." In Roland L. Warren (ed.) Politics and the Ghettos. New York: Atherton, 1969, 44-58.

3985.   Reiss, Albert J. and Howard Aldrich.   "Absentee Ownership and Management in the Black Ghetto: Social and Economic Consequences." Social Problems 18 (Winter 1971), 319-339.

3986.   Reiss, L.S. "Five Ghettos of the Modern Exodus." Survey 51 (October 1923-March 1924), 447-452.

3987.   Renshaw, Patrick. "The Black Ghetto, 1890-1940." Journal of American Studies 8:1 (1974), 41-59.

3988.   Richards, Hilda and Marionette S. Daniels. "Sociopsychiatric Rehabilitation in a Black Urban Ghetto: Innovative Treatment Roles and Approaches," American Journal of Orthopsychiatry 39

(July 1969), 662–676.

3989. Richings, G.F. Evidences of Progress Among Colored People. Philadelphia: Ferguson, 1905.

3990. "Riot Reader: A Collection of Recent Material Dealing with the Causes of Ghetto Unrest, Possible Remedies -- and Probable Consequences of Continued National Neglect," The City 2 (January 1968), 13–28.

3991. Rist, Ray C. "Student Social Class and Teacher Expectations: The Self-Fulfilling Prophecy in Ghetto Education." Harvard Educational Review (August 1970), 411–451.

3992. Rodman, H. "Family and Social Pathology in the Ghetto." Science 161 (August 23, 1968), 756–762.

3993. Rose, Harold M. "The All-Black Town: Suburban Prototype or Urban Slum?" People and Politics in Urban Society. Beverly Hills: Sage (1972), 397–431.

3994. Rose, Harold M. The Black Ghetto as a Territorial Entity. Special Publication No. 3, Department of Geography, Northwestern University, 1969.

3995. Rose, Harold M. The Black Ghetto: A Spatial Behavioral Perspective. New York: McGraw-Hill, 1971.

3996. Rose, Harold M. "The Development of an Urban Subsystem: The Case of the Negro Ghetto." Annals of the Association of American Geographers (March 1970), 1–17.

3997. Rose, Peter I. The Ghetto and Beyond: Jewish Life in America. New York: Random House, 1969.

3998. Rosen, S.M. "Better Mousetraps: Reflections on Economic Development in the Ghetto." Urban Review 4 (May 1970), 14–18.

3999. Rossi, Peter H., et al. "Between Black and White -- The Faces of American Institutions and the Ghetto." In Supplemental Studies for the National Advisory Commission on Civil Disorders, July 1968.

4000. Rossi, Peter H. (ed.) Ghetto Revolts. Chicago: Aldine, 1970.

4001. Rossi, Peter H. and Richard A. Berk. "Local Political Leadership and Popular Discontent in the Ghetto." Annals of the American Academy of Political and Social Science 391 (September 1970), 111–127.

4002. Rossi, Peter H., et al. The Roots of Urban Discontent. Public Policy, Municipal Institutions and the Ghetto. New York: Wiley, 1974.

4003. Rothman, Jack. "The Ghetto Makers." Nation (1961), 222-25.

4004. Rouse, James W. and Nathaniel S. Keith. No Slums in Ten Years, a Workable Program Urban Renewal. Report to the Commissioners of the District of Columbia, January 1955.

4005. Rustin, Bayard. "A Way Out of the Exploding Ghetto." New York Times Magazine (August 13, 1967).

4006. Rustin, Bayard. "The Watts 'Manifesto' and the McCone Report." Commentary (March 1966), 30.

4007. Rushin, Bayard. "Way Out of the Exploding Ghetto." Harvard Review 4 (1968), 31-40.

4008. Sager, Clifford J., et al. The Black Ghetto Family in Therapy: A Laboratory Experience. New York: Grove Press, 1970.

4009. Salisbury, Howard G. "The State Within A State: Some Comparisons Between the Urban Ghetto and the Insurgent State." Professional Geographer 22 (April 1971), 105-112.

4010. Sanders, Ralph A. Spatial Trends in Age Structure Changes within the Cleveland Ghetto: 1940-1965. Master's Thesis, Pennsylvania State University, 1968.

4011. Sanders, Ralph A. and John S. Adams. "Age Structure in Expanding Ghetto Space, Cleveland, Ohio, 1940-1965." Southeastern Geographer 11 (November 1971), 121-132.

4012. Sands, Gary. "Ghetto Development in Detroit" in Joe T. Darden (ed.) The Ghetto Readings With Interpretations. Port Washington, New York: Kennikat, 1981, 89-108.

4013. Sands, Gary. "Ghetto Development in Detroit." In Robert D. Swartz (ed.) Metropolitan America: Geographic Perspectives and Teaching Strategies, 175-197. Oak Park: National Council for Geographic Education, 1972.

4014. Santiestevan, Henry. "The Union to End Slums is Waging a Campaign Against Chicago's Slumlords: Fresh Wind in the Ghettos." IUD Agenda 3 (February 1967), 9-12.

4015. Saunders, Marie Simmons. "The Ghetto: Some Perceptions of a Black Social Worker". Social Work 14 (October 1969), 884-88.

4016. Savich, Harold. "Powerless in an Urban Ghetto: The Case of Political Biases and Differential Access in New York City." Policy 5 (Fall 1972), 19-56.

4017. Schnare, Ann and Raymond J. Struyk. "An Analysis of Ghetto Housing Prices Over Time." In G. Ingram (ed.) The Economics of Residential Location and Urban Housig Markets. New York:

National Bureau of Economic Research Conference on Income and Wealth, May 1975.

4018. Schorr, Alvin Louis. "Slums and Social Security," In Jewel Bellush and M. Hausknecht (eds.). Urban Renewal: People, Politics, and Plannings. New York: Anchor Books, 1967, 415-24.

4019. Schorr, Alvin Louis. Slums and Social Insecurity, an Appraisal of the Effectiveness of Housing Policies in Helping to Eliminate Poverty in the United States. Washington, D.C.: Government Printing Office, 1963.

4020. Schulman, Jay. "Ghetto-Area Residence, Political Alienation and Riot Orientation." In Louis H. Masetti and Don Bowen (eds.) Riots and Rebellion: Civil Violence in the Urban Community, 261-284. Beverly Hills: Sage, 1968.

4021. Schulz, David A. Coming Up Black: Patterns of Ghetto Socialization. Englewood Cliffs, New Jersey: Prentice-Hall, 1969.

4022. Schulz, David A. "Some Aspects of the Policeman's Role as it Impinges Upon Family Life in a Negro Ghetto." Sociological Focus 2 (Spring 1969), 63-72.

4023. Schuman, Howard and Barry Gruenberg. "Dissatisfaction with City Services: Is Race an Important Factor?" in Joe T. Darden (ed.) The Ghetto: Readings with Interpretations. Port Washington, New York: Kennikat Press, 1981, 159-173.

4024. Seig, Louis. "Concepts of Ghetto: A Geography of Minority Groups." Professional Geographer 23 (January 1971), 1-4.

4025. Sengstock, Mary C. "The Corporation and the Ghetto: An Analysis of the Effects of Corporate Retail Grocery Sales on Ghetto Life." Journal of Urban Law 45 (1968), 673-703.

4026. Sexton, Donald E. Groceries in the Ghetto. Lexington, Mass.: D.C. Heath, 1973.

4027. Shapiro, Linda G. Relative Deprivation Examined as an Explanation of Ghetto Violence. M.A. Thesis, University of North Carolina, Chapel Hill, NC., 1975.

4028. Skolnick, Jerome H. "The Police and the Urban Ghetto," in Charles E. Reasons and Jack L. Kuykendall (eds.). Race, Crime and Justice. Pacific Palisades, California: Goodyear Publishing Co., 1972, 236-58.

4029. Slum Removal Study, New York City. Division of Housing and Community Renewal, New York, February 1968.

4030. Smith, Christopher J. "Being Mentally Ill in the Asylum of the

Ghetto." _Antipode_ 7 (September 1975), 53-59.

4031. Smolensky, Eugene, et al. "The Prisoner's Dilemma and Ghetto Expansion." _Land Economics_ 44 (November 1968), 419-430.

4032. Solomon, Daniel, et al. "Family Characteristics and Elementary School Achievement in an Urban Ghetto." _Journal of Consulting and Clinical Psychology_ 39 (1972), 462-466.

4033. Soskin, William F. "Riots, Ghettos and the Negro Revolt," in Arthur M. Ross and Herbert Hill (eds.), _Employment, Race and Poverty_. New York: Harcourt, Brace and World, 1967, 305-333.

4034. Sowell, Thomas. "A Neo-Mercantilist Model for Maximizing Ghetto Income." _The Review of Black Political Economy_ 1 (1971), 22-27.

4035. Spear, Allan. "The Institutional Ghetto". In John Bracey, et al. (eds.) _The Rise of the Ghetto_. Belmont: Wadsworth Publishing, 1971, 170-174.

4036. Spear, Allan. "The Origins of the Urban Ghetto, 1870-1915." In Nathan Huggins (ed.) _Key Issues in the Afro-American Experience_. New York: Harcourt Brace Jovanovich, 1971, 153-166.

4037. Spear, Allan H. _Black Chicago: The Making of a Negro Ghetto, 1880-1920._ Chicago: University of Chicago Press, 1967.

4038. Steiss, Alan W., et al. _Dynamic Change and the Urban Ghetto._ Lexington, Mas.: D.C. Heath, 1975.

4039. Strauss, A. "Medical Ghettos." _Transaction_ (May 1967), 7-16.

4040. Sturdivant, Frederick D. "Better Deal for Ghetto Shoppers." _Harvard Business Review_ 46 (March-April 1968), 130-139.

4041. Sturdivant, Frederick D. (ed.) _The Ghetto Marketplace._ New York: Free Press, 1969.

4042. Suttles, Gerald D. _The Social Order of the Slum: Ethnicity and Territory in the Inner City._ Chicago: University of Chicago Press, 1968.

4043. Suttles, Gerald D. "Anatomy of a Chicago Slum." _Trans-Action,_ 6 (February 1969), 16-25.

4044. Tabb, William R. "Black Power-Green Power: The Economics of the Ghetto." In John L. Sullivan (ed.) _Explorations in Urban Land Economics._ Hartford: University of Hartford, 1970, 56-80.

4045. Tabb, William R. "A Cost-Benefit Analysis of Location Subsidies for Ghetto Neighborhoods," _Land Economics_ 48 (1972),

45-52.

4046. Tabb, William R. The Political Economy of the Black Ghetto. New York: W.W. Norton, 1970.

4047. Taber, Richard. "A Systems Approach to the Delivery of Mental Health Services in Black Ghettos." American Journal of Orthopsychiatry 40 (1970), 702-709.

4048. Tata, Robert J., et al. "Defensible Space in a Housing Project: A Case Study from a South Florida Ghetto." Professional Geographer 27 (August 1975), 297-303.

4049. Tebbel, Robert. The Slum Makers. New York: Dial, 1963.

4050. "Techniques for Breaking Up America's Racial Ghettos: Many Private, Voluntary Devices are Being Tried as Supplements to Public Action." Journal of Public Housing 24 (October 1967), 505-10.

4051. "The Tough New Breed: Ghetto Black Under 30." Newsweek (June 30, 1969), 4-5.

4052. Tucker, Sterling. Why the Ghetto Must Go. New York: Public Affairs Committee, 1968.

4053. U.S. Bureau of the Census. The Social Economic Status of the Black Population in the United States. Washington, D.C.: Government Printing Office, 1979.

4054. U.S. Commission on Civil Rights. A Time to Listen . . A Time to Act . . Voices from the Ghettos of the Nation's Cities. Washington, D.C.: Commission on Civil Rights, November 1967.

4055. U.S. Commisson on Civil Rights. Equal Opportunity in Suburbia. Washington, D.C.: Government Printing Office, 1974.

4056. U.S. Massachusetts Advisory Commission. Voice of the Ghetto: Report on Two Boston Neighborhood Meetings. Washington, D.C.: U.S. Government Printing Office, 1967.

4057. U.S. Congress. House. Special Committee on East St. Louis Riots. East St. Louis riots. Report of the Special Committee Authorized by Congress to Investigate the East St. Louis Riots. Washington, D.C.: Government Printing Office, 1918.

4058. Vernarelli, M. Joseph. Locational Distortion and Black Ghetto Expansion. Unpublished Ph.D. Dissertation. State University of New York at Binghamton, 1978.

4059. Vietorisz, B. Harrison. "Ghetto Development, Community Corporations, and Public Policy." Review of Black Political Economy 2 (Fall 1971), 28-43.

4060. Walden, Theodore. "Intervention by a Jewish Community Relations Council in a Negro Ghetto: A Case Illustration." Journal of Jewish Communal Service 44 (Fall 1967), 49-63.

4061. Walker, Williams. "Cleveland's Crisis Ghetto." Trans-Action 4:9 (September 1967), 4-12.

4062. Ward, David. "The Emergence of Central Immigrant Ghettos in American Cities, 1840-1920." Annals of the Association of American Geographers 58 (1968), 343-359.

4063. Warner, Sam Bass and Colin B. Burke. "Cultural Change and the Ghetto." Journal of Contemporary History 4 (1969), 173-188.

4064. Warren, Donald I. Social Structural Processes Related to the Ghetto. NIMH Research Grants of the Center for Minority Group Mental Health Programs, RO 1 16403, June 30, 1971.

4065. Warren, Roland L. (ed.) Politics and the Ghetto. New York: Atherton Press, 1969.

4066. Wassenich, Mark. New Towns from the Point of View of the Ghetto Resident: Phase II. Chapel Hill: University of North Carolina, Center for Urban and Regional Studies, 1970.

4067. Weaver, Robert C. The Negro Ghetto. New York: Harcourt, Brace, 1948.

4068. Weaver, Robert C. "Non-White Population Movements and Urban Ghettos." Phylon 20 (Autumn 1959), 235-241.

4069. Weiss, Nancy J. "Building the Black Ghetto." Review in American History 5:1 (1977), 83-91.

4070. Weller, Charles Frederick. Neglected Neighbors: Stories of Life in the Alleys, Tenements and Shanties of the National Capital. Philadelphia: John C. Winston, 1965.

4071. Wheeler, James O. "Transportation Problems in Negro Ghettos." Sociology and Social Research 53 (1969), 171-179.

4072. Wheeler, James O. "Work Trip Length and the Ghetto." Land Economics 44 (1968), 107-112.

4073. Wheeler, James O. and Stanley D. Brunn. "An Agricultural Ghetto: Negroes in Cass County, Michigan, 1845-1968." Geographical Review 59 (July 1969), 317-329.

4074. Wieand, K. "Housing Price Determination in Urban Ghettos." Urban Studies 12 (1975), 193-204.

4075. Williams, Joyce. Black Community Control: A Study of Transition in a Texas Ghetto. New York: Praeger, 1973.

4076. Williams, Walter. "Cleveland's Crisis Ghetto." In Peter Rossi (ed.) Ghetto Revolts. Chicago: Aldine, 1970, 13-31.

4077. Wilson, Robert A. "Anomie in the Ghetto: A Study of Neighborhood Types, Race, and Anomie." American Journal of Sociology 77 (1971), 66-68.

4078. Wilson, William. "Race Relations Models and Explanations of Ghetto Behavior." In Peter Rose (ed.) Nation of Nations: The Ethnic Experience and the Racial Crisis. New York: Random House, 1972, 259-275.

4079. Wirth, Louis. "The Ghetto" in Joe T. Darden (ed.) The Ghetto: Readings with Interpretations. Port Washington, New York: Kennikat, 1981, 15-26.

4080. Wirth, Louis. The Ghetto. University of Chicago Press, 1956.

4081. Wolfe, Joseph A. Increasing Black Enterpreneurship in the Ghetto: An Exploratory Study of a Management Training Program for Harlem Blacks. Ph.D. Dissertation, New York University Graduate School of Business Administration, 1971.

4082. Wolpert, Elaine and Julian Wolpert. "From Asylum to Ghetto." Antipode 6 (1974), 63-76.

4083. Wood, Edith. Slums and Blighted Areas in the United States. Washington, D.C.: Government Printing Office, 1935.

4084. Wood, Robert C. "The Ghettos and Metropolitan Politics." In Roland L. Warren (ed.) Politics and the Ghetto. New York: Atherton, 1969, 59-70.

4085. "Writing a Policy for the Ghetto." Business Week (September 9, 1967), 34.

4086. Wye, Christopher G. Midwest Ghetto: Patterns of Negro Life and Thought in Cleveland, Ohio, 1929-1945. Ph.D. Dissertation, Kent State University, 1973.

4087. Young, Whitney M. "Central-City Ghettos Need an Operation Urban Survival." Business Economics 2 (Spring 1967), 34-36.

4088. Young, Whitney M. "Ghetto Power". Business Today (Summer 1969), 1-10.

4089. Zangwill, Israel. Children of the Ghetto: A Study of a Peculiar People. New York: Grosset and Dunlap, 1895.

4090. Zangwill, Israel. Dreamers of the Ghetto. New York: Harper and Row, 1898.

4091. Zangwill, Israel. Ghetto Comedies. New York: Maximillan,

1907.

4092. Zangwill, Israel. Ghetto Tragedies. London: McClure and Co.,
      1893.

4093. Zeublin, Charles. "The Chicago Ghetto." In Hull House Maps
      and Papers. Chicago: Thomas Y. Cromwell, 1895, 91-111.

CHAPTER 6

Suburbanization and Reurbanization

4094. Agrocs, C. "Who's in American Dream? Ethnic Representation in Suburban Opportunity Structure in Metropolitan Detroit, 1940–1970." Ethnic Groups 4:4 (1982), 239-54.

4095. Alexis, Marcus." The Economic Status of Blacks and Whites" American Economic Review 68:2 (May, 1978), 179-85.

4096. Alfred, Stephen J. and Charles R. Marcoux. "Impact of a Community Association on Integrated Suburban Housing Patterns." Cleveland State Law Review 19 (January 1970), 90-99.

4097. American Academy of Political and Social Science, Racial Desegregation and Integration. Philadelphia; American Academy of Political and Social Science, 1956.

4098. Armstrong Association of Philadelphia. A Study of Living Conditions Among Colored People in Towns in the Outer Part of Philadelphia and in Other Suburbs Both in Pennsylvania and New Jersey. Philadelphia, 1915.

4099. Bacon, Margaret H. "The White Noose of the Suburbs." Progressive 24 (October 1969), 37-38.

4100. "Benign Quotas: A Plan for Integrated Private Housing." Yale Law Journal 70 (November 1966), 126-134.

4101. Bergman, E.M. Eliminating Exclusionary Zoning: Reconciling Workplace and Residence in Suburban Areas. Cambridge, Massachusetts: Ballinger, 1974.

4102. Berry, Brian J.L. et al. "Attitudes Towards Integration: The Role of Status in Community Response to Neighborhood Change". In Barry Swartz (ed.) The Changing Face of Suburbs. Chicago: University of Chicago Press, 1976, 221-64.

4103. Bittker, B.I. "The Case of the Checker-Board Ordinance: An Experiment in Race Relations." Yale Law Journal 71 (July 1962), 1387-1423.

4104. Blumberg, Leonard and Michael Lalli. "Little Ghettoes: A Study of Negroes in the Suburbs." Phylon 27 (Summer 1966), 117-131.

4105. Butterfield, Fox. "The Exodus of Newark" in Louis H. Masotti and Jeffrey K. Hadden (eds.) Suburbia in Transition. New York: New Viewpoints, 1974, 78-81.

4106. Caldwell, Earl. "The Problems of a Black Suburb" in Louis H. Masotti aand Jeffrey K. Hadden (eds.) Suburbia in Transition. New York: New Viewpoints, 1974, 78-81.

4107. Campbell, Carlos C. "Musings on Suburbia: Seeds of Rebellion and Concentric Ring of Slums." City: Magazine of Urban Life and Environment 5:1 (January-February 1971), 51-53.

4108. Clark, Dennis. "Strategy in Suburbia." Interracial Review 35 (July 1962), 160, 164-167.

4109. Clark, Thomas A. Blacks in Suburbs: A National Perspective. New Brunswick, New Jersey: Center for Urban Policy Research, 1979.

4110. Clark, Thomas A. Race, Class, and Suburbanization: Prior Trends and Policy Perspectives. Unpublished paper. New Brunswick, New Jersey: Rutgers University, Department of Urban Planning and Policy Development, 1979.

4111. Clay, Phillip L. The Process of Black Suburbanization. Cambridge, Massachusetts: M.I.T., Department of Urban Studies and Planning, Ph.D. Thesis, 1975.

4112. Clay, Phillip L. "The Process of Black Suburbanization." Urban Affairs Quarterly 14:4 (1979), 405-424.

4113. Coe, Paul F. "Non-White Population Increases in Metropolitan Areas." Journal of American Statistical Association 50 (June 1955), 283-308.

4114. Connally, Harold X. "Black Movement to the Suburbs: Suburbs Doubling Their Black Population During the 1960's." Urban Affairs Quarterly 9:1 (1973), 91-111.

4115. Connecticut, State of. Commission on Civil Rights. Racial Integration in Private Residential Neighborhoods in Connecticut. Hartford: Research Division, 1957.

4116. Cottingham, Phoebe H. "Black Income and Metropolitan Residential Dispersion." Urban Affairs Quarterly 10 (1975), 273-96.

4117. Cowgill, Donald O. "Segregation Scores for Metropolitan Areas." _American Sociological Review_ 27 (June 1962), 400-402.

4118. Culver, Lowell W. "Changing Settlement Patterns of Black Americans, 1970-1980. _Journal of Urban Affairs_ 4:4 (Fall 1982), 29-48.

4119. Damerell, Reginald G. _Triumph in a White Suburb_. New York: William Morrow, 1968.

4120. Danielsen, Michael N. "The Politics of Exclusionary Zoning in Suburbia". _Political Science Quarterly_ 91:1 (Spring, 1976), 1-18.

4121. Darden, Joe T. "Blacks in the Suburbs: Their Number is Rising but Patterns of Segregation Persist." _Vital Issues_ (December 1977), 1-4.

4122. Davidoff, Linda, et al. "The Suburs Have to Open Their Gates" _New York Times Magazine_ (November 7, 1971), 40-50.

4123. Davis, Dewitt and Emilio Casetti. "Do Black Students Wish to Live in Integrated, Social Homogeneous Neighborhoods? A Questionnaire Analysis." _Economic Geography_ 54:3 (1978), 197-210.

4124. Delaney, Paul. "Black Middle Class Joining the Exodus to White Suburbia." _New York Times_ (January 4, 1976), 1-10.

4125. Delaney, Paul. "Negroes Find Few Tangible Gains." in L.H. Masotti and J.K. Hadden (eds.), _Suburbia in Transition_. New York: New Viewpoints, 1974, 278-82.

4126. Deskins, Donald R. _Residential Mobility of Negroes in Detroit, 1837-1965._ Ann Arbor, Michigan: Department of Geography, University of Michigan, 1972.

4127. DeVise, Pierre. "The Status of Integration in Suburban Chicago." _Focus Midwest_ 61 (1974), 10-18.

4128. DeVise, Pierre. "The Suburbanization of Jobs and Minority Employment." _Economic Geography_ 52:4 (1976), 348-62.

4129. Donaldson, Scott. "Should the Suburbs Plead Guilty?" _City: Magazine of Urban Life and Environment_ 6:1 (January-February 1972), 57-59.

4130. Downs, Anthony. _Opening Up the Suburbs._ New Haven: Yale University Press, 1973.

4131. Dudas, John L. and David B. Longbrake. "Problems and Future Directions of Residential Integration: The Local Application of Federally Funded Programs in Dade County, Florida."

Southeastern Geographer 11:2 (1971), 157.

4132. Duncan, Beverly and Philip M. Hauser. Housing a Metropolis: Chicago. Glencoe, Illinois: Free Press, 1961.

4133. Duncan, Otis and Beverly Duncan. The Negro Population of Chicago: A Study of Residential Succession. Chicago: University of Chicago Press, 1957.

4134. Eisenberg, Lawrence D. "Uncle Tom's Multi-Cabin Subdivision - Constitutional Restriction on Racial Discrimination by Developers." Cornell Law Review 53 (January 1968), 314-324.

4135. Farley, Reynolds. "Components of Suburban Population Growth." In Barry Schwartz (ed.) The Changing Face of the Suburbs. Chicago: University of Chicago Press, 1976, 3-38.

4136. Farley, Reynolds. "The Changing Distribution of Negroes within Metropolitan Areas: The Emergence of Black Suburbs." american Journal of Sociology 75 (January, 1970), 512-529.

4137. Farley, Reynolds, et al. "'Chocolate City, Vanilla Suburbs': Will the Trend Toward Racially Separate Communities Continue?" Social Science Research 7 (December 1978), 319-44.

4138. Farley, Reynolds, et al. "The 1960's: A Decade of Progress for Blacks" Demography 9 (August, 1972), 353-370.

4139. Felder, Henry E. "Black Family Income, 1960-1980" Focus 11:8 (August, 1983), 3.

4140. Frey, William H. "Black Movement to the Suburbs: Potentials and Prospects for Metropolitan-Wide Integration." In Frank D. Bean and W. Parker Frisbie (eds.), The Demography of Racial and Ethnic Groups. New York: Academic Press, 1978, 79-118.

4141. Frey, William H. Black Movement to the Suburbs: Potentials and Prospects for Metropolitan-Wide Integration. Discussion Paper No. 452-77. Madison: University of Madison, Institute for Research on Poverty, December 1977.

4142. Frieden, Bernard J. "Blacks in Suburbia: The Myth of Better Opportunities." in L. Wingo (ed.), Minority Perspectives. Baltimore: Johns Hopkins University Press, 1972, 31-49.

4143. Geale, Paul E. Suburbanization Process in a Black Community: Pecoima, A Case Study. Los Angeles: California State University, M.A. Thesis, 1971.

4144. Glazer, Nathan. "On 'Opening Up' the Suburbs." The Public Interest 37 (Fall 1974), 89-111.

4145. Glazer, Nathan. "Race and the Suburbs" Habitat International

5:1-2 (1980), 175-180.

4146. Goering, John M. "Neighborhood Tipping and Racial Transition: A Review of Social Science Evidence." Journal of the American Institute of Planners. 44:1 (1978), 68-78.

4147. Goldblatt, Harold S. Westchester Real Estate Brokers, Builders, Bankers and Negro Home Buyers: A Report to the Housing Council of the Urban League of Westchester County, Inc. on Opportunities for Private Open-Occupancy Housing in Westchester, New York, 1954.

4148. "Government's Plan to Desegregate The Suburbs." U.S. News and World Report (October 10, 1966), 76-78.

4149. Grabow, Steve. Migration of Blacks and Whites: A Focus on Outlying Neighborhoods of Cincinnati, Ohio. Cincinnati, Ohio: University of Cincinnati, M.A. Thesis.

4150. Greenfield, Robert W. "Factors Associated with Attitudes Toward Desegregation in a Florida Residential Suburb." Social Forces 40 (October 1961), 31-42.

4151. Grier, Eunice. Black Suburbanization in Metropolitan Washington. Report No. 1: Characteristics of Blacks Suburbanites. Washington, D.C.: The Washington Center for Metropolitan Studies, October 1973.

4152. Grier, Eunice and George Grier. Black Suburbanization of the Mid-1970's. Washington, D.C.: Center for Metropolitan Studies, April 1978.

4153. Grier, Eunice and George Grier. In Search of Housing: A Study of Experiences of Negro Professional and Technical Personnel in New York State. New York: State Commission Against Discrimination, 1958.

4154. Grier, George with Eunice Grier. The Impact of Race on Neighborhood or the Metropolitan Setting. Washington, D.C.: Washington Center for Metropolitan Studies, May 1961.

4155. Grodzins, Morton. "Metropolitan Segregation." Scientific American 197 (October 1957), 24, 33-41.

4156. Guest, Avery M. "The Changing Racial Composition of Suburbs, 1950-1970." Urban Affairs Quarterly 14 (December 1978), 195-206.

4157. Guest, Avery M. "Patterns of Suburban Population Growth, 1970-1975." Demography 16 (August, 1979), 401-415.

4158. Haar, Charles Monroe. Housing the Poor in Suburbia: Public Policy at the Grass Roots. Cambridge, Massachusetts:

Ballinger, 1973.

4159. Haar, Charles Monroe and D.S. Iatridis. Housing the Poor in Suburbia: Public Policy at the Grass Roots. Cambridge, Massachusetts: Ballinger, 1974.

4160. Harrison, Bennette. Urban Economic Development: Suburbanization, Minority Opportunity and the Condition of the Central City. Washington, D.C.: The Urban Institute, 1974.

4161. Hart, John Fraser. "The Changing Distribution of the American Negro." Annals of the Association of American Geographers 50 (September, 1960), 242-66.

4162. Henry, Curtis Charles. The Spatial Integration of Black Families in Suburban Cities in the Bay Area: A Study of Black Subsytem Linkages. Ph.D. Dissertation, University of California, Berkeley, CA., 1978.

4163. Hermalin, Albert and Reynolds Farley. "The Potential Poor Residential Segregation in Cities and Suburbs: Implications for the Busing Controversy." American Sociological Review 38 (October 1973), 595-610.

4164. Hmes, Joseph S. "Some Characteristics of the Migration of Blacks in United States." Social Biology 18:4 (December, 1971), 360-62.

4165. Ibom, Godfrey Gamali. A Dynamic Quasi-Stochastic Model for Forecasting Population Distribution of Residential Black Pupils in Suburbia. Ph.D. Thesis, The Ohio State University, 1973.

4166. Jakubs, John Francis. Ghetto Dispersion and Suburban Reaction. Ph.D. Thesis, The Ohio State University, Columbia, Oh., 1974.

4167. Johnson, J.W.C. "Youth Gangs and Black Suburbs." Pacific Sociological Review 24:3 (1981), 355-75.

4168. Kain, John F. "Housing Segregation, Negro Employment and Metropolitan Decentralization." Quarterly Journal of Economics 82 (May 1968), 175-197.

4169. Kaplan, Samuel. "Them Blacks in Suburbia." New York Affairs 3 (Winter 1976), 20-41.

4170. King, William M. Ghetto Riots and the Employment of Blacks: An Answer to the Search for Black Political Power? Unpublished Ph.D. Thesis, Syracuse University, 1973.

4171. Klein, Frederick C. "Urban Irony: Some Integrated Towns Draw Five for Efforts to Keep Racial Balance: Chicago Suburbs and Sued by Real Estate Industry: Some Blacks See Quotas" Wall Street Journal (8 January, 1979).

4172. Klove, Robert C. "Urban and Metropolitan Population Trends and Patterns." Annals of the Association of American Geographers 44 (1954), 222.

4173. Krueger, Robert O. "Business, Jobs and the Ghetto," Pittsburgh Business Review 39 (April 1969), 1-7.

4174. Lake, Robert W. The New Suburbanites: Race and Housing in the Suburbs. New Brunswick: Rutgers University Center for Urban Research, 1981.

4175. Lake, Robert W. "Racial Transition and Black Homeownership in America Suburbs" Annals of the Academy of Political and Social Science 441 (January 1979), 142-156.

4176. Lake, Robert W. and Sue C. Cutler. "Typology of Black Suburbanization in New Jersey Since 1970." Geographical Review 70 (1980), 167-181.

4177. Larry, Long and Diana DeAre. "The Suburbanization of Blacks," American Demographics, (September 1981), 17-21.

4178. Laska, S.B. and D. Spain (eds.). Back to the City. Elmsford, New York: Pergamon, 1980.

4179. Lazare, Dan. "Suburbia Agonizing Over Desegregation" The New Brunswick Home News (January 29, 1979).

4180. Lee, George A. "Negroes in a Medium-Sized Metropolis: Allentown, Pennsylvania - A Case Study." Journal of Negro Education 37 (Fall 1968), 397-405.

4181. Levin, Mark A. "A Comprehensive Approach to the Challenge of Integration." Public Manafencent 59:11 (November, 1977), 24-25.

4182. Lieberson, Stanley A. "Suburbs and Ethnic Residential Patterns" American Journal of Sociology 68 (1963), 673-81.

4183. Logan, John R. "The Disappearance of Communities from National Urban Policies." Urban Affairs Quarterly 19:1 (September 1983), 75-90.

4184. Logan, John R. and O. Andrew Collver. "Residents: Perception of Suburban Community Differences." American Sociological Review 48 (June 1983), 428-433.

4185. Logan, John R. and Mark Schneider. "Racial Segregation and Racial Change in American Suburbs, 1970-1980." American Journal of Sociology 89:4 (January 1984), 874-888.

4186. Logan, John R. and Linda Brewster Stearns. "Suburban Racial Segregation as Non-Ecological Process." Social Forces 60:1 (September 1981), 61-73.

4187. Logan, John R. and Linda Brewster Stearns. Trends in Racial Segregation: A Caution on the Index of Dissimilarity. American Sociological Association, August, 1980.

4188. Long, Larry. Interregional Migration of the Poor. Some Recent Changes. Washington, D.C.: Government Printing Office, 1978.

4189. Long, Larry and Diana DeAre. "The Suburbanization of Blacks: 1980 Census Trends." American Demopgrahics 3:8 (September, 1981), 16-21.

4190. Marshall, Harvey H. "Black and White Upper Middle-Class Suburban Selection: A Casual Analysis". Pacific Sociological Review 25:1 (January, 1982), 25-27.

4191. Marshall, Harvey H. and John M. Stabura. "Determinents of Black Suburbanization: Regional and Suburban Size Category Patterns". The Sociolgocial Quarterly 20:2 (Spring, 1979), 237-53.

4192. Marshall, Harvey H. and John M. Stahura. "Black and White Population Growth in American Suburbs: Transition or Parallel Development?" Social Forces 58:1 (September, 1979), 305-28.

4193. Marshall, Harvey H. and John M. Stahura. "The Impact of Racial Composition and Racial Transition on the Status of American Suburbs." Sociological Inquiry 50:1 (1980), 75-82.

4194. Maxwell, Neil. "Black Flight: Much Like Whites, Many Blacks Move to the Suburbs: They Seek Cheaper Housing, Better Schools: But Often They Run Into Hostility." Wall Street Journal (August 20, 1979).

4195. Meadow, Kathryn P. "Negro-White Differences Among Newcomers to a Transitional Urban Area." Journal of Intergroup Relations 3 (Fall 1962), 320-330.

4196. Midura, Edmund M. Blacks & Whites: The Urban Communication Crisis. Washington, D.C.: Acropolis, 1971.

4197. Miller, Loren. "The Changing Metro-Urban Complex." Journal of Intergroup Relations 3 (Winter 1961-1962), 55-64.

4198. Miller, J.S. "Factors Affecting Racial Mixing in Residential Areas" in A. Hawley and U. Rock (eds.) Segregation in Residential Areas. Washington, D.C.: National Academy of Sciences 1973, 148-71.

4199. Moorhead, James William. Negro Suburban Migration: 1955-1960. Brown University. Unpublished Ph.D. Thesis, 1971.

4200. Muller, P.O. The Outer City: Geographical Consequences of the Urbanization of the Suburbs. Washington, D.C.: Resource Paper

No. 75-2, Association of American Geographers, 1976.

4201. Nelson, Kathryn P. Recent Suburbanization of Blacks: How Much, Who and Where. Washington, D.C.: Office of Policy Development and Research, U.S. Department of Housing and Urban Development, 1979.

4202. Nelson, Kathryn P. "Recent Suburbanization of Blacks: How Much, Who, and Where"? Journal of American Planning Association 46:3 (July, 1980), 287-300.

4203. Nichols, W.W. "Community Safety and Criminal Activity in Black Suburbs." Journal of Black Studies 9:3 (March, 1979), 311-333.

4204. Newman, Dorothy K. "The Decentralization of Jobs: Job Opportunities Multiply in the Suburbs, Out of Reach of the City-Center Poor," Monthly Labor Review 90 (May 1967), 3-13.

4205. New York, State of. Non-Whites in New York's Four "Suburban" Counties: An Analysis of Trends New York. Albany, New York: New York State Commission Against Discrimination, 1959.

4206. Orshansky, Mollie. "The Poor in City and Suburb, 1964," Social Security Bulletin 29 (December 1966), 22-37.

4207. Pendleton, William W. "Blacks in Suburbs." In Louis H. Masotti and Jeffrey K. Hadden (ed.) The Urbanization of the Suburbs. Beverly Hills: Sage, 1973, 171-184.

4208. Phillips, Barbara E. and Richard T. LeGates. "Suburbia: A Photoessay" in E. Barbara Phillips and Richard T. LeGates (eds.) City Lights: An Introduction to Urban Studies. New York: Oxford University Press, 1976.

4209. Pierce, P. "Crime in the Suburbs," Ebony 20 (August 1965), 167-172.

4210. Rabinovitz, Francine F. and William J. Siembieda. Minorities in Suburbs: The Los Angeles Experience. Lexington, Massachusetts: Lexington Books, 1977.

4211. Rapkin, Chester and William G. Grigsby. The Demand for Housing in Racially Mixed Areas: A Study of the Nature of Neighborhood Change. Beverly Hills: University of California Press, 1960.

4212. Roof, Wade Clark and Daphne Spain. "A Research Note in City-Suburban Socio-Economic Differences Among American Blacks". Social Forces 56:1 (September, 1977), 15-20.

4213. Rose, Harold. "The All-Black Town: Suburban Prototype or Urban Slum". People and Politics in Urban Society. Beverly Hills, Sage, 1972, 397-431.

4214. Rose, Harold M. "The All-Negro Town: Its Evolution and Function". The Geographical Review 55 (July, 1965), 362-431.

4215. Rose, Harold. Black Suburbanization, Access to Improved Quality of Life or Maintenance of Status Quo. Cambridge, Massachusetts: Ballinger, 1976.

4216. Rose, Harold M., et al. "Neighborhood Reactions to Isolated Negro Residents: An Alternative to Invasion and Succession." American Sociological Review 18 (October 1953), 497-507.

4217. Rose, Jerome G. After Mount Laurel: The New Suburban Zoning. New Brunswick: Rutgers University, Center for Urban Policy Research, 1977.

4218. Rubinowitz, Leonard S. Low-Income Housing: Suburban Strategies. Cambridge, Massachusetts: Ballinger, 1974.

4219. Rubinowitz, Leonard S. "A Question of Choice: Access of the Poor and Black Suburban Housing" in Louis H. Masotti and Jeffrey K. Hadden (eds.) The Urbanization of the Suburbs. Beverly Hills: Sage, 1973, 329-66.

4220. Schechter, Alan H. "Impact of Open Housing Laws on Suburban Realtors." Urban Affairs Quarterly 8 (June 1973), 439-63.

4221. Schneider, Mark and John R. Logan. "Suburban Racial Segregation and Black Access to Local Public Resources." Social Sciences Quarterly 63:1 (December 1980), 762-770.

4222. Schneider, Mark and John R. Logan. "Fiscal Implications of Class Segregation: Inequalities in the Distribution of Public Goods and Services in the Suburban Municipalities." Urban Affairs Quarterly 63 (December, 1982), 762-70.

4223. Schnore, Leo F. Class and Race in Cities and Suburbs. Chicago: Markham Publishing Co., 1972.

4224. Schnore, Leo F., et al. "Black Suburbanization, 1930-1970," in Barry Schwartz (ed.) The Changing Face of the Suburbs. Chicago: University of Chicago Press, 1976.

4225. Sharp, Harry and Leo F. Schnore. "The Changing Color Composition of Metropolitan Areas." Land Economics 38 (May 1962), 169-85.

4226. Smith, Lella. Apartment Integration in Suburban Washington: A Survey of the Effect of Admitting Negro Tenants to Apartments Previously Closed to Them. Washington, D.C.: Metropolitan Washington Housing Program, American Friends Service Committee, June 1967.

4227. Smith, Ralph V., et al. Community Interaction and Racial

Integration in the Detroit Area: An Ecological Analysis.
Ypsilanti, Michigan: Eastern Michigan University, 1967.

4228. Smith, Richard A. "An Analyusis of Black Occupancy of Mobile
Homes." Journal of the American Institute of Planning 42:4
(October, 1976), 410-18.

4229. Spain, Daphne, et al. Housing Successions Among Blacks and
Whites in Cities and Suburbs. U.S. Bureau of the Census,
Current Population Reports, Special Studies, Series P-23, No.
101. Washington, D.C.: Government Printing Office, 1980.

4230. Statura, John M. "Status Transition of Blacks and White in
American Suburbs" Sociological Quarterly 23:1 (Winter, 1982),
79-93.

4231. Statura, John M. "Determinants of Change in the Distribution
of Blacks Across Suburbs." Sociological Quarterly 24:3 (1983),
421-433.

4232. Sternlieb, George and Robert W. Lake. "Aging Suburbs and Black
Home-Ownership." Annals of the American Academy of Political
and Social Science 422 (November 1975), 105-17.

4233. Straits, Bruce C. "Residential Movement Among Negroes and
Whites in Chicago." Social Science Quarterly 49 (December
1968), 573-592.

4234. Sutker, Solomon and Sara Smith Sutker (eds.). Racial
Transition in the Inner Suburb: Studies of the St. Louis Area.
New York: Praeger, 1974.

4235. Taeuber, Karl E. and Alma F. Taeuber. "White Migration and
Socioeconomic Differences Between Cities and Suburbs."
American Sociological Review 29 (October 1964), 41-53.

4236. Thomas, William V. "America's Changing Suburbs." Editorial
Research Reports (August 17, 1979), 583-600.

4237. Tyler, Poyntz. City and Suburban Housing. New York: H.W.
Wilson, 1957.

4238. U.S. Commission on Civil Rights. Equal Opportunity in
Suburbia. Washington, D.C.: U.S. Commission on Civil Rights,
1974.

4239. Veena, Sneh Bebarta. The Movement of Blacks from Central
Cities to Rings in the Metropolitan Areas of the United States.
Unpublished Ph.D. Thesis, University of Georgia, 1979.

4240. Vrooman, John and Stuart Greenfield. "Are Blacks Making it in
the Suburbs: Some New Evidence on Intra-Metropolitan Spatial
Segmentation." Journal of Urban Economics 7:2 (March, 1980),

155-67.

4241. Weissboard, Bernard. Segregation, Subsidies, and Megalopolis.
Santa Barbara, California: Center for the Study of Democratic
Institutions, 1964.

4242. Weston, Martin V.B. "Tales of the Suburbs: Warren Keeps Most
of Its Castle Intact." City: Magazine of Urban Life and
Environment 5:1 (January-February 1971), 77-80.

4243. White, Michelle J. "Job Suburbanization, Zoning and the
Welfare of Urban Minority Groups." Journal of Urban Economics
5 (1978), 219-40.

4244. Whitehead, John S. Ida's Family: Adaptations to Poverty in a
Suburban Ghetto. Yellow Springs, Ohio: Antioch College, 1969.

4245. Aickmund, Joseph and Deborah Ellis Deurs (eds.). Suburbia: A
Guide to Information. Detroit: Gale Research Company, 1979.

4246. Zschock, Dieter. "Black Youth in Suburbia." Urban Affairs
Quarterly 7:1 (September 1, 1971), 61-74.

4247. Zschock, Dieter K. "Poverty Amid Affluence in Suburbs" in D.K.
Zschock (ed.) Economic Aspects of Suburban Growth: Studies of
the Nassau-Suffolk Planning Region. Stony Brook, New York:
Economic Research Bureau, 1969, 64-88.

CHAPTER 7

Geography and Rural Studies

4248. Abrahams, Roger D. "Negro Stereotype: Negro Folklore and the Riots," Journal of American Folklore, 83 (April 1970), 229-258.

4249. Abrahams, Roger D. Positively Black. Englewood Cliffs, New Jersey: Prentice-Hall, 1970.

4250. Abrams, Charles. "The Time Bomb that Exploded in Cencero," Omentary, 12 (November 1951), 407-414.

4251. Adams, John S. "The Geography of Riots and Civil Disorders in the 1960's." Economic Geography, 48 (January 1974), 24-42.

4252. Adams, Samuel C. The Changing Organization of a Rural Negro Community and its Implication for Race Accommodations. Chicago: Chicago University Press, 1953.

4253. Agresti, B.F. "The First Decades of Freedom: Black Families in a Southern County, 1870-1885." Journal of Marriage and the Family 40 (November 1970), 697-706.

4254. Aiken, Charles S. Transitional Plantation Occupance in Tate County, Mississippi. Master's Thesis, University of Georgia, 1962.

4255. Aiken, Charles S. Transitional Plantation Occupance in Tate County, Mississippi. Master's Thesis, University of Georgia, 1962.

4256. Alexis, Marcus. Consumption by the Poor, paper presented at the Conference on Research on Urban Poverty held by the Social Science Research Council, the Woodrow Wilson School and the Industrial Relations Section, Princeton University, May 23, 1969.

4257. Allen, Vernon L. "Towards Understanding Riots: Some Perspectives," Journal of Social Issues, 26:1 (Winter 1970), 1-18.

4258. Allport, Gordon W. The Nature of Prejudice. Garden City, New York: Doubleday, 1958.

4259. Altshuler, Alan A. Community Control: The Black Demand for Participation in Large American Cities. Indianapolis: Bobbs-Merrill, 1970.

4260. "Anatomy of a Riot." Journal of Urban Law, 45 (Spring-Summer 1968), 1-5.

4261. "Anatomy of a Riot: An Analytical Symposium of the Causes and Affects of a Riot." Journal of Urban Law, 45 (Spring-Summer 1968), 5-10.

4262. Anderson, Bernard E. "Economic Patterns in Black America," in James D. Williams (ed.), The States of Black America, New York: National Urban League, 1982, 1-32.

4263. Anderson, Theodore R. "Intermetropolitan: A Correlation Analysis." American Journal of Sociology, 61 (March 1956), 59-62.

4264. Aptheker, Herbert. American Negro Slave Revolts. New York: International Publishers, 1970.

4265. Aptheker, Herbert. A Documentary of the Negro People in the United States. New York: Citadel, 1951.

4266. Astin, Alexander. Minorities in American Higher Education. San Francisco: Jossy-Bass, 1982.

4267. Babchuk, Nicholas and Ralph V. Thompson. "The Voluntary Association of Negroes," American Sociological Review. 27 (October 1962), 647-655.

4268. Bacon, Lloyd. "Migration, Poverty, and the Rural South." Social Forces 51, 3 (1973), 348-354.

4269. Bailer, Lloyd H. "The Negro in the Labor Force of the United States." Journal of Negro Education 22:3 (1953), 297-306.

4270. Balmer, Gary L. A Spatial Analysis of Racially Mixed Voting Behavior. Master's Thesis, University of Pennsylvania, 1970.

4271. Barbour, Floyd B. The Black Power Revolt: A Collection of Essays. New York: Collier Books, 1969.

4272. Bardolph, Richard. The Negro Vanguard. New York: Holt, Rinehart and Winston, 1959.

4273. Barth, Ernest A.T. and Baha Abu-Laban. "Power Structure and the Negro Sub-Community," _American Sociological Review,_ 24 (February 1959), 69-79.

4274. Basso, Hamilton. "The Riot of 1935," _The New Republic,_ (April 3, 1935), 209-210.

4275. Batchelder, Alan. "Poverty-the Special Case of the Negro," _American Economic Review,_ (May 1965), 1-19.

4276. Bates, Timothy. "Effectiveness of the Small Business Administration in Financing Minority Business," _The Review of Black Political Economy_ 11:3, (1981), 321-366.

4277. Bates, Timothy and Alfred E. Osbourne. "The Perverse Effects of SBA loans to Minority Wholesalers," _Urban Affairs Quarterly_ 15:1 (1979), 87-98.

4278. Bauer, Catherine. "Good Neighborhoods," _Annals of the American Academy of Political and Social Science,_ November 1945, 104-15.

4279. Bean, F.D. "The Negro in American Agriculture." In John P. Davis (ed.) _The American Negro Reference Book._ Englewood Cliffs, New Jersey: Prentice-Hall, 1965.

4280. Beardwood, Robert. "Southern Roots of Urban Crisis: Forced Off The Farms into Destitution, Thousands of Negroes Migrate to Northern Slums." _Fortune_ 78 (August 1968), 80-84.

4281. Becker, Gary S. _Economics of Discrimination._ Chicago: University of Chicago Press, 1957.

4282. Bedell, Mary S. "Employment and Income of Negro Workers -- 1940-52," _Monthly Labor Review_ 76:6 (June 1963), 596-601.

4283. Bell, Dean. _Busing as Related to Desegregation of Schools in the Rural South._ M.A. Thesis, University of Cincinnati, Cincinnati, 1974.

4284. Bennett, Don C. "Segregation and Racial Interaction." _Annuals of the Association of American Geographers_ 63:1 (1973), 48-57.

4285. Bennett, Lerone. _Before the Mayflower: A History of the Negro in America, 1619-1962._ Chicago: Johnson, 1962.

4286. Bennett, Lerone. "How to Stop Riots," _Ebony_ 22 (October 1967), 29-32.

4287. Bennett, Lerone. _Confrontation: Black and White._ Baltimore: Pelican Books, 1965.

4288. Bensman, Joseph and Emanuel Tobier. "Anti-Poverty Programming: A Proposal." _Urban Affairs Quarterly_ 1:1 (September 1965), 54-

665.

4289. Bergman, Peter M. The Chronological History of the Negro in America. New York: Harper and Row, 1969.

4290. Bernard, Jessie. Marriage and Family Among Negroes. Englewood Cliffs, New Jersey: Prentice-Hall, 1968.

4291. Bernstein, Saul. Alternatives to Violence: Alienated Youth and Riots, Race and Poverty. New York, Associated Press 1967.

4292. Berry, Brian J.L. Comparative Mortality Experience of Small Business in Four Chicago Communities. Background Paper No. 4, Small Business Relocation Study, Center for Urban Studies, University of Chicago, 1966.

4293. Berry, Brian J.L., et al. "Attitudes Towards Integration: The Role of Status in Community Response to Neighborhood Change," in Barry Schwartz (ed.), The Changing Face of the Suburbs. Chicago: University of Chicago Press, 1976, 221-64.

4294. Berry, Mary Frances and John W. Blassingame. Long Memory: The Black Experience in America, New York: Oxford University Press, 1982.

4295. Bevel, James. "The Sickness in America Today," in Jim Chard and Jon York (eds.). Urban America: Crisis and Opportunity. Belmont, California: Dickerson, 1969, 95-102.

4296. Billingsley, Andrew. Black Families in White America. Englewood Cliffs, New Jersey, Prentice-Hall, 1968.

4297. Billington, Ray Allen. The Journal of Charlotte Forten: A Free Negro in the Slave Era. New York: Cromwell-Collier, 1961.

4298. Binkin, Martin and Mark F. Eitelberg. Blacks and the Military. Washington, D.C.: Brookings Institution, 1982.

4299. Bird, Alan R. Poverty in Rural Areas of the United States: Agricultural Economic Reports 63. Washington, D.C.: Government Printing Office, 1965.

4300. Birdsall, Stephen S. "Introduction to Research on Black America: Prospects and Preview." Southeastern Geographer 11 (November 1971), 85-89.

4301. "The Black and the Jew: A Falling Out of Allies." Time 94 (January 31, 1969), 55-56.

4302. Black, Blanton E. The Impact of Extension Education Program on Rural Negroes in Georgia, 1914-1964. Master's Thesis, University of Georgia, 1971.

4303. Black Enterprise. "Swimming Against the Tide," Black Enterprise 10 (June 1980), 76-82.

4304. Black Enterprise 100: "A Decade of Study Progress," Black Enterprise 12:11 (June 1982), 76-79.

4305. Blackett, R.J.M. "...Freedom, or the Martyr's Grave": Black Pittsburgh's Aid to the Fugitive Slave." Western Pennsylvania Historical Magazine 61:2 (1975), 117-134.

4306. Blair, Lewis H. A Southern Prophecy: The Prosperity of the South Dependent Upon the Elevation of the Negro (1889). Boston: Little Brown, 1964.

4307. Blalock, H.M. "Percent Non-White and Discrimination in the South." American Sociological Review 22:6 (1957), 677-682.

4308. Blalock, H.M. Economic Discrimination and Negro Increase. American Sociological Review 21 (1957), 527-528.

4309. Blalock, H.M. Towards A Theory as Minority Group Relations. New York: Wiley, 1967.

4310. Blauner, Robert. "The Dilemma of the Black Revolt." Journal of Housing 24 (December 1967), 603.

4311. Blauner, Robert. "Whitewash over Watts: The Failure of the McCone Commission Report." Trans-action 3 (March-April 1966), 3-9.

4312. Blauner, Robert. "Black Culture: Lower-Class Result or Ethnic Creation," in Lee Rainwater (ed.) Black Experience, Soul. New Brunswick: Transaction Books, 1970, 143-180.

4313. Bloombaum, Milton. "The Conditions Underlying Race Riots as Portrayed by Multidimensional Scalogram Analysis: A Reanalysis of Lieberson and Silverman's Data" American Sociological Review 33 (February 1968), 76-91.

4314. Blume, Frank Reinhart. The Effect of Negro Pictorial Material on Racial Attitudes. Unpublished Ph.D. Thesis, Claremont Graduate School, 1966.

4315. Bodnar, John E. and Peter C. Blackwell. "The Negro Community of Steelton, 1880-1920". Pennsylvania Magazine of History and Biography 97:2 (1973), 199-209.

4316. Bonacich, E. "A Theory of Ethnic Antagonism: The Split Labor Market." American Sociological Review 37 (1972), 547-559.

4317. Bonacich, E. "Advanced Capitalism and Black-White Race Relations in the United States: A Split Labor Market Interpretation." American Sociological Review 41 (1970), 34-

51.

4318. Bonnett, Aubrey W. Group Identification Among Negroes: An Examination of the Soul Concept in the United States of America. Sarasota: Century Twenty-One, 1980.

4319. Bourdon, E. Richard, et al. Economic Prospects for Blacks in the 1980's. Report No. 81-278E. Washington, D.C.: Congressional Research Service, 1981.

4320. Brawley, Benjamin. A Social History of the American Negro London: Collier-Macmillan Ltd., 1970.

4321. Brenner, Bernard. Racial Integration and City Planning, unpublished Master's Thesis, Massachusetts Institute of Technology, Department of City and Regional Planning, 1958.

4322. Brimmer, Andrew F. "The Negro in the National Economy," in John P. Davis (ed.), The American Negro Reference Book. Englewood Cliffs, New Jersey: Prentice-Hall, 1966.

4323. Brimmer, Andrew F. and H.S. Terrell. The Economic Potential of Black Capitalism. Presented at the Eighty-Second Annual Meeting of the American Economic Association, New York, December 29, 1969.

4324. Brink, William and Louis Harris. Black and White: A Study of U.S. Racial Attitudes Today. New York: Simon and Schuster, 1967.

4325. Brodber, Erna and Nathaniel Wagner. "The Black Family, Poverty and Family Planning: Anthropological Impressions," The Family Coordinator. 19:2 (1967), 14-27.

4326. Brookfield, H.C. and Tatham, M.A. "The Distribution of Racial Groups in Durham." The Geographical Review 47(January 1960), 14-27.

4327. Broom, Leonard and Norval Glenn. Transformation of the Negro American. New York: Harper and Row, 1965.

4328. Broude, Jeffrey E. A Survey of 1960 Negro Occupational Patterns in Standard Metropolitan Statistical Area by Region, Total Population, and Percentage Negro. Master's Thesis, University of California, Los Angeles, 1971.

4329. Brown, Claude. Manchild in the Promised Land. New York: The New American Library, 1966.

4330. Brown, Richard Maxwell. American Violence. Englewood Cliffs, New Jersey: Prentice-Hall, 1970.

4331. Brown, William H. Education and Economic Development of the

Negro in Virginia. Charlotteville, VA.: University of
Virginia, 1923.

4332. Brown, William H. Class Aspects of Residential Development and
Choice in the Oakland Black Community. Ph.D. Dissertation,
University of California, Berkeley, CA, 1970.

4333. Brunn, Stanley D. "Geography and Black America. Geographical
Record." Geographical Review. 64:3 (1974), 423-25.

4334. Bryant, Nathaniel H. Black Migration and the Settlement of the
Puget Sound Country. Master's Thesis, University of
Washington, 1972.

4335. Buford, Carolyn B. The Distribution of Negroes in Maryland,
1850-1860. Master's Thesis, Catholic University of America,
1956.

4336. Bunche, Ralph J. "The Negro in the Political Life of the
United States." The Journal of Negro Education 10 (July 1941),
579-81.

4337. Buni, Andrew. The Negro in Virginia Politics, 1902-1965.
Charlottesville,: University of Virginia Press, 1967.

4338. Buntzman, Gabriel F. Negro Voting in the Electoral Geography
of Raleigh, North Carolina. Master's Thesis, University of
North Carolina, 1970.

4339. Cable, George W. The Negro Question: A Selection of Writings
on Court Rights in the South. Garden City, New York:
Doubleday, 1958.

4340. Cairnes, John Elliot. The Slave Power: Its Character, Career
and Probable Designs: Being an Attempt to Explain the Real
Issues Involved in the American Contest. New York: Harper and
Row, 1969.

4341. Calef, Wesley C. and Howard J. Nelson. "Distribution of Negro
Population in the United States." The Geographical Review 44
(January 1956), 82-97.

4342. Campbell, Angus. White Attituds Toward Black People. Ann
Arbor, Michigan: Institute for Social Research, University of
Michigan, 1971.

4343. Campbell, Byram. Race and Social Revolution: Twenty-One Essays
on Racial and Social Problems. New York: Truth Seeker, 1958.

4344. Campbell, Rex R. "The Changing Distribution of Negroes Within
Five Metropolitan Areas: The Emergence of Black Suburbs.
American Journal of Sociology. 75: 4 (January 1970), 512-29.

4345. Campbell, Rex R. and Peter R. Robertson. Negroes in Missouri: A Compilation of Statistical Data from the 1960 United States Census of Population. Jefferson City, Missouri: Missouri Commission on Human Rights, 1967.

4346. Carlson, David B. "The New Urbanities: Nature and Dimensions." Architectural Forum (June 1960), 1-7.

4347. Carter, Bernard. An Investigation of the Black Population Concentration in the Ohio-Mississippi River Confluence Area of Illinois. Master's Thesis, Southern Illinois University, Carbondale, 1969.

4348. Cassity, Michael J. Chains of Fear: American Race Relations Since Reconstruction. Westport, Conn.: Greenwood Press, 1984.

4349. Chachere, Bernadette P. "The Medical Program: The Low-Income Health Care Subsidy," The Review of Black Political Economy. 11:1 (Fall 1980), 80.

4350. Chambers, Bradford. Chronicle of Negro Protest. New York: Parents Magazine Press, 1968.

4351. Chicago, City of. Commission on Race Relations. The Negro in Chicago. Chicago: University of Chicago Press, 1922.

4352. Chicago, City of. Commission on Race Relations. The Negro in Chicago: A Study of Race Relations and a Race Riot in 1919. New York: Arno Press and the New York Times, 1968.

4353. Christensen, David E. "The Negro's Changing Place in Southern Agriculture." In The Negro in American Society. Tallahassee: Florida State University, 1958.

4354. Christian, Charles M. The Impact of Industrial Relations from the Black Community upon Job Opportunities and Residential Mobility of the Central Workforce. Ph.D. Dissertation, University of Illinois, Urbana, IL, 1975.

4355. Chudacoff, Howard P. "A New Look at Ethnic Neighborhoods: Residential Dispersion and the Concept of Visibility in a Medium-Sized City." Journal of American History, 60:1 (1973), 76-93.

4356. Clark, Kenneth B. "Group Violence: A Preliminary Study of the Attitudinal Pattern of Its Acceptance and Rejection -- A Study of the 1943 Harlem Riots," Journal of Social Psychology 19 (August 1944), 319-337.

4357. Clark, Kenneth B. Dark Ghetto. New York: Harper and Row, 1965.

4358. Clark, Kenneth B. and Talcott Parsons. The Negro American.

New York: Houghton Mifflin, 1966.

4359. Claspy, Everett. The Negro in Southwestern Michigan, Negroes in the Northern Rural Environment. Dowaglae, Michigan, The Author, 1967.

4360. Clawson, Edward Clyde. A Study of Attitudes of Prejudice Against Negroes in an All-White Community. Ed.D. Thesis, The Pennsylvania State University, 1968.

4361. Cleeland, H.F. "Black Belt of Alabama in Maps." Geographical Review 10 (1920), 375-87.

4362. Cloward, Richard A. and Frances F. Piven. "Corporate Imperialism for the Poor." The Nation 20:12 (October 16, 1967).

4363. Coates, B.E., et al. Geography of Inequality. Oxford: Oxford University Press, 1977.

4364. Cobb, Robert W. Black Settlement in Silverton, Ohio, 1960-1967. A Spatial Diffusion Process. Ph.D. Dissertation, State University of New York at Buffalo, 1971.

4365. Cogdell, Roy and Sybil Wilson. Black Communication in White Society. Sarasota: Century Twenty-One, 1980.

4366. Cohen, Jerry. Burn, Burn, Baby. New York: Dutton, 1966.

4367. Cohen, Oscar. "The Case for Benign Quotas in Housing," Phylon 21:1 (Spring 1960), 35-40.

4368. Cohen, Saul, et al. "The Geography of Afro-America: The Anatomy of a Graduate Training Curriculum Development Project." Journal of Geography. 70 (1971), 465-472.

4369. Cohen, W. "Riots, Racism, and Hysteria: The Response of the Federal Investigative Officials to the Race Riots of 1919," Massachusetts Review 13 (Summer 1972), 373-400.

4370. Coleman, James S. Equality of Educational Opportunity, U.S. Department of Health, Education and Welfare. Washington, D.C.: Document OE-38001. 1966.

4371. Coley, James E. "Slavery in Connecticut," Magazine of American History 21:6 (1891), 1-5.

4372. Coman, Katherine. "The Negro as a Peasant Farmer." American Statistical Association 9 (1904), 39.

4373. Comer, J.P. The Black Family: An Adaptive Perspective. New Haven: Child Study Center, Yale University, mimeo., 1970.

4374. Conzen, Kathleen Neils. "Immigrants, Immigrant Neighborhoods, and Ethnic Identity: Historical Issues." Journal of American History 66:3 (1979), 603-615.

4375. Corkey, E. "A Family Planning Program for the Low-Income Family," Journal of Marriage and the Family. 26 (November 1964), 38-45.

4376. Cortese, Charles F. and J.E. Leftwitch. "A Technique for Measuring the Effects of Economic Base on Opportunity for Blacks." Demography 12:2 (1975), 325-239.

4377. Cortese, Charles F., et al. "Further Considerations on the Methodological Analysis of Segregation Indexes." American Sociological Review 41 (1976), 630-637.

4378. Coser, Lewis A. "Some Social Functions of Violence," Annals of the Association of American Geographers 366 (March 1966), 8-18.

4379. Coser, Lewis A. "The Sociology of Poverty," Social Problems. 13:2 (Fall 1965), 14-18.

4380. Cottingham, Phoebe H. "Black Income and Metropolitan Residential Dispersion." Urban Affairs Quarterly 10 (1975), 273-96.

4381. Courant, Paul N. and John Yinger. "On Models of Racial Prejudice and Urban Residential Structure," Journal of Urban Economics 4 (1977), 272-91.

4382. Cowhig, James D. and Clavin Beale. "Socioeconomic Differences Between White and Nonwhite Farm Populations of the South." Social Forces 42:3 (1964), 354-362.

4383. Cox, D.C. "The Negroes' Use of their Buying Power in Chicago as a Means of Securing Employment." Crisis (July 1931), 39-42.

4384. Cox, D.C. "Sex Ration and Marital Status Among Negroes," American Sociological Review. 5 (1940), 937-947.

4385. Craig, William. Weekend and Recreational Behavior of a Negro Community in Louisiana: A Spatial Study. Ph.D. Dissertation, University of Michigan, 1968.

4386. Crossland, William A. Industrial Conditions Among Negroes in St. Louis. St. Louis: Press of Mendle Printing Co., 1914.

4387. Crow, Jeffrey J. and J. Hatley Flora. Black Americans in North Carolina and the South. Chapel Hill: University of North Carolina Press, 1984.

4388. Curtis, Thomas B. Supplementary View, in the U.S. Congress, Senate Joint Economic Committee, Report: Employment and

Manpower Problems in the Cities--Implication of the Report of the National Advisory Commission on Civil Disorders, 90th Congress, 2nd Session, Report No. 1568. U.S. Government Printing Office, Washington, D.C., September 16, 1968.

4389. Cybriwsky, Roman A. "Social Aspects of Neighborhood Change." Annals of the Association of American Geographers 68:1 (1978), 17-33.

4390. Dahlke, H.O. "Race and Minority Riots--A Study in Typology of Violence," Social Forces 30 (May 1952), 419-425.

4391. Dannenbaum, Jed. "Immigrants and Temperance: Ethnocultural Conflict in Cincinnati, 1845-1860." Ohio History 87:2 (1978), 125-139.

4392. Darden, Joe T. "Black and White Difference in Unemployment in The United States" in R.A. Obudho (ed.) Afro-Americans and the City. Albany, New York: State University of New York Press, 1984.

4393. Darden, Joe T. "Black Inequality and Conservative Strategy" in Wilbur Brookover, et al. (eds.) Readings in Sociology. New York: Thomas Cromwell Co., 1974, 653-663.

4394. Darden, Joe T. "Racial Differences in Unemployment: A Spatial Perspective", The Review of Black Political Economy 12:3 (Spring 1983), 93-99.

4395. Davenport, Frances Garron. Ante-Bellum Kentucky: A Social History 1800-1860. Westport, Conn.: Greenwood Press, 1970.

4396. Davis, Allison, et al. Deep South, A Social Anthropological Study of Caste and Class. Chicago: University of Chicago Press, 1941.

4397. Davis, David B. The Problem of Slavery in Western Culture. Ithaca: Cornell University Press, 1966.

4398. Davis, Dewitt and Emilio Casetti. "Do Black Students Wish to Live in Integrated Socially Homogeneous Neighborhoods? A Questionnaire Analysis." Economic Geography. 54:3 (1978), 197-210.

4399. Davis, George and Fred Donaldson. Blacks in the United States: A Geographic Perspective. Boston: Houghton Mifflin Co., 1975.

4400. Davis, Jane E. "Over-Crowded and Defective Housing in the Rural District." Southern Workman 44 (1915), 454.

4401. Davis, John P. (ed.) The American Negro Reference Book. Englewood Cliffs, New Jersey: Prentice-Hall, 1966.

4402. Day, C.B. and E.A. Hooton. A Study of Some Negro and White Families in the United States. Cambridge: Peabody Museum, Harvard University, 1932.

4403. Day, Judy and M. James Kedro. "Free Blacks in St. Louis: Antebellum Conditions, Emancipation, and the Postwar Era." Missouri Historical Society Bulletin 30:2 (1974), 117-135.

4404. Daymont, Thomas N. Parameters of Racial Discrimination in the Late 1960's. Unpublished Ph.D. Dissertation. The University of Wisconsin, Madison, 1978.

4405. Degler, Carl. R. Neither Black Nor White: Slavery and Race Relations in Brazil and the United States. New York: Macmillan Co., 1971.

4406. DeLong, Gordon F. and George A. Muillery. Kentucky's Negro Population in 1960. Lexington, Kentucky: University of Kentucky, Department of Rural Sociology, 1965.

4407. Department of Social Relations, Johns Hopkins University. The Employment Situation of White and Negro Youth in the City of Baltimore. Baltimore, Maryland, 1963.

4408. Deskins, Donald R. Negro Settlement in Ann Arbor. Unpublished M.A. Thesis, University of Michigan, 1963.

4409. Deskin, Donald R. "Race as an Element in the Intra-City Regionalization of Atlanta's Population." Southeastern Geographer. 11:2 (1971), 90-100.

4410. Deskin, Donald R. and Linda Speil. "The Status of Blacks in American Geography." Professional Geographer. 23:4 (1971), 283-289.

4411. Deutsch, Morton and Mary Evans Collins. Interracial Housing. Minneapolis: The University of Minnesota Press, 1951.

4412. Dobson, Kenneth E. Journey to Work Patterns of Black Federal Employees in Early Twentieth Century Washington, D.C. M.A. Thesis, University of Maryland, College Park, MD., 1975.

4413. Dollard, John. Caste and Class in a Southern Town. New Haven: Yale University Press, 1937.

4414. Donald, Henderson H. The Negro Freedman. New York: Henry Schuman, 1952.

4415. Donaldson, O. Fred. "Geography and the Black American: The White Papers and the Invisible Man." Antipode. 1:1 (1969), 17-33.

4416. Donaldson, O. Fred. "Geography and the Black America: The

White Papers and the Invisible Man." Journal of Geography. 7:3 (1971), 138-149.

4417. Donaldson, O. Fred. "The Geography of Black America: Three Approaches." Journal of Geography. 71:7 (1971), 414-420.

4418. Donaldson, O. Fred and Richard Morris. "Geographical Perspectives on the History of Black America." Economic Geography. 48:1 (January 1972), 1-24.

4419. Doran, Michael. "Negro Slaves of the Five Civilized Tribes." Annals of the Association of American Geographers. 68:3 (1968), 335-350.

4420. Douglass, Joseph H. "The Urban Negro Family," in John P. Davis (ed.) American Negro Reference Book. Englewood, New Jersey: Prentice-Hall, 1966.

4421. Douglass, Joseph H. The Negro Family's Search for Economic Security. Washington, D.C.: U.S. Department of Health, Education, and Welfare, July 1956.

4422. Down, Anthony. "The Anatomy of Racism," City: Magazine of Urban Life and Environment 4,:1 (1970), 21-24.

4423. Downes, Randolph. "Negro Rights and White Backlash in the Campaign of 1920," Ohio History 75 (Spring-Summer 1966), 85-107.

4424. Doyle, Bertram W. The Etiquette of Race Relations in the South. Port Washington, New York: Kennikat Press, 1968.

4425. Drake, St. Clair. "Recent Trends in Research on the Negro in the United States," International Social Science Bulletin, UNESCO, 9 (1957), 475-92.

4426. Drake, St. Clair. "The Social and Economic Status of the Negro in the United States," Daedalus. 94:4 (Fall 1965), 771-814.

4427. DuBois, W.E.B. The Negro American Family. Atlanta: Atlanta University Press, 1908.

4428. DuBois, W.E.B. The Philadelphia Negro. Philadelphia: Publications of the University of Pennsylvania, 1899.

4429. DuBois, W.E.B. The Souls of Black Folk: Essays and Sketches. Chicago: McClung, 1903.

4430. DuBois, W.E.B. "The Negro in the Black Belt: Some Social Sketches." Bulletin Department Labor 22 (1902), 401-17.

4431. DuBois, W.E.B. "the Negro Landholder of Georgia." Bulletin Department of Labor 35 (1901), 647-777.

4432. DuBois, W.E.B. "The Rural South". American Statistical Association Publishers (1912), 80-84.

4433. Dumont, Dwight Lowell. New Jersey Fair Housing Committee. Discrimination in the Twin Borroughs: A Report to the Residents and Officials of Dumont and Bergenfield, New Jersey. Milford: Fair Housing Committee of Dumont, Bergenfield, and New Milford, 1965.

4434. Dunbar, Leslie W. "Toward Equality, Toward a More Perfect Union," in James D. Williams (ed.) The State of Black America 1982. New York: National Urban League 1982, 33-79.

4435. Duncan, Beverly and Otis Dudley Duncan. "Family and Occupational Success," Social Problems. 16 (Winter 1969), 273-285.

4436. Duncan, Otis Dudley. "Inheritance of Poverty or Inheritance of Race," in D.P. Moynihan (ed.) Understanding Poverty. New York: Basic Books, 1969, 75-80.

4437. Duncan, Otis Dudley. "Patterns of Occupational Mobility Among Negro Men." Demography 5:1 (1968), 11-22.

4438. Duncan, Otis Dudley and Beverly Duncan. The Negro Population of Chicago. Chicago: The University of Chicago Press, 1957.

4439. Duncan, Otis Dudley and Beverly Duncan. "Residential Distribution and Occupational Stratification," American Sociological Review 60 (March 1955) 493-503.

4440. Duncan, Otis Dudley and Beverly Duncan. "A Methodological Analysis of Segreation Indexes," American Sociological Review 20:2 (April 1955), 491-505.

4441. Duncan, Beverly and Philip M. Hauser. Housing A Metropolis-- Chicago, Glencoe: The Free Press, 1960.

4442. Dyce, Cedric. A Geogrpahical History of the Negro Middle Class in West Balitmore, 1880-1970. M.A. Thesis, Syracuse University, Syracuse, New York 1973.

4443. Edmonds, Helen G. The Negro and Fusion Politics in North Carolina, 1894-1901. Chapel Hill: University of North Carolina Press, 1951.

4444. Edwards, Otis B. An Economic History of the Negro in Agriculture in Dallas, Macon, and Madison Counties, Alabama, 1910 to 1950. Ph.D. Thesis, The University of Nebraska - Lincoln, 1955.

4445. Ernst, Robert T. and Lawrence Huggs (eds.). Black America: Geographical Perspectives. Garden City, N.Y: Anchor, 1976.

4446. Evans, Jeanette. An Analysis of Relevance of Education in Geography to Blacks. Master's Thesis, University of Washington, 1972.

4447. "Extensive Migration of Negro Labors on the Southern States." Economic World 12 (1916), 549-50.

4448. Falk, William Warren. School Desegregation, Mobility Attitudes, and Early Attainment of Rural, Black Youth. Unpublished Ph.D. Thesis, Texas A & M University, 1975.

4449. Farley, Reynolds. "Trends in Racial Inequalities: Have the Gains in the 1960's Disappeared in the 1970's?" American Sociological Review 42 (April 1977): 189-208.

4450. Farley, Reynolds and Karl E. Taeuber. "Population Trends and Residential Segregation Since 1960." Science 159 (March 1968), 953-956.

4451. Fein, Rashu. An Economic and Social Profile of the Negro American. Washington: Brookings Institute, 1966.

4452. Fellows, Keith Donald. A Mosaic of America's Ethnic Minorities. New York: John Wiley, 1972.

4453. Ferguson, Homer L. "Negro Labor in the South." Southern Workman 49 (1920), 304.

4454. Ferman, Louis A., et al. Poverty in America. Ann Arbor: University of Michigan Press, 1965.

4455. Firestone, J.M. "Theory of the Riot Process," American Behavioral Scientist 15 (July 1972), 859-882.

4456. Fisher, James S. "Negro Farm Ownership in the South." Annals of the Association of American Geographers. 63:4 (December 1973), 478-489.

4457. Fisher, Lloyd and Joseph Weckler. The Problem of Violence. New York: American Council on Race Relations, 1946.

4458. Fisher, Sethard. Power and the Black Community: A Reader on Racial Subordination in the United States. New York: Knopf, 1970.

4459. Florin, John W. "The Diffusion of the Decision to Integrate: Southern School Desegregation, 1954-1964." Southeastern Geographer. 11:2 (1971), 139-144.

4460. Fogelson, Robert M. "From Resentment to Confrontation: The Police, the Negroes, and the Outbreak of the Nineteen-Sixties Riots." Political Science Quarterly 83 (June 1968), 217-47.

4461. Fogelson, Robert M. _Violence as Protest_. Garden City, New York: Doubleday, 1971.

4462. Fogelson, Robert M. "White on Black: A Critique of the McCone Commission Report on the Los Angeles Riots" _Political Science Quarterly_ 82 (September 1967), 337-367.

4463. Foley, Eugene P. _The Achieving Ghetto_. Washington, D.C.: National Press, 1968.

4464. Foner, Philip S. "The Battle to End Discrimination Against Negroes on Philadelphia Streetcars: Background and Beginning of the Battle." _Pennsylvania History_ 40:3 (1973), 261-292.

4465. Ford, Lawrence. _The Areal Variation in Negro Registration Levels and Changes in those Levels During the 1956-1967 Time Period in Louisiana_. Master's Thesis, Ohio State University, 1967.

4466. Fordham, Monroe. "The Buffalo Cooperative Economic Society, Inc., 1928-1961: A Black Self-Help Organization." _Niagara Frontier_ 23:2 (1976), 41-49.

4467. Forster, Arnold and Benjamin R. Epstein. _The Troublemakers: An Anti-Defamation League Report_. Garden City, New York: Doubleday, 1952.

4468. Fortune, T. Thomas. _Black and White; Land, Labor and Politics in the South._ New York: Arno Press, 1968.

4469. Foster, Badi. "Toward a Definition of Black Referents" in Vernon J. Dixon and Badi Foster (eds.) _Beyond Black or White: An Alternative America_. Boston: Little Brown, 1971, 18.

4470. Foster, L.H. "Race Relations in the South, 1960: A Tuskegee Institute Report." _Journal of Negro Education_ 30 (Spring 1961), 138-149.

4471. Fossett, M. and C.G. Swicegood. "Rediscovering City Differences in Racial Occupational Inequality." _American Sociological Review_ 47 (1982), 681-689.

4472. Franklin, Charles L. _The Negro Labor Unionist of New York_. New York: Columbia University Press, 1936.

4473. Franklin, John Hope. _The Negro Church in America_. New York: Schocken, 1963.

4474. Franklin, John Hope. _The Negro in the United States_. New York: Macmillan, 1959.

4475. Franklin, John Hope. _From Slavery to Freedom: A History of American Negroes_. New York: Knopf, 1956.

4476. Franklin, John Hope and Isidore Starr. Negro in Twentieth Century America. New York: Vintage Books, 1967.

4477. Fraser, Walter J. and Winfred B. Moore. The Southern Enigma: Essays on Race, Class and Folk Culture. Westport, Conn.: Greenwood Press, 1983.

4478. Frazier, E. Franklin. The Negro Family in the United States. Chicago: University of Chicago Press, 1966.

4479. Frazier, E. Franklin. The Free Negro Family. Nashville, Tennessee: Fisk University Press, 1932.

4480. Frazier, E. Franklin. The Negro Family in Chicago. Chicago: University of Chicago Press, 1966.

4481. Frazier, E. Franklin. Negro Youth at the Crossway. New York: Harper and Row, 1940.

4482. Frazier, E. Franklin. Black Bourgeoisie. New York: Colliers Books, 1957.

4483. Frazier, E. Franklin. The Negro in the United States. New York: Macmillan, 1949.

4484. Frazier, E. Franklin. "Family Life of the Negro in the Small Town." National Conference of Social Work 38 (1926), 84-8.

4485. Freeman, Linton C. and M.H. Sunshine. Residential Segregation Patterns. Boston: Schenkman and Company, 1970.

4486. Freeman, Richard. "Black Economic Progress Since 1964." The Public Interest 52 (Summer 1978): 52-69.

4487. Fried, Mare and Peggy Gleicher. "Some Sources of Residential Satisfaction in an Urban Slum," Journal of the American Institute of Planners. 27 (November 1961), 494-512.

4488. Frisbie, W.P. and L. Neidert. "Inequality and the Relative Size of Minority Populations: A Comparative Analysis." American Journal of Sociology 32 (1977), 1007-1030.

4489. Frissell, Hollis Burke. "Southern Agriculture and the Negro Farmer." American Statistical Association of Publishers 13 (1912), 65-70.

4490. Fujita, Kuniko. Black Worker's Struggles in Detroit's Auto Industry, 1935-1975. Sarasota: Century Twenty-One, 1980.

4491. Funnye, Clarence. "A Black View of the Hardhats March." City: Magazine of Urban Life and Environment 4:2 (August-September 1970), 45-46.

4492. Furstenberg, Frank F. "Premarital Pregnancy Among Black Teenagers," Transaction. 7 (May 1970), 52-55.

4493. Gaines, Jean Foley. An Evaluative Analysis of Job Opportunities for Negro Students of Business Education in Houston, Texas. Unpublished M. Bus. Ed. Thesis, University of Colorado, 1956.

4494. Galster, George C. Preferences for Neighborhood Racial Composition. Unpublished report prepared for the U.S. Department of Housing and Urban Development. Washington, D.C., 1978.

4495. Gans, Herbert J. "The Failure of Urban Renewal", in James Q. Wilson (ed.) Urban Renewal: The Record and the Controversy. Cambridge: The MIT Press, 1966, 14-21.

4496. Gans, Herbert J. "The Negro Family: Reflections on the Moynihan Report," Commonwealth. (October 15, 1965), 7-14.

4497. Gannett, Henry. Statistics of the Negroes in the United States. Baltimore: The Trustees, 1894.

4498. Garnett, B.P. "Mob Disturbances in the Urban States." Editorial Research Reports (October 20, 1931), 701-718.

4499. Garonzik, Joseph. "The Racial and Ethnic Make-up of Baltimore Neighborhoods, 1850-1870." Maryland History Magazine 71:3 (1976), 392-402.

4500. Garst, Eleanor. "Good Neighbors in Washington," The Progressive 28:2 (February, 1964), 1-10.

4501. Garver, John B. Selected Aspects of the Geography of Poverty. Master's thesis, Syracuse University, 1966.

4502. Genzberg, Eli. The Middle-Class Negro in the White Man's World. New York: Columbia University Press, 1967.

4503. Gerschenfeld, W.J. The Negro Labor Market in Lancaster, Pennsylvania. Unpublished Ph.D. Dissertation, University of Pennsylvania, 1964.

4504. Geschwender, James A. Black Revolt: The Civil Rights Movement. Ghetto Uprisings, and Separatism. Englewood Cliffs, New Jersey: Prentice-Hall, 1971.

4505. Gibbs, J.P. "Occupational Differentiation of Negroes and Whites in the United States." Social Forces 44 (1965), 159-165.

4506. Gibson, John William. Progress of a Race. Naperville, Illinois: J.L. Nichols and Co., 1912.

4507. Gilbert, Ben W. and The Staff of the Washington Post. Ten Blacks from the White House: Anatomy of the Washington Riots of 1968. New York: Praeger, 1968.

4508. Giles, Helen F. "Differential Life Expectancy Among White and Nonwhite Americans: Some Explanations During Youth and Middle Age," in Ron C. Manuel (ed.), Minority Aging. Westport, Conn.: Greenwood Press, 1982, 63-68.

4509. Gilliam, Dorothy. "The United States Civil Rights Commission in Transition." City: Magazine of Urban Life and Environment 6:1 (January-February 1972), 45-49.

4510. Gilroy, Curtis L. "Black and White Unemployment: The Dynamics of the Differential." Monthly Labor Review 97 (February 1974), 38-47.

4511. Ginzberg, Eli. The Negro Challenge to the Business Community. New York: McGraw-Hill, 1964.

4512. Ginzberg, Eli and Dale L. Hiestrand. Mobility in the Negro Community. Washington, D.C.: 1968.

4513. Glassgow, Douglas G. The Black Underclass: Poverty, Unemployment and Entrapment of Ghetto Youth. New York: Vintage, 1980.

4514. Glazer, Nathan. "The School as an Instrument in Planning," Journal of the American Institute of Planners 25:4 (November 1959), 1-7.

4515. Glazer, Nathan. "School Integration Policies in Northern Cities," Journal of the American Institute of Planners 30:3 (August 1964), 25-30.

4516. Glazer, Nathan and Davis McEntire. Studies in Housing and Minority Groups. Berkeley: University of California Press, 1960.

4517. Glazer, Nathan and Daniel P. Moynihan. Beyond the Melting Pot. Cambridge, Massachusetts: Harvard University Press, 1970.

4518. Glenn, N. "Occupational Benefits to Whites from the Subordination of Negroes." American Sociological Review 28 (1963), 443-448.

4519. Glenn, N. "The Relative Size of the Negro Population and Negro Occupational Status." Social Forces 43 (1964), 42-49.

4520. Glenn, N. "White Gains from Negro Subordination." Social Problems 14 (1966), 159-178.

4521. Golden, Joseph. "Desegregation of Social Agencies in the

South." _Social Work_ 10 (1965), 58-67.

4522. Goldring, Paul. _The Initial Interview with Negro Adolescents._
Unpublished Ph.D. Thesis, University of Rochester, 1969.

4523. Goldstein, Michael L. "Preface to the Rise of Booker T.
Washington: A view from New York City of the Demise of
Independent Black Politics, 1889-1902." _Journal of Negro
History_ 62:1 (1977), 81-99.

4524. Goldstein, Rhoda L. _Black Life and Culture in the United
States._ New York: Thomas Y. Crowell, 1971.

4525. Goodfriend, Joyce P. "Burghers and Blacks: The Evaluation of a
Slave Society at New Amsterdam." _New York History_ 59:2 (1978),
125-144.

4526. Goodman, L.A. "A General Model for the Analysis of Surveys."
American Journal of Sociology 77 (1972), 1035-1086.

4527. Gordon, Joan. _The Poor of Harlem: Social Functioning in the
Underclass._ New York: Office of the Mayor, 1965.

4528. Gordon, Margaret. _Poverty in America._ San Francisco: Chandler
Publishing Company, 1965.

4529. Gosnell, Harold F. _Negro Politicians: The Rise of Negro
Politics in Chicago._ Chicago: University of Chicago Press,
1935.

4530. Gourlay, Jack G. _The Negro Salaried Worker_ New York American
Management Association, 1965.

4531. Graham, Hugh Davis and Ted Robert Gurr. _Violence in America:
Historical and Comparative Perspectives._ New York: Bantam,
1969.

4532. Granger, Lester B. "Crime in Harlem." _Better Times_ (April 16,
1943), 1-7.

4533. Gray, Edgar M. _The Washington Race Riot, Its Cause and Effect._
New York: Schomburg Collection of the New York Public Library,
1919.

4534. Green, D.S. and E.D. Driver (eds.) _W.E.B. Dubois on Sociology
and the Black Community._ Chicago: The University of Chicago
Press, 1978.

4535. Green, James Alan. _Attitudinal and Situational Determinants of
Intended Behavior Towards Negroes._ Ph.D. Thesis, University
of Colorado at Boulder, 1967.

4536. Greene, Lorenzo Johnston. _Employment of Negroes in the_

District of Columbia. Washington, D.C.: Association for the Study of Negro Life and History, 1943.

4537. Greene, Lorenzo Johnson. The Negro in Colonial New England: 1620-1776. New York: Columbia University Press, 1942.

4538. Greene, Lorenzo Johnson and Carter G. Woodson. The Negro Wage Earner, Washington, D.C.: Associated Publishers, 1930.

4539. Green, McLaughlin. The Secret City: A History of Race Relations in the Nation's Capital. Princeton: Princeton University Press, 1967.

4540. Gremshaw, Allen D. A Study in Social Violence: Urban Race Riots in the United States. Unpublished Ph.D. Dissertation, University of Pennsylvania, 1959.

4541. Grenz, Suzanna Maria. The Black Community in Boone County Missouri, 1850-1900. Ph.D. Thesis, University of Missouri - Columbia, 1979.

4542. Grier, Eunice and George Grier. "Equality and Beyond: Housing Segregation in the Great Society," Daedalus. 95 (1968), 77-106.

4543. Grier, William and Price Cobb. Black Rage. New York: Basic Books, 1968.

4544. Griffin, James S. "Blacks in the St. Paul Police Department: An Eighty-Year Survey." Minnesota History 44:7 (1975), 255-265.

4545. Grimshaw, Allen D. "Actions of Police and the Military in American Race Riots," Phylon 24 (1963), 271-289.

4546. Grimshaw, Allen D. "Changing Patterns of Racial Violence in the United States," Notre Dame Lawyer 60:5 (1965), 534-548.

4547. Grimshaw, Allen D. "Factors Contributing to Colour Violence in the United States and Great Britain," Race 3 (May 1962), 3-19.

4548. Grimshaw, Allen D. "Lawlessness and Violence in the United States and Their Special Manifestations in Changing Negro-White Relationships," Journal of Negro History 44 (January 1959), 52-72.

4549. Grimshaw, Allen D. "Three Major Cases of Colour Violence in the United States," Race 5 (July 1963), 76-87.

4550. Grimshaw, Allen D. "Urban Racial Violence in the United States: Changing Ecological Considerations." American Journal of Sociology 65 (September 1960), 109-119.

4551. Gross, Barry R. Discrimination in Reverse: Is Turnabout Fair

<u>Play?</u> New York: New York University Press, 1978.

4552. Gross, J.A. <u>The N.A.A.C.P., the A.F.L.-C.I.O. and the Negro</u>
<u>Worker</u>. Unpublished Ph.D. Dissertation, University of
Wisconsin, 1962.

4553. Gunnar, Myrdal. <u>An American Dilemma</u>. New York: Harper & Row,
1944.

4554. Gurin, Gerald. <u>Inner-City Negro Youth in a Job Training</u>
<u>Project: A Study of Factors Related to Attrition and Job</u>
<u>Success</u>. Ann Arbor: Institute for Social Research, University
of Michigan, 1968.

4555. Guthrie, Patricia. <u>Catching Sense: the Meaning of Plantation</u>
<u>Membership Among Blacks on St. Helena Island, South Carolina.</u>
Ph.D. Thesis, The University of Rochester, 1977.

4556. Gutman, Herbert G. "The Negro and the United Mine Workers of
America." In Julius Jacobson (ed.) <u>The Negro and the American</u>
<u>Labor Movement.</u> Garden City, N.Y.: Doubleday, 1968, 40-50.

4557. Gutman, Herbert G. <u>The Black Family In Slavery and Freedom,</u>
<u>1750-1925.</u> New York: Vintage Books, 1977.

4558. Guzda, Henry P. "Labor Departments First Program to Assist
Black Workers," <u>Monthly Labor Review</u> 105:6 (June 1982), 39-44.

4559. Halsey, Margaret. <u>Color Blind: A White Woman Looks at the</u>
<u>Negro</u>. New York: Simon and Schuster, 1946.

4560. Hall, Charles E. <u>Negroes in the United States, 1920-1932</u>. New
York: Arno Press, 1969.

4561. Hall, Edward T. <u>The Hidden Dimension</u>. Garden City, N.Y.:
Doubleday, Books, 1966.

4562. Hamilton, Charles V. "Measuring Black Conservatism," in James
D. Williams (ed.) <u>The State of Black America, 1982</u>. New York:
National Urban League, 1982, 113-140.

4563. Hamilton, Horace. "Continuity and Change in Southern
Migration." In John C. McKinney and Edgar T. Thompson (eds.)
<u>The South in Continuity and Change</u>. Durham, N.C.: Duke
University Press, 1965.

4564. Hammond, Lily. <u>In the Vanguard of a Race</u>. New York: Council
of Women for Home Missions and Missionary Education Movement of
the United States and Canada, 1922.

4565. Hammond, George. <u>Economic Discrimination in the Negro</u>
<u>Community</u>. Unpublished Paper, Rice University, 1968.

4566. Handlin, Oscar. Race and Nationality in American Life. Boston: Little Brown, 1957.

4567. Hansberry, Lorraine. The Movement: Documentary of a Struggle for Equality. New York: Simon and Schuster, 1964.

4568. Hansberry, Lorraine. To be Young, Gifted and Black. Englewood Cliffs, New Jersey: Prentice-Hall, 1969.

4569. Hardy, Erie W. Relation of the Negro to Trade Unionism. Unpublished M.A. Thesis, University of Chicago, 1911.

4570. Hardy, John G. A Comparative Study of Institutions for Negro Juvenille Delinquents, Southern States. Madison: University of Wisconsin, 1947.

4571. Hare, Nathan. Black Anglo-Saxons. New York: Marzone and Munsell, 1965.

4572. Harper, Samuel. "Negro Labor in Jacksonville," Crisis 49 (January 1942), 11-16.

4573. Harrington, Michael. The Other America: Poverty in the United States. New York: Macmillan, 1962.

4574. Harris, Abram L. "Negro Labor's Quarrel with White Workingmen," Current History 24 (September 1926), 903-7.

4575. Harris, Abram L. "Economic Foundations of American Race Division." Journal of Social Forces 5 (1927), 468-478.

4576. Harris, Abram L. The New Negro Worker in Pittsburgh. Unpublished M.S. Thesis, University of Pittsburgh, 1924.

4577. Harris, Donald J. "Economic Growth, Structural Change, and the Relative Income Status of Blacks in the U.S. Economy, 1947-78," The Review of Black Political Economy 12:3 (Spring 1983), 75-92.

4578. Harris, Dwight N. The History of Negro Servitude in Illinois and the Slavery Agitation in that State, 1719-1861. New York: Negro Universities Press, 1969.

4579. Harris, Leroy. The Other Side of the Freeway: A Study in the Settlement Pattern of Negroes and Mexican Americans in San Diego, California. Ph.D. Dissertation, Department of Social Work, Carnegie-Mellon University, Pittsburgh, PA, 1974.

4580. Harris, Louis, et al. Black and White. New York: Simon and Schuster, 1967.

4581. Harris, M. "Great Springfield Race War," Negro Digest 8 (November 1949), 52-57.

4582. Harrison, Bennett. Education, Training, and the Urban Ghetto. Baltimore, Johns Hopkins University Press, 1972.

4583. Hart, Hornel. "Differential Negro Fertility," American Sociological Review. 18 (June 1953), 192-194.

4584. Hart, John Fraser. "The Changing Distribution of the American Negro." Annals of the Association of American Geographers 50 (1960), 242-255.

4585. Hart, John Fraser. "A Rural Retreat for Northern Negroes." Geographic Review 50 (1960), 47-68.

4586. Hartman, Chester. "The Housing of Relocated Families," in James Q. Wilson (ed.), Urban Renewal: The Record and the Controversy. Cambridge: The MIT Press, 1966, 70-82.

4587. Harvey, David. "Social Justice in Spatial Systems" in R. Peet (ed.) Geographical Perspectives on American Poverty. Worcester, Massachusetts: Clark University, Antipode Monographs in Social Geography No. 1, 1972, 87-106.

4588. Harwood, Edwin. "Youth Unemployment--A Tale of Two Ghettos," Public Interest 17 (Fall 1969), 78-87.

4589. Harwood, Edwin. "Urbanism As a Way of Life," in William McCord, et al. (eds.) Life Styles in The Black Ghetto. New York: W.W. Norton, 1969, 19-35.

4590. Hatch, John Wesley. The Black Rural Church: Its Role and Potential in Community Health Organization and Action. Unpublished Ph.D. Thesis, University of North Carolina at Chapel Hill, 1974.

4591. Hauser, Philip M. "Demographic Factors in the Integration of the Negro," Daedalus. 94 (1970), 847-877.

4592. Hauser, Robert M. and D.L. Featherman. "White-Nonwhite Differentials in Occupatioal Mobility Among Men in the United States, 1962-1972." Demography 11:2 (1974), 247-266.

4593. Hawley, Amos H. Segregation in Residential Areas. Washington, D.C.: National Academy of Sciences, 1973.

4594. Haynes, George Edmund. "Effect of War Conditions on Negro Labor," Academy of Political Science Proceedings 8 (February 1919), 299-312.

4595. Haynes, George Edmund. "Migration of Negroes into Northern Cities." National Conference on Social Work 1917, 494-7.

4596. Hazel, Joseph A. The Geography of Negro Agricultural Slavery in Alabama, Florida and Mississippi, circa 1860. Ph.D.

Dissertation, Columbia University, 1972.

4597. Heaps, Willard A. Riots, U.S.A., 1865-1965. New York: Seabury, 1966.

4598. Helfertz, Robert. "The Public Sector: Residential Desegregation and the Schools: A Case Study from Buffalo, New York." Urban Review (February 1969), 30-34.

4599. Helm, Mary. From Darkness to Light: The Story of Negro Progress Revell. New York, 1909.

4600. Helper, Rose. The Racial Practices of Real Estate Institutions in Selected Areas of Chicago. Chicago: University of Chicago Press, 1959.

4601. Henderson, Janet St. Cyr and John F. Hart. "The Development and Spatial Patterns of Black Colleges." Southeastern Geographer 11 (November 1971), 133-38.

4602. Henry, Keith S. "Language, Culture and Society in the Commonwealth Caribbean." Journal of Black Studies 7:1 (1976), 79-94.

4603. Herskovits, Melville J. The Myth of the Negro Past. Boston: Beacon Press, 1958.

4604. Herskovits, Melville J. The American Negro. New York: Harper and Bros., 1928.

4605. Hesslick, George K. Black Neighbors: Negroes in a Northern Rural Community Indianapolis: Bobbs-Merrill, 1968.

4606. Hiestand, Dale L. Economic Growth and Employment Opportunities for Minorities. New York: Columbia University Press, 1964.

4607. Higham, Robin D. S. Bayonets in the Streets: The Use of Troops in Civil Distrubances. Lawrence: University Press of Kansas, 1969.

4608. Hill, Herbert. "The Equal Employment Opportunity Acts of 1964 and 1972: A Critical Analysis of the Legislative History and Administration of the Law." Industrial Relations Law Journal 2 (Spring 1977), 1-96.

4609. Hill, Herbert. "Employment, Manpower Training and the Black Worker," Journal of Negro Education 38 (Summer 1969), 204-17.

4610. Hill, John Louis. When Black Meets White. Chicago: Argyle, 1922.

4611. Hill, Samuel S. "God and the Southern Plantation System," in Religion and the Solid South. Nashville: Abingdon Press, 1972,

68.

4612. Hill, Robert B. The Strengths of Black Families. New York:
Emerson Hall Publishers, 1972.

4613. Hill, T. Edward. The Negro in West Virginia. Charleston, West
Virginia: Bureau of Welfare, 1926.

4614. Hill, Thomas A. "The Dilemma of Negro Workers," Opportunity
(February 1926), 17-20.

4615. Himes, J.S. "Forty Years of Negro Life in Columbus, Ohio,
1900-1940," Journal of Negro History 27 (April 1942), 339-45.

4616. Himes, J.S. "Negro Labor in Columbus," Opportunity 16, 11
(November 1938), 339-41.

4617. Hine, William C. "The 1868 Charleston Streetcar Sit-ins, a
Case of Successful Black Protest." South Carolina Historical
Magazine 77:2 (1976), 110-114.

4618. Hines, Linda O. and Allen W. Jones. "A Voice of Black Protest:
The Savannah Men's Sunday Club, 1905-1911." Phylon 35:2
(1974), 193-202.

4619. Hodges, David Julian. The Cajun Culture of Southwestern
Louisiana: A Study of Cultural Isolatin and Role Adaptation as
Factors in the Fusion of Black African and French Acadian
Culture Traits. Ph.D. Thesis, New York University, 1972.

4620. Hoey, Edwin. "Terror in New York -1741." American Heritage
25:4 (1974), 72-77.

4621. Hoffecker, Carol E. "The Politics of Exclusion: Blacks in Late
Nineteenth Century Wilmington, Delaware." Delaware History
17:1 (1974), 60-72.

4622. Holland, John Ben. Attitudes Toward Minority Groups in
Relation to Rural Social Structure. Ph.D. Thesis, Michigan
State University, 1950.

4623. Holstege, Henry, Jr. Conflict and Change in Negro-White
Relations in Great Falls. Ph.D. Thesis, Michigan State
University, 1966.

4624. Homel, Michael W. "The Lilydale School Campaign of 1936:
Direct Action in the Verbal Protest Era." Journal of Negro
History 59:3 (1974), 228-241.

4625. Hope, John H. "Trends in Pattern of Race Relations in the
South Since May 17, 1954." Phylon 17 (Summer 1956), 103-118.

4626. Hope, John H. "The Employment of Negroes in the United States by Major Occupation and Industry." <u>Journal of Negro Education</u> 22:3 (1953), 307-321.

4627. Hope, Richard O. <u>Racial Strife in the United States Military</u>. New York: Praeger, 1979.

4628. Horton, James Oliver. Generations of Protest: Black Families and Social Reform in Ante-Bellum Boston. <u>New England Quarterly</u> 49:2 (1976), 242-256.

4629. Horvath, Ronald J., et al. "Activity Concerning Black America in University Departments Granting M.A. and Ph.D. Degress in Geography." <u>The Professional Geographer</u> 21 (May 1969), 137-39.

4630. Horwitz, Julius. "In One Month, 50,000 Persons were Added to the City's Welfare Roles." <u>New York Times Magazine</u> (January 26, 1969).

4631. Hostader, Richard and Michael Wallace. <u>American Violence: A Documentary History.</u> New York: Alfred A. Knopf, 1970.

4632. Hubert, Benjamin F. "What About the Rural Negro?" <u>Manhood</u> 10 (1919), 154.

4633. Hubert, James H. "Harlen Faces Unemployment," <u>Opportunity</u> 9 (February 1931), 42-45.

4634. Hunter, John M. "Teaching To Eliminate Black-White Racism: An Educational Systems Approach." <u>Journal of Geography</u> 71 (February 1972): 87-95.

4635. Hunter, Lloyd A. Slavery in St. Louis 1804-1860. <u>Missouri Historical Society Bulletin</u> 30:4 (1974), 233-265.

4636. Hunter, Charlayne. "Black and the Liberation Movement," <u>Black Politician</u> 2 (January 1971), 15, 39.

4637. Humphrey, Norman D. "Black Ghetto in Detroit," <u>The Christian Century.</u> (January 15, 1947), 78-79.

4638. Hutton, Oscar D. <u>The Negro Worker and the Labor Unions in Chicago</u>. Unpublished M.A. Thesis, University of Chicago, 1939.

4639. Hymer, B. <u>Racial Dualism in the Chicago Labor Market</u>. Unpublished Ph.D. Dissertation, Northwestern University, 1968.

4640. Illinois, State of. Chicago Commission on Race Relations. <u>The Negro in Chicago; A Study of Race Relations and a Race Riot</u>. Chicago: University of Chicago Press, 1922.

4641. Institute for the Study of Educational Policy. <u>Affirmative Action for Blacks in Higher Education: A Report</u>. Washington, D.C.: Howard University Press, 1975.

4642. Jacob, John E. and Vernon E. Jordan. "Introduction" in James
       D. Williams (ed.) The State of Black America, 1982. New York:
       National Urban League, 1982, i-x.

4643. Janowitz, Morris. Social Control of Escalated Riots. Chicago:
       University of Chicago Press, 1968.

4644. Janowitz, Morris and Charles Moskos. "Racial Composition in
       the All-Volunteer Force" Armed Forces and Society (November
       1974).

4645. January, Alan F. "The South Carolina Association: An Agency
       for Race Control in Antebellum Charleston." South Carolina
       Historical Magazine 78:3 (1977), 191-201.

4646. Jefferies, Leroy. "New York's Slave Marts," Opportunity 27
       (March 1939), 85-86.

4647. Jeffries, Vincent John. Cultural Values and Antagonism Toward
       Negroes. Ph.D. Thesis, University of California Los Angeles,
       1968.

4648. Jencks, Christopher. "Private Schools for Black Children."
       New York Times Magazine (November 3, 1968), 1-8.

4649. Jenkins, Michael A. and John W. Shepherd. "Decentralizing High
       School Administration in Detroit: An Evaluation of Alternative
       Strategies of Political Control." Economic Geography. 48
       (January 1972), 95-106.

4650. Jiobu, R.M. and H.H. Marshall. "Urban Structure and the
       Differentiation Between Blacks and Whites." American
       Sociological Review 36 (1971), 638-649.

4651. Job, Barbara Cottman. "The Black Labor Force During the 1975-
       78 Recovery" Monthly Labor Review 102 (May 1979), 3-7.

4652. Johnson, Edward Augustus. School History of the Negro Race in
       America from 1619-1890. Raleigh, North Carolina: Edward and
       Broughton, 1891.

4653. Johnson, Charles S. Growing up in the Black Belt. New York:
       Harper and Row, 1941.

4654. Johnson, Charles S. The Negro in American Civilization. New
       York: Henry Holt and Company, 1930.

4655. Johnson, Charles S. The Shadow of the Plantation. Chicago:
       University of Chicago Press, 1966.

4656. Johnson, Charles S. Patterns of Negro Segregation. New York:
       Harper & Brothers, 1943.

4657. Johnson, Guy B. "A Sociologist Looks at Racial Desegregation in the South." Social Forces 32 (October 1954), 1-10.

4658. Johnson, James Weldon. Black Manhattan. New York: Knopf, 1930.

4659. Jones, Barbara A. "Utilization of Black Human Resources in the United States." The Review of Black Political Economy 10:1 (1979), 79-96.

4660. Jones, Dennis Eugene. Spatial Patterns of Racial Participation at Previously Black State Parks in North Carolina. Master's thesis, University of North Carolina, 1972.

4661. Jones, Donald W. Migration and Urban Unemployment in Dualistic Economic Development. Chicago: Department of Geography. The University of Chicago, 1975.

4662. Jones, Mary Somerville. The Racial Factor in School Districting: The Chapel Hill, North Carolina Case. Master's Thesis, University of North Carolina, 1971.

4663. Jones, William Henry. Recreation and Amusement Among Negroes in Washington, D.C.: A Sociological Analysis of the Negro in an Urban Environment. Washington, D.C., 1927.

4664. Jones, Yvonne Vivian. Ethnicity and Political Process ina Southern Rural Community: An Examination of Black-White Articulation in Decision-Making. Ph.D. Thesis, American University, 1978.

4665. Jordan, Kenneth Allen. The Geography of Consumer Economics Among Black Americans in Oakland: A Cultural Behavioral Perspective. Ph.D. Dissertation, University of California, Berkeley, Cal., 1977.

4666. Journal of Negro History. "The Negro Migration of 1916-1918." 6 (1921), 383-398.

4667. Journal of Negro History. "The Negro in the Reconstruction of Virginia: The Migration." 11 (1926), 327-346.

4668. Kahen, Harold I. "Validity of Anti-Negro Restrictive Covenants: A Reconsideration." University of Chicago Law Review (February 1945), 198-213.

4669. Kain, John F. "The Distribution and Movement of Jobs and Industry", in J.Q. Wilson (ed.) Metropolitan Enigma: Inquiries into the Nature and Dimensions of American 'Urban Crisis'. Cambridge, Massachusetts: Harvard University Press, 1968, 1-43.

4670. Kasperson, Roger E. "Toward a Geography of Urban Politics: Chicago, A Case Study." Economic Geography 41 (1965), 95-107.

4671. Katz, William L. The American Negro: His History and Literature. Atlanta: Atlanta University Publications, 1968.

4672. Kelley, Artbell. Some Aspects of the Georgraphy of the Yazoo Basin, Mississippi. Ph.D. Dissertation, University of Nebraska, Lincoln, Nebraska, 1954.

4673. Kellogg, John. "Negro Urban Clusters in the Postbellum South." Geographical Review. 67:3 (1977), 310-321.

4674. Kennedy, Louise V. The Negro Peasant Turns Cityward. New York: Columbia University Press, 1930.

4675. Keyserling, Mary Dublin. The Negro Woman in the United States--New Roles--New Challenges. Speech before the National Association of Colored Women's Clubs Convention, Oklahoma City, Oklahoma, July 27, 1966.

4676. Keyserling, Mary Dublin. Women, Work, and Poverty, Speech before Conference of Women in the War on Poverty, Washington, D.C., May 8, 1967.

4677. Keyserling, Mary Dublin. Manpower Administration. Negro Employment in the South. Volume 2: The Memphis Labor Market. Washington, D.C.: Government Printing Office, 1971.

4678. Killian, Lewis. The Impossible Revolution: Black Power and the American Dream. New York: Random House, 1968.

4679. King, Louis Eugene. Negro Life in a Rural Community. Ph.D. Thesis, Columbia University, 1951.

4680. King, Martin Luther. Stride Toward Freedom: The Montgomery Story. New York: Harper and Row, 1958.

4681. King, William M. Ghetto Riots and the Employment of Blacks: An Answer to the Search for Black Political Power? Unpublished Ph.D. Dissertation, Syracuse University, 1973.

4682. Kinnick, Bernard Conrad. An Experimental Study and Analysis of Attitudinal Change Toward Negroes and School Desegregation Among Participants in a Summer Institute Sponsored Under the Civil Rights Act of 1964. Ed.D. Thesis, Auburn University, 1966.

4683. Klaczynska, Barbara. "Why Women Work: A Comparison of Various Groups- Philadelphia. 1910-1930." Labor History 17:1 (1976), 73-87.

4684. Klein, Herbert S. Slavery in America. Chicago: University of Chicago Press, 1967.

4685. Klove, Robert C. "Urban and Metropolitan Population Trends and

Patterns." Annals of the Association of American Geographers 44 (1954), 222.

4686. Klungness, Paul H. Negro Population Density and Agricultural Changes, The Case of North Carolina. M.A. Thesis, Syracuse University, Syracuse, New York, 1970.

4687. Knowles, Louis L. and Kenneth Prewitt. Institutional Racism in America. Englewood Cliffs, New Jersey: Prentice-Hall, 1969.

4688. Knuth, Clarence P. Early Immigration and Residential Patterns of Negroes in Southwest Michigan. Ph.D. Dissertation, University of Michigan, Ann Arbor, MI., 1969.

4689. Krant, Alan M. Crusaders and Compromisers: Essays on the Relationship of Antislavery Struggle to the Antebellum Party System. Westport, Conn.: Greenwood, 1983.

4690. Kristol, Irving. "The Negro Today is Like the Immigrant Yesterday." New York Times Magazine (September 11, 1966), 14-15.

4691. Kroll-Smith, J. Stephen. "Charisma and Breakthrough: The Role of the Black Preachers in the Sunday Morning Worship Service," Review of Afro-American Issues and Culture 2:1 (Summer, 1980), 57-75.

4692. Kuy-Rendall, Jack L. "Police and Minority Groups: Toward a Theory of Negative Contacts." Police (September-October 1970), 47-56.

4693. Lacy, Dan. The White Use of Blacks in America. New York: McGraw-Hill, 1972.

4694. Ladd, Everett C. Negro Political Leadership in the South. Ithaca, New York: Cornell University Press, 1966.

4695. Ladd, Florence C. "Research Report: Black Youths View their Enviroments: Some Views of Housing." Journal of American Institute of Planners March 1972.

4696. LaGory, M. and R.J. Magnani. "Structural Correlates of Black-White Occupational Differentiationa: Will U.S. Regional Differences in Status Remain?" Social Forces 27 (1979), 157-160.

4697. Lake, Robert W. Race, Status and Neighborhood Behavioral Aspects of the Ecology of Racial Residential Change. M.A. Thesis, University of Chicago, Chicago, IL, 1972.

4698. Lamb, Richard. Metropolitan Impacts on Rural America. Chicago: Department of Geography, The University of Chicago, 1975.

4699. Lamon, Lester C. "The Black Community in Nashville and the Fisk University Student Strike of 1924-1925." Journal of Southern History 40:2 (1974), 225-244.

4700. Lang, Marvel. Historic Settlement and Residential Segregation in Rural Neighborhoods of Jasper County, Mississipppi. Ph.D. Thesis, Michigan State University, 1979.

4701. Lang, Marvel. "Rural Settlements and Patterns of Afro-Americans: Some Historical Perspectives" in R.A. Obudho (ed.) Afro-Americans and the City. Albany, New York: State University of New York Press, 1984.

4702. Lang, William L. "The Nearly Forgotten Blacks on Last Chance Gulch, 1900-1912," Pacific Northwest Quarterly 70:2 (1979), 50-57.

4703. Larimore, Ann E., et al. "Geographic Activity at Predominantly Negro Colleges and Universities: A Survey." The Professional Geographer 21 (May 1969), 140-44.

4704. Lawrence, Charles R. "Race Riots in the United States, 1942-1946," in Jessie Parkhurst Guzman (eds.) Negro Year Book. Tuskegee, Alabama: Department of Records and Research, Tuskegee Institute, 1947, 232-257.

4705. Leacock, Eleanor, et al. The Bridgeview Study: A Preliminary Report. New York: Bank Street College of Education, 1963.

4706. Lee, Alfred McClung and Norman D. Humphrey. Race Riot. New York: Octagon, 1968.

4707. Leighton, Ann S. The Spatial Pattern of Black-Owner Businesses in Washington, D.C. M.A. Thesis, University of Maryland, College Park, MD., 1975.

4708. Levine, Marvin R. The Untapped Human Resource: The Urban Negro and Employment Equality. Morriston, New Jersey: General Learning Press, 1972.

4709. Lewinson, Paul. Race, Class & Party; A History of Negro Suffrage and White Politics in the South. New York: Russell & Russell, 1963.

4710. Lewis, Edward S. "Defense Problems of Baltimore Negroes," Opportunity 19 (August 1941), 244-46.

4711. Lewis, G.M. "The Distribution of the Negro in the Conterminous United States." Geography (November 1969), 411-416.

4712. Lewis, Hyland. "Innovations and Trends in Contemporary Southern Community." Journal of Social Issues 10 (January

1954), 19-21.

4713. Lewis, Hyland and Hill Mozell. "Desegregation, Integration, and the Negro Community." Annals of the American Academy of Political and Social Science 204 (March 1956), 116-23.

4714. Lewis, Lawrence Thomas. "The Geography of Black America: the Growth of A Sub-Discipline." Journal of Geography 73:9 (1974), 38-43.

4715. Lewis, Pierce F. Geography in the Politics of Flint. Ph.D. Dissertation, University of Michigan, 1957.

4716. Lewis, Pierce F. "Impact of Negro Migration on Electoral Geography in the Northern City." Annals 53 (December 1963), 604.

4717. Lewis, Pierce F. "Impact of Negro Migration on the Electoral (Geography of Flint, Michigan, 1932-1962: A Cartographic Analysis." Annals LV (March 1965), 1-25.

4718. Lieberson, Stanley. "Generational Differences Among Blacks in the North." American Journal of Sociology 79 (1973), 550-565.

4719. Lieberson, Stanley. "Suburbs and Ethnic Residential Patterns." American Journal of Sociology 22 (May 1962), 673-681.

4720. Lieberson, Stanley and Glenn V. Fugitt. "Negro-White Occupational Differences in the Absence of Discrimination." American Journal of Sociology 73 (1967), 188-200.

4721. Lieberson, Stanley and Arnold R. Silverman. "The Precipitants and Underlying Conditions of Race Riots." American Sociological Review 30 (December 1965), 887-898.

4722. Light, Ivan H. Ethnic Enterprise in America: Business and Welfare of Chinese, Japanese and Blacks. Berkeley: University of California Press, 1972.

4723. Lipsel, Seymour M. and Reinhard Bendix. Social Mobility in Industrial Society. Berkeley, University of California Press, 1959.

4724. Lipsky, Michael and David J. Olson. "Riot Commission Politics," Trans-action 6 (July-August 1969), p. 8-21.

4725. Litwack, Leon F. North of Slavery. Chicago: University of Chicago Press, 1961.

4726. Lloyd, Kent. "Urban Race Riots vs. Effective Anti-discrimination Agencies: An End or a Beginning?" Public Administration 45 (Spring 1967), 43-45.

4727. Locke, Alain. "Enter the New Negro." The Survey 53:11 (March 1, 1925), 631-34.

4728. Locke, Alain. The New Negro. New York: Alert and Charles Boni, 1925.

4729. Logan, Rayford W. and Irving S. Cohen. The American Negro. Boston: Houghton, Mifflin, 1947.

4730. Lord, J. Dennis. "School Busing and White Abandonment of Public Schools." Southeastern Geographer 15:2 (1975), 81-92.

4731. Loth, David and Harold Fleming. Integration North and South. New York: The Fund for the Republic, 1956.

4732. Lowry, March II. "Race Socioeconomic Well-Being: A Geographical Analysis of the Mississippi Case." The Geographical Review 40 (October 1970), 511-28.

4733. Lowry, March II. "Racial Segregation: A Geographical Adaptation and Analysis." Journal of Geography 71 (January 1972), 28-40.

4734. Lowry, March II. "Schools in Transition." Annals of the Association of American Geographers 63:2 (1973), 167-180.

4735. Luna, Teleforo W. Changes in the Distribution Pattern of Negro Population in the United States. Master's Thesis, Clark University, 1956.

4736. Lurie, Melvin and Elton Rayack. "Employment Opportunities for Negro Families in Sattelite Cities," Southern Economic Journal 36 (October 1969), 191-95.

4737. MacGee, Jane. Politico-Geographic Implications of School Busing. Ph.D. Dissertation, University of Kansas, Lawrence, Kansas, 1974.

4738. Mack, Raymond W. Race, Class and Power. New York: American Book, 1968.

4739. Magubane, Bernard. The American Negro's Conception of Africa: A Study in the Ideology of Pride and Prejudice. Ph.D. Thesis, University of California, Los Angeles, 1967.

4740. Marge, Gail B. A Functional Analysis of Land Use Patterns in the Negro Shopping Areas of Raleigh and Charlotte, North Carolina. Master's Thesis, University of North Carolina, 1969.

4741. Markley, Oliver Wendel. Having a Negro Roommate as an Experience in Intercultural Education. Ph.D. Thesis, Northwestern University, 1968.

4742. Marr, Paul D. "Functional and Spatial Innovation in the Delivery of Govermental Social Services." In Harold M. Rose (ed.) Geography of the Ghetto, Perspectives in Geography. Vol. II. Dekalb, Illinois: Northern Illinois University Press, 1972.

4743. Marx, Gary Trade. Protest and Prejudice: A Study of Belief in the Black Community. New York, 1969.

4744. Marx, Gary Trade. Protest and Prejudice: The Climate of Opinion in the Negro American Community. Ph.D. Thesis, University of California, Berkeley, 1966.

4745. Massey, David. "Class, Racism, and Busing in Boston." Antipode 8:2 (1976), 37-49.

4746. Masotti, Louis H. and Don R. Bowen. Riots and Rebellion: Civil Violence in the Urban Community. Beverly Hills: Sage, 1968.

4747. Matthews, Donald R. and James W. Prothro. Negroes and the New Southern Politics. New York: Harcourt, Brace and World, 1966.

4748. Mays, Benjamin Elijah and Joseph W. Nicholson. The Negro's Church. New York: Institute of Social and Religious Research, 1933.

4749. Mayo, S.C. and C. Horace Hamilton. "Current Population Trends in the South." Social Forces 42 (October 1963), 77-88.

4750. Mayo, S.C. and C. Horace Hamilton. "The Rural Negro Population of the South in Transition." Phylon 24 (1963), 160-171.

4751. McAllister, Ronald J., et al. "Residential Mobility of Blacks and Whites: A National Longitudinal Survey." American Journal of Sociology 77 (1972), 445-55.

4752. McCullock, James E. "Another View of the Washington Riots." Outlook 123 (1919), 28-95.

4753. McCutcheon, Murry K. Racial Geography in the Twentieth Century. Master's Thesis, University of Toronto, 1951.

4754. McKinney, John C. and Linda Brookover Bourque. "The Changing South: National Incorporation of a Region." American Sociological Review 36 (June 1971), 399-411.

4755. McMillan, George. "Race Violence and Law Enforcement." New South 18 (November 1960), 4-32.

4756. McNeal, Alvin. The Distribution of Store-Front Churches in the Greater Cincinnati Area. M.A. Thesis, Department of Geography, University of Cincinnati, 1969.

4757. McPherson, James M. Anti-Negro Riots in the North. New York, 1969.

4758. McWilliams, Carey. "Watts: the Forgotten Slum." Nation 201 (August 30, 1965), 89-90.

4759. Meir, August and Elliott Rudwick. From Plantation to Ghetto. New York: Hill and Wang, 1970.

4760. Meier, August and Elliott Rudwick. "Negro Boycotts of Segregated Streetcars in Virginia, 1904-1907." Virginia Magazine of History and Biography 81:4 (1973), 479-487.

4761. Meier, August and David Lewis. "History of the Negro Upper Class in Atlanta, Georgia, 1890-1958." Journal of Negro Education (Spring 1959), 479-488.

4762. Meltzer, Milton. In their Own Words, A History of the American Negro, 1865-1916. New York: Thomas Y. Crowell, 1965.

4763. Mendelson, Wallace. Discrimination. Englewood Cliffs, New Jersey: Prentice-Hall, 1962.

4764. Metcalfe, Ralph H. "Chicago Model Cities and Neocolonization." The Black Scholar 1:6 (April 1970), 23-30.

4765. Meyer, David R. Spatial Variation of Black Households in Cities Within a Residential Choide Framework. Ph.D. Dissertation, University of Chicago, 1970, Published as Department of Geography, Research Paper No. 129, 1970.

4766. "Migration of Negroes to Northern Industrial Centers." Monthly Labor Review 12 (1921), 201-3.

4767. "Migration to Philadelphia." Opportunity (1923), 19-20.

4768. Militancy for and Against Civil Rights and Integration in Chicago: Summer 1967. A Research Report Prepared by the Interuniversity Social Research Committee-Chicago Metropolitan Area, Report No. 1, Chicago, August 1, 1967.

4769. Miller, Herman P. Rich Man, Poor Man. New York: Thomas Y. Crowell, 1964.

4770. Miller, Herman P. Poverty American Style. Belmont, California: Wadsworth Publishing Company, 1964.

4771. Miller, Kelly. "Education of the Negro in the North." Educational Review 62:3 (October 1921), 233-38.

4772. Miller, Loren. "Restrictive Covenants Versus Democracy." Racial Restrictive Covenants. Chicago Council Against Racial and Religious Discrimination, 1946.

4773. Molotch, Harvey. Manager Integration: Dilemmas of Doing Good in the City. Berkeley: University of California, 1972.

4774. Moore, Clarence Walter. An In-Depth Exploration and Analysis of an Indigenous Predominantly Black Leadership Group in a Rural County in Georgia. Ed.D. University of Georgia, 1977.

4775. Morrill, Richard and O. Fred Donaldson. "Geographical Perspectives on the History of Black America." Economic Geography 48:1 (1972), 1-23.

4776. Morrill, Richard and Ernest Wohlenberg. The Geography of Poverty in the United States. Englewood Cliffs, New Jersey: Prentice-Hall, 1971.

4777. Moses, Earl Richard. Migrant Negro Youth: A Study of Culture Conflict and Patterns of Acommodation Among Negro Youth. University Park: University of Pennsylvania, 1948.

4778. Moses, Earl Richard. Migrant Negro Youth: A Study of Culture Conflict and Patterns of Accommodation Among Negro Youth. Ph.D. 1948 University of Pennsylvania, 1948.

4779. Moynihan, Daniel Patrick. "Employment, Income, and the Ordeal of the Negro Family." Daedalus. 94:4 (Fall 1965), 745-770.

4780. Moynihan, Daniel Patrick. The Negro Family: The Case for National Action. Washington, D.C.: Government Printing Office, 1965.

4781. Moynihan, Daniel Patrick. The Negro Family: The Case of National Action. Washington, D.C.: United States Department of Labor, 1975.

4782. Murray, Albert. The Omni-Americans: New Perspective on Black Experiences and American Culture New York: Avon Books, 1971.

4783. Muse, Benjamin. The American Negro Revolution: From Nonviolence to Black Power. Bloomington: Indiana University Press, 1968.

4784. Myrdal, Gunnar. An American Dilemma. New York: Harper and Row, 1944.

4785. Naison, Mark D. Communism and Black Nationalism in the Depression: The Case of Harlem. Journal of Ethnic Studies 2:2 (1974), 24-36.

4786. National Advisory Commisson of Civil Disorders. Report Washington, D.C.: Government Printing Office, 1968.

4787. National Association for the Advancement of Colored People. Memorandum Concerning Present Discriminatory Practices of

Federal Housing Administration October 26, 1944.

4788. National Catholic Welfare Conference. Seminar on Negro Problems in the Field of Social Action 1946.

4789. National Urban Coalition. Displacement: City Neighborhoods in Transition. Washington, D.C.: National Urban Coalition, 1978.

4790. National Urban League. Bulletin, Employment Problems of the Negro. Washington, D.C.: National Urban League Papers, 1944.

4791. National Urban League. Unemployment Among Negroes . . Data on 25 Industrial Cities. New York: National Urban League, 1930.

4792. National Urban League. Report Performance of Negro Workers in 300 War Plants. New York: National Urban League, 1944.

4793. National Urban League. Unemployment Among Negroes . . Data on 25 Industrial Cities. New York: National Urban League, 1935.

4794. National Urban Legue Report Performance of Negro Workers in 300 War Plants. New York: National Urban League, 1945.

4795. Nash, Gary B. "Slaves and Slaveowners in Colonial Philadelphia." William and Mary Quarterly 30:2 (1973), 223-256.

4796. Negro Status and Race Relations in the United States, 1911-1946. New York: Thirty-Five Year Report of the Phelps-Stokes Fund, 1946.

4797. Negro Families in Rural Wisconsin: A Study of their Community Life. Madison, Wisconsin: Governor's Commisson on Human Rights, 1959.

4798. "Negro Farmers Get Unfair Deal." Farm Journal 89 (April 1965), 75.

4799. Nelson, Irene J. "Opportunities for Geographic Research on the Role of the Negro in the Southern Economy." Economic Geography 11:2 (1971), 145-148.

4800. Nelson, Hart M. and Hugh P. Whitt. "Religion and the Migrant in the City: A Test of the Holt's Cultural Shock Thesis." Social Forces 50 (1972), 379-84.

4801. Nelson, H. Viscount. "The Philadelphia NAACP: Race Versus Class Consciousness During the Thirties." Journal of Black Studies 5:3 (1975), 255-276.

4802. Newman, Dorothy K. The Negroes in the United States, Their Economic and Social Situation. Washington, D.C.: Government Printing Office, 1966.

4803. Nichols, J.L. Progress of Race: or, The Remarkable Advance of the American Negro. Nichols, Illinois: Naperville, 1929.

4804. Nitkin, David A. Negro Colonization as a Response to Racism: an Historical Geography of the Southwestern Ontario Experience, 1830-1860. M.A. Thesis, York University, Toronto, Ontario, 1973.

4805. Noe, Kaye Sizer. The Fair Housing Movement: An Overview and a Case Study. College Park, Maryland, University of Maryland, 1965.

4806. Nolen, Claude H. The Negro's Image in the South: The Anatomy of White Supremacy. Lexington, University of Kentucky Press, 1967.

4807. Nordsiek, Evelyn M. The Residential Location and Mobility of Blacks in Indianapolis, 1850-1880. M.A. Thesis, University of Maryland, College Park, MD., 1975.

4808. Norton, E.H. Population Growth and the Future of Black Folk. Washington, D.C.: Population Reference Bureau, 1973.

4809. Northwood, Lawrence K. Urban Desegregation: Negro Pioneers and Their White Neighbors. Seattle: University of Washington, 1965.

4810. Northwood, Lawrence K. Urban Desegregation: Negro Pioneers and Their White Neighbors. Seattle: School of Social Work, Department of Sociology, University of Washington, 1966.

4811. Oblendori, George W. and William P. Kuvlesky. "Racial Differences in the Educational Orientation of Rural Youths." Social Science Quarterly 49 (September 1968), 274-283.

4812. O'Brien, John T. "Factory, Church, and Community: Blacks in Antebellum Richmond." Journal of Southern History 44:4 (1978), 509-536.

4813. Obseschall, Anthony. "The Los Angeles Riot." Social Problems 4 (Winter 1968), 322-42.

4814. One Year Later: An Assessment of the Nation's Response to the Crisis Described by the National Advisory Commission on Civil Disorders. New York: Urban American and the Urban Coalition, 1969.

4815. Orshansky, Mollie. "Counting the Poor: Another Look at the Poverty Profile." Social Security Bulletin 28 (1965), 3-29.

4816. Ovington, Mary White. Half a Man, The Status of the Negro in New York. New York: Arno Press, 1968.

4817. Palen, J.J. and Leo F. Schnore. "Color Composition and City-Suburban Status Differences: A Replication and Extension." Land Economics 41 (1965), 87-91.

4818. Palmore, Erdman. "Integration and Property Values in Washington, D.C." Phylon 27 (Spring 1966), 15-19.

4819. Parker, Elsie Smith. "Both Sides of the Color Line." Appraisal Journal (January 1943), 27-35.

4820. Parsons, Talcott and Robert F. Bales. Family Socialization and Interaction Process. New York: The Free Press, 1955.

4821. Parsons, Talcott and Kenneth B. Clark (eds.) The Negro American. New York: Houghton Mifflin, 1966.

4822. Patterson, Orlando. "Reflection on the Fate of Blacks and the Americas," in Lee Rainwater (ed.) Black Experence: Soul. New Brunswick, Transaction Books, 1970, 201-254.

4823. Patterson, Pat. "Race and the Media in the 1980's" in James D. Williams (ed.) The State of Black America 1982. New York: National Urban League, 1982, 239-263.

4824. Payne, A.A. "The Negro in New York, Prior to 1860." Howard Review I (1923), 1-64.

4825. Payne, Ethel. "The Blacks Pay the Price of Postal Efficiency." City: Magazine of Urban Life and Environment 5:6 (Winter 1971), 8-13.

4826. Pearce, Diana M. Black, White, and Many Shades of Gray: Real Estate Brokers and Their Racial Practices. Ph.D. Dissertation, University of Michigan, 1976.

4827. Pearlman, Kenneth. "The Closing Door: The Supreme Court and Residential Segregation." Journal of the American Institute of Planners 44:2 (April 1978), 160-69.

4828. Pederson, H.A. "Merchandized Agriculture and the Farm Laborer." Rural Sociology 19 (June, 1960), 14-20.

4829. Perdue, Charles L. Movie Star Woman in the Land of the Black Angries: Ethnography and Folklore of a Negro Community in Rural Virginia. Ph.D. Thesis, University of Pennsylvania, 1971.

4830. Persky, Joseph J. and John F. Kain. Migration, Emplyment and Race in the Deep South. Program on Regional and Urban Economics, Discussion Paper No. 46. Cambridge: Harvard University, 1969.

4831. Peters, Marie F. "Black Families: Notes from the Guest Editor," Journal of Marriage and the Family 40 (November

1978), 124.

4832. Pettigrew, Thomas F. A Profile of the Negro American.
Princeton, New Jersey: Van Nostrand, 1964.

4833. Pettigrew, Thomas F. "Racial Change and Social Policy."
Annals of the American Academy of Political and Social Science
441 (January 1979): 114-31.

4834. Pettigrew, Thomas F. and Robert L. Green. "School
Desegregation in Large Cities: A Critique of the Coleman 'White
Flight' Thesis." Harvard Educational Review 46:1 (1976), 1-53.

4835. Poe, Clarence H. "Rural Land Segregation Between Whites and
Negroes." South Atlantic Quarterly 13 (1914), 207-12.

4836. Polenberg, Richard. One Nation Divisible: Class, Race and
Ethnicity in the United States Since 1938. New York: Pension,
1982.

4837. Poole, Isaiah J. "Black Business: A Negative View of
Washington." Black Enterprise 12:11 (June 1982), 57.

4838. Popper, Robert J. and Michael D. Donnelly. Evaluating Transit
Service to Minorities. Blacksburg, Virginia: Virginia
Polytechnic Institute and State University, Department of
Transportation, 1976.

4839. Postell, William D. The Health of Slaves on Southern
Plantations. Baton Rouge: Louisiana State University Press,
1951.

4840. Powdermaker, Hortense. After Freedom: A Cultural Study in the
Deep South. New York: The Viking Press, 1939.

4841. Powledge, Fred. Black Power, White Resistance. New York: World
Publishing, 1967.

4842. Price, Daniel O. "Educational Differentials Between Negroes
and Whites in the South." Demography 5:1 (1968), 23-33.

4843. Price, Edward T. "The East Tennessee Melungeons: A Mixed Blood
Strain." Annals of the Association of American Geographers 39
(1949), 68.

4844. Price, Edward T. "A Geographic Analysis of White-Negro-Indian
Racial Mixtures in Eastern United States." Annals of the
Association of American Geographers 43 (1953), 138-155.

4845. Price, Edward T. "The Melungeons: A Mixed Blood Strain of the
Southern Appalachians." Geographical Review 41 (1951), 256-
271.

4846. Price, Edward T. "Mixed Blood Populations of the Eastern United States." _Annals of the Association of American Geographers_ 40 (1950), 143.

4847. Price, Edward T. "Mixed Blood Populations of the Eastern United States." _Annals of the Association of American Geographers_ 41 (1951), 175.

4848. Price, Edward T. _Mixed Blood Populations of Eastern United States as to Originals, Localizations and Persistance._ Ph.D. Dissertation, University of California, Berkeley, CA., 1950.

4849. Price, Thomas. _Negro Store-Front Churches in San Francisco: A Study of Their Distribution in Selected Neighborhoods._ M.A. Thesis, San Francisco State College, 1968.

4850. Prunty, Merle. "The Renaissance of the Southern Plantation." _Geograhical Review_ 45:4 (October 1955), 459-492.

4851. Quarles, Benjamin. _The Negro in the Civil War_. Boston: Little, Brown, 1953.

4852. Quarles, Benjamin. _The Negro in the Making of America_. New York: Collier Books, 1964.

4853. Raab, Earl (ed.) _American Race Relations Today_. Garden City, New York: Doubleday, 1962.

4854. Radford, J.P. _Patterns of Nonwhite Segregation in Washington, D.C. in the Late Nineteenth Century._ M.A. Thesis, University of Maryland, College Park, Maryland, 1967.

4855. Radzialowski, Thaddeus. "The Competition for Jobs and Racial Stereotype: Poles and Blacks in Chicago." _Polish American Studies_ 33:2 (1976), 5-18.

4856. Raines, Howell. "Whites Grow Reluctant to Back Integration Steps." _New York Times_ December 12, 1979.

4857. Raines, Howell. _My Soul is Rested: Movement Days in the Deep South Remembered_. New York: Penguin Books, 1982.

4858. Rainwater, Lee. "The Negro Lower Class Family, Crucible of Identity." _Daedalus_ (Winter 1966): 179.

4859. Rainwater, Lee and William L. Yancey. _The Moynihan Report and the Politics of Controversy_. Cambridge, M.I.T. Press, 1967, 107.

4860. Rankin, David C. "The Origins of Black Leadership in New Orleans During Reconstruction." _Journal of Southern History_ 40:3 (1974), 417-440.

4861. Rankin, David C. "The Impact of the Civil War on The Free Colored Community of New Orleans." Perspectives in American History , 11 (1977-78), 377-416.

4862. Reckford, Gordon. "The Geography of Poverty in the United States." In Saul B. Cohen (ed.) Problems and Trends in American Geography. New York: Basic Books, 1967.

4863. Record, C. Wilson. "Negroes in the California Agriculture Labor Force." Social Problems 6 (Spring 1966), 361.

4864. Reissman, Leonard. "Readiness to Succeed: Mobility Aspirations and Modernism Among the Poor." Urban Affairs Quarterly 4 (March 1969), 379-395.

4865. Report of the National Advisory Commission on Civil Disorders. Washington, D.C.: Government Printing Office, 1968.

4866. Report on the 1964 Riots. Washington, D.C.: A Report of the Federal Bureau of Investigation, September 18, 1964.

4867. Report of the National Advisory Commission on Civil Disorders. New York: Bantam, 1968.

4868. Reuter, Edward B. The Mulatto in the United States. Boston: Gorham Press, 1918.

4869. Reuter, Edward B. Race Mixture. New York: McGraw-Hill Books Company, 1931.

4870. Reuter, Edward B. The American Race Problem. New York: Thomas Y. Crowell, 1970.

4871. Rex, John and Robert Moore. Race, Community and Conflict: A Study of Sparkbrook. New York: Oxford Press, 1959.

4872. Rhee, Jong M. "The Redistribution of the Black Work Force in the South by Industry." Phylon 35:3 (1974), 293-300.

4873. Rich, Spencer. "Nearly 1 of 5 Blacks Gets Welfare: Study Reports," The Washington Post (May 22, 1982).

4874. Rich, Wilbur C. Toward A Theory of Black Voting. Detroit, Michigan: Wayne State University, 1982.

4875. Riessman, Frank L. and Hermine I. Papper. Up from Poverty. New York: Harper and Row, 1968.

4876. "Riot Reader: A Collection of Recent Material Dealing with the Causes of Ghetto Unrest, Possible Remedies--And Probable Consequences of Continued National Neglect." The City 2 (January 1968), 13-28.

4877. Rittenoure, Lynn. Negro Employment in the Federal Service in the South. Unpublished Ph.D. Thesis, University of Texas, Austin, Texas, 1960.

4878. Rivers, Marie D. "Upward Mobility Trends in Negro Housing in Selected Cities of Indiana from 1950 through the 60's." Interracial Review (January 1966), 3-13.

4879. Robinson, E.F. "The Sociology of Race Riots," Phylon 2, April 1941, 162-171.

4880. Robinson, Donald L. Slavery in the Structure of American Politics, 1756-1820. New York: Harcourt Brace Jovanovich, 1971.

4881. Robinson, Pearl I. "Black Political Power-Upward or Downward" in James D. Williams (ed.) The State of Black America 1982 New York: National Urban League 1982, 81-111.

4882. Roff, Kenneth L. "Brooklyn's Reaction to Black Suffrage in 1860." Afro-Americans in New York Life and History 2:1 (1978), 29-40.

4883. Roherer, John and Munro Edmonson. The Eighth Generation Grows Up: Cultures and Personalities of the New Orleans Negroes. New York: Harper and Row, 1960.

4884. Rose, Harold M. The Negro in America. New York: Harper, 1948.

4885. Rose, Harold M. and Carolina B. Rose. Minority Problems: A Textbook of Readings in Intergroup Relations. New York: Harper and Row, 1965.

4886. Rose, Harold M. "The Origin and Development of Urban Black Social Areas." Journal of Geography. 68 (1969), 326-33.

4887. Rose, Harold M. "The Structure of Retail Trade in a Racially Changing Trade Area." Geographical Analysis II (April 1970), 135-48.

4888. Rose, Harold M. and Harold McConnell. Perspectives in Geography #2: Geography of the Ghetto. DeKalb, Il.: Northern Illinois University, 1972.

4889. Ross, Arthur M. and Herbert Hill. Employment, Race and Poverty New York: Harcourt, Brace and World, 1967.

4890. Rubin, Morton. "Localism and Related Values Among Negroes in a Southern Rural Comunity." Social Forces 36 (March 1958), 263-267.

4891. Rubin, Morton. "Migration Patterns of Negroes from a Rural Northeastern Mississippi Community." Social Forces 39 (October

1959), 59–66.

4892. Rubin, Morton. _Plantation Country._ Chapel Hill, North Carolina: University of North Carolina Press, 1951.

4893. Rubin, Morton. "Social and Cultural Change in the Plantation Area." _Journal of Social Issues_ 10 (January 1954), 28–35.

4894. Rudwick, Elliot M. _Race Riot at East St. Louis, July 2, 1917._ Carbondale: Southern Illinois University Press, 1964.

4895. Rusco, Elmer R. _Poverty in Washoe County._ Technical Report No. 4A. Reno, Nevada: Bureau of Governmental Research, University of Nevada, 1968.

4896. Russell, James S. "Rural Economic Progress of the Negro in Virginia." _Journal of Negro History_ 11 (1926), 556–62.

4897. Russell, John H. _The Free Negro in Virginia._ Baltimore: John Hopkins University Press, 1913.

4898. Ruttan, Vernon W. "Farm and Non-Farm Employment Opportunities for Low Income Farm Families." _Phylon_ 26 (Fall 1959), 248–255.

4899. Sadezky, Hannelore. _The Geographical Patterns of School Desegretation in the South._ Master's thesis, Michigan State University, 1965.

4900. Safa, Helen Icken. "The Case for Negro Separatism: The Case of Identity in the Black Community." _Urban Affairs Quarterly_ 4:1 (September 1968), 45–63.

4901. Sager, Leon B. "Give Dollars, Give Jobs, Give a Damn." _The Center Magazine_ 2 (November 1969), 9–27.

4902. Salisbury, Harrison. "The Shook-up Generation" in Jewel Bellush and Murray Hausknecht (eds.) _Urban Renewal: People, Politics and Planning._ New York: Anchor Books, 1967, 425–36.

4903. Salisbury, Howard. "The State Within a State: Some Comparison Between the Urban Ghetto and the Insurgent State." _The Professional Geographer_ 23 (April 1971), 105–12.

4904. Salter, Paul S. and Robert C. Mings. "A Geographical Aspect of the 1968 Miami Racial Disturbances: A Preliminary Investigation." _The Professional Geographer_ 21 (May 1969), 79–86.

4905. Saltman, Juliet. "Housing Discrimination: Policy Research, Methods and Results." _Annals of the American Academy of Political and Social Science_ 441 (January 1979): 186–96.

4906. Sandburg, Carl. _The Chicago Race Riots, July 1919._ New York:

Harcourt, Brace & World, 1969.

4907. Sargent, F.O. "Economic Adjustments in Negro Farmers in East Texas." Southwestern Social Science Quarterly 42 (1961), 32-34.

4908. Scanzoni, John H. The Black Family in Modern Society. Boston: Allyn and Bacon, 1971.

4909. Scarborough, D.D. Economic Study of Negro Farmers as Owners, Tenants, and Croppers. Athens, Georgia: McGregor, 1925.

4910. Scarborough, William Sanders. "The Negro Farmer in the South." Current History 21 (1925), 565-9.

4911. Scarborough, William Sanders. "Negro Farmers in Virginia." Current History 25 (1926), 384-87.

4912. Schmid, Calvin F. and Wayne W. McVey. Growth and Distribution of Minority Races in Seattle, Washington. Seattle: Seattle Public Schools, 1964.

4913. Schulz, David. Coming up Black. Englewood Cliffs, New Jersey: Prentice-Hall, 1969.

4914. Sears, David O. Los Angeles Riot: Political Attitudes of Los Angeles Negroes. Los Angeles: Institute of Government and Public Affairs, University of California, 1967.

4915. Seman, Paul. Structure and Spatial Distribution of Black-Owned Businesses in Columbia, South Carolina, 1900-1976. M.A. Thesis, University of South Carolina, Columbia, South Carolina, 1977.

4916. Semyonov, Moshe et al. "Place, Race and Differential Occupational Opportunities" Demography 21:2 (May 1974), 259-270.

4917. Sernett, Milton C. Black Religion and American Evangelicalism: White Protestants, Plantation Missions, and the Flowering of Negro Christianity, 1787-1865. Metuchen, N.J.: Scarecrow Press, 1975.

4918. Sernett, Milton C. "Mapping Freedom's Frontier: Notes Toward an Historical Geography of Nineteenth Century African Methodism," in Report of the Conference in Black Studies, December, 1-2, 1976 Syracuse: New York State Black Studies Conference and the Office of Higher Education Management Services, New York State Education Department, 1978, 58-63.

4919. Sernett, Milton C. "The Religious Geography of Afro-Americans" in R.A. Obudho (ed.) Afro-Americans and the City Albany, New York: State University of New York Press, 1984.

4920. Shannon, Gary W. _Residential Distribution and Travel Patterns:_ _a Case Study of Detroit Elementary School Teachers._ M.A. Thesis, University of Michigan, Ann Arbor, Michigan, 1965.

4921. Shapiro, Fred G. and James W. Sullivan. _Race Riots, New York,_ _1964._ New York, Crowell, 1964.

4922. Sheldon, Marianne Buroff. "Black-White Relations in Richmond, Virginia, 1782-1820." _Journal of Southern History_ 45:2 (1979), 27-44.

4923. Shifflett, Crandall Avis. _Shadowed Thresholds: Rural Poverty_ _in Louisa County, Virginia, 1860-1900._ Ph.D. University of Virginia, 1975.

4924. Shover, John L. "Ethnicity and Religion in Philadelphia Politics, 1924-40." _American Quarterly_ 25:5 (1973), 499-515.

4925. Siegel, Paul M. "On the Cost of Being a Negro," _Sociological_ _Inquiry_ 35 (Winter 1965), 335-45.

4926. Silberman, Charles E. _Crisis in Black and White._ New York: Vintage Books, 1964.

4927. Simmons, Janet T. and Everett S. Lee. "The Extraordinary Composition of Rural Black Population Outside the South." _Phylon_ 35:3 (1974), 313-322.

4928. Simpson, George Eaton and John Milton Yinger. _Racial and_ _Cultural Minorities: An Analysis of Prejudice and_ _Discrimination._ New York: Harper and Row, 1958.

4929. Singer, Dorothy. _Interracial Attitudes of Negro and White_ _Fifth-grade Children in Segregated and Unsegregated Schools._ Ed.D. Columbia University, 1966.

4930. Sitkoff, Harvard. "The Detroit Race Riot of 1943." _Michigan_ _History_ 53 (Fall 1969), 183-194.

4931. Sly, David F. _Technology, Environment, Organization and_ _Migration: An Ecological Approach to Southern Negro Migration._ Ph.D. Brown University, 1971.

4932. Smith, Bulkeley. "the Differential Residential Segregation of Working-Class Negroes in New Haven." _American Sociological_ _Review_ 24 (August 1959), 529-533.

4933. Smith, Charles V. "Race, Human Relations and the Changing South." _Phylon_ 23 (Spring 1962), 66-72.

4934. Smith, David. _The Geography of Social Well-Being in the United_ _States._ New York: McGraw Hill, 1973.

4935.   Smith, James A. and Finis R. Welch. Race Difference in
        Earnings: A Survey and New Evidence. Santa Monica, California:
        RAND Corporation, 1978.

4936.   Smith, James P. "The Improving Economic Status of Black
        Americans." American Economic Review 68 (May 1978): 171-78.

4937.   Smith, Kelly M. "Religion As a Force in Black America" in
        James D. Williams (ed.) The State of Black America 1982 New
        York: National Urban League, 1982, 197-237.

4938.   Smith, Paul Alan. Negro Settlement in Los Angeles, California,
        1890-1930. M..A. Thesis, California State University at
        Northridge, Northridge, CA, 1973.

4939.   Smith, P.M. "Personal and Social Adjustment of Negro Children
        in Rural and Urban Areas of the South." Rural Sociology 24
        (1961), 78-7.

4940.   Smith, Peter Craig. Negro Hamlets and Gentlemen Farms: A
        Dichotomous Rural Settlement Pattern in Kentucky's Bluegrass
        Region. Ph.D. Thesis, University of Kentucky, 1972.

4941.   Smith, Peter Craig and Karl B. Raitz. "Negro Hamlets and
        Agricultural Estates in Kentucky's Inner Bluegrass,"
        Geographical Review 64 (January 1974), 217-234.

4942.   Smith, Richard A. "An Anlysis of Black Occupancy of Mobile
        Homes," Journal of the American Institute of Planners 42:4
        (October 1976), 410-18.

4943.   Smith, Stanley H. "The Older Rural Negro." in E. Grant Yeoman
        (ed.), Older Rural America. Lexington, Kentucky: University of
        Kentucky Press, 1967, 262-280.

4944.   Smith, Wallace F. Filtering and Neighborhood Change. Research
        Report No. 24. Berkeley: The University of California, The
        Center for Real Estate and Urban Economics, Institute of Urban
        and Regional Development, 1964.

4945.   Smith, Wallace F. and Karl B. Raitz. "Negro Hamelts and
        Agricultural Estates in Kentucky's Inner Bluegrass."
        Geographical Review 64:2 (1974), 217-234.

4946.   Snow, Ronald W. "Origin and Characteristics of Mississippi
        Immigrants in the Last 1970's." Southeastern Geographer 22
        (1982), 110-129.

4947.   Sorenson, Annemette, et al. "Indexes of Racial Residential
        Segregation for 109 Cities in the United States, 1940-1970."
        Sociological Focus (April 1975), 125-42.

4948.   Southern Rural Research Project. Black Farm Families, Hunger and Malnutrition in Rural Alabama: A Survey by Southern Research Project of Living Conditions in Eight Counties. Selma, Alabama: Southern Rural Research Project, 1968.

4949. Southern Rural Research Project. The Extinction of the Black Farmer in Alabama. Selma, Alabama: Southern Rural Research Project, 1968.

4950. Sowell, Thomas. "Black Excellence: The Case of Dunbar High School." Public Interest 35 (1974), 3-21.

4951. Spatta, Carolyn L. Regionalization: One Adjustment to Racial Imbalance in the Ann Arbor Schools. Master's Thesis, University of Michigan, 1968.

4952. Spear, Allan H. Black Chicago: The Making of a Negro Ghetto, 1890-1920. Chicago: University of Chicago Press, 1967.

4953. Speigner, Thodore R. "Critical Shortage of Black Geography Teachers." Journal of Geography 68 (October 1969), 388-89.

4954. Spencer, Mary E.S. The General Well-Being of Rural Black Elderly: A Descriptive Study. Ph.D. Thesis, University of Maryland, 1979.

4955. Spilerman, S. Industry Differences in Stratability of the Rate of Negro Employment. Discussion Paper #56-69. Madison, Wis.: University of Wisconsin Institute for Research on Poverty, 1969.

4956. Spilerman S. and R.E. Miller. Community and Industry Determinants of the Occupational Status of Black Males. Discussion Paper #330, Madison, Wis.: University of Wisconsin Institute for Research on Poverty, 1976.

4957. Stampp, Kenneth M. The Peculiar Institution: Slavery in the Ante-Bellum South. New York: Knopf, 1956.

4958. Staples, Robert. Introduction to Black Sociology. New York: McGraw-Hill, 1976.

4959. Staples, Robert. The Black Family: Essays and Studies. Belmont: Wadsworth Publishing Company, 1971.

4960. Staples, Robert. The Lower Income Negro Fmaily in Saint Paul. St. Paul: St. Paul Urban League, 1967.

4961. Starobin, Robert S. Industrial Slavery in the Old South, New York: Oxford University Press, 1970.

4962. Steinbrink, John E. The Effectiveness of Advance Organizers for Teaching Geography to Disadvantaged Rural Black Elementary Students. Ed.D. Dissertation, University of Georgia, 1970.

368

4963. Steptoe, R. and B. Clark. "The Plight of Rural Southern Blacks and Some Policy Implications." Bulletin of Southern University, and A & M College 55 (June 1969).

4964. Stern, Oscar I. "Long Range Effect of Colored Occupancy." Review of the Society of Residential Appraisers 11:1 (January 1946), 4-6.

4965. Stern, Oscar I. "The End of the Restrictive Covenant." The Appraisal Journal 14:4 (October 1948), 1-7.

4966. Sterner, Bernard. The Negro in Depression and War. Chicago: Quadrangle Books, 1969.

4967. Sterner, Richard M., et al. The Negro's Share: A Study of Income, Consumption, Housing and Public Assistance. New York: Harper, 1943.

4968. Stiffler, Larry Wayne. Negro Participation in Manufacturing: A Geographical Appraisal of North Carolina. M.A. Thesis, University of North Carolina, Chapel Hill, NC., 1965.

4969. Stinchcombe, Arthur and Mary M.D. Walker. "Is there a Racial Tipping Point in Changing Schools?" Journal of Social Issues 25:1 (1969), 127-36.

4970. Stolzenberg, R.M. and R.J. D'Amico. "City Differences and Nondifferences in the Effect of Race and Sex on Occupational Distribution." American Sociological Review 42 (1977), 937-960.

4971. Struhsaker, Virginia L. Stockton's Black Pioneers. Pacific History 19:4, (1975), 341-355.

4972. Sullivan, Teresa A. "Racial-Ethnic Differences in Labor Force Participation: An Ethnic Stratification Perspective." In Frank D. Bean and W.P. Frisbie (eds.) The Demography of Racial and Ethnic Groups. New York: Academic Press, 1978, 165-187.

4973. Sumka, Harold J. "Racial Segregation in Small North Carolina Cities." Southeastern Geographer 17:1 (1977), 58-75.

4974. Supplemental Studies for the National Advisory Commission on Civil Disorders. Washington, D.C.: Government Printing Office, 1968.

4975. Sutherland, Robert L. Color, Class and Personality. Princeton, New Jersey: Nostrand, 1964.

4976. Swinton and Morse. "Black Youth Unemployment," Urban Institute Research Paper. Washington, D.C.: The Urban League Institute, 1970.

4977. Taeuber, Karl F. "Racial Segregation: The Persisting Dilemma." Annals of the American Academy of Political and Social Science (November 1975), 87-96.

4978. Taeuber, Karl F. "The Effect of Income Redistribution on Racial Residential Segregation." Urban Affairs Quarterly 4 (September 1958), 51-?.

4979. Taeuber, Karl F. "Residential Segregation." Scientific American 213 (August 1965), 12-19.

4980. Taeuber, Karl F. and Alma F. Taeuber. "The Negro as an Immigrant Group Recent Trends in Racial and Ethnic Segregation in Chicago." American Journal of Sociology 69 (January 1964), 374-382.

4981. Tatum, Charles E. The Christian Methodist Episcopal Church, With Emphasis on Negroes in Texas, 1870 to 1970: A Study in Historical Cultural Geography. Ph.D. Dissertation, Michigan State University, 1971.

4982. Tatum, Charles E. and Lawrence Somers. "The Spread of the Black Christian Methodist Church in the United States, 1870-1970." Journal of Geography 74 (1975), 343-359.

4983. Taylor, Alrutheur Ambush. The Negro in the Reconstruction of Virginia. New York: Russell and Russell, 1969.

4984. Taylor, Grady W. An Analysis of Certain Factors Differentiating Successful from Unsuccessful Farm Families in Two Counties in Alabama. University of Wisconsin, 1958.

4985. Tilly, Charles, et al. Race and Residence in Wilmington, Delaware. New York: Bureau of Publications, Teachers College, Columbia University, 1965.

4986. Tindal, George Brown. South Carolina Negroes, 1877-1900. Columbia: University of South Carolina Press, 1952.

4987. Thomas, June Sheralyn Manning. Blacks on the South Carolina Sea Islands: Planning for Tourist and Land Development. Ph.D. the University of Michigan, 1977.

4988. Thomas, Norman. The Plight of the Sharecroppers. New York: League for Industrial Democracy, 1934.

4989. Thompson, Edgar and Everett Hughes. Race: Individual and Collective Behavior. New York: Free Press, 1965.

4990. Thornbrough, Emma Lou. "The Negro in Indiana," Indiana Historical Collection 37 (1957), 1-7.

4991. Thurow, Lester. Poverty in Black and White: Highlights of

Poverty and Discrimination. Washington: The Brookings Institute, 1969.

4992. Thurow, Lester. Poverty and Discrimination. Washington: The Brookings Institution, 1969.

4993. Todd, William J. Factor Analytic Black-White Polarization in Milwaukee, 1950-1970. M.A. Thesis, Indiana State University, Terre Haute, IN., 1972.

4994. Toll, William. "The Genie of 'Race': Problems in Conceptualizing the Treatment of Black Americans." Journal of Ethnic Studies 4:3 (1976), 1-20.

4995. Toll, William. Social Organization and Cultural Change: An Essay Review. Pacific Northwest Quarterly 66:1 (1975), 30-34.

4996. Tomasson, R.F. "Patterns in Negro-white Differential Mortality 1930-1957," Milbank Memorial Fund Quarterly 38 (October 1960), 362-386.

4997. Tower, J. Allen. "Cotton Change in Alabama, 1879-1946." Economic Geography 24 (January 1950), 6-28.

4998. Trubowitz, Sidney. A Handbook for Teaching in the Ghetto School. New York: Quadrangle Books, 1968.

4999. Tsong, Peter Z. "Changing Patterns of Labor Force Participation Rates of Nonwhites in the South." Phylon 35:3 (1974), 301-312.

5000. Turner, Edward Raymond. The Negro in Pennsylvania, 1639-1861. Washington, D.C.: American Historical Association, 1911.

5001. Turner, R. "The Relative Position of the Negro Male in the Labor Force of Large American Cities." American Sociological Review 16 (1951), 524-529.

5002. "U.S. Area Redevelopment Administration. Negro-White Differences in Geographic Mobility." In: Series in Economic Redevelopment Research. Washington, D.C.: Government Printing Office, 1964.

5003. U.S. Bureau of Census. The Social and Economic Status of Negroes in the United States, 1969. Washington, D.C.: Government Printing Office, 1970.

5004. U.S. Bureau of Census. The Social and Economic Status of Negroes in the United States, 1970. Washington, D.C.: Government Printing Office, 1971.

5005. U.S. Bureau of the Census. Trends in Social and Economic Conditions of Negroes in the United States. Washington, D.C.:

Government Printing Office, 1969.

5006. U.S. Bureau of Census. Recent Trends in Social and Economic Conditions of Negroes in the United States. Washington, D.C.: Government Printing Office, 1968.

5007. U.S. Bureau of Census. Educational Attainment of Nonwhite Women. Washington, D.C.: Government Printing Office, 1968.

5008. U.S. Bureau of Census. Social and Economic Conditions of Negroes in the United States. Washington, D.C.: Government Printing Office, 1967.

5009. U.S. Bureau of Census. We The Black People of the United States. Washington, D.C.: Government Printing Office, 1970.

5010. U.S. Bureau of the Census and U.S. Bureau of Labor Statistics, The Social and Economic Status of Negroes in the United States, 1969. Washington, D.C.: Government Printing Office, 1970.

5011. U.S. Commission on Civil Rights. Racism in America and How to Combat It. Washington, D.C.: Government Printing Office, January 1970.

5012. U.S. Commission on Civil Rights. Civil Rights U.S.A., Housing in Washington. Washington, D.C.: Government Printing Office, 1962.

5013. U.S. Commission on Civil Rights. The Federal Civil Rights Enforcement Effort: To Eliminate Employment Discrimination. Washington, D.C.: Government Printing Office, 1975.

5014. U.S. Department of Commerce and Labor. Conditions of Living Among the Poor, Bureau of Labor Bulletin 64. Washington, D.C.: Government Printing Office, 1966.

5015. U.S. Department of Health, Education and Welfare, Social Security Administration. The Aged Negro and His Income. Social Security Bulletin. Washington, D.C.: Government Printing Office, 1968.

5016. U.S. Department of Labor. Black Americans: A Chart Book. Washington, D.C.: Government Printing Office, 1971.

5017. U.S. Department of Labor. Labor Force Projections by Color, 1970-80. Washington, D.C.: Government Printing Office, 1981.

5018. U.S. Department of Labor. Black Americans: A Decade of Occupational Changes. Washington, D.C.: Government Printing Office, 1972.

5019. U.S. Department of Labor. Negro Employment in the South. Volume I: The Houston Labor Market. Washington, D.C.:

Government Printing Office, 1971.

5020. U.S. Department of Labor. <u>Negroes in the United States: Their</u>
       <u>Economic and Social Situation</u>. Washington, D.C.: Government
       Printing Office, 1966.

5021. U.S. Department of Labor, Bureau of Labor Statistics. <u>Black</u>
       <u>Americans- A Chartbook 1971</u>. Washington, D.C.: Government
       Printing Office, 1971.

5022. U.S. Department of Labor. <u>Black Americans: A Decade of</u>
       <u>Occupational Change.</u> Washinton, D.C.: Government Printing
       Office, 1972.

5023. U.S. Department of Labor and Department of Commerce. <u>The</u>
       <u>Social and Econoomic Status of Negroes in the United States.</u>
       Washington, D.C.: Government Printing Office, 1969.

5024. U.S. Joint Center for Political Studies. <u>Foreign Trade Policy</u>
       <u>and Black Economic Advancement</u>. Washington, D.C.: Government
       Printing Office, 1980.

5025. U.S. Manpower Administration. <u>Civil Rights in the Urban</u>
       <u>Crisis</u>. Washington, D.C.: Government Printing Office, 1968.

5026. U.S. National Advisory Commission on Civil Disorders. <u>Report.</u>
       Washington, D.C.: Government Printing Office, 1968.

5027. U.S. <u>Negroes in the United States: Their Economic and Social</u>
       <u>Situation</u>. Washington, D.C.: Government Printing Office, 1966.

5028. U.S. <u>Negro Women Worker in 1960.</u> Washington, D.C.: Government
       Printing Office, 1963.

5029. U.S. <u>Negro Women in the Population and in the Labor Force.</u>
       Washington, D.C.: Government Printing Office, 1967.

5030. U.S. <u>Negro Women in Industry in 15 States.</u> Washington, D.C.:
       Government Printing Office, 1929.

5031. U.S. <u>Nonwhite Women Workers.</u> Washington, D.C., Government
       Printing Office, 1966.

5032. U.S. <u>The Poor-Some Facts and Some Fictions</u>. Washington, D.C.:
       Government Printing Office, 1967.

5033. U.S. Senate Report No. 693, 64th Congress, 2nd Session Part 2
       as quoted in Milton Meltzer (ed.) <u>In Their Own Words: A</u>
       <u>History of the American Negro</u>. New York Thomas Y. Crowell Co.,
       1965.

5034. U.S. "Who's Who Among the Poor: A Demographic View of
       Poverty." <u>Social Security Bulletin</u>, July 1965.

5035. Urban League of Greater Cincinnati: Is Yours a Changing Neighborhood? Cincinnati: The Author, 1959.

5036. Utley, Roi and William J. Weatherly. The Negro in New York. New York: Oceana Publications, 1967.

5037. Valentine, Charles A. Culture and Poverty. Chicago: University of Chicago Press, 1968.

5038. Vandell, Kerry D. and Bennett Harrison. "Racial Transition Among Neighborhoods: A Simulation Model Incorporating Institutional Parameters." Journal of Urban Economics 5 (1978), 441-70.

5039. Vieira, Norman. "Racial Imbalance, Black Separatism and Permissible Classification by Race." Michigan Law Review 67 (1969), 1553.

5040. Violence in the City, Governor's Commission Report on the Los Angeles Riots. Sacramento: The Commission, 1965.

5041. Vose, Clement E. Caucasions Only: The Supreme Court, the NAACP and the Restrictive Covenant Cases. Berkeley: University of California Press, 1959.

5042. Wachtel, Dawn. The Negro and Discrimination in Employment, Ann Arbor: Institute of Labor and Industrial Relations, University of Michigan, 1965.

5043. Wachtel, Howard and Charles Betsey. "Low Wage Workers and the Dual Labor Market: An Empirical Investigation" Review of Black Political Economy 5 (Spring 1975): 290-322.

5044. Wadley, Janet K., et al. "Disappearance of Black Farmer." Phylon 35:3, 1974), 276-283.

5045. Wakin, E. Portrait of a Middle-Class Negro Family at the Edge of Harlem. New York: Morrow, 1965.

5046. Walls, Dwayne. The Chicken Bone Special. New York: Harcourt Brace Jovanovich, 1971..

5047. Warner, Robert A. New Haven Negroes: A Social History. Yale University Press, New Haven, 1940.

5048. Warner, W. Lloyd, et al. Color and Human Nature. Washington, D.C., American Council on Education, 1941.

5049. Warren, Donald J. Black Neighborhoods: An Assessment of Community Power. Ann Arbor, Michigan: University of Michigan Press, 1974.

5050. Waskow, Arthur I. The 1919 Race Riots: A Study in the

Connection Bewteen Conflict and Violence. University of Wisconsin, 1963.

5051. Waskow, Arthur I. From Race Riot to Sit-In: 1919 and the 1960's: A Study in Connection Between Conflict and Violence. Garden City, New York: Doubleday, 1966.

5052. Watson, Bernard C. "Public Education: A Search For Sanity and Humnanity" in James D. Williams (ed.) The State of Black America 1982. New York: National Urban League 1982, 141-170.

5053. Watts, Eugene J. "Black Political Progress in Atlanta, 1868-1895." Journal of Negro History 59:3 (1974), 268-286.

5054. Weaver, Robert C. "Negro Employment in the Aircraft Industry," Quarterly Journal of Economics 59:4 (August 1945), 597-625.

5055. Weaver, Robert C. Negro Labor: A National Problem. New York: Harcourt, Brace, 1946.

5056. Weaver, Robert C. The Urban Complex: Human Values in Urban Life. Garden City, New York: Doubleday, 1964.

5057. Weeks, Stephen B. The History of Negro Suffrage in the South. Boston: Ginn, 1894.

5058. Weisbard, R.G. "The Black Debate Begins: Quality Versus Quantity." in R.G. Weisbard (ed.) Genocide? Birth Control and Black America. Westport, Connecticut: Greenwood, 1975, 41-55.

5059. Wellenback, Shirley. Segregation 1975: Residential Patterns and Possibilities for New Negro Households in the Philadelphia Region. Philadelphia: Philadelphia Housing Association, November 1967.

5060. Wesley, Charles H. Negro Labor in the United States, 1850-1925; A Study in American Economic History, New York: Vanguard Press, 1927.

5061. Westcott, Diane Nilsen. "Blacks in the 1970's: Did They Scale the Ladder?" Monthly Labor Review (June 1982), 37.

5062. Wharton, Vernon Lane. The Negro in Mississippi, 1865-1890. New York: Harper and Row, 1965.

5063. Wheeler, James O. "The Spatial Interaction of Blacks in Metropolitan Areas." Southeastern Geographer 11 (November 1971), 101-12.

5064. Wheeler, James O. and Stanley D. Brunn. "An Agricultural Ghetto: Negroes in Cass County, Michigan, 1845-1968." The Geographical Review 59 (July 1969), 317-29.

5065. Wheeler, James O. and Stanley, D. Brunn. "Negro Migration into Southwestern Michigan." The Geograhical Review 58 (April 1968) 214-30.

5066. Wilcox, J. and W.C. Roof. "Percent Black and Black-White Status Inequality: Southern Versus Non-Southern Patterns." Social Science Quarterly 59: (1978), 422-434.

5067. Will, Robert and Harold G. Vatter. Poverty in Affluence: The Social, Political and Economic Dimensions of Poverty in the United States. New York: Harcourt, Brace and World, 1970.

5068. William, Dorothy Slade. Ecology of Negro Communities in Los Angeles, 1940-1959. Unpublished Ph.D. Thesis, UCLA, 1961.

5069. Williams, James D. The State of Black America 1982. New York: National Urban League, 1982.

5070. Williams, James D. The State of Black America 1983. New York: National Urban League, 1983.

5071. Williams, Leodrey. Factors Associated with the Effectiveness of Leaders in Black Rural Communities. Ed.D. The Louisiana State University and Agricultural and Mechanical College, 1975.

5072. Williams, Melvin D. Community in a Black Pentecostal Church: An Anthropological Study Pittsburgh: University of Pittsburgh Press, 1975.

5073. Williamson, Joel. After Slavery: the Negro in South Carolina During Reconstruction, 1861-1877. Chapel Hill, N.C. The University of North Carolina Press, 1965.

5074. Willie, Charles V. (ed.) The Family Life of the Black People. Columbus, Ohio: Charles B. Merill, 1970.

5075. Wilson, Bobby McClain. "Church Participation: A Social Space Analysis in a Community of Black In-migrants, "Journal of Black Studies, 10 (1979), 211.

5076. Wilson, Bobby McClain. The Influence of Church Participation on the Behavior in Space of Black Rural Migrants within Bedford-Stuyvesant: A Social Space Analysis. Ph.D. Dissertation, Clark University, Worcester, MA., 1974.

5077. Wilson, Bobby McClain and Herman Jenkins. "Symposium: Black Perspectives on Geography." Antipode 4 (July 1972), 42-44.

5078. Wilson, James Q. "The Negro in Politics" in Talcot Parsons and Kenneth B. Clark (eds.) The Negro American. Boston: Houghton Mifflin, 1966.

5079. Wilson, James Q. Negro Politics. New York: The Free Press,

1960.

5080. Wilson, Joseph. "Industrial Geography of Americans 1970 to 1980" in R.A. Obudho (ed.) Afro-American and the City Albany, New York: State University of New York Press, 1984.

5081. Wilson, William J. The Declining Significance of Race :Blacks and Changing American Institutions. Chicago: University of Chicago Press, 1979.

5082. Winegarden, C.R. "Barriers to Black Employment in White Collar Jobs: A Quantitative Approach," Review of Black Political Economy 2:3 (1972), 13-24.

5083. Windley, Lathan A. Runaway Slave Advertisements: A Documentary History from the 1730's to 1790. Volume I: Virginia and North Carolina; Volume II: Maryland; Volume III: South Carolina; Volume IV: Georgia. Westport, Conn.: Greenwood, 1983.

5084. Wirth, Louis. The Ghetto. Chicago, University of Chicago Press, 1928.

5085. Wittenberg, Clarissa K. An Intimate Record of How it was in Yesterday's Harlem. Smithsonian 6:3 (1975), 84-91.

5086. Wohlenberg, Ernst H. The Geography of Poverty in the United States." A Spatial Study of the Nation's Poor. Ph.D. Dissertation, University of Washington, 1970.

5087. Wolf, Eleanore Papeo. "Class and Race in the Changing City: Searching for New Solutions for Old Problems." in Leo Schore (ed.). Social Science and the City. New York: Praeger, 1968, 14-29.

5088. Wolters, Raymond. Negroes and the Great Depression. Westport, Connecticut: Greenwood, 1970.

5089. Woodson, Carter G. The History of the Negro Church. Washington, D.C.: Associated Publishers, 1921.

5090. Woodson, Carter G. The Rural Negro. Washington, D.C.: Association for the Study of Negro Life and History, 1930.

5091. Woodson, Carter G. The Negro Professional Man and the Community. Washington, D.C.: The Association for the Study of Negro Life and History, 1934.

5092. Woofter, Thomas Jackson. Negro Migration: Changes in Rural Organization and Population of Cotton Belt. New York: W.D. Grey, 1920.

5093. Wright, Richard. "With Black Radicals in Chicago." Dissent 24:2 (1977), 156-161.

5094. Wright, Robert C. A Black Perspective of Black Political Behavior in the 1961, 1965 and 1969 Mayoral Elections in Detroit, Michigan. Ph.D. Dissertation, Clark University, Worcester, MA., 1972.

5095. Yette, Samuel F. The Choice: The Issue of Black Survival in America. New York: Berkeley Publishing Corp., 1971.

5096. Zelinsky, Wilbur. "An Approach to the Religious Geogrpahy of the United Staes: Patterns of Church Membership in 1952," Annals of the Association of American Geographers 51 (1961), 139-93.

5097. Zilversmit, Arthur. The First Emancipation: The Abolition of Slavery in the North. Chicago: University of Chicago Press, 1967.

5098. Zschock, Dieter. "Black Youth in Suburbia," Urban Affairs Quarterly 7:1 (September 1, 1971), 61-74.

CHAPTER 8

Urban and Regional Planning Policies

5099.   Affirmative Discrimination: Ethnic Inequality and Public
        Policy. New York: Basic Books, 1975.

5100.   Anderson, E. Frederick. The Development of Leadership and
        Organization Building in the Black Community of Los Angeles
        From 1900 through World War II. Sarasota, Florida: Century
        Twenty-One Publishers, 1980.

5101.   Anderson, Martin. The Federal Bulldozer: A Critical Analysis
        of Urban Renewal 1949-1962. Cambridge, Massachusetts:
        Massachusetts Institute of Technology Press, 1964.

5102.   Bailey, Harry A. "Negro Interest Group Strategies," Urban
        Affairs 4: 1 (September, 1968), 26-38.

5103.   Banfield, Edward C. Politics, Planning and the Public
        Interest: The Case of Public Housing in Chicago. Glencoe,
        Illinois: Free Press, 1955.

5104.   Barresi, Charles M. and John H. Linquist. "The Urban
        Community: Attitudes Toward Neighborhood and Urban Renewal,"
        Urban Affairs Quarterly 5: 3 (March, 1970), 278-290.

5105.   Beauregard, Robert A. and Briavel Holcomb. "Enterprise Zones:
        The Non-Manipulation of Economic Space," Urban Geography;
        1984, 14-22.

5106.   Beilson, Roge. Recommendations to Promote Racial Integration
        in Housing. New York: New York Planned Communities, 1968.

5107.   Bell, D.A. "Affirmative Discrimination: Ethnic Inequality and
        Public Policy A Review of Glazer," Emory Law Journal 25
        (February 1976), 4-19.

5108. Bensman, Joseph and Emanuel Tobier. "Anti-Poverty Programming: A Proposal." Urban Affairs Quarterly 1:1 (September 1965), 54-65.

5109. Brimmer, Andrew F. "Can Enterprise Zones Work?" Black Enterprise 11:8 (1981), 71.

5110. Buchanan, Jeffrey D. "Urban Renewal in DeSoto-Carr: Citizen Participation Comes of Age." Urban Law Annual (1970), 103-132.

5111. Burges, Ernest W. "Social Planning and Race Relations." In Jitsuichm Masuaka and Preston Valien (eds.) Race Relations Problems and Theory. Chapel Hill, North Carolina: University of North Carolina Press, 1961, 4-10.

5112. Bush, Gordan. An Analysis of the First Year Action Prograam of the East St. Louis Model City Program. Master's Thesis, Southern Illinois University, Edwardsville, 1971.

5113. Catlin, Robert A. "An Analysis of the Community Development Black Grant Program in Nine Florida Cities, 1975-1979," Urban and Social Change Review 14:1 (1981), 3-11.

5114. Canter, Donald. "How Negro Removal Became Black Renewal." City: Magazine of Urban Life and Environment 4:3 (October-November 1970), 54-59.

5115. Canter, Donald. "What Is This Thing Called Urban Growth Policy?" City: Magazine of Urban Life and Environment 4:2 (August-September 1970), 31-32.

5116. Carleton, Mark T. "The Politics of the Convict Lease System in Louisiana, 1888-1901." Louisiana History (Winter 1967), 5-26.

5117. "City Planning and the Riot Torn City." Planning (1968), 19-32.

5118. Cloward, Richard A. and Frances F. Piven. "Corporate Imperialism for the Poor." The Nation 205:12 (October 16, 1967), 11-19.

5119. Collazo, Robert G. "Enterprise Zones: Trickle Down in the Big Cities?" Black Enterprise 12:12 (1982), 50-54.

5120. Comptroller General of the United States. HUD Needs to Better Determine Extent of Community Block Grants' Lower Income Benefits. Washington, D.C.: U.S. General Accounting Office, 1982.

5121. Crecine, John P. and Louis H. Masotti. Financing the Metropolis. Beverly Hills: Sage, 1970.

5122. Cross, Theodore L. Black Capitalism: Strategy for Business in the Ghetto. New York: Atheneum, 1971.

5123.   Curtis, Richard F. et al. "Prejudice and Urban Social
        Participation." American Journal of Sociology 73 (September
        1967), 235-45.

5124.   Darden, Joe T. and A.S. Tabachneck, "Algorithm 8: Graphic and
        Mathematical Descriptions of Inequality, Dissimilarity,
        Segregation, or Concentration," Environment and Planning 12
        (1980), 227-234.

5125.   Davis, James W. "Decentralization, Citizen Participation, and
        Ghetto Health Care," American Behavioral Scientist 15
        (September 1971), 94-107.

5126.   Davis, Lenwood G. and Winston Van Horne. "The City Renewed:
        White Dream-Black Nightmare?" Black Scholar 7:3 (1975), 2-9.

5127.   Denton, Herbert H. "Battle Lines Drawn Over Plan to End City
        Grant Program," Washington Post (February 10, 1981), 112.

5128.   Dobbratz, Joan. An Analysis of the Southwest Urban Renewal
        Project Area in Terre Haute, Indiana. Master's Thesis, Indiana
        State University, 1967.

5129.   Dudas, John L. and David B. Longbrake. "Problem and Future
        Directions of Residential Integration: The Local Application of
        Federally Funded Programs in Dade County, Florida." Southeast
        Geographer 11:2 (1971), 157.

5130.   Dunlap, David. "South Bronx Neighbors Hold Devastation at
        Bay," New York Times (October 10, 1982), 54.

5131.   Eisenberg, Lawrence D. "Uncle Tom's Multi-Color Subdivision -
        Constitutional Restrictions on Racial Discrimination by
        Developers." Cornell Law Review 53 (January 1968), 314-324.

5132.   Evans, Bruce. "Elwood Park and Urban Renewal." Field Notes,
        Discussion Paper 3 (1971), 50-53.

5133.   Fainstein, Norman and Susan Fainstein. Urban Political
        Movements: The Search for Power by Minority Groups in American
        Cities. Englewood Cliffs: N.J.: Prentice-Hall, 1974.

5134.   Fantini, Mario, et al. Community Control and the Urban School.
        New York: Praeger, 1969.

5135.   Frieden, Bernard J. and Nash Williams (eds.). Shaping and
        Urban Future: Essays in Memory of Catherine Bauer Wurster.
        Cambridge: MIT Press, 1968.

5136.   Frieden, Bernard J. and James Peters. "Urban Planning and
        Health Services: Opportunities for Cooperation," Journal of the

American Institute of Planners 36 (March 1970), 82-95.

5137. Fusfeld, Daniel R. The Economics of the Urban and Racial Problem. New York: Holt, Rinehard & Winston, 1972.

5138. Gans, Herbert. "Planning and the Social Life: Friendship and Neighbor Relations in Suburban Communities," Journal of the American Institute of Planners 27 (1961): 134-140.

5139. Gergen, David R. "Renewal in the Ghetto: A Study of Residential Rehabilitation in Boston's Washington Park." Harvard Civil Rights-Civil Liberties Law Review 3 (Spring 1968), 243-310.

5140. Gold, Stephen F. "Comprehensive Health Planning and Consumers of Health Serices," Journal of Urban Law 48 (1970-71), 279-290.

5141. Greenstone, J. David and Paul E. Peterson. Race and Authority In Urban Politics: Community Participation and the War on Poverty. New York: Russell Sage Foundation, 1973.

5142. Greer, Scott. Urban Renewal and American Cities: The Dilemma of Democratic Intervention. Indianapolis: Bobbs-Merrill, 1965.

5143. Grier, Eunice. Civil Rights and Land Development: Background on Housing for Negroes in Cleveland, Ohio. Washington, D.C.: Washington Center for Metrpolitan Studies, 1966.

5144. Grigsby, William G. Housing Markets and Public Policy. Philadelphia: University of Pennsylvania Press, 1963.

5145. Haar, Charles Monroe. Housing the Poor in Suburbia: Public Policy at the Grass Roots. Cambridge, Massachusetts: Ballinger, 1973.

5146. Haar, Charles Monroe and D.S. Iatridis. Housing the Poor in Suburbia: Public Policy at the Grass Roots. Cambridge, Massachusetts: Ballinger, 1974.

5147. Harrison, Bennett. Urban Economic Development: Suburbanization, Minority Opportunity and the Condition of the Central City. Washington, D.C.: The Urban Institute, 1974.

5148. Harries, Keith D. An Analysis of Inter-Ethnic Variations in Commercial Land-Use in Los Angeles. Ph.D. Dissertation, University of California, Los Angeles, 1969.

5149. Helper, Rose. Racial Policies and Practices of Real Estate Brokers. Minneapolis: University of Minnesota Press, 1969.

5150. Henderson, Lenneal J. "Energy Urban Policy and Socio Economic Development," Urban League Review (Winter 1978), 9.

5151. Hill, Robert B. _Economic Policies and Black Progress Myths and Realities._ Washington, D.C.: National Urban League, Research Department, 1981.

5152. Hill, Robert B. "The Illusion of Black Progress." _Social Policy_ (November-December 1978), 14-25.

5153. Hill, William E. "Racial Restrictive Housing Covenants." _Opportunity_ (1946), 119-21.

5154. Hogan, Lloyd. _The State of the Black Economy: Issues in Community Revitalization._ New Brunswick, N.J.: Transaction Books, 1980.

5155. Holcomb, Briavel et al. "Blacks and Urban Revitalization: Winners or Losers?" in R.A. Obudho (ed.) _Afro-Americans and the City._ Albany, New York: State University of New York Press, 1984.

5156. Holcomb, Briavel and Robert A. Beauregard. _Revitalizing Cities._ Washinton, D.C.: The Association of American Geographers, 1981.

5157. Holleb, Doris B. _Social and Economic Information for Urban Planning: Its Selection and Use._ Chicago: Center for Urban Studies, University of Chicago, 1969.

5158. Jencks, Christopher, et al. _Inequality: A Reassessment of the Effect of Family and Schooling in America._ New York: Basic Books, 1972.

5159. Jenkins, Michael A. and John W. Sheperd. "Decentralizing High School Administration in Detroit: An Evaluation of Alternative Strategies of Political Control." _Economic Geography_ 48 (January 1972), 95-106.

5160. Kaplan, Samuel. "Yonkers Debates Slum Integration: Renewal Plan Would Shift Poor to City Projects in Top Residential Areas." _New York Times_ (May 5, 1965), B 1-19.

5161. Kelley, Joseph B. "Racial Integration Policies of the New York City Housing Authority, 1958-1961." _Social Service Review_ 38 (June 1964), 153-162.

5162. Lang, Michael. _Gentrification amid Urban Decline: Strategies for America's Older Cities._ Cambridge: Ballinger, 1982.

5163. Lepper, Mark H., et al. "Approaches to Meeting Health Needs of Large Poverty Populations," _American Journal of Public Health_ 57 (July 1967), 1153-1157.

5164. Lepper, Mark H., et al. "Health Planning for the Urban Community: The Neighborhood Health Center," _Public Welfare_ 25

(April 1967), 141–149.

5165.   Levin, Melvin R.   "Planners and Metrpolitan Planning," Journal of the American Institute of Planners 33:2 (March, 1967), 5–10.

5166.   Lowe, Jeanne R.   Cities in a Race With Time: Progress and Poverty in America's Renewing Cities.   New York: Random House, 1967.

5167.   Lowi, Theodore J.   "Apartheid U.S.A.: Federally Assisted Urban Redevelopment: A Blueprint for Segregation."   Trans-action 7 (February 1970), 32–39.

5168.   Marcus, Matityahu.   "Racial Composition and Home Price Changes: A Case Study."   Journal of American Institute of Planners 34 (September 1968),   334–338.

5169.   Marcuse, Peter.   "Black Housing: A New Approach for Planners."   Connection 6 (1969),   95–125.

5170.   Marcuse, Peter.   "Integration and the Planner."   Journal of the American Institute of Planners 35 (March 1969), 113–117.

5171.   Maslen, Sidney.   "Relocation in the Southeastern Region During the Process of Urban Renewal."   Phylon 19 (Spring 1958), 70–71.

5172.   Masters, S.H.   Black-White Income Differentials: Empirical Studies and Policy Implications.   New York: Academic Press, 1975.

5173.   Mayer, Albert.   The Urgent Future: People, Housing, City, Region.   New York: McGraw-Hill, 1967.

5174.   McNeil, William H. and Ruth S. Adams.   Human Migration: Patterns and Policies.   Boston: American Academy of Arts and Science, 1978.

5175.   Metcalfe, Ralph H.   "Chicago Model Cities and Neocolonization," The Black Scholar 1:6 (April 1970), 23–30.

5176.   Metro Denver Urban Coalition.   Training for Action Strategies Against Displacement.   Denver: Report of Technical Assistance Workshop of National Urban Coalition, 1980.

5177.   "Metropolitan Segregation,"   Scientific American (October 1957), 33–41.

5178.   Meyer, David R.   "Implications of Some Recommended Alternative Urban Strategies for Black Residential Choice."   In Harold M. Rose (ed.) Geography of the Ghetto: Perspetives in Geography Vol. II.   Dekallb, Illinois: Northern Illinois University Press, 1972.

5179. Meyerson, Martin. _Housing People and Cities._ New York: McGraw-Hill, 1962.

5180. Meyerson, Martin and Edward C. Banfield. _Politics, Planning and the Public Interest: The Case of Public Housing in Chicago._ Glencoe, Illinois: Free Press, 1955.

5181. Milgram, Morris. _Developing Open Communities._ New York: Association Press, 1963.

5182. Millspaugh, Martin and Gurney Brechonfeld. _The Human Side of Urban Renewal._ New York: Ives Washburn, 1960.

5183. Mitchell, Robert E. and Richard Smith. "Race and Housing: A Review and Comments on the Context and Effects of Federal Policy." _Annals of the American Academy of Political and Social Science 441_ (January 1979): 168-185.

5184. Moran, Sara. _Can Enterprise Zones Work For Us?_ Washington, D.C.: National Urban League, 1982.

5185. Morten, Baker E. "Urban Renewal Axed." _Washington Afro-American_ (February 6, 1965), 122-4.

5186. Munski, Douglas C. and John V. O'Loughlin. "Housing Rehabilitation in the Inner City: A Comparison of Two Neighborhoods in New Orleans," _Economic Geography_ 55 (1979), 1-20.

5187. Murray, R.F.J. "The Ethical and Moral Values of Black Americans and Population Policy." In R.M. Veatch (ed.) _Population Policy and Ethics: The American Experience_. New York: Irvington, 1977, 197-209.

5188. Myers, Phyllis. "Boston's METCO: What To Do Until the Solution Arrives." _City: Magazine of Urban Life and Environment_. 5:1 (January-February 1971), 80-82.

5189. Myers, Phyllis. "What's Happening to My World?" _City: Magazine of Urban Life and Environment_ 4:1 (August-September 1970), 60-62.

5190. New York Times. "Georgetown: A Proposal for Secession." _New York Times_ (March 3, 1983), A22.

5191. Northwood, L.K. "The Threat and Potential of Urban Renewal," _Journal of Intergroup Relations_ 2:2 (Spring 1961), 1-10.

5192. Northwood, Lawrence K. _Urban Development-Implications for Social Welfare._ New York: International Conference of Social Work, 1966.

5193. O'Loughlin, John and Dale A. Berg. "The Election of Black

Mayors, 1960 and 1973." Annals of American Political Academy of Social Science 67:2 (1977), 223-238.

5194. Orfield, Gary. Toward a Strategy for Urban Integration: Lessons in School and Housing Policy from Twelve Cities. New York: Ford Foundation, 1981.

5195. Puma, John J. "Improving Negro Employment in Boston," Industrial Management Review 8 (Fall 1966), 37-45.

5196. Rapkin Chester. Market Experience and Occupancy Patterns in Interracial Housing Developments. Philadelphia: Institute for Urban Studies, University of Pennsylvania, 1964.

5197. Rapkin, Chester. "Price Discrimination Against Negroes in the Rental Housing Market." Essays in Urban Land Economics. Berkeley, California: University Graduate School of Business Administration, 1966, 323-345.

5198. Ravitz, Mel J. "Effects of Urban Renewal on Community Racial Patterns." Journal of Social Issues 13 (October 1957), 38-49.

5199. Richard, C. and J. Rowe. "Restoring a City: Who Pays the Price?" Working Papers for a New Society 4:4 (1977) 54-61.

5200. Rose, Harold M. "The Development of an Urban Subsystem: The Case of the Negro Ghetto." Annals of the Association of American Geographers 60:1 (1970), 1-17.

5201. Rose, Harold M. Social Processes in the City: Race and Urban Residential Choice. Washington, D.C.: Association of American Geographers, 1969.

5202. Rose, Harold M. "The Spatial Development of Black Residential Subsystems." Economic Geography. 48:1 (1972), 43-65.

5203. Rossi, Peter H. and Robert A. Dentler. The Politics of Urban Renewal - the Chicago Findings. New York: The Free Press, 1961.

5204. Rouse, James W. and Nathaniel S. Keith. No Slums in Ten Years, A Workable Program Urban Renewal. Report to the Commissioners of the District of Columbia, Janury, 1955.

5205. Sereno, Julian. "Enterprise Zones," Chicago Journal 1 (April 21, 1982), 6-7.

5206. Schuchter, Arnold. White Power, Black Freedom; Planning the Future of Urban America. Boston: Beacon Press, 1968.

5207. Sieverding, Herman C. Displacement in Reinvestment Neighborhoods. Cincinnati: Senior Project, Department of Urban Planning, University of Cincinnati, 1979.

5208. Sikes, James R. "Newburgh Divided in Urban Renewal Plan: Integration of Negroes is Key Issue." New York Times (May 7, 1965), 37.

5209. Silvers, Arthur H. "Urban Renewal and Black Power." American Behavioral Scientist 12 (March 1968), 43-46.

5210. Solomon, Sandra. Neighborhood Transition Without Displacement: A Citizen's Handbook. Washington, D.C.: National Urban Coalition, 1979.

5211. Specht, Harry. "Community Development in Low-Income Areas." Social Work II (October 1966), 78-91.

5212. Tobin, James. "On Improving the Economic Status of the Negro," Daedalus. (Fall 1965), 1-10.

5213. Tomlinson, T.M. "Development of a Riot Ideology Among Urban Negroes." American Behaviorial Scientist 11 (March 1968), 27-31.

5214. Tucker, Sterling. Why the Ghetto Must Go. New York: Public Affairs Committee, 1968.

5215. U.S. Senate. Problems of Dislocation and Diversity in Communities Undergoing Neighborhood Revitalization Activity. Hearings before the Committee on Banking, Housing and Urban Affairs, July 7 and 8. Washington, D.C.: Government Printing Office, 1977.

5216. U.S. Congress. Joint Economic Committee. Structural Unemployment and Urban Policy. Hearing Before the Subcommittee on Economic Growth and Stabilization of the Joint Economic Committee, 95th Congress, 2nd Session, March 17, 1978. Washington, D.C.: Government Printing Office, 1978.

5217. U.S. Department of Commerce, Minority Business Development Agency. New Directions: Goals, Strategies, Programs. Washington, D.C.: Government Printing Office, 1982.

5218. U.S. Department of Housing, Office of Minority Business Enterprise. Progress of the Minority Business Enterprise Program 1973. Washington, D.C.: Government Printing Office, 1973.

5219. U.S. Department of Housing and Urban Development, Office of Fair Housing and Equal Opportunity. Minority Business Enerprise in HUD Programs Annual Report F.Y. 1978. Washington, D.C.: Government Printing Office, 1979.

5220. U.S. Department of Housing and Urban Development, Office of Policy Development Research. An Impact Evaluation of the Urban Development Action Grant Program. Washington, D.C.: Government

Printing Office, 1982.

5221. Van Horne, Winston A. (ed.) Ethnicity, Law and The Social Good: Volume II of The Ethnicity and Public Policy Series. Madison, Wisconsin: University of Wisconsin Press, 1983.

5222. Walker, Earl. The Impact of Urban Renewal of the Los Angeles Subcommunity of Sawtelle. Master's Thesis. University of California, Los Angeles, 1968.

5223. Watts Labor Community Action Committee. "New Hope for Watts." HUD Agenda, 3 (February 1967), 13-15.

5224. Watts, Lewis G. Attitudes Toward Moving of Middle-Income Negro Family Faces Urban Renewal. Boston: Massachussetts Department of Commerce and Development, 1965.

5225. Weaver, Robert C. "Planning for More Flexible Land Use." Journal of Land and Public Utility Economics. (February 1947), 29-41.

5226. Will, Robert and Harold G. Vatter. Poverty in Affluence: The Social, Political and Economic Dimensions of Poverty in the United States. New York: Harcourt, Brace & World, 1970.

5227. Williams, J. Allen. "The Effects of Urban Renewal Upon a Black Community: Evaluation and Recommendations." Social Science Quarterly 50 (December 1969), 713-722.

5228. Wilson, Margaret Bush. "Enterprise Zones: Assessing Their Impact on Minorities," Commentary 5:3 (1981) 15-17.

5229. Wilson, Robert L. "Liability of the City: Attitudes and Urban Development," in F. Stuart Chapin and Shirley Weiss (eds.) Urban Growth Dynamics. New York: Wiley, 1962, 20-30.

5230. Wolf, Eleanor and Charles N. Lebeaux. "On the Destruction of Poor Neighborhoods by Urban Renewal." Social Problems 15 (Summer 1967), 3-8.

5231. Wood, Elizabeth. A New Look at the Balanced Neighborhood: A Study and Recommendation. New York: Citizens Housing and Planning Council of New York, 1960.

5232. Woodbury, Coleman (ed.) The Future of Cities and Urban Redevelopment. Chicago: University of Chicago Press, 1953.

5233. Woofter, Thomas Jackson. "Southern Population and Social Planning." Social Forces 14 (October 1935), 18.

5234. Young, Whitney M. Beyond Racism: Building an Open Society. New York: McGraw-Hill, 1969.

5235. Zarembka, Arlene. "The Regional Housing Mobility Program: The Government's Solution to the Urban Crisis." <u>Housing Law Bulletin</u> 3 (May/June 1980), 10-15.

INDEX

A

Abajian, James de T., 0001, 0002
Abbot, Edith H., 2139
Abbot E.M., 1196
Abernathy, R., 1197
Abolition and Emancipation Literature, 0003
About Black Americans, 0004
About 100 Books: Getaway to Better Group Understandings, 0005
Abrahams, Roger D., 4248, 4249
Abrams, Charles, 2140, 2851, 2852, 2853, 2855, 4250
Abudu, Margaret J.G., 3688
Abu-Laban, Baha, 4275
Acevedo, Z., 1198
Achembaum, Andrew, 1111
Ackerman, Susan Rose, 2856
Acquisitions in Black Material, 0006
Adair, Charles H., 2149
Adair, Thelma, 0007
Adams, Arvil V., 3689
Adams, John B., 3690
Adams, John S., 4251
Adams, Ruth S., 5174
Adams, Samuel C., 4252
Adams, Samuel L., 2857
Adamson, John C., 2142
Adamson, John S., 2141, 2721
Addo, Linda D., 0008
Adger, Robert M., 0009, 0010
Adinarayaniah, S.P., 0011
Adjei-Barwuah, Barfour, 2143, 3691, 3692
Adler, Patricia, 0012
Adrian, Charles R., 3693

Aery, William A., 0013
Affirmative Discrimination, 5099
African Bibliographic Center, 0014
Africans in the United States, 0015
Afro-American, 0016
Afro-American and Mexican American Bibliography, 0017
Afro-American Bibliography, 0018
Afro-American Books for Children, 0022
Afro-American Culture and History, 0019
Afro-American Encyclopedia, 0020
Afro-American History Week, 0021
Afro-American 1553-1906, 0023
Afro-American Resource of the El-Camino College Library, 0024
Afro-American Studies, 0025, 0026
Agelusto, M., 0027
Agrocs, S., 4094
Agresti, B.F., 4253
A Guide to Negro Periodical Literature, 0028
Airall, Jackqueline, 0029
Aiken, Richard S., 0618
Akeroyd, Richard, 0030, 0031, 0032
Akin, Edwards N., 2144
Akin, Joy, 0034
Alex, Nicholas, 2145
Alexander, Susan, 1328
Alexis, Marcus, 4095, 4256
Aldrich, Howard E., 3694, 3985
Alfred, Stephen J., 2858, 4096
Alienikoff, Alexander, 2859
Alilunas, Leo, 2146
Allard, Ursula, 0035
Allee, M.H., 0036
Allen, A., 2147
Allen, E.H., 0037
Allen, Irving Lewis, 0038
Allen, James Egert, 1199, 2148
Allen, Kathleen S., 0342
Allen, Louis L., 3695
Allen, Rodney F., 2149
Allen, Thomas H., 2150
Allen, Vernon L., 4257
Allison, Thomas W., 1200, 2151
Allport, Gordon W., 4258

All Winds Blow Free, 0034
Aloi, Frank, 2861, 2860
Alonso, W., 1201
Alston, John P., 2152
Altenderfer, Marion E., 1202
Altschuler, Alan A., 2153, 4259
American Academy of Political and Social Science, 4097
American All: An Intercultural Bibliography, 0051
American and Foreign Books and Articles Bearing on the Negro, 0039
American Association of Farmer's Institute Workers, 4216
American Jewish Committee, 0040
American Missionary Association Archives in Fisk University Library, 0041
American Studies Program, 0050
American Negro, 0046, 0047
American Negro and African Studies, 0043
American Negro: History and Achievement, 0044
American Negro in Contemporary Society, 0045
American Negro Reference Book, 1203
American Negro: Selected Bibliography, 0042
American Negro speaks to Young Americans, 0048
American Negro Writing, 0049
Amoroso, Doreen, 0052
Amos, P.E., 0053, 0054
Analytical Guide and Indexes, 0055, 0056, 0057
Anatomy of A Riot, 2154, 4260, 4261
Anchor, Shirley, 3696
Anderson, Barbara, 0058
Anderson, Bernard E., 4219
Anderson, E. Frederick, 5100
Anderson, J.E., 1204, 1205
Anderson, Marc B., 2155, 2862
Anderson, Martin, 5101
Anderson, Richard, 4262
Anderson, S.G., 1206
Anderson, Theodore R., 2156, 4263
Andrew, Ann, 0059
Andrews, Regina M., 0060

Anonymous, 1207, 1208, 1209, 1210, 1211, 1212, 1213, 1214, 1215, 1216, 1217, 1218, 1219, 1220, 1221, 1222, 1223
Another Negro Exodus to the North, 1224
Annotated Bibliography: Afro-American, Hispanio and Amerind, 0062
Ansley, Robert E., 0062
Anthony, Elizabeth V., 0063
Anthony, Ernestine, 0064
Aptheker, Herbert, 0065, 0066, 0067, 2157, 4264, 4265
Archibald, Helen A., 0068, 2158
A Report of Attitudes of Negroes in Various Cities, 2138
Arken, Charles S., 4254, 4255
Armbrister, Trevor, 3698
Armstrong Association of Philadelphia, 4098
Armstrong, B.K., 2443
Armstrong, Douglas, 0069
Armstrong, R.J., 1225
Arnold, Benjamin William, 2159
Arnold, C.B., 1226, 1227
Arter, Rhetta M., 2863
Arthur B. Spingarm Collection of Negro Authors, 0070
Ashby, William M., 2160, 2864
Ashe, C., 1228
Asher, Robert, 0071, 2161
Ashford, F.C., 0072
Asinot, E., 3699
Association for the Study of Negro Life and History, 0073
Astin, Alexander, 4266
Atelsek, Frank J., 2865
Atkins, H.D., 0074
Atkinson, Paul, 3697
Attah, E.B., 1229
Aug, R.G., 1230
Austin, D.F., 1396
Austins, Mary, 0075
Availability of Negro Source Material in Philadelphia, 0076

B

Baatz, Wilmer H., 0733
Babchuk, Nicholas, 2611, 4267
Babcock, Richard F., 2866

Bensman, Joseph, 4288, 5108
Bercouici, Konrad, 2173, 2174, 2175
Berg, Dale A., 5193
Berg, Irving, 2886
Berger, Stephen D., 2887
Bergman, E.M., 2888, 4101
Bergsman, Joel, 3708
Bergman, Peter M., 0108, 0109, 0110, 0111, 0112, 0113, 0114, 4289
Berk, Richard A., 3709, 3710, 4002
Berkowitz, William R., 3711
Bernard, Jessie, 1255, 4290
Berndt, Harry E., 3712
Bernstein, Betty J., 3713
Bernstein, I.M., 1256
Bernstein, Saul, 4291
Berry, Almedius B., 0115
Berry, Brian J.L., 1257, 2176, 2889, 2890, 2891, 2893, 3714, 3715, 4102, 4292, 4293
Berry, Edwin, 2177
Berry, Mary Francis, 4294
Berry, W.E., 1258
Berry, Theodore, 2178
Berson, Lenora E., 2179, 3716
Best, Jack L., 0116
Bethel, Elizabeth, 0117
Bethune, Mary McLeod, 2180
Bethen, Neil, 2181
Betsey, Charles, 5043
Bevel, James, 4295
Bezrry, Annie Laurie, 0663
Baxter, Camille, 0099
Bianchi, S.M., 1259
Bibliographic Guide to Black Studies, 0118, 0119, 0120, 0121, 0122, 0123, 0124, 0125
Bibliographical Suggestions for the Study of Negro History, 0126
Bibliography and Resource Guide, 0127
Biblography for Educational Integration, 0128
Bibliography for Educators, 0129
Bibliography of African and Afro-American Religions, 0130, 0131
Bibliography of Afro-American Culture, 0132

Bibliography of Bibliographies of Negro at Libraries of the University of Michigan, 0133
Bibliography of Black Studies, 0134, 0151
Bibliography of Books and Periodicals About Blacks at University of Kansas Library, 0135
Bibliography of Books By and About Negroes, 0138
Bibliography of Contributions of Negro Women to American Civilization, 0137
Bibliography of Doctoral Research on the Negro, 0138
Bibliography of Master's Thesis, 0139
Bibliography of Minorities, Blacks, and Mexican-Americans, 0140
Bibliography of Negro Life, 0141
Bibliography of Negro Nursing, 0156
Bibliography of Published Works of Robert C. Weaver, 0142
Bibliography of References and Resource Materials of Black Family Life, 0143
Bibliography of Required Materials for Teacher Training Centers, 0144
Bibliography of Resource Materials on American Negro, 0145
Bibliography of Sources on Blacks, 0146
Bibliography of Student Movements, 0147
Bibliography of Studies on Negroes, 0148
Bibliography of the Negro Press, 0149
Bibliography on Afro-American History and Culture, 0150
Bibliography on the Black American, 0160
Bibliography on Education of the Negro, 0152
Bibliography on Fair Employment Practice Law, 0153
Bibliography on Negroes, 0157
Bibliography on Negro Labor,

Blum, H.F., 1271
Blum, Zahara D., 0225, 0026, 1272
Blumberg, Leonard, 2198, 3728, 3897, 4104
Blume, Frank Reinhart, 4314
Blumer, Herbert, 0227
Blumfeld, Hans, 0228
Blumstein, B.A., 1273
Boal, F., 3404
Boddy, J.M., 1274
Bodnar, J.E., 1275, 1276, 1277, 1278, 4315
Boehnke, B., 0604
Boesel, David Paul, 3729, 3730, 3731, 3732
Bogen, David S., 2898
Boggs, James, 2199, 2200
Boggs, Vernon William, 2201
Bogue, Donald J., 1279, 1280, 1281, 1282, 1283, 1284, 2202, 2203, 2237, 3733
Bogue, Grant, 2204
Bohm, R.A., 1285
Bohrn, Harold, 0229
Bolan, Lewis, 0230
Boles, Alan, 2899
Boles, Nancy G., 0231
Bolner, James, 0232
Boner, Marian D., 0233
Bonacichi, E., 4316, 4317
Bonnett, Audrey W., 4318
Bontemps, Alan, 2900
Bontemps, Arna, 0234, 0235, 1286, 2205
Booher, D.E., 0236
Booker T. Washington, 0237
Books About Negro, 0238, 0239, 0240, 0241, 0242, 0243, 0244, 0245, 0246, 0247, 0248, 0249, 0250
Books on Minority Groups, 0251
Books Transcend Barriers, 0252
Boone, Dorothy Deloris, 0253
Booth, Robert S., 0254
Boskin, Joseph, 2206, 2207, 2208, 2209, 3734, 3735
Boswell, T.D., 2901
Boubel, Margaret, 0255
Bouknight, L. Marie, 0256
Boulding, Kenneth E., 2210
Bourdon, E. Richard, 4319
Bousefield, M.O., 1288

Bourgue, Linden Brookover, 4754
Bourne, J.P., 1287
Bowen, David Warren, 2902
Bowen, Donald R., 2604
Bowen, Harry W., 2211
Bowen, Louise D., 2212
Bowes, John Elliott, 2213
Bowles, G.K., 1289, 1692, 1693
Bowles, M.R., 0074
Boyce, Byrl N., 0257
Boyd, Sandra H., 0258
Bracey, John H., 3737
Brachet, Vivianne, 0259
Bracken, M.B., 1290
Bradburn, N.M., 2903, 2904
Bradley, F.J., 1291
Bradley, Gladyce Helene, 0260
Bradshaw, Barbara Robinson, 1502, 1503, 2905
Brandon, D.G., 1292
Branscomb, A.W., 2901
Bragaw, Donald H., 2214
Brandt, Lillian, 2215, 2216
Braun, Mary, 0261
Brawley, Benjamin, 0262, 4320
Brechonfeld, Gurney, 5182
Breckenridge, W.C., 1005
Breed, Warren, 1293
Breit, Marguerita, 0539
Brenner, Bernard, 2908, 4321
Breskiridge, Sophonisha Preston, 2907
Bressler, T., 1294
Breyfoyle, Donna, 0263
Brickman, W.W., 0264
Bridges, Hal, 0265
Bright, Thomas, 1230
Brignano, R.C., 0266
Brimmer, Andrew F., 0267, 4322, 4323, 5109
Brindley, Timothy, 2965
Brink, William, 4324
Brisbane, Robert H., 2217
Briscoe, Dorothy, 0268
Broadhead, Clare A., 0269
Brodber, Erna, 4325
Brookfield, H.C., 1296, 4326
Brooks, Alexander D., 0270
Brooks, Lester, 2677
Brooks, Michael P., 2218
Brooks, Thomas R., 2219
Broom, Leonard, 4327
Bronstein, E.S., 1295

0296, 0297, 0298
Camerota, Michael, 2248
Campbell, Agnes, 0299, 2249
Campbell, Angus, 4342
Campbell, Arthur A., 1316
Campbell, Byram, 4343
Campbell, Carlos C., 4107
Campbell, D.W., 0300
Campbell, M.V., 0301
Campbell, Rex R., 1317, 1318,
 1319, 1320, 1321, 1624, 1625,
 4344, 4345
Campbell, Robert, 3744
Canadian Black Studies
 Biliography, 0302
Canine, Helen, 0087
Canfield, Roger B., 3745
Canter, Donald, 5114, 5115
Capeci, Dominic Joseph, 2256
Caplan, Eleanor, 2925
Caplan, Nathan, 2251, 3746, 3747
Capouya, E., 0303
Cardinale, Susan, 0304
Carey, Elizabeth L., 0305
Carey, George W., 2252, 2253,
 2926, 3748
Carey, T.C., 2927
Carley, Judith, 0306
Carleton, Mark T., 5116
Carlos, Luis, 0307
Carlson, Alvar W., 0308
Carlson, David B., 2254, 2928,
 4346
Carlson, K., 0309
Carmela, Margaret, 0310, 0311,
 0312
Carney, M., 0313
Carpenter, Niles, 2255
Carper, Laura, 2929, 2930
Carr, Homer B., 3749
Carter, Bernard, 1322, 4347
Carter, Dan T., 2256
Carter, Donna K., 3250
Carter, Elmer A., 1323
Carter, Hugh, 1324
Carter, Perris M., 0314
Carter, Wilmoth A., 2257, 2258
Case, Fred E., 2259
Caselli, Ron, 0315
Casetti, Emilio, 2995, 4123,
 4398
Casey, Stephen C., 2931
Cassity, Michael J., 4348

Casstevens, T.W., 2932, 2933,
 3035
Catalogue of Books, 0317
Catalogue of Heartman Negro
 Collection, Catalog of, 0321
Catalogue of Negro Collections,
 0319
Catalogue of Old Slave Mart
 Museum and Library, 0320
Catalogue of Publications, 0318
Catalogue of the Special Negro
 and African Collection, 0322
Cates, Willard, 1325
Catlin, Robert A., 5113
Causes of Chicago Race Riot,
 2260
Cayton, Horace R., 2261, 2352,
 2934, 2935, 3782
Cervantes, Alfonson J., 3750
Citizen's Housing Council of New
 York, 2940
City Planning and the Riot Torn
 City, 5117
City-Wide Citizen's Committee on
 Harlem, 2270, 2941
Chabot, Marion J., 1326
Chachere, Bernadette P., 4349
Chambers, Bradford, 4350
Chambers, Frederick, 0323
Champion, P., 1327
Chapman, Abraham, 0326
Changing Patterns of the Negro
 America, 0325
Chandler, Sue, 0324
Charities, 2262
Charles, Alan, 1328
Chase, Helen C., 1329, 1330,
 1331, 1415
Chasteen, R.R., 1332
Cheatham, Mary L., 0327
Cherry, Frank E., 2263
Chicago Afro-American Union
 Analytic Catalogue, 0328
Chicago, City of, 2264, 2265,
 2266, 2936, 4351, 4352
Chicago Race Riot, 2267
Chisholm, Shirley, 3751
Chitoka, Richard A., 2268
Chobanian, Peter, 0329
Christams, Walter, 0330
Christensen, Carol, 0331
Christensen, David E., 4353
Christian, Charles M., 2269,

Congress of Industrial Organization, 2958
Conley, Paul B., 2300
Connally, Harold X., 3763, 4114
Connecticut, State of, 2959, 2960, 4115
Connery, Robert H., 2301
Conover, Helen F., 0355, 0356
Contant, Florence, 0357
Conant, R.R., 3862
Contemporary Negro, 0358
Conroy, Jack, 1286, 1287, 2900
Conzen, Kathleen Nelis, 4374
Cook, Katherine M., 0359
Cooke, A.L., 0360, 0361
Cooper, A.J., 1347
Cooper, John L., 3764
Cooper, Gary Douglas, 2961
Conzen, Kathleen Neils, 4351
Corsi, Jerome R., 2605
Cordasco, Francesco, 0362
Corkey, E., 4375
Cornwell, Sophy, 0363
Cortese, Charles F., 2962, 4376, 4377
Coser, Lewis A., 4378, 4379
Cosner, Eugene D., 2963
Cottingham, Clement, 2302
Cottingham, Phoebe H., 2303, 2964, 4116, 4180
Cottingham, Phoebe M., 4357
Couper, Mary, 2965
Courant, Paul J., 2304, 4381
Courant, Paul N., 2966, 2967, 2968, 4358
Courts and Coercion, 2969
Cowgill, Donald D., 2305, 2306, 2970, 2971, 2972, 2973, 4117
Cowgill, Mary S., 2973
Cowhig, James D., 1348, 4382
Cowles, Wylda, 1349
Cox, D.C., 4383, 4384
Cox, Oliver, C., 1350
Coyers, James E., 2307
Craig, Tom, 2746
Craig, William, 4385
Craigie, David William, 1351, 2308, 2309, 2974
Craven, Erma C., 1352
Crawford, Thomas J., 3765
Crawthier, Beatrice, 1202
Crayton, James E., 0364
Crecine, John P., 5121

Cressey, Paul F., 2310
Crevelling, Harold F., 2311, 2312
Crew, Spencer R., 2313
Crisis on Black and White, 0365, 0366
Crockett, Norman L., 2314
Cromwell, John W., 0367
Cromein, F., 3068, 3092
Crosby, Alexander L., 2315, 2975, 2976
Cross, Theodore L., 5122
Crossland, William A., 2316, 4386
Crouch, Barry A., 0368
Crouthamel, James L., 2317
Crouchett, Lawrence, 0369, 0370
Crow, Jeffrey, 4387
Crowe, Charles, 2318, 2319
Crumb, Laurence N., 0371
Crump, Charles, 2320
Cull, John G., 3848
Culture and Historical Contributions of American Minorities, 0372
Culver, Lowell W., 4118
Cummings, John, 1353
Cuomo, Mario, 2977
Currant, Barbara W., 2321
Current Books About Negroes, 0373, 0374
Curry, Prudence L., 0375
Curtis, C. Michael, 2322
Curtis, Richard, 5123
Curtis, Thomas B., 2323, 4388
Cushman, Marc, 0310
Cushman, William Mitchell, 0375, 0376, 2324
Cutler, W.B., 1355
Cutright, P., 1356, 1357, 1556, 1613
Curry, James P., 1354
Cybrinsky, Roman A., 2978, 4389
Czaja, Ronald, 2325

D

Daams, Gerrit, 2979
Dabney, Lillian Gertrude, 2326
Dabney, Wendell P., 2327
Dahlke, H.O., 4390
Dalquist, Janet A., 0377

Daliwal, M.S., 1358
Dalva, Harry M., 0378
Daily, E.F., 1360
Damerell, Donald O., 4119
D'Amico, R.J., 4970
Damon, A., 1360
Danaella, Rose Decarlo, 2328
Danchik, K.M., 2114
Dancy, J.C., 1361
Dandekar, D.P., 1283
Daniel, Eleanor Murphy, 0379
Daniels, Belinda S., 0425
Daniels, Charles B., 2980, 2981
Daniels, Douglas H., 2329
Daniels, John, 2330
Danielson, M.N., 2331, 2982
Danielson, Michael, 4120
Dannenbaum, Jed, 4391
Dannett, Sylvia G.L., 0382
Daniel, Walter C., 0380
Daniels, Marionette S., 3988
Danner, Vinnie M., 0381
Darden, Joe T., 0383, 0384,
    2983, 2984, 2985, 2986, 2987,
    2988, 2989, 2990, 2991, 2992,
    2993, 2994, 3767, 3768, 3769,
    3770, 3771, 4121, 4392, 4393,
    4394, 5124
Darity, W.W., 1362, 1363, 1365,
    1366, 1995, 1996
Darney, P.D., 1367, 1368
Davenport, Frances Garron, 4395
Davies, Shane, 2332, 2333, 2334,
    3772
Davidson, R.A., 1918
Davis, Allison, 4396
Davis, C.S., 1369, 1370
Davis, D., 1371
Davis, David B., 4397
Davis, DeWitt, 2995, 4123, 4398
Davis, F. James, 2996
Davis, George, 4399
Davis, Jane E., 2998, 4400
Davis, John P., 0385, 4401
Davis, J.T., 2997
Davis, James W., 3773, 5125
Davis, Lenwood G., 0386, 0387,
    0388, 0389, 0390, 0391, 0392,
    0393, 0394, 0395, 0396,
    0397, 0398, 0399, 0400, 0401,
    0402, 0403, 0404, 0405, 0406,
    0407, 0408, 0409, 0410, 0411,
    0412, 0413, 0414, 0415, 0416,

0417, 0418, 0419, 0420, 0421,
    0422, 0423, 0424, 0425, 0426,
    0427, 0466, 0644, 5126
Davis, Morris E., 0428
Davis, Nathaniel, 0429
Davis, R., 1372, 1373, 1374
Davis, Susan E., 0430
Davis, Webster D., 1611
Davison, R.B., 2999
Davison, Ruth A., 0431
Dawkins, Marvin, 1441
Dawson, John A., 0432
Day, C.B., 1375, 4402
Day, Judy, 4403
Daymont, Thomas N., 1376, 1377,
    4404
Deahn, Jean, 0433
Deakin, Nicholas, 3000
DeAre, Diana, 4177, 4198
Death, Colin Edward, 2335
Deasy, L.C., 1378
DeFriese, Gordon H., 3001
Degler, Carl R., 4405
Delaney, N.J., 3085
Delaney, Paul, 4124, 4125
DeLaubenfels, David J., 1379
Delcampo, R.L., 1380
DeLong, Gordon F., 4406
Demeny, P., 1381
Democracy Unlimited for American
    Minority, 0434
Dempsey, Travis J., 3002
Dengel, Ray E., 0435
Denham, Bernard J., 0436
Denton, John H., 3003, 3004
Denton, Herbert H., 5127
Denver, Robert A., 5203
Deodene, Frank, 0437
Department of Social Relations,
    University of Johns Hopkins,
    4407
Deskins, Donald R., 0438, 1382,
    2336, 2337, 2338, 3005, 3006,
    3007, 3774, 3775, 4126, 4408,
    4409, 4410
Detroit, City of, 2342
Detroit Bureau of Government
    Research, 2341
DeVeaux, Diane, 0439
Development of Open Occupancy
    Laws, 3011
DeVise, Pierre, 2343, 4127, 4128
Deutsch, Morton, 3008, 3009,

DuToit, Brian M., 2363
Dutton, Penny, 0492
Dvorkin, Bettifae E., 0493
Dworaczek, Marian, 0069, 0263, 0494
Dworkin, Rosalind J., 3028
Dyce, Cedric, 4442
Dyer, D.R., 1397
Dynes, Russell R., 2365, 2366
Dytkoff, E.F., 3029

E

Eason, V.T., 0495
East St. Louis Riots, 2367
Eaton, Elsie M., 0496
Eblen, J.E., 1398, 1399
Eckard, E., 1400, 1401
Economic Causes of the Negro Exodus, 1402
Edel, Matthew, 3785
Edelman, M.W., 1403
Editors of Ebony, 0497
Edmonds, Helen G., 4443
Edmonson, Munro, 4883
Edwards, G. Franklin, 1404, 1405, 1406, 1407
Edwards, Otis B., 4444
Edwards, Ozzie L., 2368, 3029,3780
Edwards, Paul K., 2369
Eggers, Frederick J., 3031
Eiben, Crowell, 3787
Eichenbaum, J.J., 1408, 2370
Eichler, Edward P., 3032
Eisinger, P.K., 2371
Eisenberg, Lawrence D., 3033, 4134, 5131
Eitelberg, Mark, 4298
Eklund, Kent, 3651
Elam, Lloyd C., 3788
Eley, L.W., 3034, 3035
Elgie, Robert, 3789
Eliot, J.W., 1578
Ellifson, K.W., 1409
Elliot,, Deborah M., 3036
Ellis, C.A., 1410
Ellis, E.M.V., 0498
Elman, Richard M., 3761
Emlet, John T., 2373, 2374
Elwang, William Wilson, 2372
Emlen, J.T., 1411

Emmer, Pietere, 0499
Employment of Minorities, 0500
Engerman, S., 1412, 1413
Epstein, Abraham, 1414, 2375
Epstein, Benjamin R., 4467
Epstein, Irene, 0501
Equal Opportunity, 0502, 0503
Erbe, B.M., 3037
Erbies, Richard A., 3038
Erhard, C.L., 1415, 1416
Erickson, Rodney A., 2376
Erikson, Conrad, 0504
Eripps, Thomas R., 3790
Ernest R. Alexander Collection of Negroana, 0505
Ernst, Robert T., 0506, 0507, 0508, 1417, 2377, 4445
Erskine, H.G., 3039
Ervin, James M., 2378
Eshelman, Sylvia N., 0509
Ethnic and Cultural Studies, 0510
Ethnic and Racial Groups, 0511, 0512
Ettore, E.M., 3791
Etzkowtiz, Henry, 2380, 3794
Evans, Bruce, 5132
Evans, Jeanette, 4446
Evans, Lelia, 3792
Evans, Lola, 0513
Evans, Williams L., 2379, 3040, 3041
Evenson, Phillip, 2729, 3495
Everett, John R., 2381, 3793
Everly, Elaine C., 051, 0515
Ewer, Gibbs J., 1418
Exodus of Negro, 1419
Extensive Migrations of Negro Labor on the Southern States, 4447
Ezzard, N.V., 1420, 1421, 1422

F

Faber, Bernard Lewis, 1423
Fainstein, Norman, 2382
Fainstein, Susan, 2382
Fairbanks, Helen, 0514
Fair Housing Council of Metropolitan Washington, D.C.,

3042
Falk, David, 3043
Falk, R., 1424, 1488
Falk, William Warren, 4448
Family Planning Digest, 1425, 1426
Fantini, Mario, 2383, 5134
Farber, Evan, 0517
Farley, Dorothy Anne, 2384
Farley, Reynolds, 1427, 1428, 1429, 1430, 1431, 1432, 1433, 1434, 1435, 1436, 1437, 1438, 1439, 1440, 2385, 2386, 2387, 2388, 2389, 3044, 3045, 3046, 3144, 4135, 4136, 4137, 4438, 4450
Farrell, Gregory R., 1441, 3795
Farrell, Walter, 3791, 3797
Faucett, Melba, 0518
Faum, S., 3047
Fauset, Arthur Huft, 2390
Fawcett, B.E., 1442
Favor, Homer Eli, 2391, 3048
Faytell, David, 3505
Feagin, Joe R., 1443, 2393, 2394, 3798, 3799, 3800, 3801
Fearney, J., 0519
Featherman, David L., 1546, 4592
Federal Fair Housing Requirements, 3049
Federal Housing Administration, 3050
Federal Public Housing Authority, 3051, 3052, 3053, 3054
Federation of Neighborhood Association of Chicago, 3055
Fedink, Simon, 0520
Fein, Rashu, 4451
Felder, Henry E., 4139
Feldstein, Sylvan G., 2392
Fellows, Keith Donald, 4452
Femley, Dianna, 0509
Ferebee, J. Boulding, 1444
Ferguson, E.L., 2115
Ferguson, Homer L., 4453
Ferman, Louis A., 4454
Fersten, Elyce Z., 1445
Fifteen Topics on Afro-American, 0521
Fine, J., 3056
Finney, James E., 0522
Fire This Time, 0523

Firestone, J.M. 4458
Fisch, Maria Alba, 1446
Fishbein, Annette, 3059
Fischer, Roger A., 3057
Fischman, S., 1447
Fisher, Edith Maureen, 0524
Fisher, Ernest McKinley, 3058
Fisher, Constance, 1448
Fisher, Isaac, 1449
Fisher, James S., 4456
Fisher, Lloyd, 4457
Fisher, R.A., 0525
Fisher, Sethart, 4458
Fisk University, 0526, 0527
Fitzgerald, A., 2064
Flacon, Richard, 2898
Flanders, Teresa, 0528
Fleischmann, Al, 0529
Fleming, Harold, 1718, 4731
Fleming, Karl Henshaw, 2395
Fleming, Robert E., 0967
Fleming, Walter L., 1450
Flesher, Lorna, 0530
Fletcher, Ruth, 0531
Fligstein, Neil David, 1451, 1452
Flora, J. Hatley, 4387
Florin, John W., 4459
Fly, Jerry, 3060
Focus on Minorities, 0532
Fogelson, Robert M., 4460, 4461, 4462
Foley, Donald, 3061
Foley, Eugene P., 3802, 4403
Foote, Nelson N., 3062, 3063
Ford, James, 3064, 3803
Ford, K., 1453, 1454, 1455, 1456
Ford, Lawrence, 3804, 4465
Ford, W. Scott, 3001
Fordham, Monroe, 4466
Foreman, Paul B., 0533, 0622
Forman, E.M.S., 3065
Forman, Robert, 3805
Forrester, Washington B., 2570
Forster, Arnold, 4467
Fort, A.T., 1389
Fortson, B., 1457
Fortune, J. Thomas, 4468
Fossett, M., 4471
Foster, Arnold, 4440
Foster, B., 4467
Foster, Joanne, 0534
Foster, L.H., 4470

Foster, Madison, 3806
Foster, William E., 0535
Found, W., 0536, 0537
Fower, Phillip S., 4464
Fowler, Gary L., 1369, 1370, 2334, 3087
Fowler, Julian S., 0645
Frank, Iiona, 0539
Frank, Myrna E., 1663
Fralken, Laurie, 0538
Frankena, F., 0540
Frankel, Barbara, 3808
Franklin, Charles L., 4472
Franklin, E. Franklin, 2400, 2401, 2403, 2404, 2405, 2406, 2407, 2408, 2409, 2410, 2411, 2412, 2413
Franklin, Hardy Rogers, 2396
Franklin, Herbert M., 3043
Franklin, John Hope, 3066, 4407, 4473, 4474, 4475, 4476
Franklin, Vincent P., 3809
Frankowiski, R.F., 1248, 1249
Fraser, James H., 0541
Fraser, Lyn, 0542
Fraser, Walter J., 4477
Frazier, E. Franklin, 1457, 1458, 1459, 1460, 1461, 1462, 2397, 2398, 2399, 2400, 2401, 2402, 2403, 2404, 2405, 2406, 2407, 2408, 2409, 2410, 2411, 4478, 4479, 4480, 4481, 4482, 4483, 4484
Freeman, Edwards Barnes, 2412, 3299
Freeman, Leah, 0543
Freeman, Linton C., 3067, 3068, 4485
Freeman, John Esten, 1464
Freeman, M.G., 1465
Freeman, Richard, 4486
Freeman, Walter E., 1101
French, William P., 0437
Frey, Williams H., 1466, 1467, 2413, 3075, 3076, 4140, 4141
Fried, E.S., 1468
Fried, Marie, 3810, 4487
Fried, Joseph P., 3069
Frieden, Bernard, 2414, 3070, 3071, 4131, 5135, 5136
Friedman, Lawrence M., 3072, 3811
Friedman, Linton C., 3073

Friend, Bruce I., 0544
Friesma, H. Paul, 2415
Frisbie, W. P., 1469, 4488
Frishman, Joshua A., 2416
Frissell, Hollis Burke, 4489
From Negro Protest to Black Revolt, 0545
From Slavery to Protest, 0546
Frueh, Linda K., 2417
Frumkin, Robert M., 2418
Fugitt, G., 4720
Fujita, Kuniko, 4490
Fuller, Ross, 2419
Fuller, Sara, 0547
Fuller, Willie J., 0548
Fulton, Robert L., 3076
Funnye, Clarence, 3812, 3813, 4491
Furniss, W. Todd, 0547
Furstenberg, Frank F., 1470, 1471, 2420, 4492
Fusfeld, Daniel R., 2421, 3814, 3815, 3816, 5137

G

Gagala, Kenneth L., 0550
Gaines, Jean Foley, 4493
Gale, Stephen, 2422
Gallagher, Eugene Francis, 2423
Gallagher, Ursula M., 1472
Gallaway, Lowell E., 1473
Galle, Omar R., 1474
Gallop Poll, 3078
Galster, George C., 3077, 4494
Gamberg, Herbert Victor, 3079
Gans, Herbert J., 2425, 3817, 4495, 4490
Gannett, Henry, 4497
Gappert, Gary, 2424
Gardner, Burleigh B., 3818
Gardner, Henry L., 0551
Gardner, Major, 3080
Garity, John T., 3819
Garland, T.N., 1949
Garn, S.M., 1475
Garnett, B.P., 4498
Garofalo, C., 0552
Garonzik, Joseph, 4499
Garoogian, Andrew, 0553, 0554
Garst, Eleanor, 4500
Garvin, Charles H., 1476

Guzda, Henry P., 4558
Guzman, Jessie P., 0588, 0589, 0590, 0591

H

Haar, Charles Monroe, 3125, 3126, 3127, 4158, 4159, 5145, 5146
Hackman, Martha, 0592
Hadden, J., 0593
Hadden, Kenneth, 3128
Hahn, Harlan, 3801, 3835, 3836, 3837, 3838
Haigler, Virgie Biggins, 0594
Hale, C.B., 1518, 1519, 1686
Hall, Beverly, 0531
Hall, Charles E., 4560
Hall, Edward T., 4561
Hall, Woodrow Wadsworth, 0595
Haller, Elizabeth S., 0596
Halliday, Thelma Y., 0597, 0598
Halsey, Margaret, 4559
Hameleth, Margaret, 2494
Hammerz, Ulf, 3839, 3840, 3841, 3842
Hamilton, Charles V., 4562
Hamilton, C.H., 1739, 1740
Hamilton, C. Horace, 1520, 1521, 1522, 1523, 1524, 4563, 4750
Hammond, Agnes, 1053, 1054
Hammond, George, 4565
Hammond, Lily, 4564
Hampton and Negro Migration, 1525
Hampton Institute, 0599, 0600, 0601
Hampton, Robert L., 1526
Handlin, Oscar, 2463, 4566
Haney, C.A., 1527, 1528
Haney, Jane B., 2993
Hansberry, Lorraine, 4567, 4568
Hannerz, Ulf, 0602
Hansell, C.R., 3843, 3844
Hansen, Ann, 0603
Hansen, Carol, 0331, 3758
Hansen, Christian M., 1529
Hansen, P.O., 0604
Hansen, H., 1530
Hansen, K.A., 1715, 1716
Harding, Robert R., 3129
Hardy, Erle W., 4569

Hardy, John G., 4570
Hardy, Richard T., 3848
Hare, Nathan H., 1531, 4571
Harig, T.J., 1532
Harlem, 2464
Harmon, John, 2465, 3130
Haro, Robert P., 0605
Harper, Harriet, 0267
Harper, Roland M, 1533
Harper, Samuel, 4572
Hargood, Hutchines, 3845, 3846, 3847
Harrier, Keith D., 1534
Harries, Keith D., 2466, 2467, 2468, 5148, 2469, 5148
Harrington, Michael H., 2469, 4573
Harris, Addie, 0606
Harris, Abraham L., 1535, 4574, 4575, 4576
Harris, Donald J., 3849, 4577
Harris, Dwight N., 4578
Harris, H.L., 1536, 1537
Harris, Leroy, 1538, 2470, 3131, 4579
Harris, Louis, 4324
Harris, M., 4581
Harris, William, 1539, 2471
Harrison, Algea, 1540
Harrison, Bennett, 3615, 3850, 3851, 3852, 3853, 4160, 4582, 5038, 5147
Harrison, N., 3854
Hart, Hormel, 4583
Hart, John Fraser, 1541, 1542, 1543, 2472, 4161, 4584, 4585
Hartman, Chester W., 3132, 3133, 3959, 4586
Harvey, Cecil, 1014
Harvey, David, 3134, 3855, 3856, 4587
Harvey, Diane, 2473
Harwood, Edwin, 2474, 3857, 4588, 4589
Hastie, W.H., 3135
Hatch, John Wesley, 4596
Hatcher, Richard G., 2475
Hauser, Robert M., 1546, 4592
Hauser, Phillip M., 1544, 1545, 1590, 1666, 3020, 3136, 4132, 4441, 4491
Havrilesky, Catherine, 0607
Hawley, Amos H., 2476, 3137,

K

Lopez, Manual M. 3258
Loth, David, 1719, 4731
Loventhal, Milton, 0816
Lovett, Edward P., 3259
Lowe, Jeanne R., 2587, 5166
Lowi, Theodore J., 5167
Lowman, Ruth M., 2588
Lowenfels; Doris B., 0786
Lowry, Ira S., 2589, 3260
Lowry, Mark, 1720, 1721, 3261,
   4732, 4733, 4734
Lubeck, Dennis Russell, 2590
Luchferhand, E., 3926
Luna, Telesford W., 1722, 4735
Lunde, A.S., 1723, 1724
Lundgren, Terry Dennis, 1725,
   3927
Lupsha, Peter A. 2591
Lurre, Melvin, 1727, 4736
Lure of the North for Negroes,
   1726
Luster, Israel A., 2549
Lusterman, Seymour, 3738
Lyells, Ruby E. Stutts, 0787
Lyle, Jerolyn R., 2591
Lyles, Lionel D., 2592, 3262
Lynch, Hollis R., 2593
Lyons, S.R., 3928
Lytle, E.E., 0788

<h2 style="text-align:center">M</h2>

MacDonald, K.I., 3263
MacErbe, Brigitt, 3264
MacGee, Jane, 4737
Mack, Raymond W. 4738
Macken, Lynn, 0465
Mackler, Bernard, 2392, 3929
Macri, J.M., 1728
Madans, J.H., 1729
Madden, J. Patrick, 3265
Maddrell, Jane G., 0789
Magnani, R.J., 4696
Magubane, Bernard, 4739
Maher, C.A., 3266
Maher, T.M., 0818
Malcolm X Bibliographies in
   Black Studies, 0790
Malone, Erwin Lionel, 1730
Mandelbaum, Joel, 3267
Mandell, Richard, 3268
Manly, A.L., 2595

Manoni, Mary, 2596
Mansfield, Stephen, 0791
Marantz, Janet K., 3269
Marcoux, Charles R., 2862, 4096
Marcum, J.P., 1247
Marcus, Burton H., 3930
Marcus, Matityahu, 5168
Marcus, Edgar K., 1848
Marcuse, Peter, 2169, 3270, 5169
March, Sue, 2874
Mare, R.D.M., 1731
Margavio, Anthony Victor, 3270
Marge, Gail B., 2597, 4740
Mark, Ber, 3931
Mark, Mary Louise, 2598
Markley, Oliver Wendel, 4741
Marko, Gayle, 0647
Marr, Paul D., 4742
Marsh, Robert E., 1732
Marshall, Charles K., 1733
Marshall, Harvey H., 1734, 3272,
   3273, 4190, 4191, 4192, 4193
Marshall, Thurgood, 2599
Marston, Wilfred George, 2605
Martin, A.J., 3274
Martin, C.T., 0083, 0792
Martin, Marcine, 3932
Martin, Peter W., 3275
Martin, R. Lawrence, 0261
Martineau, William Henry, 2600
Marx, Gary Trade, 4743, 4744
Masleo, Sidney, 3276, 5171
Masnick, G.S., 1745
Mason, Elliot James, 2603
Mason, Peter F., 3902, 3933,
   3934
Masotti, Louis H., 0593, 2604,
   2605, 4746, 5121
Massa, Ann, 2602
Massey, David, 4745
Massey, S. Douglas, 3277, 3278
Masters, Deborah C., 0793, 0794
Masters, S.H., 5172
Matre, Marc, 3279
Matsumbo, S.K., 1731
Mather, F.L., 0795
Mathieson, Moira B., 0796
Matten, Margaret, 1098
Matthews, Diller G., 1735
Matthews, Donald P., 4747
Matthews, Miriam, 0797, 0798
Maurer, Neil, 1736, 1737
Maxey, Alva, 2606

Ohio, Central State College, One Hundred Years of Freedom, 0912
Okun, Bernard, 1797
O'Laughlin, John V., 3967, 5186, 5193
Olson, David J., 4724
Omari, Thompson, 2665
Onderdonk, Dudley, 0913, 3380
One Hundred Years of Freedom, 0914
One Year Later, 4814
O'Neill, Mara, 0298
O'Neil, S.C., 1518
Openshaw, H., 3381
Oppel, W., 1798
Ordinance Segregating Blacks and Whites into Separate Communities, 3382
Orfield, Gary, 3383, 5194
Orlanski, Harold, 2666
Orshansky, Mollie, 1799, 4206, 4815
Ory, H.W., 1800, 1801
Osborn, Donald D., 2667
Osbourne, Alfred E., 4277
Osgood, F.W., 0915
Oskison, J., 2668
Osofsky, Gilbert, 2669, 3968, 3969
Ottley, Roi, 2670
Overton, Holda, 0916
Ovington, Mary White, 4802, 4816
Oxley, Lawrence A., 0917

P

Paaswell, R.E., 2671
Paderanga, Cayetano Woo, 3384
Padbury, P., 0918
Padgett, Herbert R., 1803
Page, Alfred N., 3385, 3386
Paige, Jeffrey M., 2251, 3747
Pakter, J., 1804
Palen, J.J., 4817
Palley, Marian Leif, 3970
Palmer, Dewey, 1805
Palmer, E.N., 2672
Palmer, Stuart N., 3387
Palmieri, Victor H., 2673, 2674
Palmore, Erdman, 3388, 3389, 4818
Panker, G.J., 3971

Papper, Hermine L., 4875
Park, Woo-Suh, 3390
Parker, Elsie Smith, 4819
Parker, Franklin, 0919, 0920, 0921
Parker, Russell D., 2675
Parker, Seymour, 2676
Parks, Martha, 0922
Parris, Guichard, 2677
Parson, Talcott, 1806, 4820, 4821
Partridge, William, 3972
Pascal, Anthony H., 3391, 3392
Passel, Jeffrey, 3405
Pastorette, Tomma N., 0923
Pathak, Chittaranjan, 1807
Patterson;, John, 3393
Patterson, Orlando, 4822
Patterson, Pat, 4823
Patterson, William L., 1808, 2678
Paulus, Virginia, 3394
Payne, A.A., 4824
Payne, Ethel, 4825
Peabody, Patricia, 1004
Peabody, Ruth, 0924, 0925
Peace, Glenda, 0731
Peach, Ceri, 3395
Pearce, Diana M., 3396, 3397, 4826
Pearl, R., 1809, 1810, 1811
Pearlman, Kenneth, 3398, 4827
Pearlmutter, Jane, 0298
Peathe, Lisa R., 0926
Pederson, H.A., 4828
Peebles, Joan, 0927, 0928
Peet, R., 0929
Peirce, Neal R., 1812
Pendleton, William W., 4207
Percy, Charles H., 3973
Perdue, Charles L., 4829
Persky, Joseph J., 3888, 3889, 4830
Perlman, Laura, 2679
Perry, Pennie E., 1084
Perry, Welhelmina Elaine, 2680
Peters, James, 5136
Peters, Marie F., 4831
Peterson, Paul E., 5142
Petty, John, 1815
Pettyjohn, Leonard, 2683, 2684
Pettigrew, Thomas F., 0930, 1813, 1814, 2681, 2682, 3399,

3400, 3401, 4832, 4833, 4834
Pfifer, Alan, 1816
Pflieger, E.F., 0931
Phares, Donald, 3402
Philpet, Harriet O., 1821
Philliber, S.G., 1817, 1819
Philpel, Harriet F., 1822
Phillpott, Thomas L., 3974
Phillips, Barbara E., 4208
Phillips, Coy T., 1819
Phillips, J.H., 1820
Phillips, Kenneth E., 3338
Phillips, Myrtle R., 0932
Phillis, Susan, 0683
Phinazee, Annette Hoage, 0933, 0934
Phipps, Clarie A., 0935
Piccolo, Vincent, 0936
Pick, J.B., 1822
Pickens, Williams, 1457
Pier, Helen Louis, 0937
Pierce, P., 4209
Pierce, Odessa, 2917
Pilche, W.W., 0938
Pilson, V., 2208
Pinderton, J.R., 3496
Pinkerton, J.R., 3403
Pinto, Patrick R., 0937
Piven, Francis E., 2685, 2686, 4362, 5118
Pinkney, Alphonse, 1823
Pitche, W.W., 0927
Pleck, Elizabeth H., 1824, 1825
Ploski, H., 0940, 0941
Podlish, Phillip, 0942
Poe, Clarence H., 4835
Poehlman, Dorothy, 0943
Pohlman, Vernon C., 1826
Polenberg, Richard, 4836
Polgar, S., 1827
Police and Race Relations, 0944
Pollack, Newman F., 2687
Ponza, M., 1582
Pomeroy, R., 1828
Poole, Isaiah J., 4837
Poole, James, 0916
Poole, M.A., 3404
Pope, Hallowell, 1829
Popenoe, D., 3405
Popper, Robert J., 4838
Population Reference Bureau, 1830
Porter, Dorothy B., 0945, 0946,

0947, 0948, 0949, 0950, 0951, 0952
Porter, Jack N., 0953
Porter, Nancy, 0954
Porter, William A., 2688, 3406
Portes, A., 3407
Posselt, Jane, 0955
Postell, William D., 4839
Poston, Dudley, 3408
Potomac Institute, Washington, D.C., 3409, 3410
Poulos, Angela, 0804, 0956
Poverty-Rural Poverty and Minority Groups, 0957
Powdermaker, Hortense, 4840
Powe, Alphonso S., 2689
Powell, Ronald M., 0958
Powers, Mary G., 3411
Powledge, Fred, 4841
Pratt, W.F., 1831
Pred, Allan, 2690
Preliminary List of Resource Materials on Minority Groups, 0959
President's Conference on Home Building and Home Ownership, 3412
Presser, H.B., 1307, 1837, 1838, 1839
Pressley, Milton M., 0960
Preston, Clarence Johnson, 0961
Preston, M.B., 0962
Prevention and Control of Race Riots, 0963
Prewitt, Kenneth, 4687
Price, Daniel O., 0964, 1832, 1833, 1834, 1835, 1836, 2691, 4842
Price, Edward T., 4843, 4844, 4845, 4846, 4847, 4848
Price, Thomas, 2692, 4849
Price, William A., 3975
Price, William L., 3413
Prince George's County Memorial Library, 0965
Prior, Nancy B., 0836
Property Values, 3414
Prothro, James W., 4747
Provine, Dorothy, 2693
Provisional Bibliography on Slavery, 0966
Pruitt, Shirley, 2694
Prunty, Merle, 4850

Rhee, Jong M., 4872
Rhodes, Barbara, 0993
Rhodes, Lelia, 0994
Rica-Velasco, J., 3499
Rice, R.L., 3435
Rich, J.M., 3436
Rich, Richard, 3437
Rich, Spencer, 4873
Rich, Wilbur C., 4874
Rischaner, Robert Danton, 1863
Richard, C., 5199
Richards, Eugene S., 1856
Richards, Hilda, 3988
Richardson, Ann, 3438
Richarson, J.M., 0995
Richarson, Marilyn, 0996
Richmond, Anthony, 3439
Richings, G.F., 3989
Richter, Edward, 0997
Ridley, F.R., 2705
Riemer, Robert J., 1857
Riessman, Frank L., 4875
Riis, Jacob A., 3440
Rindfuss, R.R., 1858, 1859,
    1860, 1963
Riot, Reader, 3441, 3990, 4876
Riots, 3441
Rischaner, Robert Danton, 1861
Rist, Ray C., 3991
Ritchey, P. Neal, 1862, 1863
Ritter, Fredreick A., 2706
Ritternonre, Lynn, 4877
Rivoir, Farah S., 0451
Rivers, Marie D., 4878
Rivers, N.W., 1338
Robb, Frederick H., 2707
Robertson, Peter R., 1321, 4335
Roberts, R.E., 1864
Roberts, Richard J., 3442, 3443
Robins, Lee N., 2708
Robinson, Corienne K., 0304,
    3444
Robinson, Donald L., 4880
Robinson, E.F., 4879
Robinson, Evelyn B., 0632
Robinson, Henry S., 1865
Robinson, Leonard, 2709
Robinson, Pearl I., 4881
Robinson, Welford C., 2710
Rochat, R.W., 1287, 1288, 1866,
    1867, 1868, 1869
Rock, Vincent, 2476, 3138
Rockwood, H.L., 1870

Rodman, H., 1902, 1903, 3992
Roff, Kenneth I., 4882
Roge, M.J., 1871
Roghmann, Klaus J., 1872
Roherer, John, 4883
Roland, Andrew, 0428
Roof, Wade Clark, 2711, 3445,
    3446, 3447, 3448, 3449, 3450,
    4212, 5066
Rose, Frank Alexander, 0994
Rose, G., 1873
Rose, Harold M., 1874, 1875,
    2424, 2712, 2713, 2714, 3451,
    3452, 3453, 3454, 3456, 3992,
    3993, 3994, 3995, 3996, 4213,
    4214, 4215, 4216, 4884, 4885,
    4886, 4887, 4888, 5200, 5201,
    5202
Rose, Jerome G., 4217
Rose, John Carter, 1876, 1877,
    1878, 1879
Rose, Peter I., 3997
Roseman, Curtis C., 1880
Roseman, Curtis C., 2715, 2716
Roseman, D.M., 3457
Rosen, D.H., 3458
Rosen, H.M., 3458
Rosen, R.H., 1881
Rosen, S.M., 3998
Rosenberg, Arnold, 0998
Rosenberg, Terry J., 3459, 3460
Rosenwaike, Ira, 1882
Rosenblatt, Aaron, 3935
Roshco, Bernard, 3461
Ross, Arthur M., 4889
Ross, Frank Alexander, 0999
Ross, J., 1883
Ross, Myron H., 3462
Rosser, Lawrence, 3463
Rossi, Peter H., 0225, 0226,
    3732, 3999, 4000, 4001, 4002,
    5203
Rothman, Jack, 4003
Rothney, W.B., 2112
Rothstein, F., 1827
Rountree, Louise, 1000, 1001
Rouse, James W., 4004, 5204
Rowe, J., 5199
Rowell, Gordon A., 1002
Rowley, Gwyn, 3464
Rubin, E., 1884, 1885
Rubin, Morton, 4890, 4891, 4892,
    4893

Tackle, John A., 1093

Tacoma Area Urban Coalition, 1094

Taeuber, Alma F., 1970, 1971, 1972, 1973, 2777, 2778, 3549, 3550, 3564, 4235, 4980

Taeuber, Conrad, 1966, 2776

Taeuber, Irene B., 1966, 1967, 1968, 1972

Taeuber, Karl E., 1474, 1969, 1970, 1971, 1972, 1973, 2113, 2388, 2777, 2778, 3046, 3550, 3551, 3552, 3553, 3554, 3555, 3556, 3557, 3558, 3559, 3560, 3561, 3562, 3563, 3564, 3658, 4235, 4450, 4977, 4978, 4980

Tagart, Robert, 3917

Talbot, F., 1095

Tangenyi, Z., 2779

Tannenbaum, Earl, 1096

Tanneyhill, Ann, 1097

Tarone, R., 1571

Tarver, J.D., 1289

Tata, Robert J., 3565, 4048

Tatcho, Mindiola, 3279

Tatham, M.A., 1296, 4326

Tatis, Rita M., 0796

Tatum, Charles E., 4981, 4982

Taylor, Alrutheur Ambush, 4983

Taylor, Barbara, 1098

Taylor,D. Garth, 3566

Taylor, Grady W., 4984

Taylor, David Vassar, 1099

Taylor, Henry Louis, 2548, 2780

Taylor, William L., 3567

Tebbel, Robert, 3568, 4049

Techniques of Breaking Up America's Racial Ghettos, 4050

Teele, James E., 1974

Terrell, H.S., 4323

Texas Southern University, Library Heartman Negro Collection, 1100

Thaden, J.F., 1101

The Tough New Breed: Black Ghetto, 4051

Thernstrom, Stephen, 2781

Thirty Four Percent of Suburan Black, 2782, 3569

Thiebaux, H.J., 1364, 1367

Thomas, Gerald Eugene, 2783

Thomas, Herbert A., 2784

Thomas, June Sheralyn Manning, 4987

Thomas, Norman, 4988

Thomas, Trevor, 3572

Thomas, Wesley Wyman, 1975, 1976, 3571

Thomas, William V., 2785, 3572, 4236

Thomlinson, R., 1977

Thompson, Alma, 1104

Thompson, Bryan, 1102

Thompson, Charles H., 1978

Thomspon, Edgar T., 1103, 1104, 4989

Thompson, K.S., 1979

Thompson, Lawrence Sidney, 1106

Thompson, Lucille Smith, 1102

Thompson, Marilyn, 1107

Thompson, Ralph V., 4267

Thompson, Robert A., 1981, 3573

Thompson, S.J., 1982

Thompson, M. Cordell, 1980

Thornbrough, Emma Lou, 4990

Thorne, Kathleen, 1108

Thorpe, C., 1983

Thorpe, E., 1109

Thurow, Lester, 4991, 4992

Tietze, C., 1984

Tilgham, Levin, 1110

Tillman, James, 3574, 3575

Tilly, Charles, 1985, 3576, 4985

Timosky, C., 1035

Tindal, George Brenon, 4986

Tobier, Emanuel, 4288, 5108

Tobin, James, 5212

Tobin, P., 1986

Todd, William J., 2786, 4993

Toll, William, 4994, 4995

Tolmachev, Mirjana, 1111

Tolnay, Stewart E., 1987, 1988, 1989

Tomasson, R.F., 4996

Tomlison, T.M., 2734, 5213

Tompkins, Dorothy Campbell, 1112

Torres, A., 1828

Touchstone, Blake, 0285

Tower, J. Allen, 1990, 4997

Trainor, Juliette, 1113

Trattner, W., 1114

Treadwell, Mary, 1991

Trewory, M.L., 1115

Trigg, Martelle Daisy, 1992

Trubowitz, Julius, 2787, 2788

Trubowitz, Sidney, 4998

Vieira, Norman, 5039
Viet, Jean, 1138
Vietorisz, B. Harrison, 4059
Villenneave, Paul Y., 3622
Villie, Charles Vert, 2075, 2082
Vincent, Clark E., 2076, 2077
Vinton, Warren Jay, 3623
Violence in the City, 5046
Viteritti, Joseph Peter, 2808
Vogel, Kenneth Robert, 3624
Von Furstenberg, George M., 1139, 1140
Vose, Clement E., 3625, 5041
Vroman, Mary Elizabeth, 2804
Vrooman, John, 4240

W

Wachtel, Dawn, 5042
Wachtel, Howard, 5043
Wacker, Peter O., 2078
Wacks, Edward, 3650
Wade, Mary Pius, 1142, 1143
Wade, Richard C., 2810
Wadley, Janet K., 5044
Wagner, Nathaniel, 4325
Wakin, E., 2811, 5045
Wakstein, A.M., 1143
Walden, Theodore, 4060
Walker, Earl, 2812, 5222
Walker, Cornelia A., 1144
Walker, Jack Lamar, 2813, 2814
Walker, Mary M.D., 4969
Walker, Robert A., 1145
Walker, Williams, 4061
Walkley, Rosabell, 3653, 3654
Wallace, David A., 3626
Wallace, Michael, 4631
Wallace, Patricia, 1146
Walls, Dwayne, 5046
Walsh, Robert H., 1826
Walters, Mary Dawson, 1147, 1148
Walters, Ronald, 2079
Walton, Hanes, 1149
Waltzer, K., 1150
Ward, David, 4062
Warfield, D., 2637
Warner, Robert A., 5047
Warner, Sam Bass, 4063
Warner, W. Lloyd, 5048
Warren, Donald J., 5049
Warren, Donald I., 4064

Warren, Ronald I., 4065
Washington Center for Metropolitan Studies, 2622
Waskow, Arthur I., 5050, 5051
Wassenieh, Mark, 4066
Watkins, Ralph Richard, 2815
Watson, Bernard C., 5052
Watson, Franklin J., 2080
Watson, James Milton, 2816
Watson, Ora Vesta Russell, 2081, 2817
Watts, Eugene J., 5053
Watts Labor Community Action Committee, 5223
Watts, Lewis Gould, 2818, 5224
Weatherby, Norman Lee, 3628
Weatherly, William J., 2670, 2806
Weaver, Robert C., 2082, 2083, 2084, 2819, 2820, 3629, 3630, 3631, 3632, 3633, 3634, 3635, 3636, 3637, 3638, 4067, 4068, 5054, 5055, 5056, 5225
Weber, Michael P., 3639
Weckler, Joseph, 4457
Wedd, Cindy L, 3096, 3640
Weed, Perry L., 1151, 1152
Weeds, James, 3123
Weeks, Stephen B., 5057
Weinberg, Meyer, 1153, 1154
Weininger, Andriana, 1314
Weinstein, E.A., 3641
Weintraub, Irwin, 1155
Weir, Birdie, 1156
Weisbard, R.G., 5058
Weiss, Leonard, 2094
Weiss, Nancy J., 4069
Weiss, Shirley F., 2922
Weissboard, Bernard, 2821, 3642, 4241
Weissbord, R.G., 2085, 2086, 2087, 2088, 2089, 2090, 2091, 2092, 2093
Welch, Finis R., 4935
Welch, S., 1344
Wellenback, Shirley, 3643, 5059
Weller, Charles Frederick, 2822, 3644, 4070
Weller, Robert H., 2095
Wells, Marion, 1157
Welsh, Erwin K., 0280, 1158, 1159
Werling, Thomas, 3129

ABOUT THE COMPILERS

R. A. OBUDHO is Associate Professor of African/Afro-American Studies, Geography, and Regional Planning at the State University of New York at Albany. He is the co-author (with P. P. Waller) of *Periodic Markets, Urbanization, and Regional Planning* (Greenwood Press, 1976), and the author of *Demography, Urbanization, and Spatial Planning in Kenya: A Bibliographical Survey* (Greenwood Press, 1985), *Slum and Squatter Settlement in Africa, Urbanization and Development Planning in Kenya*, and *Urbanization of Kenya*, among others. His articles have appeared in *Regional Development Dialogue, Third World Planning Review, African Urban Studies, Cahiers d'Etudes Africaines*, and *Social Indicators Research Journal*. He is also the founder and editor of *African Urban Quarterly*.

JEANNINE B. SCOTT received her M.A. in International Relations from Yale University in 1985. She has also studied at the Sorbonne, l'Institut de Science Politique and the Universite de Paris I, and the Universite de Dakar, Senegal.